Private Company Law Reform

International and European Perspectives

Private Company Law Reform

International and European Perspectives

edited by

Joseph A. McCahery
Levinus Timmerman
Erik P.M. Vermeulen

T•M•C•Asser press

ISBN 978-90-6704-251-2

PREFACE AND ACKNOWLEDGEMENTS

This collection of essays arose out of a June 2006 Conference on Private Company Law Reform hosted by the Netherlands Ministry of Justice in The Hague. Two of the editors were fortunate to have had the opportunity to work with Ellen D.G. Kiersch, of the Netherlands Ministry of Justice, in developing the themes and organizing the conference. We would particularly like to thank the speakers, commentators and chairs of the sessions for the contributions at the Conference.

We would also like to thank the authors for agreeing to contribute their work to this collection. Several of the chapters have previously been published as articles, and where the copyright is not held by the authors, we are also grateful for the publishers for permitting us to reproduce the material. In particular, we acknowledge the permission of the *German Law Journal* (Chapter 13); *Illinois Law Journal* (Chapters 9, 10 and 11) and the *Journal of Corporation Law* (Chapter 2). We gratefully acknowledge financial support from the Netherlands Ministry of Economic Affairs, the Netherlands Ministry of Justice, and the Anton Philips Fund. We owe a large debt of gratitude to James J. Risser and Natalia Escobar Meija for their excellent work in editing the chapters, and are most grateful to Philip van Tongeren and his colleagues at Asser Press for their professionalism and support of this project.

Finally, we would like to thank the Tilburg Law and Economics Center, the Erasmus University Rotterdam School of Law and the Tilburg University Faculty of Law for the stimulating research environments that they provide to the editors.

Tilburg/Rotterdam/Tilburg, September 2009

Joseph McCahery
Levinus Timmermans
Erik Vermeulen

SUMMARY OF CONTENTS

TABLE OF CONTENTS

ABBREVIATIONS

ABA	American Bar Association
AG	*Die Aktiengesellschaft*
All ER	All England Law Reports
BGBl	*Bundesgesetzblatt*
BGH	German Federal Supreme Court
BGHZ	*Entscheidungen des Bundesgerichtshof in Zivilsachen*
Bpb	Bill on private companies
CBC	Center for Business and Corporate Law
CJEC	Court of Justice of the European Communities
CLRFC	Company Legislation and Regulatory Framework Committee
CMLR	Common Market Law Reports
CREDA	*Centre de recherche sur le droit des affaires de la Chambre de commerce et d'industrie de Paris*
DCC	Dutch Civil Code
DTI	Department of Trade and Industry
EC	European Community
ECJ	European Court of Justice
ECR	European Court Reports
ECFR	European Council of Foreign Relations.
EEA	European Economic Area
EEC	European Economic Community
EEIA	European Economic Interest Association
EFTA	European Free Trade Association
EHUG	*Gesetz über das elektronische Handelsregister und Genossenschaftsregister sowie das Unternehmensregister*
EP	European Parliament
EPC	European Private Company
EU	European Union
EwiR	*Entscheidungen zum Wirtschaftsrecht*
EWS	*Europäischer Wirtschafts- und Sozialausschuss*
FCJ	Federal Court of Justice
GmbH	*Gesellschaft mit beschränkter Haftung*
GmbHG	*Gesetz über Gesellschaften mit beschränkter Haftung*
GP	General Partnership
HR	*Hoge Raad*
ICCLR	International Company and Commercial Law Review
IPO	Initial public offering
IRC	Internal Revenue Code of 1986
IRS	Internal Revenue Service

JBL	Journal of Business Law
J. Corp. L.	Journal of Corporation Law
JOR	Journal of Online Research, Journal of Oriental Research.
LLC	Limited liability company
LLP	Limited liability partnership
LLLP	Limited liability limited partnership
LP	Limited partnership
MBCA	Model Business Corporation Act
MEDEF	*Mouvement des Entreprises de France*
METI	Ministry of Economy, Trade and Industry
MSSCALA	Model Simplified Stock Corporations Act for Latin America
NASA	National Aeronautics and Space Administration
NCCUSL	National Conference of Commissioners on Uniform State Laws
NJ	*Nederlandse Jurisprudentie*
OECD	Organisation for Economic Co-operation and Development
OJ	Official Journal of the European Communities/Union
Rabels Z	*Rabels Zeitschrift fur Auslandische und Internationales Privatrecht.*
RGZ	*Entscheidungen des Reichgerichts in Zivilsachen*
RULPA	Revised Uniform Limited Partnership Act
RUPA	Revised Uniform Partnership Act
SA	*Société Anonyme*
SARL	*Société à Responsabilité Limitée*
SAS	*Société par Actions Simplifiée*
SAS	*Sociedad por Acciones Simplificada*
SEC	Securities and Exchange Commission.
S-LLP	Singapore LLP
SMEs	Small and medium-sized enterprises
SORP	Statement of Recommended Practice
S. Tex. L. Rev.	South Texas Law Review.
Stan. L. Rev.	Stanford Law Review
TVVS	*Tijdschrift voor vennootschappen, verenigingen en stichtingen*
UCLA Law Review	University of California Los Angeles Law Review
U.L.A	Uniform Laws Annotated.
ULLCA	Uniform Limited Liability Company Act
ULPA	Uniform Limited Partnership Act
UPA	Uniform Partnership Act
U.S.C.	United States Code
WLR	Weekly Law Reports
Yale LJ	Yale Law Journal
ZHR	*Zeitschrift für das gesamte Handelsrecht und Wirtschaftsrecht*
ZIP	*Zeitschrift für Wirtschaftsrecht*

LIST OF CONTRIBUTORS

Stephen M. Bainbridge is William D. Warren Professor of Law at UCLA.

Scott A. Baker is Professor of Law at Washington University School of Law.

Michael Beurskens is Assistant, Heinrich Heine University of Düsseldorf, Germany.

Robert Drury is Senior Lecturer in Law, University of Exeter; Member of CREDA/MEDEF Drafting Group for the EPC Regulation.

Henry Hansmann is August E. Lines Professor of Law, Yale Law School.

Masato Hisatake is Professor of Policy Analysis, Tohoku University School of Law.

Peter Hommelhoff is Professor of Law, University of Heidelberg.

Reinier Kraakman is Ezra Ripley Thayer Professor of Law at Harvard Law School.

Kimberly D. Krawiec is Professor of Law, Duke Law Faculty.

Maarten J. Kroeze is Dean and Professor of Company Law, Erasmus School of Law, Erasmus University Rotterdam.

Saul Levmore is Dean and William B. Graham Professor of Law, University of Chicago Law School.

Joseph A. McCahery is Professor of International Economic Law, Tilburg University Faculty of Law and Professor of Financial Market Regulation, Tilburg Law and Economics Center, Research Associate ECGI (Brussels).

Ulrich Noack is Professor of Law, Heinrich Heine University of Düsseldorf, Germany.

Richard W. Painter is S. Walter Richey Professor of Corporate Law, University of Minnesota Law School.

Francisco Reyes is Professor and Director of Graduate Program in Corporation Law, Universidad Javeriana in Colombia.

Larry E. Ribstein is Mildred van Voorhees Chair in Law, University of Illinois College of Law.

Jun Saito, member of the Executive Staff, Corporate Technology Management, Nikon Corporation, Japan.

Richard Squire is Associate Professor of Law at Fordham University School of Law.

Levinus TIMMERMAN is Professor of Company Law, Erasmus University Rotterdam; Advocate General at the Netherlands Supreme Court.

Erik P.M. VERMEULEN is Professor of Law and Management, Tilburg University Faculty of Law, Fellow Center for Company Law and Tilburg Law and Economics Center, and Legal Counsel at Philips International B.V.

Allan W. VESTAL is Dean and Professor of Law, Drake University Law School.

Jan Berend WEZEMAN is Professor of Company and Commercial Law, Faculty of Law, University of Groningen.

INTRODUCTION: PRIVATE COMPANY LAW REFORM

Joseph A. McCahery*, Levinus Timmerman** and Erik P.M. Vermeulen***

1. Introduction

This book is devoted to the most topical and important areas of company law reform, namely the revision of the corporate forms and the introduction of unincorporated entities such as partnerships and hybrid legal entities. The advantage of unincorporated business forms is that they provide important contractual provisions in advance, support the enforcement of implicit contracts and internalized norms, and supply businesses with relationship legal entity status. These features make them suitable for a wide variety of firms.

In recent years, the increased emphasis on competition between jurisdictions led US observers in the 1980s to call for the creation of a set of new types of business entities that are suitable to different types of businesses. Over the last three decades, we have witnessed the rise of the new unincorporated entities and the way they operate. The success of the new type of business associations is not accidental, however. Unsurprisingly, a large number of business parties have a preference for the new and more flexible types of entities, which have a perceived competitive advantage over corporations. Several factors contribute to the growth of these forms. First, states have responded to the needs for business structures that are more flexible contractually, which has reduced reliance on or eliminated inefficient older forms. Second, the liberalization of partnership law has been accompanied by the virtual elimination of the distinction between partnerships and corporations accompanied by a move toward the recognition of partnerships as entities. Third, the increase in the choice of new contractual limited liability entities for business has resulted in the erosion of traditional restrictions on the internal structure of legal business forms.

Since the beginning of the 1990s, some European Member States have also created a variety of flexible hybrid business forms that are designed to improve the conditions of firms doing business. For example, the 1994 introduction of the *Société par Actions Simpli-*

* Professor of International Economic Law, Tilburg University Faculty of Law and Professor of Financial Market Regulation, Tilburg Law and Economics Center, Research Associate ECGI (Brussels).

** Advocate General, The Netherlands Supreme Court, and Professor of Foundations of Company Law, Erasmus University Rotterdam.

*** Professor Financial Market Regulation, Tilburg Law and Economics Center, Professor of Law and Management, Tilburg University Faculty of Law, and Senior Legal Counsel, Corporate Legal Department, Philips International, B.V.

J.A. McCahery, L. Timmerman and E.P.M. Vermeulen (eds.), Private Company Law Reform

fiée (*SAS*) and its subsequent modification in 1999 is an example of responsive law-making in a civil law country.[1] The *SAS* is a limited liability vehicle that provides for a flexible organization and administrative structure, which restricts free transferability and the expulsion of minority shareholders. The vehicle allows parties to choose the firm's management and decision-making structure and the contents of its by-laws.

Like the United States, the competition between European jurisdictions for real inflows of capital has caused Member States to adopt a variety of new business forms designed to stem the outflow of taxable resources. The pressure of competition from other Member States, which are viewed as having more suitable closely held business forms, stimulated French lawmakers in 1999 to adopt a new organization structure with significant costs and benefits for firms. The modification proved highly successful in attracting large numbers of foreign firms to France for investment purposes. Subsequently, lawmakers set out to improve the competitive environment for investment through the introduction of a series of company law and fiscal reforms. In particular, Law n° 2008-776, *Le Roi de modernisation de l'economie* dated August 4th 2008 (loi LME), was promulgated to streamline and simplify the code offering firms, for example, with easy access to the *SAS* and a more beneficial fiscal regime for SMEs. This vehicle allows parties to choose the firm's decision-making structure and the contents of its by-laws. The *SAS* holds out the potential to provide cost-saving benefits that may attract new 'incorporations', allowing France to compete effectively with Germany, the Netherlands and the United Kingdom.

The legal reform process has also been advanced considerably by recent wave of decisions by the European Court of Justice, which has stimulated the mobility of small businesses toward the United Kingdom, and hence the introduction of various legislative strategies to meet the needs of businesses that might be lured to more attractive jurisdictions. Naturally, the increased mobility of small companies has led some European jurisdictions to be responsive. For example, lawmakers in Germany have sought to make improvements in the efficiency in their existing unincorporated business forms while seeking to minimize the cost of regulation by lowering obligations. Although some diversity can be expected, most reform activity is focused on modernization and simplification of legal business forms, rather than with the introduction of new business statutes.

From the legislator's perspective, the influence of 'legal transplants' from the United States and United Kingdom is being felt more and more in company law reform projects in Japan, Singapore, and other Asian jurisdictions such as India and Hong Kong. For example, a Limited Liability Partnerships Act 2005, inspired by the Delaware LLP, came into effect on 11 April 2005 in Singapore. The Company Legislation and Regulatory Framework Committee (CFRFC) spurred the introduction of an LLP in Singapore in order to expand the governance options to be considered by small- and medium-sized businesses, professionals and investment funds.

Japan, which has a tradition to follow Germany's company law model, has also been inspired by the success of legal innovation in the United States resulting in the introduction of two new legal forms: the J-LLP (*Yigensekinin-jigyo-kumiai*) and J-LLC (*Godo-kaisha*). The J-LLC bears a strong resemblance to the US LLC (e.g., voting and distribution rights are by default proportionate to the members' contributions), but diverges in a number of

[1] Law no. 94-1 of 3 January 1994 J.O.; Law no. 99-587 of 12 July 1999, J.O., 13 July 1999, p. 10396, D.S.L. 1999 p. 425, Art. 3.

important respects, including: (1) contributions to the J-LLC are limited to cash or property, but no services, know-how or other agreements are permitted; and (2) the J-LLC has corporate, and not pass-through, tax treatment. In contrast, the J-LLP is characterized by limited liability, a flexible organization structure, pass-through taxation, and restrictions on the free transferability of partners' interests. Despite these attractive aspects, the legislation mandates a number of highly restrictive and costly features including registration of the J-LLP agreement and disclosure of financial information at the request of creditors. These shortcomings must arguably have been responsible for the slow start of the J-LLP. Indeed, with respect to incorporations, the J-LLC has proved the more popular entity.

Unlike US and European reforms, the new Japanese business law forms were not shaped by a policy process shaped by competitive law-making and interest group pressures. Japan differs considerably from the United States by having a party-based system of law-making that is influenced by a strong bureaucracy controlled by the cabinet (or government party). In party-based systems, common in most Asian countries, interest group participation is low and, correspondingly, lawmakers have few incentives to invest in specialized legislative skills that are needed for initiating significant legal changes. This is especially true in the case of statutory business form innovations. Hence the combination of the allocation of legislative power and the key role played by the bureaucracy are the main factors affecting the innovative capacity of the party-centered systems. However, there are reasons for thinking, based on recent evidence, that party-centered systems in Asia may have higher levels of innovative capacity than earlier research suggests.

2. Issue coverage

This book is divided into four parts. It starts in Part I by analyzing the emergence of new business entities in the United States. The last three decades have been characterized as a period of rapid change and innovation in business organization law with the development of the limited liability company (LLC), the limited liability partnership (LLP), the limited liability limited partnership (LLLP) and the statutory business trust. These vehicles all combine the pattern of creditors' rights, which is traditional to the business organization, with the freedom of contract among investors and managers, which is traditional to the partnership. In their essay which opens the volume, Henry Hansmann, Reinier Kraakman and Richard Squire identify the main factors supporting the emergence of the new business entities in the United States, and argue that these statutory innovations are, in their view, best seen as a continuing development of the corporate form. Part I also takes stock of the debate on whether jurisdictional competition is an effective means to bring about more efficient rules for business formations. In Chapter 2, Larry Ribstein explains that the evolution of partnership-type vehicles in the United States was driven by competition-oriented law-making at the state level, which improved the chances for efficient rules to emerge. Analyzing the pace of evolution of partnership type structures in the United States, he suggests that jurisdictional competition is a more successful approach for European jurisdictions as the Member States seek to reform their partnership law. In identifying the factors that shape and structure the new and innovative forms, this part of the book delivers insights into how legal business entities can be adapted and reformed successfully. In his contribution, in Chapter 3, Saul Levmore explores how partnership-type statutes have so far avoided exposure to the heavy-handed US federal regulation that corporations face today, and considers the conditions and interest group pressures that could lead to increased regulation against the LLC /LLP.

Whereas Part I focuses on the introduction of new business entities in the United States, Part II evaluates the rise of new company law products in Asia, Europe and South America. In Chapter 4, Joseph McCahery, Erik Vermeulen, Misato Hisatake and Jun Saito ask why some countries have a higher capacity to innovate in developing new legal business forms while others are less successful in making drastic changes in generating alternative business forms suited to the needs of different types of firms. In his essay, Francisco Reyes, who offers a general framework for the adoption of hybrid business forms in Latin America, focuses on introduction of the Colombian Simplified Stock Company (*Sociedad por Acciones Simplificada* or *SAS*) as an example of a successful efficiency-minded law-making effort, in a Civil Law jurisdiction, to create a new business organization form. In Chapter 6, Ulrich Noack and Michael Beurskens look at the factors that stimulated the reform of the German private limited company (*Gesellschaft mit beschränkter Haftung – GmbH*), observing that the reform-bill, namely the '*MoMiG*'[2] eliminated most of the burdensome formalities and complexities of German corporate law without introducing new provisions based on British, Spanish or Danish corporate law. In Chapter 7, Maarten Kroeze and Jan Berend Wezeman focus on the reform of the Dutch *BV* which was designed, most prominently, to introduce more flexibility into private company law while reducing the regulatory burden for firms. In his chapter, Levinus Timmerman considers the questions that arise between fairness and welfare in Dutch corporate, examining the role of justice in corporate law by suggesting that the notions of reasonableness and fairness, found in Book 2 of the Dutch Civil Code and the fundamental rights of the European Convention, continue to be critical factors today in Dutch corporate law.

Part III examines limited liability and private ordering issues involving the new partnership-type business forms in the United States. In Chapter 9, Stephen Bainbridge focuses on veil piercing, showing that not only is it arbitrary, inconsistent and relatively rare in practice but will likely increase transaction costs for small businesses due to its uncertainty and lack of predictability. In the next chapter, Scott Baker and Kimberly Krawiec examine the costs and benefits of limited liability of the LLP statute for New York law firms and the factors that influenced partners to switch from a general partnership to a LLP. In Chapter 11, Richard Painter shifts the section's focus from limited liability to an account of the type of default rules that should be introduced for lawyers involved in representing unincorporated business entities. Allan Vestal, in his chapter, is skeptical of instituting a policy of private ordering for business organization forms and has sought instead to justify an approach that seeks to strike a balance between the benefits and costs of: (1) plenary private ordering of monitoring costs imposed on third parties; and (2) the search and negotiation costs imposed on participants during the formation stage.

Part IV comprises two chapters which together highlight the recent developments by the European Commission to introduce a European Private Company (EPC). In Chapter 13, Peter Hommelhoff clearly examines the practical necessity for the EPC as a supra-national legal form given the availability of closely held business forms that firms have at the Mem-

[2] *Gesetz zur Modernisierung des GmbH-Rechts und zur Bekämpfung von Missbräuchen* [Law on the modernisation of the law of private limited liability companies and to combat abuses], available on the website of the German Federal Ministry of Justice at: <http://www.bmj.bund.de/media/archive/1236.pdf>.

ber State level. In Chapter 14, Robert Drury surveys the main justifications for the introduction of the EPC, against the background of recent decisions by the European Court of Justice, and shows that the prospective benefits outweigh the costs. Drury concludes with an instructive account of the model Articles of Association, which appear in the Annex, for the EPC that were drafted by a team of top law professors from Exeter and Heidelberg.

3. Overview

Part I examines the factors that influenced the evolution of corporate law and the recent expansion of partnership type forms in the United States.

In Chapter 1, Henry Hansmann, Reinier Kraakman and Richard Squire focus on the evolution of legal organizational forms with entity-based features necessary to facilitate commercial relationships with third parties. From a law and economics perspective, legal entity status is a necessary device to define property rights over which participants in the firm can contract. In the absence of entity status, it would be practicably impossible to shield assets of the firm from the creditors of the firm's owners. The separation between the firm's assets and the personal assets of the participants inside the firm, 'affirmative asset partitioning', is viewed as the defining feature of a legal entity. However, the opposite form of asset partitioning, 'defensive asset partitioning', is not necessary for the creation of a legal entity. The entity status strengthens the firm's bargaining power *vis-à-vis* outsiders. For these and other reasons, in the early stage of development of partnership law, lawmakers in civil law jurisdictions have bestowed a weak form of entity status on commercial partnerships and, to some extent, on civil partnerships. In contrast, Anglo-American lawmakers applied common law's aggregate theory to most of the problems arising out of partnership transactions. However, it did not take the entity theory long to become embedded in practice. The entity approach increasingly mingled with the aggregate approach.

Nevertheless, the type of asset partitioning conferred on traditional partnerships differs from the strong type found in the corporate litigation process. Both types of affirmative asset partitioning assign to the firm's creditors a prior claim on the firm's assets, but, in contrast to corporations, the personal creditors of an insolvent partner can initiate the dissolution and liquidation of the partnership's assets to satisfy their claims. In the view of Henry Hansmann, Reinier Kraakman and Richard Squire, the available statutory forms for the organization of firms should reflect the degrees of entity status. The menu of business forms could be limited and adapted to the prevailing forms of asset partitioning, varying from no partitioning to super-strong asset partitioning. Given the foregoing, the development of new hybrid business forms over the last thirty years is particularly interesting because they combine the type of asset partitioning characteristic of the corporation with a flexible organizational structure and contractual freedom. The partnership type business forms cover a wide spectrum of business organizations, ranging from firms consisting of two people to large professional firms with tiers of partners and varying rights and obligations. At one end of the spectrum are organizations that are close to the boundary between firms and non-firms, and at the other end, are organizations that resemble publicly held firms. There are significant theoretical and practical disputes about how many different hybrid type business forms are required to meet the efficient contracting needs of a variety of firms.

In the next chapter, Larry Ribstein shows that the landscape of partnership law has changed dramatically over the last decade. The breakdown in uniformity led to a proliferation of new partnership variations that took place without the impetus of a uniform act. For instance, the LLP emerged in Texas in 1991 and thereafter spread rapidly from two states in 1992 to all 50 states and the District of Columbia. The development of the LLC evinces a similar development. The emergence of these new partnership forms shows that the needs of various types of firms can be met when firms can freely choose between their place of incorporation and from among the different types of business forms available within a jurisdiction. The inherent benefit of horizontal choice is that it limits states imposing strong and costly rules on firms' internal structures. Likewise, vertical choice is advantageous because a wide variety of firms and professionals can choose between alternative bundles of rules. Evidence from the United States shows that vertical competition takes place and that its effect has been to eliminate inefficient mandatory rules and promote opportunities for regulatory arbitrage. The implication of this analysis is that the benefits of the US model of horizontal jurisdictional competition could work for Europe in encouraging the development of competitive law-making for entrepreneurs, SMEs and other newly incorporating firms within the EU.

In Chapter 3, Saul Levmore asks whether the state that dominates US corporate law will also come to dominate unincorporated firms and focuses on the probability of federal intervention with respect to the conduct of the new business forms. Commentators have widely noted that Delaware is the leading state of incorporation for nearly half of corporations listed on the New York Stock Exchange and more than half of the all Fortune 500 firms. Conversely, it appears that states do not have high-powered incentives to compete for LLC or LLP incorporations because most firms tend to find the cost of forum shopping excessive and have generally preferred a home state to incorporate. Still, Delaware does seem to have some incentives to keep up with legislative innovations in the field of business organization law. While not the leading state for LLC formations, Delaware's lawmakers have every reason to increase the share in the market for large, corporate-style LLCs where Delaware is the clear market leader. Arguably, Delaware can expect that LLC formations will grow significantly in the long run due to the statute's flexibility. The inherent benefits of the LLC (and its clear advantages over the corporate form) are likely to recede, Levmore suggests, with the predictable growth in federal regulation of partnership law in response to growth in importance of the new partnership forms. In fact, it appears that Delaware may very well avoid federal regulation of partnerships in the near term because there has been far less migration to the LLC formation than anticipated, which should allow Delaware to reinforce its pre-eminence in partnership-type business forms.

While the discussion so far has focused on the importance of making available a coherent menu of standard business forms to meet the needs of different firms and professionals, Part II, in contrast, focuses on understanding the reform process and the barriers to the development of a free standing hybrid business form. The essays begin in Part II by investigating the reforms that employ a structural transplant approach, such as in Japan, Singapore and Columbia, and then move on to examine the up-grading strategy to reform legal business forms, which is common in continental Europe.

In Chapter 4, Joseph McCahery, Erik Vermeulen, Masato Hisatake and Jun Saito show that the reform of business organization forms can be understood in terms of three different strategies of reform. The first reform strategy, which is located on the left hand side of the spectrum and closest to stasis, is where virtually no effective legal changes can occur and where only the idea of reform clashes with legal tradition and standardization pressures. An example of a jurisdiction that takes this position is Germany. A second strategy, located near the mid-point of the spectrum, can be viewed as where company law changes are less impeded by tradition and standardization factors, but more influenced by interest group pressures. England occupies this position. Finally, Japan can be seen as a more adaptable jurisdiction located toward the right end of the spectrum and therefore better able to create and introduce more functional legal rules and institutions that turn the traditional view of company law around. The authors argue that Singapore is also located on the right side of the spectrum as its legislature is aware of the need to adapt the legal system to international business practices in order to develop a distinct jurisprudence, acclaimed for its efficiency and integrity, which is set apart from the English legal system.

Arguably, these reform strategies lead roughly to the emergence of three distinct statutory products. First, a legal upgrade provides an easy-to-use vehicle that supplies lawyers and firms with familiar provisions that are tried and tested and consequently offer learning and network benefits to users of the form. Second, a linked, but new, legal business form similarly holds out continued network and learning benefits along with the prospect of superior cost advantages due to better suited statutory provisions. Third, in contrast, a non-networked product holds out greater costs for adopting firms as switching costs effect prospective users negatively, and the absence of an established set of precedents – which are needed to fill the gaps in the inherently incomplete law – provide few incentives for parties to adopt an entirely new type of legal product. Against this background, what emerges is that although most jurisdictions still employ the upgrade strategy to reform, an increasing number of countries embrace a new product approach by following either the second or third reform strategies. This can be seen in the cases of the United Kingdom, Japan, Singapore and Columbia, which moved quickly into unchartered territory when embarking on a new legal reform strategy that complemented their existing upgrade legislative reform approach. Consequently, this development seems better able to ensure speedy and effective legislative action than competing approaches.

While Chapter 4 explores the different strategies of reform of closely held firms, Francisco Reyes explores and extends these findings, in Chapter 5, by showing that the use of a legal transplant is particularly effective in introducing a more effective legal business form. In this context, he addresses the question why most Latin American countries continue to follow the taxonomy of business associations inherited from the 19th century's French codification movement. He shows how the persistence of these legal and institutional barriers makes it difficult for modern firms to operate effectively in a business environment characterized by uncertainty and unpredictability. In this context, Reyes suggests that the case for developing new business forms is strong, given the need for many types of firms to engage in private ordering. However, most Latin American legislators, like their European counterparts, have been reluctant to develop new hybrid vehicles. To be sure, the pent-up demand for new business forms has recently led to several initiatives within the region. These efforts have been recently surpassed by the introduction of the *Sociedad por Acciones Simplificada* (*SAS*) or Simplified Stock Corporation in Columbia. Even though it draws upon the French *Société par Actions Simplifiée*, this entity closely resembles the hybrid business entities that have been set in place in the United Kingdom and the United States, the upshot is that the *SAS*, provides a mixture of corporate and partnership-like components that allow for significant contractual flexibility while still preserving the benefits of limited liability and asset partitioning. Ultimately, it is expected that the *SAS* will have to compete with other types of business forms.

In Chapter 6, Ulrich Noack and Michael Beurskens examine recent efforts to modernize the German private limited company (*Gesellschaft mit beschränkter Haftung*, so-called '*GmbH*'). New developments in Europe, particularly the competitive pressure arising from the UK private limited company (Limited), prompted lawmakers to consider possible reform strategies available to confront the competition by adopting provisions that are responsive to the inroads made by the UK's Limited.

Lawmakers seeking more *GmbH* incorporations have sought to introduce reforms designed to (1) introduce simplification by allowing the option of formation by an oral agreement before the notary public (who is still required to warn and explain) only when there are a maximum of three shareholders and one manager with full authority *vis-à-vis* third parties and himself; (2) retain the minimum capital requirement, but allow for a new type of *GmbH* (i.e., the *GmbH* – the *Unternehmergesellschaft (haftungsbeschränkt)* that allows for formation of a company with a minimum capital of € 1; (3) liberalize the rules for raising capital that require that shareholders must prove that at least a certain part of the full amount is available in liquid assets; (4) allows any assets given to the *GmbH* to be immediately returned to its shareholders if there is a legally and economically valid claim for their return at any given time; (5) change the rule on membership rights which will allow every shareholder to hold more than one share and the value of each part can be freely determined (in multiples of € 1); (6) modernize the system of transferring ownership rights by requiring the notary public involved in the transfer of ownership rights to update the list and send it to the register and mandating that only those shareholders on the official list are recognized in their rights; (7) introduce rules to protect the good faith purchaser who relied on the shareholder list; (8) allow German companies the freedom of choice to move their seat of administration abroad; (9) introduce some checks and balances to the extant system designed to ensure that shareholders are unable to enrich themselves at the expense of the company or its creditors by requiring the repayment of certain assets that they received out of company funds in the case of insolvency; (10) stricter liability rules strengthening liability for managers and joint personal liability upon all shareholders if they knowingly allow a disqualified director to act on behalf of their company; (11) impose new duties on shareholders by mandating a duty to file for bankruptcy if there is no management available and assigning the responsibility of receiving legally binding statements when the managers resign, die or are dismissed; and (12) introduce a new system for loans that follows the international tendency to subordinate obligations to shareholders compared to obligations to third parties only in case of bankruptcy. Such reforms are likely to streamline and attract private company law form that should limit the attractiveness of foreign forms for many German entrepreneurs.

In Chapter 7, Maarten Kroeze and Jan Berend Wezeman describe the complex reform process of Dutch private company law over the last two decades. Beginning with early academic calls for reform at the beginning of the 1990s, the authors show how the reforms were stimulated by the ECJ triad of opinions in *Centros, Überseering* and *Inspire Art* cases, which led eventually to the adoption of the internal affairs doctrine. Against this background, Dutch lawmakers have recently undertaken a series of reforms, reflected in The Private Company Law (Simplification and Flexibilization) Act, designed to increase internal flexibility, which should lead to fewer mandatory rules and the elimination of burdensome and ineffective rules. Moreover, the effect of the reform will lead to removal of the minimum capital requirement and the elimination of the corresponding provisions dealing with the circumvention of the minimum capital requirement and the strict capital protection regime. In addition to the organizational changes, the private company statute creates new classes of shares, including shares without voting rights, shares without financial rights and shares with multiple voting rights. Crucially, the new legislation eliminates the need for a share transfer restriction clause in the articles of association and introduces important changes in decision-making by the shareholders' meeting as well as amendments that allow for the introduction of a one-tier board. Despite the length and difficulties encountered in he reform process, the outcome will create greater flexibility and a create a framework that encourages more formations.

In Chapter 8, Levinus Timmerman argues that Dutch lawmakers have for several decades used the company law regime for their own policy ends. This is reflected in a variety of initiatives, such as establishing employee participation in corporate decision-making in the 1960s, which have persisted in Dutch law despite the loss in confidence in some of these measures. However, the success of the economic approach will inevitably place limits on legislative interventions by lawmakers while, at the same time, improving shareholder rights and more contractual freedom. Timmerman is not opposed to political or economically motivated corporate law reforms since he believes that this is unavoidable in a democratic society. To be sure, the implication is that corporate law will be less sacred and may become more of an instrument for the realization of social aims. It is important to recognize that the environment in which corporations operate tends to demand that the firm is efficiently organized and operated. In this context, many of the key features of the corporate form were developed in the 19th century that, to some extent, have been crucial in enhancing the economic activities of the firm. This chapter also focuses on the idea of justice in corporate law, which has a secure place given the diversity of interests and visions of the firm. By introducing a pluralistic approach, combining efficiency and justice, it is crucial that consideration be given to binding notions, such as the general interest. Justice can play a pivotal role in corporate law through the principles of reasonableness and fairness and fundamental rights. Associated with this vision, is the idea that parties are familiar with this way of thinking and that they will remain lasting concepts in the practice of Dutch company law.

Part III assesses the scope of liability protection for a member operating a firm and also the desirable amount of private ordering within partner/client relationship or when structuring a new hybrid vehicle.

In Chapter 9, Stephen Bainbridge revisits the corporate law doctrine of veil piercing, exploring whether the doctrine should, in the absence of an statutory provision, be extended to LLC context. This question is particularly relevant since courts are often found applying corporate law doctrine to the LLC and the LLC veil, in practice, may be pierced under certain circumstances. In identifying the factors that could lend support to veil piercing, Bainbridge refers to leading American case law to determine if common standards emerge for holding the LLC member to be personally liable. It seems that unless there are organizational failures regarding the operation of the firm, it is unlikely there will be sufficient basis for piercing the veil. Having reviewed the relevant American case law, Bainbridge analyzes and discusses whether there is a coherent policy justification for veil piercing.

The policy arguments (e.g., negative externalities), in turn, provide no additional support in favor of veil piercing. Consequently, since veil piercing is both dysfunctional and discourages capital formation, it seems that there are good grounds for its abolition.

In Chapter 10, Scott Baker and Kimberly Krawiec assess the respective theories concerning the costs and benefits of the LLP form. The empirical work presented is based on data collected on 147 law firms having more than 25 lawyers and their primary offices in New York City. This chapter also analyzes which firms were more likely to be transformed into an LLP or remain a GP. The theory presented suggests that the liquidity or profit sharing theories would predict that all or nearly all of the firms in the sample would have transformed into an LLP. What emerges is that a sizeable number of firms, approximately 13 percent decided to remain GPs, whereas 67 percent became LLPs. The results show that there is no significant variation based on the number of lawyers, size of offices, rate of growth, level of profits, and other factors such as level of collegiality, sophistication of practice and type of client. The data shows a lack of correlation between individual firms characteristics and the choice of business organization form. This chapter supports the claim that the choice of organization form is dependent on a number of factors. First, they postulate that, given the high number of transformations, most law firms recognize the costs of unlimited liability and thus most will eventually convert to the LLP form. Second, the data reveals that a small minority of GPs value unlimited liability notwithstanding the costs. Consequently, they conclude that the choice of organization form is viewed as determined by a variety of factors, including the conduct of other competitor firms.

In Chapter 11, Richard Painter speculates that the new age of the un-incorporation could provide both opportunities and problems for professional responsibility. This chapter takes off from the insight that, while the age of incorporation was successful in promoting clarity to the lawyer's obligation, namely by elevating a client entity above the interests of individual shareholders, directors and officers, there remain important unanswered questions along these lines in the age of the un-incorporation. Painter asks whether the supremacy of the entity as client disappear; and does it increase the possibility of the pre-incorporation ambiguity of individuals and groups of individuals behind the firm return. This chapter tackles these concerns by arguing that, in the age of the un-incorporation, the parties (lawyers, owners and managers) could define their lawyer-client relationship *ex ante* rather than rely upon public ordering (which may not be possible given the absence of authority). Given Painter's preference for private ordering, he endorses all efforts for courts and professional associations to enforce such contracts that specify the professional responsibilities of lawyers for unincorporated entities. Hence, the implication of this argument is that there will be lower litigation costs in the long run as lawyers and clients are better able to define their *ex ante* expectations more proximately through repeat contracting.

In Chapter 12, Allan Vestal challenges the orthodoxy associated with economic accounts of the success of the new unincorporated business entities, maintaining that there is a need to broaden the cost/benefit analysis by seeking to make an aggregate determination of the benefits and costs associated with the new contractual forms. The task should be to determine, as to each statutory provision, which level of private ordering is justified and in how many cases regulation may be required to correct the imbalance where private ordering is not warranted. As part of this expansive cost/benefit procedure, Vestal concludes that a determination of the how many state-based variations of each business form is needed to justify their widespread use.

Part IV is based on a set of articles focused on the draft regulation for a European Private Company. The section provides a critical and wide-ranging assessment of the need for an EPC and the prospective benefits. Importantly, the draft Articles of Association are included in the annex for review.

In Chapter 13, Peter Hommelhoff suggests, despite continuing skepticism about the relevance of this form, that there is indeed a strong demand for a supra-national legal form, such as the EPC. The author, who takes an expansive view of the need for the EU form, suggests that there is wide consensus among firms about the necessity of this new business form. In this context, there seem to be many advantages associated with the EPC, including simpler formation of subsidiaries, a single legal structure with the simplification of the internal organization structure, increased corporate mobility and reduced advisory costs. Apparently, the EPC will also contribute significantly to the formation of cross-border ventures. In terms of target firms, it seems that the EPC Regulation should be structured to meet the interests of SMEs. The EC Consultation Paper shows further the importance for protection of creditors. In this respect, the system of protection ideally should be based on limited partner liability and exclusion of liability if the shareholder's contribution has been fully paid. Moreover, it seems that more consideration must be given to the design of the asset protection system that will be implemented. Naturally certain problems emerge with the EPC statute since the litigation and insolvency law should be provided by the Member State legal system. Another problem concerns the degree of structural freedom in the EPC. In fact, the EPC consultation paper proposed a very detailed framework in which there is very little flexibility for founders and shareholders. These and other problems suggest that there are some problems with the EPC. Conversely, the EC has indicated that it favors lean and convenient set of provisions. In practice, the aim is also to introduce comprehensive rather than uniform regulation which is more effective in practice.

In the final chapter, Robert Drury argues that the EPC is especially well-placed to be used widely throughout the EU. The introduction of the EPC is likely to create significant benefits for firms that wish to incorporate, for example, a set of subsidiaries with reasonably uniform organizational structures. There are political considerations as well that support the introduction of the EPC. Specially, some lawmakers wish to have commercial vehicles of a particular size to support innovation. To be sure, there are a number of particular problems for the EPC. An especially thorny problem concerns, for example, which to apply when an issue cannot be easily determined by reference to ECP legislation. While such problems show the difficulties with developing a project of this sort within the EU, the author (along with co-draftsmen from Exeter and Heidelberg) have created a draft model Articles of Association that should make it easier for certain classification of companies to operate more effectively.

4. Conclusion

This book looks at a range of private company law forms that have emerged in the United States, Europe, Asia and South American. The contributors provide important insights into the supply and demand for these new forms. It can be expected that the expanded menu of hybrid business forms can stimulate both the competition between business forms and eliminate cumbersome and antiquated legal rules. Conversely, the reform process in the European Union is less directed toward the introduction of new self-standing forms that could satisfy the needs of professionals and many different types of firms. Not only do European firms have less freedom of choice to adopt sets of legal rules that meet their need, but the legal reform process is subject to upgrading and modernizing closely held business forms rather than creating new highly innovative forms. We also found that law reform based on legal transplants could lead to efficient business forms. Ultimately, we have seen that developments in Japan, Singapore and Columbia could produce significant economic benefits for both firms and investors.

Part I

THEORY: NEW BUSINESS ENTITIES

Chapter 1

THE NEW BUSINESS ENTITIES IN EVOLUTIONARY PERSPECTIVE

Henry Hansmann*, Reinier Kraakman and Richard Squire*****

1. Introduction

The new types of business forms that have developed over the past thirty years all combine the freedom of contracting that is traditional to the partnership with the pattern of creditors' rights that is traditional to the business corporation. Legal scholars differ on the issue of whether these new business forms are more partnership-like or corporation-like. Those taking the partnership-like view argue that the degree of freedom of contract is the essential difference between the traditional corporation and partnership forms, while those adhering to the corporation-like view argue that the pattern of creditors' rights is the essential difference. The authors support the latter view. They argue that an examination of the evolution of business entities reveals that the traditional inflexibility in corporations served importantly to protect creditors' rights, but as substitute sources developed to protect the rights of all investors, the need for inflexibility diminished and freedom of contracting in the corporate form flourished.

In this chapter, the authors first discuss the historical evolution of business entities, focusing on the primary role that creditor protection has played in that evolution. Next, the authors argue that, although legal scholars generally focus on limited liability when discussing creditor protection and the distinction between the corporation and the partnership, the principal feature distinguishing the corporation from the partnership is 'entity shielding'– a term referring to the allocation of different rights to different groups of creditors in the assets of a firm. After discussing the importance of strong entity shielding – a characteristic of the corporation but not the partnership – and how it complements limited liability, the authors conclude that the development of new business forms is the culmination of the process of extending strong entity shielding to unrestricted types of entities and, therefore, the new business forms should be viewed as generalizations of the business corporation rather than the partnership.

The many legal forms for business organizations that first appeared during the last thirty years – the limited liability company (LLC), the limited liability partnership (LLP), the

* August E. Lines Professor of Law, Yale Law School.
** Ezra Ripley Thayer Professor of Law at Harvard Law School.
*** Associate Professor of Law at Fordham University School of Law.

J.A. McCahery, L. Timmerman and E.P.M. Vermeulen (eds.), Private Company Law Reform

limited liability limited partnership (LLLP), and the statutory business trust – all combine the pattern of creditors' rights (or, as we have characterized it elsewhere, the rules of 'asset partitioning')[1] that are traditional to the business corporation with the freedom of contract among investors and managers that is traditional to the partnership. To view these new entities as partnership-like is to treat the degree of freedom of contract as the essential difference between the traditional corporation and partnership forms; to view them as corporation-like is to treat the pattern of creditors' rights as the essential difference. We believe the latter is more accurate. To be sure, both views capture important aspects of the evolution of business entities. But history shows that much of the contractual inflexibility in the traditional corporation served merely to buttress its pattern of creditors' rights, and that this inflexibility fell away upon the development of substitute sources of investor protection. The new forms are thus better understood as part of the continuing development of the corporate form rather than as entities more akin to the traditional partnership which has, in fact, been evolving in a different direction.

We develop this argument first in terms of the tradeoff between contractual freedom and the form of asset partitioning that to date has received the most scholarly attention – that is, limited liability. We then explore the evolution of the new forms from a less familiar perspective, focusing on what we term the 'entity shielding' component of asset partitioning.[2]

2. THE HISTORICAL DEVELOPMENT OF BUSINESS ENTITIES

From ancient Roman times until the end of the 19th century, the partnership was the dominant form for organizing jointly owned business firms. In fact, until the 17th century the partnership was the only form available for most types of business. Partners bore unlimited personal liability for the contractual obligations of the firm, and this was the basis for the firm's creditworthiness.

By the latter half of the 19th century, an alternative form of organization, the statutory business corporation, had also become available for most types of business activity. Because the shareholders in a business corporation had limited liability, the obligations of these companies were bonded only by the assets held in the name of the firm itself. This meant that, for the firms to be creditworthy, creditors had to have some reason to believe that the firms would generally maintain reasonable levels of assets and, in particular, that the owners of the firms would not opportunistically withdraw assets from the firms or otherwise keep firms undercapitalized.

For the small firms that dominated Western economies prior to the Industrial Revolution, a firm's owners could not credibly make such a pledge to the firm's creditors. The opportunity and incentive to siphon off assets from the firm were too great – a problem that was accentuated by poor accounting standards and weak bankruptcy procedures. Personal liability for the firm's owners was the only way to make the firm creditworthy, and thus the partnership was the dominant mode of organization.

---

1 H. Hansmann and R. Kraakman, 'The Essential Role of Organizational Law', 110 *Yale Law Journal* (2000) p. 393.

2 We draw here heavily upon our working paper, H. Hansmann, R. Kraakman, and R. Squire, *Legal Entities, Asset Partitioning, and the Evolution of Organizations* (Oct. 2004) (unpublished manuscript), which explores these themes, and the relevant history, in substantially greater depth and detail.

In general, the only means for an equity investor to achieve limited liability in a creditworthy firm was through the limited partnership – a form that has ancient roots and that became available for business of all types, at least on the European continent, beginning in the 15th century. The limited partnership obtained credibility toward creditors by permitting limited liability only for those investors who exercised no control over the firm. The advantage of this rule was that the limited partners, while having an incentive to withdraw assets from the firm opportunistically, lacked power to do so. At the same time, the general partners, who did have the power to dissipate the firm's assets, had little incentive to do so if that would threaten the firm's solvency, as they would be personally liable for any shortfall.

In short, until the rise of the business corporation, an equity investor in a firm could enjoy control with unlimited liability, or limited liability without control, but not both control and limited liability. This last combination evidently was inconsistent with making a firm creditworthy.

2.1 Formalism and creditor protection

What permitted the business corporation to succeed in combining limited liability and control? A variety of factors were evidently important, including improved accounting, larger scale for enterprise, better bankruptcy procedures, and more robust securities markets. But the business corporation also dealt with the problem of creditworthiness by adopting a formal structure that constrained shareholder opportunism toward creditors. The early general corporation statutes in the United States were principally designed for large firms with numerous shareholders of roughly equal status in terms of earnings and control rights, and with strong delegation of operational authority to an elected board. Control structures that expanded the powers normally attendant upon stock ownership, such as partnership-like arrangements that permitted shareholders to exercise control over management directly, were prohibited.[3] As a consequence, the withdrawal of assets by owners was conspicuous and easy to monitor. Also, the interests of non-controlling shareholders were largely aligned with those of creditors, so that efforts by non-controlling shareholders to protect themselves from exploitation by control persons would also redound to the benefit of the firm's creditors. Legal capital requirements were imposed and given serious effect, as they could be in such large and formal structures.

Such rigid structures were not, however, well-suited to small or closely-held firms, which required customized allocations of earnings and control. Consequently, small firms generally continued to be organized in the partnership form, in which these attributes were not just easy to establish, but were in fact the default rules.

Beginning in the late 19th century, the restrictions on the corporate form began to be relaxed, making the form increasingly suitable for – and thus increasingly used by – small-scale enterprises of the type that previously would have become partnerships. At the same time, legal capital requirements became increasingly flexible. In part this liberalization

---

[3] See J.H. Chopper et al., *Cases and Materials on Corporations* (5th edn.) (New York, Aspen Publishers 2000) pp. 18-22, 712; L.M. Friedman, *A History of American Law* (2nd edn.) (New York, Touchstone 1985) pp. 511-25; G.D. Hornstein, 'Judicial Tolerance of the Incorporated Partnership', 18 *Law and Contemporary Problems* (1953) p. 435, at pp. 439-48.

occurred through the revision of the general business statutes and their judicial interpretation, and in part through the adoption of special close corporation statutes.[4]

What accounts for this liberalization? An important factor, we suggest, was increasing sophistication in financial contracting that permitted firm creditors to evaluate, monitor, and control more precisely the creditworthiness of the firms in which they invested. Improved accounting and disclosure, the adoption of federal bankruptcy law in 1898 and its subsequent evolution, the imposition of federal corporate income taxation in 1909 (which demanded clear and accurate accounting), the growth of credit rating agencies, greater financial literacy among businesspersons, and better communications, presumably all contributed to this development. It became possible to give both control and limited liability to the owners of small firms without rendering the firms uncreditworthy.

The new entity forms of the past thirty years represent a continuation of this process. Although such entities provide limited liability, they also permit the freedom of internal structure that was long available only in the general partnership. How much of an incremental change they constitute is, to be sure, debatable; by the time they arose, there was already great flexibility available in the close corporation. In fact, the new forms were at first motivated largely by tax considerations rather than by a desire for increased flexibility in business entities. Nevertheless, the new forms now offer at least some degree of flexibility that was previously unavailable in limited liability entities. Indeed, Delaware's business trust statute of 1988[5] arguably represents the logical culmination of this evolution: by eliminating all remaining ambiguity as to the availability of limited liability for the beneficiaries of private trusts,[6] it established a limited liability form that provides nearly complete freedom of contract as to control, allocation of earnings, and even fiduciary duties.

These developments have rendered the control rule of the limited partnership anachronistic, and with the availability of the LLP and the LLLP, that rule effectively has been abandoned.[7]

3. The continuing role of the partnership

These developments do not mean, however, that the partnership has been rendered obsolete. To the contrary, the partnership remains useful for situations where the firm's own assets might not constitute a credible bond and thus the firm's owners, whether they are individuals or other firms, must pledge all of their respective assets in support of the firm's obligations to make the firm creditworthy. In fact, the partnership's suitability to this role recently was enhanced. In 1715, the Anglo-American partnership was given a modest degree of limited liability. An English court of equity ruled that year that, if a partner and his

---

[4] See Chopper et al., *supra* n. 3, at p. 712.

[5] Del. Code Ann. tit. 12, §§ 3801–3862 (2001). For a thoughtful study of the development and character of the statutory business trust, see R. Sitkoff, 'Trust As Uncorporation: A Research Agenda', *University of Illinois Law Review* (2005) p. 31.

[6] H. Hansmann and U. Mattei, 'The Functions of Trust Law: A Comparative Legal and Economic Analysis', 73 *New York University Law Review* (1998) p. 434, at pp. 474–5.

[7] This is not to say that most limited partnership statutes do not retain this rule. See, e.g., Cal. Corp. Code § 15632 (St. Paul, West 1991 & Supp. 2005); N.Y. Partnership Law § 121–303 (New York, McKinney Supp. 2005). But practically speaking, if one wants to have limited liability and also exercise all the control powers typical of a partner, one can simply form one's business as an LLP, LLLP, or statutory business trust.

partnership were both bankrupt, the partner's personal creditors enjoyed a claim prior to that of the partnership creditors to the partner's personal assets.[8] That is, partnership creditors could levy upon a partner's personal assets only if the personal creditors had already been paid in full. This rule remained in effect in the United States until 1978, when it was abandoned in favor of the rule that had prevailed for thousands of years before 1715: partnership creditors share equally with a partner's personal creditors in the partner's personal assets.[9]

Why the reversion? The evident rationale is that the 1715 priority rule worked a compromise. Partnerships of the time were creditworthy without personal liability. At the same time, efficiency considerations suggested that firm creditors could monitor firm assets more cheaply than could personal creditors, who enjoyed a corresponding advantage with respect to personal assets. So partnership creditors were given (in 1682) priority in partnership assets,[10] but were then (in 1715) subordinated in their claim to personal assets. When, however, the corporate form with its full limited liability became a feasible means of organizing small firms, there was no longer a need for the compromise of 1715. The partnership form could be tailored to those who wanted to pledge their personal assets in full to their business ventures, and the corporate form could be employed by firms whose business creditors were willing to rely solely on business assets. Positions between these extremes could be achieved by mixing or modifying the forms, or by customized contracting between the firm and its creditors.

In short, the partnership continues to play its historical role as the business form that allows owners to pledge their personal assets to bond the firm's contracts, while corporate-type entities – including each of the new forms of the past thirty years – serve to bond the firm's contracts only with the firm's own assets. The important change over time – and it has been gradual rather than sudden – has been the emergence of various economic, technological, and legal factors that broaden the set of firms whose debts can be bonded with their own assets (i.e., that have limited liability).

This view of organizational evolution suggests a reason why European jurisdictions were far ahead of US jurisdictions in adopting highly flexible limited liability forms for small businesses. The German LLC form (the *GmbH*) appeared in the 1890s, while the French LLC form (the *SARL*) dates from the 1920s.[11] Both are highly contractual limited liability vehicles for closely-held businesses. Perhaps Germany and France were offered these flexible forms so long ahead of US jurisdictions because of the pro-creditor orientation of European law as contrasted with the pro-debtor orientation of US law. The traditionally strong European creditor-protection measures – such as mandatory disclosure of financial statements by closely-held companies, minimum capital requirements, and creditor-oriented bankruptcy rules[12] – may have been the precondition for increased contractual freedom among investors.

---

8 *Ex parte Crowder*, 21 Eng. Rep. 870 (Ch. 1715).

9 The change was a result of the Bankruptcy Act of 1978. See 11 U.S.C. § 723 (2000). It has also become a substantive rule of partnership law in those states adopting the Revised Uniform Partnership Act. See generally W. Allen and R. Kraakman, *Commentaries and Cases on the Law of Business Organization* (New York, Aspen Publishers2003) pp. 56-8. The 1715 rule remains in effect in England.

10 *Craven* v. *Knight*, 21 Eng. Rep. 664 (Ch. 1682–83).

11 See J. Treillard, 'The Close Corporation in French and Continental Law', 18 *Law and Contemporary Problems* (1953) p. 546, at pp. 553–4.

12 R. Kraakman et al., *The Anatomy of Corporate Law* (Oxford, Oxford University Press 2004) pp. 97–9.

4. Entity shielding

We have spoken so far as if limited liability were the principal feature that distinguishes the corporation from the partnership. An even more important distinction, however, lies in what we have elsewhere termed 'affirmative asset partitioning',[13] and what here we simply will call 'entity shielding'.[14] In a sense, entity shielding is the reverse of limited liability: while limited liability shields the assets of a firm's owners from the claims of the firm's creditors, entity shielding protects the assets of the firm from the claims of the owners' personal creditors. Entity shielding and limited liability are forms of asset partitioning in that they allocate claims to the assets of a firm and claims to the personal assets of the firm's owners to different groups of creditors.

Entity shielding, for our purposes here, comes in two forms. 'Weak' entity shielding is what one finds in the traditional partnership: firm creditors enjoy first claim, over the owners' personal creditors, to firm assets. This has the virtue of reducing monitoring costs for firm creditors by giving them, in effect, a security interest in firm assets. 'Strong' entity shielding, in turn, is what one finds in the business corporation. It adds to weak entity shielding a rule of liquidation protection, under which neither an owner nor his personal creditors may demand unilaterally a payout of the owner's share of firm assets. In effect, with strong entity shielding an owner and his personal creditors lose the withdrawal right that characterizes the traditional partnership at will. Strong entity shielding has the advantage of protecting a firm's going-concern value (or, as economists would put it, the value of firm-specific investments).

The corporation, then, is characterized by both strong entity shielding and limited liability, while the traditional partnership lacks limited liability and has been characterized by only weak entity shielding or (prior to the 17th century) none at all. This pattern of differentiation is not accidental. Strong entity shielding and limited liability are highly complementary; the presence of one generally calls for the other. The loss of the withdrawal right that constitutes strong entity shielding would render an owner's investment in the firm illiquid if the investment were not transferable. Transferability of shares, in turn, calls for limited liability.[15] Moreover, the loss of withdrawal rights removes an important source of protection for owners of minority shares against exploitation by control persons. Limited liability has the advantage of capping the losses that minority shareholders can suffer from such exploitation.

Conversely, limited liability generally requires strong entity shielding, largely because limited liability increases the incentive for owners to withdraw from the firm when its prospects are doubtful. That incentive, in turn, creates the threat of a run on the firm's assets, which would destroy going-concern value to the detriment of both the firm's creditors and its owners.[16] By denying owners the power to withdraw unilaterally, strong entity shielding prevents such runs.

---

[13] Hansmann and Kraakman, *supra* n. 1, at p. 393.

[14] This terminology, and the concepts of weak and strong entity shielding described immediately below, are taken from Hansmann, Kraakman and Squire, *supra* n. 2.

[15] See F.H. Easterbrook and D.R. Fischel, 'Limited Liability and the Corporation', 52 *University of Chicago Law Review* (1985) p. 89, at p. 92. In fact, unlimited liability is compatible with tradable shares so long as the liability is *pro rata* rather than joint and several. See H. Hansmann and R. Kraakman, 'Toward Unlimited Shareholder Liability for Corporate Torts', 100 *Yale Law Journal* (1991) p. 1879, at pp. 1903–04.

[16] Another important reason why limited liability requires strong entity shielding is that without it firm creditors would be exposed to excessive opportunism by the firm's owners.

We have argued above that limited liability requires accounting innovations and monitoring technology that permit creditors to rely on a firm's assets. But accounting and monitoring methods for small firms, until recently, were highly imperfect with the consequence that limited liability tended to be confined to large firms with a standardized and easy-to-monitor ownership structure. Improvements in the technology of financial monitoring have permitted the extension of limited liability to smaller and more closely-controlled firms.

A similar argument can be offered for strong entity shielding. As we have noted, the loss of withdrawal rights that characterizes strong entity shielding removes an important source of protection for owners of minority shares in a firm. When general incorporation statutes were first enacted in the 19th century, the rigid structure that these statutes imposed compensated for the loss of the withdrawal right by constraining control-person opportunism toward shareholders as well as toward creditors. Important in this respect were rules designed to prevent the de-coupling of control and income rights from shareholdings, such as prohibitions on shareholder voting agreements, rigid prohibitions on self-dealing transactions, and narrow interpretations of corporate purposes. Early corporate law also forbade restrictions on the free alienability of shares, thereby ensuring that shareholders who lacked withdrawal rights might have an alternate source of liquidity.

While such rigidity mitigated governance and liquidity problems associated with strong asset partitioning, it was, as we observed above, often incompatible with the needs of small, closely-held firms, in which flexibility in allocating control and income rights, and restrictions on alienation of shares, can be essential. The relaxation of this rigidity in corporate law over the intervening century suggests that sources of protection for non-controlling owners have arisen that are superior both to the withdrawal right and to formal restrictions on the allocation of earnings and control.

In part, these new sources of protection are the same as those that redounded to the benefit of firm creditors – developments that have made it easier for outsiders to monitor a firm's financial status and performance. Another source of protection, which appears particularly important for the viability of strong entity shielding, is increased sophistication on the part of courts in evaluating the behavior of corporate insiders. This has permitted courts to employ refined fiduciary duties in place of outright bans on particular ownership structures or transaction types. Increased sophistication in valuation techniques also reduces the need to rely upon liquidation of a firm to determine the value of an owner's share if he or his creditors need to be bought out.

The new forms of the past thirty years are the culmination of this process of extending strong entity shielding to less restricted entity types. Strong entity shielding in perpetuity is available in the LLC.[17] And recent statutory changes make clear that owners may opt for

---

[17] In the Uniform Limited Liability Company Act of 1996 (ULLCA), the default regime for member withdrawal is the same as under the Revised Uniform Partnership Act: a member may withdraw, rightfully or wrongfully, at any time; if the company is at will he must be bought out immediately, but if the company is for a term then buyout need not occur until the term's expiration. Unif. Ltd. Liab. Co. Act §§ 602(a), 701(a), 6A U.L.A. 610, 614 (2003). ULLCA expressly provides, however, that most of its rules may be altered in the company's operating agreement, including those respecting a member's withdrawal voluntarily or due to his bankruptcy. Id. §§ 103, 601(1),(7), at 567–68, 608–09. Moreover, ULLCA explicitly provides that the rules for determining whether a member's withdrawal is wrongful apply only '[i]f the operating agreement has not eliminated a member's power to dissociate.' Id. § 602(b), at 610. Members of an LLC thus may contract for strong-form entity shielding and full liquidation protection in perpetuity with respect to themselves and their personal creditors. The only exception is that companies must retain procedures for dissolution or the expulsion of members upon a judicial finding of persistent misconduct or that the purpose of the company has been frustrated. Id. § 103 (5), (6), at 568.

strong entity shielding for a defined period in even the partnership by forming a partnership for a term or specific undertaking.[18] Such strong entity shielding in the partnership can be combined with limited liability through the LLP or LLLP. Finally, strong entity shielding is the default rule in the statutory business trust, with its unrestricted liberty of structure.[19]

Meanwhile, the traditional partnership still plays a role with respect to entity shielding as it does with respect to limited liability. With only weak rather than strong entity shielding, the traditional partnership-at-will continues to provide a convenient entity form for owners who wish to retain a right of unilateral withdrawal as a governing device or source of liquidity.

5. How many new forms?

In short, the new statutory forms for commercial enterprise – the LLC, the LLP, the LLLP, and the business trust – are best seen as generalizations of the business corporation. They combine the pattern of asset partitioning provided by the traditional corporation – strong entity shielding and full limited liability – with the greater flexibility in internal structure that the corporate form has evolved to offer. Meanwhile, the general partnership continues to provide a very different pattern of asset partitioning – weak entity shielding and unlimited personal liability – for those firms that require it.

How many different corporate-type forms are required for the sake of efficiency, and how these forms are best structured, are questions that remain subject to debate and experimentation. In theory, any entity that can be formed as a business corporation, an LLC, an LLP, or an LLLP could be fashioned instead as a statutory business trust, simply by specifying the necessary structure in the trust's governing instrument. If the more restricted forms continue to serve a purpose, it is perhaps that they permit types of signaling and bonding that the business trust cannot provide. Alternatively, the various alternative forms may have the virtue of offering specialized sets of default rules that are suitable to different types of firms and that, if put instead in a firm's governing instrument, might prove either too flexible or too rigid.[20] Unfortunately, we do not understand these functions of legal forms well enough to reach a consensus on their appropriate number and structure.[21] Not surprisingly, then, the new entity forms have been protean, and we can expect further sorting among them.

---

[18] See Unif. P'ship Act §§ 701(h), 801(2) (1997), 6 U.L.A. (pt. I) 189 (2001).

[19] See Del. Code Ann. tit. 12, § 3808(a)–(b) (1999 & Supp. 2004).

[20] See H. Hansmann, 'Corporation and Contract' 8 *American Law and Economics* Review (2006) p. 1.

[21] This is not to say that the new forms have not been the subject of thoughtful analysis. Their emergence has elicited insightful commentary by, in particular, Larry Ribstein, whose extensive writings on these forms provide our most substantial source of wisdom concerning them. See, *e.g.*, L. Ribstein, 'Why Corporations?', 1 *Berkeley Business Law Journal* (2004) p. 183.

Chapter 2

THE EVOLVING PARTNERSHIP

Larry E. Ribstein*

1. Introduction

The partnership form has rapidly evolved in the United States, particularly in recent years, as a result of competition between jurisdictions and among business forms. This provides an important lesson for Europe in the wake of *Centros.*[1] This chapter shows that competition creates a dynamic law that is responsive to the varied needs of modern firms. This is preferable to uniform law-making, which erroneously assumes that lawmakers can anticipate what optimal rules should be over time and across different firms.

The recent *Centros* decision raises important questions about the future of European law, particularly the law of business organizations. By characterizing a corporation as eligible for the privileges and immunities of a full-fledged citizen of its state of origin, including the right to establish a branch in a country outside its origin that is subject to home-state law,[2] *Centros* sets the stage for increased jurisdictional competition for European business law. Although *Centros* does not eliminate the rule that the law of the country in which a firm has its *real seat* or main office governs its internal affairs,[3] it invites erosion of this doctrine by giving some firms a way to avoid its effect.

---

* Mildred van Voorhees Chair in Law, University of Illinois College of Law. Versions of this paper were presented at the International Conference on Close Corporation and Partnership Law Reform in Europe and the United States, Tilburg University, May 17-18, 2001, Conference on Reform of Private Company Law, June 27, 2006, The Hague, Netherlands. An earlier version was published in 26 *Journal of Corporation Law* (2001) p. 819. The chapter has been updated to reflect current developments.

[1] Case C-212/97, *Centros Ltd.* v. *Erhvervs-og Selskabsstyrelsen*, 1999 *ECR* I-1459 (1999), 2 *CMLR* 551 (1999). See also, Case C-167/01, *Kamer van Koophandel en Fabrieken voor Amsterdam* v. *Inspire Art Ltd.*, September 30, 2003), 2003 *ECR* 2 (2003) (holding that the right of establishment in Article 48 barred the Netherlands from imposing local regulations on a company that was based locally but incorporated elsewhere solely in order to avoid these regulations); Case C-208/00, *Überseering BV* v. *Nordic Construction Company Baumanagement GmbH (NCC)* 2002 *ECR* I-9919 (2002) (denying a Dutch corporation the right to sue in Germany pursuant to the real seat rule was contrary to the right of establishment).

[2] See ibid.

[3] For discussions of the implications of *Centros*, see W.F. Ebke, '*Centros* – Some Realities And Some Mysteries', 48 *American Journal of Comparative Law* (2000) p. 623; E. Wymeersch, '*Centros*: A Landmark Decision in European Company Law', in *Festschrift für R.M. Buxbaum* (Th. Baums ed., 2000); R.J. Gilson, 'Globalizing Corporate Governance: Convergence of Form or Function' (Stanford Law and Economics Working Paper No. 192, Columbia Law and Economics Working Paper No. 174), available at <http://papers.ssrn.com/sol3/papers.cfm?abstract_id=229517>.

J.A. McCahery, L. Timmerman and E.P.M. Vermeulen (eds.), Private Company Law Reform

Centros might spur regulators either to more aggressive efforts to harmonize European business law,[4] or to embrace jurisdictional competition for business law. This chapter advocates the latter approach. Focusing on US partnership law, which has developed recently in a setting of open competition among the fifty-one US jurisdictions, this chapter demonstrates that jurisdictional competition is preferable to a regime in which firms must comply with the rules of all states in which they do business, or in which a single law-making body provides all the rules.

Until recently, partnership law was uniform across US jurisdictions, all but one of which had adopted the 1914 Uniform Partnership Act almost verbatim. During this stable era of partnership law, the partnership form was characterized by decentralized management directly by the owners, personal liability of members, and dissolution upon dissociation of a member. These features kept partnerships closely held, predominantly family affairs.

But partnership has always contained within it powerful seeds for change. Partnerships have been governed mostly by contract, unlike corporations, which are constrained by the concept of *state creation*. These seeds have now germinated. The stable era of partnership ended in the United States around 1988 and was replaced by a period of rapid development and change. Partnership law itself is now non-uniform across US jurisdictions. More importantly, the partnership form itself has split into sub-forms, including the limited liability company (LLC) and the limited liability partnership (LLP), that provide a continuous spectrum of forms.

This recent history in the United States holds important lessons for Europe as it embarks on partnership law reform. A single set of business association rules issued by a central planner cannot meet the needs of various types of firms or respond to firms' changing business needs. Central planning is hostage both to inherent limits on human knowledge and foresight and to interest group politics. Rather, firms should be able to pick suitable rules by making both *horizontal* choices among the various jurisdictions and *vertical* choices among business forms available within jurisdictions. Moreover, more efficient rules can emerge from jurisdictional competition for business formations, and from an evolutionary process in which more efficient forms become more prevalent and less efficient forms fall into disuse.[5] The primary engine of efficiency is the parties' ability to contract for the applicable law, including selection of a firm's internal governance rules through choice of the state of organization.[6] There is significant evidence that permitting horizontal and vertical choice of business forms produces efficient outcomes.[7] In particular, the recent, rapid changes in partnership and related business forms in the United States, discussed above, provide a kind of laboratory in which to test the efficiency of various regulatory approaches. New and more efficient legal structures have evolved that regulators could not have envisioned only a few years ago. Moreover, the *lock-in* effects that some theoreticians imagined have not impeded the evolution of business forms. Instead of being locked in, inefficient old forms have been swept away. This is the world that *Centros* potentially opens to Europe.

---

[4] This is the approach recommended by Ebke, *supra* n. 3.

[5] See *infra* text accompanying nn. 78-82; L.E. Ribstein and B.H. Kobayashi, 'Economic Analysis of Uniform State Laws', 25 *Journal of Legal Studies* (1996) p. 131, at pp. 149-150.

[6] See E.A. O'Hara and L.E. Ribstein, 'From Politics to Efficiency in Choice of Law', 67 *University of Chicago Law Review* (2000) p. 1151, at pp. 1152-53; L.E. Ribstein, 'Choosing Law by Contract', 18 *Journal of Corporation Law* (1993) p. 245.

[7] See *infra* Section 3.3.5.

This chapter proceeds as follows. Section 2 broadly describes partnerships, contrasting the traditional and new varieties and contrasting the partnership form with the corporate form. Section 3 discusses the forces that have shaped partnership in the United States, primarily firms' ability to engage in horizontal choice among jurisdictions and vertical choice among business forms. Section 4 discusses the evolution in partnership terms wrought by these competitive forces. This process suggests that optimal partnership rules defy top-down theorizing and planning. Section 5 presents some implications of the analysis, particularly for present and future European law. Section 6 presents concluding remarks.

2. The nature of partnership

This section broadly describes the subject of this chapter.[8] Section 2.1 shows that the partnership form, though mutable, is essentially defined by its contrast with the corporate form. Section 2.2 and 2.3 describe the beginning and ending points of the evolutionary process discussed below in Section 2, while Section 3 provides more detailed descriptions of specific partnership issues.

2.1 Partnership v. corporation

The partnership is fundamentally a contractual entity. Courts and commentators often describe partnership as proceeding from contract,[9] and as arising from the intent of the purported partners.[10] In contrast, the corporation is often described as a state-created legal 'person'.[11] The most famous expression of that view is in *Trustees of Dartmouth College* v. *Woodward*,[12] which characterized a British crown charter granted to Dartmouth College as 'a contract, on the faith of which, real and personal estate has been conveyed to the corporation'[13] and thus entitled to protection under the contract clause of the US Constitution.[14] Constitutional protection came as part of a Faustian deal by which the firm recognized the state (in this case, the Crown) as its creator. According to Chief Justice Marshall, the corporation was a 'mere creature of law',[15] suggesting that it had rights that private contract could not create. This characterization reflects entrepreneurs' early practice of obtaining special state charters that granted permission to incorporate. However, special chartering was replaced long ago by general incorporation, in which the state's only involvement in creating the corporation is accepting the articles of incorporation for filing.[16]

---

8 For another general description, see L.E. Ribstein, 'Partnership', in P. Newman (ed.) *New Palgrave Dictionary of Economics and the Law* (Hampshire, Palgrave Macmillan 1998) vol. 3, at pp. 10-13.

9 See, e.g., *Bradley* v. *Bradley*, 554 N.W.2d 761, 765 (Minn. Ct. App. 1996); A.R. Bromberg and L.E. Ribstein, *Bromberg and Ribstein on Partnership* (Denver, Aspen Publishing 1988 and Supp. 2001) § 2.05(d).

10 See Bromberg and Ribstein, *supra* n. 9, at § 2.05(a); *H.T. Hackney Co.* v. *Robert E. Lee Hotel*, 300 S.W. 1, 2 (Tenn. 1927) ('A partnership can only arise by a voluntary contract of the parties').

11 See L.E. Ribstein, 'The Constitutional Conception of the Corporation', 4 *Supreme Court Economic Review* (1995) p. 95 (discussing various constitutional implications of the entity view).

12 17 U.S. (4 Wheat.) 518 (1819).

13 Ibid., at p. 644.

14 US Const. Art. I, § 10, cl. 1.

15 *Trs. of Dartmouth Coll.*, 17 U.S. at 627.

16 For a discussion of the evolution of American corporate law from special to general incorporation, see H.N. Butler, 'Nineteenth Century Jurisdictional Competition in the Granting of Corporate Privileges', 14 *Journal of Legal Studies* (1985) p. 129.

Although the advent of general incorporation reinforced the view of the corporation as a contract among the parties to the firm, vestiges of the corporate person theory survive through shareholders' limited liability for torts and the special corporate choice of law rules. With respect to tort liability, it might seem that, because the firm's owners cannot insulate themselves from tort creditors solely by contracting among themselves, limited liability is a state privilege, and the firm is to some extent a creation of the state rather than of private contract. This is inaccurate because limited liability is simply a feature of a particular type of contract.[17] More importantly, limited liability provided an excuse for distinguishing corporations from other types of contracts that did not apply to partnerships. Similarly, the corporate person theory supports the *internal affairs* choice of law rule that applies the law of the incorporating state to certain legal issues. Without this rule, corporations would be subject to the vagaries of enforcement of contractual choice of law. By contrast, a state-created corporate entity, like any other state citizen, is subject to the protection of the creating state. Again, the apparent distinction between corporations and other contracts, though illusory,[18] shaped the different legal treatment of corporations and partnerships. In short, incorporated firms exchanged their autonomy as contractual entities for favors accorded state-created entities. This gave states a reason to apply special restrictions to corporate contracting that they would not apply to ordinary contracts.

Partnerships, by contrast, never made this Faustian deal. Traditionally, partners are vicariously liable for debts of the firm. Moreover, while they can select the law of a particular state to govern their contract (and in the United States courts normally enforce these clauses),[19] enforcement is not as invariable as the application of the incorporation state's law under the US internal affairs rule.

Distinctions between partnerships and corporations seem to be diminishing. Partnership-type businesses, such as LLCs and LLPs, have limited liability based on state filings and are subject to corporate-type internal affairs rules.[20] There is an increasing trend toward recognition of partnerships as entities.[21] However, the entity characterization is simply a way to summarize the effect of partnership law for various (although not necessarily

[17] See Ribstein, *supra* n. 11, at pp. 101-03. By the same token, limited liability is a feature of a creditor's contract with the firm *vis-à-vis* other creditors. The fact that a state filing is a prerequisite to enforcing limited liability does not make the term non-contractual, anymore than does the filing requirement for secured credit. Nor does the fact that limited tort liability may create an externality, which is true of other types of contracts, or that it is infeasible to opt into or out of this rule by private contract, which reflects Coase's insight that legal rules matter in the presence of transaction costs. See R.H. Coase, 'The Problem of Social Cost', 3 *Journal of Law and Economics* (1960) p. 1. Whether or not limited liability involves a special type of contracting problem which justifies special regulation, as argued in J. Armour and M.J. Whincop, 'An Economic Analysis of Shared Property in Partnership and Close Corporation Law', 26 *Journal of Corporation Law* (2001) p. 101, the main point in the text is that regulation cannot properly be justified simply by designating the relationship as 'non-contractual.'

[18] See Ribstein, *supra* n. 6 (comparing enforcement of contractual choice of law for corporations and for other types of contracts).

[19] See generally Bromberg and Ribstein, *supra* n. 9, at § 1.04.

[20] See generally A.R. Bromberg and L.E. Ribstein, Bromberg and Ribstein on Limited Liability Partnerships and the Revised Uniform Partnership Act (Denver, Aspen Publishing 2001) ch. 6; L.E. Ribstein and R.A. Keatinge, Ribstein and Keatinge on Limited Liability Companies (Colorado Springs, Shepards/McGraw-Hill 1992 and Supp. 2001) ch. 13.

[21] See, e.g., Rev. Unif. P'Ship Act § 201 (amended 1997), 6 U.L.A. 55 (Supp. 2001).

all) purposes, and does not change the fundamental nature of partnership.[22] Partnerships remain contractual despite these corporate trappings.[23]

2.2 The traditional partnership

Although partnerships have remained true to their basically contractual nature, the specific rules of partnership have changed significantly. That change and its explanations are the focus of this chapter. The basic model of the partnership set forth in the Uniform Partnership Act (UPA) is for a very closely held and informal firm. Each partner has, by default, an equal power to control the business and to share in profits, irrespective of his capital investment.[24] Thus, each partner is both a co-principal and an agent in a principal-agent relationship. As an agent, a partner can bind the business to acts within the scope of the agency[25] while, as a principal, a partner is personally liable for the acts of the firm's other partners and employees.[26] It follows from their role as co-principals that each partner can veto important acts, such as amending the partnership agreement and admitting new partners.[27] It follows, in turn, from these significant management powers and partner liability that partners cannot freely transfer all of their partnership rights.[28] Instead, they exit by cashing out of or liquidating the firm, in either case through at least a technical dissolution.[29]

2.3 The new partnership

Many of these basic default rules have carried over into modern US law, including the Revised Uniform Partnership Act of 1994 (RUPA), but with some important modifications. Partners now can limit the agency power of non-managing members, at least in real estate transactions.[30] The partners' personal liability for the debts of the firm has been qualified by requiring creditors to first exhaust partnership assets, even in tort cases.[31] Exit provisions have been significantly revised to eliminate the absolute requirement of dissolution upon partner dissociation.[32]

Even more important than these changes in general partnership law, the partnership form has splintered into other forms. This, in effect, reserves general partnerships only for the most informal relationships. LLCs, while having many partnership characteristics, have

---

[22] For a discussion of the many cases applying both entity and aggregate characteristics of partnership, see Bromberg and Ribstein, *supra* n. 9, at § 1.03. It is not clear the extent to which section 201 of the Revised Uniform Partnership Act (RUPA) will change the results in these cases. For a criticism of the RUPA provision on this basis, see Bromberg and Ribstein, *supra* n. 20, at § 8.201.

[23] See generally L.E. Ribstein, 'Fiduciary Duty Contracts In Unincorporated Firms', 54 *Washington and Lee Law Review* (1997) p. 537.

[24] See Unif. P'ship Act § 18(a), (e) (1914), 6 U.L.A. 526 (1995).

[25] Id. §§ 9-14, 6 U.L.A. 400-454 (1995).

[26] Id. § 15, 6 U.L.A. 456 (1995).

[27] Id. § 18(g)-(h), 6 U.L.A. 526 (1995).

[28] Id. § 27, 6 U.L.A. 736 (1995).

[29] Unif. P'ship Act §§ 29-31, 38 (1914), 6 U.L.A. 752-71, 880 (1995).

[30] See Rev. Unif. P'ship Act § 303 (amended 1997), 6 U.L.A. 63-64 (Supp. 2001).

[31] See ibid., at § 307, 6 U.L.A. 73-74 (Supp. 2001); *infra* Section 4.1.1.

[32] See Rev. Unif. P'Ship Act. § 103 (amended 1997), 6 U.L.A. 44-45 (Supp. 2001) (permitting partnership agreement to waive provisions of act except for those listed); id. § 801, 6 U.L.A. 108-09 (Supp. 2001) (providing for continuation of the firm in certain situations); *infra* Section 4.6.

the corporate features of limited liability, an option for centralized management, and even – under many statutes – restrictions on dissociation of members.[33] LLPs are essentially general partnerships with limited liability. This allows firms to eliminate vicarious liability while retaining the general partnership form, which may be advantageous in complying with regulations and facilitating the transition from general partnership. As discussed below, these changes resulted from jurisdictional competition in the US federal system and have made the partnership form more adaptable to business needs.

3. COMPETITION AND CHANGE

This section discusses the principal force that produced the changes discussed above – jurisdictional competition within the US federal system. As previously discussed, other forces also played a role in the change, including contractual avoidance and external shocks such as tax law changes.[34] This chapter emphasizes jurisdictional competition in order to focus on the potential effects of the *Centros* case. Sections 3.1 and 3.2 distinguish two forces of jurisdictional competition: *Horizontal* choice among jurisdictions, and *vertical* choice among the various business forms available in each jurisdiction. Section 3.3 discusses the effects of competition, particularly eroding formerly mandatory state and federal rules. These limits on firms' ability to avoid mandatory rules indicate that jurisdictional competition constrains regulation without eliminating government's power to regulate efficiently.

Before beginning this analysis, it is important to note the significant difference between horizontal and vertical choice discussed here and an alternative menu-type approach to business association statutes that offers firms choices with respect to each of several issues. Although jurisdictions might compete to provide different menus, menu options, in themselves, are not comparable to horizontal choice because a single rulemaker determines the options. Nor are menus comparable to vertical choice, because menu options arise in a single business form rather than offering choices among distinct business forms. This issue relates to the costs and benefits of linkage, discussed below.[35]

3.1 Horizontal choice

Horizontal choice arises in the United States because firms can choose the rules that govern their internal structure at low cost by organizing under the rules of any *incorporation* state while doing business or locating assets in one or more *host* states. Thus, horizontal choice arises by contract alone, unconstrained by the firm's location. Firms' ability to contract for any state's internal rules prevents states from imposing strong and costly regulation on firms' internal structures. While this rule initially applied mainly to corporations, more recently it has spread to unincorporated firms such as the LLC and LLP, which permit corporate-type choice through filings in the state of organization.[36] Until recently, general partnerships had less flexibility because they were subject to general choice of law rules

---

[33] See generally Ribstein and Keatinge, *supra* n. 20, at ch. 8, at pp. 11-12.

[34] See L.E. Ribstein, 'Politics, Adaptation and Change in Corporate Law', 8 *Australian Journal of Corporate Law* (1998) p. 244.

[35] See *infra* Section 4.8.

[36] See *supra* n. 20 and accompanying text.

and because the UPA had been adopted in fifty of the fifty-one US jurisdictions. However, general partnership moved closer to other business associations with the promulgation of RUPA in 1994 by the National Conference of Commissioners on Uniform State Laws (NCCUSL), and the spread of LLP provisions. RUPA introduced to US partnership law both non-uniformity and explicit recognition of contractual choice of law.[37] LLP provisions, which have been adopted in every state and were added to RUPA in 1997, accelerated these changes by permitting general partnerships to select governing state law through corporate-type filings.[38]

Because this chapter seeks to offer lessons from the United States for Europe, it would be useful to briefly describe the conditions that create jurisdictional choice. To begin with, it has been thought that constitutional protection under the Commerce Clause and Privileges and Immunities Clause of the US Constitution enabled interstate competition for corporate governance.[39] But the Constitution has played a smaller role in facilitating this competition than these commentators suppose. Because corporations are *artificial* persons, they are not protected by the Privileges and Immunities Clause.[40] Thus, their ability to do business outside their states of incorporation under the formation state's rules, including rules regarding limited liability, depends solely on comity between host and incorporation states rather than the Constitution.[41] Nor does the Dormant Commerce Clause[42] of the US Constitution support horizontal choice. Although the clause theoretically might be interpreted to compel a state to enforce a firm's internal rules in order to permit it to do business in several states, in fact states can protect local creditors and shareholders and other internal interests as long as they do not discriminate against foreign corporations.[43] Finally, the Full Faith and Credit Clause of the US Constitution[44] does not in itself require states to give full effect to other states' laws, as distinguished from judicial decrees or other state acts.

More critical to horizontal competition in the United States are the constitutional rules and cultural and institutional factors that provide an environment conducive to interstate competition.[45] The Commerce Clause at least forbids states from imposing trade barriers against out of state firms by discriminating against them merely because they are not incorporated locally. More importantly, firms are subject to constitutional protections such as

---

[37] See Rev. Unif. P'ship Act §§ 103, 106 (amended 1997), 6 U.L.A. 44, 53 (Supp. 2001) (providing that governing law under section 106 is subject to contractual variation under section 103).

[38] See ibid., at § 103(b)(9), 106(b) (amended 1997), 6 U.L.A. 45, 53 (Supp. 2001) (providing that any such filing supersedes any contradictory choice of law selected in the agreement).

[39] See Butler, *supra* n. 16.

[40] See *Paul* v. *Virginia*, 75 U.S. (8 Wall.) 168, 181 (1869) (stating corporations are 'mere creation of local law' and therefore have no constitutional right under the Privileges and Immunities Clause to do business outside their states of incorporation).

[41] Ibid. By contrast, the European constitution applied in *Centros* characterizes a corporation as eligible for the privileges and immunities of a full-fledged citizen of its state of origin. See Case C-212/97, *Centros Ltd.* v. *Erhvervs-og Selskabsstyrelsen*, 1999 *ECR* I-1459 (1999), 2 *CMLR* 551 (1999).

[42] US Const. Art. I, § 8, cl. 3 (providing that Congress has the power '[t]o regulate Commerce … among the several States').

[43] See Ribstein, *supra* n. 6, at pp. 287-94.

[44] US Const. Art. IV, § 1 ('Full Faith and Credit shall be given in each State to the public Acts, Records, and judicial Proceedings of every other State. And the Congress may by general Laws prescribe the Manner in which such Acts, Records and Proceedings shall be proved, and the Effect thereof').

[45] See B.H. Kobayashi and L.E. Ribstein, 'Contract and Jurisdictional Freedom', in F.H. Buckley (ed.) *The Fall and Rise of Freedom of Contract* (Durham, Duke University Press 1999) p. 325.

due process wherever they do business in the United States. Apart from the Constitution, firms can do business in every state under the same basic legal institutions and language. Thus, firms' mobility is not inhibited by significant variations in the business environment among the states.

The ability to conduct interstate business, in turn, gives host states incentives to recognize incorporation state rules. Interest groups in each state stand to gain or lose in the resulting interstate competition. Accordingly, they push for rules that make their jurisdictions inviting to, or at least do not repel, interstate firms.[46] In particular, lawyers gain from promoting the use of the state's courts and of their own expertise as business planners.[47] State legislators may therefore stand to gain more from welcoming interstate firms and offering them friendly terms than by appeasing groups that would gain from the application of local law.

A Europe governed by a strong application of the *Centros* decision is both more and less conducive to jurisdictional competition than the United States. It is more conducive in the sense that it offers constitutional protection for foreign incorporation.[48] On the other hand, it is less conducive because the basic structures, such as common language and institutions, make it harder for multi-jurisdictional firms to operate in Europe than in the United States. This difference makes constitutional protection of foreign incorporation even more important in Europe than in the United States. Moreover, as discussed below in Section 5, this difference ultimately may prevent US-style jurisdictional competition from arising in Europe and may necessitate changes in how the competition model should be applied in this context.

3.2 Vertical choice: choice of form

Firms can choose rules not only from among states, but also from among a variety of business forms within each state. A multiplicity of statutory forms provides different sets of default rules for different types of firms, which are valuable where the costs of customized contracting are high.[49] Among other things, these rules serve to form the basis of interpretive networks of cases and forms.[50] Although private organizations can generate forms, statutory promulgation is often helpful in generating networks and in providing enforcement mechanisms.[51]

Multiple business forms are beneficial because they offer alternative coherent bundles of rules for different types of firms.[52] The traditional partnership form, discussed above,

---

[46] See ibid.

[47] See L.E. Ribstein, 'Lawyers as Lawmakers: A Theory of Lawyer Licensing', 69 *Missouri Law Review* (2004) p. 299; L.E. Ribstein, 'Delaware, Lawyers and Contractual Choice of Law', 19 *Delaware Journal of Corporate Law* (1994) p. 999, reprinted in 37 *Corporate Practice Commentator* (1995) p. 151. See also J.R. Macey and G.P. Miller, 'Toward an Interest-Group Theory of Delaware Corporate Law', 65 *Texas Law Review* (1987) p. 469 (discussing the role of lawyers in corporate context).

[48] See *supra* n. 41 and accompanying text.

[49] See L.E. Ribstein, 'Statutory Forms for Closely-held Firms: Theories and Evidence from LLCs', 73 *Washington University Law Quarterly* (1995) p 369, at pp. 380-83.

[50] See M. Klausner, 'Corporations, Corporate Law, and Networks of Contracts', 81 *Virginia Law Review* (1995) p. 757; Ribstein, *supra* n. 49, at 378.

[51] See ibid., at pp. 378-80.

[52] See ibid., at pp. 380-83.

offers one such bundle in the sense that strong co-management and at-will dissolution naturally complement partners' personal liability.

Even more importantly, multiple forms within each state provide an additional dimension of regulatory competition that can break down inefficient mandatory rules. Multiple forms offer opportunities for regulatory arbitrage.[53] Consider, for example, the role of multiple business forms in facilitating moves from mandatory fiduciary duties to enforcement of fiduciary waivers or from vicarious partnership liability to limited liability. Legislators may resist such moves either because of opposition from strong interest groups such as trial lawyers, or because of genuine policy concerns about the costs of permitting free bargaining. But permitting the move in one of several standard forms may not trigger the same level of opposition because the new rule will apply only to firms that are willing to incur the switching and other costs of adopting liberal business forms[54] thereby limiting the number of firms likely to seek the benefits of the rule. In this way, partnership-type business forms can be used as proving grounds to test increased flexibility in internal governance rules.[55]

3.3 **Effects of choice**

This section discusses the effects of horizontal and vertical choice in eroding mandatory rules and contributing to the evolution of the partnership form. Sections 3.3.1 and 3.3.2 discuss the erosion of state and federal rules. Section 3.3.3 discusses the advantages of offering different forms for different types of firms. Section 3.3.4 shows that choice does not necessarily lead to chaos, but instead may lead to convergence on uniform rules where efficient. Finally, Section 3.3.5 shows evidence of the effectiveness of choice of law and choice of form, notwithstanding the *lock-in* effect some commentators have feared.

3.3.1 *Erosion of state restrictions*

There have been two eras in which horizontal competition among states and vertical competition among forms eroded traditional restrictions on the internal structure of business associations. Innovations spread from single states and business forms, leading to a gradual process of nationwide recognition. These developments demonstrated the power of horizontal and vertical competition in breaking down state-imposed barriers to contractual freedom.

In the first era, competition broke down the practice of special chartering involving state legislators' sale of charters to individual firms.[56] Beginning with New Jersey and Delaware, states passed general incorporation statutes, and other states gradually recognized the firms formed under these statutes.

---

[53] See P.H. Huang and M.S. Knoll, 'Corporate Finance, Corporate Law and Finance Theory', 74 *Southern California Law Review* (2000) p. 175, at p. 190 (discussing regulatory arbitrage as a respect in which capital structure may add value to the firm).

[54] See *infra* Section 3.3.5.

[55] See J.A. McCahery and E.P.M. Vermeulen, 'The Evolution of Closely Held Business Forms in Europe', 26 *Journal of Corporation Law* (2001) p. 857 (discussing the possibility of regulatory arbitrage in Europe through the introduction of a new LLC business form).

[56] See *supra* n. 16 and accompanying text.

The second era is the recent history of the partnership form. Even after the spread of general incorporation, closely held firms that wanted limited liability had to be satisfied with unaccommodating corporate default and mandatory rules. For example, centralized management through a board of directors, restricted transferability of ownership interests, voting according to ownership interests, and continuation of the firm following a member's exit are all provisions unsuited to closely held firms. Corporations' contracts for partnership-type governance rules were sometimes strictly interpreted or simply not enforced.[57] While states adopted statutory and judicial rules for *incorporated partnerships*, firms that adopted such forms remained exposed to the default rules of the chosen corporate form beyond the specific partnership-type provisions they agreed to.

The logical response to this situation was giving firms the option to adopt partnership-type business forms that included limited liability. But US tax law reduced the benefits of adopting limited liability partnership-type forms by essentially applying two-tier corporate taxation to such firms. The next section discusses the change in federal tax law that accommodated the development of partnerships with limited liability. That change unleashed state competition regarding partnership-type limited liability forms. The LLC spread rapidly from two states in 1988 to all fifty-one jurisdictions only six years later. As LLCs evolved, they became more flexible and better adapted to closely held firms' needs.[58]

These new forms not only brought new flexibility in themselves, but also helped loosen the rules of existing forms. States developed LLPs and changed the older limited partnership form. Moreover, the greater contractual freedom permitted in the partnership form appears to be spreading back to the traditionally more constrained corporate form. Some states, particularly Delaware, recognized the contractual nature of partnership by passing statutes that explicitly provided for enforcement of broad fiduciary duty waivers.[59] This provided a precedent for dropping restrictions on corporate waivers.[60]

3.3.2 *Erosion of federal rules*

A federal system subordinates state law to federal law in some respects. This would seem to significantly constrain state competition.[61] However, it is important to keep in mind that state law often defines the terms and the contexts in which federal law operates. Thus, changing state rules can reduce the impact of federal constraints.

A good example of this process concerns federal tax constraints on state business forms. Federal tax law once restricted the availability of limited liability by using this feature as an important part of the test for determining whether a firm was subject to corporate tax treat-

---

[57] See generally L.E. Ribstein and P.V. Letsou, *Business Associations*, 4th edn. (New York, Matthew Bender 2003) ch. 5.

[58] See *infra* Section 4.

[59] The first such statute was appended to Delaware's limited partnership statute. See Del. Code Ann. tit. 6, § 17-1101(c)-(d) (1999).

[60] See L.E. Ribstein, 'Unlimited Contracting in the Delaware Limited Partnership and its Implications for Corporate Law', 16 *Journal of Corporation Law* (1991) p. 299. Indeed, one possible result is Delaware's recent authorization of charter provisions permitting contracting with regard to corporate opportunities, similar to provisions in LLC and partnership statutes. See Del. Code Ann. tit. 8, § 122(17) (1999).

[61] The constraint is not necessarily inefficient. In some situations federal law might provide a vertical dimension of jurisdictional competition that disciplines inefficient state law. See A. Breton and P. Salmon, 'External Effects of Domestic Regulations: Comparing Internal and International Barriers to Trade', 21 *International Review of Law and Economics* (2001) p. 135.

ment.[62] Although the Internal Revenue Service (IRS) nominally applied a four-factor test that required at least two corporate characteristics in addition to limited liability to hold that a firm was a *tax corporation*, it had signaled that limited liability alone could cause a firm to be considered a corporation by initially proposing that the first LLCs be taxed as corporations.[63]

While the IRS was pondering LLCs, state legislatures and businesses were changing the limited partnership form.[64] Businesses formed limited partnerships with corporate general partners, thereby giving firms virtually complete limited liability. Also, state legislatures eroded the 'control rule' pursuant to which limited partners who participated in control took on the personal liability of general partners. This forced the IRS to make increasingly fine distinctions in order to maintain the tax distinction between corporations and partnerships. The IRS also had to choose between greatly broadening the corporate tax and making official what the changes in the limited partnership form now implied. In 1988, the IRS chose to classify a Wyoming LLC as a partnership for tax purposes.[65] This led to the rapid development and spread of LLC statutes[66] and the development of the LLP.[67]

3.3.3 *Variation and adaptability*

Increased choice of form not only eroded federal and state restrictions on form, but also allowed firms to customize their contracts to suit their individual needs. As discussed in more detail below, the currently available range of business forms suits firm-specific preferences in such respects as degree of formality and centralization of management. State laws offering several different sets of default rules allow a firm to adopt a set of rules that

[62] For a discussion of the policy arguments for basing tax classification on limited liability and a history of the erosion of this approach, see J.A. Maine, 'Linking Limited Liability and Entity Taxation: A Critique of the ALI Reporters' Study on the Taxation of Private Business Enterprises', 62 *University of Pittsburgh Law Review* (2000) p. 223. Maine notes that the IRS ultimately accepted a broader-based entity approach to classification that led to reduction and eventual elimination of a limited liability test, but does not explain why this occurred. For arguments against this approach to tax classification, see L.E. Ribstein, 'The Deregulation of Limited Liability and the Death of Partnership', 70 *Washington University Law Quarterly* (1992) p. 417, at p. 456.

[63] See 45 Fed. Reg. 75,709 (1980). Although the Service later withdrew the regulations (I.R.S. News Release IR-82-145 (Dec. 16, 1982); I.R.S. Announcement 83-4, 1983-2 I.R.B. 30 (Jan. 14, 1983)), it issued a private letter ruling classifying an LLC as a corporation (Priv. Ltr. Rul. 83-04-138 (Oct. 29, 1982)) and decided that it would not issue additional private rulings concerning LLC classification (Rev. Proc. 83-15, 1983-1 C.B. 676).

[64] See Ribstein, *supra* n. 62, at p. 426. This activity was at least partly attributable to the Tax Reform Act of 1986, which, among other things, caused top corporate tax rates to exceed top individual rates and eliminated the lower tax on capital gains.

[65] Rev. Rul. 88-76, 1988-2 C.B. 360.

[66] See L.E. Ribstein, 'The Emergence of the Limited Liability Company', 51 *Business Lawyer* (1995) p. 1. A court recently noted the effect of the change in tax classification rules on the development of LLC law: 'The Virginia statutory requirement that prevented the continuity of life corporate attribute from attaching to Virginia limited liability companies necessarily permitted events over which the company had no control to jeopardize its very existence, potentially in the prime of its economic life. With the change in the IRS regulations, it was no longer necessary to avoid this corporate attribute. Potentially serious problems could be avoided by eliminating dissolution upon enumerated unforeseen events. As of July 1, 1998, a Virginia limited liability company may have, effectively, perpetual existence. The same Act that gave Virginia limited liability companies perpetual existence also added § 13.1-1040.1 which addressed events causing a member's dissociation. The events that previously led to the dissolution of the company now result in the member's dissociation.' *In re Garrison-Ashburn, L.C.*, 253 B.R. 700, 706-07 (Bankr. E.D. Va. 2000).

[67] See generally L.E. Ribstein, 'Possible Futures for Unincorporated Firms', 64 *University of Cincinnati Law Review* (1996) p. 319 (discussing history and development of LLP form).

is coherent (in the sense that the different rules work together), that invites efficient gap-filling by courts, and that helps ensure efficient application of regulatory provisions.[68] This permits more efficient matching of default rules with various types of firms.

Consider, for example, the choices offered by the three leading partnership-type business forms. The general partnership form suits very closely held firms managed directly by their owners not only in terms of its default management rules,[69] but also its rules regarding owners' power to bind the firm.[70] In contrast, management and control are sharply separated in limited partnerships, as exemplified by the limited partnership 'control rule' which penalizes limited partners who participate in management.[71] The LLC falls between these extremes, offering a choice between centralized and decentralized management, multiple sets of fiduciary and agency rules to suit both options, and more ambiguous treatment under regulatory statutes.[72]

3.3.4 *Evolution of business forms*

The important question about the erosion of regulation and the variations in state statutes is whether these changes efficiently meet firms' needs. Some might argue that, on the *supply side* of regulation, legislators are not adequately motivated to make efficient changes that do not serve the objectives of powerful interest groups.[73] Indeed, powerful groups might actively oppose changes that erode existing regulation favored by these groups. There is also arguably a *demand side* problem in that firms will be impeded from making choices among laws and forms that optimally suit their needs because they are locked into existing forms.[74] Some might claim that state competition will produce a *race-to-the-bottom*, where firms perversely choose statutes that are socially inefficient, perhaps because they hurt creditors.

Several arguments, however, support the proposition that business forms will evolve efficiently. First, with respect to the role of interest groups, there is strong reason to believe that lawyers can be the engines of efficiency. Transactional lawyers have much to gain from promoting efficient business laws in their states.[75] Such laws give firms incentives to physically locate in the enacting state and to hire local lawyers who are proficient in the local law. The potential free-rider problem is ameliorated by state lawyer licensing laws that exclude lawyers from some of the benefits of practicing under the law of a state in which they are not licensed and by the fact that lawyers earn individual reputational benefits from participating in law reform efforts.[76] These factors help solve problems on the

---

[68] See Ribstein, *supra* n. 49, at pp. 380-83.

[69] See Unif. P'ship Act § 18 (1914), 6 U.L.A. 526 (1995); Rev. Unif. P'ship Act § 401 (amended 1997), 6 U.L.A. 77-78 (Supp. 2001).

[70] See Unif. P'Ship Act § 9 (1914), 6 U.L.A. 400-01 (1995); Rev. Unif. P'ship Act § 301 (amended 1997), 6 U.L.A. 60 (Supp. 2001).

[71] See Rev. Unif. Ltd. P'ship Act § 303 (amended 1985), 6A U.L.A. 144-45 (1995).

[72] See generally Ribstein and Keatinge, *supra* n. 20; Ribstein, *supra* n. 66.

[73] For discussions of the supply-side problem, see I. Ayres, 'Judging Close Corporations in the Age of Statutes', 70 *Washington University Law Quarterly* (1992) p. 365; D.J. Cumming and J.G. MacIntosh, 'The Role of Interjurisdictional Competition in Shaping Canadian Corporate Law', 20 *International Review of Law and Economics* (2000) p. 141.

[74] See *infra* text accompanying nn. 83-86.

[75] See *supra* text accompanying nn. 46-47.

[76] See Ribstein, Lawyers' Licensing, *supra* n. 47.

supply-side of regulation[77] by giving a particular interest group the incentive to drive efficient law reform.

A second argument for efficient evolution is that, as Armen Alchian has observed, even if legislators lack knowledge, motivation, and foresight to supply efficient laws, such laws may nevertheless emerge through the *adaptive mechanism* of the marketplace.[78] Evolution through experimentation is consistent with Hayek's observation that 'if left free, men will often achieve more than individual human reason could design or foresee.'[79] These insights are relevant to both common[80] and statutory[81] law. In other words, it is necessary to look beyond the actions of individual participants in the process to the outcome of the process itself. For example, although particular firms or interest groups caused enactment of the first LLC and LLP statutes,[82] these statutes are best viewed merely as mutations that spurred evolution. The ultimate form and success of LLCs and LLPs depended on the ensuing process of jurisdictional competition rather than on the circumstances in which these business forms were born.

Third, there are strong arguments against *lock-in* or *path dependence* as constraints on efficient evolution of statutory forms. These terms can be taken to refer to individuals' or firms' inability to adopt terms that, but for lock-in, would optimally suit their needs.[83] The most coherent explanation of lock-in is *network externalities*, which asserts that, because individual economic actors do not internalize all network benefits, the most efficient products are not necessarily the ones that succeed in the market.[84] This theory has been applied to business association standard forms,[85] which depend on networks of users to create beneficial features such as case law and expertise. But there are several problems with this

[77] See *supra* text accompanying n. 73.

[78] See A. Alchian, 'Uncertainty, Evolution, and Economic Theory', 58 *Journal of Political Economy* (1950) p. 211. See also M. Vihanto, 'Competition between Local Governments as a Discovery Procedure', 148 *Journal of Institutional and Theoretical Economics* (1992) p. 411 (showing how jurisdictional competition can produce unexpected discoveries).

[79] F.A. Hayek, 'Individualism: True and False', in *Individualism and Economics Order* (Chicago, University of Chicago Press 1948) p. 1 and p. 11.

[80] See, e.g., P.H. Rubin, 'Why is the Common Law Efficient?', 6 *Journal of Legal Studies* (1997) p. 51.

[81] See B.H. Kobayashi and L.E. Ribstein, 'Evolution and Uniformity', 34 *Economic Inquiry* (1996) p. 464, reprinted in J. Lott (ed.) *Uncertainty and Economic Evolution* (London, Routledge 1997).

[82] In the case of LLC statutes, a single firm, Hamilton Brothers Oil Company, and its lawyers and accountants, caused the adoption of the initial Wyoming statute. For accounts of the history of the LLC, see W.J. Carney, 'Limited Liability Companies: Origins and Antecedents', 66 *University of Colorado Law Review* (1995) p. 855; C.R. Goforth, 'The Rise of the Limited Liability Company: Evidence of a Race Between the States, But Heading Where?', 45 *Syracuse Law Review* (1995) p. 1193; S.P. Hamill, 'The Origins Behind the Limited Liability Company', 59 *Ohio State Law Journal* (1998) p. 1459. LLP statutes were instigated to protect Texas law firms against liability in connection with the collapse of savings and loan institutions. See Bromberg and Ribstein, *supra* n. 20, at § 1.01; S.S. Fortney, 'Seeking Shelter in the Minefield of Unintended Consequences – The Traps of Limited Liability Law Firms', 54 *Washington and Lee Law Review (*1997) p. 717; R.W. Hamilton, 'Registered Limited Liability Partnerships: Present at the Birth (Nearly)', 66 *University of Colorado Law Review* (1995) p. 1065, at pp. 1068-74.

[83] For discussions of alternative meanings of lock-in, see S.J. Liebowitz and S.E. Margolis, 'Path Dependence, Lock-in, and History', 11 *Journal of Law, Economics, and Organization* (1995) p. 205, at pp. 206-12; Ribstein, *supra* n. 34, at p. 247; M.J. Roe, 'Chaos and Evolution in Law and Economics', 109 *Harvard Law Review* (1996) p. 641, at pp. 646-53.

[84] See generally J. Farrell and G. Saloner, 'Standardization, Compatibility, and Innovation', 16 *Rand Journal of Economics* (1985) p. 70, at pp. 70-72; M.L. Katz and C. Shapiro, 'Systems Competition and Network Effects', 8 *Journal of Economic Perspectives* (1994) p. 93.

[85] See Klausner, *supra* n. 50.

theory. Among other things, it is not clear what should be considered an *externality*, because market actors can internalize the benefits from creating networks, and it will rarely be clear whether a product or business form has failed because of its inherent defects or because of network externalities.[86]

Fourth, a race-to-the-bottom is unlikely to occur with respect to closely held firms. Unlike publicly held corporations, legislators would not be competing for franchise fees.[87] Indeed, it has been argued that, because of this, there would be inadequate supply-side competition to provide closely held business forms.[88] But as noted above, transactional lawyers help drive this competition, and they do not have strong incentives to promote business forms that hurt creditors. Moreover, the strong trial lawyer bar has incentives to protect their tort creditor clients.

The recent history of unincorporated business forms in the United States strongly supports efficient evolution through horizontal and vertical choice. First, and perhaps most strikingly, the LLC form has evolved rapidly since 1988 into a dynamic entity offering such features as flexible management and corporate-type continuity, rather than locking in the early Wyoming version of the LLC, which was based closely on the limited partnership.[89]

Second, LLC statutes have spontaneously evolved toward uniformity with respect to the types of provisions for which uniformity is most efficient.[90] This compares favorably with the effects of the *official* Uniform Limited Liability Company Act promulgated by the NCCUSL.[91]

Third, there is evidence specifically refuting the role of network externalities in the development of unincorporated business forms. The LLP is very similar to the LLC except that it is designed to overcome network effects by permitting partnerships to access the existing network of general partnership case law and forms while opting into limited liability. If network externalities really did impede efficient evolution, partnership-type firms likely would opt for the LLP rather than the LLC form. In fact, the opposite has occurred, and firms' choices between forms depend on state-specific regulatory and tax considerations rather than network effects.[92]

This evidence suggests what might happen in a post-*Centros* Europe in which firms have greater ability to make horizontal and vertical choices. Indeed, there is direct evidence against a race-to-the-bottom in both Europe and the United States showing that firms tend to choose high-quality securities regimes even when they can choose lower-quality regimes.[93]

---

[86] For a summary of alternative explanations for apparent network externality phenomena, see L.E. Ribstein and B.H. Kobayashi, 'Choice of Form and Network Externalities', 43 *William and Mary Law Review* (2001) p. 79.

[87] For the leading franchise-fee-competition explanation of corporate law, see W.L. Cary, 'Federalism and Corporate Law: Reflections Upon Delaware', 83 *Yale Law Journal* (1999) p. 663.

[88] See Ayres, *supra* n. 73.

[89] See generally Ribstein, *supra* n. 49; Ribstein and Kobayashi, *supra* n. 86.

[90] See Kobayashi and Ribstein, *supra* n. 81. For example, uniformity is most efficient and prevalent in transactions involving third party creditors who deal with many different firms and therefore face high potential information costs of sorting out the rules applicable to each firm. Ibid., at p. 468.

[91] See generally L.E. Ribstein and B.H. Kobayashi, 'Uniform Laws, Model Laws and ULLCA', 66 *University of Colorado Law Review* (1995) p. 947.

[92] See Ribstein and Kobayashi, *supra* n. 86.

[93] See S.J. Choi, 'Assessing the Cost of Regulatory Protections: Evidence on the Decision to Sell Securities Outside the United States', 2 *Theoretical Inquiries in Law* (2001) p. 613 (showing that firms that had been sued under the securities laws and investigated by the Securities and Exchange Commission tend to make US-regulated

All of this is not to say that business forms that evolve from horizontal and vertical choice necessarily are optimal. Firms may encounter some friction, including the effect of local regulations that firms can avoid only by locating their physical business elsewhere, which may limit firms' mobility enough to prevent development of optimal forms. For example, law firms necessarily are subject to ethical rules of the profession that apply in each state in which the firm practices. This keeps firms from avoiding inefficient ethical rules, such as rules that restrict non-competition agreements and that therefore help prevent opportunistic exit.[94] The main point is not that evolution operates perfectly, but that offering some jurisdictional choice is likely to yield more efficient results – at least in the context of business forms – than rules promulgated by a single rulemaker.

3.3.5 *Competition and regulation as a dynamic process*

Critics of jurisdictional choice might argue that many of the effects described in Section 3.3.4 are inefficient, particularly the erosion of federal and state regulation. However, it is important to keep in mind that erosion and evolution do not sweep away all regulation. With respect to state regulation, for example, professional firms must comply with substantial local regulations even if they can operate under the *internal affairs* rules of any state's business association statute.[95] Avoidance of regulation involves such difficulties as choosing contractual terms that would not be optimal but for the regulation, the need to vote and revise existing agreements when switching forms, and the extra costs of organizing under the law of a favorable jurisdiction and then doing business as a *foreign firm* in the home state. Thus, regulation will continue to be effective even with jurisdictional choice except to the extent that firms derive strong net benefits from avoiding the regulation even taking into account market constraints. Moreover, it is important to keep in mind that firms have market-based incentives to serve customers' needs even if they legally could adopt the rules of a lax jurisdiction.

4. The Output of the Process: The Elements of Partnership

This section discusses the specific effects of the processes described in Section 3. It shows the extent to which partnerships have been engaged in a continuous process of change that has increased partnership-type business firms' adaptation to their needs. The following

securities offerings rather than foreign offerings, indicating that they are using US federal securities laws to allay investor mistrust); J.C. Coffee, Jr., 'The Coming Competition Among Securities Markets: A Path Dependent Perspective' Columbia Law and Economics Working Paper No. 192 (2002) available at <http://ssrn.com/abstracts=283822>; H.E. Jackson and E.J. Pan, 'Regulatory Competition in International Securities Markets: Evidence from Europe in 1999 – Part I', 56 *Business Lawyer* (2001) p. 653, at p. 691 (finding that the market demanded more securities disclosures than required by the minimum standards in EU Directives, and noting that 'market developments in European capital markets to date do not offer support to critics of regulatory competition who claim that the issuer choice proposals would prompt a race to the bottom in international securities regulation'); I.G. MacNeil, 'Competition and Convergence in Corporate Regulation: The Case of Overseas Listed Companies' (2001), available at <http://ssrn.com/abstract=278508>.

[94] See L.E. Ribstein, Ethical Rules, 'Law Firm Structure, and Choice of Law', 69 *University of Cincinnati Law Review* (2001) p. 1161. For a discussion of opportunistic exit in law firms, see generally R.W. Hillman, 'Professional Partnerships, Competition, and the Evolution of Firm Culture: The Case of Law Firms', 26 *Journal of Corporation Law* (2001) p. 1061 (discussing adverse effects of partnership law on firm stability).

[95] This will also be true under *Centros* which explicitly preserved a role for professional regulation. See Case C-212/97, *Centros Ltd.* v. *Erhvervs-og Selskabsstyrelsen*, 1999 *ECR* I-1459 (1999), 2 *CMLR* 551 (1999).

sections review features of the general standard partnership form introduced in Section 2 and show both the theoretical uncertainty concerning what these features should look like and how experimentation in the *laboratory* of state laws has responded to this uncertainty.

4.1 Partner liability

Vicarious liability of partners for the firm's debts is still the default rule for US partnerships.[96] This reflects partners' incentives as profit-sharers and co-managers to monitor the firm and the potentially high moral hazard from limited liability when owner-managers deal with creditors.[97] Because creditors in these circumstances usually demand personal guarantees from owners,[98] making vicarious liability the default rule for contracts economizes on transaction costs. Owners of very closely held firms would gain little from tort limited liability because the firm's torts can often be attributed to the owners' acts.[99]

Nevertheless, as discussed in the following sections, it is not clear that vicarious liability should be the default rule for some, or even any, partnership-type firms. This uncertainty is reflected in variations in partner liability between the extremes of limited and vicarious liability.

4.1.1 *Limited liability for closely held firms*

Even if vicarious liability is efficient for some firms, particularly owner-managed partnerships, limited liability may be an efficient default rule for other firms. Although commentators have highlighted the advantages of limited liability in facilitating public trading of shares,[100] limited liability may also be valuable in some closely held firms, particularly where ownership and management are specialized and even in some cases where owners manage the firm.[101] If this is the case for many closely held firms, it follows that limited liability should be available as a default rule rather than forcing firms to enter into non-recourse contracts with casual trade creditors and forcing their owners to bear vicarious liability in tort suits where non-recourse contracts are not feasible. Alternatively, it may be efficient to adopt modified forms of limited liability, such as focusing vicarious liability on managers or providing for limited liability only for certain types of debts. Indeed, as discussed below in this section, various forms of vicarious and limited liability have been tested in the laboratory of state law.

---

[96] See Unif. P'ship Act § 15 (1914), 6 U.L.A. 456 (1995); Rev. Unif. P'ship Act § 306 (amended 1997), 6 U.L.A. 69 (Supp. 2001).

[97] For analyses of vicarious liability based on the principal's ability to monitor, motivate or select agents, see L.A. Kornhauser, 'An Economic Analysis of the Choice Between Enterprise and Personal Liability for Accidents', 70 *California Law Review* (1982) p. 1345; A.O. Sykes, 'The Economics of Vicarious Liability', 93 *Yale Law Journal* (1984) p. 1231.

[98] See R.J. Mann, 'The Role of Secured Credit in Small-Business Lending', 86 *Georgetown Law Journal* (1997) p. 1, at pp. 26-37 (showing evidence that most small firm debt is backed by the owners' personal guarantees).

[99] See R.B. Thompson, 'Unpacking Limited Liability: Direct and Vicarious Liability of Corporate Participants for Torts of the Enterprise', 47 *Vanderbilt Law Review* (1994) p. 1.

[100] See F.H. Easterbrook and D.R. Fischel, 'Limited Liability and the Corporation', 52 *University of Chicago Law Review* (1985) p. 89; S. Woodward, 'Limited Liability in the Theory of the Firm', 141 *Journal of Institutional and Theoretical Economics* (1985) p. 601.

[101] See Ribstein, *supra* n. 62, at pp. 428-38.

It has been argued that shareholder limited liability for corporate torts is inefficient[102] and therefore is not part of the essential role of business forms.[103] From the standpoint of the present chapter's analysis, the main question is whether this assertion about inefficiency can be refuted by every state's acceptance of tort limited liability, including in closely held firms. One commentator has suggested that states' adoption of limited liability business forms is not evidence of efficiency because the forms were adopted over a brief period, without significant public debate, and primarily at the behest of lawyers.[104]

In order to establish the inefficiency of the spread of LLC statutes, critics must ask why business lawyers were able to steamroll over all other interest groups in all fifty-one US jurisdictions. States could have prevented the spread of limited liability within their borders, had they chosen to do so, simply by failing to recognize the LLC liability limitation.[105] Nor did LLC statutes move in under cover of night. The process took eight years from the time of the tax ruling that made LLCs viable until the last LLC statute was passed, during which time Westlaw reports that 350 law review articles were published with *limited liability company* in the title.[106] And trial lawyers, who long have vigorously pressed for extension of tort liability and opposed attempts to reform state tort and professional liability laws, lobbied hard against LLC statutes in several states, including Missouri, Ohio, Tennessee, Washington and Oklahoma,[107] as well as against the California LLP act.[108] Finally, between the 1977 passage of the Wyoming law and the 1988 tax ruling, LLC statutes faced the significant federal tax classification hurdle, during which time opponents of limited liability might have prevailed at the federal level.[109]

A benign explanation of the spread of LLC statutes is that they reflected closely held firms' increasing need for limited liability because of the increase in tort and malpractice exposure. Thus, LLC statutes represented a reverse swing of the tort pendulum after the tort revolution in the United States had left firms exposed to excessive tort risk. The statutes spread so quickly because, by the time of the 1988 tax classification rule, the need for them was well-recognized. In other words, the rapid spread of LLC statutes indicates the inefficiency not of the new rule, but rather of the pre-1988 tax rules that had constrained the passage of LLC statutes prior to that date.[110] It also shows how a dynamic system is able to react to inefficiency by providing an opportunity for regulatory arbitrage.

---

[102] H. Hansmann and R. Kraakman, 'Toward Unlimited Shareholder Liability for Corporate Torts', 100 *Yale Law Journal* (1991) p. 1879.

[103] See H. Hansmann and R. Kraakman, 'The Essential Role of Organizational Law', 110 *Yale Law Journal* (2000) p. 387, at p. 431. Hansmann and Kraakman distinguish limited liability from 'affirmative asset partitioning', or shielding the entity's assets from claims by owners' creditors. Ibid., at pp. 394-96. See also Armour and Whincop, *supra* n. 17 (analyzing the 'essential' role of affirmative asset partitioning in a broader framework of business organization rules); *infra* n. 162 and accompanying text (discussing variations in the degree of affirmative asset partitioning between partnership-type and corporate-type firms, particularly regarding 'liquidation protection' of the firms from owners' individual creditors).

[104] See J.W. Callison, 'Federalism, Regulatory Competition and the Limited Liability Movement: The Coyote Howled and the Herd Stampeded', 26 *Journal of Corporation Law* (2001) p. 951.

[105] For a discussion of the conflict of laws issue, see Ribstein and Keatinge, *supra* n. 20, at § 13.04.

[106] The Westlaw search was 'TI (limited liability company!)' in the 'All Law Reviews and Journals' (TP-ALL) database.

[107] See Goforth, *supra* n. 82, at pp. 1271-75, 1279-81.

[108] See B. Ainsworth, 'Trial Lawyers Learn to Live with Limited Liability', *Recorder* (June 26, 1995) p. 2.

[109] See *supra* n. 62 and accompanying text.

[110] See Ribstein, *supra* n. 62.

4.1.2 *Exhaustion of firm assets*

Owner liability rules do not involve a choice simply between the extremes of vicarious and limited liability. One option is requiring creditors to sue the partnership and exhaust its assets before they can recover from partners. Under US partnership law, partners traditionally are directly liable only to tort-type creditors such as accident victims. However, several US jurisdictions, including those adopting RUPA,[111] require both contract and tort creditors to exhaust partnership assets. The exhaustion rule is consistent with the so-called 'dual priorities' rule of the UPA, which gives partnership creditors priority only in the assets of the partnership and not in those of individual partners.[112] This form of limited liability represents a compromise between full-fledged corporate-type limited liability and full-fledged vicarious liability. The US rule contrasts with partners' joint and several liability for all partnership debts in most other countries.[113]

These alternative rules raise the issue of which is best for partnership. The exhaustion rule obviously raises collection costs for creditors, while lifting partners' burden of paying creditors and then seeking indemnity from the firm. Creditors' costs arguably would exceed those of partners, who deal regularly with the firm.[114] On the other hand, the exhaustion rule may be a reasonable compromise for some firms between vicarious and full-fledged limited liability where personal liability addresses moral hazard problems but creditors' costs of suing the firm are not much higher than those of owners.

Because the efficiency of the exhaustion rule is unclear from the standpoint of pure theory, it should be tested in the laboratory of state laws. With NCCUSL's promulgation of across-the-board exhaustion in RUPA, coupled with increased availability of contractual choice of law in general partnerships,[115] states can accept or reject the RUPA rule, and firms can choose from among the various state rules. If states tend to adopt, say, the RUPA across-the-board exhaustion rule, and if firms tend to choose these statutes, this would indicate that this rule is efficient for most partnership-type firms.

The problem with a competition solution to these issues, however, is that federal bankruptcy law in the United States stifles full-fledged competition regarding the nature of limited liability. Bankruptcy law, among other things, overrules the dual priorities rule by providing for direct access by partnership creditors – through the bankruptcy trustee – to assets of bankrupt individual partners, and bankruptcy courts have enjoined creditors' actions against non-bankrupt partners.[116] All firms are subject to these rules in federal bankruptcy proceedings regardless of the otherwise applicable state law.[117]

---

[111] See Rev. Unif. P'ship Act § 307 (amended 1997), 6 U.L.A. 73-74 (Supp. 2001).

[112] See Unif. P'ship Act § 40(i) (1914), 6 U.L.A. 902 (1995).

[113] See J. Heenen, 'Partnership and Other Personal Associations for Profit', in *International Encyclopedia of Comparative Law* (Hamburg, Martinus Nijhoff Publishers 1975) vol. 13, pp. 97, 140-44.

[114] See Ribstein, *supra* n. 62. Conversely, it has been argued that, because a universally available corporate form 'captures all of the creditor-monitoring economies available under the old U.P.A. priority rules for partners' creditors ... the partnership form retains value only as an unlimited liability alternative to the corporate form, which implies that the claim of partnership creditors should be strengthened—they should have the same claim on the assets of individual partners as do individual creditors.' Hansmann and Kraakman, *supra* n. 103, at p. 428 n. 60.

[115] See *supra* text accompanying nn. 37-38.

[116] For discussions and criticisms of these and other effects of bankruptcy law on partnerships, see L.E. Ribstein, 'Partner Bankruptcy and the Federalization of Partnership Law', 33 *Wake Forest Law Review* (1998) p. 795; L.E. Ribstein, 'The Illogic and Limits of Partners' Liability in Bankruptcy', 32 *Wake Forest Law Review* (1997) p. 31.

4.1.3 *Limited liability for torts only*

Another possible approach to owner liability would be a rule of personal liability for contract but limited liability for torts. This approach would address the infeasibility of contracting out of vicarious liability as to tort creditors while providing by default for the liability that most contract creditors of closely held firms apparently want.[118] On the other hand, vicarious liability may not be the efficient default rule for contract claims, and distinguishing two sets of creditors imposes extra transaction costs on the firm.[119] Although the original Texas rule distinguished contract and tort claims,[120] less than a third of the LLP statutes now take this approach.[121] Thus, the laboratory of state laws generally has rejected what appears to be an inefficient liability rule.

4.1.4 *Limited liability in limited partnerships and the control rule*

A third approach to owner liability is the mixed liability rule for limited partnerships, in which general partners have vicarious liability but limited partners have limited liability unless they participate in control.[122] This rule can be rationalized as a way to permit limited liability investments in an unincorporated firm, while minimizing the potential moral hazard problem with limited liability in closely held firms[123] by giving managers an incentive to act in creditors' interests.[124] The control rule no longer unduly restricts limited liability, as it did when firms had few other limited liability options, now that firms can combine separation of ownership and control and limited liability by forming LLCs.

The main counter-argument is that too few firms would opt for this approach to justify continuing to offer it. As with the other issues discussed in this chapter, the best way to answer this question is through the laboratory of state competition. State law and contractual variations have made vicarious liability in limited partnerships vestigial. Limited partners' control liability under the existing version of the Revised Uniform Limited Partnership Act (RULPA) has been reduced – through an extensive safe harbor for permissible control acts – to a type of partnership by estoppel based on misrepresentation of general partner status.[125] At the same time, general partners can avoid liability by the simple expedient of incorporating.

---

[117] It has been argued that the transaction costs of entering into contracts regarding creditors' access to separate pools of owner and firm assets make legal default rules on such matters particularly important and binding. See Hansmann and Kraakman, *supra* n. 102. But this does not preclude variation in these rules. Indeed, as transaction costs make legal default rules more valuable, they should also increase the value of competition and evolution regarding such rules in order to help ensure the rules' efficiency. Uniformity may be efficient if the rules are complex, entailing learning costs by third party creditors. See Kobayashi and Ribstein, *supra* n. 81 (showing evidence that LLC rules regarding matters of this sort are, indeed, more uniform). However, the efficiency of uniformity does not necessarily follow from high costs of contracting around the default rule.

[118] See *supra* text accompanying n. 98.

[119] See Bromberg and Ribstein, *supra* n. 20, at § 3.02; L.E. Ribstein, 'Possible Futures for Closely-held Firms', 64 *University of Cincinnati Law Review* (1996) p. 319, at pp. 329-31.

[120] See Bromberg and Ribstein, *supra* n. 20, at §1.01(a).

[121] See ibid., at tbl.3-1.

[122] See Rev. Unif. Ltd. P'ship Act § 303 (amended 1985), 6A U.L.A. 144-45 (1995).

[123] See *supra* text accompanying n. 97.

[124] See L.E. Ribstein, 'Limited Partnerships Revisited', 67 *University of Cincinnati Law Review* (1999) p. 953, at p. 979.

[125] See Rev. Unif. Ltd. P'ship Act § 303 (amended 1985), 6A U.L.A. 144-45 (1995).

The advent of the LLP continued this evolutionary process. Several states explicitly permit limited partnerships to organize as limited liability limited partnerships (LLLPs) and thereby eliminate the vicarious liability of general partners and, in some cases, also of limited partners who participate in management.[126] LLLPs raise still further questions. On the one hand, now that limited partnerships can easily opt into full-fledged limited liability, the limited partnership statute arguably should tighten the control rule and general partner liability for the general partners that do not make the election, thereby preserving two distinct alternatives. On the other hand, because most limited partnerships will elect LLLP status if it is available, the statute arguably should eliminate vicarious liability for limited partnerships as simply a trap for the unwary, thereby making the LLLP in effect the default limited partnership. This issue was debated in the context of NCCUSL's revision of RULPA.[127] The final version of this provision provides for default personal liability of general partners.[128] However, the Reporter reflected the confused history of the revision on this issue in the following note to the April 2001 draft:

> 'Having consulted severally with a majority of the Commissioners on the Drafting Committee, the Reporter believes that the Committee will vote to 'flop' on the 'flip' – i.e., to provide that, as a default rule, the general partner of a limited partnership is liable for the debts of the entity. If the Reporter's prediction is wrong (not an unprecedented event), the changes indicated above (and elsewhere) will simply be removed.'[129]

This suggests that uniform vicarious liability rule for limited partnerships was determined by how a particular committee felt at a particular time. But the laboratory of state legislatures considering whether to adopt the revision ultimately will, and should, determine the law on this issue.

4.1.5 *Limited liability as a default rule for all partnerships*

Limited liability in limited partnerships raises an additional question about the future of vicarious liability in general partnerships. If the state laboratory ultimately should decide that vicarious liability is simply a trap for limited partnerships, why not for general partnerships as well? One might respond that general partnerships are the default entity, unlike limited partnerships which the parties must commemorate by a state filing. But limited liability, like vicarious liability, can also be seen as a prescribed legal consequence of a particular relationship. The decision by the vast majority of firms to opt for limited liability arguably suggests that this is the efficient rule and that the legal consequence of forming a partnership should change accordingly. Full-fledged vicarious liability may not be an efficient default rule for a significant number of firms because the collection costs of actions against individual partners and the increased monitoring costs of both partners and creditors under a vicarious liability rule probably exceed any benefits to creditors from the

[126] See Bromberg and Ribstein, *supra* n. 20, at ch. 5.
[127] See Ribstein, *supra* n. 124, at p. 971.
[128] See Unif. Ltd. P'Ship Act (2001) § 404(a).
[129] Nat'l Conference of Comm'rs of Unif. State Laws, Proposed Revisions of Uniform Limited Partnership Act (1976) with 1985 Amendments §404 note 9 (April 2001), available at <http://www.law.upenn.edu/bll/ulc/ulc_frame.htm>.

availability of a direct action.[130] Once again, this is a complex issue that is best decided in the laboratory of state law.

4.2 Partners' financial rights

There are several theoretically possible default rules for partners' shares in profits and losses, including equally (*per capita*), according to partners' financial contributions (*pro rata*), and *per capita* or *pro rata* by class of holder depending on their liability for the firm's debts and management responsibilities. As discussed below, these default rules reflect varying assumptions concerning firms' management and liability structures. As with the other issues discussed in this chapter, the appropriate rule or mix of rules is difficult to determine as a matter of *a priori* theory.

US partnership law provides that partners share equally in profits and losses after paying non-partnership creditors.[131] Indemnification by the partnership and contribution by individual partners reconciles partners' loss shares with their vicarious liability for all partnership debts. Partnership statutes also deny partners interest and rent in addition to their profit shares except where they specifically contract to loan or lease property to the firm.[132] These rules contrast with the *pro rata* sharing rule for corporations and with the partnership rule in some non-US jurisdictions.[133]

The partnership equal sharing rule raises significant policy issues.[134] Fred C. Dobbs (Humphrey Bogart) observed in *The Treasure of the Sierra Madre* that 'in any civilized place the biggest investor gets the biggest return'.[135] The rule might be defended as based on the assumption that, in the absence of contrary agreement, the partners' profit share compensates them for all of their investments in the firm, including their credit contribution to a vicarious liability firm. This would explain why this default rule does not apply in limited liability firms and is so often varied by contract in firms where the equal-contribution assumption does not hold.[136] The default rule applies even to firms where the parties' contributions are not in fact equal but the parties have not contracted around the rule. But to what extent should this result prevail even in the face of clear expectations to the contrary in particular firms? For example, should partnership law provide for a different default rule in LLPs where the assumption of credit contributions does not hold?[137] A rigid default rule

---

[130] See Ribstein, *supra* n. 62, at pp. 428-33.

[131] Unif. P'ship Act § 18(a) (1914), 6 U.L.A. 526 (1995); Rev. Unif. P'ship Act § 401(b) (amended 1997), 6 U.L.A. 77 (Supp. 2001).

[132] See Unif. P'Ship Act § 18(c), (f) (1914), 6 U.L.A. 526 (1995); Rev. Unif. P'ship Act § 401(d), (h) (amended 1997), 6 U.L.A. 77 (Supp. 2001).

[133] For example, German law provides for sharing on the basis of capital shares. See Heenen, *supra* n. 113, at p. 108.

[134] This markedly contrasts with one commentator's peculiar view, based on evolutionary biology, that the rule plays an essential role in partnership. See T.A. Smith, 'Equality, Evolution and Partnership Law', University of San Diego Law and Economics Research Paper No. 11, University of San Diego Public Law Research Paper No. 20, 2001, available at <http://ssrn.com/abstract=262407>. The paper ignores considerations underlying default rules as distinguished from actual contracts in particular firms, variations across types of partnership-like firms, cross-country differences and, in general, the adaptability of business forms.

[135] *The Treasure of the Sierra Madre* (Hollywood, Metro-Goldwyn-Mayer 1948).

[136] Indeed, courts may often assume a contrary agreement in this situation. See, e.g., *Warren* v. *Warren*, 784 S.W.2d 247 (Mo. Ct. App. 1989) (holding that partners who provided substantial time and vital services deserved extra compensation).

[137] See Bromberg and Ribstein, *supra* n. 20, at § 4.04(a).

would encourage costly contrary agreements, seemingly inconsistent with the transaction-cost-reducing function of default rules. On the other hand, a flexible rule, or applying many different default rules, imposes information costs on firms.[138]

Again, the laboratory of state laws should resolve these issues through horizontal and vertical competition. States can offer hybrid or variant business forms that provide alternatives to some of the general partnership default rules, including those regarding allocation of financial rights, without increasing general partners' information costs or uncertainty. For example, limited partnership statutes[139] and most LLC statutes[140] provide for *pro rata* financial rights.

4.3 Management and control

Management and control default rules theoretically vary on a continuum according to their flexibility or rigidity, from rules providing for equality among partners with fixed categories of authority, to those creating classes of owners and managers with particular levels of authority. The more flexible the members' default authority, the greater the uncertainty costs associated with determining that authority and the need to allocate those costs between the firm and third parties.

Default partnership rules treat all partners equally regarding management and control: Partners participate directly in management;[141] each partner has one vote rather than apportioning votes by the value of money contributions as under corporate law;[142] and all partners vote on the firm's decision, with a majority vote required to approve all ordinary decisions and unanimity required for extraordinary decisions, including amendment of the agreement and admission of new partners.[143]

Equality rules for management, like those for financial rights discussed above, suit very closely held firms in which the partners' combinations of capital, service, and credit contributions can be assumed to equalize. At the same time, majority-vote rules avoid the high coordination costs of requiring unanimity on ordinary decisions.[144] The rules regarding a partner's power to bind the firm in transactions with third parties reflect this equal allocation of power. Under US law any partner normally can bind the firm in ordinary business transactions with third parties.[145] Similarly, because the default rules assume that partners are full-time co-managers, their acts in the ordinary course of business trigger partnership tort liability, as do acts by full-time employees of other types of firms.

---

138 Moreover, the 'linkage' of general partnership default rules with LLPs is arguably an advantage of LLPs. See generally Ribstein and Kobayashi, *supra* n. 86.

139 See Rev. Unif. Ltd. P'ship Act § 503 (amended 1985), 6A U.L.A. 209-10 (1995).

140 See Ribstein and Keatinge, *supra* n. 20, at app. 5-1 (tabulating statutes).

141 See Unif. P'ship Act § 18(e) (1914), 6 U.L.A. 526 (1995); Rev. Unif. P'ship Act § 401(f) (amended 1997), 6 U.L.A. 77 (Supp. 2001).

142 See Unif. P'ship Act § 18(e) (1914), 6 U.L.A. 526 (1995); Rev. Unif. P'ship Act § 401(f) (amended 1997), 6 U.L.A. 77 (Supp. 2001).

143 See Unif. P'Ship Act § 18(h)-(i) (1914), 6 U.L.A. 526 (1995); Rev. Unif. P'ship Act § 401(i)-(j) (amended 1997), 6 U.L.A. 77-78 (Supp. 2001).

144 See generally J. Buchanan and G. Tullock, *The Calculus of Consent* (Ann Arbor, University of Michigan Press 1962) (describing optimal voting rules). Armour and Whincop argue that decisions should be made by at least a majority vote. See Armour and Whincop, *supra* n. 17, at 994. However, the parties might decide to reduce the costs of consensus through sub-majority voting and delegation.

145 See Unif. P'ship Act §§ 9-13 (1914), 6 U.L.A. 400-44 (1995); Rev. Unif. P'ship Act §§ 301-305 (amended 1997), 6 U.L.A. 60-68 (Supp. 2001).

But even many closely held firms do not fit the model of active worker-management. For example, larger partnerships need to centralize authority to minimize decision-making costs. Because of the basic partner equality assumption, the firm bears the burden of notifying third parties of limitations on partners' authority to bind the firm.[146] RUPA makes only a slight concession to this problem by providing a mechanism for binding third parties in real estate transactions where third parties can easily check a central record.[147]

There is, therefore, a need for default rules that suit centralized management even in partnership-type firms. The limited partnership was once the only alternative set of default rules that US law offered for closely held firms. The traditional limited partnership form clearly delineates classes of managing general partners, who have vicarious liability for the debts of the firm and can bind the firm in transactions with third parties, and non-managing limited partners, who have limited liability – unless they participate in control[148] – and no power to bind the firm.[149]

The traditional limited partnership does not, however, suit the many closely held firms in which investor-employees want substantial say even if they do not exercise day-to-day control. State statutes initially accommodated this need by diluting the limited partnership control rule and permitting limited partners to participate more actively in management without losing their limited liability. These state statutory developments were reflected in 1976 and 1985 versions of the Uniform Limited Partnership Act (ULPA), which offered increasing levels of management flexibility.[150] The recent revision of ULPA has now completely eliminated the *control rule*.[151] However, eliminating the clear demarcation between general and limited partners simultaneously raises general partnership type problems of third party uncertainty in determining member authority.

The LLC offers a compromise form of *chameleon* management: the firm can choose either direct partnership-type control by the members or centralized control by managers that is closer to, but not as rigid as, the limited partnership format.[152] With this greater flexibility comes greater uncertainty for third party creditors than in limited partnerships as to whether particular individuals have authority to bind the firm. For example, limited partnership statutes generally provide that the certificate is notice to third parties that those designated therein as general partners are such.[153] LLC statutes generally do not have comparable provisions.[154] Thus, under most statutes courts would apply agency rules that would require the firm to notify third parties which non-managing members lack binding authority.[155] However, some states, particularly including Delaware, make the operating agree-

---

[146] See Unif. P'ship Act § 9 (1914), 6 U.L.A. 346 (1995); Rev. Unif. P'ship Act § 301 (amended 1997), 6 U.L.A. 60 (Supp. 2001).

[147] Rev. Unif. P'ship Act § 303 (amended 1997), 6 U.L.A. 63-64 (Supp. 2001).

[148] See Unif. Ltd. P'ship Act § 7 (1916), 6A U.L.A. 336 (1995); Rev. Unif. Ltd. P'ship Act § 303 (amended 1985), 6A U.L.A. 144-45 (1995).

[149] See Rev. Unif. Ltd. P'ship Act § 403(a) (amended 1985), 6A U.L.A. 177 (1995) (providing that a general partner in a limited partnership has the same rights and powers as a general partner in a general partnership).

[150] Compare Rev. Unif. Ltd. P'ship Act § 303 (1976), 6A U.L.A 144-45 (1995), with Rev. Unif. Ltd. P'ship Act § 303 (amended 1985), 6A U.L.A. 144-45 (1995).

[151] See Nat'l Conference of Comm'rs of Unif. State Laws, *supra* n. 129 at § 303.

[152] See Ribstein and Keatinge, *supra* n. 20, at app. 8-1 (summarizing and tabulating state statutes).

[153] See Rev. Unif. Ltd. P'Ship Act § 208 (amended 1985), 6A U.L.A. 134 (1995).

[154] See Ribstein and Keatinge, *supra* n. 20, app. 4-1.

[155] See ibid., at § 8.05.

ment binding as to members' and managers' authority, thereby effectively requiring third parties to check this agreement when dealing with the firm.[156]

The main point is that the laboratory of state law, and not uniform law drafters, has produced governance structures that efficiently reflect the variety of firms' needs. Even where rules are embodied in NCCUSL's uniform partnership, limited partnership, and LLC acts, NCCUSL generally has followed rather than led the process.[157] For example, the LLC chameleon management structure had evolved in many state statutes before being included in ULLCA.[158]

4.4 Partner's property rights in the firm

Partners have the right to sell or otherwise alienate their rights to distributions, unlike corporate shareholders, however, they cannot transfer their rights to participate in control without their co-partners' consent.[159] Like the other partnership default rules, this assumes that each partner is a co-manager and therefore is not fungible with other investors, as are corporate shareholders.

These rights raise at least two important issues. First, to what extent should partners be able to protect their interests in the firm from their individual creditors? The rights of partners' creditors must be balanced against those of the non-debtor owners to continue to exercise their substantial management rights free from creditors' interference. These owner and creditor rights may collide in partnerships. Unlike in a publicly held firm, an individual partner may be able to exercise significant control over the partnership and thereby restrict distributions that creditors otherwise would be able to reach by levying on the partner's interest. Moreover, unlike in a corporation, the creditor who levies on, or 'charges, a partnership interest cannot, by foreclosure, take over the voting power of the stock because the charging creditor is no more than a transferee of the partner's financial rights.'[160] Instead, the creditor's rights are subject to those of the owner, including the debtor himself.

The laboratory of state law has dealt with this issue. State general partnership statutes vary as to whether a charging creditor can foreclose on the debtor's partnership interest.[161] This is a significant issue under general partnership law because foreclosure permits the creditor to obtain a judicial dissolution and liquidation of a partnership without an unexpired term.[162] Foreclosure and dissolution rights may or may not carry over from general to the limited partnership statutes under current law. Although these statutes do not explicitly provide for dissolution by members' creditors,[163] they incorporate general partnership terms

---

156 See ibid., at app. 8-1 (summarizing state statutory provisions).

157 See Ribstein and Kobayashi, *supra* n. 91.

158 See Ribstein, *supra* n. 66, at p. 2.

159 See Unif. P'ship Act § 27 (1914), 6 U.L.A. 736 (1995); Rev. Unif. P'ship Act § 503 (amended 1997), 6 U.L.A. 91 (Supp. 2001).

160 See Unif. P'ship Act § 28 (1914), 6 U.L.A. 744 (1995); Rev. Unif. P'ship Act § 504 (amended 1997), 6 U.L.A. 92-93 (Supp. 2001).

161 See Bromberg and Ribstein, *supra* n. 9, at § 3.05(d)(3)(v); see also ibid., at § 3.05(d)(3)(i) (discussing whether charging order is creditor's exclusive remedy).

162 See Unif. P'ship Act § 32 (1914), 6 U.L.A. 803 (1995); Rev. Unif. P'ship Act § 801(6) (amended 1997), 6 U.L.A. 108-09 (Supp. 2001). This means that a partnership's creditors, unlike those of a corporation, do not have the type of 'affirmative asset partitioning' that gives them 'liquidation protection' against owners' creditors. See Hansmann and Kraakman, *supra* n. 103, at p. 394.

163 See Rev. Unif. Ltd. P'ship Act § 801 (amended 1985), 6A U.L.A. 240-41 (1995).

to the extent that these are not inconsistent with the limited partnership statute.[164] This raises the question whether the general partnership provision on the assignee's right to compel dissolution is 'inconsistent',[165] as one leading case has held.[166] The ULPA revision clarifies that issue through a special limited partnership provision that permits judicial dissolution actions only by a partner.[167] On the other hand, ULLCA provides both for foreclosure of LLC interests and for judicial dissolution on application by transferees of interests.[168] These variations set the stage for evolution and competition among both states and business forms on this issue.

The second issue regarding partner property rights concerns free transferability of management rights. Because restricted transferability assumes that members are co-managers, it arguably follows that the default rule should differ in firms where that assumption does not hold. Partnership-type statutes that include rules based on centralized management arguably should provide for free transferability of management rights for non-managing members. Yet restricted transferability of management rights is still the rule for all interests in partnership-type firms. This may be because such transferability is the tax and regulatory dividing line between corporate-type and partnership-type firms.[169] This may also be an example of tax and regulation trumping efficient state law evolution of business forms. On the other hand, a transferability-based distinction among business forms may be more efficient than other bases because it is less likely to induce firms to make inefficient tax or regulation-induced adjustments in form.[170]

4.5 **Fiduciary duties**

Because fiduciary duties minimize agency costs associated with the separation of ownership from management rights, they arguably should apply only when partners act as agents.[171] Indeed, imposing fiduciary duties when partners act as owners to protect their interests – for example, by voting on partnership transactions, selling their ownership interests, exiting the firm, or expelling other partners – actually could increase agency costs by inhibiting partners from monitoring managers. It follows that fiduciary duties should not apply, or at least not strictly require unselfish conduct, when partners act as owners rather than as managers or agents. Apart from optimal default rules, fiduciary duties are part of the contract among the partners and therefore should be subject to contrary agreement.[172] Finally, the statutes should provide some mechanism for enforcing fiduciary duties, again subject to contrary agreement. The following subsections raise issues concerning fiduciary duties that can be, and have been, addressed in the laboratory of state laws.

---

[164] See id. § 1105, 6A U.L.A. 302 (1995).

[165] See L.E. Ribstein, 'Linking Statutory Forms', 58 *Journal of Law and Contemporary Problems* (1995) p. 187 (discussing general linkage issue).

[166] *Baybank* v. *Catamount Constr., Inc.*, 693 A.2d 1163 (N.H. 1997).

[167] See Unif. Ltd. P'Ship Act (2001) § 802.

[168] See Unif. Ltd. Liab. Co. Act § 504(b), §801(5) (amended 1996), 6A U.L.A 107 (Supp. 2001) (discussing foreclosure and dissolution, respectively).

[169] See 26 U.S.C. § 7704 (1994) (providing that partnerships with freely transferable shares are subject to double corporate taxation). Prior to check-the-box, transferability also was one of the attributes that distinguished corporations from partnerships under the classification rules. See Treas. Reg. § 301.7701-2(a)(2) (1994).

[170] See Ribstein, *supra* n. 62, at pp. 469-70.

[171] See L.E. Ribstein, 'Are Partners Fiduciaries?', *Illinois Law Review* (2005) p. 209.

[172] See F. Easterbrook and D. Fischel, 'Contract and Fiduciary Duty', 36 *Journal of Law and Economics* (1993) p. 425; Ribstein, *supra* n. 23.

4.5.1 *Managers v. owners*

To what extent should default duties reflect degrees of centralization of management? This issue mirrors those regarding financial rights, agency, and transferability discussed above. Given the model of co-equal ownership in the general partnership, it would seem to follow that partners would not have default fiduciary duties when they are acting solely as owners rather than as managers. That is, in this situation, partners would be able to act selfishly, subject to general contract and good faith principles. This is consistent with UPA section 21, titled *Partner Accountable as a Fiduciary*,

> 'which requires partners to "account to the partnership for any benefit and hold as trustee for it any profits derived by him without the consent of the other partners"'

from partnership transactions.[173] Despite its title, this provision simply forbids a partner from taking more from the partnership than the partners have agreed. To be sure, the classic statement of partners' fiduciary duties, by Justice Cardozo in *Meinhard* v. *Salmon*,[174] seems to go much further:

> 'Not honesty alone, but the punctilio of an honor the most sensitive, is then the standard of behavior. As to this there has developed a tradition that is unbending and inveterate. Uncompromising rigidity has been the attitude of courts of equity when petitioned to undermine the rule of undivided loyalty by the 'disintegrating erosion' of particular exceptions. [citation omitted] Only thus has the level of conduct for fiduciaries been kept at a level higher than that trodden by the crowd. It will not consciously be lowered by any judgment of this court.'[175]

But close analysis of partnership cases reveals that courts, consistent with the language of UPA section 21, attend to the nature of specific contracts in applying fiduciary duties.[176]

RUPA confuses the law by generally characterizing partners as fiduciaries and then ambiguously qualifying this characterization. RUPA section 404 defines 'general standards of partner's conduct', to include an explicit 'duty of loyalty' and a 'duty of care'.[177] In order to deal with the many cases referred to above in which partners were held not to be acting as fiduciaries, RUPA section 404 qualifies these general duties as follows:

> '(e) A partner does not violate a duty or obligation under this [Act] or under the partnership agreement merely because the partner's conduct furthers the partner's own interest.
> (f) A partner may lend money to and transact other business with the partnership, and as to each loan or transaction, the rights and obligations of the partner are the same as those of a person who is not a partner, subject to other applicable law.'[178]

These provisions are unclear.[179] At their broadest, they can be taken to negate the general 'standards' elsewhere in section 404. The most straightforward interpretation is that part-

---

[173] Unif. P'Ship Act § 21 (1914), 6 U.L.A. 608 (1995).
[174] 164 N.E. 545 (N.Y. 1928).
[175] Ibid., at p. 546.
[176] See Ribstein, *supra* n. 23.
[177] Rev. Unif. P'ship Act § 404 (amended 1997), 6 U.L.A. 83 (Supp. 2001).
[178] Ibid.
[179] See L.E. Ribstein, 'The Revised Uniform Partnership Act, Not Ready for Prime Time', 49 *Business Lawyer* (1993) p. 45, at pp. 54-55.

ners are not subject to a fiduciary duty when they are not acting as fiduciaries. This can be reconciled with the remainder of section 404, which does not impose a fiduciary duty on all partners, but literally only defines the 'only fiduciary duties a partner owes to the partnership'[180] – that is, when one is owed.

Because of its ambiguity, RUPA section 404 eliminates whatever advantage might otherwise have been derived from statutory definition of partners' duties. This problem is exacerbated by the limited waivability of fiduciary duties under RUPA discussed below. Unfortunately, many of the states that have adopted RUPA, which now exceed a majority of US jurisdictions, are taking along with it these undesirable features. This illustrates the potential harm that can be caused by promulgation of uniform law proposals.[181]

Horizontal and vertical choice and statutory and common law evolution, however, mitigate the harm caused by RUPA. In particular, many LLC statutes clearly separate the fiduciary duties of managing members from the looser, good faith duties of non-managing members.[182] A similar rule is emerging in limited partnership case law[183] and is included in the revised ULPA.[184] Statutory provisions explicitly authorizing fiduciary duty contracts, discussed in the next subsection, further mitigate problems under standard form provisions.

Questions concerning the consequences of centralization of management also arise regarding disclosure duties. It has been argued that, when ownership and management are separated, the non-managing owners should have relatively weak access to information to reflect their weak fiduciary duties regarding use of the information they obtain.[185] But it also could be argued that isolation from control creates a greater need for information and therefore justifies stronger information rights. Indeed, courts follow this approach when determining the applicability of the US securities laws.[186]

These questions are best resolved through firm-specific contracts that reflect variations concerning the potential for member abuse of information and through evolution of statutory default provisions in different states and business forms. For example, perhaps the information rights of limited partners, who are completely locked out of control by the limited partnership *control rule*, should differ from those of non-managing LLC members who are not similarly impeded. Even within a given business form there is room for several different approaches. Reflecting these uncertainties concerning the optimal rule, US jurisdictions have shown remarkable variability regarding members' information rights in LLC statutes.[187]

---

180 Rev. Unif. P'ship Act § 404 (amended 1997), 6 U.L.A. 83 (Supp. 2001).

181 See Ribstein and Kobayashi, *supra* n. 5, at pp. 146-48 (discussing the potential of uniform law proposals to spur adoption of inefficient statues).

182 See Ribstein and Keatinge, *supra* n. 20, at app. 9-1 (describing and tabulating statutes).

183 See Bromberg and Ribstein, *supra* n. 9, at § 16.07(a).

184 See Unif. Ltd. P'Ship Act (2001) § 305 (describing limited duties of limited partners). The Comment to section 30 makes clear that '[t]he obligation of good faith and fair dealing is not a fiduciary duty, does not command altruism or self-abnegation, and does not prevent a partner from acting in the partner's own self-interest.' Ibid.

185 J.W. Callison and A.W. Vestal, '"They've Created a Lamb with Mandibles of Death": Secrecy, Disclosure, and Fiduciary Duties in Limited Liability Firms', 76 *Indiana Law Journal* (2001) p. 271.

186 These laws apply to the offer or sale of a *security*, the existence of which has been held to depend significantly on whether the investor's participation in management was significant in producing the expected return. See generally L.E. Ribstein, 'Private Ordering and the Securities Laws: The Case of General Partnerships', 42 *Case West Reserve Law Review* (1991) p. 1 (discussing the application of this case law to partnerships).

187 For a summary of LLC statutory variations, see Callison and Vestal, *supra* n. 184, at pp. 287-91. Callison and Vestal demonstrate significant jurisdictional variation despite the existence of a uniform law and condemn

4.5.2 *Waiver of fiduciary duties*

Whatever the statutory rules concerning fiduciary duties in partnership-type firms, they clearly should be, and essentially are, subject to contrary agreement.[188] There are strong policy reasons for permitting contractual tailoring of duties to particular relationships. Among other things, there may be considerable costs associated with empowering partners to sue under broad and ambiguous fiduciary duty rules.[189] The arguments against enforcement of fiduciary duty waivers are based mainly on the contracting parties' inability to protect themselves against oppressive contracts or to foresee potential harm. These arguments should have no more traction in business association contracts than in contracts generally.[190]

In any event, because partnerships, like other business associations, clearly are voluntary relationships, contracts inevitably will hold sway. If a state forbids waivers in one or more forms, the parties can contract for a different business form or type of relationship, or for application of the law of another state. The issue, therefore, is not whether the law forbids fiduciary duty waivers, but how costly it makes them.

Delaware has taken the lead in enacting legislative provisions that explicitly permit contracting around partnership-type fiduciary duties. These provisions first entered Delaware's limited partnership act,[191] and now are also found in Delaware's LLC[192] and general partnership[193] acts. Several LLC statutes provide for broad power to waive fiduciary duties.[194] Courts have interpreted these provisions expansively to give full range to freedom of contract, subject to reasonable interpretation of fiduciary duty provisions, including general contractual good faith duties.[195] A few other states also permit full waiver of fiduciary duties in partnership-type limited liability firms.[196]

Should statutes give parties the same freedom to waive fiduciary duties in all types of partnership-type firms? One might argue that there should be more stringent limits on contracting in general partnership – which is the default form for very informal firms – than in LLCs and limited partnerships that require a filing and are usually done with the advice of counsel. On the other hand, because fiduciary duties may be inappropriate for closely held, owner-managed general partnerships,[197] restrictions on waiver may be most costly for such firms. Again, these issues arguably are appropriate for resolution in the state law laboratory. If, despite competition among forms, firms continue to form partnerships that are subject to anti-waiver rules, this provides some evidence that firms forming general partnerships prefer to be bound by restrictions on waiver.[198]

---

that law's approach. Ibid., at pp. 279-80. Oddly enough, they nevertheless advocate that this issue be dealt with in uniform laws. Ibid., at pp. 291-92.

[188] See Ribstein, *supra* n. 23.

[189] See L.E. Ribstein, 'Law v. Trust', 81 *Boston University Law Review* (2001) p. 553, at pp. 577-79.

[190] See generally H.N. Butler and L.E. Ribstein, 'Opting Out of Fiduciary Duties: A Response to the Anti-Contractarians', 65 *Washington Law Review* (1990) p. 1; Easterbrook and Fischel, *supra* n. 172.

[191] See *supra* n. 59 and accompanying text; see also Ribstein, *supra* n. 60.

[192] Del. Code Ann. tit. 6, § 18-1101 (1999).

[193] See ibid., at § 15-103(b)(8).

[194] See Ribstein and Keatinge, *supra* n. 20, at app. 9-1.

[195] See Bromberg and Ribstein, *supra* n. 9, at § 16.07(h)(5); Ribstein and Keatinge, *supra* n. 20, at § 9.04, at 11 (Supp. 2001).

[196] See Bromberg and Ribstein, *supra* n. 20, at § 8.103 (discussing general partnership provisions); Ribstein and Keatinge, *supra* n. 20, at app. 9-1 (tabulating LLC provisions).

[197] See *supra* Section 4.5.1.

[198] However, an informal firm that a court deems to be a partnership may not realistically be said to be choosing its business form or applicable law.

A corollary to the point that partnership fiduciary duties are essentially contractual and subject to testing and evolution through competition and variation in state laws is that any excessive or inadequate fiduciary duties are attributable to restrictions on competition and variation. For example, attorney ethical rules in the United States are not subject to competitive forces.[199] In particular, ethical rules constrain law firms from restricting opportunistic exit and competition,[200] thereby leading to the sort of conduct Professor Hillman condemns in his article for this Symposium.[201]

4.5.3 *Enforcement of duties*

Partners have rights against the partnership for their shares of profits or other compensation and indemnification, and against individual partners for contribution toward partnership losses or for damages for breach of fiduciary duty. US law traditionally held that partners could not enforce these rights except in an action called an *accounting*, generally brought on dissolution, that resolves all of the partner's rights and obligations in a single proceeding.[202] However, some cases recognized partners' rights to sue without an accounting,[203] and RUPA explicitly permits partners to use non-accounting actions to enforce partnership rights.[204]

Although the RUPA approach seems sensible, it is not free from doubt. Given the potential for litigation to disrupt the partnership relationship, the partnership default rule arguably should restrict such suits until global resolution on dissolution and winding up, when there is no more relationship to preserve.[205] That seems particularly logical in the very closely held general partnership. However, in firms with centralized management, partner suits may be needed as a way to police the firm's agents. Once again, this issue is appropriate for resolution in the laboratory of state laws. There is, in fact, variation among the states, particularly regarding explicit recognition of derivative suits in LLCs.[206]

4.6 **Dissociation and dissolution**

As with other partnership issues, there is a range of policy choices regarding partner exit from the firm. On the one hand, given the restricted transferability of and limited market for partnership interests, partners need to be able to either dissolve the firm or sell interests back to the firm (or the other partners) in order to have a viable ability to exit the firm. Partner exit rights give partners control over their investments and thereby constrain copartners' opportunism more effectively than the weaker powers to vote or to sue for copartner misconduct.[207] Moreover, the stronger the partners' ownership rights in the firm's

---

199 See Ribstein, *supra* n. 94.

200 See L.E. Ribstein, 'Ethical Rules, Agency Costs and Law Firm Structure', 84 *Virginia Law Review* (1998) p. 1707, at pp. 1735-38 (discussing how these restrictions may injure clients).

201 See Hillman, *supra* n. 94, at 1062.

202 See Bromberg and Ribstein, *supra* n. 9, at § 6.08(c) (discussing accounting 'exclusivity' rule).

203 The leading case is *Sertich* v. *Moorman*, 783 P.2d 1199 (Ariz. 1989).

204 Rev. Unif. P'ship Act § 405 (amended 1997), 6 U.L.A. 87-88 (Supp. 2001).

205 See S. Levmore, 'Love It or Leave It: Property Rules, Liability Rules, and Exclusivity of Remedies in Partnership and Marriage', 58 *Law and Contemporary Problems* (1995) p. 221.

206 See Ribstein and Keatinge, *supra* n. 20, at app. 10-1 (tabulating statutes).

207 See Levmore, *supra* n. 205, at pp. 237-39.

assets, the stronger their incentives to participate in developing these assets.[208] On the other hand, partner exit rights invite opportunistic conduct in the form of withdrawing property that is the product of joint investment, or threatening to do so in order to extort a payoff from their co-partners. This risk of opportunism, in turn, dilutes the partners' incentives to invest in the firm.[209] In general, the problem is one of finding the appropriate balance between these costs of exit and of continuity.

Partnership law in the United States began with the single UPA rule that each partner can dissolve the firm at will, even if contrary to the partnership agreement.[210] This sort of strong exit rule is appropriate for very closely held firms that consist of particular individuals making unique contributions and that change fundamentally when one individual leaves. However, the rule probably does not suit many partnerships that want rules that encourage the partners to stay.[211] Partners always have been able to contract around the UPA default rule by entering into a partnership agreement in which they agree to continue the firm notwithstanding a partner's exit.[212] The UPA also provides a kind of default continuation agreement for partners who agree to a partnership for a particular term or undertaking, pursuant to which the leaving partner must pay damages and is not entitled to share in the goodwill of the continuing firm.[213] Under either type of agreement, partner dissociation would cause only a technical dissolution after which the business of the firm would continue. But these agreements may not provide enough continuity for many firms because strong default exit rules may be traps lying in wait for partners who have neglected to provide for continuity in a particular situation. Moreover, even a technical dissolution may raise questions concerning the continuity of the partnership's rights and obligations in contracts with third parties.[214]

RUPA eliminates even technical dissolution in the event of certain types of partner dissociation, as where the partner dissociates wrongfully or by death or bankruptcy[215] – the sorts of sudden departure where forcing buyout or liquidation can wreak the most havoc. Thus, the states now offer a choice between UPA and RUPA exit rules.[216]

Even more importantly, states have developed additional variations through LLC and limited partnership statutes. In particular, some statutes have eliminated not only default dissolution upon member dissociation, but also the right to dissociate, meaning that members can take their services elsewhere, but may not be able to remove their investments from the firm.[217] This evolution was driven to some extent by the federal tax law changes

---

[208] See generally S.J. Grossman and O.D. Hart, 'The Costs and Benefits of Ownership: A Theory of Vertical and Lateral Integration', 94 *Journal of Political Economy* (1986) p. 691.

[209] For discussions of the opportunism problem in closely held firms, see L.E. Ribstein, 'A Statutory Approach to Partner Dissociation', 65 *Washington University Law Quarterly* (1987) p. 357; E.B. Rock and M.L. Wachter, 'Waiting for the Omelet to Set: Match-Specific Assets and Minority Oppression in Close Corporations', 24 *Journal of Corporate Law* (1999) p. 913.

[210] See Unif. P'ship Act §§ 31, 38 (1914), 6 U.L.A. 771, 880 (1995).

[211] See Ribstein, *supra* n. 209.

[212] See Bromberg and Ribstein, *supra* n. 9, at § 7.13.

[213] Unif. P'ship Act §§ 31, 38 (1914), 6 U.L.A. 771, 880 (1995).

[214] See Bromberg and Ribstein, *supra* n. 9, at § 7.14(b) (discussing effect of dissolution on partnership's executory contracts).

[215] Rev. Unif. P'ship Act § 801 (amended 1997), 6 U.L.A. 108 (Supp. 2001).

[216] See Bromberg and Ribstein, *supra* n. 20, at ch. 8 (summarizing state variations on RUPA provisions).

[217] See Bromberg and Ribstein, *supra* n. 9, § 17.01(c) n.19 (listing limited partnership provisions); Ribstein and Keatinge, *supra* n. 20, at app. 11-1 (tabulating LLC statutes).

that allowed much more flexibility in the types of firms that are entitled to elect partnership-type taxation.[218] It has also been affected by estate tax laws that impose higher taxes on interests in firms governed by state laws that provide by default for liquidation on partner dissociation.[219]

Has state competition produced an optimal mix of exit rules? Eliminating partners' default exit right swings the pendulum toward permitting oppression of locked-in partners. Indeed, close corporations were long plagued by such problems, which triggered complex and unpredictable judicial remedies to relieve minority oppression.[220] The application of estate tax rules irrespective of the rights provided for in the agreement may have encouraged legislatures to provide for a higher level of default continuity than would have been the case apart from tax considerations. State competition and evolution arguably produced an optimal mix of rules if tax considerations are taken into account.

4.7 Switching and changing forms

The many new forms that have been developed, and the changes within forms discussed above, raise problems as well as benefits. The basic issue is how to balance the benefits of legal evolution against the need to protect the rights of parties who are caught up in the changes.[221]

To begin with, the proliferation of standard statutory forms creates a need for procedures that simplify the task of moving from one form to another. The traditional method in a general partnership was to dissolve and liquidate the firm, triggering tax and other costs of discontinuity. But the states have reduced switching costs by providing merger and conversion procedures that allow partnerships to combine with or become other types of entities without dissolving.[222] This promotes legal evolution by encouraging existing firms to move to the new forms. On the other hand, the ability to switch easily into limited liability forms may hurt third party creditors of the original business, among others.

This raises the broader topic of the effect of changes within statutory forms. Again, while these changes are an inherent part of the beneficial evolution described above, they may frustrate the expectations of those who have relied on the existing rules. For example, members or partners may have relied on dissolution and dissociation at will, and therefore may be hurt by changing the rules to restrict these rights.

Case law applying common law creditor-protection rules or the contract clause of the US Constitution[223] may protect parties' expectations. The problem with these approaches, however, is that they are applied *ex post* by courts, and therefore may frustrate the expectations of some parties while attempting to protect those of others. Here, too, it is worth considering what the laboratory of state laws might accomplish regarding, for example, rules specifying prospective application of changes in dissociation and dissolution provisions.

---

218 See *supra* Section 3.3.2.

219 See Ribstein and Keatinge, *supra* n. 20, at ch. 18.

220 See generally Ribstein and Letsou, *supra* n. 57, at § 5.05(c).

221 See L.E. Ribstein, 'Changing Statutory Forms', 1 *Journal of Small and Emerging Business Law* 11 (1997), reprinted in 39 *Corporate Practitioner Commentator* (1998) p. 703.

222 See Ribstein and Keatinge, *supra* n. 20, at § 11.16.

223 See *supra* n. 14 and accompanying text.

4.8 The limits of variation in business forms

How many different business forms should there be? Here, too, important policy choices lie along a spectrum and are best addressed through state law competition and variation. There are costs to 'linking' business forms or adopting 'unified' business entity laws and thereby foregoing the advantages of facilitating regulatory arbitrage and providing different business rules to suit different types of firms.[224]

On the other hand, linkage does have the important benefit of permitting firms to use case law, customs, and forms associated with both of the linked forms that aid in the application and interpretation of the statute and private agreement, thereby encouraging the development and use of new business forms.[225] The greater the number of forms, the greater are owners' and third parties' information costs of selecting and dealing with firms, and the less the potential for standardization and development of private forms and case law interpretations. This suggests that standard forms should not provide every feasible combination of default rules.

Because the current menu of choices has emerged from substantial state competition and evolution over the past few years, there is reason to believe that it efficiently reflects firms' needs. However, from a theoretical standpoint there is an additional option the states might consider – an open-ended *contractual entity* that enables firms to have the advantage of limited liability without having to confine themselves to an existing set of default rules.[226] This device might *incubate* new standard forms by encouraging parties to enter into new types of contracts.

5. Implications of the analysis

The above analysis holds lessons for statutory law development, including those underway in Europe. Most importantly, this chapter demonstrates the benefits of *horizontal* jurisdictional competition to facilitate market-testing, variety, and evolution of laws. In this respect, the United States may have an inherent advantage over individual European countries where there are no significant subordinate political entities. It has been pointed out that '[f]or most of the last 300 years, the richest nation in the world has had a federal structure.'[227] In other words, federal systems are likely to beat unitary jurisdictions in international competition.

The US model also might work for Europe as a whole. The disappearance of international trade barriers may reduce the significance of whether countries are allied in a US-style federal system. This suggests that the best path for Europe is to facilitate competition regarding business association laws rather than eliminating competition through *harmo-*

---

[224] See L.E. Ribstein, 'Making Sense of Entity Rationalization', 58 *Business Lawyer* (2003) p. 1023.

[225] See Ribstein and Kobayashi, *supra* n. 86; Ribstein, *supra* n. 165.

[226] See generally L.E. Ribstein, 'Limited Liability Unlimited', 24 *Delaware Journal of Corporate Law* (1999) p. 407.

[227] B. Weingast, 'The Economic Role of Political Institutions: Market-Preserving Federalism and Economic Development', 11 *Journal of Law, Economics, and Organization* (1995) p. 1, at p. 3. For other historical and comparative discussions of different federal systems, see W. Riker, *Federalism: Origin, Operation, Significance* (New York, Little, Brown and Company 1964); F.A. Hayek, *The Economic Conditions of Interstate Federalism* (Chicago, University of Chicago Press 1939), in F. Hayek, *Individualism and the Economic Order* (Chicago, University of Chicago Press 1948) ch. 12.

nization. To the extent that centralizing law-drafting functions is desirable, it can be best accomplished through promulgation of *model* laws rather than by compelling uniformity through federal mandates.[228]

There may be, however, significant differences between Europe and the United States that prevent the development of US-style competition in Europe. This difference is not constitutional, because there may be a firmer constitutional basis for jurisdictional competition in post-*Centros* Europe than in the United States.[229] Rather, inherent legal, cultural, language, historical and other differences among European countries may play a greater role in constraining firms' ability to choose from among different jurisdictions. Also, jurisdictional competition in Europe must overcome the *real seat* choice of law rule, which *Centros* has not necessarily displaced.[230] Moreover, lawyers may not be able to take the lead in law reform in Europe as they have in the United States[231] because of differences between lawyers' role and the structure of the bar in the two contexts. All of this is not to say that jurisdictional competition cannot arise in Europe. For example, LLP legislation in England apparently was provoked by competition from Jersey.[232] Moreover, the *Centros* line of cases may bring the end of the real seat rule as new firms establish in the United Kingdom to avoid the rule.[233] However, jurisdictional competition in Europe may never take the full-fledged US form.

These differences suggest that it may be appropriate to design legal rules to compensate for the reduced feasibility of competition in the European context. These rules might mimic competition by providing for menus of business features within individual statutes.[234] Although a menu offered by a single lawmaker is not equivalent to jurisdictional choice, menus may be a viable, second-best alternative to facilitate adaptation and variation given inherent constraints on jurisdictional competition.

Europe may differ from the United States not only in terms of the competitive dynamic, but also in terms of the optimal rules and, therefore, the likely outcome of an efficient competition. In particular, there may be less need for limited liability for small firms given the reduced threat of tort liability in Europe as compared to the United States. The growth of limited liability in the United States may be partly attributable to the revolution in tort liability.[235] In Europe, by contrast, limited liability in small firms arguably adds little protection because owners of small firms would be liable for their own acts in any case, and most of their remaining business and personal liability would be insurable or subject to limitation by contract.[236]

---

228 See Ribstein and Kobayashi, *supra* n. 91.

229 See *supra* Section 3.1.

230 See text accompanying *supra* n. 3.

231 See *supra* text accompanying n. 47.

232 See McCahery and Vermeulen, *supra* n. 55, at 866 n. 50

233 See M. Becht, C. Mayer and H.F. Wagner, Corporate Mobility and the Costs of Regulation, ECGI – Law Working Paper No. 70/2006, available at <http://ssrn.com/abstract=906066> (finding an increase in UK incorporations of firms not physically located in the UK, mostly coming from other EU countries subject to the *Centros* rule).

234 A menu approach has been recommended for the American system to deal with the supposed problems created by network externalities. See Klausner, *supra* n. 50. However, network externalities probably do not impede jurisdictional competition in the United States sufficiently to justify reliance on this method there. See *supra* n. 86 and accompanying text.

235 See *supra* Section 4.1.1.

236 See *Williams* v. *Natural Life Health Foods Ltd*, 1 *WLR* 830, 2 *All ER* 577 (1998), in which the House of Lords held that an employee of a limited company was not personally liable for his own negligent misstatement

6. Concluding remarks

As this chapter shows, enforcing jurisdictional choice can have profound benefits for the evolution of business law. Because humans cannot accurately foresee and provide for the future, a market-oriented evolutionary process is preferable to government-imposed rules. Markets, not governments, have the wisdom necessary to guide firms in an uncertain world. Thus, policymakers should be wary of top-down planning and the hegemony of theory untested in the markets. Policy reform should focus on the mechanisms of legal evolutions and markets for law rather than on the substantive provisions of business law. These lessons have important implications for Europe as it enters the post-*Centros* age.

because, under *Hedley Byrne and Co Ltd.* v. *Heller and Partners Ltd.*, there was an absence of reliance sufficient to create a special relationship between plaintiff and defendant that would justify liability for negligent misrepresentation. This is a contract-type privity argument that may not have held up against wide-open tort theories in the United States.

Chapter 3

UNCORPORATIONS AND THE DELAWARE STRATEGY

Saul Levmore*

1. INTRODUCTION

Will jurisdictions that dominate corporate law dominate partnership law, and other 'uncorporate' (non-corporate) forms, as well? Should we anticipate federal legislation with respect to partnerships, limited liability companies, and other 'uncorporations', to recapitulate federal involvement in corporate law? These are important questions without obvious answers. These questions are avoided, or perhaps simply not confronted, in the academic literature, which is otherwise rich in its discussion of incorporation and alternatives to it. In this essay, I set out a few claims with respect to these matters, and then a blueprint for future work. The first of these claims is that, contrary to conventional wisdom which depicts federal intervention as arising where there is a regulatory vacuum, national regulation often follows substantial state regulation. The second is that it is useful to think of Delaware as pursuing a distinct strategy with respect to corporations and uncorporations. The nature of this strategy and the thinking behind it is, however, open to interpretation, as the Delaware strategy is consistent with a variety of policies and assumptions about competitive behavior.

This chapter draws on two important articles as starting points for these inquiries. One is a paper by Professor Larry Ribstein on the puzzle of the dominance of the corporate form,[1] and the other is one by Professor Mark Roe on the importance of federal-state, as opposed to interstate, competition in the regulation of corporations.[2] Section 2 offers a brief review of these contributions, with some critical reactions. Section 3 incorporates an argument about the role of crises in bringing about federal incursions into business law. This evolutionary explanation makes it possible to weave together the pattern of federal-state competition for corporate law with notions about the competition, if it can be called that, between corporate law and partnership (and other 'uncorporate') law. Section 4 brings on the puzzle of Delaware's own corporation-uncorporation strategy. Section 5 concludes with some ideas for future work.

---

* Dean and William B. Graham Professor of Law, University of Chicago Law School. I am grateful for suggestions received from Kevin Blackman, John Coates, and Larry Ribstein, and from participants at the University of Illinois UNCORPORATION Symposium in April 2004.

[1] L.E. Ribstein, 'Why Corporations?', 1 *Berkeley Business Law Journal* (2004) p. 183.

[2] M.J. Roe, 'Delaware's Competition', 117 *Harvard Law Review* (2003) p. 588.

J.A. McCahery, L. Timmerman and E.P.M. Vermeulen (eds.), Private Company Law Reform

2. The popularity of the corporate form and its regulation

2.1 Why corporations or uncorporations?

Professor Ribstein first asks why corporations remain so popular and then declines to accept conventional – and inadequate – answers.[3] The question arises because uncorporations' income is generally taxed less, which is to say once rather than twice, and because they offer substantial flexibility for co-venturers who want to blaze their own path even as there are default rules for those who want tried and true rules to govern their principal-agent, formation, dissolution, and other arrangements.[4] A sophisticated observer might insist that businesses prefer the corporate form, and especially Delaware's version of it, because there is a great deal of experience and settled law for such entities.[5] The default rules for corporations may often be more mandatory than default in character, but they provide predictability, or at least a kind of mainstream solidity, that can be attractive to investors. If investors choose non-waivable, clear rules of engagement over flexible, and even less expensive material, we might simply recognize this preference for experience and certainty. There is much more to be said about Delaware's advantage, but this is hardly the place to tweak conventional wisdom on that subject. I will proceed with the shared and common understanding that, at present, Delaware is simply immensely popular, perhaps because of network effects (with so many corporations arranged there, it is convenient to share in the pool of law and practitioners operating in that stew) or reliability.[6] Delaware is also said to be beholden to corporations which provide it with substantial tax revenue,[7] though that claim is a more vulnerable one, and is touched on below.[8]

Twenty years ago it may have been convincing to claim that the prevalence of corporations in the business sector could be explained by the fact that the law surrounding these entities was more certain, and that legal certainty or even network effects explained the dearth of partnerships and other forms. But time has weakened that explanation, for the intervening years and potential profit have not done much to stimulate change.[9]

There is no shortage of attempts to explain the dominance of the corporate form. Thus, one contrarian approach is to argue that the apparent tax disadvantage of two-tier corporate taxation is actually an advantage because it puts all investors on equal footing with respect

---

[3] Ribstein, *supra* n. 1, at pp. 196-99.

[4] In the spirit of this Symposium, I endeavor to use the terms *uncorporations* and *uncorporate law* interchangeably with expressions such as non-corporate forms, or partnership law and limited liability company law, meaning always to refer to the law enabling and regulating non-corporate forms of business activity.

[5] Alternatively, attorneys may be continuing to guide clients towards corporate forms because they are familiar with the legal implications of different strategies under corporate law. This trend may be due to risk aversion on the part of attorneys, or to the lower transaction costs associated with the use of familiar, corporate law.

[6] See R.J. Gilson, 'Globalizing Corporate Governance: Convergence of Form or Function', 49 *American Journal of Comparative Law* (2001) p. 329, at p. 350 (noting that the aggregation of public companies in Delaware creates a 'de facto national corporate law'); E. Kamar, 'A Regulatory Competition Theory of Indeterminacy in Corporate Law', 98 *Columbia Law Review* (1998) p. 1908, at pp. 1910-11 (discussing Delaware's sources of competitive advantage).

[7] R. Romano, 'Law as a Product: Some Pieces of the Incorporation Puzzle', *Journal of Law, Economics, and Organization* (1985) p. 225, at p. 276.

[8] See *infra* n. 27 and accompanying text.

[9] L.E. Ribstein, 'The Evolving Partnership', 26 *Journal of Corporation Law* (2001) p. 819, at p. 833: 'If network externalities really did impede efficient evolution, partnership-type firms likely would opt for the LLP rather than the LLC form. In fact, the opposite has occurred....'

to an enterprise's disposition decisions.[10] It is thus possible that corporations are popular because tax law, combined with the structure of the corporation, facilitates the pooling of capital.

But these ideas are clever after-the-fact attempts to explain the world that we know, a world in which the corporate form dominates. They are hardly neutral reactions or assessments of the likely impact of legal rules. One suspects that if partnership law or limited liability law became as dominant and well settled as corporate law is at present – though it should be noted that corporate law is not that stable when all is said and done[11] – it would in fact be easier to explain the evolutionary success of those systems. Nor is any perceived advantage or disadvantage to the early-mover sufficient to explain the world of business law that we know.[12] A variety of forms has been tried, and the returns to successful innovation (along with the benefits available to states and law firms that facilitate such success) are so great as to make a first-mover argument implausible. At least where large enterprises with pooled capital are concerned, uncorporations are common only in a small set of industries.[13] A fair-minded observer must surely find the dominance of the corporate form a bit puzzling. In any event, Professor Ribstein devotes some space to conventional responses to the *Why Corporations*? question,[14] and I will proceed under the assumption that this is not the place to try out other ideas or counterarguments. Professor Ribstein's readers are, as usual, safe in his hands.

For the purposes of the present essay, I follow most observers in focusing not on the tax bite associated with corporations but rather on the cost of the corporate form in terms of managerial flexibility. Mandatory governance rules may be attractive to many businesses because they provide commonly understood default rules that investors can count on. An enterprise that sought new capital, and disclosed that it would announce at some future time what governance rules apply to it, would surely need to pay more for capital than if it

---

[10] H. Kanda and S. Levmore, 'Taxes, Agency Costs, and the Price of Incorporation', 77 *Virginia Law Review* (1991) p. 211, at pp. 234-36 (arguing that the two-tier tax causes investors in different tax brackets to be single-minded about disposition decisions within the corporation, though differing about distribution decisions out of the corporation).

[11] Delaware's fluctuating takeover law in the mid-1980s is such a case. The Delaware 'court decisions zig-zagged' during this period, giving little guidance to future litigants. See Roe, *supra* n. 2, at p. 626. Students of corporate law are also familiar with changes, or even unpredictability, in Delaware law with respect to corporate law issues such as special litigation committees and sale-of-control issues.

[12] A state that was an early-mover might gain some business either because it signalled its reliability in seeking to accommodate business and its perceived needs, or simply because firms would migrate in response to an innovation and then have no need to migrate away. On the other hand, first-movers can make drafting errors, and second-movers can gain a reputation for reliably imitating good innovations. Somewhat similarly, at the level of the firm rather than the state, first-movers might be disadvantaged by the higher transaction or information costs associated with the use of a new form. The market may trade new uncorporations at a discount because of uncertainty about the qualities of the untested form. Managers may, therefore, have little incentive to choose an uncorporate form before it is well-known and, in turn, it is possible that it will not become well-known. In the long run, with so much money at stake, it is hard to believe that the 'best' forms will not emerge and win out. Cf., D.S. Goldberg, 'Choice of Entity for a Venture Capital Start-up: The Myth of Incorporation', 55 *Tax Lawyer* (2002) p. 923, at p. 950 (stating that the LLC will be the 'best' choice in most start-up situations because of its tremendous flexibility).

[13] The location of uncorporations is not well explained. Conventional wisdom is that tax law explains the emergence and even prevalence of public limited liability companies (LLCs) in the real estate and natural resources industries. These businesses are able to identify more than 90% of their income as passive income and thus enjoy single-tier, pass-through taxation. See IRC § 7704 (2000).

[14] See Ribstein, *supra* n. 1, at pp. 187-89.

offered the investors some certainty about the rules of the game. On the other hand, there must be many businesses that would prefer to, and would do better if they could, contract out of or simply avoid much of the corporate law that Delaware, or another state, imposes. Professor Ribstein emphasizes that partnership-like forms are more flexible in this regard,[15] and I will follow his lead and use the word 'flexible' to mean capable of contractual design in a way that is inconsistent with, and more liberal than, that required of Delaware corporations by that state's legislature and courts. The idea is that courts will second-guess corporate managers, even as they allow partner-ship-like entities to be governed by the firm-specific rules drafted by their clever lawyers, most often in the context of *ex ante* contractual agreements.[16]

The overall picture is one in which, setting tax considerations aside, the partnership form (along with other uncorporate forms) is superior for many sophisticated investors. Anything a corporation can do, a partnership can do better. The partners can contract, or select defaults, to be like corporations in terms of governance norms. But when they want something different, perhaps because their own principal-agent relationships will thrive with different rules, they can simply contract for that as well. Viewed this way, corporations are certainly more rigid than partnerships.

Put somewhat differently, or at least in more illustrative terms, corporate law emphasizes, encourages, and to some extent mandates the primacy of the board of directors (though it is apparent that managers can influence and anoint these directors to a large degree) and the power of courts to respond to and encourage shareholder lawsuits interpreting the managers and directors' fiduciary duties. This regulatory framework may not be optimal for all firms and shareholders, and one solution is to offer an alternative regime or simply to allow shareholders the right to cash out.[17] In some sense this is precisely what partnership law offers. Readers who prefer a non-business analogue might think about the realm of politics, where many of our rules are mandatory.[18] Some citizens might prefer significantly more direct democracy than is permitted in our federal political system, for example. Direct democracy, of a sort, is much more easily integrated into a partnership than it is into a corporation, because the latter requires intermediation by the board of directors.[19]

Professor Ribstein's own attempt to explain the evolutionary success of the corporate form is rather pessimistic in nature and gives a nod to the importance of tax law (which I, too, have tried to set aside) and center stage to the concept of rent-seeking (by which is meant the fact that while managers profit from being in control, they also service legislators, and waste resources in the process, in order to protect their comfortable positions). The argument is that corporations offer managers insulation from displacement; there is,

[15] See Ribstein, *supra* n. 1, at pp. 216-23 (emphasizing the flexibility of partnership and other uncorporate law with reference to case law and also to parties' power to avoid some federal law).

[16] Delaware has embraced freedom of contract in partnerships. Ribstein, *supra* n. 1, at p. 213: ('At least in the leading state of Delaware, the [partnership] agreement may modify both loyalty and care duties, not merely the duty of care as in Delaware corporate law.').

[17] Ribstein stresses the utility of giving owners the right to cash out. Ibid., at p. 216.

[18] Citizens might prefer direct election of the President, or the power to introduce and enact federal legislation directly through plebiscite, but such preferences would require constitutional amendments to be effected. Somewhat similarly, shareholders have no simple way of bypassing or avoiding the board of directors of their corporation.

[19] Another example of flexibility relates to federal law. Partnerships, and their close relatives, may be able to avoid some federal securities law by structuring their contracts around the definition of 'security' that triggers federal law.

after all, not much in the way of direct democracy and there is a fair incentive to retain earnings if only to avoid dividend taxation. Law thus works to freeze corporations in place, and managers have no reason to push for changes in these legal rules because their well-compensated positions go along with the insulated character of the firm. The very inflexibility associated with the corporate form begets rent-seeking. The picture is one in which federal and state governments get to regulate corporations, in large part because of the corporations' inflexibility and inability to escape the regulation, and in which corporate managers become further insulated from their shareholders.

2.2 State-federal competition

But what exactly is this federal regulation, for it must be obvious that interstate competition for corporations, or at least for their chartering and governance regulation, affects state regulation in ways that it cannot possibly affect federal regulation? It is this federal-state competition that intrigues Professor Mark Roe, who points to the rather considerable volume of federal regulation – in the form of securities laws (including insider trading laws), takeover law, Sarbanes-Oxley's impact on governance law, corrupt practices sanctions, and more – and then also to the idea that states must see that the federal government is at least as important a competitor as is any other state.[20]

At one level, Professor Roe delivers an important educational message:

The most common conception of corporate law, not to mention the way in which we educate new lawyers, is fundamentally misguided. Academic commentary (and virtually every casebook and hornbook) focuses entirely on interstate competition.[21] Delaware's dominance at the state level may only be weakly understood and explored, but it is the center of activity. I suspect that most students of corporate law would be surprised to learn that Delaware also dominates the market for partnerships;[22] this importance undermines, or at least complicates, Professor Roe's excellent argument. Indeed, Delaware's success in the partnership law field weakens much of the conventional wisdom about the nature and cause of its success in corporate law.

---

[20] See Roe, *supra* n. 2, at pp. 603-34.

[21] The only debate, if it is that, is whether there is any remaining competition, or perhaps whether the competition is for law firm and other business. See M. Kahan and E. Kamar, 'The Myth of State Competition in Corporate Law', 55 *Stanford Law Review* (2002) p. 679, at pp. 687-700 (arguing that only Delaware structures its taxes to raise money and gain directly from incorporations).

[22] 'Dominates' is probably not the right word, and there is something of an apples-and-oranges comparison here because of the role of the Uniform Partnership Act and other uniform acts. Still, Delaware's legislature and courts (and law firms) are, undeniably I think, disproportionately important in uncorporate law. 'As in corporate law, Delaware has frequently amended its version of R.U.L.P.A. to accommodate newly perceived needs of organizers and managers . . . . Thus, Delaware will often be the first choice for a limited partnership that is to be formed somewhere outside its main place of operation.' See A.R. Bromberg and L.E. Ribstein, *Bromberg and Ribstein On Partnership* (Denver, Aspen Publishing 1998) § 12.25(C). Note that Delaware has experienced growth in LLCs from 67,000 in 1998 to 222,000 in 2003. By way of (virtually random) comparison, in 2003, Delaware had seven times the number of corporations, six times the number of LLCs, and two and one-half times the number of LPs as Texas; these ratios have remained roughly stable in the past five years, though the absolute number of LLCs has of course grown. E-mail from Tina Passell, Manager for Public Information and Technology, Corporations Section of the Secretary of State, State of Texas, to Kevin Blackman (July 26, 2004, 15:34:51 CST) (on file with author); E-mail from Nicole Hall, Department of State: Division of Corporations, State of Delaware, to Kevin Blackman (July 22, 2004, 09:00:01 CST) (on file with author). These illustrative data do not differentiate between public and private entities and do not tell us anything about state revenues.

At another level, Professor Roe's thesis, that Delaware's real competitor is in Washington D.C., can be understood as an evolutionary argument. It is that Delaware's corporate law is crafted with an eye toward maintaining its position not just with respect to other states, for that is the least of it (or so he holds), but especially with respect to the federal government. A strong form of this argument would be that Delaware – which is to say some combination of its legislature, bar, and judiciary – works anxiously so that the federal government does not offer federal charters for corporations or simply pre-empt and take over the chartering function, for that would really put Delaware out of business. A more modest form is that Delaware suffers a loss each time the federal government pre-empts, or takes for itself, part of the regulatory domain. Thus, when the federal government intervened with the 1933 Securities Act, with insider trading regulation, with takeover legislation and, most recently, with Sarbanes-Oxley, Delaware lost some of its market. In each case, some state law was trivialized or supplanted. Its law became less relevant and, presumably, some of the state's law business moved not only to federal courts and agencies but also to out-of-state law firms. In turn, with each bite by the federal government, Delaware's legislators became a bit less important to interest groups. Of course, Professor Roe's argument is that even if there were no federal legislation of the kind just listed, though there is of course plenty of it, the threat of federal corporate law has a strong influence on Delaware law. State law changes in fear of anticipated federal law, some of which can be avoided by the right moves at the state level in advance of any federal incursion.

It is possible to take issue with this view of state-federal competition.

Contrary to Professor Roe, and perhaps to common sense, Delaware might be indifferent to, or even welcoming of, federal intervention, though surely not total pre-emption of a kind that would take place if there were large-scale federal chartering of corporations. Assuming that Delaware's goal is to dominate the interstate market for corporate law, because it enjoys and protects either the corporate franchise tax revenues that are associated with its market position or the legal business generated by Delaware corporations, or both, then it is plausible that Delaware protects its position best if there is less terrain on which other states can innovate.

The question is empirical because in theory the impact of federal regulation (or the thinking in Delaware) could go either way. Beginning on the smug side, Delaware might reason that the more the federal government takes over, so that fewer issues remain contested among the states, the more the state's dominant position in corporate law is secure. If there is some fear at present that a competitor state will develop new and better default rules at a lower price (either in terms of corporate taxes or the cost of legal services), then this fear must diminish with fewer possible rules or subjects regarding which states could differentiate. Similarly, as the domain of state law shrinks because of federal incursions, there is less need for Delaware to fear that another state will prove superior at appealing to corporations by finding the optimal balance (from the hungry states' point of view) between captivating managers and attracting shareholders. With too much managerial slack, corporations will stay away from the state or allow share prices to drop; excessively anti-managerial rules will reduce flexibility and interfere with profit-making or simply encourage managers, who are not perfectly responsive to their investors, to lead their firms elsewhere. In short, we can go forward thinking about Delaware's strategy in a world in which Delaware seeks to avoid federal incursions, but we can also ponder its strategic thinking in an atmosphere in which it benefits from some federal incursions, especially if these limit the competitive capacity of its state competitors.

3. Federal incursions and the flexibility of uncorporations

It should be noted that Professor Roe does not offer a theory as to when we, or state lawmakers, might expect federal intervention, perhaps because he would say that there is always the threat of federal intervention. In any event, there is no reason to expect federal lawmakers to be any more or less public-regarding than state legislators. Indeed, federal lawmakers may be less so because they face less horizontal competition than do their state counterparts. But we might simply think of federal politicians and regulators as episodically interested in corporate law. They are presumably motivated by organized interest groups, either because there is private gain from responding to interest groups or because these groups bring information and focus to what lawmakers might do.

I would emphasize the role of crises, or even simple newsworthiness, in stimulating federal law. When a market crash or serious corporate scandal dominates the news, opportunistic (or responsive) politicians will be drawn to the matter and inclined to act. Sophisticated citizens might see that a dark event, and even an avoidable one, is not necessarily a sign of under-regulation, but the need or perceived need for regulation is less a matter of science than one of politics. Moreover, a major and newsworthy disappointment is often good evidence of the need for change, or it may help overcome barriers to change that were not easily overcome in the past. Much as a space shuttle explosion occasions changes at NASA and new safety rules, so too an Enron or Arthur Andersen collapse will bring about something on the order of Sarbanes-Oxley. A shuttle explosion does not prove that new safety steps were needed, but in a Bayesian manner each striking piece of evidence does change the probability that new safety steps are desirable. It is also plausible that there is a large set of cost-benefit justified regulations that could be enacted, and that a jolt simply causes politicians to reach into this set and draw out a few that can now be installed because of the altered political climate. Politics and change thrive on crisis. An even better analogy is offered by the likely federal response, to what is otherwise a matter for the states, after a major earthquake or flood or terrorist attack. The intervention may bring federal relief (and for this the states are supplicants rather than competitors), but it is also likely to beget regulation in the form of new building codes, insurance requirements, or direct precautionary steps.[23] Corporate scandals are not terribly different, even if the victims are not nearly so successful in gaining federal relief.

Viewed through such a lens, it follows that there may not be much states can do to avoid federal intervention, other than try to prevent salient events, or crises, in the first place. This is difficult, or even hopeless, not only because the best regulatory systems, like the best traffic laws, will not aim to prevent all losses, but also because federal intervention will follow a shocking scandal even if only one state could have saved the day with regulation. A state may have a terrific strategy for preventing blow-ups, and it may even be motivated by the desire to avoid federal regulation, but another state's lax enforcement or regulatory structure may cause a crisis that brings on nationwide federal intervention. Meanwhile, the zealous state might lose some corporate law business if managers prefer more flexible states.

---

[23] See S. Levmore, 'Coalitions and Quakes: Disaster Relief and Its Prevention', 34 *University of Chicago Law School Roundtable* (1996) p. 1, at pp. 32-34; S. Levmore and K.D. Logue, 'Insuring Against Terrorism – and Crime', 102 *Michigan Law Review* (2003) p. 268, at pp. 278-79.

One way or the other, we should expect an increasing amount of federal corporate law, precisely as we have experienced over the last seventy years. Crises are simply inevitable even in the face of overregulation (by state or federal power) and, as just argued, it is possible that states see little point in aggressive regulation in which case crises might happen more quickly still.[24] In the very long run, it is possible that the cost of overregulation will become apparent – perhaps through a different sort of crisis – and a national politician will benefit by deregulating this sector of the economy. This phase of the regulation cycle seems so far off at present that I will focus here only on the state-federal competition to regulate (rather than deregulate), and leave for another day the longer term view in which deregulation is a federal strategy, as it has been in other law.

If the connection between crises and federal intervention is correctly understood, then it should be noted that it is possible, though I think quite unlikely, that states, in a quest for more corporate law activity in their jurisdictions, under-regulate with the idea of allowing crises to develop – and then profiting from the predictable increase in federal regulation. This could be a winning strategy for states other than Delaware if the federal intervention did indeed take away much of Delaware's advantage. In contrast, it could, I suppose, be a strategy for Delaware to follow, if federal intervention removed opportunities for insurgent states to innovate.[25]

4. Delaware's strategy

There is much more to be said about all this state-federal competition, especially if we think of it as essentially Delaware-federal competition. But rather than pursuing various lines opened here, I turn to the particular question of Delaware's strategy with respect to the development of partnership, limited liability company, and other uncorporate law. We can think of this development as one part of Delaware's competition strategy with the federal government, not to mention with other states. We normally think of the growth of uncorporate law as something that is generated by private enterprises gravitating toward that business form. We are accustomed to asking why business firms migrate to, or begin with, the corporate form or with an alternative form, and less accustomed to asking when a state will see fit to encourage firms to undertake such migration. The firm is not the only active participant in the process. A state can affect results by making new law that investors (or managers) will find relatively attractive, by lowering the franchise and other tax costs associated with uncorporations, and by making the corporate form relatively less attractive – in the expectation that firms will migrate to the uncorporate side of the state, so to speak, rather than to other jurisdictions.

All of this takes on importance when we recognize that Delaware is significant, and perhaps as important, for partnerships and limited liability companies as it is for corporations. Whatever the source of its dominance in corporate law, that atmosphere, reliability, human capital, or political will carries over to uncorporate law. Delaware was not the first state to offer a limited liability company or limited liability partnership statute, but once

---

[24] I do not mean to imply that we are overregulated but rather that even if states sought simply to discourage federal intervention by regulating matters they thought would, if unchecked, lead to such regulation, there would inevitably be some crises anyway.

[25] See *supra* text accompanying n. 22.

Wyoming or Texas innovated, Delaware was among those states quickest to follow. Delaware was able not only to imitate and respond, but also to capture more than its share of the new market.[26] I will ignore for now the question of whether this market success shows that commentators put too much weight on Delaware's corporate franchise tax revenues when explaining its dominant position in corporate law.[27] Delaware's fees for partnerships and the like are extremely low, and yet investors (or their lawyers) seem to feel safe in Delaware's hands.[28] For now the point is simply that we must combine our understanding of state-federal competition with that of the choice of corporate form; Professors Ribstein and Roe cast light on different aspects of a single phenomenon, even though that would hardly be apparent on first reading.

If we add to this the notion that federal corporate law follows crises, either because perceived need breeds legal solutions or because politicians go where the news cameras are to be found, then it should also be clear that the distance between corporate and uncorporate law is bound to narrow. Professor Ribstein's case for uncorporations rests largely on the observation that corporate law is much more regulated, with uncorporate law significantly more flexible.[29] Principals and agents who seek to profit by delegating more flexibility to the agents than Delaware's courts have in mind for corporations, can choose to be governed by partnership law, for example. Partnership law is in this way said to be more flexible than corporate law, where default rules are more often mandatory rules.

But as more uncorporations arise, and as (or if) they occupy significant parts of the economy, then it is inevitable that newsworthy crises will draw these entities, and the forms that make them possible, into the political wringer. Federal law will grow to regulate partnerships and other forms, either with the claim that unsophisticated investors and pension funds and the like need protection or with the intent of avoiding the costs of federal bailouts – for there will be pressure for such bailouts when various interest groups lose fortunes in the wake of partnership collapses. If these uncorporate enterprises grow in importance, then the pattern that brought federal law-making to corporations will bring federal law-making to limited liability companies and their cousins. One conclusion of this essay, therefore, is that the relative flexibility of uncorporations is likely to be a short term state of affairs.

This claim, that both federal regulation of uncorporations and the narrowing of the corporation-uncorporation regulatory gap are to be expected, will seem less surprising if we think of business law as not terribly unlike other law. Federal law followed state regulation

---

26 See R.W. Hamilton, 'Entity Proliferation', 37 *Suffolk University Law Review* (2004) p. 859, at pp. 864, 870–71; Kahan and Kamar, *supra* n. 21, at p. 742 (noting Delaware's theory incentive to imitate); L.E. Ribstein and B.H. Kobayashi, 'Choice of Form and Network Externalities', 43 *William and Mary Law Review* (2001) p. 79, at p. 86.

27 I do not mean to minimize Delaware's revenues or reliance. In 2003, it collected $448 million, or 18.4% of its total revenue, from the corporate franchise tax, and just $66 million, or 2.7% of total revenue, from the corporate income tax, which is of course collected on the basis of a multi-state formula and not affected by the place of incorporation. Delaware Department of Finance, Fiscal Notebook: State General Fund (2003), available at <http://www.state.de.us/finance/ publications/fiscal_notebook_03/Section02/sec2page24.pdf> (last visited September 28, 2004).

28 Delaware limited liability companies are subject to a flat annual fee of $200 as compared to its corporations which pay, in what might be described as an old-fashioned or charming manner, based on the number of authorized shares or assumed no-par capital, a minimum of $35 to a maximum franchise tax of $165,000. Del. Code Ann. tit. 6, § 18-1107, tit. 8, § 503 (2003).

29 Ribstein, *supra* n. 1, at p. 230.

in such areas as workplace safety, highway regulation, environmental regulation, and even primary education. If partnerships grow in importance and if their mistakes or misfortunes create groups of disappointed citizens, then there is every reason to expect increased federal regulation. The difference in flexibility between corporate law and uncorporate law may be a function of the increased federal presence in corporate law – and along with it, the steps states have taken to prevent further incursions.

I am describing the growth of federal regulation of uncorporations as inevitable, but I should be more cautious. So long as partnerships and other uncorporations are the projects of relatively sophisticated investors, at least as compared to the large publicly held corporations, a scandal or major loss associated with an uncorporation may not bring on federal regulation the way it would for a corporation. Conventional, unsophisticated investors are the stuff of the evening news, as well as the cause of protective political reactions. On the other hand, pension funds and other intermediaries are better equipped to lobby for protection and for bailouts than are unsophisticated corporate shareholders, so that the case for expecting federal intervention in uncorporate law may gain as much force from interest groups as it loses from the characteristics of the likely investors.

The narrowing of the regulatory gap between corporations and uncorporations may come from state lawmakers rather than federal lawmakers, so long as the threat of federal intervention is on the horizon. It is the states that might bring about the end of uncorporations' ability to accommodate almost any bargain that investors or promoters advance. After all, if states do dread federal intervention, then we should expect state law in advance of anticipated federal law except, as before, where the state gains little from leading the pack because federal law is inevitable, as when crises are unpreventable or arise in more lax states. One way or the other, if uncorporations continue to grow in significance, then more opportunities for political intervention will arise in association with uncorporations – and increased regulation is sure to follow. The gap between corporations and uncorporations will narrow or disappear.

A very different, but related, conclusion concerns the pattern of Delaware law. Why does Delaware allow uncorporations such relative flexibility? And why does it tax uncorporations modestly? Delaware must fear migration to uncorporate forms because it has no reason to think that it can retain its strong competitive advantage once the boundaries of corporate law are breached.[30] Perhaps Delaware hopes to build up human capital and reputation in the partnership area (and with respect to other uncorporate law) before there is a large shift across the nation away from corporate law. If and when such a migration occurs, Delaware will be ready and attractive to the migrants. This view is consistent with the low franchise taxes that Delaware presently associates with uncorporations. With little established advantage in non-corporate business law, Delaware cannot afford to extract the revenues that it attracts from corporations. But as it builds up an advantage in partnership and in other non-corporate law, then we can expect increased franchise taxes for uncorporations, not to mention revenue through legal and other services provided in Delaware to enterprises that are, at least on paper, located in Delaware and subject to its courts and legislature.

---

[30] Delaware, of course, is not a single-minded 'it'. A state's laws are the product of disparate political forces, legislative and judicial minds, and interest groups. But the singular image is convenient. A state can, after all, have a strategy.

Even if Delaware sees that its own light-handed regulation of uncorporations makes federal regulation more likely in the future, it must fear competing with, or obviating, federal intervention now because individual firms will then migrate from Delaware corporate status to uncorporation status in other states. Delaware law can thus be understood as in transition. What we observe is consistent with a dominant player hoping to extend its position to a new market which is, in this case, uncorporate law.

Meanwhile, Delaware has little to fear. The migration to uncorporate status has been slow, somewhat to Professor Ribstein's surprise and in part, perhaps, because (federal) corporate tax rates have declined. At this pace, large-scale, uncorporate scandals that would bring about federal intervention may be some time off and Delaware can in the interim build up an advantage in uncorporate law. And, in the long run, Delaware can do just fine alongside active federal law-making, raising tax revenues and business from partnerships, much as it derives these from corporations today.

5. Conclusion and future inquiries

This chapter has made two claims, one about the inevitable coming of federal (and therefore state) regulation of uncorporations, and the other about Delaware's strategy in this regard. In future work, I plan to explore the question of whether increased federal regulation does indeed diminish Delaware's regulatory dominance or whether perhaps a reduced state domain leaves the leading state better off, or perhaps as well off as before. That question surely bears on the practical question of a state's best law-making strategy.

The second question for state lawmakers is what to do in their partnership and other uncorporate codes. Once it is clear that competition, to use an inaccurate word, comes not only from other states and not only from federal regulation, but also from other business forms, this question is an interesting and difficult one. Moreover, the nature of interstate competition must also be re-examined. Small states (in business terms) can attract firms with tax breaks for factories and the like, and the question is how they might attract corporations and uncorporations to make their legal homes in particular jurisdictions or whether the larger point is simply that it is unwise for eager states to go this route because of the threat of federal law. These questions are left for another effort.

Part II

PRIVATE COMPANY LAW REFORM IN EUROPE AND ASIA

Chapter 4

THE NEW COMPANY LAW: WHAT MATTERS IN AN INNOVATIVE ECONOMY

Joseph A. McCahery*, Erik P.M. Vermeulen, Masato Hisatake*** and Jun Saito******

1. Introduction

Ideally new company law vehicles are the result of legislative processes that are initiated for the most part to create mechanisms designed to reduce agency costs and satisfy the contracting interests of business parties, such as investors, firm founders and joint venture partners.[1] The voluminous literature on law and society explains that lawmakers are public regarding actors who will identify which rules are efficient across different firms and time, and replace inefficient rules accordingly. Thus conceived, the ideal and actual function of law-making is to attempt to increase social welfare by correcting market failures. Lawmakers supposedly regulate company forms in the public interest.[2]

Criticism of this public interest theory of law-making has largely focused on two shortcomings. First, legislation is not primarily the result of efficiency considerations. Second, despite similar external market pressures, differences in company law forms continue to persist. Even though there have been recent instances of formal legal convergence, current law-making procedures and pre-existing conditions tend to lock the evolution of company law structures into a particular path, thereby maintaining diversity between individual jurisdictions.[3]

* Professor of International Economic Law, Tilburg University Faculty of Law and Professor of Financial Market Regulation, Tilburg Law and Economics Center, Research Associate ECGI (Brussels).

** Professor of Law and Management, Tilburg University Faculty of Law, Fellow Center for Company Law and Tilburg Law and Economics Center, and Legal Counsel at Philips International B.V.

*** Professor of Policy Analysis, Tohoku University School of Law.

**** Executive Staff, Corporate Technology Management, Nikon Corporation, Japan.

[1] See R. Kraakman, et al., *The Anatomy of Corporate Law: A Comparative and Functional Approach* (Oxford, Oxford University Press 2004).

[2] This view corresponds to the 'public interest theory'. The public interest paradigm of lawmaking emphasizes the government's role in correcting market imperfections such as monopoly pricing and pollution. See J-J. Laffont and J. Tirole, *A Theory of Incentives in Procurement and Regulation* (Cambridge, MIT Press 1993) p. 475.

[3] Gilson distinguishes between functional convergence (when existing institutions are flexible enough to respond to the demands of changed circumstances without altering institutions' formal characteristics) and formal convergence resulting in legislative action necessary to alter the existing institutions. See R.J. Gilson, 'Globalizing Corporate Governance: Convergence of Form or Function', 49 *American Journal of Comparative Law* (2001) p. 329.

J.A. McCahery, L. Timmerman and E.P.M. Vermeulen (eds.), Private Company Law Reform

At the other end of the spectrum is the view that competitive pressures induce lawmakers to adopt the company law rules that are value-increasing. Under these circumstances, lawmakers, eager to please investors and other businesses parties, identify practices seen as enhancing firms' economic performance, will introduce company law reforms that have the potential to be more cost-effective, and suitably adapted to firms' changing business needs. Firms and their internal participants are viewed as consumers in a market for company law, in which lawmakers seek to design a predictable legal product that reduces firms' costs.[4]

Consequently, as national boundaries are of diminishing significance, the cross-fertilization of legal concepts is not so much a choice as a necessity. In many countries there is a revival of interest in company law reform projects and the introduction of new hybrid governance structures that presumptively could lead to formal convergence, as reform projects spread around the world through a combination of outright borrowing and more subtle imitation. Due largely to the worldwide development of the Internet, it is relatively easy for lawmakers to take notice of foreign legal business forms that have already been tried and tested in a legal system with similar business, social and political dimensions. If we take this a step further, the drive towards new company law at all business levels could eventually lead to more efficiency, as countries adopt rules and institutions representing the best possible outcome. This theory is based on the premise that unless a country's lawmakers consider foreign legislative approaches and solutions, the domestic economy will fall behind its competitors.

Indeed, as the influence of *legal transplants* from the United States is felt more and more in company law reform projects in both Europe and Asia, it might be expected that non-US jurisdictions will eventually display similar patterns of legal evolution as we currently see in the United States. For instance, the last decade has witnessed the rise of new legal entities and US transplants in countries that represent both common law and civil law traditions. In the United Kingdom, the promulgation of the Limited Liability Partnership (LLP) was prompted by competition from offshore LLP statutes, particularly that of Jersey where Price Waterhouse and Ernst & Young promoted the new legislation based on a similar law enacted in State of Delaware. The Department of Trade and Industry (DTI), which was directly involved in the introduction of the LLP in the United Kingdom, did not, however, just adopt the US LLP – which simply added the limited liability feature to its general partnership law provisions. Ultimately, the DTI created a stand-alone, hybrid company form that is situated between a partnership and a corporation.

Similarly, a Limited Liability Partnerships Act 2005, inspired by the Delaware LLP, came into effect on 11 April 2005 in Singapore. The Company Legislation and Regulatory Framework Committee (CLRFC) spurred the introduction of an LLP in Singapore in order to expand the governance options to be considered by small- and medium-sized businesses, professionals and investment funds. Importantly, Japan, which has a tradition to follow Germany's company law model, has recently been inspired by the success of legal innovation in the United States and the United Kingdom, resulting in the introduced two new legal forms: the LLP (*Yugensekinin-jigyo-kumiai*) and LLC (*Godo-kaisha*). These hybrid entities, which are intended to supply Japanese firms with more contractual flexibility, are arguably more suitable for firms involved in multinational joint ventures in the human capital intensive and financial services sectors.

---

[4] See R. Romano, *The Genius of American Corporate Law* (Washington, American Enterprise Institute 1993).

As politicians and business groups across Asia reflect on the changes in Japanese company law, which are seen as offering organizational advantages to firms in knowledge intensive industries, lawmakers in other Asian competitive countries, such as India and China, are already sequencing reforms that will lead to the introduction of the LLP. To the extent that India, for example, is a latecomer in adopting LLP legislation, the delay seems to have provided opportunities for lawmakers to learn from the tried and tested experiences in other jurisdictions. Effort to improve on the LLP structure, based on learning outcomes in other countries, may well benefit Indian professional firms, who are increasingly involved in international transactions, by giving them a business form that is adaptive to their competitive and litigious environment. The reform is seen as desirable, moreover, as it can help induce the introduction of more business start-ups. Similar arguments are used to the same effect by the Chinese Standing Committee of the National People's Congress, which already adopted major revisions to China's company law on 27 October 2005, including the introduction of one-person companies, lower capital requirements,[5] improved information rights and other corporate governance techniques. This laid the basis for China's top legislature to open the discussion, in April 2006, on introducing LLPs in order to stimulate venture capital investment and create a level-playing field to facilitate a competitive advantage for Chinese professional firms that increasingly operate in the global market. Importantly, the type of reforms proposed in Asia point to significant inherent benefits in terms of increased flexibility for the firms that adopt new hybrid legal forms. As they are cheaply available and combine the best of the partnership and corporate world, these flexible legal forms contain features that make them better suited to professional firms, start-ups, small family firms, and financial funds.

These developments suggest that there may be significant benefits for businesses and investors in jurisdiction that make available more productive business forms. Why do we not see a proliferation of new hybrid business forms in continental Europe? After all, the European Court of Justice decisions in the *Centros*, *Überseering* and *Inspire Art* only recently set in train the basis for the cross-border movement of administrative headquarters and the migration of new firms to more favorable jurisdictions. The ECJ case law has improved corporate mobility dramatically as a large number of continental European privately held firms have been influenced, by the absence of minimum capital requirements, to incorporate in the UK as limited companies.[6] We have to keep in mind, however, that those European firms incorporating in the UK are mostly 'round-trippers', which means that a large percentage of businesses in continental Europe could benefit directly from the development of more efficient hybrid entities in their own jurisdiction. But, they need a coalition of groups to crack open the policy-making agenda and induce national legislatures to introduce new limited liability vehicles. These reasons may be enough to explain that the impact of the ECJ's decisions has only led to patching-up initiatives in most Member States, influencing some legislatures to eliminate or reduce minimum capital for pri-

[5] For limited liability companies, the minimum capital has been decreased from RMB 100,000 to RMB 30,000 (approx. $ 3,750). A one-person company could be set up with a minimum capital of approx. $ 12,500.

[6] See M. Becht, C. Mayer and H. Wagner, 'Where Do Firms Incorporate? Deregulation and the Cost of Entry', 14 *Journal of Corporate Finance* (2008) p. 241.

vate companies. As a consequence, the demand for upgraded company law unhindered by capital maintenance requirements is relatively high across the European Union, while the introduction of new hybrid business forms is mainly viewed as unnecessary since they contribute to increased costs attributed mainly to transition issues and enhanced choice.[7]

As we will see in Section 3 of this chapter, there are three main implications for a theory of legal evolution that significantly shape the landscape of and influence the debate on company law reforms. First, the predominance of particular legal elites or traditions in the field of company law restricts the evolution of the law rather than enhancing its development.[8] Second, the standardization of legal business forms confers large increasing returns benefits to the users and their legal advisers, arguably limiting the development of modern innovative business forms. Most legal advisers tend to rely on standard legal rules, which reduce costs as most parties are familiar with them, irrespective of the cumbersome and inefficient nature of many of the standard statutory provisions. Proponents of traditional rules argue that, even if a firm has additional incentives to use an innovative legal form, they are generally unlikely to select the vehicle, despite its potential, due to the lack of certainty about its legal provisions. Third, start-up and smaller firms have considerable financial and organizational constraints that do not allow them to influence the legislature to adopt business form statutes that match their needs. Even if the existing menu of business forms imposes considerable costs on firms which are required to either comply with highly formalistic and technical regulations or contract around obsolete provisions, these firms are usually not able to run up against the presence of concentrated interest groups defending the *status quo*. Hence, even if incentives to overhaul company law are clearly present, the reform process is belated by sources of path dependence that inhibit the evolution of innovative legal business forms.

Nevertheless, if we compare and weigh up the competing interests on the supply and demand sides of legislation, we cannot predict with certitude the effects of path dependence on legal change in a particular jurisdiction. The outcome will depend largely on the effect that each interest has on the evolutionary process. If certain pressures are not present in a jurisdiction, or are mitigated by unspecified reactions and forces, the influence of path dependence factors on business forms is likely to be commensurately weaker. The application of the idea of path dependence to law shows that legal institutions evolve along a historical path and can therefore become locked-in and resistant to change. In turn, this inflexibility often leads to inefficiencies, as legal rules fail to respond to changes in the underlying social and economic conditions.

That is not to say that new hybrid business forms provide efficient and all-encompassing governance frameworks and solutions, but they arguably can play a pivotal role in transaction planning and cooperative bargaining among business participants. Opponents to new legal forms attempt to frustrate and ridicule the need of new company law. One common view is that a firm can tinker with the existing legal framework by simply adjusting the statutory provisions or combining existing legal forms to a structure that is respon-

[7] See J. Freedman, 'The Quest for an Ideal Form for Small Businesses – A Misconceived Enterprise?', in B.A.K. Rider and M. Andenas (eds.), *Developments in European Company Law Volume 2/1997: The Quest for an Ideal Legal Form for Small Businesses* (Amsterdam, Wolters Kluwer 1999).

[8] Clark distinguishes among three approaches to lawmaking: (1) contractual rulemaking; (2) elite rulemaking; and (3) traditional rulemaking. See R.C. Clark, 'Contracts, Elites, and Traditions in the Making of Corporate Law', 89 *Columbia Law Review* (1989) p. 1703.

sive to its needs. The balance of evidence suggests, however, that substantially modifying the company law statutes involves significant costs (e.g., increased information costs and uncertainty, distortions in the signaling function of business forms, decreased coherence of terms, erroneous gap-filling by courts and other negative spill-over effects) that outweigh possible benefits. In this chapter, we show how new separate business statutes are or should be more efficient in providing firms, at different levels, with a legal structure that does not impose burdens or create distortions and, hence, would have significant cost advantages.

This chapter provides an analytic framework for the development of new legal forms for closely held professional and business firms. Thus, we interpret how differences in legal forms may persist across jurisdictions, and offer some predictions on the evolution of new legal forms. In interpreting the process by which business forms have evolved so far, this chapter seeks to identify the parties that help to set the agenda for the reform of company law, and which considerations have been instrumental in stimulating the recent instigation of new law reform strategies. In order to clear up the common misconception that the law evolves towards efficiency, this chapter applies concepts of comparative law, economics, and political science to legal evolution of closely held forms.

The next section begins by examining the contractual theory of the firm. The contractual theory gives important insights into the legal structure of business organizations. Not only does this approach have the capacity to point to common problems that arise in this environment, but it also emphasizes the key function of law in defining the governance structure of the firm, supplying important contractual provisions *ex ante*, and supporting the enforcement of implicit contracts and internalized norms *ex post*. From this perspective, statutory and judicial company law should offer standardized, contractual, products that help to economize on transaction costs, such as drafting, information and enforcement costs, and to limit opportunism and fill gaps in the business context. In other words, efficient company law offers models that cover the relationships between the business participants inside the firm and the representation of the firm in its dealings with outside participants, such as creditors. Company law statutes act thus as a set of *off-the-rack* terms upon which business participants can fall back when establishing the distribution and allocation of powers and responsibilities for varying levels of control and commitment.[9] Finally, the theoretical and empirical contributions to the literature on incomplete contracts emphasizes that providing a set of default rules that deal with every possible contingency is a complex and uncertain process. Building on this literature, economic theories of the firm suggest that, besides the statutory and judicial default rules, the incentive and ownership structure of company law forms and the interaction between explicit and implicit contracts help the parties and institutions involved in filling the inherent gaps in the relationship, thereby preventing possible conflicts.

Although the function of company law as a means for incentive design and transaction planning appears to be underrated by lawmakers and academics,[10] the introduction of new hybrid business forms indicates that contractual rule-making sometimes prevails over so-called elite and traditional rule-making.[11] In that case, Section 3 argues that the path depen-

---

[9] See F.H. Easterbrook and D.R. Fischel, *The Economic Structure of Corporate Law* (Cambridge, Harvard University Press 1991).

[10] See J. Friedman, 'Limited Liability Partnerships in the United Kingdom: Do They Have a Role for Small Firms', in J.A. McCahery, et al., *The Governance of Close Corporations and Partnerships: US and European Perspectives* (Oxford, Oxford University Press 2004).

[11] See Clark, *supra* n. 8.

dence story does not necessarily imply that legal innovations are inherently inefficient. We argue that devising new and separate company law forms is more efficient as they offer distinct sets of rules and norms for businesses. Indeed, a separate set of legal arrangements has substantial contracting benefits for the firm's participants by allowing them to define their expectations *ex ante* – less hindered by existing doctrines and traditions – and, hence, assist judiciaries in solving governance problems and other conflicts *ex post*. As a matter of fact, practicing lawyers and business advisors appear to be willing to embrace new company law convinced that from both a tax and business perspective these hybrid business forms obtain the most efficient result. Section 4 provides empirical evidence for the popularity and effectiveness of new legal products in the United States, Europe and Asia. It seems that the selection of legal entities requires balancing, on the one hand, limited liability protection against, on the other hand, tax benefits, and contractual freedom to organize and structure the firm. Empirical research from the United States confirms the importance of forms that combine limited liability with partnership-type taxation and flexibility. The recent developments in Asia suggest that lawmakers and academics cannot afford to remain in denial of the fact that the 'new company law' will eventually prevail over the existing partnership and corporate forms. Section 5 concludes.

2. Company law as product

It is often said that economic concepts are fundamental to the analysis of company law reform. This approach casts a different light on the role and function of company law than traditional theories of law and society. Understanding these concepts, as adapted to company law, helps lawmakers to identify the needs and requirements of the participants in business firms, but also to define the role of the law in offering an effective governance structure for business parties to pursue economic objectives. The contractual theory of the firm, which dominates the thinking of efficiency-minded lawmakers, can assist lawmakers in identifying the central problems that business parties encounter, and the role that company law plays in helping to resolve these problems. In a Coasean world with complete and perfect information, and no transaction costs, we do not need to worry about company law. The business parties will be able to contract into the most efficient governance structure themselves. In the real world, however, lawmakers could approximate the hypothetical world by offering legal products, in the form of default and possibly mandatory rules, that minimize transaction costs and remove impediments to private ordering arrangements between the business parties.

In this section, we explore the extent to which lawmakers are able to draft comprehensive and self-explanatory legal provisions that stipulate each party's rights and obligations in each state of the world. We argue that while the standard terms of company law statutes can resolve governance problems, companies must often rely on behavioral rules and norms to resolve contractual incompleteness and other intra-corporate conflicts. Consequently, for a variety of reasons, it is submitted that company law is intrinsically incomplete. This section shows that efficiency-minded lawmakers should assist parties in selecting an appropriate set of governance rules which best suit their business needs by supplying standard contractual forms that develop litigation and case law and thereby increasing legal certainty and enhancing the effectiveness of law enforcement.

2.1 Why is company law inherently incomplete?

Proponents of the contractual theory view company law as a nexus of contracts. The nexus of contracts theory treats business forms as products that serve as a nexus for a set of relational contracts among its participants.[12] From this perspective, the contractual theory of the firm is arguably an appropriate and socially desirable concept, since it draws attention to the variety of needs, i.e., rights and duties, of participants involved in different firms.[13] Nonetheless, the nexus of contracts theory of the firm only partially explains why firms require a particular type of product. Moreover, the theory's narrowly conceptualized assumptions – i.e., that: (1) the firm is best viewed as a set of incentive contracts; (2) the function of the legal system is to supply rules and standards that are *ex ante* efficient; (3) rationally informed firm participants will bargain themselves into efficient governance structures; and (4) the firm's contracts are self-enforcing and do not require judicial enforcement – are successfully challenged.

In general, the complaint against the nexus of contracts theory is not that relational contracts are irrelevant to understanding the internal organization of the firm, but that it is difficult and costly to write *ex ante* complete contracts inside the firm. For one thing, people intend to act rationally, but they are simply not able to foresee and describe all future contingencies in a contract. Economists claim that people are 'boundedly rational'.[14] More importantly, even if contingencies can be dealt with contractually, information asymmetries and strategic bargaining often prevent efficient and complete contracts from emerging.[15] In short, relational contracts are often incomplete due to the difficulties to: (1) foresee some contingencies at the outset of the relationship; (2) specify all contingencies in the contract; (3) monitor the performance of the other participants; and (4) enforce the relational contracts.

Viewing the firm as an incomplete contract thus provides a broader understanding of the legal mechanisms required for the optimal production and design of company law and governance frameworks, and, more significantly, of the importance of having a variety of frameworks in general. Incomplete contract theories, which in many ways build on and formalize the concepts and ideas of transaction costs economics, attempt to explain how structuring as a particular type of firm helps to prevent opportunistic behavior. Indeed, when parties can simply write a complete contract, they specify in full detail what each party must do in each state of the world and how the surplus should be shared. In practice, bounded rationality and private information inevitably entail contractual incompleteness. Consequently, firm participants may have to renegotiate the contract to react to unforeseen contingencies, which may lead to an opportunistic attempt by one of them to obtain more of the ex post return on investment.

In line with the incomplete contract paradigm, a company law framework could be viewed as a product, i.e., a 'standard set of governance rules', that represents different points on the continuum of types of firms. This continuum ranges from an organization in which the owners themselves retain substantial autonomy to organizations that involve an

---

12 See C. Jensen, and W.H. Meckling, 'Theory of the Firm: Managerial Behavior, Agency Costs and Ownership Structure', 3 *Journal of Financial Economics* (1976) p. 305.

13 See O. Hart, *Firms, Contracts, and Financial Structure* (Oxford, Oxford University Press 1995).

14 See O.E. Williamson, *The Economic Institutions of Capitalism* (New York, Free Press 1985).

15 See P. Bolton and M. Dewatripont, *Contract Theory* (Cambridge, MIT Press 2005).

increasing surrender of 'individual autonomy' in favor of reciprocity and *firm autonomy*. On the scale of firmness, autonomy seems to shift from relational contracts with self-interested owners to organizations in which self-interest becomes more subordinate to the firm's collective interest. It is argued that organizational arrangements that have more firmness rank higher in terms of autonomy and, in traditional legal terms, are more easily perceived as entities.[16] In this view, close corporations have relatively more firmness than general partnerships. In comparison with general partnerships, close corporations have governance structures which are more based on hierarchy than consensus, *lock-in* firm specific assets and, hence, decrease an individual's ability to engage in opportunistic behavior by threatening to break up the business relationship. At the same time, however, individuals may have information and skills to pursue their personal interest and to compete against the firm, whereas general partnership law contains provisions prohibiting individual partners from competition against the firm. It follows that legal business forms present different solutions to the failings of the firm as an autonomous organization, and so rate differently on the scale of firmness.

In the second best world of incomplete law,[17] lawmakers do not supply business forms that offer comprehensive and unambiguous guidance in all future contingencies, but determine, among other things, in company law statutes how control over the firm's resources is allocated, how hierarchy is created within the firm, and which implied fiduciary terms and principles will assist courts in filling possible future gaps in the relational business contract. Company law thus acts as a facilitator, enabling business participants to move towards the most optimal governance equilibrium within a firm. To see this, let us consider some of the key features of a corporation, which is the main choice of governance mechanisms for listed firms: (1) a corporation is a legal entity that holds the firm's assets; (2) a corporation creates centralized management, to which the shareholders delegate important control rights;[18] and (3) the limited liability feature allows shareholders, many of whom are wealth constrained and risk-averse, to diversify their risks. These principles facilitate the separation of ownership and control, thereby reducing agency costs associated with the delegation of control rights. In a typical publicly held corporation the shareholders are too small and numerous to exercise the residual rights of control. It would be too costly if all of them were involved in decision management. Moreover, the shareholders, who are only interested in the company's share price, lack the expertise and competency to take part in decision-making process. As a consequence, the incomplete contracts theory of the firm recognizes that delegating residual control rights is necessary to facilitate management's participation in the firm and to give management sufficient incentives to undertake relationship-specific investments as well as to fill possible gaps in the corporate contract.

---

16 See N.R. Lamoreaux, 'Partnerships, Corporations, and the Theory of the Firm', 88 *American Economic Review* (1998) p. 66.

17 See K. Pistor and C. Xu, 'Fiduciary Duty in Transitional Civil Law Jurisdictions Lessons from the Incomplete Law Theory', ECGI – Law Working Paper No. 01/2002 (2003), available at <http://www.ssrn.com/abstracts=343480>.

18 The centralized management feature is not only necessary to facilitate management's participation in the firm, but also to attract specialized and competent managers and, more importantly, to give them sufficient incentives to encourage innovation and wealth creation.

2.2 A critique of a 'one-size-fits-all' company law

As we have seen, the corporation is best viewed as a particular standard form contract which offers limited liability, continuity, transferability of interests and, most importantly, centralized management.[19] Whilst the corporation may provide an effective nexus for implicit and explicit contracts and market relationships between shareholders, managers, creditors and other stakeholders, it does not, correspondingly, offer a clear solution for the problems that occur in multi-owner closely held companies in which the identity of the shareholders is a much more important characteristic due to: (1) the relatively small number of shareholders; (2) no ready market for the corporate stock; and (3) substantial (majority) shareholder participation in management, direction and operation of the firm. First, the centralized management feature is poorly tailored to fit the governance needs of closely held firms. When ownership and control are typically not completely severed, as is the case in these firms, the delegation of control rights is not so important and precarious as in publicly held companies. Second, the majority rule and statutory norms of centralized management, which characterize the corporate form, creates an opportunity to oppress minority shareholders by, among other things, appropriating corporate opportunities and distributing cash and property to majority shareholders. Figure 1 depicts some instances in which the majority shareholder may assume voting control. Even if shareholders, ostensibly, have no majority stake in a corporation's equity, dual class shares and pyramid structures often serve the purpose of remaining in control.

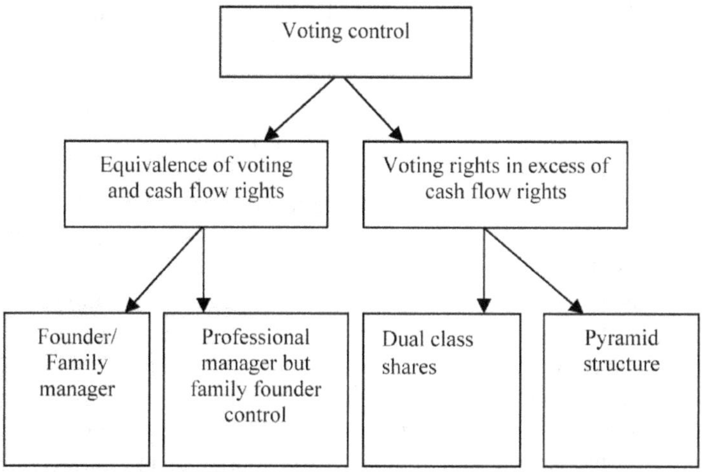

Figure 1. Voting control within the firm

Source: P. Halpern, 'Systematic Perspectives on Corporate Governance Systems', Working Paper, University of Toronto (1999)

The fact that we observe numerous multi-ownership structures employing the corporate form suggests that company law rules may, in general, be trivial in the sense that these

[19] See E.B. Rock and M.L. Wachter, 'Corporate Law as a Facilitator of Self Governance', 34 *Georgia Law Review* (2000) p. 529.

firms are able to effectively contract around and adapt the corporate governance structure as they deem fit. In fact, the close corporation accounts for more than 55% of registered businesses and 90% of output in OECD countries. This is largely due to the positive externalities that arise as a consequence of firms having selected the closely held corporation for tax and liability reasons. Moreover, the widespread use of this structure reinforces and even strengthens the use of this form, arguably excluding the choice for other business forms. Nevertheless, the success story of the close corporation in many jurisdictions could give eloquent testimony to the fact that business participants often neutralize the law's detrimental effect by either relying on *ex post* gap-filling by courts or by making contractual adjustments *ex ante*.[20] Hence, the rules of company law appears not to matter, since deviations from statutory provisions are common and often predictable in the event of the corporation being employed by firms seeking only legal entity status and limited liability protection.

In this view the corporate form may function effectively and appropriately in an incomplete contracting setting. Legal entity status, for instance, is necessary to define the property rights over which participants within a firm can contract. In the absence of entity status, it would be practicably impossible to shield the assets of the firm from creditors of the firm's owners. First, the transaction costs of drafting and inserting provisions in all contracts between the participants inside the firm and the firm creditors on the one hand and their personal creditors on the other will be prohibitively high. Second, the firm participants, including the business creditors, would face a moral hazard problem, as it is virtually impossible to assure the business creditors of the existence of the necessary agreements with the personal creditors.[21] The second (and secondary) purpose for choosing the corporate form is the limited liability feature. Its function is to protect owners by limiting creditors of the entity to pursue claims on the owners' individual and separate assets. Limited liability promotes partnerships and inter-firm cooperation by limiting monitoring costs, externalizing risk and facilitating the sectorial and geographical diversification of business projects.

In closely held businesses, however, corporate rules may be insufficient to provide an adequate basis to govern relations between the majority and minority and the firm itself. Suppose, for example, that the majority shareholders take the decision to eliminate certain minority interests under the principle of majority rule thereby assuming complete control and squeezing out their views and wishes. Although this is a standard corporate transaction, no doubt many minority shareholders, who consider themselves partners in the enterprise with equal say and decision-making powers, will be unhappily surprised.

Similarly, while most closely held firms are governed by extra-legal mechanisms, corporate law rules could be used opportunistically encouraging disputes and litigation when the rules do not match expectations of investors. Indeed, the weight of economic evidence

---

[20] See A.K. Dixit, *Lawlessness and Economics, Alternative Modes of Governance* (Princeton, Princeton University Press 2004).

[21] Hansmann and Kraakman call the separation between the firm's assets and the personal assets of the participants inside the firm affirmative asset partitioning. They view affirmative asset partitioning as the core defining characteristic of a legal entity. That is not to say that there are no other transaction cost advantages attached to the use of the corporate form that is bestowed with legal entity status. The entity status strengthens the firm's bargaining power *vis-à-vis* outsiders. Creditors and other outsiders can deal with the firm as a unit rather than with the individual members. See H. Hansmann and R. Kraakman, 'The Essential Role of Organizational Law', 110 *Yale Law Journal* (2000) p. 387.

seems to confirm the view that business parties may be loath to bear the transaction costs of contracting around inadequate statutory terms.[22] Studies from the United States illustrate that even though business participants would theoretically be better off opting into specifically available close corporation rules, in practice these opt-in provisions have not been widely used. The standardization of the general corporation statute due to network and learning effects suggested lower legal formation and operation costs than the not yet standardized *innovations* with respect to close corporations. To be sure, judges and arbitrators could offer a solution to a puzzling and disturbing gap in the corporate contract, such as an easy buyout right for the dissatisfied partner, if the incomplete contract makes the minority vulnerable to opportunistic exploitation by the majority.[23] However, judicial gap-filling is not only costly and time-consuming, but may also be prone to error. Judicial intervention can create a potential judicial wild card that creates costly uncertainty.[24] It is submitted that whilst intra-firm controversies are often observable to the exasperated parties, they may not be easily verified by a judge or arbitrator, and even less so when personal relationships in the family or between friends are involved.[25] As a consequence, many analysts think the judicial role should be limited, in the case of contractual incompleteness, to the selective enforcement of contracts according to their written terms. Indeed, the difficulty in predicting the judicial outcome explains why relatively few disputes seem to end up in court.[26]

In light of the foregoing discussion, the absence of statutory guidance, which could be adopted *ex ante*, may have a detrimental effect on both the firm and its participants. As participants in a firm tend to react strategically to rules, the wrong rule could produce significant inefficiencies much greater than the nominal costs of contracting around a rule.[27] For instance, the supply of the inefficient default rule could have a detrimental effect on relational arrangements in firms that are mainly governed by extra-legal and social norms. Even if the parties are completely unaware of the default rules *ex ante* and start their business on the basis of trust and reputation, midstream awareness of the legal rules might crowd out interpersonal trust and replace it with institutional trust in the legal system. Moreover, overconfidence, over-optimism and excitement about the prospects of a new business venture prevent participants from engaging in business planning and contemplating methods for addressing future conflicts of interest. Because participants must either trust each other or forgo the deal, they often avoid tailoring their business arrangement, thereby intentionally leaving gaps in their relational contract. Furthermore, bargaining theory

---

[22] An empirical survey in the United States found that deviations from state-supplied default settings are uncommon. See W.S Hochstetler and M.D. Svejda, 'Statutory Needs of Close Corporations – An Empirical Study: Special Close Corporation Legislation or Flexible General Corporation Law?', 10 *Journal of Corporation Law* (1985) p. 849.

[23] See D.A. Oesterle, 'Subcurrents in LLC Statutes: Limiting the Discretion of State Courts to Restructure the Internal Affairs of Small Business', 66 *University of Colorado Law Review* (1995) p. 881.

[24] See P.G. Mahoney, 'Trust and Opportunism in Close Corporations', National Bureau of Economic Research (NBER) Working Paper 6819 (1998).

[25] O'Neill illustrates the artificiality of the family/market dichotomy with a US case, *United States* v. *Chestman*, 947 F.2d 551 (2d Cir. 1991), in which the Second Circuit surprisingly ruled that marriage creates a confidential business relationship See T.A. O'Neill, 'Reasonable Expectations in Families, Businesses, and Family Businesses: A Comment on Rollock', 73 *Indiana Law Journal* (1998) p. 591.

[26] Easterbrook and Fischel note that the available economic models of litigation indicate that the more trouble parties have in predicting how a judge will decide, the less likely they are to resolve their differences short of litigation, even when there are only two parties See Easterbrook and Fischel, *supra* n. 9.

[27] See I. Ayres, 'Default Rules for Incomplete Contracts', in P. Newman (ed.), *The New Palgrave Dictionary of Economics and the Law* (London, Macmillan Reference Limited 1998) vol. 1.

in law and economics recognizes that even if the contract parties are willing to accept the challenge of drafting an agreement and transaction costs are marginal, information asymmetries and strategic behavior could prevent them from bargaining their way to the optimal governance structure.[28]

The upshot is that governmental lawmakers, i.e., legislatures, should implement, administer and enforce business form legislation. There are several advantages in putting the responsibility of business form design in governmental hands. In addition to economies of scale, the publicity of the legislative process reduces the information costs for potential users of the statutes. Moreover, new networks are arguably more likely to arise around legislative products. It is, therefore, suggested that the legislatures and courts should resolve the high costs of internal and external rules not only by adopting a deregulatory policy towards the laws relating to the governance of closely held business firms, but also by introducing an alternative legal vehicle between the existing partnership and corporate forms. To take the example of the close corporation, one is inclined to point to the troublesome nature of *over-regulation* with respect to multi-ownership arrangements. The corporate form usually does not give unlimited freedom of contract in devising the ownership and governance structure of the firm. The mandatory and formal nature of provisions in the corporate statute could trump the terms set forth in the agreement between the participants, thereby making the enforceability of the contractual provisions a cumbersome process.

Central to this view is the claim that relaxing the provisions of investor and creditor protection will provide a clear set of benefits to the participants in closely held firms. The goal of regulatory reform must be to balance the interests of third parties and the benefits to firms of modifying the statutory structure of close corporations so as to meet the interests of, for instance, entrepreneurs and joint venturers. To be sure, domestic legislators and judges have offered several judicial and statutory solutions to meet the special needs of the variety of closely held firms. Even though the framework of corporate law is not optimal for these types of firms, courts have attempted to resolve intra-firm conflicts by reference to partnership law principles. However, an acknowledged problem with this approach to the legal control of closely held firms is the risk of ignoring the needs of other types of firms that operate as close corporations. It is well-known that legal rules for firms with capital symmetry should differ from the rules for those without. For instance, equal rights in management, automatic buyout rights and broad fiduciary duties that govern *partnership corporations* are not automatically suitable for start-up corporations financed by venture capital.[29] The deregulatory approach tends to increase the cost of statutory ambiguity, including legal research, litigation and judicial system costs.[30] A more efficient regulatory response, which involves determining the appropriate level of regulation, ultimately requires cost-benefit decisions to ascertain the necessary policy changes. In pursuing this goal, lawmakers should, as we have seen, view legal business forms as products and focus on designing legislation that contains clear and simple fall-back provisions tailored to the requirements of firms characterized by multi-ownership. Because participants in these firms

---

[28] It might be argued that the cost of drafting a customized agreement is minimal, because forms for special clauses abound in libraries and lawyers' files. See Oesterle, *supra* n. 23, at p. 920. However, the internal participants in many closely held firms seem, nevertheless, to be reluctant to deviate from statutory default rules.

[29] See E.B. Rock and M.L. Wachter, 'Waiting for the Omelet to Set: Match-specific Assets and Minority Oppression in Close Corporations', 24 *Journal of Corporation Law* (1999) p. 913.

[30] See I. Ramsay, 'Corporate Law in the Age of Statutes', 14 *Sydney Law Review* (1992) p. 474.

sometimes start their business ventures with a handshake rather than an articulate agreement,[31] a business form statute should ideally supply a set of default terms that the majority of parties would have bargained for in a costless world.[32] By doing so, lawmakers not only help to minimize transaction costs for firms that wish to enter into customized agreements, but also reduce the costs of statutory ambiguity.

2.3 The rise of new 'company law' products

In the previous subsection, we explored the limitations of arguments in support of the one-size-fits-all approach. It is our contention that the problem with this approach stems from the inability of a single set of statutory measures to govern the needs of many types of firms. Indeed, the shift away from the extant partnership and corporate forms as a business vehicle for closely held firms in jurisdictions that introduced new company forms is not surprising. The effect is most obvious in the United States where the relatively simple landscape of company law has changed dramatically over the last two decades. For instance, the LLP emerged in Texas in 1991 to provide *peace of mind* insurance for innocent partners. Thereafter, the LLP spread rapidly from two states in 1992 to all 50 states and the District of Columbia by 2001. In the original Texan conception of the LLP, general partners in professional firms were allowed to avoid joint and several malpractice liabilities. As the LLP evolved, most states expanded the scope of this business form by allowing non-professional firms to use the statute. In addition, most states expanded the original shield of limited liability protection beyond malpractice or other torts of their fellow partners to include all liabilities of the firm, whether based on tort, contract or other basis.

The LLC is yet another, and more successful, legal production that combines partnership features with corporate characteristics. The introduction of the LLC bundled together limited liability, a flexible governance structure and preferential tax treatment and also require less ongoing paperwork than corporations. Also, it provides an almost total shield against personal liability without cumbersome formation and capital maintenance rules. In 1977, the first modern LLC statute was promulgated in Wyoming at the behest of lawyers and accountants acting as a lobby group for an oil company wishing to combine limited liability and pass-through tax treatment.[33] Before the Internal Revenue Services (IRS) generally secured the favorable partnership taxation for this new business form, Florida was the only other state that enacted LLC legislation, which it did in 1982 so as to attract foreign investors, particularly from South and Central America. However, the uncertainties with respect to the tax treatment of the new business form severely hampered the rush to conduct business under this new statute, and consequently did not lead to the expected upsurge of economic activity in Florida. As late as 1988, the IRS clarified the tax treatment of the LLC by issuing a ruling stating that the eligibility for partnership tax treatment is

---

[31] Even billion-dollar joint ventures often operate under a short and simple agreement. See J.D. Lewis, *Trusted Partners; How Companies Build Mutual Trust and Win Together* (New York, The Free Press 1999).

[32] See Easterbrook and Fischel, *supra* n. 9.

[33] In 1975, lawyers and accountants advising Hamilton Brothers Oil Company devised the *limited liability company*, resembling the Panamanian *limitadas*. After a failed legislative effort in Alaska, they lobbied successfully for enactment of the LLC statute in Wyoming. In 1980 only, the IRS issued a favorable private letter ruling to Hamilton Brothers Oil Company regarding its Wyoming LLC structure. See R.W. Hamilton, 'Professional Partnerships in the United States', 26 *Journal of Corporation Law* (2001) p. 1045.

conditional upon the business form's corporate features.[34] If the LLC lacked two of the four corporate characteristics considered by the IRS to be crucial (continuity of life, centralization of management, limited liability and free transferability of interests), then the Treasury regulations would treat the LLC as a partnership for tax purposes.[35] After this ruling, other states jumped on the LLC bandwagon, slowly and hesitantly at first, but after 1990, LLC legislation swept rapidly through the United States, largely because of competitive pressures and domestic interest groups, especially legal practitioners who viewed the LLC as better-suited to the needs and expectations of their clients. LLC provisions have been adopted in all 51 US jurisdictions by the close of 1996 (see Table 1).

The emergence of and experimentation with the LLC forced the tax authorities to explain in more detail the distinction between partnership and corporate tax treatment, which eventually led to a new federal 'check-the-box' tax rule. Under the IRS *check-the-box* regulations, which became effective on 1 January 1997, *unincorporated* associations are taxed as partnerships unless they affirmatively elect to be taxed as corporations.[36] The *check-the-box* regulations triggered yet a third wave of amendments of the LLC statutes, thereby encouraging the development of corporate-type LLCs and the adoption of a wide variety of LLC statutes. Table 1, for example, shows the variety in enactment dates and the type of fiduciary duties regime. In terms of fiduciary duties, the table distinguishes between: ULLCA §409 (Uniform Limited Company Act) which mandates the duty of loyalty and care in a member-managed company; UPA §21 (Uniform Partnership Act), which requires the members to act as a trustee for any profits derived without the consent of other partners; 8 Delaware Code §144 authorizes that the company is bound by the transactions entered into by directors and officers; MBCA §8.30 (Model Business Corporation Act) which provides the standards of duty of faith and duty of care for directors; and RULPA §107 (Revised Uniform Limited Partnership Act) which does not bind parties to fiduciary duties. Table 2 compares the LLP – as regulated in RUPA (Revised Uniform Partnership Act) – and the LLC – as it appears in the Uniform Limited Company Act and the Delaware Limited Liability Act.

If we agree that company law is incomplete and view lawmakers as just another producer in the overall economy, the introduction of the hybrid business forms appears to be nothing more than product innovation based on the compelling logic of firms seeking easy access to a range of governance structures designed to have limited liability protection, reduce complexity and limit transaction costs. However, it follows from the above discussion that new business forms do not immediately provide business parties with an optimal and comprehensive governance structure. In fact, the analysis in the next section shows that competing legal elites and traditions, incumbent interest groups, and other path dependence factors tend to significantly shape the landscape of legal business forms and

---

[34] Revenue Ruling 88-76 (1988).

[35] The test for determining entity classification was set out in § 301.7701-2 of the Treasury regulations, known as the *Kintner regulations*. These regulations had a profound influence on the development of the early LLC statutes. A so-called *bulletproof* statute was designed so that the entity would be treated as a partnership for federal income tax purposes.

[36] The partnership taxation – pass-through tax treatment – is based on the assumption that a partnership is a mere aggregate of individual partners who re-distribute profits among themselves. Consequently, LLC income is treated as if it were personal income realized by the members, and is taxed to the members as individuals. In contrast, corporate income is taxed first to the corporation and later, if it is distributed as dividend, to the shareholders individually.

Table 1. The Development of LLC Legislation, in particular fiduciary duties, in the United States

State	Enacted	Adopted ULLCA	ULLCA § 409	UPA § 21	8 Del. Code § 144	MBCA § 8.30	RULPA § 107 3rd Party Analogy
Alabama	1993	Yes	Yes				X
Alaska	1994				X	X	
Arizona	1993						X
Arkansas	1993			X			
California	1994			X			
Colorado	1990					X	
Connecticut	1993			X		X	
Delaware	1992						X
Florida	1982				X	X	
Georgia	1994					X	
Hawaii	1997	Yes	Yes				
Idaho	1993			X			
Illinois	1994	Most	Yes, but not exclusive				
Indiana	1993			X			
Iowa	1992				X	X	
Kansas	1990						X
Kentucky	1994			X			
Louisiana	1992			X	X	X	
Maine	1994			X		X	
Maryland	1992						X
Massachusetts	1995						
Michigan	1993			X		X	
Minnesota	1993				X	X	
Mississipi	1994					X	X
Missouri	1993			X		X	
Montana	1993	Yes					
Nebraska	1993						
Nevada	1993						
New Hampshire	1993			X			
New Jersey	1993						X
New Mexico	1993			X	X		
New York	1994				X	X	
North Carolina	1993			X		X	
North Dakota	1993				X	X	
Ohio	1994				X	X	
Oklahoma	1992			X		X	
Oregon	1994		X			X	
Pennsylvania	1995			X			
Rhode Island	1992			X		X	
South Carolina	1994	Yes	Yes				
South Dakota	1993	Yes	Yes				
Tennessee	1994			X	X	X	
Texas	1991				X		
Utah	1991						
Vermont	1996	Yes	Yes				
Virginia	1991					X	X
Washington	1994			X			
West Virginia	1992	Yes	Yes				
Wisconsin	1999				X		
Wyoming	1977						
Washington DC	1994						X

Source: Adapted from <www.LLCweb.com> and Murdoch 2001 (Limited Liability Companies in the Decade of the 1990s)

Table 2. Comparison US LLP and US LLC

Characteristic	LLP (RUPA)	LLC (ULLCA)	LLC (DEL. LLC)
Legal Personality	Yes	Yes	Yes
Management	Decentralized	Decentralized (default) Centralized (opt-in)	Decentralized (unless otherwise provided in the LLC agreement, the management is vested in LLC members in proportion to the then current percentage or other interest of members in the profits)
Formation	Informal by two or more partners	Public filing of the articles of organization with the secretary of state (one or more members)	In order to form an LLC, one or more authorized persons must execute a certificate of formation, which must be filed in the office of the Secretary of State
Autonomy of Articles of Organization	Partnership: relationship governed by written and oral agreements	If operating agreement is inconsistent with the Articles of Organization: (1) the operating agreement controls the internal affairs, (2) the Articles control as to third parties who reasonably rely on the Articles (the Articles must set forth only a limited and specific information, such as the name of the company and the address of the initial designated office)	It is the policy to give maximum effect to the principle of freedom of contract and to the enforceability of limited liability company agreements
Notarization of Articles of Incorporation	No	No	No
Fiduciary Duties	Duties of loyalty and care. Obligation of good faith and fair dealing	Duties of loyalty and care. Obligation of good faith and fair dealing	Access to in formation and records
Financial Rights	Equal sharing (default rules)	If no agreement, sharing in proportion to the members' contribution to capital	If no agreement, profits and losses will be allocated on the basis of the agreed value of the contributions
Transferable Interests	Generally, no	Yes, restrictions are imposed by the Act, securities laws and operating agreement	Yes, restrictions are imposed by the Act, securities laws and operating agreement
Continuity of Life	Withdrawal does not automatically dissolve the LLP	Withdrawal does not automatically dissolve the LLC	Possibility to resign from an LLC is limited; resignation does not automatically dissolve the LLC
Limited Liability	Yes	Yes	Yes
Financial Statements	No need to disclose records publicly; partners have access to records	Members have access to records. No mandatory disclosure	Members have access to records. No mandatory disclosure
Taxation	Pass-through ('check-the-box')	Pass-through ('check-the-box')	Pass-through ('check-the-box')
Linkage	Linked to general partnership form	Some provisions are similar to RUPA	De-linked

influence the debate about the introduction of innovative company law. We will focus on the main components of the legal production process in order to show some of the deficiencies in new modern business forms in the United States, Europe and Asia. The extent to which some aspects of the 'elite law-making' and 'traditional law-making' processes pervade the entire law-making structure will be evaluated.

3. THE PRODUCTION OF COMPANY LAW: THREE REFORM STRATEGIES

This section introduces three law-making strategies that are often deployed by policymakers in company law reform projects. The first strategy involves legislative and political processes that result in a mere updating of the existing company law statute. It is predicted that, in general, lawmakers are not likely to engage in innovative rule-making, but will supply only a superficial 'upgrade' in the existing legal product range. As this strategy is motivated by concerns to mimic results achieved by reforms to business forms in other competitive jurisdictions, as witnessed in continental Europe, these revisions are not likely to implicate the interests of the controlling elites and interest groups. A second strategy, involving the introduction of a new business form explicitly linked to the traditional company law framework can lead to genuine change that will increase the overall quality of law for firms generally. As will be discussed, the difference between the first and second strategy is that the reforms yielded by the latter strategy may hold out potential costs savings for several classes of firms. Finally, the third strategy is moved by exogenous and interest groups pressures with the effect of the promulgation of a new innovative legal statute. It is important to recognize that jurisdictions can use any combination of the above-referred strategies when considering reforms, and that there may be additional incentives not mentioned above that motivate legislative outcomes.

Rather than making a strict distinction between the different reform strategies, that could be used to explain the multiple paths of company law development, this section argues that reform measures undertaken by national level governments are best seen in terms of a spectrum of possible reform paths. It ranges from countries that belong to a strong legal tradition that curb deviations from the existing regime *via* countries with weakly organized centralized governments and strong organized pressure groups that break down the resistance to legislative change to competitive and entrepreneurial jurisdictions that attempt to offer an up-to-date legal product range. On the one end of the spectrum, reformers find it difficult to make changes due to the high switching costs and institutional rules and political mechanisms that effectively define and control the items on the legislative reform agenda. On the other side of the spectrum, there is the presence of incentives to innovate and the type of institutional infrastructure under which we can expect pressure groups to have agenda-setting powers may well explain the result of new company forms. Illustrations of recent national company law reforms allow us to see how the trajectory of trends tends to map on to the spectrum of legal reform.

3.1 The first strategy: 'patching-up' revisions

The first strategy only leads to legal upgrades leaving the core of the company law system untouched. In this part, we seek to understand the variations in national legal rules and structures that are responsible for the persistence of inefficient company law rules and structures that policymakers cannot simply alter. It seems that the inferior outcome could largely be explained by strong path dependence factors, such as the influence of legal elites and traditions, and the effect of increasing returns on the law-making process. Naturally there are varying degrees of path dependence which are reflected in the diversity of recent company law developments. However, in terms of generalization, strong path dependence is a common phenomenon in legal systems that are dominated by legal elites and traditions bereft of the *law-as-a-product* dimension. Ironically, if legal products – like regular products – gain popularity and expand utilization, increasing returns can magnify the benefits of defending the *status quo*, resulting in a similar evolution pattern. This partly explains why European jurisdictions are still loath to overhaul their company laws even though the ECJ, as noted above, has opened the door towards a market for company law products After a short discussion about what causes the strong path dependence, the chapter will turn to introduce factors that have proven to be effective in changing the company law reform path.

3.1.1 *Elites and traditions in company law*

In this part we show how lawmakers traditionally shape and structure the company law reform process. It is submitted that legislators, judges, practitioners, regulatory agencies, professional groups and legal scholars constitute an elite law-making group that is responsible for interpreting, preserving and developing the law.[37] These legal professionals produce different kinds of texts, such as statutes, judicial decisions and scholarly writings, which one school of comparative law academics calls 'legal formants'.[38] The law does not consist solely of these texts, but should instead be viewed as a series of formulations that complement each other.[39] Still the law and its evolution appears more like a battleground on which law-making elites compete for hegemony than a system of checks and balances.[40]

What are the factors that tend to reinforce legal rules and institutions that are in place? Generally, there are two factors which operate to make law conservative. First, the law-making elite treats the law as existing in its own right. In this view, the law is largely autonomous and operates in its own sphere.[41] As one commentator puts it:

> '[t]he means of creating law, the sources of law, come to be regarded as a given, almost as something sacrosanct, and change in these even when they are obviously deeply flawed is extremely difficult to achieve.'[42]

Second, the law is justified in its own terms. Lawmakers, i.e., persons trained in law and nothing else, search for the legitimacy of legal change, which makes the law typically

[37] See A. Watson, *The Evolution of Law* (Baltimore, Johns Hopkins University Press 1985).

[38] See R. Sacco, 'Legal Formants: A Dynamic Approach to Comparative Law', 39 *American Journal of Comparative Law* (1991) pp. 1-34; 343-402; P.G. Monateri and R. Sacco, 'Legal Formants', in Newman, *supra* n. 27. The theory of legal formants, as suggested by Rodolfo Sacco, views the law as a social activity in which lawmaking elites compete to provide legal doctrines.

[39] See R.B. Schlesinger, H.W. Baade, P.E. Herzog and E.M. Wise, *Comparative Law, Cases-Text-Materials* (New York, Foundation Press 1998).

[40] See P. Bourdieu, 'The Force of Law: Toward a Sociology of the Juridical Field', 38 *Hastings Law Journal* (1987) p. 805 (Translator's Introduction by R. Terdiman).

[41] See H. Kelsen, *Pure Theory of Law* (Berkeley, UC Berkeley Press 1967).

[42] See Watson, *supra* n. 37.

backward-looking. To a large extent, this insulates legal evolution from social and economic change and it therefore displays a serious degree of path dependence.

To what extent does the evolution of the legal rules and institutions reflect social and economic change? Lawmakers, who genuinely disagree as to which rules and institutions are *best*,[43] could be viewed as legal elites that produce competing legal formants. It is possible to distinguish between conservative and reform-minded legal elites. Because the law is viewed as autonomous, lawmakers historically employ two strategies when entering the competitive arena of legal reform. On the one hand, conservative lawmakers deploy the existing legal doctrines, principles and culture to protect the *status quo* and thwart reform. On the other hand, reform-minded lawmakers traditionally make reference to foreign rules and institutions to propose legal change and to induce the controlling elite of the receiving system to believe that the offered model meets their expectations.[44]

If we take this a step further, it could be argued that the development of the law takes place mainly by transplantation of legal rules. Yet in order to be effective, a borrowed legal rule or institution must be understood and appreciated by the dominant, and usually conservative, law-making elite. Indeed, it is submitted that a legal transplant increases its own receptivity when adaptations to the domestic formal and informal legal order are made or the borrower is already familiar with basic legal principles of the donor jurisdiction.[45]

It is in the legal actors' nature to attach considerable importance to authority in the transplanting process. It is often very difficult for a law reformer to *sell* his ideas without the support of some kind of authority whose expertise is widely recognized by the legal community.[46] That authority could be inherent in a foreign legal system or institution due to its prestige, common legal tradition or high accessibility. Reform-minded lawmakers attempt to convince the controlling elite that borrowing should occur by juxtaposing black-letter law reports, and consulting intuition and any available facts to show the foreign legal system's supremacy.[47] Yet, the results of comparative legal studies often lack a clear theoretical or empirical explanation of why a particular foreign system or institution is the most suitable model, given the needs of the social and economic environment. When legal parochialism is strong and jurisdictions are largely resistant to transplants (which is often the case where jurisdictions are convinced of the effectiveness of their own legal system), reform-minded elites adopt a different strategy. They deny the fact that a model is borrowed, and use local authority to bolster their opinion.[48] In this view, legal change could be

[43] See L.A. Bebchuk and M.J. Roe, 'A Theory of Path Dependency in Corporate Ownership and Governance', 52 *Stanford Law Review* (1999) p. 127.

[44] See A. Watson, *Legal Transplants, An Approach to Comparative Law* (Charlottesville, The University Press of Virginia 1974).

[45] See D. Berkowitz, K. Pistor and J-F. Richard, 'Economic Development, Legality, and the Transplant Effect', 47 *European Economic Review* (2003) p. 165.

[46] Sacco argues that a legal innovation that does not originate from an authority is often viewed as an *error*. See Sacco, *supra* n. 38, at p. 400.

[47] See A.I. Ogus, 'Law-and-Economics from the Perspective of Law', in Newman, *supra* n. 27. Prestige seems to be the key word. As a consequence, 'it is unlikely that a European country will imitate an African model, that the United States will imitate a Venezuelan model, that the Scandinavian countries will imitate an Italian model, and so forth'. Sacco, *supra* n. 38, at p. 399. Fanto gives an analysis of psychological factors used by reform-minded lawmakers to make a persuasive case for reform. See J.A. Fanto, 'Persuasion and Resistance: The Use of Psychology by Anglo-American Corporate Governance Advocates in France', Working Paper (2002), available at <http://www.ssrn.com/abstracts=304050>.

[48] See U. Mattei, 'Efficiency in Legal Transplants: An Essay in Comparative Law and Economics', 14 *International Review of Law and Economics* (1994) p. 3.

explained largely by *hidden* transplants, which are a mixture of foreign and indigenous doctrines and principles.[49]

However, it might be argued that if a jurisdiction becomes part of a common market like the United States or the European Union, convergence of important principles of company law is likely to become greater, as the number of firms that not only do business in more than one state, but have among their members residents of different states, increases. In this context, national level company law reforms in the European Union (EU) have been encouraged by changes in European Court of Justice case law, which have encouraged firm mobility for start-ups, giving reform-minded lawmakers an incentive to intensify their efforts to modernize their domestic company laws.[50] But, as noted earlier, the dominant reform strategy of most national level policymakers is still influenced by a 'patching up' approach designed to ensure prevalence of the *status quo*.[51]

For instance, the elimination of the capital maintenance rules for private companies appears relatively easy. These rules, where the content is less important than their uniformity,[52] had already been applied to public corporations and subsequently were harmonized by the European Commission to reduce costs for third parties transacting with the firm.[53] Having served simply as an authoritative focal point rule for legislators engaged in company law reform, the decision to eliminate the rule for private companies – in light of the ECJ's triad of judgments on free mobility – is hardly surprising as it could be accomplished without causing too much disturbance of existing expectations of the controlling and conservative law-making elite. In this view, the array of mandatory legal capital rules only seems to benefit several interest groups.[54] In fact, incumbent management may have influenced the EU legislature to supply provisions that limit dividend payments and share repurchases so as to obtain more leeway to reinvest firm's profits. Accountants, who play a pivotal role in the required valuation, also have a substantial interest in exerting influence on the legislative outcome.

But also members of the law-making elite, such as lawyers and other legal practitioners, seem to benefit from guiding their clients through the complicated harmonized rules.[55] Thus, since legal elites that benefit from the existing legal rules arguably have incentives to block innovative measures, reform-minded groups are confronted with the daunting task of replacing the existing legal rules with new measures and techniques.[56] Still, it is not sur-

[49] See D.L Horowitz, 'The Qur'an and the Common Law: Islamic Law Reform and the Theory of Legal Chance', 42 *American Journal of Comparative Law* (1994) p. 233.

[50] Case C-212/97 *Centros Ltd* v. *Erhvervs- og Selskabsstryelsen* [1999] *ECR* I-1459; Case C-208/00 *Überseering BV* v. *Nordic Construction Co Baumanagement GmbH*; Case C-167/01 *Kamer van Koophandel en Fabrieken voor Amsterdam* v. *Inspire Art Ltd.*

[51] See J.A. McCahery and E.P.M. Vermeulen, *Understanding (Un)incorporated Business Forms* (Amsterdam, Amsterdam Center for Corporate Finance 2005).

[52] See D. Charny, 'Competition among Jurisdictions in Formulating Corporate Law Rules: An American Perspective on the "Race to the Bottom" in the European Communities', 32 *Harvard International Law Journal* (1991) p. 423.

[53] For the most part, harmonized rules for legal capital tended to benefit publicly-listed firms engaged in cross-border transactions. See P Leleux, 'Corporation Law in the United States and in the E.E.C., Some Comments on the Present Situation and the Future Prospects', 5 *Common Market Law Review* 6 (1967) p. 133.

[54] See W.J. Carney, 'The Political Economy of Competition for Corporate Charters', 26 *Journal of Legal Studies* (1997) p. 303.

[55] See L. Enriques and J.R. Macey, 'Creditors *versus* Capital Formation: The Case against the European Legal Capital Rules', 86 *Cornell Law Review* (2001) p. 1165.

[56] As discussed, the blocking power of the conservative lawmaking elite differs from country to country. For instance, the French legislature reacted immediately to the possibility of losing new incorporations to England by

prising that bringing about change can be more troublesome than merely having to protect the incumbent interests. This partly explains the inherent shortcomings of this legal reform strategy.

3.1.2 *Increasing returns*

This subsection surveys another factor of path dependence that is responsible for creating barriers that hinder reform-minded lawmakers from persuading the legislature to adopt effective company law forms. This factor of path dependence, which is generally labeled as increasing returns, can explain the survival of particular institutions and traditions that were once effective in solving serious problems in the business environment, but no longer provide strong support of lawmakers given changing economic and social circumstances.

It is now commonplace that if firms use a particular business form more frequently, its value increases, thereby decreasing incentives to introduce legal reform. Increasing returns engender the standardization of rules and institutions over time.[57] Standardization, in turn, accounts for the lock-in to a sub-optimal framework.[58] The increasing returns approach corroborates the hypothesis that lawmakers are prone to inertia and inflexibility. The models pertaining to the appearance of increasing returns are often used to explain why the widespread adoption of products and technologies that become more valuable as their use (or the use of compatible products) increases could lead to a sub-optimal outcome.[59] When increasing returns are associated with competing products, inferior products may prevail over products that are inherently better. More importantly, they may stand in the way of innovations.

The literature points to the success of the QWERTY keyboard, VHS video recorder and DOS operating system over allegedly superior alternatives.[60] Three related but conceptually different mechanisms are responsible for the possible dominance of increasing returns over inherent benefits: (1) sunk costs; (2) learning effects; and (3) network effects. The end result is that if new adopters of a product or technology are only interested in their own benefits without any consideration of the effect of their decision on other *network users*, the development of new products and technologies will be impeded, thereby fostering lock-in to the inferior standard.

---

reducing the minimum capital requirement to € 1. On the other hand, the German legislature, as we will see, which experiences a much higher number of businesses opting for the English limited, seems only to be able to agree on a compromise which lowers the capital requirement from € 25,000 to € 10,000.

[57] See M. Kahan and M. Klausner, 'Path Dependence in Corporate Contracting: Increasing returns, Herd Behavior and Cognitive Biases', 74 *Washington University Law Quarterly* (1996) p. 347.

[58] Bebchuk and Roe state that 'rules might be path-dependent because the identity of the locally efficient legal rule – the rule efficient for a given country – might depend on the rules and structures that the country had at earlier times.' Bebchuk and Roe, *supra* n. 43, at p. 155.

[59] See W.B. Arthur, *Increasing Returns and Path Dependence in the Economy* (Ann Arbor, University of Michigan Press 1994); see also ibidem., 'Increasing Returns and the New World of Business', 74(4) *Harvard Business Review* (July-August 1996) p. 100.

[60] See M.L Katz and C. Shapiro, 'Technology Adoption in the Presence of Network Externalities', 94 *Journal of Political Economy* (1986) p. 822. These allegedly superior products are the Dvorak Simplified Keyboard (DSK), Sony's Beta format and Philips V2000 format for VCRs and Apple's Macintosh system respectively. But Liebowitz and Margolis demonstrate that the evidence for the superiority of a particular product is weak and, hence, the extent of network effects may be much more limited than is commonly assumed. See S.J. Liebowitz and S.E. Margolis, 'Path Dependence, Lock-In, and History', 11 *Journal of Law, Economics, and Organization* (1995) p. 205; and ibidem., 'Network Effects and Externalities', in Newman, *supra* n. 27, vol. 2.

Unsurprisingly, law and economics scholars have asserted that similar increasing return mechanisms help to explain inertia and momentum in the evolution of legal rules and institutions.[61] Comparable increasing return effects appear to play a pivotal role, especially in the field of business forms, which, as we have seen, should be viewed as legal products traded in a market.[62] Consider, for example, statutory provisions and cases under company laws. In most western jurisdictions, the majority of firms are organized under the provisions of a corporate statute. Such statutes not only confer substantial network effects to users of those statutes, but firms also expect to obtain further benefits as new enterprises incorporate. Unlike the fax machine, which became more valuable as more and more people possessed one,[63] the use of the corporate statute could be valuable to a particular firm, regardless whether other firms have incorporated under the same statute. All the same, widespread use of the corporate form could have network effects analogous to those of the QWERTY keyboard. As more firms adopt the corporate form, networks of legal actors specializing in this particular business form (e.g., lawyers and legal scholars) will develop, thereby offering legal services of a higher quality and lower cost. Furthermore, firms may choose the corporate form to attract and accommodate investors who expect firms to use it.[64]

Learning effects further reinforce the application of increasing returns processes to business forms, including legal doctrines, statutory provisions and case law.[65] These effects, which come from the use of the corporate law statute, for instance, also explain why most of the parties that originally opted into the corporate form have an incentive to continue to use the regime. Factors that arguably add to the value of the traditional corporate form include avoidance of formulation errors, ease in drafting relational agreements, availability

---

[61] See M. Klausner, 'Corporations, Corporate Law, and Networks of Contracts', 81 *Virginia Law Review* (1995) p. 757; Kahan and Klausner, *supra* n. 57. But see C.P. Gillette, 'Lock-In Effects In Law and Norms', 78 *Boston University Law Review* (1998) p. 813; M.A. Lemley and D. McGowan, 'Legal Implications of Network Economic Effects', 86 *California Law Review* (1998) p. 479; L.E. Ribstein and B.H. Kobayashi, 'Choice of Form and Network Externalities', 43 *William and Mary Law Review* (2001) p. 79.

[62] See R.A. Posner, 'Economics, Politics, and the Reading of Statutes and the Constitution', 49 *University of Chicago Law Review* (1982) p. 263. Banoff gives an overview of the literature that uses the product metaphor. See B.A. Banoff, *Company Governance Under Florida's New Limited Liability Company Act*, Florida State University College of Law Public Law and Legal Theory Working Paper No. 43 (2001), available at <http://www.law.fsu.edu/Journals/lawreview/downloads/295/banoff.pdf>.

[63] The value of the fax machine depends heavily on the number of other users. See, e.g., Katz and Shapiro, *supra* n. 60.

[64] See Klausner *supra* n. 61, at pp. 785-86 argues that where information asymmetries exist and signaling is costly, marketing network externalities may exist. Network effects provide a purely academic explanation for the fact that US high-tech start-ups are structured predominantly as public corporations, despite tax disadvantages. Venture capitalists would rather avail themselves of the predictable corporate form, for which many contractual mechanisms have been developed and standardized, than rely on new customized governance and organizational structures.

[65] See W.W. Bratton, 'Game Theory and the Restoration of Honor to Corporate Law's Duty of Loyalty', in L.E. Mitchell (ed.), *Progressive Corporate Law* (Greeley, Westview Printing 1995). If, for instance, case law creates a legal rule that goes beyond the statute, such as enhanced fiduciary duties for close corporations, increasing returns derive directly from precedent and the doctrine of *stare decisis*. See O.A. Hathaway, 'The Path Dependence of the Law: The Course and Pattern of Legal Change in a Common Law System', 86 *Iowa Law Review* (2001) p. 601; E. Rasmussen, 'Judicial Legitimacy as a Repeated Game', 10 *Journal of Law, Economics, and Organization* (1994) p. 63; A.S. Sweet. and M. McCown, *Path Dependence, Precedent, and Judicial Power*, Paper prepared for delivery at the 2001 Annual Meeting of the American Political Science Association, San Francisco, California, 30 August – 2 September 2001.

of case law on the interpretation of the statute, and the familiarity to legal actors.[66] If these benefits are taken into account, newly formed businesses are likely to migrate to the business corporation statutes that confer these benefits to the user. This will mean that demand will be higher than it otherwise might be, which in turn will lead to the supply of standardized statutory terms, rather than customized ones that benefit a particular firm in a particular situation. Because standardized terms offer certainty,[67] when advising their clients about incorporation decisions, business lawyers will recommend a standardized term – even if it is sub-optimal – rather than draft a customized term that could lead to a higher expected value for a client.

The result of network and learning effects is that continuous use of the dominant business form, even if it is not ideally suited to some firms, will reduce the incentives for lawmakers to innovate. As in other areas of law reform, the reluctance to diverge from the existing framework means that even if new business forms were created, parties might be unwilling to substitute the standard form for non-standard terms. In short, the benefits that accrue to a standardized regime may be sufficient to outweigh the benefits that firms could gain by shifting to a new or modernized statute. Also, because potential first-users of new business forms do not have the advantage of future network benefits, such new forms may only emerge if the inherent benefits are of paramount importance.

These 'switching costs', i.e., the costs of switching from a standardized form to a new or innovative business form, constitute yet another reason for conservative lawmakers to defend the *status quo* or only engage in patching-up reforms.[68] The uncertainty about the future benefits of the introduction of new legal business forms leads to the persistence of traditional rules and governance structures, and delays genuine legal innovation.[69] Like R&D investments into high-tech products and technologies, initial law-making costs are partially sunk costs. In this respect, legal intervention is costly, not only due to the research, legislative and publication costs of new law, but also because various legal actors must invest substantial amounts in human capital and modes of operation that *fit* the new rules and institutions. If the new legal regime proves to be undesirable over time, these costs cannot easily be recovered.

3.1.3 *GmbH reform: an example of 'patching-up' provisions*

In the context of company law, the ingredients of strong path dependence may involve externalities that lock firms into an inferior business form and make it very difficult for the

---

66 See Clark, *supra* n. 8.

67 See C.J. Goetz and R.E. Scott, 'The Limits of Expanded Choice: An Analysis of the Interactions between Express and Implied Contract Terms', 73 *California Law Review* (1985) p. 261.

68 Research in behavioral psychology has indicated that people in general show a natural bias toward the *status quo*, in that, they have a tendency to prefer to leave things as they are. Moreover, evidence from laboratory experiments shows that people exhibit a so-called endowment effect: people often demand significantly more to give up an object than they would be willing to pay to acquire it, even when the transaction costs associated with reacquiring a similar object are very low. See J. Arlen, 'Comment: The Future of Behavioral Economic Analysis of Law', 51 *Vanderbilt Law Review* (1998) p. 1765.

69 See F. Parisi, V. Fon, and N. Ghei, 'The Value of Waiting in Lawmaking', 18(2) *European Journal of Law and Economics* (2004) p. 131; Department of Trade and Industry (DTI) argues that in light of the opposition from special interests, professional advisers and network externalities, introducing a new statute is of no value unless it will be widely used. See Department of Trade and Industry, *The UK Consultation Document from the Company Law Review Steering Group, Modern Company Law for a Competitive Economy, The Strategic Framework* (London, DTI 1999) at pp. 64-65.

reform-minded to convince the controlling elite of the merits of offering a new menu of legal business forms. To explain this, let us look at the current reform situation in Germany to see how resilient these mechanisms have been in facing off challenges to reforms that might have allowed firms more organizational choice. For example, despite competitive and interest group pressures to reform the German close corporation, the *GmbH,* along the line of the British Ltd., German legislators have largely resisted taking actions that would challenge the *status quo*. To be sure, proposals have been advanced to reform the *GmbH* in order to stem the flow of German firms using the British Limited. Figure 2 shows that in the first eight months of 2005 23,496 new *GmbHs* were formed against 3,195 Ltds, which counts for fourteen percent of the newly incorporated firms.

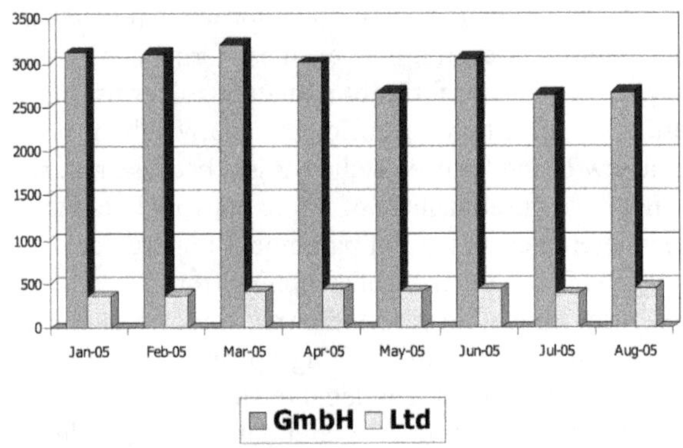

Figure 2. Comparison Newly Incorporated *GmbHs* versus Ltds

Source: Adapted from *Deutscher Bundestag (BT) – Drucksache* 16/283 – 16.12.2005 – *Auswirkungen und Probleme der Private Limited Companies in Deutschland*

However, economic and political pressures have not built up sufficiently to force through German legislative action that would involve substantial costs to incumbent groups. For example, it has been proposed that changes involving the reduction of minimum capital requirement (involving a reduction from € 25,000 to € 1), the transplant of the British *wrongful trading rule,*[70] and the option allowing firms to choose a single layer member-managed *GmbH*, would lead to a more flexible and lower cost structure and thereby over-coming the path dependence forces which have successfully blocked he introduction of a more market friendly structure so far.[71] The German legislature had a two-phased reform in mind, first, a compromise proposal would have lowered the capital requirement from € 25,000 to € 10,000. Subsequently, a more fundamental reform would have further adjusted the *GmbH* legislation to the social and economic changes. However, due to the change in government after the federal election in September 2005, the proposed reform path has not seen the light of day. The point here is that not only have reform groups failed to

[70] The *wrongful trading regulation* requires directors to monitor the firm's health and, if necessary, to take some remedial or preventive measures that prevent their firms from sliding into insolvency.

[71] To be sure, the German legislature a professional limited liability partnership. (*Partnerschaftgesellschaft)* in 1995 and updated the legislation in 1998. However, the procedures involving the formation and operation of this partnership form appear too costly and cumbersome to economic actors. For instance, the *Partnerschaftgesellschaft* statute is linked awkwardly to both the civil and commercial partnership rules.

overcome the system's barriers, but they have also failed to effectively alter society's perceptions about the need for legislative change in this field. Major reforms that involve deviations from the current rules on the preservation of the share capital and the notarial deed requirement for the transfer of the shares are unlikely to find support in the near future. Indeed, in order to limit the increasing popularity of the limited, a new proposal to introduce a modernized *GmbH* was published on 29 May 2006.[72] The proposed act – *Gesetzes zur Modernisierung des GmbH-Rechts und zur Bekämpfung von Missbräuchen (MoMiG)* is built on three main functions of the *GmbH* law: (1) The incorporation of a *GmbH* should be fast, cheap and simple; (2) the new *GmbH* should offer a transparent shareholder structure; and (3) creditors should be better protected against illicit exploitation and rent seeking strategies of the owners of a *GmbH*.

The reform measures serve to simplify the registration system, making a fast and electronic registration with the Chamber of Commerce possible for *GmbHs*. The availability of a public shareholders' list at the Chamber of Commerce emphasizes the importance of the electronic registration as such an up-to-date list should help prevent the acquisition of the company from non-shareholders. It is the intention of the new Act to consider only registered persons as shareholders In order to make the *GmbH* an attractive export product, the new Act proposes to abolish the requirement that the registered office of a firm is located in the same country as its corporate seat. Surprisingly, however, the upgraded *GmbH* would still require a minimum capital of €10,000 (see Table 3). Moreover, as a trade-off for the reduction of the minimum capital requirement, the legislature proposes to increase the managing director's liability in the event of the firm's insolvency. It seems that Germany's law-making elite endeavors to secure the popularity of the *GmbH* by enacting a compromise legislation that mainly focuses on the relations of shareholders and managers to persons dealing with the *GmbH*.

Table 3. Legal Characteristics 'new' *GmbH* (Germany)

Characteristic	**GmbH (revised)**
Legal Personality	Yes
Management	At least one managing director
Formation	Articles of Incorporation + notarial deed + registration at the Registry of Commerce + audit by the Local Court + publishing in a legal gazette
Autonomy of Articles of Incorporation	Some provisions are only valid if they are included in the Articles. Agreements and resolutions with effect for the future or that lack the agreement of all shareholders are null and void or voidable
Notarization of Articles of Incorporation	The Articles must be recorded in a notarial deed, otherwise the Articles are null and void
Fiduciary Duties	Statutory shareholder's right to information/case law duty of good faith and loyalty
Financial Rights	Shareholders have a right to share profits in proportion of their investment
Transferable Interests	No public offerings allowed; a transfer of shares requires a notarial deed in order for the transfer to be valid
Continuity of Life	Yes
Limited Liability	Yes, minimum capital requirement of EUR 10,000
Financial Statements	Mandatory disclosure
Taxation	Corporate taxation
Linkage	Management structure of public corporation (*Aktiengesellschaft, AG*)

72 See <http://tinyurl.com/yv2wnn>.

The above example shows that the legislative inertia resulting from both elite and traditional rule-making as well as the standardization-effect arguably leads to strong-form path dependence in Germany, which hampers innovation despite serious competitive pressures from the English Limited. The next section, however, will discuss how competitive pressures could instigate reforms despite the presences of considerable path dependence effects. It seems that the influence of high-powered, reform-minded interest groups is pivotal to the direction of change in company law reform.

3.2 The second strategy: responding to reform-minded interest group pressures

The evolution of company law may well generate a new transformation if national lawmakers find a compelling reason to abandon the defense of well-entrenched legal forms and increasing returns that reinforce their position and block the diffusion of new innovative legal rules and institutions. Studies on the political determinants of legislative change have examined the connection between public welfare and legislative outcomes, calling into question the motivation of lawmakers to undertake reforms on this basis. Given this, the introduction of new company law forms in response to social and economic concerns would seem unlikely. Nevertheless, the recent emergence of new business forms strongly suggests the presence of some kind of incentive to innovate.

A general implication for a broad theory of legal evolution is that lawmakers do not always dominate the law-making process. This is especially true of company law, which is influenced not only by lawmakers, but also by politicians and – more importantly – interest groups.[73] To fully explore this phenomenon, this section discusses the incentives for the introduction of new legal forms. This analysis builds on the economic theory of legislation, which assumes that legal rules are demanded and supplied in much the same way as other products. Legislation ensues from the jointly maximizing relationship between interest groups and political actors. Promising political or personal support,[74] interest groups persuade political members of the legislature, and specifically those who run the supply and demand process of legal products, to pass or veto legislation.[75]

A key question concerns the identification of which groups of firms are able to lobby successfully for business organization law reform and the prospect of success. Within the economic theory of legislation, legislatures have no incentive to adopt efficient provisions for firms that lack sufficient resources to lobby for laws.[76] Generally, the legislature, consist-

[73] See G.S. Becker, 'A Theory of Competition Among Pressure Groups for Political Influence', 98 *Quarterly Journal of Economics* (1983) p. 371; G. Grossman and E. Helpman, *Special Interest Politics* (Cambridge, MIT Press 2001).

[74] Interest groups have several means of influencing the so-called *brokers* of legislation. For instance, they can offer hoped-for future employment. Another pervasive means is political support, i.e., monetary contributions to political campaigns and votes. In addition, personal relationships make members of the legislature particularly responsive to interest groups. See Laffont and Tirole, *supra* n. 2; R.E. McCormick and R.D. Tollison, *Politicians, Legislation, and the Economy, An Inquiry into the Interest-Group Theory of Government* (Boston, Martinus Nijhoff Publishing 1981). Because politicians care about their re-election, they seek information on how their position on a particular issue will affect the outcome of the next election. As a result, it is submitted that 'lobbying and information provision by interest groups to politicians is the most important factor in explaining governmental policy outcomes'. See J.M. de Figueiredo, 'Lobbying and Information in Politics', 4 *Business and Politics* (2002) p. 125.

[75] See R.D. Tollison, 'Public Choice and Legislation', 74 *Virginia Law Review* (1988) p. 339.

[76] See M McCubbins and T. Schwartz, 'Congressional Oversight Overlooked: Police Patrols *versus* Fire Alarms', 28 *American Journal of Political Science* (1984) p. 165.

ing of risk-averse politicians and conservative lawmakers, tries to avoid innovations. Yet if powerful interest groups demanded that provisions of business forms be changed, political pressures within the legislature would attempt to satisfy the demand with beneficial legislation.[77]

In terms of assessing the likelihood of the enactment of modernized or new business forms into national law, there are several classes of firms that might be directly attracted by the cost-saving benefits. The first class is made up of prospective firms that will only come into existence if modern, flexible and responsive business vehicles are available. For instance, it is expected that simplicity and low formation costs will not only appeal to firms, but will also encourage the formation of joint ventures and other combinations. The second class consists of future start-ups which would use either the traditional partnership or close corporation form. For the most part, these start-ups are small, closely held firms that would not consider the law *ex ante*, but may unwittingly fall foul of unexpected and disruptive rules *ex post*. The third class is made up of potential portfolio firms that will convert into the newer business form in order to have a chance of attracting outside capital. A fourth and related class consists of existing firms for which cost savings will accrue in the event of reorganization to a new business form, with the savings exceeding the cost of reorganization. This class includes professional service firms which, but for a limited liability partnership form, would continue to use a traditional partnership form.

A wide array of business firms may deviate from the *status quo* to demand a new company law form. Economic evidence shows that only certain firms will have sufficient influence to achieve positive legislative results, either because they are more powerful than others or because they perform collective lobbying through a common body which gives them an advantage over other firms in the procurement of favorable legislation.[78] Small- and medium-sized enterprises (SMEs), for instance, are not likely to play a featured role in the development of business organization legislation. While this type of firm could derive much benefit from legal changes that dispose of the cumbersome formation and operation requirements, information and organization costs arguably inhibit its efficacy in attaining its preferred legislative goals.[79] In the event of SMEs making the lobbying effort independently, they must first incur information costs in discovering the effects of the choice of business forms on their own welfare.[80] Consequently, since SMEs may be severely budget-constrained in their ability to influence the legislature,[81] they have incentives to join up with firms with whom they share common interests so as to lobby for legislation. The organization costs (i.e., the costs of identifying other similarly situated firms) must not exceed the overall benefits from lobbying. This is especially true if firms encounter collective action problems. Rational firms have incentives to free-ride on the costly lobbying efforts of others. Attempts to engage in collective lobbying will therefore fail if a few firms bear the entire cost, but receive only a portion of the benefits.[82] Additionally, even if small-

---

77 See Bratton *supra* n. 65.

78 See J.R. Macey, 'Public Choice and the Law', in Newman, *supra* n. 27.

79 See McCormick and Tollison, *supra* n. 74.

80 As small firms are unlikely to consider business organization laws, except in major relational crises, it is costly to ascertain the effects of different rules and provisions in advance.

81 See J.M. de Figueiredo and E.H. Tiller, 'The Structure and Conduct of Corporate Lobbying: How Firms Lobby the Federal Communication Commission', 10 *Journal of Economics and Management Strategy* (2001) p. 91.

82 See M. Olson, *The Logic of Collective Action* (Cambridge, Harvard University Press 1965).

and medium-sized firms can overcome these problems and have adequate resources to lobby legislatures, they are likely to expend their efforts on more pressing operational and special considerations relating to a particular industry.

It can therefore be predicted that company laws will not adequately reflect the needs of SMEs. But even if this class of firms has high-powered incentives to lobby for innovative business forms,[83] their efforts might not be successful. In terms of assessing the prospect of success, two factors may play a crucial role. First, legislative procedures and political processes reduce the stakes interest groups have in regulation. Legislatures have developed administrative structures and mechanisms (e.g., the political and regulatory institutions, voting rules, rules of order) to control the opportunistic conduct of politicians and legislators who are sensitive to lobbying.[84] As a result, the supply side plays a decisive role with respect to company law reform.[85] Second, although amendments to the menu of business forms would arguably make smaller firms more efficient, it may not be in the interests of other more powerful lobby groups to modify the law to allow new legal forms to emerge. Consequently, legislatures are likely to respond by failing to adopt value-increasing legislation.

Consider, for instance, the notaries (lawyers who specialize in incorporations and are qualified to issue a notarial deed) who could organize themselves as a significant interest group, blocking innovative measures and frustrating attempts to effectively implement the easy availability of limited liability for small businesses.[86] In continental Europe, a notarial deed is usually required for all incorporations (see also Table 3). Given the importance that firms attach to the regulation and cost of market entry,[87] the extension of limited liability protection to partnership forms would preferably not require the issuance of such a deed. Yet, if a limited liability partnership were to gain adherence amongst investors and popularity with entrepreneurs,[88] the notaries' fee revenues might drop substantially. If their losses are more acute than the possible gains of business lawyers who would be involved in

---

[83] Bernardo and Welch argue that overconfident entrepreneurs are relatively less likely to imitate their peers and more likely to explore the environment leading them to adopting new innovations. See A.E. Bernardo and I. Welch, 'On the Evolution of Overconfidence and Entrepreneurs', 10 *Journal of Economics and Management Strategy* (2001) p. 301.

[84] See M.D. McCubbins, R.G. Noll and B.R. Weingast, 'Structures and Process, Politics and Policy: Administrative Arrangements and the Political Control of Agencies', 75 *Virginia Law Review* (1989) p. 431; A. Schwartz and R.E. Scott, 'The Political Economy of Private Legislatures', 143 *University of Pennsylvania Law Review* (1995) p. 595.

[85] See Laffont and Tirole, *supra* n. 74.

[86] It might be argued that the persistence of the system of notaries is an example of the path dependence role of interest groups as a serious source of path dependence. In the 12th and 13th century, the function of notaries was to register long-term contracts, including relational contracts – such as partnerships. Apparently, the merchants used notaries when 'reputation via word of mouth alone was insufficient to support honest behavior and that a third party without any binding authority to enforce obligations was nonetheless quite valuable for promoting honest exchange.' P.R. Milgrom, D.C. North and B.R. Weingast, 'The Role of Institutions in the Revival of Trade: the Law Merchant, Private Judges, and the Champagne Fairs', 2 *Economics and Politics* (1990) p. 6. In continental European jurisdictions, the formal use of lawyers as notaries evolved into a requirement to obtain legal personality.

[87] See S. Djankov, R. La Porta, F. Lopez-de-Silanes and A. Shleifer, 'The Regulation of Entry', 117 *Quarterly Journal of Economics* (2002) p. 1.

[88] It is submitted that the developments with respect to the 'quasi-partnership' close corporation demonstrate the demand for business forms that combine the combination of partnership and corporate features. See L.E. Ribstein, 'Statutory Forms for Closely Held Firms: Theories and Evidence from LLCs', 73 *Washington University Law Quarterly* (1995) p. 369.

the formation process of a new limited liability vehicle, the notaries will have a particularly high-powered incentive to block such a new form.

That is not to say that legal professionals will not lobby for modernized company law legislation. Indeed the US experience points in the opposite direction. As experts in law with a well-entrenched position and proximity to the law-making process, they have a strong ability to influence the legislature.[89] As noted, the increase in recent years of the number of hybrid entities offering limited liability can be attributed to the legislatures' responsiveness to the interest group activities of professional services actors. Well-organized professional firms may lack enough choice to shield their liability, giving them adequate incentives to exercise political influence over legislatures to enact an LLP-type form.[90] In addition, innovative legal professionals who seek to design and implement new arrangements for their clients may have a financial incentive to persuade the legislature to enact a new business form.[91] If the existing menu of business forms does not satisfy a pent-up demand for firms to employ new and improved frameworks,[92] 'innovative form entrepreneurs' will endeavor to capture the market, thereby increasing their fee revenues.[93] In the event of these professionals strongly favoring reform, given both types of incentives, the legislature is likely to respond by referring back to, and evolving from, existing doctrines and rules. For instance, they will bear in mind the key role of the notaries in the formation and operation of business forms. In fact, the current role of the notaries in business formations makes it likely that they will be able to defend the *status quo*, or expand their power in the future.

The upshot is that the political economy of new company law statutes tends to reflect the compromise between the legislature and powerful organizations of professional lawyers. It is by no means certain that a new framework that meets the perceived interests of professionals is efficient and equally beneficial to other business firms, SMEs in particular. Nevertheless, legislatures are likely to allow these other firms to use such a framework without the value of corresponding advantages for these firms.

To illustrate these points, let us consider the introduction of the LLP in the United Kingdom. While the decision to introduce an LLP was motivated by diverse factors, including election politics, which contributed to its speedy passage, the Department of Trade and Industry (DTI) was directly involved in the establishment of the LLP. The DTI, which was motivated by the threat of regulatory competition from offshore LLP statutes, particularly that of Jersey,[94] promulgated the Limited Liability Partnership Act

---

89 See L.E. Ribstein, 'Lawyer Licensing and State Law Efficiency', Working Paper (Draft of March) (2002).

90 The professional lobbies could be very powerful if they are in fact the by-products of organizations that obtain their strength and support because they perform some functions in addition to lobbying for collective goods. Because membership is in fact mandatory, the organization can overcome information, organization and collective action problems. See Olson, *supra* n. 82.

91 The role of business lawyers as interest groups is of course closely related to their role as lawmakers in the arena of legal formants.

92 Since there is a prevailing view that tax issues play a crucial role in choice-of-business-form decisions, innovative lawyers are inclined to design statutes or combinations of statutes with a view to helping firms obtain favorable tax treatment. Section 4 of this paper shows that there are other choice of business form drivers, such as contractual flexibility and the autonomy of firm participants in structuring, free from court interference, the internal affairs of the firm. See Oesterle, *supra* n. 23.

93 See Banoff, *supra* n. 62.

94 Limited Liability (Jersey) Law, 1996. Motivated by liability and tax considerations, British accountants (in particular Ernst & Young and Price Waterhouse) provided a wholly crafted statute to the Jersey legislature, a largely passive and accessible body that decided to enact the statute. In speedily adopting the LLP, Jersey signaled

in 2001.[95] The legislation introduced a new limited liability vehicle that has legal personality, a partnership governance structure, and partnership tax treatment.[96] In drafting this legislation, DTI responded to the pent-up demand from multinational professional service firms wishing to transfer to LLP status.[97] Importantly, the reform-minded law-making elite, side-stepping traditional elites, exploited the lobby groups' pressures to extend the scope of the UK LLP to other non-professional firm. In this view, the linkage of the UK LLP to the corporate law provisions, such as the requirement to comply with many of the provisions of the Companies Act and Insolvency Act, constituted a trade-off for gaining access to limited liability. Equally, conservative lawmakers made it mandatory that accounts must be audited to show a 'true and fair' view under UK GAAP.[98] The Consultative Committee of Accountancy Bodies published its Statement of Recommended Practice (SORP) on accounting by Limited Liability Partnerships (LLPs).[99] SORP confirms that UK LLPs must disclose their financial statements in line with those of limited companies. Table 4 gives an overview of the most important legal features of the UK LLP.

Table 4. Legal Characteristics UK LLP

Characteristic	UK LLP
Legal Personality	Yes
Management	Decentralized; in absence of agreement every partner may take part in management, however designated members have particular responsibility for certain statutory requirements
Formation	Registration at Companies House on a prescribed form LLP2 together with a statutory fee – two or more partners
Autonomy of Articles of Incorporation	N/A
Notarization of Articles of Incorporation	No
Fiduciary Duties	No general duty of good faith; specific duties in the regulations to account for competing activities and use of partnership property
Financial Rights	In absence of agreement equal sharing rights
Transferable Interests	No public offerings allowed
Continuity of Life	Change in membership of partners does not lead to dissolution
Limited Liability	Yes
Financial Statements	An annual return and annual statutory accounts must be filed
Taxation	Pass-through taxation
Linkage	Linked to corporate law provisions

its commitment to a comprehensive set of business forms for foreign organizations. However, high switching costs and doubts about the prospective benefits of incorporating as a Jersey LLP may explain Jersey's failure to capture a share of the UK partnership market.

95 The Limited Liability Partnerships Act 2000, The Limited Liability Partnerships Regulations 2001, and Limited Liability Partnerships (Fees) (No. 2) Regulations 2001 came into force on April 6, 2001.

96 The Limited Liability Partnership Act 2000 and the Finance Act 2001 provide that LLPs are classified as partnerships for tax purposes.

97 In its draft Regulatory Impact Assessment, the DTI made a 'tentative estimate' that around 60,000 regulated firms might eventually become LLPs.

98 There are exemptions from audit for LLPs with turnover up to a certain threshold. On 26 May 2000, this threshold was set at an amount of 1 million Pounds.

99 See SORP Accounting by limited liability partnerships at <http://www.ccab.org.uk>.

It follows that innovative change differs across systems depending on the organization of reform-minded interest groups, and the accessibility and responsiveness of legislative bodies. In fact, these features help explain the capacity of the US and UK legal systems to establish hybrid legal vehicles for different forms of business relationships and professional firms. The next section suggests that legal evolution is also not immune to exogenous shocks, such as social and economic changes, international competition and foreign pressures, which may be sufficient to trigger a new company law statutes.[100]

3.3 The third strategy: responding to exogenous pressures

In this section, we discuss how existing institutional arrangements may be called into question by economic shocks, increasing global competition or war.[101] The large scale effects of these events can lead to reversals of expectations and consequently supply incentives and opportunities for reform-minded groups to create new legal rules and institutions. Even though there are few genuine exogenous shocks in history, it is generally recognized that the Asian economies experienced a major financial crisis in 1997 which, combined with earlier underlying weaknesses, prompted policymakers to consider altering the taken-for-granted institutional arrangements. A most conspicuous example of external-shock induced organizational changes is the corporate governance and securities law reforms in Japan, which were introduced by governmental regulators in response to the so-called lost decade of the 1990s.

Japan has a long history of responding to external threats. Consider the period before the Meiji reforms when Japan was essentially a closed country and carried out only limited commercial and cultural exchanges with the Hollanders.[102] At the end of the Edo period (1603-1867), the Japanese government responded to the external shock of confronting new social and economic pressures of the Russians, and later Europeans and Americans, which attempted to establish trade contracts with Japan. Yet, it was only in 1854 that Japan ratified the Japan-US treaty of peace and amity forced by Commodore Perry of the US Navy. But, it took some time for the trade, which remained very limited until the beginning of the Meiji period (1868-1912), to develop. Foreign nations demanded the ratification of treaties, which provided for immunity for foreigners from Japan's existing penal system. At the same time, these treaties granted foreign traders economical and legal advantages over domestic business people. In order to regain independence and dignity in their own coun-

---

[100] Initially there was significant resistance to the UK government mandating financial disclosure for LLPs. Many commentators assumed that the high cost of disclosure and privacy issues would limit the interest in the LLP. The Limited Liability Partnerships Regulations and accounting standards require that the financial statements should include, unless exempted by the requirements of the Companies Act 1985 as modified by the Regulations, the following items: (1) profit and loss statement, consolidated in the case of a group preparing accounts; (2) a statement of total recognized gains and losses pursuant to FRS 3, consolidated in the case of a group preparing accounts; (3) cash flow statement pursuant to FRS 1, consolidated in the case of a group preparing accounts; (4) a balance sheet, and a consolidated balance sheet in the case of a group preparing accounts; and (5) notes to the financial statements disclosed.

[101] See M.J. Roe, 'Legal Origins and Modern Stock Markets', 120 *Harvard Law Review* (2006) p. 460, available at <http://www.harvardlawreview.org/issues/120/dec06/roe.shtml>; R.G. Rajan and L. Zingales, *Saving Capitalism from Capitalists: Unleashing the Power of Financial Markets to Create Wealth and Spread Opportunity* (New York, Crown Publishing Group 2003).

[102] The Meiji period (1868-1912) is known for bringing about the modernization of Japanese economic, political and social institutions.

try, Japan reacted, among other things, by adopting legal reforms, including a legislative regime to govern the internal affairs of companies, inspired by German law. The transplantation of a civilized, Western-style legal system was viewed as the only rapid and effective solution to force the foreign powers to abrogate the treaties.

Thus, company law in Japan could be viewed as a German transplant.[103] Despite the 1950-amendments introduced during the American occupation, the general corporate form (*Kabushiki Kaisha*) remained relatively formal and later reforms continue to show a tendency to transplant German legal rules.[104] For instance, the enactment of the *Yugen Kaisha*, a closely held business form based on the German *GmbH* in 1938, reflects the German legacy.

Subsequently, radical attempts to change Japan's company law system emerged in the late 1990s. In general this period is considered to be a 'lost decade' as Japan experienced a long-lasting severe recession that followed the burst of the preceding bubble economy. The Japanese economy was hit hard as large corporations defaulted and banks suffered under an increasing weight of non-performing loans. The *shock* not only hit the financial economy but also destroyed Japan's self-esteem as a *technopower*. The weakening of domestic confidence, manifested in the involvement of the Japanese bullet train, *Shinkansen* – once a symbol of the reliability of Japan's technological superiority – in multiple accidents in 2000, has become increasingly important for Japan. Moreover, large firm confidence was further weakened by the successful commercial strategies of European and American high-tech companies, collaborating through US hybrid entities, that have eroded the position of many Japanese technology-oriented firms.

All of this raised concerns about the rigidities and shortcomings of Japanese law. The growing emphasis on institutional reform and change, in response to globalization and the corresponding competitive pressures, has been stimulated by a new constellation of interest groups which have significant political clout to bring about a variety of reforms, including the facilitating of stock options, to spur the knowledge-based sector and encourage investment.

Besides traditional governance measures, policymakers have focused on creating hybrid business forms, similar to those developed earlier in the US and UK, that offer more flexibility in the decision-making structure and governance framework as well as resource management mechanisms needed to support the efforts of firms working in the human capital intensive sector. Moreover, there are numerous indications that policymakers have devoted considerable attention to the concerns of the largest and most established companies seeking to develop new technology, spin-off new opportunities and intellectual property, and which can form the basis of joint ventures and alliances.[105] Thus, by 2003, the Ministry of Justice had established a number of priorities involving the amendment of the

[103] See C.J. Milhaupt, 'In the Shadow of Delaware? The Rise of Hostile Takeovers in Japan', 105 *Columbia Law Review* (2005) p. 2171.

[104] Such as strengthening the statutory auditors' powers.

[105] In 2002, realizing this adverse change in the competitive situation, Japan used its prior and existing 'Research Association for Mining and Manufacturing Technology Law' (*koukougyo gijutsu kenkyuu kumiai hou*), and established 'EUVA' (EUV association, 2002-2008) aiming at catching up to the EUV-LLC, but so far, this effort has not born fruit. To worsen the situation, the US-European group has just initiated their stage by starting the INVENT partnership (2005-2012) to which IBM, AMD, Infineon, and Micron Technology have contributed roughly ¥ 70 billion (about $ 700 million) which is also a closely held firm aimed at carrying out similar R&D activities (similar to EUV-LLC) on technologies to form a super-fine semiconductor integrated circuit by using extreme ultra violet (EUV) light.

Commercial Code. The end result was a package of legislative reform measures, comprised in The New Company Law, which were submitted to the Diet in March 2005.

Generally, the New Company Law (*Kaisha Ho*) abolishes the *Yugen Kaisha* (*YK*), the close corporation, and leaves a modernized *Kabushiki Kaisha* (*KK*) in place (grandfathering the existing *YK*s). The *KK* regulation is liberalized through the relaxation of the minimum capital requirements (reducing the threshold from net assets of ¥ 10M to ¥ 3M). Further, closely held *KK*s, which restricts in its articles of association the free transferability of shares, will only require one director to be appointed instead of three. The appointment of a statutory auditor for the *KK* is not mandated if an officer is appointed who has the qualifications of tax accountant or accountant. While a suitably modernized *KK* will surely attract a number of closely held firms, the legislature acknowledged that the amendments introduced will not be sufficiently attractive to those individuals or established companies that are interested in selecting a more flexible business form.

It is therefore not surprising that the New Company Law provides for the introduction of a new company law form, the Limited Liability Company (LLC) or *Godo Kaisha*. The LLC is a partnership-type form that bundles together limited liability, decentralized management by default, unanimous consent to transferability of members' interests, fiduciary duties and no requirement to audit and disclose financial records. The Japanese vehicle bears a strong resemblance to the US LLC (e.g., voting and distribution rights are proportionate to the members' contributions), but diverges in a number of important respects, including: (1) contributions to the LLC will be limited to cash or property, but no services, know-how or other agreements are permitted; and (2) the LLC will receive corporate, but not pass-through, tax treatment.

It may be that the adoption of a US-style LLC can be seen as the effect of a strong triggering event, which is the determinative force of domestic institutional change. It is difficult at this juncture, however, to be certain that these changes are only the result of such an exogenous trigger. Moreover, it is hard to distinguish between endogenous and exogenous pressures as the determinative force of institutional change. In any event, it could be argued that the sequence of institutional changes marked by the new hybrid entities is ultimately the result of both pressures. On the one hand, the effects of decreasing returns on key actors within commercial system, notably through the growth and internationalization of the financial system and the integration of product markets as a whole, actually influences the course of legal and institutional development, undermining complementary institutions and policies. Further, pronounced disruptions to the existing path not only altered intrinsically the interests of key pressure groups, but also modified their incentives to invest in the development of new types of legal institutions and rules. That said, the scope for both exogenous and endogenous pressures to bring about major structural reforms in Japan is evidently great.

On the other hand, controlling legal elites and incumbent interest groups were initially strongly resistant, regardless of the pressures, to adopt a business form that combines important attributes of the corporate form and the partnership form, such as limited liability, flexibility and pass-through taxation. In order to overcome resistance to change, the Ministry of Economy, Trade and Industry (METI) stepped in and submitted, subsequent to the introduction of the *Godo Kaisha*, the Limited Liability Partnership Bill to the Diet in February 2005. As a consequence, the LLP or *Yugen Sekinin Jigyou Kumiai* came into effect on 1 August 2005 to encourage the creation of new business ventures, joint ventures and other strategic partnerships between high tech companies and research institutions. The LLP Law provides for the introduction of a vehicle that is characterized by limited liability, a flexible organization structure, pass-through taxation, and restrictions on the free transferability of partners' interests. Despite these attractive features, the legislation mandates a number of highly restrictive and costly features including: (1) registration of the LLP agreement; (2) disclosure of financial information including the profit and loss statements and the balance sheet upon the request of creditors; (3) the mandatory obligation of partners to participate in LLP management and its operation; and (4) the right of partners to exit at will. Notwithstanding these arguable shortcomings, which reflect political compromises, the LLP may, as will be discussed in the next section, provide significant cost advantages to firms.

Viewed from the perspective of an entrepreneurially government faced with exogenous pressures, such as global competition,[106] rapid changes in technologies and evolving market conditions, it is more likely to promote the competitiveness of indigenous industries through adoption of a cost-effective, reliable and flexible legal regime. If the future brings a substantial increase in business activity, a shift in interest group pressures for efficiency-based law-making could well be expected. Such a jurisdiction may consider entering the competitive law-making environment for the supply of law as product. In the company law context, a jurisdiction could reap the benefits by coming forward with a set of contractual-based rules ideally suited to closely held firms. If this jurisdiction would engage in a law reform process along such lines, it could very well create a focal point leading to a significant number of domestic and even foreign firms to select this legal innovation.

Singapore is an example of an entrepreneurial jurisdiction. As a result of increased competition in Asia and the rapid development of China and the increase of Chinese firms being engaged in cross-border activities, the Singapore legislature enacted, among other things, an LLP (which came into effect on 11 April 2005). This evolution reflects

> 'the acute awareness of the need to recognize and accommodate current international business and commercial practices.'[107]

The Singapore LLP (S-LLP) is a new type of business vehicle in Singapore based on the Delaware LLP and to a less extent the UK LLP. An S-LLP is a legal entity that can sue and be sued and acquire and hold property. Like the Japanese counterpart, it offers a flexible management structure and pass-through taxation. The LLP is a stand-alone business form explicitly de-linked from the existing partnership law.[108] The partners are not personally liable for the firm's debts and obligations.[109] This protection shall not effect the personal liability of a partner in tort for his own wrongful act or omission. The internal relationship between the partners is governed by the limited liability partnership agreement. In the absence of an agreement or when the agreement is silent, the First Schedule, which acts as a model agreement, will apply. Although the S-LLP is required to keep accounts and other records, it is not necessary to prepare profit and loss accounts or balance sheets or to have them audited and disclosed. Table 5 provides a comparative overview the revised and introduced business forms in Japan and Singapore.

---

[106] See W.W. Bratton and J.A. McCahery, 'An Inquiry into the Efficiency of the Limited Liability Company: Of Theory of the Firm and Regulatory Competition', 54 *Washington and Lee Law Review* (1997) p. 629.

[107] See <www.singaporelaw.sg>.

[108] See § 6 of the Limited Liability Partnerships Act 2005.

[109] The LLP may recover distributions from partners that know or ought to have known that the LLP was insolvent or the distributions caused insolvency of the LLP.

Table 5. Comparison – New Company Law in Japan and Singapore

Characteristic	KK (new)	J-LLC	J-LLP	S-Private Company	S-LLP
Legal Personality	Yes	Yes	No	Yes	Yes
Management	Corporate structure (shareholders-board of directors)	Flexible – no restriction	Flexible – mandatory participation of all partners	Corporate structure (shareholders-board of directors)	Flexible – default: partnership like management structure
Formation	Registration of the articles of incorporation with the Legal Affairs Bureau (*hômukyoku)* – registration fee = JPY 150,000	Formed by articles of incorporation signed between members – registration of operating agreement and corporate seal with the Legal Affairs Bureau (*hômukyoku)* – registration fee = JPY 60,000	Registration and disclosure of the LLP agreement with the Legal Affairs Bureau (*hômukyoku)* – registration fee = JPY 60,000	Registration of the Memorandum (subscribed by at least 1 person) and the articles of association	Online Registration at www.bizfile.gov.sg / Registration Fee is S$ 165 / Registration takes 15 minutes
Autonomy of Articles of Incorporation	Yes	Operating agreement	LLP agreement	Yes	LLP agreement
Notarization of Articles of Incorporation	Yes – notarization fee = JPY 50,000	No	No	No	No
Fiduciary Duties	Directors must act in good faith	Managers have similar duties to legal duties of KK directors	Defined by LLP agreement (Incomplete law)	Duties of directors: (1) to act honestly; (2) duty to disclose shareholdings; (3) duty to convene general meetings	Defined in LLP agreement or, if the agreement is silent, the provisions in the First Schedule (full disclosure of relevant information and non-compete clause)
Financial Rights	Distribution of profits and losses allocated according to equity participation ratio (however, distributions of profits require net assets of at least JPY 3 million)	Profits and losses may be allocated at a different rate from equity participation rate if specified in operating agreement	Profits and losses may be freely allocated with the unanimous approval of partners	Dividends shall be apportioned and paid proportionately to the amounts paid or credited as paid on the shares during any portion or portions of the period in respect of which the dividend is paid;	Defined in LLP agreement or, if the agreement is silent, the provisions in the First Schedule (equal sharing rule)

Table 5. Cont.

Characteristic	**KK (new)**	**J-LLC**	**J-LLP**	**S-Private Company**	**S-LLP**
Transferable Interests	Shares are freely transferable. Restrictions (by making transfer subject to board approval) in the articles possible	Members' unanimous approval required	Partners' unanimous approval required (mandatory rule)	A private company restricts the right to transfer its shares	LLP agreement – default: assignment of financial rights
Continuity of Life	Yes	Yes – even with one member	Yes, but minimum of two partners	Yes	Yes – the Court may order the winding up if the LLP carries on business with less than two partners for more than two years
Limited Liability	Yes, no minimum capital requirement, but in practice some paid-in capital is necessary	Yes	Yes	Yes	Yes (claw-back provision for distributions made three years before insolvency)
Financial Statements	Disclosure of annual balance sheet	No disclosure of annual balance sheet – financial statements must be made available to members and creditors	LLP must disclose its balance sheet and profit and loss statement to creditors (upon request)	Submission of an audited profit and loss account and balance sheet at a general meeting	Accounts and other records should be kept and retained for seven years. No mandatory audit and disclosure requirements
Taxation	Corporate	Corporate	Pass-through	Corporate	Pass-through
Linkage	Company Law	Company Law	Law Concerning Limited Liability Partnership Agreements	Companies Act	Non-applicability of partnership law clause

Source: Adapted from <www.singaporelaw.sg> and <www.jetro.go.jp>

The transformation described above provides a framework to evaluate the economic role of new hybrid business forms. On this basis, the next section will evaluate the new legal entities that emerged in the US, UK and Asia and are attracting more and more businesses to their relatively new network. It is suggested that these hybrid business forms, compared to the traditional menu, can provide effective choices for controlling opportunism while limiting transaction costs. Three fundamental questions will be asked: (1) whether closely held firms would prefer to select a new, redesigned hybrid legal entity, which sets forth the joint ownership structure and provides important contractual provisions in advance; (2) whether new business forms ideally suited to particular businesses are better positioned to offset the inefficiencies resulting from the lock-in effects and path dependence factors; and (3) how many products a menu of legal business forms should contain.

4. New product selection

The three reform strategies roughly lead to the emergence of three distinct statutory products. First, a legal up-grade arguably provides an easy-to-use vehicle that supplies lawyers and firms with familiar provisions that are *tried and tested* and consequently offer learning and network benefits to users of the form. Second, a linked, but new, legal business form similarly holds out continued network and learning benefits along with the prospect of superior cost advantages due to better suited statutory provisions. Third, in contrast, a non-networked product holds out greater costs for adopting firms as switching costs effect prospective users negatively, and the absence of an established set of precedents – which are needed to fill the gaps in the inherently incomplete law – provide few incentives for parties to adopt an entirely new type of legal product.

It would not be surprising that, given the relative cost advantages of upgrading, that the first approach is the obvious alternative. A modified statute could be attractive as there are no new learning costs involved. Because there are usually few alterations needed, it is easier for practitioners and business parties to adjust to the new round of changes. Given that the changes are unlikely to touch the core components of the legal tradition and its legitimating features, parties will have an incentive to learn the new rules. Nevertheless, the up-grade model has been criticized for not only making innocuous, albeit necessary, changes but for being out of step with innovative social and economic change. Although the up-grade approach seems attractive, particularly if the existing statutory framework is functionally obsolete, it is unlikely to benefit users unless accompanied by genuine cost saving changes.

Despite the apparent ease for jurisdictions to engage in producing statutory upgrades, this phenomenon has proved more costly and time-consuming than anticipated. This is evidenced by: (1) the difficulty in the design of acceptable upgrades; and (2) the reluctance of lawmakers to agree and quickly implement the proposed changes. Apparently, lawmakers when committed to incremental reform are less concerned with the pace and practical consequence of legislative change.

Even though most jurisdictions still employ the up-grade strategy to reform, an increasing number of countries embrace a new product approach by following either the second or third reform strategies as described in the previous section. This can be seen in the cases of the UK, Japan, and Singapore which moved quickly into unchartered territory when embarking on a new legal reform strategy that complemented their existing upgrade legislative reform approach. Surprisingly, this development seems better able to ensure speedy and effective legislative action. The length of time to develop and reform new company statutes is reflected in Figure 3.

It follows from Figure 3, that it is probably easier for lawmakers to understand and appreciate the alleged benefits of the new forms across political systems. The complex tax and doctrinal issues that can hamper and delay law reform projects are more effectively avoided when a new vehicle is proposed which leaves untouched the existing company law framework. Reforms along these lines, moreover, are supported by interests groups due to the measurable benefits they yield, including a new business form's (1) greater flexibility; (2) response to specific market problems and pressures; (3) ability to resolve conflicts between agents; and (4) value-added features in the structuring of transactions and business planning. Thus seen, the introduction of new legal products results in inherent benefits for businesses leading to major changes in the bargaining environment in which firms operate.

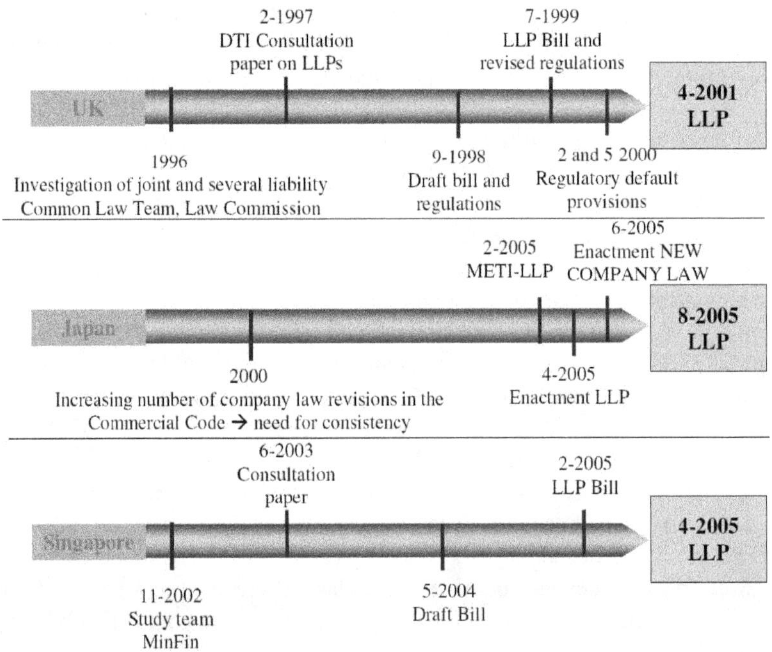

Figure 3. The time needed to introduce the LLP

4.1 Inherent benefits of new statutory products

4.1.1 *Limited liability and pass-through taxation*

New statutory products often involve an optimal mix of legal and fiscal attributes.[110] Empirical research supports the view that a new legal product eventually outweighs the ben-

[110] See R.B. Thompson, 'The Taming of Limited Liability Companies', 66 *University of Colorado Law Review* (1995) p. 921.

efits that arise due to learning and network effects.[111] While there is great appeal to the utilization of existing frameworks, firms are now more inclined to structure their business in a framework that is largely free from legal oversight and allows experimentation. Figure 4 shows the number of LLP formations in the United Kingdom for the period 2001-2005.

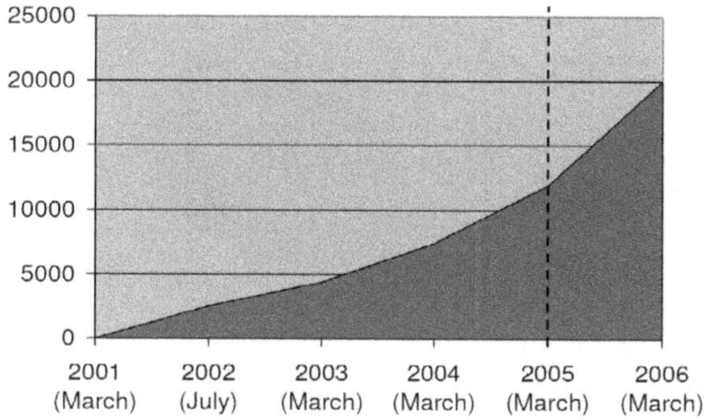

Figure 4. Total Number of LLPs in the UK

Source: Companies House (20,000 LLPs on March 2006 is an estimated figure)

Figure 5 and Figure 6 below show respectively the categories of businesses that have adopted the S-LLP and J-LLP.

Rather than the professional firms that the LLP form was initially designed for, there are numerous other categories of businesses which, due to a variety of drivers, have selected this new form. There are a number of common factors that induce firms to choose hybrid

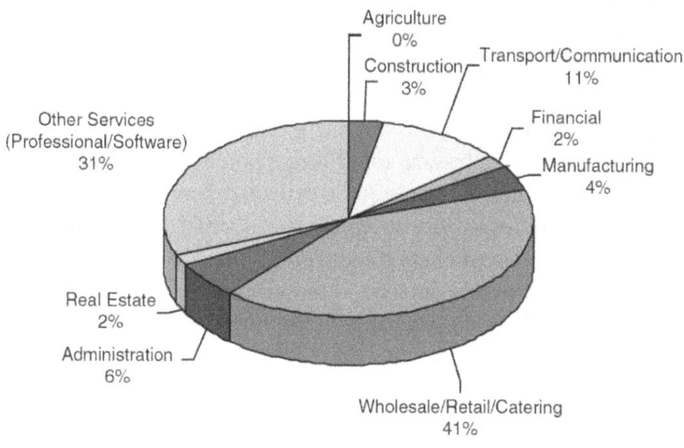

Figure 5. LLPs in Singapore

Source: BizFile Singapore

[111] See Ribstein and Kobayashi *supra* n. 61.

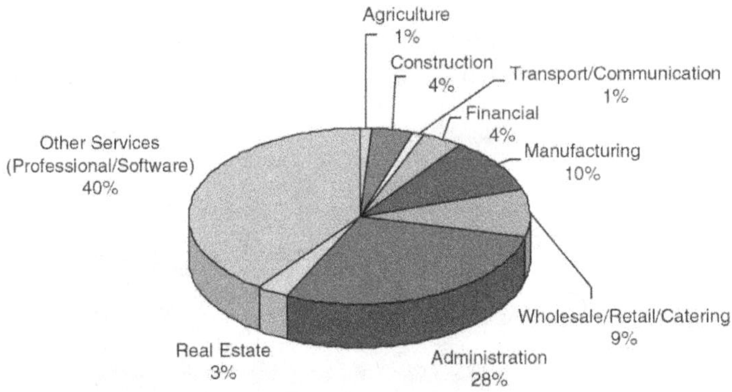

Figure 6. LLPs in Japan

forms (e.g., limited liability and tax advantages). Limited liability is the most important attractor of businesses to the hybrid entities. Surprisingly, empirical research shows that, despite tax benefits, the emergence of the LLC did not affect the total number of new incorporations. It appears that the first LLC-statutes were not able to attract firms that typically incorporated.[112] Observers questioned, for example, why high-tech start-up firms chose to forgo tax savings by selecting the public corporation.

Naturally, it is difficult to give a clear-cut answer, as the factors prompting start-ups to prefer the corporate legal form to other vehicles, is the subject of considerable controversy. Commentators have argued that the network effects and conversion costs, rather than the pass-through tax treatment and its lower tax rate, is the main considerations for selecting the corporate form.[113] The reluctance on the part of venture-capital backed start-ups to choose the LLC is explained in terms of a preference to save on transaction costs and time in the course of the venture capital cycle. By forming a public corporation, for instance, they would avoid the costs of converting the LLC into the corporate form before an initial public offering (IPO).[114] Indeed, conversion to a corporation remains necessary as long as underwriters in the United States are loath to support hybrid business forms that issue equity interests.[115] To be sure, it is only to be expected that the popularity of the US LLC will increase when it becomes a more accepted instrument for initial public offerings. Even though the US LLC allows for publicly traded *units* – that are nothing more than depository receipts for the owners' property interest – the efficiency of selling units is called into question because underwriters are probably unwilling to employ *units* on a large scale.

---

112 Ibid.

113 See J. Bankman, 'The Structure of Silicon Valley Start-ups', 41 *UCLA Law Review* (1994) p. 1737; Klausner *supra* n. 61.

114 Although the laws regarding the conversion of LLCs to corporations are usually very flexible in the United States, such a conversion could nevertheless, depending on the number of investors, be surrounded by cumbersome barriers in terms of finances and resources.

115 See Bankman, *supra* n. 113, at pp. 1749-50. Issuing interests to the public dissipates the tax advantage because most publicly traded business forms are taxed as corporations under § 7704 of the Internal Revenue Code.

Nevertheless, the popularity of the LLC in the fastest growing business segment of the market in the United States is increasing. Approximately 30% of the 100 fastest growing firms in the United States are structured as LLCs. These companies are less than five years old, but their annual sales exceed $ 1 million.[116] This trend is to some extent driven by the recent tendency of venture capital and private equity funds, faced with an ever-growing fierce and global competition, to embrace complex structures that help optimize the financial results for each group of investors. Figure 7 below shows, for instance, how the pass-through feature of the LLC, in combination with a corporate blocker, could increase the options for fund managers to better tailor the tax structure to the needs of their investors.

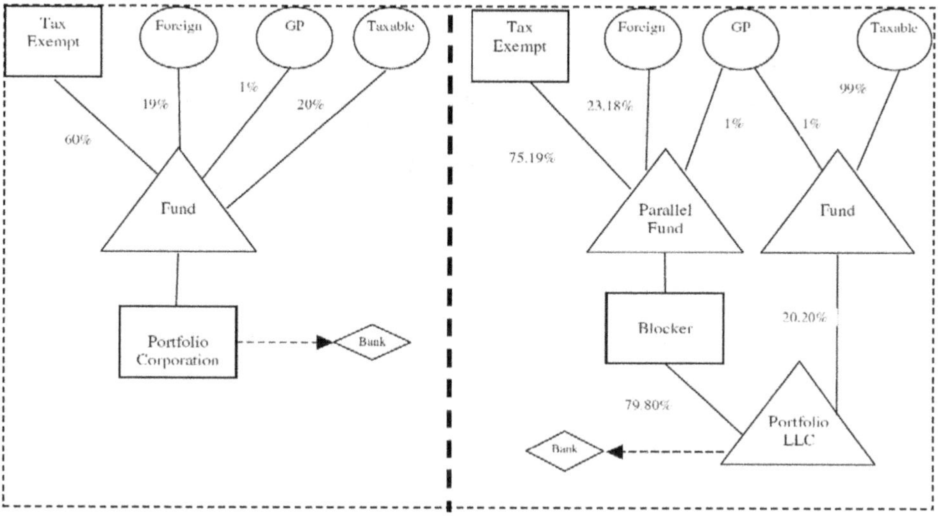

Figure 7. Tax-driven business planning

Source: Blashek and McLean (2006)

Certainly, there is some evidence that similar flow-through vehicles, such as the Canadian Business Income Trust, Energy Trusts and Real Estate Investment Trust, are associated with tangible tax benefits that attract a significant number of firms.[117]

While the Canadian vehicles, for example, can be employed more widely than in other jurisdictions, their enhanced popularity, compared to similar vehicles in the US, seems mainly related to the fact that an IPO does not effect their tax treatment. In contrast, US listed entities are by definition taxed as corporations. A similar pattern would likely emerge if US tax authorities were to adopt the same fiscal measures. Such a development would naturally tip the balance in favor of the LLC since the possible benefits of incorporation, like network effects, would not weigh-up against the advantages of hybrid forms.

There is already a trend which shows a high number of firms selecting the LLC over the corporate form in the US. The decrease in new incorporations is not only attributed to tax

---

116 See <http://www.entrepreneur.com/hot100>. These 100 firms had a total sales of $ 1.7 billion in 2005 and employed a total number of 6,920 people.

117 Consultation Paper by the Department of Finance Canada – Tax and Other Issues Related to Publicly Listed Flow-Through Entities (Income Trusts and Limited Partnerships).

Table 6. Comparison of the Taxes Paid Under Different Structures

	Corporate Structure	Income Trust	Limited Partnership
Entity Level	$35.00	NIL	N/A
Investor Level			
Taxable Canadian	$5.70	$14.82	$14.82
Non-Resident	$2.15	$3.30	$8.36
Tax-exempt	N/A	N/A	N/A
Total Tax	$42.85	$18.12	$23.28

Source: Department of Finance Canada (2005)

advantages, but also to the flexibility surrounding the formation and operation of an LLC as well as the higher costs associated with satisfying corporate governance mandates arising from the Sarbanes-Oxley Act.[118] Figure 8 shows that the number of new corporations in the US declined while the LLC continues to gain in popularity.

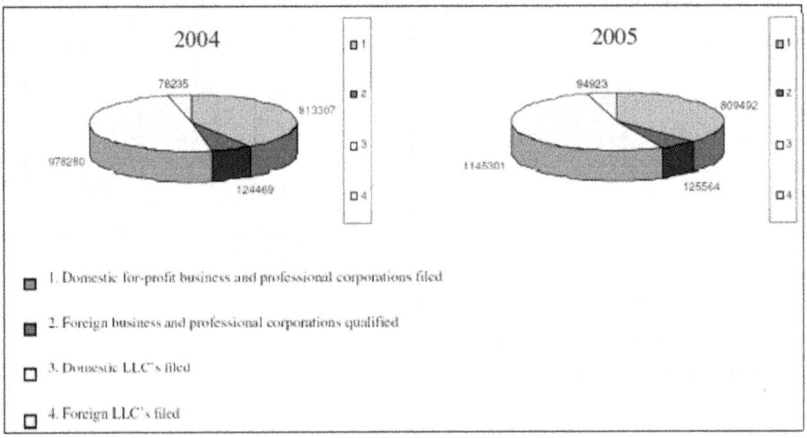

Figure 8. New Filings of Corporations and LLCs in the United States

Source: 2005 IACA Annual Report of Jurisdictions

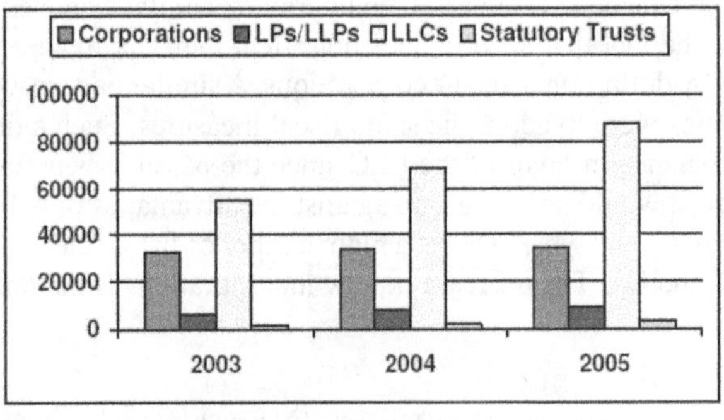

Figure 9. New Business Formation in Delaware (2003-2005)

Source: 2005 Annual Report, Delaware Department of State, Division of Corporations

LLCs are now widely employed for real estate and energy ventures, the exploitation of patents, corporate joint ventures, acquisition vehicles, and venture capital and private equity funds as well as high tech start-ups. As a matter of fact, the 2005 increase of revenues collected by the Delaware Division of Corporations – from $ 612.8 million to $ 626.1 million – is mainly due to the increase in LLC tax collections and filing fees (see Figure 9).

4.1.2 *Limited liability and private ordering*

It is a common refrain in the evolution of the corporate form that firms, in exchange for certain privileges, go through a number of formalities to incorporate their businesses, varying from, at first, the governmental approval of a corporate charter to the obligation to abide by the terms and provisions of the corporate statute, particularly the rules surrounding the separation of ownership and control. Before the Industrial Revolution the privileges consisted mostly of a monopoly over trade or the exclusive right to act on behalf of the government in developing a country's infrastructure. With the growth of commercial and industrial activity, the pressures from politically influential industrialists to abandon the specific governmental approval of a corporate charter grew steadily. By 1890, the statutes providing for incorporation by simple registration prevailed throughout the United States. The introduction of a relatively simple incorporation procedure in France in 1867 had already resulted in the rapid proliferation of general incorporation statutes in continental Europe.

In its developed form with fully-fledged limited liability protection, the corporation was the choice-of-business form for large-scale firms which were compelled to amass substantial sums of equity capital in order to give effect to capital-intensive industrial and technological innovations. The principle of limited liability was widely acclaimed as an industrial breakthrough and it took only until the late 19th century that the corporate limited liability feature became available to smaller, closely held firms. In this respect, two legal developments could be distinguished. First, a separate close corporation form, the *Gesellschaft mit beschränkter Haftung (GmbH)*, was enacted in Germany in 1892. Another, second, development demonstrates the importance of case law in furnishing smaller firms with the much-coveted limited liability feature. A decision of the House of Lords in *Solomon* v. *Solomon & Co. Ltd* overturned the assumption that only passive investors were granted limited liability under the Companies Act of 1862. These developments gained a widespread popularity across jurisdictions.[119] To date, most countries recognize a form of close corporation which, although they become increasingly flexible in terms of permissible deviations from the statutory provisions, are still modeled on the public corporations and its capital-oriented management structure.[120]

This raises the question as to whether corporate-type business forms, without the pass-through tax treatment (as discussed in the previous section), but with the partnership-type feature to devise the most efficient management and governance structure, would gain a

---

118 See L.E. Ribstein, 'Why Corporations?', 1 *Berkeley Business Law Journal* (2004) p. 183.

119 See McCahery and Vermeulen, *supra* n. 51

120 See M. Lutter, 'Limited Liability Companies and Private Companies', in D. Vagts (ed.), *Business and Private Organizations, International Encyclopedia of Comparative Law* (Boston, Martinus Nijhoff Publishing 1998) vol. 13, ch. 2.

foothold in the modern business environment. The answer to this question can be found in France. Recent data concerning the use of the French *société par actions simplifiée* (*SAS*), a limited liability vehicle that is considered to be the most flexible company form in France, which allows parties to freely contract into an optimal decision-making arrangement, indicates that not only tax, but also contractual flexibility is a main driver for business form selection.

Table 7. Comparison – French Business Forms

	Société Anonyme (SA)	**Société à Responsabilité Limitée (SARL)**	**Société par Actions Simplifiée (SAS)**	**Most advantageous**
Minimum capital	€37,000	No	€37,000	SARL
Minimum number of shareholders	7	1	1	SARL - SAS
Management structure	3-18 board members (mandatory) – the president must be an individual person	One or more managing directors who must not be corporate entities	Flexible – at least one president	SAS
Tax	Corporate	Corporate	Corporate	SA – SARL - SAS
Transfer of shares	Free transferability	Restricted	Free, but Articles may restrict	SAS
Limited Liability	Yes	Yes	Yes	SA – SARL - SAS
Accountant	Mandatory	Exempted below a certain threshold	Mandatory	SARL

Source: No. 222 April 2004 L'Entreprise

Table 7 shows the eschewal of tax as the driver for hybrid forms. Clearly, this runs against commentators' expectations that tax considerations predominately explain entity selection.[121] Obviously, the driving force behind *SAS* is the freedom of contract which enables firms, in an incomplete contracting world, to adapt to changing market circumstances and increased global competition.

That said, the key driver behind the success of the new hybrid business forms, such as the LLPs and LLCs, is the concept of maximum flexibility and autonomy of firm participants to structure the firm's internal affairs free from legal principles and doctrine.[122] It seems that, even though economic and path dependence factors prevent the emergence of complete law, the extended private ordering principles enhance the ability of business parties to experiment with these new forms. Businesses in need of debt and equity capital cannot therefore be expected to be tied up with corporate or partnership forms that only offer costly and burdensome statutory measures, such as mandatory management and deci-

[121] See Ribstein, *supra* n. 88. That is not to say that tax issues do not play a pivotal role in choice of entity decisions. See, for example, T. Petska, M. Parisi, K. Luttrell, L. Davitian and M. Scoffic, *An Analysis of Business Organizational Structure and Activity From Tax Data* (Washington, Internal Revenue Service 2005), available at <http://www.irs.gov/pub/irs-soi/05petska.pdf>.

[122] See Oesterle, *supra* n. 23.

sion-making structures (in the case of the corporation) or broad fiduciary duties (in the case of partnerships). This is especially true if these business forms – explicitly – fail to allow for the possibility to waive or contract around statutory rules and standards. For instance, the fact that parties may be subject to broad fiduciary duties, which may require a party to forgo personal interests, appears to act as a deterrent to venture capitalists and joint venturers. If parties are allowed to bring an action based on a breach of fiduciary duty when their high-risk gamble does not pay off, thereby circumventing the contractual mechanisms put in place to overcome information problems, the transaction costs arising from legal uncertainty and statutory ambiguity will increase significantly.[123]

To be sure, a new hybrid business form has the potential drawback of being a relatively untested entity that has not yet generated a large body of case law and academic research. The fact that company law is inherently incomplete and the parties are boundedly rational inevitably necessitates the involvement of the judiciary in the resolution of intra-firm disputes.[124] Indeed, it might be argued that new legal products only survive because the judiciary plays an important role in *ex post* dispute resolution and the development of legal precedent. Empirical research indicates that new business forms create a new network of cases dealing with, among other things, the nature of new business forms, formation requirements, fiduciary duties, limited liability and veil piercing, transfer of interests, and dissolution.[125] However, given the spur for new company law products that offer the maximum contractual flexibility, courts should 'permit persons or entities to join together in an environment of private ordering'.[126] In order to enhance legal certainty, courts should first respect the contractual arrangements. Only if both the statute and agreement are silent should courts endeavor to fill the contractual gap by looking at the parties' intentions *ex ante*.

That is not to say that greater contractual flexibility will automatically lead to efficiency. It follows from the discussion in Section 2 that an efficiency-minded legislature has the task to develop improved statutory default rules when enhanced certainty and guidance are needed. In order to increase the success of new business forms, legislators are advised not only to keep the statute up to date, but must also ensure it meets the coveted social and economic requirements over time. For instance, if the mandatory participation provision in the Japanese LLP entails problems for the internal stability of firms, the legislature may eventually offer new rules that are clearer and give better guidance on dealing with agency problems in a business environment. In this context it is worth noting that Delaware legislature strives to maintain legislative preeminence by periodically amending, among other things, the Delaware Limited Liability Company Act. Table 8 highlights the amendments to the Act in 2003, 2004 and 2005.

Table 8 shows that Delaware frequently updates the LLC-Act to give maximum effect to the principle of freedom of contract and to the clarification of default rules. We should point out that interest group pressures mandate the introduction of amendments facilitating domestication of and conversion to Delaware law. If we take this point a step further, it is

---

[123] See S.W. Stevenson, 'The Venture Capital Solution to the Problem of Close Corporation Shareholder Fiduciary Duties', 51 *Duke Law Journal* (2001) p. 1139.

[124] See Bratton and McCahery, *supra* n. 106.

[125] See E.S. Miller, *The Emerging LLC and LLP Case Law: A Survey of Cases Dealing with Registered Limited Liability Partnerships and Limited Liability Companies, ABA Partnerships and LLCs – Important Case Law Developments* (Chicago, American Bar Association 2003).

[126] See *Elf Atochem North America, Inc.* v. *Jaffari*, 727 A.2d 286 (Del. 1999).

Table 8. Amendments to the Delaware LLC-Act

	2004	2005	2006
Number of sections in the amendment	15	18	38
Amendment:			
Freedom of Contract	7	–	–
Clarification of Default Rules	3	10	6
Domestication/Conversion	4	6	26
Effective Date of the Amendment	1	1	1
Other amendments	–	1	5

Source: General Assembly of the State of Delaware

not difficult to explain the importance of the clarification of the default rules. Since the selection of business forms is a choice made *ex ante*, interest groups, e.g., business lawyers, have an interest to inform the legislature of shortcomings in existing provisions and provide technical support in devising amendments.

As we have seen, the freedom of contract is a priority of Delaware lawmakers and in this respect it could be argued that amending the LLC statue into an all-purpose *contractual entity* is necessary to confront the technological advances and the internationalization of the economy. There is something to the introduction of a *contractual entity* that can be tailored to the business needs and expectations of each type of firm. Parties in joint ventures, for instance, are likely to reduce agency problems and contract into the preferred structure of their particular relationship even if business form statutes do not contain any default rules. Still, the function of statutory company law – as a standard form contract – must not be underestimated. In the context of non-listed firms, company law should first offer a relatively small group of unsophisticated – and often unmotivated – business parties a ready-made business contract. Second, company law should give statutory guidance to mostly larger firms that do not fare well when ownership and control are integrated.

Table 8 also reflects Delaware's concern about emphasizing the importance of offering a coherent and consistent set of provisions. By continuously updating its legislation, Delaware signals to investors and creditors what they can expect in terms of the internal decision-making process and external representation model of a company. The foregoing discussion suggests that, given the importance of statutory guidance and the two types of governance structure – integrated and differentiated – a menu of business forms should contain at least two closely held limited liability entities, a manager-managed entity and a member-managed business form.

5. Conclusion

In this chapter, we have distinguished three different positions along the reform strategy spectrum of company law. The first position is located on the left side of the spectrum and closest to stasis – where virtually no effective legal changes can occur and where only the idea of reform clashes with legal tradition and standardization pressures. An example of a jurisdiction that takes this position is Germany. Along or near the mid-point of the spectrum, where company law changes are less impeded by tradition and standardization factors, but more influenced by interest group pressures. We see England occupying this position. Japan can be seen as a more adaptable jurisdictions located toward the right end of the spectrum and therefore better able to create and introduce more functional legal rules and institutions that turn the traditional view of company law around. It is submitted that Singapore is located on the right side of the spectrum as its legislature is aware of the need to adapt the legal system to international business practices in order to develop a distinct jurisprudence, acclaimed for its efficiency and integrity, which is set apart from the English legal system.

As we have seen in the case of the introduction of new hybrid business forms, traditional law-making elites are often out of step with the dominant vectors of economic and cultural change in society. As a consequence, this can open up opportunities for reform-minded lawmakers previously blocked in their efforts to undertake legislative reforms. This does not imply, however, that reform-mined legislators will create first-best measures that satisfy the demands of users. Yet, despite certain inefficiencies identified in this chapter, there are some inherent benefits for firms in employing the new hybrid business forms. Besides pass-through taxation, the hybrid vehicles offer parties the freedom to contractually establish the rights and obligations within the organizational structure. They combine the corporate feature of fully-fledged limited liability with the partnership law principles of flexibility and informality. In this respect, the 'new company law' ushers in a new era in which the statement *when in doubt, don't incorporate* is increasingly applicable to innovative businesses. The introduction and popularity of *new company law* as depicted in this chapter is but a small step in that direction.

Chapter 5

MODERNIZING LATIN AMERICAN COMPANY LAW: CREATING AN ALL-PURPOSE VEHICLE FOR CLOSELY HELD BUSINESS ENTITIES

Francisco Reyes*

The wave of corporate governance reforms that has permeated most major systems of Latin America has not significantly impacted the legislation applicable to closely held companies. This appears to be a misdirected approach since the region's economic reality is characterized by family control and concentrated ownership. Even listed corporations are generally subject to a block-holding structure. Policymakers have not given enough weight to these factors when determining the current legislative agenda in Corporate Law. Surprisingly most legal reforms in this field have targeted agency problems more commonly arising in the context of dispersed equity ownership models. Corporate governance reforms such as mandatory independent directors, auditing committees and certification of financial statements have become common place in the securities regulations across the region. Albeit important in improving the legal framework of listed companies, most of these legal reforms disregard the basic underlying agency problem between controlling shareholders and their minority counterparts. Regulatory provisions for non-listed firms impose severe restrictions on private ordering and prevent parties from contracting around cumbersome imperative norms. These suboptimal approaches are justified on the grounds of public policy and defended at any cost by local legal operators. In several cases path dependence in Company Law represents an unsurpassable obstacle for the adoption of modern rules suitable for market economies. Company Law in most of Latin American jurisdictions continues to follow the taxonomy of business associations inherited from the nineteenth century's French codification movement. Such business forms generally lack the necessary flexibility to cope with new economic realities due to obsolescence and rigidity. New hybrid business forms appear to be an appealing solution to deal with closely held firms in the region. However, attempts to undertake legal reform in this field must follow a structural transplant approach; namely, it cannot be restricted to the simple adoption of substantive law provisions.

This chapter is intended to provide an analytical framework for the adoption of a hybrid business form as a model law for closely held firms in Latin America. It is suggested that the advantages of flexibility and freedom of contract make such business form especially

* Professor and Director of Graduate Program in Corporation Law, Universidad Javeriana in Colombia. Has been a Visiting professor at Louisiana State University, Stetson College of Law, Agostinho Neto de Angola and Universidad Católica Argentina.

suitable for family-owned firms, start-ups, professional undertakings, and all sorts of small- and medium-sized firms within this region. The introduction in December 2008 of the Colombian Simplified Stock Company (*Sociedad por Acciones Simplificada* or SAS) is an example of a successful efficiency-minded law-making effort in a Civil Law jurisdiction. The SAS is aimed at providing its users with flexibility in organization and capitalization, complete freedom of contract and full-fledged limited liability. The Colombian example proves that even in the absence of competition for corporate charters it is possible to undertake structural transplants of company law with extraordinary results. The enthusiasm with which entrepreneurs have greeted the new legal development is reflected in the high number of SAS formations occurred after its inception. Within the first six months after the statute was passed, more than 5,000 simplified stock companies were created, outnumbering every other form of company.

Section 1 addresses the basic types of business associations that exist in the major jurisdictions in the area; Section 2 analyses some of the basic problems ensuing from the current regulation for closely held firms as it appears in codes and statutes across the region; Section 3 assesses the advantages of a simplified stock corporation and the Annex contains a model act on simplified stock corporations for Latin America.

1. Business associations in Latin America

In December of 2008, the Congress of the Republic of Colombia enacted a new law creating a new form of hybrid-business entity referred to as the Simplified Stock Corporation (*SAS*).[1] Following an Anglo-American approach to corporate law, this act reduced all formalities for incorporation to a simple registration before a public registry. It also ameliorated expenses associated with the formation and operation of boards of directors, fiscal auditors, multiple managers and other formalistic requirements. The Act made it plain that shareholders would be shielded from any liability concerning any obligations arising from the business activities of the corporation. Furthermore, it reduced old-fashioned prohibitions regarding the activity of shareholders and managers and, above all, introduced a straightforward and effective principle of freedom of contract. Following a *structural transplant* approach, the new law introduced an innovative enforcement environment in which arbitration and administrative adjudication superseded and inefficient judiciary of that country. Only six months after the enactment of this law, more than 5,000 simplified stock corporations had been created. All kinds of business enterprises, irrespective of their size or activities, took quick advantage of the multiple innovations offered by the SAS. Corporate groups rushed to convert their previous subsidiaries into the new flexible business form. More significantly, all the types of business associations that existed before the enactment of this law rapidly fell behind, and in only four months the SAS was the number one business entity, as measured by the amount of new incorporations. The revered and highly valued limited liability companies (*sociedad de responsabilidad limitada*) and stock corporations (*sociedad anónima*) were rapidly defeated in this race for new incorporations. This rather unusual experiment may evidence that the anachronistic *status quo* of company law in Latin America can be successfully challenged.

---

[1] Law 1258 of 2008.

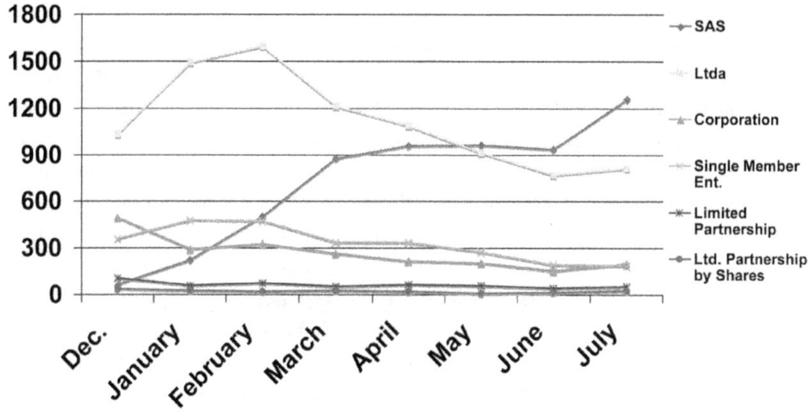

Table 1. Incorporation of new Simplified Stock Corporations (SAS)

Notwithstanding characteristic skepticism, backward approaches by legal elites and path dependence, efficiency-minded legislators could easily enact statutes such as the one mentioned above on other major Latin American jurisdictions. Latin American countries could certainly benefit from a more progressive and investor-friendly corporate form. The following description of existing business forms in the region will provide a clear evidence of the urgent need to update the legal framework for company law in Latin America.

The company law systems of Latin America share a rather homogenous taxonomy of business associations. The point of departure for these systems can be found in the 19th century codifications in which the basic types of companies were included. With the exception of the closely held corporation (*sociedad de responsabilidad limitada*), the basic business forms already existed in those codes.[2] Accordingly, most countries in the region have regulated four basic types of business associations: (1) Stock corporations (*sociedades anónimas*); (2) Partnerships (*sociedades colectivas*); (3) Limited partnerships (*sociedades en comandita*), and (4) Closely held corporations (*sociedades de responsabilidad limitada*).[3]

The traditional classification is closely linked with a distinction between business entities the nature of which is mostly related to the identity of the associates (*intuitus personae*) and the importance of capital contributions that are given by the parties (*intuitus pecuniae*). Both legal approaches fall under the ancient notion of *societas* that encompasses all the different forms of business entities. This taxonomy is somewhat advantageous, as it allows for the existence of general legal principles applicable to all the different forms of business associations. Within these general principles (*general part*) there are common rules for several different aspects such as company formation, causes for nullification, legal capacity of shareholders and partners, capital contributions, profit allocation, amendments to the company's by-laws, structural changes, mergers, split-ups, dissolution, and liquidation.[4]

---

[2] The 'srl' was introduced in Brazil after the Portuguese '*sociedade por quotas*' of 1905. The same type of business entity was brought to other Latin American countries after the enactment of the Spanish statute of 1927.

[3] For a detailed analysis of the main traits of Latin American business forms, see J. W. Fernández, et al., 'Corporate Caveat Emptor: minority shareholder rights in Mexico, Chile, Brazil, Venezuela and Argentina', 32 *University of Miami Inter-American Law Review* (2001) p. 157.

[4] See, for instance, Law 19.550 for Argentina, the Colombian Commercial Code, the company law of Ecuador, and the general law of Commercial Companies of Mexico.

The typification of each business entity requires that there exists a *special part* within these company law statutes, dealing with the specificities concerning each one of the business forms provided therein. The two extremes of the continuum are the partnership (*sociedad colectiva*) that is characterized by the highest relevance given to the *intuitus personae* element. On the other side of the continuum there is the stock corporation (*sociedad anónima*) that is usually depicted as the quintessential capitalist business entity. There is a middle ground between those two extremes in which the rules for composite business entities are laid out. In this type of companies elements of a personal nature are mingled with capitalist ingredients to create a syncretism usually devised for small- or medium-sized entities. These mixed entities include the limited liability company (*sociedad de responsabilidad limitada*) and the limited partnerships (*sociedad en comandita*). Within this last form there are in turn two separate species: the limited partnerships by quotas and the limited partnership by stocks. The obvious difference between these two forms lies with their differing capital structure. As a consequence, the former is assimilated partially to the *limitada*, whereas the latter partly resembles the *anónima*.

1.1 Partnerships (*Sociedad colectiva*)

A *sociedad colectiva* is very similar to a partnership and can even be defined in a similar way as a contract between two or more persons that make contributions in cash, in labor or in-kind with the purpose of carrying on a business for profit. The partners are jointly and severally liable for all debts and obligations in which the partnership may incur. As different to Common Law systems, partnerships in Latin America are generally subject to the same formalities that are required in order for any other company to operate regularly. Therefore, it is usual for the law to require that a public deed be granted as well as a registration for public record before a mercantile registry. In the absence of such formalities, the partnership will not form a legal entity separate and distinct from its partners (i.e., it will lack legal personality).

There is an emphasis of a personal trait (*intuitus personae*) that permeates the partnership's structure, inner workings, operation and even its dissolution. The partners enjoy a high degree of contractual flexibility. Consequently, it is generally possible to provide for very restrictive constraints to the partners, including, for instance, the inability to compete with the business activities of the partnership as laid out in the purpose clause or the possibility to expel partners if certain obligations set up in the constitutional documents are not met. Control over the businesses and assets of the partnership is exercised directly by the partners, who are entitled to represent the business entity *vis-à-vis* third parties unless such representation is delegated in a centralized administrative body or manager.

Even if this contractual flexibility appears to be highly convenient – since it allows the partners to provide sophisticated internal governance mechanisms – such advantage is offset by the unlimited liability regime to which the partners are exposed.

As a result, the number of *colectivas* that are formally created tends to be extremely low. As an alternative to the regular partnership (i.e., formally created), the parties who purport to carry out a certain business can generally opt to create the so-called *sociedad de hecho* (literally a *de facto* partnership) in which no formalities whatsoever are required. Consequently, the mere consent – even tacitly granted – of the partners suffices for the legal existence of the *de facto* partnership. The only difference in terms of liability between a *de facto* partnership and a regular partnership is normally related to the secondary nature of the liability of the latter as compared to the direct and personal exposure of the former.

1.2 Stock corporation (*Sociedad anónima*)

On the other end of the spectrum, the *sociedad anónima* (stock corporation) epithomizes the prevalence of the *intuitus pecuniae* namely the higher weight that is given to capital contributions over the identity of the individuals forming the business entity. This feature normally identifies the *sociedad anónima* with large dimension undertakings. *Anónimas* are the appropriate vehicle for an enterprise to go public. In fact, securities regulation and stock exchange rules generally restrict IPOs to companies formed as *anónimas*. Nevertheless the *anónima* is also very popular among small- and medium-sized enterprises.

The bureaucratic structure that is usually required in order to set up an *anónima* is much more complicated than the one necessary to run any other business association. In fact, pursuant to corporate statutes in the region it is normally needed, in addition to the shareholders' assembly, to appoint a board of directors, managers (legal representatives), mandatory auditors, regardless of whether the company is listed or not. Even if this cumbersome structure is clearly excessive for small enterprises, many businesspeople are forced to use it in small and medium undertakings only to achieve the benefits of full limited liability. As a result of this choice, entrepreneurs could be subject to high transaction costs when using this form.

In most jurisdictions the *anónimas'* capital is divided into shares of stock that are freely negotiable unless a right of first refusal is set forth in the corporation's by-laws. Normally, the business of the corporation is carried out under a board of directors that in turn appoints officers and managers who undertake its day-to-day operations. Such centralized management is usually characterized by an election system with proportional representation such as cumulative voting, so as to allow minority shareholders to directly participate in management. Liability is restricted to each shareholder's capital contribution and, thus, there is affirmative and defensive asset partitioning. In some Latin American jurisdictions piercing the corporate veil doctrines have been incorporated in statutory provisions. Nonetheless its actual enforceability is very limited, showing a great disparity between law-in-the-books and law-in-action.

1.3 Limited liability company (*Sociedad de responsabilidad limitada*)

A highly popular form of business association is the *sociedad de responsabilidad limitada* (limited liability company), which exists in all Latin American jurisdictions and closely resembles the original model of the German *GmbH* of 1892 and the *société a responsabilité limité* introduced in France in 1927. The original 19th century European LLC model is an attempt to reconcile the basic feature of limited liability provided for stock corporations and the broader level of flexibility allotted to partnerships.[5] In that sense, it was originally a *hybrid* business form that was transplanted into Latin American legislations under a similar conception.

[5] P. Ulmer, *Principios fundamentales del Derecho alemán de sociedades de responsabilidad limitada* (Madrid, Editorial Civitas 1998) pp. 22-23.

A caveat must be made concerning the significant difference that exists between the United States LLC and the Latin American *limitada*. To be sure, even if the first LLC statute enacted in the state of Wyoming is said to have been crafted along the lines of the Panamanian *limitada*,[6] present American LLC's are very distant from their originating model.[7]

While a process of modernization has taken place in the United States over the past three decades, the Latin American *limitadas* are still linked to their early 20th century European model. For this reason, this type of entity is characterized by all kinds of formalistic proceedings that make it a highly rigid business form. As an example, it is interesting to highlight, *inter alia*, the cumbersome proceedings for the processes for incorporation, conveyance of quota shares, by-law amendments, capital contributions, and right of first refusal.

1.4 Limited partnership (*Sociedad en comandita*)

The *sociedad en comandita* (limited partnership) is one of the oldest forms of business association dating back to medieval times, when the famous *commenda* was created as a contract between a person who made a contribution in labor (*tractator*) and another who would make contributions in money or in-kind (*commendator*). The latter is usually referred to as a dormant partner, for he was not entitled to participate in the proposed business. The *commendator* was shielded from liability *vis-à-vis* third parties concerning any unsatisfied that could arise from the venture. The *tractator* carried on the business and representative activities and, as a result, was personally liable for all debts and obligations incurred in the course of the undertaking. This structure was disseminated through all European countries and served as the basis for the modern *sociedad en comandita* as it exists in European and Latin American jurisdictions.[8]

The *sociedad comanditaria* is characterized by the presence of a general partner (*socio gestor*) who conducts the affairs of the company and is subject to unlimited liability for all obligations arising in connection with the undertaking. General partners are governed under the laws applicable to *sociedades colectivas* (general partnerships). Limited partners provide capital contributions and are precluded from engaging themselves in managing the company. As a result of such management system, limited partners, as a general rule, do not

---

6 See J.A. McCahery, E. Vermeulen, et al., *The New Company Law: What Happens in an Innovative Economy*, SSRN Id. No. 942993.

7 The tax-driven legislative process carried out in the US for the inception of the LLC was aimed at obtaining a pass-through treatment to overcome double taxation for a vehicle endowed with limited liability. Therefore, the new business entity had to meet the four-prong test set up by the Internal Revenue Service in order not to be treated as a corporation. Consequently, while the original model granted limited liability it lacked continuity of existence, centralized management and free transferability of shares. Opting these three elements out of the IRS' four-item test for corporations, required to use a rather anachronistic approach in which shareholders had the direct administration of the LLC's day-to-day affairs, a term of fixed duration was mandatory in the organizational documents and a right of refusal was also included as an imperative stipulation. The newer US statutes on LLCs are of a facilitating nature and therefore the Wyoming model has been upgraded through enabling provisions in a manner in which regulatory rules are exceptional. Robert R. Keatinge, 'The Limited Liability Company, A Study of the Emerging Entity', 47 *The Business Lawyer* (1992) p. 378.

8 According to Folsom and Levasseur, the US regulation concerning Limited Partnerships can be traced back to the Civil Law *sociedad en comandita*. 'This business form was first introduced in the United States via a 1822 statute enacted in the state of New York' (R.H. Folsom and A.A. Levasseur, *Pratique du droit des affaires aux États-Unis* (Paris, Ed. Dalloz 1995) p. 250.

incur liability for the company's debts beyond the amounts that they have infused into the venture. Profits are allocated between the general and limited partners in the proportions laid out in the organizational documents or by-laws. It is usually possible for a limited liability company or a stock corporation to be a general partner within a limited partnership. In this manner, the effect of unlimited liability is offset due to the usual undercapitalization of the vehicle appointed as a general partner.

This business association is divided into two separate sub-species that depend on the manner in which the company's capital is divided. In accordance with this classification, there is a first type in which the capital is divided into quotas. This entity is referred to as simple limited partnership (*sociedad en comandita simple*). In the second type the capital is divided into shares of stock; the resulting company is called limited partnership by stock (*sociedad en comandita por acciones*). This entity is more suitable for larger enterprises since it allows for a more expeditious capitalization. Both sub-types of limited partnerships are particularly suitable for family businesses due to the ability to separate the roles of founding partners – who have the direct administration of the company's business – from those pertaining to limited partners – who are excluded from management.

It follows from the previous analysis of existing business associations in Latin America that the legislative approach is rather restrictive. This is partly due to the fact that the legal framework was conceived along the lines of company law theories developed in 19th century European codifications and their progeny. Reluctance by traditional legal scholars and legislators in the region to switch to a more advanced conception of company law has prevented the inception of more flexible rules and regulations for company law.

2. Basic problems in current legislative approaches

2.1 Codification of company law

All Latin American countries belong to the Civil Law tradition. Its most salient features are evident: prevalence of legislative law-making processes over judge-made law, deductive methods of reasoning on the judicial adjudication process and codification. Civil and Commercial Codes define the backbone of private law across the region. Given the influence of European scholarship since colonial times, there is a continued reliance on the evolution of French and Spanish legislations.[9] Such dependence is still significant today in the field of company law.[10]

Although there are advantages to codification, such as the systematic organization of

[9] For an explanation regarding the codification movement in 19th century Latin America see B. Kozolchyk, *La contratación comercial en el derecho comparado* (Madrid, Editorial Dykenson S.L. 2006), at pp. 130-133. This author describes the so-called Latin American codification family, which encompasses three master codes drafted by great jurists: D. Vélez-Sársfield (1800-1875) for Argentina, Andrés Bello (1781-1865) for Chile, and Augusto Teixeira de Freitas (1816-1883) for Brazil.

[10] Regarding codification in Latin America see, generally, J.H. Merryman, et al., *Comparative Law: Western European and Latin American Legal Systems, Cases and Materials* (Charlottesville, The Michie Company 1978), at pp. 208-220. Schlesinger points out to the so-called exogenous influence, which is particularly noticeable in instances in which legislators have resorted to the *wholesale importation* of foreign law. 'Most of the codes presently in force in Latin America are the result of extensive comparative study and eclectic choice among European models' (R. Schlesinger, et al., *Comparative Law, Cases-Texts-Materials,* 6th edn. (New York, The Foundation Press 1998) at p. 11). Schlesinger also adds that this process involves the danger – evident in Latin America – that foreign institutions may be copied without sufficient adaptation to local conditions (id.).

legal provisions, it is obvious that codes also create a rigid framework that is difficult to update due to the implications regarding multiple rules directly or indirectly related to those to be amended. In practice, the fear of desynchronizing the code structure usually results in delays concerning any legislative reform. The idea that any code reform affects legal certainty is always a good one to prevent the modernization of private law in Latin America. The so-called *numerus clausus* approach inherited from Roman Civil Law also contributes to the stiffness of legal institutions. To be sure, such rigid classifications are based upon elements deemed to be essential to each contract. Legislative innovation and change are hindered by this Aristotelic approach in which all too often a *substance* represents an unsurpassable theoretical obstacle to the modernization of business law rules.

Breaking company law dependence on Civil and Commercial Codes should be of paramount importance in order to set up a flexible environment for legal reform in the region. One avenue for change consists of creating separate statutes dealing with each business law subject matter individually. The usefulness of such an approach is evidenced by a higher level of flexibility to amend statutory provisions without affecting provisions regarding other legal matters. There basically are two ways of severing the company law from the Civil and Commercial Codes. The first approach recommends the creation of a statute containing *general company law* in which both general principles and specific provisions for each type of entity coexist. A separate and independent statute for each form of business entity is another legislative possibility.

2.2 Regulatory nature of company law provisions

A considerable deterrent to business activities is related to the regulatory nature of a substantial part of company law provisions. The 'public policy' and 'public order' character of such regulations is usually argued to be one of the main reasons to maintain the legislative *status quo* in Latin American codes and statutes. The highly protective nature of these provisions is intended to protect investors mostly in the field of publicly held corporations. However, since most of the business entities in the region operate outside the stream of the securities market, the applicable company law rules become unnecessarily restrictive and cumbersome.

Paradoxically, Civil and Commercial Codes across the region embrace the principles of 19th century liberalism, including freedom of contract. Lip service is paid to the latter principle to the extent that almost every company law treatise includes explicit reference regarding its supposed application.

Some company law statutes contain specific provisions regarding the freedom of contractual stipulation, although limited by the typology of business association forms. For instance, Article 110-14 of the Colombian Commercial Code relating the public deed of association determine the basic contents of such instrument, including 'all other arrangements which might be set forth by the associates to regulate the relations arising from the contract, provided that they are compatible with each type of association.'

Notwithstanding the apparent flexibility of the quoted provision, it is obvious that the 'compatibility' issue results in a significant deterrent to private ordering. The existence of public policy provisions is always a good argument to prevent parties from opting out of an imperative statutory rule. This legal rigidity also impacts the way in which by-laws and other constitutional documents are drafted. In fact, standardization – characterized by the propagation of boiler-plate corporate forms – hinders innovation and deters transaction cost-effective legal engineering.

In contrast, corporate law systems such as the ones prevailing in other jurisdictions including the United States provide a set of enabling non-regulatory corporate statutes. Parties, therefore, are entitled to bargain for the most appropriate contractual framework to deal with the problems arising from a specific business arrangement. Accordingly, these statutes provide off-the-rack housekeeping rules that can be opted out by the parties. In the absence of negotiation, the legal provisions contained in the corporate statute are applicable by default.[11] Certainly, such flexible system requires the parties to ideally negotiate a comprehensive contractual framework by addressing *ex ante* all relevant matters from which a conflict may arise.[12]

2.3 The dichotomy of corporation law in Latin America

The anachronistic dichotomy of Private Law is an all-pervasive phenomenon in Latin America. In fact, most codes and corporation statutes in the region have maintained a differentiation between civil and commercial companies. Following the French 19th century model, separate substantive rules apply according to the nature of the business company. In order to determine such nature it is usually necessary to undertake an analysis of the purpose clause as laid out in the company's by-laws. Through the application of this *objective* approach the concerned entity can be labeled commercial or civil. Accordingly, a commercial company will be such entity that has been set up for the purpose of undertaking *commercial acts* pursuant to the list contained in the relevant statutory provision.[13] Conversely, a civil company will be the one created to carry out acts not contained in such list of commercial acts. The legal consequences ensuing from the private law dichotomy are not irrelevant. They range from mere substantive law provisions to procedural aspects as well as tax treatments and other matters. Even formation proceedings may differ to the extent that commercial firms are generally subject to higher standards as compared with civil companies. Such differences are not exclusively related to formation requirements, but also include aspects such as tax rates, disclosure of information and other matters.

This two-fold regulatory scheme creates significant transaction costs and legal uncertainty. In several cases it is not easy to determine the nature of a business entity. Complex or multiple purpose clauses are difficult to read in light of the dichotomy. The analysis is not prone to error and usually submitted to difficult analytical assessment and subjective interpretation.

Even in continental European countries where the dichotomy subsists a solution has been crafted for business associations. It basically consists in creating a *typical* criterion to

---

[11] Statutory provisions are said to reflect a *hypothetical bargaining* in which all the constituencies' interests are considered by the legislator. Therefore, the legislator's role is to provide an optimal set of rules, which should reflect a balance between the parties' expectations.

[12] These careful and sometime costly negotiations may not always be feasible for the incumbent parties. It is true that this kind of statutes require the parties to carefully negotiate the terms and conditions of their specific arrangements. The flexibility provided to contracting parties may cause an increase of negotiation expenses to opt out default rules. Pursuant to Bainbridge, lack of appropriate negotiation may result in future conflicts between shareholders (Cf., S. Bainbridge, *Corporation Law and Economics* (New York, Foundation Press 2002) p. 9).

[13] Commercial Codes list all acts and enterprises that are considered as mercantile. Within those acts, there are basic intermediation transactions, leasing activities, engineering, banking, insurance, etc. The same Codes regulate non-commercial (i.e., civil) acts, including the exercise of professional activities, agricultural business carried out by an individual, etc.

define the firm's nature. Such criterion is more readily defined in terms of the *type* of business association at stake. Instead of defining the civil or commercial nature of a business association depending on the scope of their purpose clause or activity, the assessment is made on the grounds of the form adopted by the business entity. Normally stock companies, closely held corporations and limited partnerships are deemed to be commercial entities irrespective of the activities set forth in their purpose clauses. Therefore, the civil company arises as an isolated business entity of a limited usefulness. This is the approach adopted for instance by the French and Spanish legislations.

Another approach – which appears to be highly recommendable – would consist of the eventual suppression of the civil company in favor of a fully unified system of company law characterized by a unique substantive and procedural regulation such as the one that exists in the corporate statutes of the United States.

2.4 The contractual nature of company law in Latin America

The Roman law concept of *societas*, which was later developed into different forms of business entities, was strongly grounded upon a contractual scheme. The French Commercial Codes maintained the idea whereby all forms of business associations arise out of an agreement between two or more persons.[14] The adoption of Commercial Codes and company law statutes in Latin America, allowed for the inception of a full fledged contractual theory all over the region.[15] Such an all-pervasive concept is relevant to define requirements for the creation and maintenance of new companies in the area. The idea of a multi-owner entity as the basis for legal personality and limited liability represents a deterrent to admit single member corporations and wholly owned subsidiaries.

Therefore, most countries in this region have rejected legislation suppressing multi-ownership requirements. In some cases the statutes are so stringent that two shareholders do not suffice for the purpose of incorporation. Obviously this restrictive approach creates severe transaction costs, for it forces entrepreneurs either to undergo joint ventures or to create simulated and often illegal contracts in which strawmen act as shareholders for the sole purpose of fulfilling a formalistic requirement.

A sound solution adopted in continental Europe after the issuance of the Twelfth Communitary Directive (regarding single member entities) was to allow companies to be formed through contracts or 'unilateral acts'. The implementation of this directive in the European Union allowed for the presence of one-person stock corporations.

2.5 Reluctance to provide full enforcement to shareholders' agreements

There has been a traditional reluctance in the Latin American company laws to recognize and enforce shareholders' agreements. This lack of recognition disregards the importance

---

[14] An advantage of the contractual approach is that all regulations regarding obligations and contracts contained in Civil and Commercial Codes will be automatically applicable. Case law and doctrine regarding these rules and principles will also be invoked.

[15] Art. 98 of the Colombian Commercial Code: 'By means of the Company Contract two or more persons undertake to make a contribution in cash, work or in other goods representing currency, for the purpose of sharing in the profits derived from their enterprise. On legal formation of a company, it will turn into a juridical person distinct from each individual shareholder.'

of private ordering which is central to foster innovation and creativity. The Brazilian corporate law is certainly an important exception to this rule. Certainly, after the enactment of Law 10.303 of 2001, various legal devices were created to allow for the enforceability of this kind of agreements. The general disregard of such important contractual devices hinders the development of more flexible and useful schemes for firms characterized by a multi-ownership structure.

2.6 Exceptions to limited liability

The influence of new political constitutions and Constitutional Courts in Latin American countries has created several piercing the veil hypotheses grounded on causes outside the scope of corporate law. Further tax, labor and environmental regulations set up numerous causes of action that allow a plaintiff to request that the legal entity be disregarded. Aside from the cases of general and limited partnerships, in which there has been a traditional liability extension in the event of bankruptcy, there is no justification for such a broad extension of liability.[16] Such written rules and judicial precedents discourage local and foreign investment leading to simulation or otherwise wrongful configuration of the corporate contract. Parent companies are exposed to excessive risks in which piercing the veil becomes tantamount to strict liability.[17] Defending weak creditors through expeditious writs – in which the true merits of each case are not carefully assessed by constitutional courts – affects certainty and reliance on the legal systems.

Piercing the veil has been justifiably criticized in common law systems due to legal uncertainty concerns. However, such judicial solution has enjoyed support in the United States for it is decided on a case-by-case basis under an inductive method in which facts are carefully scrutinized by each court.

2.7 Excessive legal formalities for incorporation

Legal formalities for incorporation constitute one of the most significant entry barriers for entrepreneurs in Latin America. Forming a regular business entity may cost hundreds of dollars and require the fulfillment of time-consuming and cumbersome steps. Some of these proceedings are reminiscent of ancient institutions, many of which are kept mainly due to pressure groups that can hinder legal reform. The necessary participation of a notary public in the process of incorporation is a good example of such widespread formalism. Notaries are well-paid bureaucratic officers whose income is mainly associated with the so-called 'public faith' that is given to contracts and other instruments once their authorized stamp and signature have been apposed onto a document. Aside from notaries, other professionals such as attorneys and certified accountants may also have a part in the process of incorporation, not to mention the requirement to obtain certain governmental authorizations as well as to publish excerpts of the articles of incorporation in official gazettes.

---

[16] Even in these forms of business associations it is viable to provide for a limitation on the liability of general partners. New forms of entities have arisen such as the Limited Liability Partnership (LLP) and Limited Liability Limited Partnership (LLLP). These business associations combine the advantages of partnerships and limited partnerships with the benefits of business corporations, i.e., they add to a person-based business entity, the useful feature of limited liability.

[17] See for instance Decision SU-1023 of 2001 rendered by the Colombian Constitutional Court holding a parent company liable on the grounds of the simple fact of being the parent.

Paradoxically, this formalistic approach represents a significant obstacle for the formalization of business enterprises. There is empirical evidence that the most flexible legal systems are more suitable to attract investment and, correspondingly, to obtain higher income arising from registration of new companies. It is a fact that the citizens of Delaware are subject to a lower income tax due to the amounts that are contributed by corporations in the form of franchise taxes. In fact the so-called franchise tax represents almost a fifth of the overall revenue gathered by the State of Delaware. Of course there are several factors that characterize the institutional framework that is needed to administer such an important body of law. It is not only the substantive regulation that makes Delaware so attractive for corporations, the judiciary and even the specialization of the state's bar also play a significant role.[18]

Conversely, those systems that make it difficult for business people to create corporations tend to fall behind. In the recent competition for corporate chartering taking place in Europe, burdensome legal provisions, such as minimum capitalization requirements, two-tiered corporate governance structures, the participation of notaries as well as other bureaucratic authorizations have created a new market in which some businesspeople will prefer to incorporate in the United Kingdom, where the processes seem to be simpler. After *Centros*,[19] several businesses have fled to London, taking advantage of the great flexibility offered by British company law. Migration of business and capital propelled by the new market has created a unique economic incentive for company law reform in Europe. In fact, some of the company laws of France have been overhauled apparently reflecting new trends in the regulation of business associations.

It is to no avail to maintain a formalistic approach in which useless and burdensome formalities are still needed to set up a business entity. To be sure, public deeds granted before public notaries, registration before a mercantile registry, authorization granted by a governmental office, publication in an official gazette could be reduced to a single act of registration before a company's office or a similar agency.

2.8 The limited role of the mercantile registry

The so-called *commercial publicity* is an important factor in the configuration of company law in civil law jurisdictions. Pursuant to a general rule, any act or contract that is duly registered before a mercantile registry will be deemed to have legal effects. This concept is relevant in company law, for it provides legal certainty for third parties, who can rely upon the information certified by the mercantile registrar. Due to purely theoretical reasons, it has been held that the only function performed by the registry is to provide publicity. Thus, the possibility of allowing registration to become a determinant factor for the legal formation of companies has been generally denied by most systems in Latin America. A more practical approach is offered by the corporate laws of the different American states in which the existence of the corporation is conclusively presumed upon the filing of the articles of incorporation before the relevant governmental office (i.e., the Secretariat of State) (See, Revised Model Business Corporation Act).

---

[18] A. Palmiter and F. Reyes, *Arbitraje Comercial y Otros Mecanismos de Resolución de Conflictos Societarios en Estados Unidos,* (Bogotá, Cámara de Comercio, 2001) pp. 77-87.

[19] Case C-212/97, *Centros Ltd.* v. *Erthvers-og Selbskabssyrelsen*, 1999 *ECR* I-1459 (1999).

On the other hand, the registrar is usually deprived of the ability to scrutinize the legal foundations of any act or contract that is subject to registration. As a result, a company that has been duly registered is still subject to challenges that may arise from several different factors. Virtually any person that proves a legitimate interest has standing to sue and request that the corporation contract be set aside on the grounds of non-compliance with certain formalities.

Alternatively, it would be useful to introduce in the different jurisdictions of Latin America the so-called *constitutional* mercantile registry. Under this system, registration provides legal certainty regarding the existence of the corporation as well as all validity of business transactions been carried out by its officers and directors after such registration has taken place. This principle can be expressed in simple terms such as a straightforward provision whereby the company's legal personality arises after the formation documents have been filed before the relevant office. Furthermore, such system of registration ameliorates the problems associated with so-called *de facto* corporations. Certainly, where the law only requires a single act for the creation of a company the difficulties arising out of pre-incorporation transactions tend to be significantly reduced. The unpredictability and uncertainty concerning the validity of acts undertaken by a company in formation disappears under such *constitutional* registration system. At the same time, the liabilities of directors, officers, and shareholders are clearly defined as of the moment in which the formation documents are filed before the mercantile registry. Obviously, this recommendation is closely linked with the suppression of any notarial intervention in the formation process. A simple private document, duly executed by the relevant parties should suffice for the purposes of registration.

2.9 Overreaching causes for nullification

Several causes for the nullification of the corporate contract can be found within commercial codes and corporate statutes. These regulations allow any party to challenge the existence of the corporation. Through the so-called absolute and relative nullification regime, company law provisions contribute to create legal uncertainty and instability of existing business entities. These regulations are inconsistent with modern trends in which the causes for nullification are reduced to a minimum. The first European Community directive regarding disclosure, *ultra vires* and nullity adopts a restrictive approach in this respect. Pursuant to this directive nullity can only be decided through a judicial proceeding. Therefore, a court can declare that a company is void provided that the restrictive grounds specified in Section 2 are fully proven. Such grounds include, *inter alia*, that no instrument of formation was executed, that certain required legal formalities were not fulfilled, or that specific requirements provided for under the national legislation were not complied with. The European directive is intended to provide legal certainty and protection to third parties dealing with the company. By restricting the grounds upon which a person can challenge the act of incorporation, the validity of the legal entity is enhanced and the chances for opportunistic challenges are severely reduced.

2.10 Regulatory nature of most company law rules

Company law statutes and codes are mostly of a regulatory nature. Provisions concerning all aspects of corporate governance, minority shareholders rights, structural changes, mergers, dissolution and liquidation are overwhelming. Regulations concerning the basic contents of the articles of association or by-laws tend to be comprehensive and imperative. To be sure, company law statutes contain lists of clauses that have to be included within the by-laws of any company that is created. Failure to provide any of those required clauses may result in the nullification of the entire contract. In contrast with modern corporate law in which most provisions are not regulatory, the approach in this region is increasingly complex and stringent. The approach existing in all American jurisdictions characterized by enabling statutes has not been followed in Latin America. Notwithstanding the well-known and highly publicized principle of freedom of contract imbedded in 19th century codifications, the flexibility afforded to shareholders at the moment of drafting or amending the company's constitutional documents is insignificant.

Such cumbersome regulation hinders the economic activity, creates transaction costs, and prevents the parties from reaching adequate agreements concerning the basic elements of the business association. As it has been said before, these restrictions are particularly detrimental as they regard the closely held corporation. Most of these imperative legal provisions appear to be designed to deal with the problems arising in the context of publicly held entities. They are needed to protect a myriad of anonymous and dispersed shareholders and to resolve problems associated with collective action. These situations obviously demand a comprehensive legal framework. The extant regulation of shareholders' meetings as well as rules on quorum, election of board members, structural changes, appraisal remedies, forceful dissolution, etc., are appropriate to protect investors undertaking securities transactions in stock exchanges.

However, the closely held corporation constitutes an altogether different scenario. The specific problems that are germane to this form of private association require flexibility in order for the concerned parties to be able to lay down appropriate rules to govern their business relationships. Private ordering is an essential element without which the company law system cannot respond effectively to the challenges arising from the different interests that shareholders may have.

Therefore, reduction of unnecessary mandatory provisions constitutes a natural step in the modernization of Latin American company law. Specifically, the reduction in the number of imperative clauses that have to be included within the constitutional document could provide enable the parties to freely define the framework within which the company will operate. At the same time, such flexibility will foster the drafting of shareholders agreements, which – at least for the time being – are usually unenforceable *vis-à-vis* the corporation.

2.11 The negative impact of the *ultra vires* theory

The so-called *specialty theory* whereby the company's legal capacity depends upon the business activities provided for under the purpose clause in the corporation's by-laws is an anachronistic reminiscence of the concepts that were in vogue in the beginning of the 20th century. The purported advantages that arise from this theory in terms of protection to the shareholders are overshadowed by its detrimental impact on third parties. The latter are clearly affected due to the uncertainty concerning the validity of business transactions carried out by the corporation. Under the general approach existing in Latin America, it is obvious that the corporation can easily find a way out from inconvenient contracts through the simple expedient of showing that the relevant act is *ultra vires*.

This theory has been abolished in most advanced legal systems. The movement began in the United States, where old state legislation used to embrace the theory. The difficulties arising from its application caused the state legislators to repeal it altogether from all corporate statutes. Also, the requirement to include a fully defined purpose clause in the articles of incorporation by describing the business activities to be carried out by the business entity was also repealed. Such an important legislative step weakened the *ultra vires* theory by enhancing the legal capacity of the corporation and its ability to carry out any lawful legal transaction.

From the moment in which the First Communitary Directive was enacted, a similar approach was undertaken for European company law. Even if the directive departs from the fact that the corporation's legal capacity is defined by the purpose clause as it has been laid out in the articles of Association, it is also said held that third parties shall be protected concerning the validity of any *ultra vires* business transaction to which they were a party, provided that they did not know that the corporation lacked sufficient capacity to undertake such transaction. Pursuant to the same directive, bad faith will not be presumed on the grounds that the relevant party had access to a certificate rendered by the relevant company's registrar, in which the purpose clause may appear.

2.12 Rigid regulations regarding capital contributions

An excessive reverence is given to the concept of legal capital and par value. There is almost an obsession with the so-called integrity and maintenance of legal capital. Some regulations even provide that a corporation shall be dissolved whenever losses affect its capital (i.e., whenever, as a result of losses, the corporation's equity falls below the amount of subscribed paid in capital). Under a related provision contributions cannot be made for any amount below the par value set up at the inception of the corporation contract. This rule clearly contradicts the economic reality where the corporation's equity value has been reduced as a result of losses. The only exception to this drastic rule requires an amendment of the articles of association to reduce the shares' par value.

Likewise, various legal provisions concerning the terms and conditions for the payment of capital contributions tend to reduce the corporation's ability to attract capital, particularly when it is undergoing financial stress. In-kind contributions are in many cases subject to several different formalities, including requirements such as independent appraisal, governmental authorization, and even imposing unlimited liability for those who make the contribution. These obstacles for capitalization are notoriously inconvenient for companies seeking to expand operations or to carry out financial reorganization. Furthermore, these cumbersome regulations are a source of transaction costs and protracted litigation.

Some of these provisions contradict contemporary financial theories in which it is usually more important for a company to have substantial cash flows to pay all debts as they become due, rather than to show a fixed amount of subscribed paid in capital in the balance sheet.

2.13 Lack of an effective judicial control on business associations

Some of the most relevant authors in the field of legal transplant in corporate law (e.g., Katarina Pistor), have stressed the importance of the so-called structural transplants. This concept refers specifically to the adoption of substantive legal rules which are suitable to be applied and enforced by the judicial and administrative authorities of the country to which the legal principle is being transplanted. Thus, it is generally acknowledged that it does not suffice to introduce appropriate substantive rules, but it is also necessary to emulate the institutional framework for the enforcement of such legal provisions that exist in the jurisdiction from which rules are being transplanted. Therefore, the determination of legal proceedings and judicial actions as well as the strengthening of the institutions are essential aspects without which legal reform becomes effective.

Latin American procedural law is characterized by a formalistic approach in which several different instances are granted to challenge every single decision rendered by the court. As a result, most processes tend to be lengthy and bureaucratic. Protracted litigation is, therefore, the rule. A peculiar system for adjudication that exists in some Latin American countries is based upon the granting of quasi-judicial powers to administrative agencies. Entities such as the General Inspection of Justice in Argentina or the Superintendency of Companies from Colombia have proven to be useful for the purpose of providing expeditious and more technical solutions to conflicts arising in the field of corporate law.

Several procedural and even substantive regulations create obstacles that make it difficult for shareholders and other stakeholders to pursue legal actions before courts. Cumbersome regulations of this sort represent an entry barrier for litigation. Furthermore, the lack of predictability and the expectation of long-lasting and expensive processes are serious deterrents for the creation of a scenario, where shareholders' rights would find adequate development.

Luca Enriques argues that the creation of an effective company law framework relies heavily upon the so-called good corporate law judge.[20] Such concept features several different attributes, including a clear understanding of the core problems that underlie the corporate conflict as well as a non-formalistic approach and a serious concern for the precedential value of any decision rendered in this field.

The simplification of the legal process has been achieved in several Latin American countries through the consecration of the writ of constitutionality (*amparo, tutela* or *mandado de segurança*). These legal actions can be easily filed, are not subject to complicated formalities and can be handled through an expeditious and prioritary proceeding. This model provided for the defense of constitutionality-protected individual rights could be adapted for shareholder suits. The creation of a specific proceeding to deal with conflicts related to company law is a solution that has been recently adopted in Italy, through the so-called *rito societario*.

3. The simplified stock corporation as an optimal business form for Latin American systems

The optimal corporate law model depends on the specific conditions of a relevant system. Substantial differences in the economic models, as well as the legal traditions give rise to different approaches and various ways to deal with agency problems. However, the common core of Latin American Law, its shared colonial heritage and the existence of a com-

[20] L. Enriques, 'Off the Books but on the Record: Evidence from Italy on the Relevance of Judges to the Quality of Corporate Law', in *Global Markets. Domestic Institutions, Corporate Law and Governance in a New Era of Cross-Border Deals* (New York, Columbia University Press 2003) at pp. 258 et seq.

paratively homogenous culture, provide an appropriate scenario to set up a level field for most of the jurisdictions in this area.

The preliminary aspect that must be taken into account refers to the priority areas of legal reform. Thus far most efforts have focused in the field of publicly held corporations, and the manner in which the securities markets' liquidity could be improved across Latin America. For this purpose, a wave of corporate governance reforms fostered specially by the OECD has affected the regulations of company law in all major Latin American jurisdictions. The consequences of these new regulations are still to be assessed. However, recent empirical research suggests that such regulatory changes have had little or no impact in the number of listed companies. Furthermore, securities exchange activity measured through the number of IPOs and other significant transactions proves that no substantial change has taken place after those corporate governance reforms took place.[21]

On the other hand, the regulation of corporations contained in Commercial Codes and business associations' statutes prevailing in the Latin American region cannot be blamed for the reduced development of the local stock markets. The widespread use of the *sociedad anónima* (joint stock company) as the vehicle to undertake public issuances of securities bears no relationship whatsoever with the structural *path dependence* factors that determine the lack of a robust and efficient market. In fact, modern corporate governance provisions resemble the regulatory nature of Latin American corporate law. The long lasting tradition of several rules of a mandatory nature, including those regarding notices for annual meetings, voting rights, inspection and information rights, cumulative voting, compulsory auditing officers and various types of dissenting remedies make of the *anónima*, a classical business entity for publicly held entities. In theory, only a few changes are needed to adapt this traditional form of business entity to modern corporate governance standards (e.g., including independent directors in the boards of listed companies).

Therefore the slowdown in the Latin American stock markets should suggest a strategic turnaround in *enforcement intensity*, instead of focusing on rather useless substantive changes like those introduced in corporate regulations across the region during the previous decade at the OECD's request. Other structural factors such as tax evasion in closely held companies, costs of compliance with securities regulations, and the consequent reduction in the spread between financial credit and the cost of capital, represent a discouraging factor for new listings. Furthermore, the low number of listed companies gives rise to low liquidity and the inapplicability of the efficient market hypothesis.

The São Paulo stock exchange has devised a different approach to the securities market by creating a multi-tier system in which the corporate governance standards vary from one level to another. In the so-called *novo mercado* (or new market) the corporate governance standards applicable to corporations listed in this segment have been raised in order to reduce the perception of risk among investors. Although this measure has been useful for the purposes of increasing the amount of listed companies, it is still uncertain whether increased costs of compliance may offset the reduction in the cost of capital. The ability of this new market to survive in times of crisis is also a matter of debate.

Segmenting the market in accordance with different levels of corporate governance intensity seems to be a sensible solution as it may provide an interesting testing scenario regarding the usefulness of various corporate governance devices.

---

[21] There were no IPOs or public issuances of stocks of any listed company in the Colombia stock exchange in 2008. In the same year such exchange experienced a reduction of 12% of listed companies (See Financial Superintendency, Resolution of January 2009).

In any event, the amount of resources that has been spent in the perceived need to foster new listings and enhance the liquidity of securities markets in Latin America has not only been excessive, but it may not be conducive to a substantial improvement in the financial conditions of countries that have adopted recommendations ensuing from the proposed amendments to the securities market legal infrastructure.

To be sure, Professor Robert Cooter has suggested that stock issuances and secondary market trading of these securities is not a necessary factor for development in poor countries. Based upon the Chinese and Indian experiences, Cooter concludes that economic development in the private sector can be sufficiently financed by banks and other financial institutions (private financing), even in the absence of a developed and liquid stock market.[22]

It is striking, on the other hand, to realize that only small efforts have been made to amend or repeal the laws and regulations concerning the closely held corporation still anchored in 19th century notions. From a practical standpoint, it is obvious that non-listed companies are not only the broad majority of all business associations operating in Latin America, but also the most powerful instrument to create employment in developing economies.

3.1 Structural transplants and the good corporate judge

The rule of thumb for the importation of corporate law provisions has been referred to by certain authors as the *structural legal transplant*. For example, Katharina Pistor argues that it is not sufficient for the importation of a rule to merely incorporate into the borrowing country the substantive principles or provisions that work properly in the foreign lending jurisdiction. Along with such substantive norms it is also necessary to incorporate the rules (procedural or otherwise) and factors that cause such provisions to operate properly, including all circumstances that determine its efficiency and enforceability.[23]

Therefore, any corporate law reform in which a legal transplant is involved should encompass all substantive, procedural and institutional legal and factual circumstances that are necessary to make the institution work efficiently in the foreign recipient country. Rafael La Porta argues that the honesty of judges and their efficiency (measured in terms of enforceability of their final decisions) are necessary elements for a corporate law system to be effective.[24] The increasing amount of substantive (non-structural) corporate legal transplants constitutes a serious problem, particularly in developing countries.[25] Transplanting substantive legal provisions without importing the corresponding operational and institutional structure will at best a deceptive illusion of a significant change in the legal system.

Luca Enriques has analyzed the features that in his opinion constitute the so-called *good*

---

[22] Robert Cooter and Hans-Bernd Schäfer discuss the importance for innovation and economic development of three separate stages of finance (relational, private and public). The second stage is referred to as *private* because it comes from a small group of experts in evaluating innovations in an early stage of development (*Solomon's Knot, How Law Can End the Poverty of Nations*, Draft February, 2009, pp. 8-9).

[23] K. Pistor, et al., 'Fiduciary Duty in Transitional Civil Law Jurisdictions', in *Global Markets. Domestic Institutions, Corporate Law and Governance in a New Era of Cross-Border Deals* (New York, Columbia University Press 2003) at pp. 77-106.

[24] Quoted by Enriques (2003) at pp. 258-259.

[25] Buscaglia and Daklias, quoted by Enriques (2003), at p. 259.

corporate judge. The theory is based on the assumption that in order for corporate law to be as useful *on the books* as in real life, it is crucial for a system to have highly qualified judges available. Such qualification is not restricted to basic legal training in the general areas of procedural and private law, but specifically, in the field of corporate law in theory and practice. Independence is also a very significant aspect that Enriques emphasizes. In summary, specialized professional qualifications and independence are necessary factors for the corporate judge to apply a comprehensive body of modern corporate law.[26]

These and other features are supposed to enable the judge to detach herself from the imbedded formalism that characterizes some of the most backward systems pertaining to the civil law tradition. Professor Enriques also points out to the fact that certain legal systems of continental Europe, such as the Swedish and other northern European countries are efficient in the prevention of value shifting transactions and other fraudulent schemes that occur in corporate practice. Opportunistic behavior undertaken by agents (officers, directors and controlling shareholders) cannot be counteracted only by permanent monitoring, but also requires prompt availability of a *good corporate judge* before whom the abuse can be denounced for the purpose of obtaining an expeditious and final decision.

A similar theory has been held by prominent scholars such as Robert Cooter for whom 'high quality judges have good education, understand business and markets, do not take bribes, and do not bend to political influence. The power to interpret contracts' flexibility works better in their hands than in the hands of judges without these strengths.'[27]

Within the common law tradition, one of the best examples of a *good corporate judge* is the judicial system of the State of Delaware, which along with the substantive provisions contained in the Delaware General Corporation Law, and a qualified bar of corporate lawyers constitutes a highly reliable framework to generate confidence in the business entities incorporated in that State.[28] The corporate law jurisdiction of the State of Delaware is, therefore, one of the most specialized corporate law judiciaries in the world. The effectiveness of this corporate law judge is measured by two factors: (i) the knowledge and skills in solving complex corporate law problems; and (ii) the ability to produce final decisions within a reasonable timeframe.

For the sake of comparison, it is fair to say that the formalistic procedural and bureaucratic operation of the civil law jurisdictions of Latin America epitomizes the general lack of a *good corporate judge* in the region.[29] With the amount and length of procedural obstacles existing in the area, the expectation of a prompt, technical and reasonable resolution becomes elusive. In several jurisdictions in the region the number of corporate law complaints filed before civil courts is insignificant as compared with, for instance, processes for collection of promissory notes filed before the same jurisdictions.

---

[26] Enriques, at pp. 257-294.

[27] R. Cooter and H.-B. Schäfer, *Solomon's Knot: How Can Law End the Poverty of Nations* (February 2009).

[28] See A. Palmiter and F. Reyes (2001), at pp. 77-90 and R. Romano, *The Genius of American Corporate Law* (Washington D.C., The AEI Press 1993).

[29] R. Cooter provides an example of a jurisdiction that has devised a system to ameliorate the presence of bad judges. 'The judges in India's Supreme Court and the High Court are well educated and independent. They have authority to use the principle of good faith to develop law. In contrast, the lower court judges are poorly educated and too often corrupt. They are not allowed to use the principle of good faith to develop law' (See Cooter and Schäfer, at p. 16).

However, the Delaware case does not suggest the need for a division of the ordinary jurisdiction to split up a specialized commercial law judicial branch for Latin American countries. The creation of specialized courts severed from the ordinary jurisdiction normally leads to the same inefficiency and lack of qualification that characterizes the latter.

The enormous obstacles to improve the access to justice in corporate law matters, has forced certain jurisdictions in the area to adopt alternative systems for corporate dispute resolution. The Chilean Corporate Law 20.190 of 2007 sets forth the obligation to subject any dispute arising in the context of this law to corporate arbitration.[30] Therefore, the ordinary courts are inhibited to adjudicate in corporate law disputes involving stock corporations (*sociedades por acciones*). It is that same statute that deprives the ordinary courts of the power to decide any cases regarding *sociedades por acciones*. Even if this solution may appear to have extreme consequences, it is only a response to the need for an effective system of justice to which complicated corporate cases can be submitted. Under this recent regulation, the arbitration panel seems to be a *good corporate judge* or at least a *better* court than the ordinary civil jurisdiction.

The suggested Model Simplified Stock Corporations Act for Latin America (MSSCALA) provides that dispute resolution can only be handled by a specialized corporate law court of an administrative nature or, alternatively, by corporate arbitration in the manner provided for under the corporate by-laws. There are previous examples of this kind of a successful delegation of judicial functions in administrative authorities, such as the Superintendency of Companies in Colombia and to a lesser extent the General Inspection of Justice in Argentina. Due to the obvious risks associated with the concession of judicial functions to officers pertaining to the executive branch of government, it is recommendable to provide specific entry requirements based upon experience and independence for the purposes of appointment and tenure.

3.2 Path dependence and company law reform

In order to define an appropriate model after which the business associations law could be overhauled, it is important to bear in mind the practical implications of *path dependence*. Professors Lucian Bebchuk and Mark Roe describes this theory under two separate concepts: (i) structural path dependence; and (ii) rule-driven path dependence. The former refers to the 'the direct effect of initial ownership structures on subsequent ownership structures'; the latter is associated with all pre-existent rules applicable to corporations.[31] The first category is related to analyzing the manner in which *corporate ownership structures* are preserved. Pursuant to this theory, there are five factors that allow for the continuing preservation of an existing economic system. According to Bebchuk and Roe those factors are:

---

[30] 'All conflicts among shareholders, among shareholders and the corporation, its managers or liquidators, or among the corporation and its managers or liquidators, shall be addressed through arbitration(...)' (Art. 441 of the Chilean Commercial Code, as amended by Law 20.190 of 2007).

[31] The initial structure of an economic system has a direct influence on the subsequent choices regarding the prevailing property structures. Two basic factors can be identified with such structural dependence: the first one is based on efficiency; the second relates to rent seeking (L. Bebchuk and M.J. Roe, *A Theory of Path Dependence in Corporate Ownership and Governance*, 1999, SSRN Id. No. 202748).

(i) *sunk adaptive costs*, i.e., expenses in which firms have incurred in order to adapt with a given set of practices, rules and institutions;
(ii) *complementarities*, which relate to the existence of an integrated system of institutions, practices and skills, the value of which could be lost if a significant change were to take place;
(iii) *network externalities*, which can be explained as the benefits that stem out of the use of a practice or institution by a significant amount of people. This common use implies a relevant advantage in terms of a reduction of expenses and other costs;
(iv) *endowment effects*, which are associated with the overestimation given to existing institutions and practices by their users. 'Players' having control under an existing structure might affect their valuation of having such control, which would in turn affect the total value that alternative structures would produce'; and
(v) *multiple optima*, which relates to the possibility of operating under several different ownership structures that could yield equally optimal results in each given context.[32]

Besides the previously mentioned five factors, there is another one referred to as *rent seeking*. Such concept is closely associated to the economic benefits that some individuals obtain as a consequence of the preservation of certain ownership structure. Since such individuals have the power to make the relevant decisions that could determine a change in the ownership structure, the possibility of such a change is, at best, remote. This factor alone may be responsible for the persistence of an economic model (concentrated or diffuse ownership). Even if the initial model is not optimal in terms of benefits for all shareholders, rent-seeking may cause it to remain unaltered as long as controlling stockholders retain the power to extract private benefits of control (in excess of the rights conferred by law). In the context of dispersed ownership, directors' rent seeking is associated with their ability to remain indefinitely in their posts and to enjoy the corresponding corporate perks.

The authors also suggest that rent seeking by controlling majority stockholders in concentrated ownership systems makes it difficult to migrate to a system characterized by diffused stockholding. As a consequence, a majority shareholder who enjoys private benefits of control will be obviously reluctant to undertake an IPO, due the imminent loss of such benefits. In fact, there will be no incentive for the controlling shareholder (within a corporation characterized by concentrated ownership) to make decisions leading the corporation towards a system of dispersed ownership. The parties in charge of the decision-making machinery will retain all private benefits of control.

It must be taken into account that a concentrated ownership structure is not necessarily inefficient from the economic standpoint as long as there are advantages to offset the drawbacks arising from such concentrated ownership structure.[33] However, if the advantages arising from a concentrated ownership structure (extraction of private benefits of control) exceed reasonable limits and offset all possible economic benefits for the corporation, the system becomes inefficient.

---

[32] Id.

[33] According to McCahery and Vermeulen, such advantages are related with strong ties to local governments and local communities, centralized and efficient decision-making processes, reduction of monitoring expense for minority shareholders (i.e., agency costs), etc. See J.A. McCahery, E. Vermeulen, *Understanding Unincorporated Business Ventures* (Amsterdam, Center for Corporate Finance 2005) No. 12.

Excessive extraction of private benefits of control is pervasive in the so-called inefficient corporate law systems.[34] Such excessive shifting of value by controlling shareholders or directors does not depend exclusively on the absence of legal protections contained in substantive provisions, but also on the enforcement intensity of such legal rules. For instance, a comparison between European and Latin American civil law countries may show significant differences in terms of institutional framework and enforceability of corporate laws. Such differences also reflect the existence of controls – or lack thereof – regarding the extraction of private benefits of control.[35]

Certain forms of path dependence lay out the basis for some degree of stability in a legal system. This is due to the burdensome processes that are required to introduce radical reforms. In fact, it has been held that such forms of path dependence may give rise to competitive financial and economic systems even under divergent economic circumstances.[36] A good example of such efficiency is given by the models of dispersed ownership prevailing in the United Kingdom and the United States, where substantive regulations have been crafted to deal with agency problems arising from the separation between ownership and control.[37] Positive and negative incentives are set into play in order to align the interests of shareholders and directors. Those devices tend to reduce monitoring expenses, bonding costs and residual losses stemming from *adverse selection* and *moral hazard*.[38] The latter situations are associated, in turn, with the information asymmetries present in agency relationships. Such agency relationships must be structured in a manner in which the agent has the appropriate incentives to enhance the principal's wealth. In the absence of these incentives it is possible for the agent to act opportunistically. This propensity may be caused by the uncertainty regarding the future activity that the agent must undertake, as well as the principal's inability to closely monitor the agent's performance. The basic agency problem arising in the context of dispersed ownership between shareholders and management is usually reflected, among other wrongful activities in the possibility of obtaining corporate perks, insider trading, excessive executive compensation and the usurpation of corporate opportunities.

As it will be explained in further detail below, the above-mentioned agency problems are different to the ones existing between majority and minority shareholders. One of those distinctions can be analyzed from the changes in incentives that take place whenever the majority's control block is reduced. This reduction takes place when the controlling shareholder obtains additional cash through sales of shares in the corporation. According to Jensen and Meckling, as the controlling block shrinks the incentives of the agent (i.e., the

---

[34] R. Gilson, *Controlling Shareholders and Corporate Governance: Complicating the Comparative Taxonomy*, August 2005, SSRN Id. No. 784744.

[35] Id., at 9.

[36] See, for instance, J.C. Coffee, 'Law and Market: The Impact of Enforcement', *Columbia Law and Economics Working Paper No. 304*, March 2007 (holding that France – a Civil Law system with concentrated ownership – has at least matched the UK's – a Common Law system with share ownership dispersion – economic performance over the last century).

[37] A. Berle and G. Means, *The Modern Corporation and Private Property* (New York, Transaction Publishers 1991).

[38] See M. Jensen and W. Meckling, *Theory of the Firm: Managerial Behavior, Agency Costs and Ownership Structure*, 1976, SSRN Id. No. 94043. According to these authors, the scope of agency costs may vary from one corporation to another since they depend on factors such as directors' preferences, the discretionary authority that has been granted to them (as opposed to the maximization of the corporation's value), monitoring expenses, bonding expenses, etc.

controlling shareholder) to search for new opportunities and to engage in creative activities will be hindered due to the corresponding reduction of private benefits of control. The owner-manager will avoid these stressful efforts that usually include learning new technologies and other time-consuming activities. In doing so, the agent will avoid these personal costs generating an additional profit. This reduced activity on the part of the agent will lead in turn to a substantial loss of value to the corporation and its minority stockholders.[39]

On the other hand, certain Western European countries in which capital concentration takes place have achieved high levels of economic development comparable to that existing in dispersed ownership systems.[40] A plausible explanation for this development lies in the existence of effective legal mechanisms for counteracting the specific agency problems that arise in countries with concentrated ownership. Henry Hansmann and Reinier Kraakman have emphasized on the specific nature of the agency problems arising in the context in which there is no separation of ownership and control (*concentrated* or *block-ownership systems*).[41] Obviously, in the event of concentrated ownership the basic agency problem concerns the tensions between majority and minority stockholders (not between director and shareholders as a class). Consequently, specific mechanisms must be devised in order to align, through several different incentives, the interests of majority and minority stockholders.

The previously mentioned assertions can also be linked with the already mentioned theory of *multiple optima*, whereby competing ownership structures might have equally positive results in different countries.[42] Moreover, every system has an optimal regulatory degree that could be inadequate if it is applied haphazardously to any other economic system. It follows that there might be multiple adequate levels of regulations according to the specific features of each system. This explains why countries with diverging economic models have attained comparable high levels of economic development.

Most efforts in company law reform in Latin America during the last decade have been aimed at improving the framework for publicly-held corporations in the expectation of creating a better regulatory environment for a deep and liquid securities market. The wave of corporate reform for publicly-held corporations has resulted in the overhaul of securities regulation in most major jurisdictions in the area. However, even if the OECD White Paper on Corporate Governance in Latin America has been partially implemented in these countries, the results of such implementation have been at best innocuous and at worst detrimental to the securities markets in the area. The increases in costs of compliance for listed corporations far exceed the reductions in the cost of capital. This is due in part to the formalistic nature of these recommendations and the lack of enforcement mechanisms that could foster their actual compliance. The basic criticism to these corporate governance

---

[39] Id. According to Jensen and Meckling, the loss of value stemming out of directors' opportunism will only be sub-optimal or inefficient when compared with a *Coasean World* – in which the agent's performance is complete, without the need to incur in monitoring expenses – or when compared with a hypothetical world in which agency costs were effectively lower than in reality. Nevertheless, all these costs (monitoring, bonding and residual losses) are an inevitable result in any agency relationship.

[40] See Coffee, 'Law and the Market', *supra* n. 36.

[41] Henry Hansmann, Reinier Kraakman, et al., *The Anatomy of Corporate Law: A Comparative and Functional Approach* (Oxford, Oxford University Press 2004), pp. 21-29.

[42] L. Bebchuk and M.J. Roe, *supra* n. 31.

reforms is based on the extrapolation of a model devised to deal with agency problems arising in the context of ownership dispersion, to countries with highly concentrated capital. The argument draws from the substantial differences between the agency problems that arise between shareholders and directors as compared to the relationships between majority and minority stockholders.[43] This misguided legislative agenda for corporate law disregards a conspicuous economic reality in which closely-held corporations normally dominate the landscape of business in these countries. A high level of concentrated-ownership in Latin America – which has been described as the highest in the world[44] – cannot be counteracted with formalistic recommendations that bear no relationship with the agency problems identified for the area. This is particularly true absent an institutional framework which can be used to increase enforcement intensity. An adaptation of the theory of path dependence provides an insightful tool to analyze corporate law reform for Latin America. Realizing that even in the context of concentrated ownership there can be significant economic growth may be a valuable step towards shifting legislative efforts to the closely-held corporation. This will necessarily require a reshuffling of priorities in the policy agenda aimed at a complete overhaul of the business association's regulation contained in anachronistic company law codes and statutes.[45] An upgrade in this area can easily be achieved by the introduction of a multifunctional hybrid business form that could coexist and compete with previously created company types. The successful Colombian example regarding the SAS speaks loudly of the benefits that could be obtained if such a step were to be taken.

3.3 The impact of corporate law for economic development

Ownership patterns (dispersed or concentrated) are not the only factors that have to be taken into account for the purposes of comparative company law. A substantial amount of recent academic production on the economic analysis of law draws from the econometric studies of Rafael La Porta, Florencio López-de-Silanes, Andrei Shleifer and Robert Vishny (also known as LLSV). LLSV attempted to demonstrate through empirical analysis that the main differences regarding the protection afforded to investors in multiple jurisdictions could be attributed to the legal tradition that each country had inherited (*legal origins theory*).[46] In articles published in 1997 and 1998 these authors held the controversial theory whereby those countries belonging to the common law tradition were better endowed with investor protection mechanisms as compared to their civil law counterparts.[47] After analyzing samples taken in 49 countries, LLSV showed that there was a direct statistical correlation between the legal tradition existing in each nation and its level of financial

[43] For an explanation as to the shortcomings of these corporate governance reforms and the inadequacy of many of the solutions recommended by the OECD, see Francisco Reyes, 'Corporate Governance in Latin America: A Functional Analysis', in *Inter-American Law Review*, Vol. 39, No. 2, Winter 2008.

[44] José Antonio Ocampo and Juan Martín (eds.), Economic Commission for Latin America and the Caribbean (ECLAC), 2003.

[45] Professor Robert Cooter and Hans-Bernd Schäfer have recently held that a publicly traded market for stock is not essential for the economic development of poor countries, *supra* n. 22.

[46] R. La Porta, F. López-de-Silanes, A. Shleifer and R. Vishny, *'Law and Finance', Journal of Political Economy*, Vol. 106, No. 6, December 1998.

[47] LLSV found a negative correlation between the degree of ownership concentration and the protection afforded to investors in each of the concerned countries. Based on such correlation they concluded that those systems that lacked a sufficient protection were not suitable to support a fully developed securities market.

development. Not only did they divide the world into three separate categories, i.e., (1) common law; (2) German and Scandinavian civil law; and (3) French civil law, but they rated the countries included in the first category as number one and assigned the last position to French civil law systems.[48] According to this research, common law origin countries had grown at a higher rate (4.3% per capita) in comparison with French civil law countries (3.18%).[49] The study suggested the convenience of transplanting common law-type legal provisions into civil law countries. In their opinion, the importance of legal origins in defining investor protection suggests that many rules must be changed in order for an inefficient legal system to adhere to best practices.[50]

Notwithstanding LLSV's significant contribution, their conclusions have been vigorously challenged. Although the proposition whereby *law matters* is broadly acknowledged, the legal tradition may not be all that important as the LLSV texts suggest. John C. Coffee points out to the following five factors that can be used to challenge the legal origins theory: (i) Even if the analysis assumes the inefficiency of the French legal system, France has experienced a higher economic growth than the United Kingdom during most of the period that runs from 1820 until today. French civil law appears to have been efficient, at least for France; (ii) The statistical data that have been used to prove that common law countries have outperformed civil law countries is due to a high extent to the spectacular failure of Latin American countries during the last century. Even the assertion that Latin American systems belong to the French civil law tradition is highly debatable; (iii) The statistical analysis used by LLSV is suspect to the extent that certain critics have held that it has been unduly applied; (iv) There are important examples regarding countries that have reached rapid economic development irrespective of their civil law tradition. Alternatively, there are common law countries that have not been able to reach a high level of economic development; and (v) some authors debate the assertion whereby law could have an importance even comparable to structural factors such as geography, free trade or colonial heritage.

Coffee concludes, ironically, that the failure of French civil law may have arisen from its inception in too many tropical climates, as compared with the common law that was received in more temperate countries.[51] It is his opinion that a legal system has an impact on economic growth as long as substantive norms are supplemented by an appropriate level of enforcement intensity. Such intensity can be measured both at the level of public and private enforcement. The most accurate way to undertake such measurements is by con-

---

[48] 'Legal rules protecting investors vary systematically among legal traditions or origins, with the laws of Common Law countries (originating in English Law) being more protective of outside investors than the laws of Civil Law countries (originating in Roman Law) and particularly French Civil Law'. Rafael La Porta, Florencio López-de-Silanes and Andrei Shleifer, *The Economic Consequences of Legal Origins*, November 2007, at p. 2.

[49] La Porta, et al., quoted by John C. Coffee, Jr., *Law and the Market: The Impact of Enforcement*, April 2007, p. 21.

[50] It follows from this analysis that it would be convenient to undertake the transplant of legal provisions regarding investor protections originating in common law countries. However, Holger Spamann has held that the analysis should not be approached from the standpoint of the legal tradition from which the rules are borrowed. In his opinion, the differences between the civil law and its common law counterpart are not as relevant as the nature of the jurisdiction. For this purpose, the author classifies legal systems between so-called *core* and *peripheric* jurisdictions. In the former, the legislative-making process is endogenous whereas in the rest of the countries the process is exogenous, namely, it is achieved through the importation of legal rules designed in core jurisdictions (Holger Spamann, *Contemporary Legal Transplants: Legal Families and the Diffusion of Corporate Law*, 2006).

[51] J.C. Coffee, Jr., *supra* n. 48.

sidering the amount of resources allocated to governmental enforcement agencies (*inputs*) and compare it with the consolidated amounts that are collected by such agencies (*outputs*). As enforcement intensity increases the quality of corporate law is also upgraded.[52]

3.4 Proposals for Latin American company law reform

3.4.1 *Publicly held corporations*

As a general rule, economic growth can be assessed through the measurement of capital market development and the creation of new businesses. However, Professor Robert Cooter has held that a vigorous stock market is not necessarily an essential factor for the economic development of poor countries. Using specific examples from economies in transition such as India and China, the author points out to the significant growth attained in those countries within the last decade. In determining the manner in which financing has taken place in these jurisdictions he has concluded the relative absence of highly operational systems for publicly traded stocks.[53]

A brief review of statistical data regarding stock exchanges in Latin America reveals how the stock markets are comparatively depressed as compared with those existing in developed economies (see Table 3, showing the number of listed corporations per million inhabitants in Latin America). The amount of IPOs and other public offerings is limited and the market capitalization of listed companies is relatively small as a percentage of GDP (see Table 4) and the number of issuers of securities is small.[54]

Under the international benchmark method, a comparison is made between GDPs for the some of the largest economies in Latin America and market capitalization in each of their national stock exchanges.

Table 3. Number of listed corporation per million inhabitants in major Latin American jurisdictions

Position	Country	Number of listed companies	Population	No. of listed corporations per million inhabitants
1.	Chile	246	16.134.219	15,24709687
2.	Perú	221	28.302.603	8,691780046
3.	Argentina	106	40.927.301	6,010657776
4.	Colombia	94	44.593.035	5,516556565
5.	México	335	107.449.525	2,289447068
6.	Brazil	350	190.078.227	1,294203991

52 Id. An objective criterion to assess enforcement intensity in securities markets is closely linked to the so-called bonding premium that arises in the context of cross-listings, where an issuing corporation undergoes an IPO in a foreign country with better quality corporate and securities law. There is a direct correlation between the higher or lower enforcement intensity and the amount of the bonding premium. If, for instance, the issuing corporation is originally listed in a jurisdiction with poor corporate and securities laws, listing its securities in the New York Stock Exchange will result in a high premium that can be assessed through event studies after information on the cross-listing has been disclosed.

53 See Cooter and Schäfer (2009).

54 As an example, there are only 94 corporations registered in the Colombian Stock Exchange. Only shares of stock issued by 22 of these companies have significant liquidity. Moreover, no IPOs or any other public issuance of stock took place during 2008. Transactions regarding stock represent only 2% of the total amount of securities traded in the Colombian stock exchange.

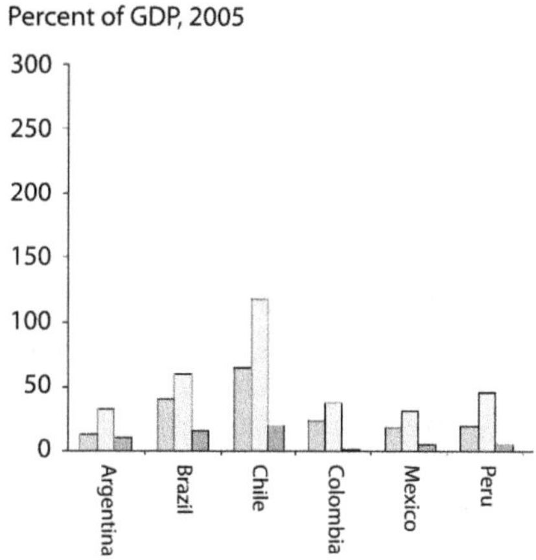

Table 4. Percentage of GDP made up by market capitalization

Source: Augusto de la Torre, *Latin American Capital Markets*, The World Bank, 2007

There appears to be an unfortunate coincidence between the wave of corporate governance reforms and the significant decrease in the number of listed firms in all major Latin American jurisdictions (see Table 5 showing the number of firms listed in domestic in Latin American domestic stock exchanges). Aside from other macroeconomic factors a hypothesis can be ventured regarding the increasing costs of compliance (mostly due to multiple requirements of a formalistic nature) without any positive impact on investor confidence. Therefore, these reforms have not resulted in a reduction in the cost of capital.

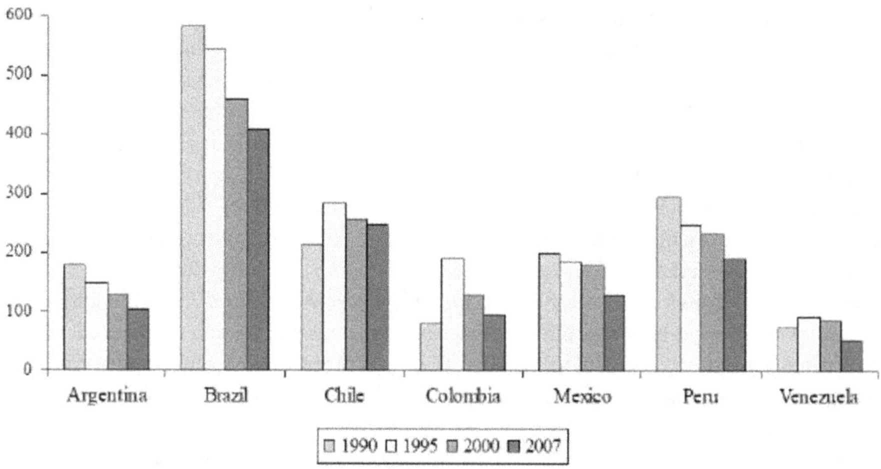

Table 5. Number of firms listed in domestic in Latin American domestic stock exchanges

Source: Augusto de la Torre, *Latin American Capital Markets*, The World Bank, 2007

These data suggest that a listing may not entail a significant reduction in the cost of capital or, worse yet, other factors such as tax evasion (which would have to be reduced after listing due to higher disclosure requirements) represent a negative incentive to list a corporation in a Latin American stock market. Furthermore, this suggests shifting the corporate law agenda towards the improvement of the legal framework for closely-held corporations instead of devoting additional resources to the development of a publicly-held corporation the future of which is at best uncertain.

3.4.2 *Closely-held corporations*

As a general rule, Latin American corporate statutes for closely-held corporations lack relevant innovation present in most modern jurisdictions. The incidence of outmoded notions such as the lack of single member companies, a strict *ultra vires* doctrine, a fixed term of duration, the existence of several formalistic prohibitions supposedly aimed at the protection of shareholders and a plethora of regulatory provisions better suited for publicly-held entities than for small and medium family businesses, are only but a few of the features characterizing an anachronistic regime that needs to be torn down.

The Colombian system in which corporate law reform has been underway for the last 15 years, is a good example of a shifting from the rigidities of an *ancien régime* such as the one described above to a reform agenda prioritizing flexibility, contractual freedom and limited liability. The goals advanced in the recent act introducing the simplified stock corporation (*sociedad por acciones simplificada*) in 2008 match the contemporary policy agenda which gives prevalence to the so-called hybrid business forms, also known as uncorporations.[55] The ability of hybrid business forms to operate as all-purpose vehicles has led to their introduction in common law and civil law jurisdictions across the board, as well as in certain Asian countries.[56]

3.4.3 *The draft legislation on simplified stock corporations for Latin America*

The case for developing new business forms is a strong one in Latin America. Family-owned businesses and closely-held companies abound in the region, creating significant demand for entities that allow parties to engage in extensive private ordering. Existing business forms have proven to be inflexible to suit the needs of family-owned and multi-owner firms. However, most Latin American legislators – much like their European counterparts – have been reluctant to develop new hybrid vehicles. Increasing entrepreneurial demand for reform has only recently spurred several initiatives within the region. Such statutory enhancements are currently being outmatched by the introduction of a new business form: the *Sociedad por Acciones Simplificada* (*SAS*) or Simplified Stock Corporation. Even though it draws upon the French *Société par Actions Simplifiée*, this entity closely resembles the hybrid business entities that have been set in place in the United Stated and the United Kingdom. By providing a mixture of corporate and partnership-like components, the SAS allows for significant contractual flexibility, while still preserving the benefits of limited liability and asset partitioning.

The model act on Simplified Stock Corporations for Latin America – crafted after the Colombian example – is not intended to serve as an amendment of traditional business

---

[55] See draft legislation for the *SAS*, prepared by Francisco Reyes in 2006. For the original draft that gave rise to the Colombian law on simplified stock corporations, see *Gaceta del Congreso* No. 111, Bogotá, April 11 of 2007, at pp. 1-6.

[56] J.A. McCahery and E. Vermeulen, *Corporate Governance of Non-listed Companies* (Oxford, Oxford University Press 2008) at p. 54.

forms contained in national codes and statutes. Instead, it is recommended that its enactment take place on a separate legislation that could be linked to the existing system.[57] In this manner, the SAS should have to compete with other types of business forms. The first advantage of this legislative system is that it avoids cumbersome and lengthy discussions with regressive-minded legal operators and other agents that favor ancient local corporate law traditions. Included within these operators, McCahery and Vermeulen mention judges, notary publics, law professors, etc.[58] The second advantage of this approach refers specifically to the creation of an internal competition among different business entities. This exercise allows to observe entrepreneurial preferences when they choose among the items in the company law menu.[59] The *SAS* is expected to gain a hefty advantage in this competition, owing to its swift process for incorporation and its ample private ordering potential. This competition could ultimately lead to the undoing of the most conservative approaches to company law, as *status quo* advocates are forced to relent in their positions when confronted with incontestable economic realities.

(a) *General aspects*

The basic framework for this proposed legislation is based upon the following five pillars: (i) full-fledged limited liability; (ii) simple incorporation requirements; (iii) contractual flexibility; (iv) supple organizational structure; and (v) single level tax structure.

Under the simplified stock corporation, shareholders acquire broad flexibility to freely regulate their relationships pursuant to a set of enabling provisions containing off-the-rack housekeeping rules. Therefore, shareholder protection can be achieved through devices of a contractual nature. In this manner, the antagonism between majority and minority shareholders may be ameliorated through *ex ante* negotiations. For this purpose, the model act not only proposes facilitating provisions, but also enhances the enforceability of shareholders' agreements. Through the latter device, it is possible to reach certain equilibrium between stockholders by means of sophisticated mechanisms in which rights and obligations can be used to carefully determine *a priori* expectations of all corporate participants. Following the incomplete contracts theory, this enhanced freedom of contract complemented by gap-filling through an efficient adjudication process is intended to provide an improved conflict-resolution scenario for shareholders.

Following the theory of *structural transplants*, the remedy of specific performance is introduced to allow for the adequate enforcement of these agreements in the event of default. Furthermore, the model act incorporates a comprehensive regulation on the *abus de droit* (abuse of rights) theory, which is extrapolated from the French jurisprudence on corporate law. Under this theory, shareholders have the ability to bring judicial actions or arbitration complaints not only on the grounds of abuses of controlling shareholders, but also concerning the same conduct where it has been deployed by minority shareholders and also in the event of abuse in symmetrical block shareholdings (i.e., dual ownership on a 50% – 50% distribution). The abuse of right action may give rise to damages for the aggrieved party, as well as rescission of the abusive act. Fiduciary duties of care and loyalty

---

57 See McCahery and Vermeulen, *supra* n. 56.

58 See McCahery and Vermeulen, *supra* n. 6.

59 This competition is already taking place in Colombia after the inception of Law 1258 of 2008 regarding the simplified stock corporation (*SAS*).

can also be applicable to the officers and directors of the *SAS*. To complete the scenario of corporate law protections, the model act allows for the application of the shadow director doctrine, by means of which any person who intrudes in a positive management activity, without being a legally appointed manager or director, can be disciplined under fiduciary duties as if she were acting in such managerial capacity.

The *SAS* is as useful for local businessmen as it is for foreign investors. This usefulness is especially significant to structure corporate groups in which the *SAS* can be used to incorporate wholly-owned subsidiaries, irrespective of their size or business activity. This light structure substantially reduces transaction costs and facilitates their operation.

The Model Act for the Simplified Stock Corporation seeks to remedy the legislative void existing throughout the region concerning hybrid business forms as well as to reduce transaction costs and provide entrepreneurs with enough flexibility to allow for private ordering in a multi-functional business form, suitable for all kinds of undertakings.

(b) *Specific aspects of the SAS Model Act*

The proposed draft legislation is based on a basic principle: granting ample freedom to entrepreneurs in structuring their relationships through contractual provisions. And yet, when parties are loath to incur the costs of contractual bargaining, the Model Act sets forth ready-made provisions to govern intra-firm relationships. These off-the-rack rules have been laid down following a two-tier system. The first regulatory tier is comprised of provisions designed specifically for the Simplified Stock Corporation. The second one remands parties to the statutory rules governing the standard corporate form, as it exists in the corresponding State of incorporation.

Some of the most salient features of the *SAS* can be summarized as follows:

(i) formation by one or more shareholders;
(ii) incorporation by simple private or electronic document (as opposed to granting a public deed for incorporation);
(iii) simple registration before a Mercantile Registry;
(iv) full limited liability, with the exception of piercing the veil for fraud or abuse of the corporate form;
(v) abolition of the *ultra vires* doctrine;
(vi) unlimited corporate duration;
(vii) full contractual freedom for corporate organization;
(viii) suppression of superfluous internal controls such as statutory auditors;
(ix) admission of several different classes of stock including shares with multiple voting rights;
(x) simple majority to make corporate decisions;
(xi) waiver of notice for shareholders' meetings;
(xii) specific regulation for abuse of rights;
(xiii) flexibility to define subscribed capital (without minimum capitalization requirements);
(xiv) long term for the effective contribution of paid-in capital;
(xv) ample contractual freedom to execute shareholders' agreements;
(xvi) remedy of specific performance to enforce shareholders' agreements in the event of default;

(xvii) dividend distribution and regulation detached from regulatory thresholds or mandatory minimum proportional allocation of profits;
(xviii) freedom to provide for arbitration for all kinds of conflicts (including disputes among shareholders or with management);
(xix) restrictions on the free transferability of shares (beyond the right of first refusal);
(xx) possibility to squeeze-out shareholders in the event of changes of control or merger (provided that an appropriate compensation at market value is granted);
(xxi) definition of the sale of all or substantially all assets;
(xxii) introduction of triangular mergers and full dissenters' remedies.

Even if limited liability is one of the main features of the *SAS*, the model act provides for piercing the corporate veil in order to extend liability to controlling shareholders in the event of fraud or abuse of the corporate form. Such mechanism has to be brought before a specialized jurisdiction or an arbitration panel that will guarantee a more technical and expedited resolution for aggrieved creditors.

4. Conclusion

Understanding the underlying economic model in Latin American countries allows for the determination of the most frequent agency problems present in business corporations in the region. Taking into account the high degree of concentrated ownership that prevails across Latin American countries, solutions should be devised in order to counteract the potentiality for oppression of minority shareholders at the hands of blockholders. The theory of structural transplants is useful for the introduction of a system that is based upon two pillars. The first pillar is composed of enabling statutes that allow parties to opt-out of default legal provisions. Private ordering facilitates the creation of tailor-made rules appropriate for closely held entities. Such freedom of contract contributes to achieving a higher degree of completeness in the corporate contract. The second pillar concerns procedural provisions that are intended to increase the degree of enforcement intensity so that gap-filling by arbitrators, judicial authorities and other entities is facilitated. The model act on simplified stock corporations for Latin America is an attempt to incorporate modern trends into legal systems characterized by a formalistic and backward structure in which regulatory provisions prevail to an overwhelming extent. The extremely successful, empirically measured result of Colombian Law 1258 of 2008 – with more than 6,000 simplified stock corporations created in eight months – clearly suggests that businesspeople prefer flexibility to old fashioned misguided paternalism. The widespread adoption of the model act would not only allow for a certain degree of convergence in countries that require a higher level of legal integration, but also could foster innovation and foreign investment. Overall, statutes such as the model act are aimed at the increase of economic development and welfare-enhancement. To sum, the rules included within the Model Act are meant to foster innovation and entrepreneurship throughout the region.

Section 4

Model Act on the Simplified Stock Corporation

Chapter I
General Provisions

Section 1. Nature. – The simplified stock corporation is a for profit legal entity by shares, the nature of which will always be commercial irrespective of the activities set forth in its purpose clause.

Section 2. Limited Liability. – The simplified stock corporation may be formed by one or more persons or legal entities.

Shareholders will only be responsible for providing the capital contributions promised to the simplified stock corporation.

Except as set forth in Section 41 of this Act, shareholders will not be held liable for any obligations incurred by the simplified stock corporation, including but not limited to labor and tax obligations.

There shall be no labor relationship between a simplified stock corporation and its shareholders, unless an explicit to that effect has been executed to that effect.

Section 3. Legal Personality. – Upon the filing of the formation document before the *Mercantile Registry [include the name of corresponding company registrar's office]*, the simplified stock corporation will form a legal entity separate and distinct from its shareholders.

Section 4. Inability to Become a Listed Entity. – The shares of stock and other securities issued by a simplified stock corporation shall neither be registered within a stock exchange, nor traded in any securities market.

Chapter II
Formation and Proof of Existence

Section 5. Contents of the Formation Document. – A simplified stock corporation will be formed by contract or by the individual will of a single shareholder, provided that a written document is granted. The formation document shall be registered before the *Mercantile Registry [include the name of corresponding company registrar's office]*, and set forth:

(1) Name and address of each shareholder;
(2) The name of the corporation followed by the words "simplified stock corporation" or the abbreviation "S.A.S.";
(3) The corporation's domicile;
(4) If the simplified stock corporation is to have a specific date of dissolution, the date in which the corporation is to dissolve;
(5) A clear and complete description of the main business activities to be included within the purpose clause, unless it is stated that the corporation may engage in any lawful business;
(6) The authorized, subscribed and paid-in capital, along with the number of shares to be issued, the different classes of shares, their par value and the terms and conditions in which the payment will be made;
(7) Any provisions for the management of the business and for the conduct of the affairs of the corporation, along with the names and powers of each manager. A simplified stock corporation shall have at least one legal representative in charge of managing the affairs of the corporation in relation with third parties.

No additional formalities of any nature shall be required for the formation of the simplified stock corporation.

Section 6. Attestation. – The *Mercantile Registrar [include the name of corresponding company registrar's office]* shall attest to the legality of the provisions set forth in the formation document and any amendments thereof. The Registrar shall only deny registration where the requirements provided under Section 5 have not been met. The decision rendered by the Registrar shall be issued within three days after the relevant filing has been made. Any decision denying registration will only be subject to a rehearing conducted by the Registrar.

Upon the approval of a formation document by the Mercantile Registrar, challenges will not be heard against the existence of the simplified stock corporation and the contents of the formation document will constitute the simplified stock corporation's by-laws.

Section 7. Assimilation to Partnership. – Where a formation document has not been duly approved by the *Mercantile Registrar [include the name of corresponding company registrar's office]* the purported corporation will be assimilated to a partnership. Accordingly, partners will be jointly and severally liable for all obligations in which the partnership is engaged. If the partnership has only one member, such member will be held liable for all obligations in which the partnership is engaged.

Section 8. Proof of Existence. The certificate issued by the *Mercantile Registrar [include the name of corresponding company registrar's office]* is conclusive evidence as regards the existence of the simplified stock corporation and the provisions set forth in the formation document.

Chapter III
Special Rules Regarding Subscribed, Paid-in Capital and Shares of Stock

Section 9. Capital Subscription and Payment. – Capital subscription and payment may be carried out under terms and conditions different to those set forth under the *Commercial Code [include the name of the relevant Code, Decree, Law or Statute]*. In any event, payment of subscribed capital shall be made within a period of two years to be counted from the date in which the shares were subscribed. The rules for subscription and payment may be freely set forth in the by-laws.

Section 10. Classes of Shares. – The simplified stock corporation may issue different classes or series of shares, including preferred shares with or without vote. Shares may be issued for any consideration whatsoever including in-kind contributions or in exchange for labor pursuant to the terms and conditions contained in the by-laws.

Any special rights granted to the holders of any class or series of shares shall be described or affixed upon the back of the stock certificates.

Section 11. Voting Rights. – The by-laws shall depict in full detail the voting rights corresponding to each class of shares. Such document shall also determine whether each share will grant its holder single or multiple voting rights.

Section 12. Share Transfers to a Trust. – Any shares issued by a simplified stock corporation may be transferred to a trust provided that an annotation is made in the corporate ledger concerning the trustee company, the beneficial owners and the percentage of beneficial rights.

Section 13. Limitation on the Transferability of Shares. – The by-laws may contain a provision whereby the shares may not be transferred for a period not to exceed ten years to be counted from the moment in which the shares were issued. Such term may only be extended by consent of all the holders of outstanding shares.

Any such limitation on share transferability shall be described or affixed upon the back of the stock certificate.

Section 14. Authorization for the Transfer of Shares. – The by-laws may contain provisions whereby any transfer of shares or of any given class of shares will be subject to the previous authorization of the shareholders' assembly granted by majority vote or by any supermajority included in the by-laws.

Section 15. Breach of Restrictions on Negotiation of Shares. – Any transfer of shares carried out in a manner inconsistent with the rules set forth in the by-laws shall be null and void.

Section 16. Change of Control in a Corporate Shareholder. – The by-laws may impose upon an incorporated shareholder the duty to notify the simplified stock corporation's legal representative about any transaction the effect of which may cause a change in control regarding such shareholder. Where a change in control has taken place, the shareholders' assembly by majority decision shall be entitled to exclude the corresponding incorporated shareholder.

Aside from the possibility of being excluded, any breach of the duty to inform changes in control may subject the concerned shareholder to a penalty consisting of a 20% reduction of the fair market value of the shares, upon reimbursement.

In the event set forth in this article all decisions concerning the exclusion of shareholders as well as the determination of any penalties shall require an approval rendered by the shareholder's assembly by majority vote. The votes of the concerned shareholder shall not be counted for the adoption of these decisions.

Chapter IV
Organization of the Simplified Stock Corporation

Section 17. Organization. – Shareholders may freely organize the structure and operation of a simplified stock corporation in the by-laws. In the absence of specific provisions to this effect, the shareholders' assembly or the sole shareholder, as the case may be, will be entitled to exercise all powers legally granted to the shareholders' assemblies of stock corporations, whilst the management and representation of the simplified stock corporation shall be granted to the legal representative.

Where the number of shareholders has been reduced to one, the subsisting shareholder shall be entitled to exercise the powers afforded to all existing corporate organs.

Section 18. Meetings. – Meetings of shareholders may be held at such place as may be designated by shareholders either within or without the corporation's domicile. For any of these meetings, the regular quorum provided in the by-laws will suffice pursuant to Section 22 hereof.

Section 19. Meetings by Technological Devices or by Written Consent. – Meetings of shareholders may be held through any available technological devices or by written consent. The minutes of such meetings shall be drafted and included within the corporate records no later than 30 days after the meeting has taken place. These minutes shall be signed by the legal representative or, in the absence of the former, by any shareholder that participated in the meeting.

Section 20. Notice of Meeting. – In the absence of stipulation to the contrary, the legal representative shall convene the shareholders' assembly by written notice addressed to each shareholder. Such notice shall be made at least five days in advance to the meeting. The agenda shall in all cases be included within any notice of meeting.

Whenever the shareholders' assembly is called upon to approve financial statements, conversion of the corporation into another form, mergers or split-off proceedings, shareholders will be entitled to exercise information rights concerning any documents relevant to the proposed transaction. Information rights may be exercised during the five days prior to the meeting, unless a longer term has been provided for in the by-laws.

Any notice of meeting may determine the date in which Second Call Meetings will take place, whenever quorum is insufficient to hold the first meeting. Second Call Meetings shall take place at any date following the next 10 days after the first meeting should have taken place. This Second Call Meeting shall not take place later than 30 days following the date of the failed meeting.

Section 21. Waiver of Notice. – Shareholders may at any point in time submit written waivers of notice whereby they forego their right to be convened to a meeting of the shareholders' assembly. Shareholders may also waive in writing any information rights granted under Section 20.

Even in the absence of a notice of meeting, the attendees in a given shareholders' assembly will be deemed to have waived the right of being convened, unless such shareholders make a statement to the contrary before the meeting takes place.

Section 22. Quorum and Majority. – A majority of the shares entitled to vote, present in person o represented by proxy, shall constitute a quorum at a meeting of shareholders, unless the by-laws specify otherwise.

The affirmative vote of the majority of shares present in person or represented by proxy at the meeting shall be the act of the shareholders, unless the by-laws contain supermajority provisions.

The sole shareholder of a simplified stock corporation may adopt any and all decisions within the powers granted to the shareholders' assembly. The sole shareholder will keep a record of such decisions in the corporate books.

Section 23. Vote Splitting. – Shareholders may split their votes during cumulative voting proceedings for the election of directors or the members of any other organism.

Section 24. Shareholders' Agreements. – Agreements entered into between shareholders concerning the acquisition or sale of shares, preemptive rights or rights of first refusal, exercise of voting rights, voting by proxy or any other valid matter shall be binding upon the simplified stock corporation, provided that such agreements have been filed with the corporation's legal representative. Shareholders' agreements will be valid for any period of time determined by the relevant agreement, not exceeding 10 years, upon the terms and conditions stated therein. Such 10 year term may only be extended by unanimous consent.

Shareholders that have executed an agreement shall appoint a person who will represent them in receiving notices from the corporation and providing any information that could be requested. The simplified stock corporation may request in writing to such representative clarification as regards any provisions set forth in the agreement. In this event, the response shall be provided also in writing within the five days following the request.

Subsection 1. – The President of the shareholders' assembly or of the concerned corporate organ shall exclude any votes cast in a manner inconsistent with the terms set forth under a duly filed shareholders' agreement.

Subsection 2. – Pursuant to the conditions set forth in the agreement, any shareholder shall be entitled to demand the specific performance of any obligation arising under such agreement, before a court with jurisdiction over the corporation.

Section 25. Board of Directors. – The simplified stock corporation is not required to have a board of directors, unless such board is mandated in the by-laws. In the absence of a provision requiring the operation of a board of directors, the legal representative appointed by the shareholders' assembly shall be entitled to exercise any and all powers concerning the management and legal representation of the simplified stock corporation.

If a board of directors has been included in the formation document, such board will be formed with one or more directors for each of whom an alternate director may also be appointed. All directors may be appointed either by majority vote, cumulative voting or by any other mechanism set forth in the by-laws. The rules regarding the operation of the board of directors may be freely established in the by-laws. Lacking a specific provision on the by-laws, the board will be governed under the relevant statutory provisions.

Section 26. Legal Representation. – The legal representation of the simplified stock corporation will be carried out by an individual or legal person appointed in the manner provided in the by-laws. The legal representative may undertake and execute any and all acts and contracts included within the purpose clause as well as those which are directly related to the operation and existence of the corporation.

Section 27. Liability of Directors and Managers. – All Commercial Code *[include the name of the relevant Code, Decree, Law or Statute]* provisions relating to the liability of directors and managers may also be applicable to the legal representative, the board of directors and the managers and officers of the simplified stock corporation, unless such provision is opted-out in the by-laws.

Subsection 1. – Any individual or legal entity who is not a manager or director of a simplified stock corporation that engages in any trade or activity related to the management, direction or operation of such corporation shall be subject to the same liabilities applicable to directors and officers of the corporation.

Subsection 2. – Whenever a simplified stock corporation or any of its managers or directors grants apparent authority to an individual or legal entity to the extent that it may be reasonably believed that such individual or legal entity has sufficient powers to represent the corporation, the company will be legally bound by any transactions entered into with third parties acting in good faith.

Section 28. Auditing Organs. – A simplified stock corporation shall not, in any case, be legally mandated to establish or provide for internal auditing organs *[include the name of corresponding auditing entity e.g. fiscal auditor, auditing committee, etc.]*.

Chapter V
By-Law Amendments and Corporate Restructurings

Section 29. By-law Amendments. – Amendments to the corporate by-laws shall be approved by majority vote. Decisions to this effect will be recorded in a private document to be filed with the *Mercantile Registry [include the name of corresponding company registrar's office].*

Section 30. Corporate Restructurings. – The statutory provisions governing conversion into another form, mergers and split-off proceedings for business associations will be applicable to the simplified stock corporation. Dissenters' rights and appraisal remedies shall also be applicable.

For the purpose of exercising dissenters' rights and appraisal remedies, a corporate restructuring will be considered detrimental to the economic interests of a shareholder, *inter alia*, whenever:

(1) The dissenting shareholders percentage in the subscribed paid-in capital of the simplified stock corporation has been reduced;
(2) The corporation's equity value has been diminished, or
(3) The free transferability of shares has been constrained.

Section 31. Conversion into Another Business Form. – Any existing business entity may be converted into a simplified stock corporation by unanimous decision rendered by the holders of all issued rights or shares in such business form. The decision to convert into a simplified stock corporation shall be registered before the *Mercantile Registry* [*include the name of corresponding company registrar's office*].

A simplified stock corporation may be converted into any other business form governed under the *Commercial Code [include the name of the relevant Code, Decree, Law or Statute]* provided that unanimous decision is rendered by the holders of all issued and outstanding shares in the corporation.

Section 32. Substantial Sale of Assets. – Whenever a simplified stock corporation purports to sell or convey assets and liabilities amounting to 60% or more of its equity value, such sale or conveyance will be considered to be a substantial sale of assets.

Substantial sales of assets shall require majority shareholder approval.

Whenever a substantial sale of assets is detrimental to the interests of one or more shareholders, it shall give rise to the application of dissenters' rights and appraisal remedies.

Section 33. Short-form Merger. – In any case in which at least 90% of the outstanding shares of a simplified stock corporation is owned by another legal entity, such entity may absorb the simplified stock corporation by the sole decision of the boards of directors or legal representatives of all entities directly involved in the merger.

Short-form mergers may be executed by private document duly registered before the *Mercantile Registry [include the name of corresponding company registrar's office].*

Chapter VI
Dissolution and Winding Up

Section 34. Dissolution and Winding Up. – The simplified stock corporation shall be dissolved and wound up whenever:

(1) An expiration date has been included in the formation document and such term has elapsed provided that a determination to extend it has not been approved by shareholders, before or after such expiration has taken place;
(2) For legal reasons or otherwise, the corporation is absolutely unable to carry out the business activities provided under the purpose clause;
(3) Compulsory liquidation proceedings have been initiated;
(4) An event of dissolution set forth in the by-laws has taken place;
(5) A majority shareholder decision has been rendered or such decision has been made by the will of the sole shareholder;
(6) A decision to that effect has been rendered by any authority with jurisdiction over the corporation, and

Whenever the duration term has elapsed, the corporation shall be dissolved automatically. In all other cases, the decision to dissolve the simplified stock corporation shall be filed before the *Mercantile Registry [include the name of corresponding company registrar's office]*.

Section 35. Curing Events of Dissolution. – Events of dissolution may be cured by adopting any and all measures available to that effect, provided that such measures are adopted within 1 year following the date in which the shareholders' assembly acknowledged the event of dissolution.

Events of dissolution consisting in the reduction of the minimum number of shareholders, partners or members in any business form governed under the *Commercial Code [include the name of the relevant Code, Decree, Law or Statute]* may be cured by conversion into a simplified stock corporation, provided that unanimous decision is rendered by the holders of all issued shares or rights or by the will of the subsisting shareholder, partner or member.

Section 36. Winding Up. – The simplified stock corporation shall be wound up in accordance with the rules that govern such proceeding for stock corporations. The legal representative shall act as liquidator, unless shareholders appoint any other person to wind up the company.

Chapter VII
Miscellaneous Provisions

Section 37. Financial Statements. – The legal representative shall submit financial statements and annual accounts to the shareholders' assembly for approval.

In the event that there is a single shareholder in a simplified stock corporation, such person shall approve all financial statements and annual accounts and will record such approvals in minutes within the corporate books.

Section 38. Shareholder Exclusion. – The by-laws may contain causes by virtue of which shareholders may be excluded from the simplified stock corporation. Excluded shareholders shall be entitled to receive a fair market value for their shares of stock.

Shareholder exclusion shall require majority shareholder approval, unless a different procedure has been laid down in the by-laws.

Section 39. Conflict Resolution. – Any conflict of any nature whatsoever, excluding criminal matters, that arise between shareholders, managers or the corporation may be subject to arbitration proceedings or to any other alternative dispute resolution procedure. In the absence of arbitration, the same disputes will be resolved by (*include specialized judicial or quasi-judicial tribunal*).

The decisions rendered by the tribunal are final and shall not be subject to appeals before any court.

Section 40. Special Provisions. – The legal mechanisms set forth under Sections 13, 14, 38 and 39 may only be included, amended or suppressed from the by-laws by unanimous decision rendered by the holders of all issued and outstanding shares.

Section 41. Veil Piercing. – The corporate veil may be pierced whenever the simplified stock corporation is used for the purpose of perpetrating fraud. Accordingly, joint and several liability may be imposed upon shareholders, directors and managers in the case of fraud or other wrongful acts done in the name of the corporation.

Section 42. Abuse of Rights. – Shareholders shall exercise their voting rights in the interest of the simplified stock corporation. Votes cast with the purpose of inflicting harm or damages upon other shareholders or the corporation or the intent of unduly extracting private gains for personal benefit or for the benefit of a third party shall constitute an abuse of rights. Any shareholders who act abusively may be held liable for all damages caused, irrespective of the judge's ability to set aside the decision rendered by the shareholders' assembly. A suit for damages and nullification may be brought in case of:

(1) Abuse of majority;
(2) Abuse of minority, and
(3) Abusive deadlock caused by one faction under equal division of shares between two factions.

Section 43. Cross-References. – The simplified stock corporation shall be governed:

(1) By this Law;

(2) By the formation document, as amended from time to time, or

(3) By statutory provisions contained in the *Commercial Code [include the name of the relevant Code, Decree, Law or Statute]* governing stock corporations.

Section 44. Promulgation. – This Act shall be effective as of the date of its promulgation and repeals any and all statutes, acts, codes, decrees or provisions of any nature that are inconsistent with this Act.

Chapter 6

OF TRADITION AND CHANGE – THE MODERNIZATION OF THE GERMAN *GmbH* IN THE FACE OF EUROPEAN COMPETITION

Ulrich Noack* and Michael Beurskens**

1. A LOW-SPEED RACE TO AN UNKNOWN DESTINATION

At 10:35 a.m. on 26 June 2008 the German parliament voted upon the most fundamental reform of the *GmbH* since its inception in the 19th century. The reform-bill called '*MoMiG*'[1] was introduced by the government more than one year before in May 2007,[2] following an internal proposal introduced in 2006. Even that draft was actually the government's second try at a reform. The previous attempt, the *Mindestkapitalgesetz*,[3] proposed in 2004, was only targeted at the minimum capital issue (by lowering the amount and requiring disclosure of registered capital in all written documents) and was not considered a sufficient solution to the numerous problems plaguing current practice.

Will the aforementioned event be remembered as an historical, or even dramatic change to German corporate law? Will it give rise to a new generation of young, dynamic businesses who profit from a superior corporate structure? The long preparations and the sheer number of changed articles might suggest that something big is afoot. Points raised in the ongoing debate regarding the *Societas Privata Europea*[4] and the contents of the recent proposal by the European Commission[5] seem to indicate that modern European (not only German) businesses require different structures than those presented in a statute dating from the late 19th century.

To understand the significance of the reform bill, one therefore has to acquire basic knowledge of the fundamentals of the *GmbH*, which have remained largely unchanged

---

* Professor of Law, Heinrich Heine University of Düsseldorf, Germany.

** Assistant, Heinrich Heine University of Düsseldorf, Germany.

1 *Gesetz zur Modernisierung des GmbH-Rechts und zur Bekämpfung von Missbräuchen* [Law on the modernisation of the law of private limited liability companies and to combat abuses], available on the website of the German Federal Ministry of Justice at <http://www.bmj.bund.de/media/archive/1236.pdf>.

2 *Regierungsentwurf* of 23 May 2007.

3 *Gesetz zur Bekämpfung von Mißbräuchen, zur Neuregelung der Kapitalaufbringung und zur Förderung der Transparenz im GmbH-Recht* [Law to combat abuses, to restructure the raising of capital and to strengthen transparency in the law of private limited liability companies], draft of 30 November 2004.

4 Recently at a conference on the European Private Company Statute of March 10, 2008 as well as a public consultation in 2007.

5 COM(2008) 396/3.

J.A. McCahery, L. Timmerman and E.P.M. Vermeulen (eds.), Private Company Law Reform

since their inception in 1892.[6] The *GmbH* was and is *not* simply a modified version of the *Aktiengesellschaft*, that is to say, the German (public) corporate form, but a distinct type of business organization designed for small and medium-sized enterprises.[7] As an *alternative* to the German public corporation,[8] it was specifically designed to provide a simple route to limited liability for small and medium-sized enterprises.[9] In this regard, German law differs significantly from the British and traditional US systems, in which 'private limited companies' are only a special type of corporation largely subject to the same rules as public or even listed companies.[10]

In how far should the rules for private companies differ from those on public or even listed corporations? The German legislator in the late 19th century followed a simple rule – leave the internal structure of closed companies to the shareholders, but enforce a strict regime of binding law with little room for freedom of contract on larger companies. Thus, unlike the *Aktiengesetz*,[11] the internal structure of a *GmbH* is largely left to its shareholders. While the *Aktiengesellschaft* features the oft-criticized distinction of a supervisory board and an executive board, the *GmbH* is generally based on a single-tiered management system, omitting the need for a supervisory board.[12] Furthermore, the shareholders may exercise direct control over the management and discharge them without cause.[13]

The other core distinction between the 'small', closed *GmbH* and the 'large', freely tradable or even listed *Aktiengesellschaft* lies with the capital system. A *GmbH* requires a lower minimum capital to be raised that is half the amount necessary for a public corporation (*Aktiengesellschaft*).[14] Similarly, there are fewer restrictions on distributions of assets

---

[6] This is in stark contrast to the law of corporations, which was not only fundamentally revised in 1937 and 1965 but has also been undergoing a 'permanent reform' (see W. Zöllner, 'Aktienrechtsreform in Permanenz – Was wird aus den Rechten des Aktionärs?', 39 *AG* (1994) p. 330 et seq.) since 1994 : *Gesetz für kleine Aktiengesellschaften und zur Deregulierung des Aktiensrechts* (1998); *Gesetz zur Kontrolle und Transparenz im Unternehmensbereich, Bundesgesetzblatt Jahrgang* 1998 Teil I Nr. 24 p. 786 (27 April); *Gesetz zur Namensaktie und zur Erleichterung der Stimmrechtsausübung, Bundesgesetzblatt Jahrgang* 2001 Teil I Nr. 4 p. 123 (16 January); *Gesetz zur weiteren Reform des Aktien- und Bilanzrechts, zu Transparenz und Publizität im Unternehmen, Bundesgesetzblatt Jahrgang* 2002 Teil I Nr. 50 p. 2681 (25 July); and *Gesetz zur Unternehmensintegrität und Modernisierung des Anfechtungsrechts, Bundesgesetzblatt Jahrgang* 2002 Teil I Nr. 60 p. 2802 (27 September).

[7] Cf., I.L. Lenhardt, 'The Corporate and Tax Advantages of a Limited Liability Company: A German Perspective', 64 *University of Cincinnati Law Review* (1996) p. 551. Admittedly, however, rules and ideas from one corporate form are often drawn upon to close gaps in the regulation of the other, for example regarding the voidability of decisions at shareholder meetings (skeptical: W. Zöllner in A. Baumbach and A. Hueck, *GmbH-Gesetz*, 18th edn. (Munich, Beck 2006) Anh. § 47, para. 3 et seq.) or groups of companies.

[8] R.B. Schlesinger, H. Baader, M. Damaska and P. Herzog, *Comparative Law*, 5th edn. (Mineola, Foundation Press 1988) p. 801 et seq.

[9] See M. Peltzer, J.P. Brooks, T. Hopcroft, and E.A. Voight, *GmbH-Gesetz – German Law Pertaining to Companies with Limited Liability*, 4th edn. (Köln, Otto Schmidt Verlag 2000) p. 1.

[10] U. Seibert, 'The Law Governing Capitalised Corporations in the Federal Republic of Germany (the AG and GmbH)', in J. Fade (ed.), *Basics of German Commercial and Economic Law* (Moscow, Beck 1994).

[11] § 23, para. 5 AktG prohibits deviations from the statute unless expressly allowed.

[12] Though such a board may be constituted voluntarily (§ 52 GmbHG) or might be required due to codetermination for over 500 employees (see *Drittelbeteiligungsgesetz, MitbestG, MontanMitbestG and MitbestErgG*) or due to special investor's needs (§ 5, para. 2 InvestmG).

[13] In the *Aktiengesellschaft*, decisions by the shareholders' meeting on management issues are expressly prohibited, § 119, para. 2 AktG.

[14] See § 5, para. 1 GmbHG; see also J. Armour, 'Legal Capital: An Outdated Concept?', 7 *European Business Organization Review* (2006) p. 5; H. Eidenmüller, B. Grunewald and U. Noack, 'Minimum Capital in the System of Legal Capital', in M. Lutter, *Legal Capital in Europe* (Berlin, De Gruyter 2006).

to the shareholders.[15] However, it is noteworthy that *limited* liability in the term *Gesellschaft mit beschränkter Haftung* is subject to certain reservations.[16] Specifically, the personal liability of (even good-faith) shareholders for violations of the capital rules by other shareholders is far stricter than in an *Aktiengesellschaft*. To compensate for that higher risk, fungibility of shares is severely limited by requiring supervision and explanation of the transfer-process by legally educated (and not entirely inexpensive) notary publics to protect less sophisticated investors.[17] The articles may, and often will, require a transfer to follow stricter requirements still, especially with regard to consent of all shareholders or compliance with rights of first refusal.[18]

In the last century, the *GmbH* became one of Germany's most famous legal exports[19] and was adopted in substantively similar forms by many countries around the world.[20] In this regard, it seemed that the *GmbH* was able to fulfil the hopes of its creators.[21] The peculiar blend of ideas from partnership law and corporate law as well as the high flexibility evidently not only interested German entrepreneurs, but also attracted the interest foreign legislators. In 2006, there were approximately 996,000 registered *GmbHs* – compared to an estimated amount of 7,000 registered[22] branches of British private limited companies in Germany.[23] According to a parliamentary inquiry, 23,496 new *GmbHs* were formed in 2005, while only 3,195 subsidiaries of English limited companies entered the public registers.[24]

Yet, as soon as the sturdy legal walls keeping out foreign European business forms fell,[25] the *GmbH* was subjected to increasingly less favorable comparisons to the British

---

[15] Compare § 30 GmbHG to § 57 *Aktiengesetz*.

[16] According to § 31, para. 1a, distribution to any shareholder lowering assets below the stated capital leads to a duty to return such distributions immediately. Furthermore, the *other shareholders* (even if they were in good faith!) are liable according to § 31, para. 3 if the beneficiary is unable to perform that obligation. Furthermore, under § 24 GmbHG, shareholders are also liable for the full payment of the registered share capital *by their co-investors* (!) although their liability is only subordinate.

[17] See § 15, paras. 3 and 4 GmbHG.

[18] See § 15, para. 5 GmbHG.

[19] See M. Lutter, 'Zur Entwicklung der GmbH in Europa und in der Welt', 96 *GmbH-Rundschau* (2005) p. 1, and the essays in M. Lutter, *100 Jahre GmbH-Gesetz* (Köln, Otto Schmidt Verlag 1992); see Schlesinger, et al., *supra* n. 8, at p. 830; see in detail B.W. Meister and M.H. Heidenhain, *The German Limited Liability Company*, 5th edn. (Frankfurt am Main, Fritz Knapp Verlag 1988) p. 24; J. Thiessen, '*Transfer von GmbH-Recht im 20. Jahrhundert—Export, Import, Binnenhandel*', in V. Duss, N. Linder, K. Kastl, C. Börner, F. Hirt and F. Züsli, *Rechtstransfer in der Geschichte* (Munich, Meidenbauer/Martin 2006) p. 446 et seq.; see also the comparative documentation by R. Süß and T. Wachter, *Handbuch des internationalen GmbH-Rechts* (Angelbachtal, Zerb Verlag 2006).

[20] Even the Limited Liability Company (LLC) adopted in many States of the United States is heavily influenced by the German *GmbH*, see Lenhardt, *supra* n. 7, p. 562, though it admittedly goes further in providing for optional member management and partnership like taxation. Interestingly, the US model replaced the German influenced GmbH structure in Japan, see A. Kaiser, 'Die Regelung der Hybridgesellschaft (godo kaisha) im japanischen Gesellschaftsgesetz', 53 *Recht der Internationalen Wirtschaft* (2007) p. 16.

[21] Wilhelm von Oechelhäuser, the 'father' of the GmbH-Statute in 1892 is quoted as saying: '*Das Land, welches die sichersten, einfachsten und mannigfaltigsten Rechtsformen für die Vereinigung von Kapital und Personen bietet, muss wirtschafthlichen Vorsprung gewinnen.*' [The country with the most secure, simplest and most varied choice of legal designs for incorporating money and persons must gain economic advantages.]

[22] In accordance with the Eleventh Company Law Directive of 21 December 1989 (Directive 89/666/EEC).

[23] U. Kornblum, 'Bundesweite Rechtstatsachen zum Unternehmens- und Gesellschaftsrecht, Stand 01.01.2006', 98 *GmbH-Rundschau* (2007) p. 25.

[24] *BT-Drucks*, 16/283.

[25] At the very latest due to the ECJ's aforementioned *Inspire Art* decision, see C. Jaehne and J. Henning, 'The European Court of Justice and the Future of the German Private Company (*Gesellschaft mit beschrankter Haftung*)

private company limited by shares.[26] While it is widely accepted that competition of regulators, like any kind of competition, is beneficial to the market participants,[27] the German legislature opted against a 'panic reaction'[28] to the newly discovered freedom of movement for European business organization forms.[29] Quite in the opposite both the drafting stage and the legislative process took longer than many businessmen (and lawyers) would have liked. While one might assume that such a long process will almost certainly result in significant changes, an overly drastic reform would have deterred investors and eliminated the advantages of existing case law, treatises and other literature. Thus, the mere duration of the process cannot serve as an indicator to the quality or size of its final results.

It also bears emphasising, that no empiric studies were undertaken in order to determine the demands of entrepreneurs and investors or even to determine the actual competitive situation *vis-à-vis* the British private company limited by shares. There were two separate and independent official reasons given for the reform.

For one, the *MoMiG* will follow the example set by other EU Member States (including Great Britain[30]) in lowering entry hurdles. While one might refer to this as a 'race to the bottom',[31] it is in accordance with oft-cited studies, which suggest that small and medium-sized enterprises select their form of incorporation based almost exclusively on base of cost of formation.[32] On this point, no public consultations took place before the introduction of the draft bill. Discussion only occurred on the basis of the governmental proposal which appeared largely 'out of the blue'. This is quite different from the approach taken, for example, on the European level, where public consultations and conferences tend to occur

– Editorial', 28 *Comparative Law* (2007) p. 33; but see also B. Angelette, 'The Revolution That Never Came and the Revolution Coming – *De Lasteyrie du Saillant, Marks & Spencer, SEVIC Systems* and the Changing Corporate Law in Europe', 92 *Virginia Law Review* (2006) p. 1189, at p. 1203 et seq. (noting that those decisions have not led to the predicted flood of foreign entities and a race-to-the-top/bottom).

26 Cf., most recently, H-F. Müller and S. Weiß, 'Die private limited company aus Gläubigersicht', *Anwaltsblatt* (2007) p. 247; V. Römermann, 'Die Limited in Deutschland—eine Alternative zur GmbH', 59 *Neue Juristiche Wochenschrift* (2006) p. 2065; V. Triebel and S. Otte, '20 Vorschläge für eine GmbH-Reform – Welche Lektion kann der deutsche Gesetzgeber vom englischen lernen?', 27 *Zeitschrift für Wirtschaftsrecht* (2006) p. 311.

27 See the detailed analysis of M. Ventoruzzo, ''Cost-Based' and 'Rules-Based' Regulatory Competition: Markets for Corporate Charters in the U.S. and in the E.U.', 3 *New York University Journal of Law and Business* (2006) p. 91.

28 Or as U. Seibert, 'Close Corporations – Reforming Private Company Law: European and International Perspectives', 8 *European Business Organization Review* (2007) p. 83, at p. 85 puts it: 'If you can't beat them – join them'.

29 Unlike France, Sweden and Spain, see T. Karst, 'Die GmbH französischen Rechts', *Zeitschrift für die notarielle Beratungs- und Beurkundungspraxis* (2006) p. 119; M. Wiberg, 'Sweden: Company Law – Reform', 21(3) *Journal of International Banking Law and Regulation* (2006), p. 19; C. Sverniov, 'Sweden: Company Law – Reform', 15(6) *ICCLR* (2004) pp. 55-6.

30 This is one of the main goals of the recent Company Law Act 2006, for example by dropping the requirement for a company secretary, annual general meetings, written decisions by simple majority and electronic communications. See UK Department of Trade and Industry, 'Companies Act 2006 – A Summary of What It Means for Private Companies' (February 2007), available at <http://www.dti.gov.uk/files/file37956.pdf>.

31 Further suggestions regarding competition between company law regulators can be found in C. Kirchner, R.W. Painter and W.A. Kaal, 'Regulatory Competition in EU Corporate Law after *Inspire Art*: Unbundling Delaware's Product for Europe', *European Company and Financial Law Review* (2005) p. 159 et seq.; H-J. de Kluiver, 'Inspiring a New European Company Law? Observations on the ECJ's Decision in *Inspire Art* from a Dutch Perspective and the Imminent Competition for Corporate Charters between EC Member States', *European Company and Financial Law Review* (2004) p. 121.

32 E.g., M. Becht, C. Mayer, and H.F. Wagner, 'Where Do Firms Incorporate?', ECGI Law Working Paper No. 70/2006 (September 2006), available at <http://ssrn.com/abstract=906066>.

before even the first draft is produced. Even in Germany such consultations or even expert groups are oft-employed, for example in the (failed) plans for a fundamental rewrite of the *GmbH*-statute in the 1980s. This may have contributed to the long delay between the first draft of the *MoMiG* and the eventual passing of the final reform bill.

In addition to competition,[33] the domestic desire for increased creditor protection was of at least comparable importance. As early as 2003, the government publicly asked for suggestions to prevent the oft-cited abuse of limited liability in practice.[34] If nothing else, this second reason for reform shows the questionable value of the current minimum capital requirement of € 25,000 at a time when many *GmbHs* enter bankruptcy with debts of € 700,000 or more.

The most visible changes of the reform bill deal with the *financial structure* of the *GmbH*.[35] Specifically, the introduction of the *'Unternehmergesellschaft (haftungsbeschränkt)'*[36] constitutes a visible step towards the demise of the minimum capital requirement.[37] On the other hand, the core elements of the *GmbH*'s *organisation* remain largely unchanged.[38] Still, a lot of window-dressing is bound to happen, including the elimination of superfluous rules,[39] the implementation of descriptive headings for all sections and some clarifications in the wording of the statute.[40] Insofar the 'modernisation' of the *GmbH* statute recalls the reform of the obligation rules in the German Civil Code in 2002.[41] Some of the changes introduced by the *MoMiG* do not only affect the *GmbH* but also apply to the (public) corporation (*Aktiengesellschaft*) and (according to the government's reasoning) also to the bankruptcy of foreign entities.[42] This chapter will examine the reform bill in three parts:

1. The first part will discuss changes intended to make the *GmbH* more competitive in Europe. These fall into two large groups: changes regarding formation and (smaller) modifications to the operation of the company.
2. Afterwards, the focus will shift to those changes meant to protect creditors in times of crisis. They are designed to prevent some forms of abuse and try to clear up some issues regarding financing through loans (or comparable actions) by shareholders.

---

[33] This goal is also emphasized by D. Leuering, 'Die GmbH und der internationale Wettbewerb der Rechtsformen', 39 *Zeitschrift für Rechtspolitik* (2006) p. 201.

[34] See U. Seibert, 'Die rechtsmissbräuchliche Verwendung der GmbH in der Krise – Stellungnahmen zu einer Umfrage des Bundesministeriums der Justiz', in G. Crezelius, H. Hirte and K. Vieweg (eds.), *Festschrift für Volker Röhricht* (Cologne, Schmidt 2005) p. 588 et seq.

[35] For more details on the current capital structure of the GmbH, see F. Dornseifer, 'Germany', in F. Dornseifer (ed.), *Corporate Business Forms in Europe*, 1st edn. (Berne, Staempfli 2005) p. 311 et seq. It is only slightly more flexible than the system for public corporations under the Second Directive that was largely modelled after German public corporation law.

[36] A new type of *GmbH* with a minimum stated capital of € 1, *infra* Section 2.1.2.2.

[37] See the essays in Lutter, *supra* n. 14 (dealing with public corporations) and the essays in 7(1) *European Business Organization Review* (2006).

[38] See Seibert, *supra* n. 28, p. 84.

[39] E.g., § 36 GmbHG, which exactly mirrored a rule under § 164 of the German Civil Code (BGB) but was deemed necessary in 1892, eight years before Germany even received a Civil Code.

[40] E.g., the term *Stammeinlage*, referring to the value of the share of the total capital held by a shareholder, will be replaced by the term 'share' or 'share value' respectively.

[41] Cf., *Gesetz zur Modernisierung des Schuldrechts* of 26 November 2001, BGBl. I 2001, 3138.

[42] Including the incompatibility rules regarding managers (*infra* Section 3.1.1), international mobility (*infra* Section 2.3), increased management liability for distributions to members/shareholders (*infra* Section 3.1.1) and rules regarding loans by members/shareholders (*infra* Section 3.2).

3. Finally, there will be a brief evaluation of the suggested changes and an outlook to the future.

2. Strengthening the competitiveness of the *GmbH*

Currently, the *GmbH* is only participating in a national competition. Since running a *GmbH* without any connection to Germany is impossible,[43] an entrepreneur is unable to select a *GmbH* for an enterprise operating exclusively on foreign soil. Similarly, even a German company may not employ a *GmbH* for its subsidiaries exclusively conducting business in the United Kingdom. While the *Cartesio* decision might change this, the current interpretation seems in line with ECJ case law, as *Daily Mail* seems to indicate that it is still in a state's authority to prevent entities from *leaving* their home country.[44]

The lack of foreign competitors worked both ways before the ECJ's *Überseering*[45] and *Inspire Art*[46] decisions. Without any alternatives, the *GmbH* had to be a success – if a German businessman desired limited liability, the *GmbH* was the cheapest choice available on the national menu of organizational forms. Nowadays, the *GmbH* seems to be losing ground to entities like the British private company limited by shares even on its national home field.[47] The reform bill puts the *GmbH* on the field of global competition for organisational forms and ease some of the long-standing formal requirements.[48]

With regard to its internal structure, few if any changes were deemed necessary. The *GmbH* has always been one of the most flexible entities in the world – requiring no 'secretary' or annual meetings and granting the shareholders almost infinite options in terms of structure (including, for example, the choice whether or not to create a supervisory board). The *GmbH* is also popular as part of corporate groups and can be (more or less) easily upgraded to a public corporation, that is to say, an *Aktiengesellschaft*.

2.1 Formation, especially the raising of minimum capital

In 2006, when the first draft was introduced, the process of forming a *GmbH* was not only deemed slow and tedious compared to the British system but was also unable to measure up against other recently reformed systems, for example in Spain.[49] Furthermore, the felt costs

---

43 See § 4a, para. 2 GmbHG (before the reform act), requiring the seat to be the place of actual operations; for a more detailed analysis, see *infra* Section 2.3.

44 ECJ, Case 81/87 *The Queen* v. *H.M. Treasury and Commissioners of Inland Revenue, ex parte Daily Mail and General Trust plc*. decision of 27 September 1988, *OJ* 1988, [1988] *ECR* 5483, at para. 24: '… Articles 52 and 58 of the Treaty cannot be interpreted as conferring on companies incorporated under the law of a Member State a right to transfer their central management and control and their central administration to another Member State while retaining their status as companies incorporated under the legislation of the first Member State.'

45 ECJ, Case C-208/00 *Überseering BV* v. *Nordic Construction Company Baumanagement* decision of 5 November 2002 – *OJ* C 323, 21.12.2002, p. 12.

46 ECJ, Case C-167/01 *Kamer van Koophandel en Fabrieken voor Amsterdam* v. *Inspire Art*, decision of 30 September 2003, *OJ* C 275, 15 November 2003, p. 10.

47 At least this result is implied by various authors emphasising the need for adaptation to English company law (see *supra* n. 26).

48 This is also emphasised by Seibert, *supra* n. 28.

49 Indeed, the formation of a Spanish *SLNE* (*sociedad limitada nueva empresa*) is supposed to take no more than 48 hours. Critics have argued that formation of a *GmbH* might take months – this is however only the case in complex constellations, including contributions in kind which require review by the courts. Following the general introduction of electronic registers in 2007, easy cases can and will be registered in a few days at most.

of formation are a decisive factor for small and medium-sized enterprises in selecting the legal regime for incorporation.[50] Thus, there was reason to fear that entrepreneurs might eventually take the 'cheap' route and prefer the fresh and modern British limited company to the established and venerable German *GmbH.*

The cost difference experienced by small- and medium-sized enterprises stems from two major factors:

- Firstly, the act of formation is subject to certain formalities, including the involvement of the aforementioned notary public.[51] The charter (*Gesellschaftsvertrag*) is reviewed by the court operating the public register.[52] Furthermore, companies in certain fields of business, including, for example, restaurants or repair shops, were only registered after official licences have been granted.[53] This amounts to a rather lengthy procedure from the initial planning to the availability of an operating entity with limited liability. However, for the period between inception and registration, the shareholders of the *GmbH* cannot rely on limited liability and risk personal responsibility for all debts incurred.[54]
- The second key hurdle is the necessary minimum capital. The shareholders of a German *GmbH* currently have to obtain a minimum of € 25,000.[55] However, only half of that amount has to be made available to the *GmbH* immediately before formation.[56] If there is only one shareholder, he must provide bank guarantees, mortgages or similar securities for the remaining amount.[57] There are special rules regarding the provision of capital by any means other than cash ('contributions-in-kind', *Sacheinlage*).[58]

Under the influence of the quick and easy formation of the British limited company, both lawyers and businessman have started to question these financial and administrative barriers imposed on limited liability. Nevertheless, the majority view of legal professionals[59] and also certain parts of the industry support the current system. Registration in public registers, and the filing of documents[60] and the certification of the corporate charter by a notary public only cause actual costs of about € 300. In comparison, a German employing a service provider to form a British limited private company limited by shares[61] will generally be required to pay approximately € 260 *plus* annual service fees of a similar amount for running a registered office in Britain.[62] Additional costs arise for filing annual reports and possibly tax documents. Furthermore, the German 'branch' of the British private com-

---

[50] E.g., a study by Becht, *supra* n. 32; see also Seibert, *supra* n. 28, at p. 85.

[51] § 2 GmbHG.

[52] § 9c GmbHG.

[53] § 8, para. 1, No. 6 GmbHG.

[54] Cf., § 11 GmbHG.

[55] § 5, para. 1 GmbHG.

[56] § 7, para. 2, sentence 2 GmbHG.

[57] § 7, para. 2, sentence 3 GmbHG.

[58] § 7, para. 3, § 5, para. 4 and § 9, para. 1, sentence 2 GmbHG.

[59] As evidenced in the decisions of the *Deutsche Juristentag*, see *supra* n. 4.

[60] In accordance with the First Council Directive 68/151/EEC of 9 March 1968 on coordination of safeguards which, for the protection of the interests of members and others, are required of companies (Directive 61/151/EEC as amended by Directive 2003/58/EC), thus similar to the other European Union Member States.

[61] See, for example: <http://www.go-limited.de>, <http://www.Limited24.de> and <http://www.limited 4you.de>.

[62] See <http://www.go-limited.de/preise/preise-und-agb.html>.

pany limited by shares must be registered in Germany,[63] leading to costs comparable to the registration of a German entity. A reasonable businessman will further look at hidden costs, including the availability of legal expertise and competent and speedy judicial decisions. Both of these factors work in favor of the long-established and well-accepted domestic form.[64] It has indeed been suggested to simply wait and see what happens, as in the light of these considerations only 'unreasonable' enterprises would elect to incorporate as a British limited company.[65] Since many dubious businesses have chosen a British limited company (due to its cheap formation), the foreign business form is beginning to suffer from a worsening reputation.

Nevertheless, the reform bill introduces a number of changes that will enable entrepreneurs to form a *GmbH* within a week by visiting a notary public and paying as little as € 1 plus the necessary fees (of the notary and the court).

2.1.1 *Formalities*

There was some debate as to whether formation should be possible by means of a mere written or even oral agreement.[66] The involvement of notary publics (who are educated as lawyers in Germany and bear public responsibility and liability for the *contents* of documents they draft) ensures a higher quality of the by-laws/articles of organization and provides sufficient warning to the future shareholders.[67] While this makes the process slower and more expensive, it serves to protect both creditors and shareholders.[68]

On that basis, it was somewhat surprising that the official government draft of the *MoMiG* seemed to introduce the new option of formation by mere written agreement in § 2, para. 1a of the *GmbH* statute. Thus, the eventual watering down of that idea in the final version of the bill was to be expected. While the idea of an easier and cheaper formation was tempting, the time was evidently not yet ripe for a mere written agreement without any explanations or warnings given by a legal professional. Much like medication limited liability seems to be made available only upon expert advice.

Still, the idea of simplification somehow prevailed. Instead of a written contract, explained by and signed before a legally trained notary public, an oral (!) agreement before the notary public (who is still required to warn and explain) is now sufficient in a very limited case (§ 2, para. 1a of the reformed *GmbH* statute). Those rules only apply when there are a maximum of three shareholders and only one manager with full authority *vis-à-vis* third parties and himself. Furthermore, the founders have to agree on certain standardized terms attached to the statute *without any amendment or modification.* Finally, a transfer of shares or any amendment to the articles requires full involvement of a legally trained notary public even in such a small and standardized entity.

---

63 As required by the Eleventh Company Law Directive of 21 December 1989 (Directive 89/666/EEC).

64 In this regard, it remains to be seen whether there is indeed room for a 'Delaware effect' regarding small enterprises or whether the traditional domestic systems will eventually be upheld. Fundamental reforms like the *MoMiG*, however, might eliminate the advantages of tradition and case law, see *infra* Section 4.

65 See Seibert, *supra* n. 28, at p. 85.

66 Like in Switzerland, where a recent reform replaced notarisation by a mere written agreement.

67 Unlike most LLC statutes in the United States, German law does not distinguish between the bylaws and articles of organisation. A single document discussing both the core elements and the details of internal structures (*Satzung*) is filed with the State and published according to the First Directive.

68 While others might argue that the notaries were only successful in their lobbying efforts.

The potential gain from this 'simplification' is questionable. The idea of a 'standard contract' is evidently a nod to the British limited company, which has provided prepared articles for quite a while, and the Spanish SLNE, which provides for formation under a check-the-box form. However, as so often, the version of that rule 'implanted' into the German system does not fit: while the *costs* of formation using standard terms are slightly (not significantly) lower, the *time* needed for formation will not decrease. While other states are moving ahead and allowing for formation online, Germany ignores modern communications altogether – even though authentication should not be an issue.[69] On the other hand, standardization would have been a strange criterion to eliminate the advice of a notary public – the formation of an *Aktiengesellschaft*, which under German law has very little freedom regarding its structure, should be easier as well.

While earlier drafts allowed for a check-the-box-choice among broadly stated corporate purposes ('Provision of services', 'Production of Goods', 'Resale of Goods'), the final reform bill returned to the level of specificity required under previous law. The decreasing importance of such statements in general[70] was deemed irrelevant.

The requirement for a substantive review of the formation procedure by the courts was not called into question at any point in the debate.[71] Formation within a day or less is possible only in the most basic cases.[72] The only (yet minor) change deals with the presentation of public licences. Indeed, such licences are needed for everyday businesses such as restaurants and property developers, as well as for other forms of trade, including car maintenance or handcraft.[73] As administrative proceedings in Germany (like in many other countries) can be slow, the previous rule linked formation to another, even slower procedure and prevented registration (and thereby limited liability) before those proceedings were finished. While the first draft required the court keeping the register to acquire proof 'within a reasonable period of up to three months', the final amendment eliminated the need for licences altogether. Therefore, such businesses are able to acquire the protection of limited liability earlier than before. The change is consistent with the modern view that the formation of an entity with limited liability and the acts of such an entity after formation are completely unrelated to each other. Even if an entity might act illegally after formation, that fear alone should not prevent formation from occurring.

Some acceleration may also be attributed to the introduction of electronic registers in early 2007.[74] While this is unlikely to provide a competitive advantage *vis-à-vis* other European entities,[75] it certainly eliminated certain delays. However, if any assets other

---

[69] See Directive 1999/93/EC of the European Parliament and of the Council of 13 December 1999 on a Community framework for electronic signatures.

[70] In the United States, it is customary to state the purpose as 'to engage in any lawful act or activity for which corporations may be organised and to exercise powers granted under corporate law.'

[71] In fact, a proposal shifting the burden of review upon the notaries was clearly declined at the *Juristentag*, see *supra* n. 4.

[72] This was and is the core argument for the introduction of the new SLNE in Spain, see F. Juan-Mateu, 'The Private Company in Spain—Some Recent Developments', 1 *ECFR* (2004) p. 60.

[73] § 1, para. 1 *Handwerksordnung* [Trade Regulation]; § 2, para. 1 *Gaststättengesetz* [Law on the regulation of inns and pubs].

[74] *Gesetz über elektronische Handelsregister und Genossenschaftsregister sowie das Unternehmensregister* (EHUG) [Act on electronic registers of trade and co-operative societies and company registers], *BGBl.* I 2006, 2553.

[75] As all Member States are required to provide such electronic registers under Directive 2003/58/EC of 15 July 2003 amending Council Directive 68/151/EEC as regards disclosure requirements in respect of certain types of companies, *OJ* 2003 L 221/13.

than cash are provided as part of the stated capital, the existing requirement for a (time-consuming) review by the court remains.

One might summarize that even though the draft took a brave, but insufficient step forward, the final version reduced this to almost nothing. Formation of a *GmbH* remains complicated compared to both the European competition and the commission proposal for the SPE (which would only allow for *either* involvement of a notary public or court review – but not both and specifically allows for on-line formation).

2.1.2 *Minimum capital*

One of the core issues subject to modernization was the need for a minimum capital.[76] To a (hypothetical) reasonable businessman, a requirement of € 25,000 does probably not seem a lot, considering the fact that *any enterprise* needs some operating assets.[77] Since the registered capital is money invested in the business; it cannot be regarded as 'bureaucratic costs' but is instead meant to ensure new companies a minimum foundation for their healthy operation or provide an entry hurdle regarding their seriousness of doing business. This position seems to be shared by the European Parliament in its resolution with recommendations to the Commission on the European private company statute, which also proposes a minimum capital.[78] The Commission itself however disagreed and did not implement such a requirement in their final proposal.

The amount actually required it is only half the amount necessary for public corporations,[79] and since it has not been increased for twenty years is worth significantly less in real value. Looking even further back in history, the drafters of the original *GmbH* statute envisioned a rather significant sum. In 1892, 25,000 *Reichsmark* was sufficient to buy a luxury home or employ ten teachers for a whole year.[80] On the other hand, lower entry barriers for limited liability inevitable draw people to a certain entity. The *GmbH* only grew in popularity after the huge inflation of the early 20th century, when it became cheap to form a *GmbH* and limited liability suddenly became an option for even the smallest entrepreneur.

The discussion of the minimum capital requirement in Germany mirrors the ongoing debate at the European level.[81] A strongly-voiced minority demanded the complete abolishment of the minimum capital requirement. They emphasized that other EU Member States grant limited liability without any or a negligible amount of capital.[82] It was also

---

[76] In fact, it was the core change proposed in the earlier draft of a reform bill of 2005, upon which the final version of the *MoMiG* is based.

[77] W. Zöllner, 'Konkurrenz für inländische Kapitalgesellschaften durch ausländische Rechtsträger, insbesondere durch die englische Private Limited Company', 97 *GmbH-Rundschau* (2006) p. 1, at p. 5; W. Happ and L. Holler, 'Limited statt GmbH?', 42 *Deutsches Steuerrecht* (2004) p. 732; R. Wilhelmi, 'Das Mindestkapital als Mindestschutz – eine Apologie im Hinblick auf die Diskussion um eine Reform der GmbH angesichts der englischen Limited', 97 *GmbH-Rundschau* (2006) p. 13, at p. 21 et seq.

[78] T6-0023/2007 of 1 February 2007.

[79] Under the Second Company Law Directive, this requirement is common to all EU Member States.

[80] See H-J. Priester, *'Mindestkapital und Sacheinlageregeln'*, in P. Behrens, P. Hommelhoff and D. Joost (eds.), *Die GmbH-Reform in der Diskussion. Sondertagung der Gesellschaftsrechtlichen Vereinigung (VGR) (Broschiert)* (Köln, Otto Schmidt Verlag 2006).

[81] See Lutter, *supra* n. 14.

[82] United Kingdom (Ltd), Ireland (PLC) and France (*SARL*) – both the Netherlands and Spain intend to follow suit.

pointed out that the current amount of € 25,000 in Germany is insufficient to provide any meaningful protection to creditors, while creating a serious hurdle for small enterprises.[83]

2.1.2.1 The correct amount

The government proposal initially opted for a conservative approach. The requirement of a minimum capital would remain; however, the amount required would be changed.[84] The explanation of the draft emphasized that the minimum capital would not only provide some form of protection to creditors but also impose a hurdle, an 'entry charge', for the privilege of immunity from (personal) liability.[85] This also guarantees that a *GmbH* will not be used as a liability shield for purely private conduct.[86] A non-insignificant amount of minimum capital is also supposed to signal quality and integrity to business partners and in this sense provides an acceptable substitute for personal liability.[87]

Even though a complete abolishment was therefore not the path that the legislator decided to follow, the right sum was subject to some debate. While it was suggested to increase (!) the amount in order to compensate for inflation and ensure better creditor protection,[88] another extreme proposal sought to have it reduced to a merely nominal amount (e.g., € 1).[89] Finally, the draft proposed a *slight reduction* to the 'European average'[90] of € 10,000. It was also identical to the amount required before the *GmbH* reform of 1980 (DM 20,000). The reasoning referred to *GmbHs* exclusively providing services and consequently needing less operating capital.[91] Indeed, a self-employed software developer may actually be content with an operating capital of € 10,000 (of which only € 5,000 has to be made available immediately).

The legal committee of the German parliament disagreed, however. Thus, the amendment of the *GmbH* statute voted upon in German parliament did not include any changes to the minimum capital. Instead of following the EC-wide tendency to lower the required amount,[92] the members of the German legislature agreed with industry representatives that

---

[83] In fact, it has been argued that the amount should therefore have been (significantly) increased, see Priester, *supra* n. 80, at p. 1 (extrapolating 25,000 *Reichsmark* in 1892 to its current value).

[84] See § 5, para. 1 *GmbHG* as amended by the *MoMiG.*

[85] See, e.g., B. Grunewald and U. Noack, 'Zur Zukunft des Kapitalsystems der GmbH – Die Ein-Euro-GmbH in Deutschland', 96 *GmbH-Rundschau* (2005) p. 189, at p. 190; see also the opinion of Advocate General Alber in *re Inspire Art* (ECJ, Case 167/01) para. 142: '[M]inimum capital rules … deter individuals from light-headedly forming companies'.

[86] See J. Vetter, 'Reform des gesellschaftsrechtlichen Gläubigerschutzes', in *Beratungen des 66. Deutschen Juristentages* (Munich, Beck 2006) p. 82.

[87] Eidenmüller, *supra* n. 14, at pp. 17, 23 et seq.

[88] H. Altmeppen, 'Änderungen der Kapitalersatz- und Insolvenzverschleppungshaftung aus 'deutsch-europäischer' Sicht', 58 *Neue Juristiche Wochenschrift* (2005) p. 1911, at p. 1912; H.-J. Priester, 'Die deutsche GmbH nach 'Inspire Art': brauchen wir eine neue? Bemerkungen zur 'Entrümpelungs'-Debatte' (EuGH, U. v. 30.09.2003 – Rs. C-167/01), 58 *Der Betrieb* (2005) p. 1315, at p. 1317; Priester, *supra* n. 80.

[89] See H. Eidenmüller, 'Die GmbH im Wettbewerb der Rechtsformen', 36 *Zeitschrift fur Unternehmens und Gesellschaftsrecht* (2007) p. 168; Triebel and Otte, *supra* n. 26; T. Drygala, 'Stammkapital heute—Zum veränderten Verständnis von System des festen Kapitals und seinen Konsequenzen', *Zeitschrift fur Unternehmens und Gesellschaftsrecht* (2005) p. 587, p. 598 et seq.; Eidenmüller, Grunewald and Noack, *supra* n. 14, at pp. 189, 193.

[90] Seibert, *supra* n. 28, at p. 87; it is also identical to the amount proposed for the EPC by the European Parliament in its Resolution with recommendations to the Commission on the European private company statute, T6-0023/2007 of 1 February 2007.

[91] W. Niemeier, 'GmbH und Limited im Markt der Unternehmensrechtsträger. Marktdaten zur Reformdebatte', 27 *Zeitschrift für Wirtschaftsrecht* (2006) p. 2237.

[92] See Seibert, *supra* n. 28, at p. 89 mentions France and Spain as examples.

any reduction would hurt the reputation of existing companies. Insofar they decided to keep the amount unchanged. The purpose of the minimum capital requirement to provide a buffer to liability and a barrier to formation remains intact. While a lower minimum capital might have removed some *psychological* disincentives, the € 12,500 seemed not to be overly burdensome.

Thus, the minimum capital remains unchanged even after the reform. While some might lament that this spells out as its 'failure', it is in fact not the most significant step taken to increase competitiveness. This is simply due to the fact that the normal *GmbH* might not even be the 'version' employed by young entrepreneurs – since the reformed statute provides for a completely new way to *start* business without following the minimum capital requirement.

2.1.2.2 *Unternehmergesellschaft* – A tricky alternative

The government draft of the *MoMiG* surprised everyone by introducing a completely new type of *GmbH* – the *Unternehmergesellschaft (haftungsbeschränkt)* (probably best translated as 'entrepreneur company with limited liability'). This gem, hidden in § 5a of the reformed *GmbH* statute turns the traditional system on its head and allows for formation of a company with a minimum capital of € 1. Unlike the reduction of the minimum capital for existing companies and the *GmbH* as a whole, this change made it through parliamentary procedures and might well be the most significant change in the *GmbH* statute up to now. While there was quite some debate regarding alternatives to the *GmbH* for tiny enterprises,[93] the *Unternehmergesellschaft (haftungsbeschränkt)* is a *GmbH* subject only to three modifications:

First of all, while a *GmbH* always carries the abbreviation *GmbH* in its name, the new subform are required to include *Unternehmergesellschaft (haftungsbeschränkt)* or the abbreviation *UG (haftungsbeschränkt)* in its name. It is noteworthy that the term *haftungsbeschränkt* (referring to limited liability) may not be abbreviated, thus reminding the public of the British limited company. The modified name distinguishes the *GmbH* (with a minimum capital of € 10,000) from its subform (with a minimum capital of € 1) and makes the different structure transparent to third parties.

Secondly, the *UG (haftungsbeschränkt)* does not require any minimum capital as such, but since all shares have to be worth € 1 the factual minimum is that amount (for a single-shareholder entity). While the incorporators are free to designate any appropriate amount below € 10,000, it is most likely that they will try to minimize costs and stay with € 1 per shareholder. The money has to be made available in cash to the future company; contributions in kind are not allowed.

Finally (and this is the tricky part), while the *UG (haftungsbeschränkt)* is not subject to strict rules on the upbringing and upholding of raising and maintaining a minimum capital (as there is no such protected capital), it is required to save 25% of its profits every year in order to raise its capital to an amount at least equal to € 10,000. As soon as it does so, it may call itself a *GmbH*. In other words, there is a mandatory saving requirement in order to eventually acquire the status of a 'full *GmbH*'. Before that time, those savings serve as a

---

[93] The reform was influenced by a draft bill suggested (though never formally introduced) by Jürgen Gehb (MP), see <http://www.gehb.de/positionen/ugg/Arbeitsentwurf-UGG.pdf>.

buffer for creditor protection, as they may not be distributed to the shareholders nor used for any purpose but covering losses.

Apart from these three modifications, the *UG (haftungsbeschränkt)* is a fully-grown *GmbH*: the rules of the *GmbH* statute apply directly and without any restriction. It is noteworthy that there are no specific liability rules or other precautions involved. Even under the different name – *UG* – the protection provided to creditors is no different from the rules associated with a 'grown up' *GmbH*.

The drastic departure from the minimum capital requirement regarding the *UG* shows that the days of such requirements are really running out. If the *UG* is able to work without any minimum stated amount, why should a 'grown-up' *GmbH* be a 'better' alternative only by requiring € 25,000? By giving entrepreneurs a choice between the two forms and allowing a *UG* to eventually grow into a *GmbH* (which will easily happen if annual profits cannot be discounted below € 100,000), German corporate law has opened itself up to a future without any minimum capital requirement. The lack of *additional* liability rules seems surprising – there is even no sanction attached to the distribution of the statutory savings amount. In this regard, further changes are likely to be forthcoming.

2.1.2.3 Procedure for raising capital

The complex system of raising the capital and not being able to remove assets from the *GmbH* up to the amount of the stated capital seems to remain intact. Still, a number of alterations regarding the procedure for raising the necessary capital are on the agenda. These seemingly small changes redefine the procedure to a point where it is almost completely different.

Currently, the shareholders must prove that at least a certain part of the full amount is available in liquid assets (i.e., in cash or in a bank account). If only a single person acts as a shareholder that individual has to provide guarantees for the remaining sum. Those guarantees are no longer be required under the reformed statute.[94] In other words, the requirements are lowered to the minimum level allowed for by the Twelfth Directive.[95]

If shareholders want to base their legal capital on anything but the aforementioned liquid assets (*Bareinlage*), they have to undergo complex and expensive procedures for the valuation of assets.[96] Finally, if any assets are lost (e.g., due to operating the business but also due to natural devaluation) between the agreement on the organizational contract (at the notary public) and registration, the shareholders are personally liable to the *GmbH* for that amount.[97] However, the registration of a *GmbH* may only be declined if there is a 'significant' difference between the alleged and the actual value of the items provided.[98] It seems likely that a lower minimum capital requirement might eliminate the need to provide assets in any form other than cash (i.e., 'contributions-in-kind').[99] As a result, a review would be avoided and formation could proceed faster.

---

[94] § 7, para. 2 will be completely eliminated.

[95] Twelfth Council Company Law Directive 89/667/EEC of 21 December 1989 on single-member private limited-liability companies, *OJ* 1989 L 395/40.

[96] § 5, para. 4 GmbHG; § 9c, para. 1, sentence 2 GmbHG.

[97] Since BGH case no. II ZR 54/80 of 3 September 1981.

[98] § 9c GmbHG.

[99] See Seibert, *supra* n. 28, at p. 89.

Two tiny amendments turn out to be revolutions, however. Firstly, § 19 para. 5 of the new *GmbH* statute allows any assets given to the *GmbH* to be immediately returned to its shareholders if there is a legally and economically valid claim for their return at any given time and the whole idea is explained at registration of the *GmbH*. This small change turns the idea of making contributions available to the *GmbH* upside down. While the current formalistic system is based on the provision of cash without any possibility of return, the new system corresponds to an economic approach, in essence taking the same approach one would take on a balance sheet. The actual form of assets is irrelevant as long as the assets are available at all, while a claim is sufficient as long as it is valid.

The traditional system invited circumvention. By actually requiring the provision of cash or, alternatively, a complex and expensive evaluation of the contributed items, the choice seemed clear. Many incorporators provided money and had their managers use that money to buy goods from them (as agreed upon earlier). Under the current system, the courts would generally require the tricky incorporator to return his cash contribution in full in exchange for the return of the goods. In bankruptcy, however, the incorporator's claim against the *GmbH* would in effect be worthless, while the *GmbH*'s claim would be quite valid. The new *GmbH* statute tries to balance the sanctions: Instead of requiring a return of the contribution in full, the incorporator (or shareholder) is only liable for the difference.[100] However, while the initial proposal simply considered the circumvention as a valid provision of the necessary assets, the final reform specifically considers it illegal and only allows for a reduction by the value of the assets actually provided.

2.1.2.4 Capital maintenance

In general, stated capital only gains relevance if it is connected to rules preventing the money from being distributed to the shareholders. Consequently, distributions are prohibited if they lower the company's assets below the stated capital.[101]

Under the new, relaxed standard, managers are allowed to provide assets to shareholders lowering the assets below the stated capital, *if* there is a valid counterclaim for their return (or a contractually agreed upon corporate group). This is the case if an eventual benefit of the same amount will be made available in the future.[102] This is meant to provide more flexibility to corporate groups by expressly allowing 'cash-pooling'. In a corporate group, a parent company will often 'pool' liquidity from subsidiaries by transferring money from them. The available assets of the subsidiary are thus effectively reduced, but the subsidiary retains a claim against its parent in return, thereby making the whole process cost neutral in theory. Nevertheless, the German Federal Supreme Court (BGH) questioned such actions on the basis of the aforementioned rules on capital maintenance, which generally prohibit any distribution to shareholders (including the parent company) that would lower the total amount of assets below the sum of the stated capital and any obligations.[103] The new statute overrules this case law. Since the sum on the balance sheet does not change, the transaction is considered irrelevant with regard to corporate assets and is therefore legal.

---

[100] § 19, para. 4 GmbHG.
[101] § 30, para. 1 GmbHG.
[102] § 30, para. 1 GmbHG, as amended by the reform bill.
[103] BGH case no. II ZR 171/01 of 24 November 2003.

2.2 Modernization of *GmbH* shares and transfer of membership rights

2.2.1 *Nature of shares*

Ownership in a *GmbH* is designed quite differently from as compared to a German public company (*Aktiengesellschaft*). There are no tangible or standardised 'shares' and there is no 'share register'. A 'shareholder' of a *GmbH* holds a part of the company capital (*Geschäftsanteil*) of € 100 or more, with a value divisible by 50.[104] Voting is *pro rata*. As there are no 'shares', the size of these parts of capital differs. To further complicate things, a shareholder may not hold more than one of these capital parts at the time of formation.[105] Dividing existing parts is subject to special rules.[106] The current system seems to be heavily influenced by partnership law.

The reform bill changes these requirements to make the current 'membership rights' conform more closely to shares. Under the reformed statute, every shareholder may hold more than one share and the value of each part can be freely determined (in multiples of € 1).[107]

2.2.2 *Transfer of membership rights*

Transferring membership rights (i.e., 'parts of the capital') in a *GmbH* is a complex procedure. Unlike shares, such membership rights cannot be transferred by trading certificates.[108] Even a written agreement between a shareholder and a purchaser is insufficient.[109] Both parties have to go to a notary public both to create an obligation to transfer and to perform the transfer itself.[110] The *MoMiG* does not change the fundamental way the ownership in a *GmbH* is transferred. The idea is to ensure that a purchaser is warned by a neutral person (i.e., the notary) before entering into an unknown business that might even give rise to personal liability under certain circumstances. It is also meant to prevent a 'grey market' for *GmbH* shares that would compete with public corporations traded on stock exchanges.

The transfer of ownership as such is not registered with public registers. However, the managers of a *GmbH* are required to file a list of shareholders with the registers at the penalty of personal liability to any creditor adversely affected.[111] This list is now available *via* online registers[112] to anyone willing to pay € 4.50.[113] However, even though courts

---

[104] § 5, paras. 1 and 3 *GmbHG*.

[105] § 5, para. 2 *GmbHG*.

[106] § 17 *GmbHG*.

[107] By eliminating the aforementioned rules regarding formation in § 5 *GmbHG* and simplifying the procedure for splitting shares in § 17 *GmbHG*.

[108] See official report on the *GmbHG* of 11 February 1892: '*... denn die formalen Voraussetzungen der Uebertragung müssen in erster Linie Gewähr dafür bieten, daß die Anteilsrecht der neuen Gesellschaften nicht zu einem Gegenstande des Handelsverkehrs werden.*' ['... the formal requirements on transfer must primarily warrant that the shares of the new companies do not become a subject of trade.']

[109] This was recently changed in Switzerland, see M. Abrell, 'Die Schweiz ermöglicht privatschriftliche Verfügungen über Geschäftsanteile', *Neue Zeitschrift für Gesellschaftsrecht* (2007) p. 60.

[110] See § 15, paras. 3 and 4 *GmbHG*.

[111] § 40 *GmbHG*.

[112] The central search mechanism of the commercial registers administered by the *Länder*, available at <http://www.handelsregister.de>; the central federal register, providing access to the commercial registers, available at <http://www.unternehmensregister.de>.

[113] § 7b JVKostO in connection with part 4 of the attached fee schedule.

may enforce the director's duty, current practice is rather lax. As a result, many *GmbHs* do not provide a current list of their shareholders.

The legislator is trying to reinforce the duty by providing stronger incentives. First of all, the notary public involved in the transfer of ownership rights is required to update the list and send it to the register (§ 40 para. 2 of the reform bill). Secondly, as in the case of the shareholder register of a corporation, only those shareholders on the official list are recognised in their rights.[114] Therefore, until the list has been updated and filed with the public register, the purchaser of membership rights is treated as a non-shareholder. It is assumed that this will cause the purchaser to force the directors to quickly file an amended list.

2.2.3 *Protection of good faith purchasers*

Currently, any new shareholder bears the risk that the seller was not in fact a shareholder and was therefore unable to transfer anything. This means that a purchaser always runs the risk that the seller has previously sold and transferred shares to a third party and was consequently unable to provide the promised shares. Even examining all previous deeds, that is to say, following the trail back to the formation of the *GmbH* (which might be as early as 1900), would not help him because there might still be a third party who purchased rights before the alleged owner.[115] Since there is no statute of limitations (insofar as the ownership of intangible, absolute rights is concerned) the danger of losing (assumed) ownership rights would exist perpetually.

The reform bill tries to protect a good faith purchaser if he relies on the shareholder list.[116] Consequently, an inaccurate list would prove a basis for reasonable reliance and the buyer could simply acquire the rights from the (listed) seller.

However, things are not quite that simple, as another layer of complexity was required to protect the (erroneously or fraudulently) unlisted shareholder. Firstly, any person may have an objection entered into the public register, thus preventing a loss of rights.[117] Additionally, reliance is only considered reasonable if the shareholder list was wrong for at least three years before the transactions or if the erroneous list may somehow be attributed to the rightful owner. Thus, a list remaining wrong for three years leads to the irrebuttable presumption of a mistake attributable to the shareholder. Therefore, any transaction within those three years eliminates the protection of the buyer. The only way to achieve at least partial protection is through the inclusion of indemnification and possible warranties combined with a penalty clause in the sales contract for the membership rights.

In sum, the changed rules might provide increased protection to the buyer under certain circumstances, but the situation is far from the complete reliance accepted in public registers such as the commercial register (*Handelsregister*) or the register of land titles (*Grundbuch*). The legislator (rightfully?) distrusts a shareholder list kept by the managers of small private companies. Even the amended duties of the notary public as such are

---

114 § 16, para. 1 GmbHG, as amended by the reform bill.

115 See Seibert, *supra* n. 28, at p. 90.

116 § 16, para. 3 GmbHG, as amended by the reform bill; highly sceptical: C. Peetz, 'Anmeldung einer Anteilsübertragung – eine eher unscheinbare Norm', *GmbH-Rundschau* (2006) p. 852.

117 § 16, para. 3, 2nd alternative GmbHG, evidently trying to copy the idea of the real estate registers (*Grundbuch*).

insufficient to approximate the authority of a true public register. Whether the amended rules really benefit the practice of mergers and acquisitions is questionable.[118]

2.3 Free movement of entities

As pointed out before, the *GmbH* has been one of the best-exported German legal constructs. Up to now, 'export' referred to the assimilation of core ideas of German law. Nowadays, under the interpretation of the EC Treaty's basic freedoms by the ECJ, German entities themselves are able to move abroad, that is to say, be 'exported'.[119] There are two legal hurdles hindering the (theoretical) free movement of German entities under the current law. German law does this in two core ways:

- On a corporate law level, each *GmbH* or *Aktiengesellschaft* currently has to register its 'real seat'.[120] That seat should generally be the center of administration, that is to say, the place where the corporate headquarters are located and decisions are made. Since only German registers allow for 'proper' registration of German associations, this essentially requires the seat to be in Germany. In 1998, the legislator amended specific rules stating the requirement of a seat in Germany.[121]
- On a conflict of laws level, Germany follows the 'real seat theory'.[122] Therefore, the law applicable to a company is determined by the place of the main administration or the center of business activities ('real seat' as opposed to 'statutory seat', see also Article 7 of the Statute for a European Company).[123] If a company has its main offices (i.e., the 'seat' used in conflict of laws) outside Germany's borders, foreign law will be applied. It is possible to apply the rules of the German *GmbH* or *Aktiengesellschaft* only if the main offices are in Germany.[124]

The *MoMiG* removed the *first* of these limitations. It eliminates the rules added in 1998 and allows both *GmbHs* and *Aktiengesellschaften* to register at any place they see fit. If they operate from another State, they are required to provide a contact address in Germany. One

---

118 See M. Schockenhoff and A. Höder, 'Gutgläubiger Erwerb von GmbH-Anteilen nach dem MoMiG: Nachbesserungsbedarf aus Sicht der M&A-Praxis', 27 *Zeitschrift für Wirtschaftsrecht* (2006) p. 1841 et seq. (discussing a previous draft).

119 It is debatable whether the EC Treaty does in fact provide for the freedom to move a corporation to another Member State if that State does not expressly allow it, see ECJ, Case 81/87 *The Queen* v. *H.M. Treasury and Commissioners of Inland Revenue, ex parte Daily Mail and General Trust plc.* decision of 27 September 1988, *OJ* 1988, [1988] *ECR* 5483, at para. 24: '... Articles 52 and 58 of the Treaty cannot be interpreted as conferring on companies incorporated under the law of a Member State a right to transfer their central management and control and their central administration to another Member State while retaining their status as companies incorporated under the legislation of the first Member State.'

120 See already, e.g., RGZ 7, 69 f; 88, 55; 107, 97; BGHZ 19, 105; BGHZ 29, 328.

121 § 4a, para. 2 GmbHG; § 5 *Aktiengesetz*.

122 See K. Baelz and T. Baldwin, 'The End of the Real Seat Theory (*Sitztheorie*): The European Court of Justice Decision in *Ueberseering* of 5 November 2002 and its Impact on German and European Company Law', 3 *German Law Journal* (2002).

123 Council Regulation (EC) No. 2157/2001 of 8 October 2001 on the Statute for a European company (SE), *OJ* L 294, 10.11.2001, p. 1: 'The registered office of an SE shall be located within the Community, in the same Member State as its head office. A Member State may in addition impose on SEs registered in its territory the obligation of locating their head office and their registered office in the same place.'

124 See N. Preuß, 'Die Wahl des Satzungssitzes im geltenden Gesellschaftsrecht und nach dem MoMiG-Entwurf', 98 *GmbH-Rundschau* (2007) p. 57.

necessary modification for such 'delocalized' companies is the new requirement of a registered office within Germany, where court actions against the company may be filed.[125]

The *second* hurdle is not directly affected by the *MoMiG*. Germany generally still follows the real seat theory; however the reformed *GmbH* statute impliedly abolishes the real seat theory for German entities operating on foreign soil. As long as the foreign state follows the incorporation theory, the reform works out well.

This holds especially true on the European continent: Articles 43 and 48 of the EC Treaty and ECJ case law require Member States to accept entities from another Member State 'as such', that is to say, apply their domestic law, thus in fact requiring these Member States to abolish the real seat theory in favor of the incorporation theory for such entities. Since the free movement of entities is also available in the EFTA States, a similar principle applies to Iceland, Liechtenstein, Norway and Switzerland. Similarly, the United States and various other countries are obliged to accept a *GmbH* due to bilateral treaties.

It is noteworthy, however, that there is a government draft intent upon abolishing the real seat theory in favor of the incorporation theory. Even though there are certain reservations and modifications, this statute (if passed) would finally allow any company from any country to move to Germany and operate exclusively from there. Of course this poses risks to creditors, employees and other third parties coming into contact with such entities – yet in an open market a protectionist approach can not and will not prevail forever.

The changes are of special importance to German corporate groups operating in foreign countries, which up to now had to adopt foreign entities for their subsidiaries.[126] This causes significant costs and legal risks that could be avoided by employing the well-known and established German *GmbH*. Furthermore, forming *GmbH*s with their registered seat in Germany will also lead to international jurisdiction of German courts,[127] thereby turning them into a well-known forum. Whether this is an advantage (as it would be an *additional* forum to the place of the registered office) is subject to debate.[128] It remains to be seen, however, if this change will also cause foreigners to adopt the *GmbH*, much like Germans have embraced the British Limited company.

3. Creditor protection

As shown, the reform does not eliminate most of the complex formalities created by the 100-year-old *GmbH* statute. Instead, the legislator is trying to focus on one of the core benefits of the current structure by strengthening the rules of creditor protection.[129] While not competing for the 'cheapest entity', the *GmbH* might inspire more trust in creditors and thereby eventually protect their shareholders better than competing forms.

Even now, a complex system of statutory and case law rules seeks to ensure that shareholders are unable to enrich themselves at the expense of the company or its creditors by

---

[125] § 4a, para. 1 GmbHG, as amended by the reform bill.

[126] See U. Noack and D. Zetzsche, *Germany's Corporate and Financial Law 2007: (Getting) Ready For Competition*, Center for Business and Corporate Law (CBC) Working Paper No. 28 (2007), available at <http://ssrn.com/abstract=986357>.

[127] See Articles 2(1) and 60 of Council Regulation (EC) No. 44/2001 of 22 December 2000 on the jurisdiction and the recognition and enforcement of judgments in civil and commercial matters.

[128] Highly skeptical: Eidenmüller, *supra* n. 89, at p. 205 et seq.

[129] See § 33 of the reformed GmbHG.

requiring the repayment of certain assets that they received out of company funds in the case of insolvency. The reform bill adds some additional checks and balances to that system. Even more complex rules govern corporate groups, but these are beyond the scope of this chapter.

3.1 Stricter liability rules

3.1.1 *Increased manager responsibility*

The managers of a *GmbH* are required to file for bankruptcy if the company is unable to meet its obligations or if its debts exceed available assets.[130] If they do not act immediately, they will become liable for any losses caused thereby.[131] The reform bill adds further liability for payments (eventually) leading to an inability to pay debts as they fall due, that is to say, insolvency.[132]

If such payments are made, even if there was an obligation to do so, the manager becomes personally liable. This is comparable to the 'solvency test' under British law,[133] but it is not quite a 'wrongful trading rule'. In case of doubt, the manager might even be required to leave office in order to evade the (all but impossible) choice of not following (theoretically binding) orders or violating the duty to protect the *GmbH*'s assets in favor of its creditors. There was a voluntary decision against a full wrongful trading rule, as such a rule causes unnecessary disputes and provides little certainty and protection to the directors. Even so, some legal scholars criticize the newly introduced combination of preventive creditor protection by the fixed capital system with conduct-oriented protection provided by flexible liability rules.[134]

The strengthened responsibility of the directors is further emphasized by extended grounds for disqualification that also apply to directors of branches of foreign entities, for example of a British limited company.[135] In addition, the new statute imposes joint personal liability (!) upon all shareholders if they knowingly allow a disqualified director to act on behalf of their company.

3.1.2 *Shareholder's responsibilities*

The reform bill also seeks to impose new duties upon the shareholders of a *GmbH*.[136] Under the current law, duties are generally imposed only upon the managers but not the shareholders. A conflict arises, however, if the shareholders instruct managers not to file for bankruptcy and even threaten them with liability for breach of fiduciary duties. Not too surprisingly, managers have occasionally escaped this predicament by fleeing the country.

---

130 § 64 GmbHG.

131 See BGHZ 29, 100, 102 ff.; BGHZ 138, 211, 214.

132 Seibert, *supra* n. 28, at p. 92.

133 However, replacing the strict formal rule of § 30 GmbHG, which prohibits any distribution that would lower available assets below the stated capital, with a flexible solvency test is also not planned and was actually voted down by a strong majority at last year's meeting of German legal professionals (*Deutscher Juristentag*).

134 Eidenmüller, *supra* n. 89, at p. 182, assumes two strictly alternative systems without any reason for combination.

135 Seibert, *supra* n. 28, at p. 92.

136 Since the rule is implemented in the Bankruptcy Code (*Insolvenzordnung*), it will similarly apply to the *Aktiengesellschaft* and any other legal entity operating in Germany.

The reform bill tries to solve the problem by imposing a duty to file for bankruptcy on the *shareholders* if (and only if) there is no management available.[137] The new amendment does not distinguish minority shareholders from influential participants. Furthermore, it is up to each shareholder to prove that he did not know of either the insolvency or the lack of a manager who could be reached. Current case law imposes personal (!) liability on managers for any obligations incurred after insolvency.[138] The courts will probably impose similar consequences on shareholders violating their duty under the new rule.

These rules are complemented by general provisions assigning the responsibility of receiving legally binding statements to the shareholders when the managers resign, die or are dismissed (§ 35, para. 1, sentence 2 et seq. of the reformed *GmbH* act). While early drafts also dealt with cases where managers simply 'disappeared', those rules have not become part of the final statute and are left to the courts to decide.

3.2 Loans by shareholders

Loans provided by shareholders to their company pose a regulatory challenge in a fixed capital system. One may treat such loans by shareholders exactly like loans by third parties, that is to say, one may require the *GmbH* to return the funds in full on demand (or the full quota in case of bankruptcy). However, it might be beneficial to actually prohibit such business relations with shareholders to force them to provide sufficient operating capital. Some States even have special statutes on such loans.[139]

Originally, the German Federal Supreme Court (BGH) regarded returning loans to shareholders in times of crisis as a breach of the manager's duty to protect the stated capital from being returned to the shareholders.[140] If the shareholders had not provided capital to the *GmbH* when a proper businessman would have done so, their loans were treated as part of the stated capital. In the 1980s, the legislator created special rules for such loans[141] that were connected to the hard-to-determine requirement of a 'crisis'.

The reform bill replaces these rules with a simpler codification in bankruptcy law.[142] The new solution tries to avoid the lack of clarity and complex case law of the previous system.

The new system follows the international tendency to 'subordinate' obligations to shareholders compared to obligations to third parties (only) in case of bankruptcy.[143] If a shareholder grants the company a loan when he should have provided it with capital instead, he will not be treated like a third-party creditor in bankruptcy. Instead, the obligation will be *subordinated* to almost every other creditor. Even if money was given in 'good times', the money is lost in insolvency if it was not returned to the shareholder in the year preceding bankruptcy.[144]

---

[137] § 15a *Insolvenzordnung* [Bankruptcy Code], as introduced by the reform bill.

[138] Both *vis-à-vis* the company and directly to corporate creditors (as a special form of pre-contractual liability since the creditors only contracted with the GmbH due to the assumption that it was not insolvent).

[139] Cf., Austrian law: *Eigenkapitalersatz-Gesetz* of 28 October 2003.

[140] See *supra* Section 2.1.2.4.

[141] Sects. §§ 32a and 32b GmbHG.

[142] § 39, para. 1, no. 5 *Insolvenzordnung*.

[143] As opposed to the current system, which is actually based on the (vague) concept of a 'crisis' and therefore theoretically provides protection even before insolvency.

[144] BGHZ 75, 334; BGHZ 127, 335, 340 et seq.

The new rules greatly simplify the system by eliminating the need for the rules developed in case law[145] and by regulating bankruptcy issues in bankruptcy law (and not in corporate law). The reformed rules no longer differentiate between shareholder loans replacing equity capital and other loans.[146] Furthermore, the removal of these rules from the specific context of *GmbH* law and placing them in general bankruptcy law is supposed to make them equally applicable to *all entities* with limited liability, including foreign companies that have their centre of business in Germany.[147]

Even cancelling the loans and thereby achieving a pay out *before* filing for bankruptcy does not protect the shareholders either. Any payments on such loans within one year must be returned to the *GmbH* in case of insolvency.[148] However, this is not up to the company's creditors: the assets must instead be returned to the insolvent firm at the request of the bankruptcy administrator. Thus, the approach avoids unnecessary litigation and the associated costs.

The current rules dealing with times of crisis beyond insolvency are abolished. However, this is at least partially compensated for by the new prohibition on distributions that might lead to an inability to pay obligations as they fall.[149]

The new rules might seem especially risky for smaller investors. However, the statute maintains special provisions in favor of minority shareholders holding less than 10% of the membership – not voting! – rights. Similar rules are introduced in the laws on public corporations. On this basis, a shareholder owning 10% or more of a public corporation might be unable to ask for payments on its loans in the case of insolvency. Another provision protects shareholders that enter a company during a crisis while trying to save the company by granting loans (*Sanierungsprivileg*).

4. Goal accomplished?

In November 2004 the German legislator officially started a reform process limited to the reduction of the minimum legal capital. Four years later a reform bill changes many details of the *GmbH* statute – yet the minimum capital remains unchanged at € 25,000. These are simple observations – but what can we make of them? Did the reform 'fail' or did it accomplish or even exceed the expectations of both legal scholars and businesspeople? Any analysis of the reform would be premature before seeing its effects in practice. Still, some general words are in order.

The magnitude of changes can be subject to some controversy: on one hand one might emphasize that no other reform act ever has changed so many parts of the *GmbH* statute – almost no article was left unchanged. A closer look reveals, on the other hand, that many of

145 See M. Lutter and P. Hommelhoff, *GmbH-Gesetz. Kommentar*, 16th edn. (Cologne, Schmidt 2004) § 32a, para. 10.

146 Skeptical, e.g., P.O. Mülbert, 'A Synthetic View of Different Concepts of Creditor Protection, or: A High-Level Framework for Corporate Creditor Protection', 7 *European Business Organization Review* (2006) p. 357, at p. 397 et seq.; H. Eidenmüller, 'Gesellschafterdarlehen in der Insolvenz', in A. Heldrich, et al. (eds.) *Festschrift für Claus-Wilhelm Canaris*, Book 2 (Munich, Beck 2007) p. 49; T. Bezzeberger, 'Kapitalersetzende Gesellschafterdarlehen im Recht der GmbH', in H.P. Westermann and K. Mock, *Festschrift für Gerold Bezzenberger zum 70. Geburtstag* (Berlin, De Gruyter 2000) p. 23.

147 See Seibert, *supra* n. 28, at p. 91.

148 § 135 *Insolvenzordnung*, as amended.

149 See *supra* Section 3.1.1.

the changes are mere window-dressing (or even window-cleaning). The new *GmbH* statute keeps most of what people love and hate. This is well in line with public opinion: At the 2006 annual conference of German legal professionals (*Deutscher Juristentag*) a clear majority opposed the introduction of new organizational forms.[150] The reasoning behind this approach is that the current system generally works out well and any innovative system designed on the drawing board would have to be subjected to years of court cases to finally reach a sufficiently certain state. The *GmbH* is a form of business organization supported by strong case law, legal writing and expertise. A new legal entity would have diverted the legal focus and, in consequence, decreased transparency. Instead of creating internal competition, the legislator chose (in line with many scholars) to focus on optimising existing legal forms.[151]

The 'interesting' changes deal with the capital structure. Each of the three pillars of the traditional financial structure of German closed companies was subjected to close review and changed.

The *Unternehmergesellschaft (haftungsbeschränkt)* requiring only an amount of € 1 per shareholder (i.e., a single person entity requires exactly € 1) is a radical departure from the *minimum capital requirement.* It is an experiment to see, whether it is feasible to allow anyone to easily acquire limited liability and whether legal forms of this type provide sufficient creditor protection. A 'clean slate' reform might have dropped the requirement for the *GmbH* as such – including any existing entities. But such a radical departure was politically impossible.

The strict requirements on the *raising of the initial capital* have been eased. While the traditional reading would have required the shareholders to provide the necessary sum in cash (without any way to get their money returned before liquidation), the new statute significantly modifies that rule: as long as the shareholders have sufficient funds and are required to provide these at any time there is no need to (permanently and actually) provide funds to their company. Once again, the reform bill did not implement that idea as a clean slate approach would have, however: it is still impossible to form a company based on the mere guarantee of funds (with liability only to the company) – instead the funds have to be provided once and returned thereafter. Similarly, the strict rules on contributions in kind still apply (and are even subject to criminal sanctions) – but carry no civil law consequences as long as the assets provided reach or exceed the value of the agreed upon contribution. This does not only seem confusing – but does in fact put the *director* of a *GmbH* at unnecessary risk of personal liability.

Finally, the rules *prohibiting the distribution of assets* were restricted to cases where the shareholder will not be required or will be unable to return those distributions. Again this seems to be a logical step – the exact position of the assets on the balance sheet is irrelevant as long as the sum remains the same. And as above the director is the person required to take responsibility if things turn out unexpectedly – he has to ensure that the shareholder will be able to return the distributions (even if he knows nothing about their personal situation and is dependent upon their vote to remain in office).

Even today, more than a hundred years after the original inception of the *GmbH*, the precise needs of legal entities for small- and medium-sized enterprises remain unclear. This

---

150 See *supra* n. 4.

151 Eidenmüller, *supra* n. 89, at p. 181 et seq.

lack of clarity affects both sides: the investors, entrepreneurs or shareholders on one hand and the creditors, employees and the public on the other.

The reform bill builds on an established legal form that has traditionally protected creditors (against total losses) as well as shareholders (against personal liability). As a result, the *GmbH* will remain a trusted and well-accepted entity even after the reform. The formula is simple: '*Never (fundamentally) change a running system*'. Critics may argue that at its core the *MoMiG* is only a (partial) revocation of case law and prior statutory changes. The prohibition on returning shareholder loans in times of crisis, introduced in 1980, will be abolished in favor of special rules of bankruptcy law. The express statutory requirement to have a seat in Germany, introduced in 1998, will be replaced by rules expressly allowing *GmbH*s to have a seat in another country. In addition, years of case law limiting distributions to shareholders will be eliminated.

Even after the reform, formation will remain complex and expensive. However, these deficiencies have been and will be compensated for by a high level of flexibility during operation. The established system of creditor protection combined with the planned improvements will guarantee a certain level of trust exceeding that of many foreign entities. In addition, the lowered entry 'price' of limited liability might attract new small and medium-sized enterprises. While some businesses might still dislike the *GmbH* (even after the reform), it is not quite clear whether it would be advantageous to orient the corporate system on the basis of their needs.

Maybe the perspective of flat-out competition between all legal forms and legislators is erroneous in itself altogether. If the Darwinian theory of evolution prevails,[152] legislators might do best to seek specific niches and make their entities fit there, instead of trying to satisfy *everyone's* needs. Insofar the *GmbH* would fill a gap between expensive and complex public entities and cheap entry-level entities for tiny enterprises.

The core advantage of domestic forms remains[153] – there is little qualified legal advice available for foreign entities. Furthermore, cross-border operations still incur higher administrative costs. Many creditors and third parties will doubt any foreign concepts (as indicated by their respective firms) and consider such entities less trustworthy. In fact, even the *GmbH* was subject to considerable scepticism at the time of its inception, even being called a *Gesellschaft mit beschränkter Hochachtung* (a 'limited respectability' company).[154] Thus, while it is hard to grasp such prejudices by means of simple statistics, it is unclear whether the competition between legal forms across Europe will indeed work out as fairly as hoped. There is a risk that many parties will refuse to deal with unknown entities or that lawyers will advise against foreign forms due to lack of experience.[155] This leads to a demand for higher personal guarantees from managers and shareholders, which might ultimately drain away the benefits of limited liability.

Thus, the reform cut out (seemingly) unnecessary formalities and complexities from German corporate law, while not turning traditional German law into a clone of British,

---

[152] In its original sense, 'survival of the fittest' means that the creature best suited to a certain situation will prevail under those conditions, leading to a distribution of numerous beings and not a single dominant species.

[153] Sceptical: Triebel and Otte, *supra* n. 26.

[154] As translated by Lenhardt, *supra* n. 7, at p. 553.

[155] This is also an oft-quoted reason for the lack of importance of the CISG in legal practice, see J.E. Murray, Jr., 'The Neglect of CISG: A Workable Solution', 17 *Journal of Law and Commerce* (1998) p. 365: 'Reflecting on the experience under CISG, we now face the reality that it suffers from neglect, as well as ignorance and even fear.'

Spanish or Danish law. It will probably not make British entrepreneurs opt for a *GmbH*, nor will it convince every German businessman that paying the higher entry costs (compared to a British limited company) is worthwhile. However, the *MoMiG* is more than mere window dressing but constitutes a brave experiment in German corporate law reform. It remains to be seen to what extent comparable efforts in Denmark and the Netherlands will follow the German example[156] or introduce better, innovative ideas.

[156] As Germany did in partially considering the recent reforms in Spain and France as well as British company law.

Chapter 7

REFORM OF DUTCH PRIVATE COMPANY LAW

Maarten J. Kroeze* and Jan Berend Wezeman**

1. INTRODUCTION

The Dutch private company ('*besloten vennootschap*' or '*BV*') was introduced in the Netherlands in 1971. An important reason for the introduction of the private company statute was to avoid – at least temporarily – the applicability of a European directive forcing Dutch companies to publish financial statements and to avoid the applicability of future directives.[1] As a consequence, the Dutch private company has never had a clear profile. The private company statute was, and still is, an almost 100% copy of the public company statute (a public company is in Dutch '*naamloze vennootschap*' or '*NV*').

In the decades after 1971 the Dutch legislator had no ambition to give the private company a character of its own. On the contrary: the European directives for the public company were implemented on a voluntary basis in the private company statute and it remained a mere copy of the public company statute. The private company statute functioned well and (almost) no complaints were heard. Apparently there were no outside economic or social forces that urged a reform. This has changed, however, in the last decade.

First there were Dutch scholars who argued for a more flexible private company statute.[2] They argued that private companies – due to their *intuïtus personae* character – had more in common with partnerships and that the private company statute should therefore not resemble the rigid public company statute. These arguments started a slow change of opinion among Dutch lawyers and state officials. Then there was the case law from the European Court of Justice in the *Centros*, *Überseering* and *Inspire Art* cases,[3] which gave a strong impetus to the adoption of the internal affairs rule in Europe. As a result, competi-

* Dean and Professor of Company Law, Erasmus School of Law, Erasmus University Rotterdam.

** Professor of Company and Commercial Law, Faculty of Law, University of Groningen.

[1] *Bundel Naamloze en Besloten Vennootschap (documentatie en systematische gerangschikte wetsgeschiedenis)*, edited by J.M.M. Maeijer, Ixc-a (Collected Parliamentary Papers; loose-leaf). At the time, the Netherlands was the only country in the European Economic Community without a limited company resembling, e.g., the German *GmbH* or the French *SaRL*. See W. Westbroek, 'Is een nadere profilering van de b.v. wenselijk', *De besloten vennootschap* (Deventer, Kluwer 1985).

[2] For example: M.J.G.C. Raaijmakers, *Rechtspersonen tussen contract en instituut* (Deventer, Kluwer 1987); L. Timmerman, 'Is versoepeling van het Nederlandse n.v./b.v.-recht wenselijk?', *TVVS* (1992) p. 163; H.J. de Kluiver, 'Het vennootschapsrecht dient te worden versoepeld … en verscherpt', *TVVS* (1992) p. 174.

[3] CJEC 9 March 1999, case C-212/97, *ECR* 1999, p. I-1459 (*Centros*); CJEC 5 November 2002, case C-208/00, *ECR* 2002, p. I-9919 (*Überseering*); CJEC 30 September 2003, case C-167/01, *ECR* 2003, p. I-10155 (*Inspire Art*).

J.A. McCahery, L. Timmerman and E.P.M. Vermeulen (eds.), Private Company Law Reform

tion between company statutes of the member states in the European Union was further stimulated.[4] This case law was the immediate cause of the reform of Dutch private company law by the Dutch Ministry of Justice and Ministry of Economic Affairs. Since May 2007, a Bill to amend the private company statute (the 'Private Company Law (Simplification and Flexibilization) Act') is pending before the Dutch Parliament and subject to debate in Parliament.[5] The Ministries of Justice and of Economic Affairs hope that this Bill will be passed by Parliament in 2010. The *Private Company Law (Simplification and Flexibilization) Act* will lead to changes in Book 2 of the Dutch Civil Code (hereafter: DCC), which regulates legal persons.

A consequence of the fact that the private company statute was established in 1971 for reasons other than a specific need for a flexible private company (as a business form complementary to the public company and the partnership) was that a real debate on the basic assumptions for a private company statute has never been held in the Netherlands. And even now, on the eve of a new Dutch private company statute, the debate focuses mainly on practical issues and not on basic assumptions. In this contribution we will start with some thoughts on the functions of private company statutes (Section 2) and the characteristics of the typical private company (Section 3). We will then highlight the most important features of the new private company statute (Section 4). These features illustrate that the new Dutch private company statute will be much better suited to the functions a private company statute ought to have than our current private company statute. These features are also much more attuned to the characteristics of the typical private company. We end this contribution with some short remarks on the position of the Dutch private company in a competitive European legal environment (Section 5) and with some concluding remarks (Section 6).

At this moment there is also a Dutch Bill on partnerships pending before Parliament.[6] The new Dutch law on partnerships will presumably enter into force in 2010 or 2011. Because the Dutch private company can be structured more like a partnership under the new private company statute the legal form of the private company and the legal form of the partnership will converge in the future. This effect will be enhanced by the possibility to establish a Dutch partnership with legal personality under the new Partnership Act. Partners in a partnership with legal personality do not, however, have the advantage of limited liability. They are fully liable for the obligations of the partnership. In the view of the Minister of Justice, legal personality will mainly simplify the internal property structure in a partnership. Furthermore, the new Partnership Act will make it possible to convert a partnership with legal personality into a private company and *vice versa*. Therefore there will be a more fluent spectrum of legal forms for businesses in the Netherlands. The Minister of Justice announced some time ago that he is not in favor of adopting a Dutch form of

---

[4] Report-De Kluiver (Vereenvoudiging en flexibilisering van het Nederlandse BV-recht), pp. 181-182, F.J.P. van den Ingh, and R.G.J. Nowak (eds.), *Vereenvoudiging en flexibilisering BV-recht, deel I, De pre-parlementaire geschiedenis* (Deventer, Kluwer 2006).

[5] Parliamentary Papers II 2006/07, 31 058, no. 1-3 (the Bill is published on <www.overheid.nl > officiële publicaties > kamerstukken>). See H.E. Boschma, M.L. Lennarts and J.H. Schutte-Veenstra, 'The Reform of Dutch Private Company law: New Rules for the Protection of Creditors', 8 *European Business Organization Law Review* (2007) 567 p. See also the special issue on the reform of the Dutch private company law of the legal journal *Ondernemingsrecht* (2007-9). Important additional changes in this Bill are proposed by Ministerial memorandum of amendments of 24 October 2008 (31 058 no. 7) and 3 February 2009 (31 058, no. 8).

[6] Parliamentary Papers nos. 28 746 and 31 065.

the LLC or LLP.[7] We will not discuss the new Partnership Act in this contribution. We think, however, that it is good to know that Dutch partnership law and private company law will both be changed in the near future.

2. Functions of private company statutes

We will use an interesting phrase in the famous book *The Morality of Law*, written by Lon Fuller, as a starting point in this contribution. This phrase reads as follows:

> 'In one aspect our whole legal system represents a complex of rules designed to rescue man from the blind play of chance and to put him safely on the road to purposeful and creative activity.'[8]

This one aspect of our whole legal system is also relevant for a small part of the legal system. The phrase guides us in the direction of what we consider to be the two important functions of a private company statute. A private company statute has to put man '*on the road to purposeful and creative activity*'. It has to serve economic activities and purposes. In this instrumental role a private company statute will contribute to economic welfare. The second function of a private company statute is – in the words of Fuller – '***to rescue man from the blind play of chance*** *and to put him* ***safely*** *on the road to purposeful and creative activity*'. A private company statute has to serve legal certainty and has to protect justified interests of persons involved in a private company. This protection is not necessarily limited to the protection of minority shareholders and creditors. Majority shareholders too have interests that are worth protecting. As a generalization one could say that this second function serves fairness.

In a private company statute the function of fairness ultimately serves welfare. When creditors and minority (and majority) shareholders know that their justified interests will be protected under a statute they are less reluctant to do business with a private company or to become involved in a private company.

In general these two functions result in two types of rules in a private company statute: rules serving welfare and rules serving fairness (which indirectly serves welfare). Rules for private companies serving welfare are usually non-mandatory. Rules serving fairness are usually mandatory.

3. Characteristics of a private company

It is important to take a closer look at the private company as object of these rules. We will mention some characteristics of the typical private company that are relevant for a private company statute.[9]

---

7 Parliamentary Papers II 2007/08, 28 752, no. 6.

8 L.L. Fuller, *The Morality of Law* (rev. edn.) (New Haven, Yale University Press 1969) p. 9.

9 See for some of these characteristics: O'Neal and Thompson's *Close Corporations and LLCs: Law and Practice* (rev. 3rd edn.) (St. Paul, MN, Thomson/West Publishing 2008) § 19 ('Normal attributes of close corporation').

A first important characteristic is that the average private company has a limited number of shareholders. Shareholders know each other well, are active in the business of the company and usually hold a position as a director. The internal relations in a private company resemble that of a partnership.

A second characteristic is that earnings of a private company are not only distributed to shareholders by dividends but also in the form of salaries and, indirectly, in the form of social security premiums. Shareholders are often employees of the private company.

A third characteristic is that private companies as a rule do not have recourse to the capital market. As a result, there is no established market for the shares of a private company. The shareholders are stuck with each other by the impossibility of an easy escape.

A fourth characteristic is that the market for control and the media do not function as a corrective mechanism for the behavior of (mostly) majority shareholders and directors.

A fifth characteristic is that a private company has legal personality and that the shareholders of a private company – in the same way as shareholders in a public company – have limited liability.

To summarize: The private company has internal characteristics resembling those of a partnership and the external characteristics of a corporate personality. Shareholders are financially and personally deeply involved in the private company and have no easy exit.

4. Consequences for a Dutch private company statute

The functions mentioned in Section 2 and the characteristics mentioned in Section 3 should be determinative for a private company statute. We will take a closer look at the features of the new Dutch private company statute to see how these functions and characteristics have found a place in the new statute.

4.1 Internal characteristics: purposeful and creative activity

The fact that a private company has internal characteristics resembling those of a partnership justifies a flexible and enabling statute for private companies for matters concerning the internal structure of the private company. This gives shareholders the opportunity to organize the internal structure of their company to their needs. These are the rules that put shareholders in a private company on the road to purposeful and creative activity. As we wrote in Section 2 this is an important function of a private company statute.

The explanatory memorandum to the new private company statute mentions more internal flexibility as one of the important goals of the new statute. This internal flexibility should come with fewer mandatory rules and the abolishment of unnecessarily restrictive and ineffective rules.[10] We will highlight the most important changes contributing to more internal flexibility. Some of these changes are also determined by the aspiration of the Dutch government to have a competing legal form for the private company in Europe.

4.1.1 *Legal capital*

At present the Dutch private company has a compulsory minimum capital requirement of € 18,000. As a consequence of this minimum capital requirement the current private com-

[10] Parliamentary Papers II 2006/07, 31 058, no. 3, p. 3.

pany statute has (i) many sections dealing with the prevention of circumvention of this minimum capital requirement; and (ii) a strict capital protection regime. For example, there are strict rules for consideration in kind, for the division of dividends, for capital reduction and for the purchase by the company of its own shares. The issuance of shares for a consideration received in-kind (contribution in property or other non-cash items) is only possible when a description and a valuation by the founders or the board of directors of the property and other non-cash items has been made and an independent expert audited the result of this description and valuation and declared that the value of the consideration in kind was at least equal to the promised consideration.

These cumbersome rules will all belong to the past once the new private company statute enters into force.[11] Although the nominal value of shares will remain as a unit of account, the minimum capital requirement will be abolished. The consequence of this abolishment is that shares can have a nominal value of € 0.0001.[12] It is even possible to have a nominal value expressed in a foreign currency such as the American dollar or the British pound.[13] Because the minimum capital requirement will be abolished, the sections dealing with prevention of circumvention of the minimum capital requirement and the strict capital protection regime will be superfluous and likewise be abolished. This leads to a simple statutory regime for the private company and to more flexibility for founders to choose their most ideal internal capital structure. It will most probably also lead to a cost reduction. A report by a financial expert is no longer required when shares are issued for a consideration in kind. A capital contribution statement by the bank is no longer necessary when shares are issued against consideration in cash. In addition to these simplifications of legal capital rules the possibilities for a private company to buy its own shares will be broadened. The same applies to the possibilities for a private company to give financial assistance in connection with share transactions in its own shares. At present, financial assistance in this situation is not allowed (section 207c Book 2 DCC).

We consider the abolishment of the minimum capital requirement for private companies as a step forward in the development of Dutch company law. It is in a sense also a step back in history. In the past, before the EEC harmonization programme and the second EEC directive on capital maintenance, the concept of a minimum capital requirement was unknown in Dutch law.

The Minister of Justice and the Minister of Economic Affairs have considered the introduction of no par value shares.[14] These will not be introduced for practical reasons. The introduction of no par value shares would involve the amendment of large parts of Dutch company law and would possibly delay the entering into force of the new private company statute. The Ministers of Justice and of Economic Affairs made public that the introduction of no par value shares could be reconsidered for the public company as well as for the private company in the near future.[15]

---

[11] See B. Bier, 'Het verleden, heden en de toekomst van kapitaalbescherming', *De vereenvoudigde BV, Preadvies van de Vereeniging 'Handelsrecht'* (Deventer, Kluwer 2006) p. 181.

[12] Parliamentary Papers II 2007/08, 31 058, no. 3, p. 26.

[13] Remarkably, in a Dutch private company only one foreign currency is allowed. See B. Bier, 'Kapitaal en kapitaalbescherming', *Het nieuwe BV-recht voor de praktijk, preadvies Koninklijke Notariële Beroepsorganisatie* (Deventer, Kluwer 2008) p. 184.

[14] See on this subject the report written by J.H. Schutte-Veenstra, H.E. Boschma, M.L. Lennarts, *Alternative Systems for Capital Protection* (Deventer, Kluwer 2005) p. 37.

[15] Parliamentary Papers II 2006/07, 31 058, no. 3, pp. 22-23.

4.1.2 *Shares*

A lot of flexibility will be added to the internal structure of the private company by the new rules concerning shares.[16] The new private company statute introduces shares without voting rights, shares without financial rights (and with restricted financial rights) and shares with multiple voting rights. Section 228 paragraph 5 of the Bill on private companies (hereafter: Bpc) introduces shares without voting rights. Under the current statute it is in fact already possible to create shares without voting rights through voting trusts (*via* the issuance of depositary receipts to the provider(s) of capital (the beneficial owner(s) of the shares) by a foundation (the legal owner of the shares)). These constructions are less cost-efficient.[17] The introduction of shares without voting rights is therefore a step forward in our opinion. According to section 228 paragraph 5 in conjunction with section 216 paragraph 5 Bpc shares without voting rights must have full financial rights attached to them.[18] Otherwise the 'shares' will not be acknowledged as shares according to section 190 Bpc. The holders of shares without voting rights are allowed to attend the shareholders' meeting and to address the general meeting. According to section 24d paragraph 2 Bpc the shares have to be taken into account for the thresholds of some important minority rights. See, e.g., section 220 Bpc (right to convene a shareholders' meeting), section 224a Bpc (right to put items on the agenda) and section 346 DCC (right to start inquiry proceedings).

Section 216 paragraph 5 Bpc introduces shares without financial rights. The current private company statute does not allow this kind of shares. In partnership law it is not allowed to deny one of the partners any share of the profits. This so-called *Societas Leonina* will now be allowed for private companies. The explanatory memorandum gives as an example of the use of shares without financial rights a father who wants to leave all the profits in a family business to his children, but still wants a formal position to co-decide on business issues.

The current private company statute has a rather restrictive regime for shares with multiple voting rights. According to section 228 paragraph 4 Bpc this regime will be less restrictive in the future. The articles of association of a private company can stipulate that shares of a certain class have 100 voting rights and shares of another class only 10 (or even 1,000 to 1).[19] Section 228 paragraph 4 Bpc does not, however, allow a restriction of the voting rights attached to shares. The articles of association cannot restrict the voting rights, for instance, to a certain category of resolutions. A last change concerning shares is the extension in section 192 Bpc of the possibility to attach additional obligations to shares (for example obligations *vis-à-vis* shareholders or *vis-à-vis* third parties).

---

[16] See on this subject: T.P. van Duuren, 'De structuur en interne organisatie van de flexibele BV', *De vereenvoudigde BV, Preadvies van de Vereeniging 'Handelsrecht'* (Deventer, Kluwer 2006).

[17] Parliamentary Papers II 2007/08, 31 058, no. 3, p. 12. Also: H.J. Portengen, 'Naar contractsvrijheid voor de BV en haar statutaire inrichting', *De vereenvoudigde BV, Preadvies van de Vereeniging 'Handelsrecht'* (Deventer, Kluwer 2006) p. 99; and E.P.M. Vermeulen, 'De plaats en inrichting van een nieuw BV-recht in een innovatieve economie', *De vereenvoudigde BV, Preadvies van de Vereeniging 'Handelsrecht'* (Deventer, Kluwer 2006) p. 173.

[18] We do not understand why shares without voting rights and with only restricted financial rights are not allowed under the new private company statute. See also G.M. Portier, 'Stemrecht en certificering', *Het nieuwe BV-recht voor de praktijk, preadvies Koninklijke Notariële Beroepsorganisatie* (The Hague, SDU Fiscale & Financiële Uitgevers 2008) p. 235.

[19] See J.A.M. ten Berg, 'Aandelen in de bv-nieuwe stijl: stemrecht en stortingsplicht', *Ondernemingsrecht* (2007) p. 338.

4.1.3 *Transfer of shares*

According to section 195 Bpc a share transfer restriction clause in the articles of association is no longer compulsory (as it is under the current statute).[20] A share transfer restriction clause restricts the transfer of shares by introducing a pre-emption right for the other shareholders, unless the articles of association stipulate otherwise (for example by abolishing any share transfer restriction or introducing an approval rule or other methods of restricting the transfer of shares). In our opinion this system is superior to the one that was included in a preliminary draft of the new private company statute. In that system there was no share transfer restriction at all included in the statute. We think it is more cost-efficient to have a non-mandatory share transfer restriction clause in place, with the possibility to deviate (for example when a restricted circle of shareholders is not an issue for the founders/shareholders). Section 195 Bpc also introduces the possibility to exclude the transferability of shares for a certain period (for example a lock-up period of 5 years). Share transfers in breach of this exclusion are invalid.

4.1.4 *Shareholders' meeting*

Some important changes to the private company statute concern decision-making by the shareholders' meeting. First of all, it will be easier to adopt resolutions by the shareholders without holding a formal meeting. An explicit clause in the articles of association that allows decision-making outside the shareholders' meeting is no longer prescribed. A resolution can also be adopted outside a formal meeting by a majority vote. Unanimity is no longer required, although section 238 Pbc prescribes that all shareholders should approve decision-making without a formal meeting. Another improvement is that the obligatory *annual* general shareholders' meeting can be held without a formal meeting (section 218 Bpc). Especially private companies with a few shareholders, with shareholders in foreign countries and companies which are 100% subsidiaries in a group of companies will probably use these facilities for easier decision-making. Worth mentioning is that the articles of association can stipulate that the place to hold a shareholders' meeting is outside the Netherlands, and that the period of notice for convening a meeting is reduced from 15 to 8 days.

4.1.5 *Directors*

An important amendment to the Dutch private company statute is the introduction of a one-tier board structure in Dutch law. According to Dutch company law public companies and private companies have a two-tier board structure; with a board of executive directors and a separate supervisory board. Recently, a Bill, separate from the Bill regarding the new private company statute, according to which public companies and private companies will be allowed to choose for a one-tier structure with executive and non-executive directors, was sent to Parliament.[21] This will lead to more flexibility regarding the internal structure of Dutch companies. The Bill also regulates some liability issues that are connected with

---

[20] See P.J. Dortmond, 'Flexibel aandeelhouderschap', *Ondernemingsrecht* (2007) p. 352.

[21] Parliamentary Papers II 2008/09, 31 763, nos. 1-3. See F.J. Oranje, 'Orgaanstructuur en bevoegdheden', *Het nieuwe BV-recht voor de praktijk, preadvies Koninklijke Notariële Beroepsorganisatie* (The Hague, SDU Fiscale & Financiële Uitgevers 2008) p. 74.

the introduction of the one-tier board structure. Under Dutch law directors are jointly and severally liable for mismanagement. The liability standard for executive and non-executive directors in a future one-tier board will have to take into account the different tasks assigned to each class of directors and exoneration by non-executive directors for mismanagement by the executive directors should be feasible.

A supervisory board is not prescribed by law in a normal private company. Under Dutch law there is a special regime (the '*structuurregime*') for large private companies (and also for public companies). This special regime is applicable when for a period of at least three years (i) the equity capital and the reserves amount to at least € 16 million; (ii) there are at least 100 employees in the Netherlands; and (iii) a compulsory works council has been established (section 263 Book 2 DCC). Only under this special regime is a supervisory board mandatory. The supervisory board in a company under this special regime is authorized to appoint and remove the members of the managing board of directors. This special regime will not be amended under the new private company statute. The way managing directors and (non-mandatory) supervisory directors are appointed in normal private companies will, however.

At present, managing directors and supervisory directors are appointed and can be removed by the general meeting (section 242 and 244 Book 2 DCC (members of the managing board) and section 252 and 254 Book 2 DCC (members of the supervisory board). The articles of association may stipulate that one or more members of the supervisory board (with a maximum of a third of the total number of supervisory board members) can be appointed by others than the shareholders' meeting (section 253 Book 2 DCC). These others can, for example, be financial institutions, the government or the supervisory board itself. Under the new private company statute these rules will remain in place. New is the possibility to stipulate in the articles of association that managing directors or supervisory directors can be appointed by holders of shares of a certain class (section 242 and 244 Bpc (managing directors) and section 252 and 254 (supervisory directors)). This will allow partners in a joint venture company each to appoint and remove their own managing or supervisory directors.

A much-debated change is included in section 239 paragraph 4 Bpc. According to this section a corporate body designated by the articles of association (probably in most cases the shareholders' meeting) can give binding instructions to the board of directors on specific issues. The board is obliged to follow these instructions, unless this would be 'to the detriment of the company and its business'. This last phrase implies that the board of directors has a separate duty to assess whether a given instruction is to the detriment of the company and its business. The board of directors will therefore be fully accountable and liable for its decisions and actions even when these were taken on the basis of an instruction given by another corporate body.

We regret that the private company without a formal board of directors and with the shareholders as governing body is not allowed.[22] The argument in the explanatory memorandum that shareholders cannot be guardians of the interest of the company has in our view limited value.[23] We do not believe that decisions in a shareholder-governed private company will differ from decisions in a private company that is governed by a board of

[22] Parliamentary Papers 2006/07, 31 058, no. 3, p. 10. Under Dutch-Antillean law, for example, a shareholder-governed private company is allowed.

[23] Parliamentary Papers 2006/07, 31 058, no. 3, p. 10.

directors. This is because the directors in the typical private company are also shareholders and because there is only a theoretical difference between the interest of the company and the interest of the shareholders in most private companies.[24] Moreover, the argument of the interest of the company has not been used for *partnerships* with legal personality and private companies resemble partnerships internally. We think that the other arguments in the explanatory memorandum that the shareholder-governed company would lead to complex questions of transitory law and would raise difficulties as to the position of shareholders who are not directors could be overcome.

4.2 Internal characteristics: rescue from the blind play of chance

As we remarked in Section 2, another important function of a private company statute is to serve legal certainty and to protect justified interests of persons involved in a private company. This function is guaranteed in private company statutes by mandatory rules serving fairness. These mandatory rules are often of a procedural nature. They prescribe how certain decisions should be taken or they provide a procedural solution to disputes. In Section 4.1 we discussed changes that contribute to flexibility and to purposeful and creative activity in the Dutch private company. In this section we will discuss how Dutch private company law rescues man from the blind play of chance and puts him safely on the road to purposeful and creative activity.

The characteristic that the shareholders are financially and personally deeply involved in the private company and have no easy exit, justifies mandatory rules that protect the interests of shareholders.[25] However, a starting point should be that every shareholder has to bear the consequences of his consent with the internal structure or with agreements between shareholders. Even a non-consenting shareholder who is outvoted by the majority has to bear the consequences of being outvoted. It was his choice to become a shareholder in a private company and one of the consequences of that choice is that decisions are in principle taken by majority vote.[26]

An exception to this general principle is justified when relevant circumstances have altered in such a way that the expectations of a shareholder (usually a minority shareholder) justify protection. An example is the shareholder who is dismissed as a director. He is financially deeply involved in the private company and without the salary as a director he may not be able to have a reasonable return on his investment and make a living. Another exception is justified when a shareholder is deprived without consent of some essential rights attached to his shares. Another exception is justified when a shareholder is the victim of fraud, misbehavior or a breach of fiduciary duties by one or more of the other shareholders (usually holding the majority of the shares).

In general the current private company statute gives adequate protection to shareholders. We will give a description of the current protection that will not be amended when the new private company statute enters into force and of the additional protection that the new

---

[24] See also F.J. Oranje, 'Orgaanstructuur en bevoegdheden', *Het nieuwe BV-recht voor de praktijk, preadvies Koninklijke Notariële Beroepsorganisatie* (The Hague, SDU Fiscale & Financiële Uitgevers 2008) p. 22.

[25] See for a different approach: H.J. Portengen, *De vereenvoudigde BV, Preadvies van de Vereeniging 'Handelsrecht'* (Deventer, Kluwer 2006) p. 69.

[26] See HR (Supreme Court) 17 May 1991, *NJ* 1991, 645 (*Tonnema*) and HR (Supreme Court) 14 September 2007, *JOR* 2007/237 (*Versatel*).

private company statute has to provide due to the more flexible and enabling new private company statute. We will first focus on protection that is provided by legal proceedings and then on protection that is provided by substantive rules of company law; mostly rules on decision-making.[27]

4.2.1 *Protection through legal proceedings*

First of all, shareholders can request the District Court of the domicile of the company to nullify resolutions of the board of directors, the shareholders' meeting or any other corporate body. The most important grounds for nullification of a resolution are: (i) that the resolution was taken in breach of statutory procedural requirements or procedural requirements prescribed by the articles of association; and (ii) that the resolution is in breach of the standard of reasonableness and fairness (section 15 Book 2 DCC). An example of the first category is a resolution that was taken in a meeting that was convened without proper and timely notice. An example of the second category is a resolution taken by the majority shareholder to reserve all the profits for the fifth consecutive year without a financial necessity to do so. Another example is the resolution to remove a director without hearing the arguments of the director against this removal. Resolutions that are in breach of substantive rules of law or contrary to morality are null and void *ab initio* without any judicial intervention (section 14 Book 2 DCC).

An important procedure in Dutch company law is the so-called 'inquiry procedure' (section 344-359 Book 2 DCC).[28] Shareholders holding – alone or together – 10% of the shares or shares with a nominal value of € 225,000 have a right to initiate the inquiry procedure by an application addressed to the Dutch Enterprise Division, a specialized branch of the Amsterdam Court of Appeal. The Enterprise Division may order an inquiry if there appear to be well-founded reasons to doubt the correctness of the policies or the conduct of a company. If there are well-founded reasons to doubt the correctness of the policies or the conduct of the company, the Enterprise Division will appoint one or more investigators. These investigators are usually independent experts, lawyers or auditors. The inquiry will lead to a report. This report brings the first part of the proceedings to an end. The objective of this first part is to disclose the policies and conduct of the company and – if relevant – to disclose who has been responsible for incorrectness of these policies and for misconduct of the company.[29] Sometimes parties are satisfied with this first part and everything ends there.

The second part of the proceedings is again initiated with an application. In this second stage the applicant asks the Enterprise Division to establish whether there has been misconduct on the basis of the report, to establish who has been responsible for misconduct and if

[27] See for an instructive article on minority rights in the Netherlands: L. Timmerman and A. Doorman, 'Rights of Minority Shareholders in the Netherlands', vol. 6.4 *Electronic Journal of Comparative Law* (December 2002), available at <http://www.ejcl.org/64/art64-12.html>.

[28] See M.W. Josephus Jitta, 'Procedural Aspects of the Right of Inquiry', *The Companies and Business Court from a comparative law perspective* (Deventer, Kluwer 2004) pp. 1-42; M.J. Kroeze, 'The Companies and Business Court as a Specialized Court', *The Quality of Corporate Law and the Role of Corporate Law Judges* (Amsterdam, ACCF/NMEA/OECD 2006) pp. 143-154; and L. Timmerman, A. Doorman, 'Rights of Minority Shareholders in the Netherlands', vol. 6.4 *Electronic Journal of Comparative Law* (December 2002), available at <http://www.ejcl.org/64/art64-12.html>.

[29] HR (Supreme Court) 10 January 1990, *NJ* 1990, 466 (*Ogem II*).

appropriate to order measures. The Enterprise Division has broad authority in ordering measures: such as declaring resolutions void, the suspension or dismissal of board members, the temporary appointment of board members, the temporary derogation from the articles of association, the temporary transfer of shares to a nominee and the dissolution of the company. The objective of this second part of the proceedings is to reorganize the company, to restore the company to a healthy state and to state who has been responsible for the misconduct of the company.[30] More than 90% of the inquiry proceedings deal with disputes in private companies. Many of these disputes are settled under the guidance of the Enterprise Division.[31] These settlements often involve an exit of one of the shareholders. The inquiry procedure is therefore an important safeguard in Dutch private company law and an important remedy to solve disputes in private company settings. It fills a gap caused by the absence of a market for control for private companies and by a lack of interest by the media as corrective mechanisms for the behavior of (mostly) majority shareholders and directors.

In addition to the successful inquiry procedure, Dutch law has an expulsion and exit procedure (section 335-343 Book 2 DCC).[32] A shareholder has a right to exit the company when his rights or interests are unfairly prejudiced by other shareholders. One or more shareholders representing alone or together at least one-third of the issued share capital can force a shareholder to exit the company if this shareholder unreasonably infringes on the interests of the company. The current expulsion and exit procedure is almost a dead letter. This failure is a consequence of the very, very long time the proceedings take. Parties can litigate in three instances (District Court, Enterprise Division, Supreme Court) separately on the question whether expulsion or exit is allowed and on the issue of the valuation of the shares. The new private company statute will amend the expulsion and exit procedure to make it more practical and user-friendly. This is achieved by abolishing interim appeal rights and concentrating litigation on the expulsion or exit and the valuation of the shares, by giving authority to the judge to declare the judgment on exit or expulsion (including the valuation of the shares) provisionally enforceable, by creating the possibility to skip litigation at the level of the District Court and by giving authority to the judge to decide not to appoint financial experts for the valuation of the shares. This can be done, for example, when parties already have agreed on the valuation criteria for the shares beforehand. As a safeguard section 340 paragraph 3 Bpc stipulates that a judge does not have to follow an agreement on the valuation criteria by the parties beforehand when this would lead to a manifestly unreasonable price for the shares. When establishing the value of the shares the new exit procedure also gives the judge the authority to take into account the harm done to the company (and reflected in the value of the shares held by the shareholder who makes the exit) by the other shareholder(s) or by others (section 343 paragraph 4 Bpc). In a speech given in 2007 the president of the Enterprise Division was highly critical about the new procedure. He predicts on good grounds that the amended expulsion and exit procedure

---

30 Ibid.

31 For exact figures see K. Cools, P.G.F.A. Geerts, M.J. Kroeze, A.C.W. Pijls, *Het recht van enquête, Een empirisch onderzoek*, February 2009, available at <http://www.justitie.nl/actueel/persberichten/archief-2009/90305ingrijpen-ondernemingskamer-bij-rechtspersoon-voorziet-in-behoefte.aspx>.

32 A.E. Driessen, 'Regulation of disputes in companies in the Netherlands', in *The Companies and Business Court from a Comparative Law Perspective* (Deventer, Kluwer 2004) pp. 125-144. See for the new expulsion and exit procedure: C.D.J. Bulten, 'De gewijzigde geschillenregeling', *Ondernemingsrecht* (2007) p. 360.

will not be successful, just like the current procedure.[33] We agree with his suggestion to introduce the possibility of exclusion and exit as one of the measures that can be taken in the more successful inquiry procedure. Because there is no market for shares in a private company, because shareholders depend in many occasions on the revenues of their investment in the companies' capital or their labor for the company and because nothing can be so financially devastating as an ongoing dispute in a private company, a practicable exit procedure is in the interest of all parties involved in a private company.

Finally, we mention that there is no such thing as derivative action in the Netherlands. According to section 9 Book 2 DCC directors are jointly and severally liable to the company for damage resulting from a breach of company law, from violation of the articles of association and, in general, from any form of negligent or deliberate mismanagement.[34] The action by the company has to be initiated by the board of directors. In practice, it is for the majority of the shareholders or the supervisory board to decide whether to initiate an action for redress. Individual shareholders generally cannot initiate proceedings against a director. Claims for damages against directors of private companies for mismanagement are consequently relatively rare and are usually filed by trustees in bankruptcy. We think it might be worthwhile to consider the introduction of a derivative action in Dutch law.[35] Especially where there is no supervisory board – as is the case in most Dutch private companies – a derivative action would be a good additional instrument for the protection of the interests of (minority) shareholders. Under current law an individual shareholder who suffers loss as a result of mismanagement can only consider holding a director liable in tort under section 162 Book 6 DCC. Usually such a tort action is bound to fail, as damage suffered by a shareholder is in most cases considered to be only 'second level' damage, reflecting only the direct loss which has been inflicted on the company.[36]

4.2.2 *Protection through substantive rules of company law*

Important substantive rules of company law that protect the interest of shareholders are rules regarding decision-making. The current private company statute gives rules that guarantee a proper decision-making process. For some far-reaching decisions the private company statute requires a supermajority of the votes and a certain percentage of the shareholders attending the shareholders' meeting (quorum). The articles of association can introduce these kind of safeguards for any decision within the company. The new private company statute introduces some new decision-making rules. When shares with voting rights are converted into shares without voting rights all shareholders concerned have to give their approval to this conversion (section 228 paragraph 5 Pbc). A comparable safeguard applies to decisions concerning shares without financial rights or with restricted financial rights (section 216 paragraph 6 Bpc) and to decisions introducing temporary non-transferable shares (section 195 paragraph 3 Bpc). For the introduction of multiple voting rights section

[33] J.H.M. Willems, 'Geschillen en exitmogelijkheden', *Flexibele rechtsvormen* (Deventer, Kluwer 2008) p. 79.

[34] See Jan Berend Wezeman, 'European Company Law and Protection of Minority Shareholders and Creditors in the European Union', *The Legal Borders of the EU, The Riga Papers* (Amersfoort, SDU Fiscale & Financiële Uitgevers 2007) p. 39.

[35] See also M.J. Kroeze, *Afgeleide schade en afgeleide actie* (Deventer, Kluwer 2004).

[36] See, e.g., HR (Supreme Court) 2 December 1994, *NJ* 1995, 288 (*Poot/ABP*) and HR (Supreme Court) 2 May 1997, *NJ* 1997, 662 (*Kip/Rabo*).

228 paragraph 4 Bpc even requires unanimity of votes in a shareholders' meeting where all shareholders are present.

Interesting is the protection of the position of shareholders who voted against a proposal to attach some additional obligations to shares according to section 192 Bpc.[37] A resolution introducing additional obligations can be adopted by a simple majority vote. However, the shareholders who voted against the proposal are not bound by the additional obligations. This right is personal and ceases to exist when the shares are transferred to a third party. Section 192a Bpc introduces an exit procedure for a shareholder who is not able to transfer his shares, or is only able to transfer his shares at an unreasonable discount, due to the attachment of additional obligations to the shares as soon as the transfer is effected. The company has to designate a prospect who wants to buy the shares at a price estimated by an independent expert. If a prospect has not been designated within three months, the shareholder is free to transfer his shares to another party within six months without the attachment of additional obligations to the shares. A similar exit procedure applies to a shareholder who opposes to the prescription of a certain quality for shareholders by the articles of association. If the company does not designate a prospect within three months the shareholder is no longer bound by the quality requirement and can transfer his shares to a party who will also not be bound by the quality requirement.

The decision rules described in this paragraph can, of course, seriously impair the internal flexibility of the private company in the future. However, we do think these rules are justified given the important rights these decisions can take away from individual shareholders. It is important for founders of a private company to bear in mind that the benefits of the enhanced flexibility of the new private company statute should be obtained at the moment the private company is incorporated. Changing the internal structure during the existence of the private company might be much more difficult than one would presume on the basis of the goals of the new private company statute.

4.3 External characteristics: corporate personality

We have described how the internal organization of a Dutch private company can be adapted to the needs of the founders or shareholders under the new private company statute. We have also described the necessary safeguards that form a counterbalance to more flexibility. We concluded that a private company has the internal characteristics of a partnership, but at the same time the external characteristics of a corporate personality. This combination of internal flexibility and external corporate personality justifies rules that do not burden third parties with extensive investigations into the internal organization of any given private company. The outside world should not have to bother about the inside world.

We therefore recommend as a change to the pending Bill that stating a purpose in the articles of association should be non-mandatory and that the external effect of an *ultra vires* act should be deleted. This suggestion has been made a few times by other authors, but was not followed by the Ministers of Justice and of Economic affairs in the Bill concerning the private company statute.[38] An improvement will be brought by the same Bill that will

---

[37] See P.J. Dortmond, 'Flexibel aandeelhouderschap', *Ondernemingsrecht* (2007) p. 350.

[38] See for example Th. Groenewald, *Doeloverschrijding bij NV en BV* (Deventer, Kluwer 2001) p. 195. Also Report-De Kluiver (Vereenvoudiging en flexibilisering van het Nederlandse BV-recht), F.J.P. van den Ingh and R.G.J. Nowak (eds.), *Vereenvoudiging en flexibilisering BV-recht, deel I, De pre-parlementaire geschiedenis*, (Deventer, Kluwer 2006) p. 261.

introduce the one-tier board structure in Dutch company law.[39] In the near future the external effect of representation by directors with a conflict of interest will be abolished. According to section 256 Book 2 DCC a director with a conflict of interest is in principle not authorized to represent the company. The supervisory board, if it exists, is authorized to represent the company in this situation. The company is not bound to an agreement if a director with a conflict of interest represented the company. This implies that third parties have to investigate to some extent whether the director has a conflict of interest. This rule will be replaced by a conflict of interest regime that is not applicable to the representation phase but to the preceding decision-making phase. The director with conflicting interests on certain issues should abstain from decision-making on these issues. Under the new rules, conflicts of interest can lead to nullity of resolutions and/or to personal liability of directors towards the company under section 9 Book 2 DCC, but it will as a rule not affect the representative authority of the directors. A third party, therefore, is no longer involved in the internal affairs concerning the conflicts of interests of directors. Under exceptional circumstances the principle of reasonableness and fairness can justify a correction to the internal effect. An example is where a director enters into an agreement that is detrimental to the company and the other party is acting in bad faith (for example because the other party is dominated by the director).[40]

The corporate personality of a private company provides the shareholders (and directors) with the advantage of limited liability. This advantage shifts business risks and other financial risks to the creditors of the private company. Therefore some thought has to be given to the position and the protection of creditors. This is particularly important given the fact that the new private company statute will abolish the current legal capital rules, which were originally intended to protect the interests of the creditors. In the explanatory memorandum to the new private company statute ample attention is given to the position of creditors and to an alternative system for creditor protection.[41] Initially, section 216 paragraph 2 Bpc demanded a decision by the board of directors that dividends could be distributed to the shareholders. The board had to withhold consent to the distribution of dividends when the board knew, or ought to have concluded at that moment, that the company would not be able to pay her due debts after the distribution of dividends. Directors who would not withhold consent to the distribution of dividends in this situation would be jointly and severally liable for the total amount of the distribution. In the most recent proposal of February 2009 these rules were abandoned. Section 216 paragraph 2 Bpc now only stipulates that the *beneficiaries* of the distribution who knew or ought to have concluded that the company would not be able to pay her due debts after the distribution of dividends are obliged to pay back the dividends they received insofar as the company cannot pay her due debts. The same rule applies to the reduction of capital followed by a distribution to the shareholders (section 208 paragraph 6 Bpc). There is still some discussion in Parliament about Section 216 paragraph 2 Bpc. A proposal to put the original version of Section 216 paragraph 2 Bpc back in the Bill was brought before Parliament by some influential politicians. There is a considerable chance that this proposal will get a majority in Parliament. If that happens Section 216 paragraph 5 and 6 Bpc (as described by us in this contribution) will be renumbered to paragraph 7 and 8.[42]

---

[39] Parliamentary Papers II 2008/09, 31 763.

[40] HR (Supreme Court) 17 December 1982, *NJ* 1983, 480 (*Bibolini*).

[41] Parliamentary Papers 2006/07, 31 058, no. 3, pp. 22-34 and 2008/09, 31 058, no. 8, pp. 3-4.

[42] See for the proposal: Parliamentary Papers 2009/10, 31 058, no. 12.

In our opinion liability for unfair distribution of dividends will only apply to a limited number of cases due to precautionary actions by those involved in the company. Shareholders will rely on the statements made by the auditor or the board of directors. The directors will verify with the company auditor whether or not they can take the practical steps necessary to distribute the dividends. In uncertain financial situations directors will probably wait for a certain period with the actual distribution of the dividends. The directors might still be liable – although a formal consent is no longer prescribed – if they take the practical steps necessary to distribute dividends when they knew, or ought to have concluded at that moment, that the company would not be able to pay her due debts after the distribution of dividends.[43]

In case of bankruptcy the trustee in bankruptcy will probably make more effective use of section 248 Book 2 DCC which gives the trustee the authority to hold *company directors* on behalf of all the creditors of the estate of the company jointly and severally liable in case of manifest mismanagement. This liability arises when the directors have clearly failed to perform their duties properly, which is a significant ground for the bankruptcy. As a result, the directors (including *de facto* directors) are liable to the estate for the whole amount of the deficit. It is not very clear what type of behavior can be qualified as improper performance. Surely this is not only the case if the trustee can prove willful misconduct harming the creditors, but also in the event of obvious mismanagement (e.g., negligence of the company's credit position; negligence in taking measures against high financial risks; failure to obtain sufficient advice in important transactions; undertaking irresponsible expensive investments without adequate preparation). The legislator, however, provided some presumptive evidence rules in section 248 paragraph 2 Book 2 DCC. If the management failed to comply with its obligations with respect to proper bookkeeping or failed to comply with its obligation to publish the annual accounts of the company, it is established that the directors have not performed their duties properly. It will then be presumed that the improper performance of duties is an important cause of the bankruptcy. Almost all cases brought under section 248 Book 2 concern private companies. We estimate that in approximately 90% of these cases the presumptive evidence rules were invoked because proper bookkeeping was absent or the annual accounts were not published properly.

5. Some aspects of competition in Europe

We started this contribution with the remark that competition is an important rationale for changing the Dutch private company statute. Enacting an attractive company statute is not enough. The costs of incorporation and other administrative costs are also important factors for the success of the new private company statute. If someone incorporates an English limited company he has to pay around € 50 (and annually some administrative costs). If someone wants to incorporate a Dutch private company he has to go to a civil-law notary. The cheapest civil-law notary on the Internet will incorporate a Dutch private company for approximately € 850. If the shareholders want to amend the articles of association they have to go to the civil-law notary again and pay a similar amount of money. The same applies if shareholders want to sell their shares or if the company wants to issue shares to a future shareholder-partner. A Dutch private company is an expensive affair. The burden of

[43] P.J. Dortmond, 'De tweede Nota van Wijziging bij het wetsvoorstel flexibilisering BV-recht', *Ondernemingsrecht* (2009-4).

these costs also seriously impairs the internal flexibility of the private company and can be a reason for Dutch businesses to choose a legal form without all these costs attached to it.[44]

In the debate on the new private company statute and in the explanatory memorandum, hardly any attention is given to the role of the civil-law notary and the costs connected with that role.[45] We would like to emphasize that we consider the role of the civil-law notary to be very valuable, but that is not the issue. The issue is that when a jurisdiction wants to be competitive it is forced by the market to cut down on the costs connected to incorporating and maintaining a private company. The Netherlands does not have to be the cheapest if it offers more than others (for example legal certainty through the assistance of the civil-law notary), but as long as the costs of incorporation stay at their current level we do not expect a significant decline in the number of English limited companies active in the Netherlands and we do not expect that the Dutch private company will become as popular as it could be for small, starting enterprises. Possible solutions could be: (i) the introduction of an administrative incorporation process by filing some key elements of the private company (name, seat, purpose, incorporators) and applying model articles of association when no choice for another regime has been made; (ii) giving the possibility to adopt and change the internal structure in the articles of association without intervention of professionals; (iii) facilitating share transfers and the issuance of shares by a registered deed executed privately. We hope a discussion on the role of the civil-law notary will take place during the debates in Parliament on the pending Bill. There is one remark we should make to put things into perspective and that is that the choice for the actual place of business is hardly influenced by the applicable legal rules concerning legal business forms. Tax, commercial and infrastructural considerations primarily determine the actual place of establishment. A country that really wants to win the competition as place of establishment must therefore be especially attractive in other areas.[46]

6. Concluding remarks

In this contribution we have identified the functions and characteristics of private company statutes. We have illustrated that these functions form the foundations of the new Dutch private company statute. The statute is more flexible and gives more possibilities to founders and shareholders to adopt an internal organization that suits the needs of a specific private company. These rules have mostly a non-mandatory character. In addition, the statute provides mandatory rules that protect the justified interests of shareholders and others involved in a private company. The new private company statute takes into account the characteristics of the typical private company; for example, by enhancing flexibility because a private company has the internal characteristics resembling those of a partnership. Many of the mandatory rules in the new private company statute are drafted with the characteristic in mind that there is no established market for shares in a private company and

---

[44] Some argue that these costs function as a useful obstacle which distinguishes the serious entrepreneurs from the too adventurous ones. There is no Dutch word for this function of high costs of incorporation; in German this is called the '*Ordnungspolitische Funktion*'. We think that high costs of incorporation do not provide the best way to distinguish between serious entrepreneurs and too adventurous ones.

[45] Also: E.P.M. Vermeulen, 'De plaats en inrichting van een nieuw BV-recht in een innovatieve economie', *De vereenvoudigde BV, Preadvies van de Vereeniging 'Handelsrecht'* (Deventer, Kluwer 2006) p. 122.

[46] See also M.J. Kroeze, H.M. Vletter-van Dort, 'History and Future of Uniform Company Law in Europe', 5(3) *European Company Law* (2008) p. 114.

that shareholders have no easy exit. The inquiry procedure fulfils the function of a corrective mechanism for the behavior of shareholders and directors and fills the gap caused by the absence of a market for corporate control, by a lack of interest by the media for private companies and by the rare occasion of liability proceedings against directors outside a situation of bankruptcy.

Our expectation is that fiduciary duties and the rule of reasonableness and fairness will become more important between shareholders in Dutch private companies. When the public company statute and the private company statute are no longer similar in the near future and are construed on different basic assumptions, the interpretation of statutory rules for public companies and private companies by judges will diverge. Rules of tort law will become more important between shareholders and directors on the one side and creditors on the other side. This is a direct consequence of the choice to delete *ex ante* rules of capital requirements and capital maintenance.

In our opinion the Ministries of Justice and of Economic Affairs have done much good and important work. It is not always easy to have far-reaching legal reform accepted by Parliament.[47] For this reason it can be understood that some controversial themes, such as the position of the civil-law notary, are left out of the Bill concerning private company law. There are some people who would like to see that the proposals went much further. Notwithstanding the fact that revolutionary proposals could lack political support, it is important to emphasize that there are already 600,000 private companies that will also be governed by the new statute. If revolutionary concepts are necessary it would be more sensible to introduce additional new legal business forms than to change the private company statute in a revolutionary way.

[47] The attempts to reform Dutch company law at the end of the 19th and the beginning of the 20th century started with a first Bill in 1871 and were only to be completed in 1928 after various totally rewritten Bills for a new Dutch company law.

Chapter 8

WELFARE, FAIRNESS AND THE ROLE OF COURTS IN A SIMPLE AND FLEXIBLE PRIVATE COMPANY LAW

Levinus Timmerman*

1. Introduction

Over the last few decades, one of the most noticeable traits of Dutch corporate law is the fact that the legislator uses corporate law to realize certain political goals. In the 1960s, for example, one of the key policy-making goals was to establish employee participation in the corporate decision-making process. In the Netherlands, the pursuit of this idea – or better yet ideal – has been rather successful. By the 1970s, a supervisory board with a complicated system of workers' representation was introduced in Dutch corporate law.[1] This arrangement remains in force, despite having been modified by amendment. Today, these provisions cause us some trouble, because we have for several reasons lost faith in the effectiveness of the participation of Dutch employees in the corporate decision-making process. Thus, our concern nowadays is how to abolish these complicated rules on worker participation in a decent way. We have relatively little experience with such matters.

About a decade ago, it occurred to the Dutch legislator and many other legislators that corporate law could be used to enhance economic activity and entrepreneurship. Not only did this view lead to an endeavor to restrict the possibility of using anti-takeover measures for a company when faced with a hostile bidder, but, even more importantly, it has given rise to reform of Dutch corporate law, which seeks, among other things, to make Dutch private company law more simple and flexible.[2]

Ultimately, I expect the result of such an economically inspired approach to corporate law reform to lead to improved shareholders' rights, especially for minority investors, and more freedom of contract, and that our legislator will to a certain extent retreat from the corporate law domain.[3] In effect, the company will become a less regulated entity with more autonomy for its shareholders, especially the majority shareholder. In my opinion, this result can be traced back to the influence of neo-classical economic thinking. Indeed,

* Professor of Company Law, Erasmus University Rotterdam; Advocate General at the Netherlands Supreme Court. This chapter was originally a speech delivered at a conference on Comparative Private Company Law organised by the Dutch Ministry of Justice in June 2006.

1 Sections 152-164 and sections 262-274 of Book 2 of the Dutch Civil Code.

2 I refer to the various drafts which have been published by the Ministry of Justice, available at <http://www.minjus.nl>.

3 On this topic, see K. Dau-Schmidt and C.L. Brun, 'Lost in Translation: The Economic Analysis of Law in the United States and Europe', 44 *Columbia Journal of Transnational Law* (2006) p. 606.

J.A. McCahery, L. Timmerman and E.P.M. Vermeulen (eds.), Private Company Law Reform

this highly abstract theory still dominates economic thinking. From this perspective, the point of departure is the autonomy of shareholders and faith in market efficiency. The bottom line, then, is that the autonomy of the shareholders and market efficiency create a stronger demand for as much freedom of contract in company law as possible.

In my view, not many objections can be raised against the use of corporate law for the realization of political or economic goals that the legislator deems appropriate at a certain time for the general well-being of our society. In the longer run, such a use of company law seems unavoidable in a democratic society, particularly where economic considerations have become more and more important in many fields, including healthcare and education. So what is the result? The cost of this trend could be that corporate law will lose some of its original sacredness and timelessness and that the law-making process becomes a tool for social engineering. Although skeptics may doubt the wisdom of this new direction in the corporate law-making process, I do not think this is wrong in itself.

In addition to the above considerations, it is worth remembering that companies traditionally function in an environment that requires management to act efficiently. Predictably, this makes it necessary for companies to be efficiently organized. This explains why, around the globe, the corporate lawyers who produced the legal framework for companies created certain features in order to make the company form more attractive for use in business. Some of these features were developed in the 19th century. In the 20th century, others were eventually added. The main features include: the concept of legal personality, limited liability for shareholders, the transferability of shares, centralized and autonomous management, profit rights for shareholders, a certain say for shareholders in the company, the admission of the concept of groups of companies and the freedom to reorganize companies, *inter alia*, by means of mergers, split-ups and conversion. It is widely acknowledged that these features have contributed greatly to promoting economic activity in the form of a company.[4] The success of the company around the globe during the last 150 years can be traced back to these features of the company.

2. Beyond economic efficiency

Although corporate law may function as an instrument to enhance economic activity, it should in my view always guarantee an acceptable level of integrity. This would effectively establish the idea of justice in corporate law. Even though this may seem self-evident, however, I doubt whether this is really the case. Let me quote the first sentence of an American book that has recently been published:

> 'Our thesis is that social decisions should be based exclusively on the welfare of individuals – and, accordingly, should not depend on notions of fairness, justice or cognate notions.'[5]

[4] See, for instance, J. Micklethwait and A. Wooldridge, *The Company: A Short History of a Revolutionary Idea* (London, Phoenix 2005) at p. xv: 'The most important organization in the world is the company: the basis of the prosperity of the West and the best hope for the future of the rest of the world', and at p. xxi: 'The limited liability corporation is the greatest single discovery of modern times.' For an older book in which the importance of the company was underlined, see G. Ripert, *Aspects juridiques du capitalisme moderne* (Paris, Librairie Générale de Droit et de Jurisprudence 1946). See especially chapter II: *l'ère des sociétés par actions*.

[5] See L. Kaplow and S. Shavell, *Fairness versus Welfare* (Cambridge, MA, Harvard University Press 2002). A well-known comparative law book – R. Kraakman's, *The Anatomy of Corporate Law: A Comparative and*

It may not be surprising that, as an old fashioned Dutch – or worse European – corporate lawyer with a predilection for a systematically practised law, I do not agree with this thesis. On that basis, we need a corporate law regime that is more than just economically efficient. There is not one universal model of corporate law, particularly where the interests and visions of people differ greatly within our society and from society to society. Clearly, the interests of a majority shareholder will not be the same as the interests of minority shareholders, and these differences must consequently be taken into account, for example, when structuring best practice codes. Irrespective of how economically sound and efficient certain decisions may be, it is precisely this wide diversity of interests and visions which demands that the decisions of a corporation should be subject to a test of fairness and carefulness. Hence, corporate law should, in my view, be based on a pluralistic approach, embracing the overarching principles of economic efficiency and justice. In addition to this, I would like to argue that our type of society, with its emphasis on efficiency and individualism, requires binding notions such as the general interest, the interest of the company and justice in order to continue to function satisfactorily.[6]

In this essay, I would like to highlight the pivotal role of justice in corporate law. I would like to focus on two legal concepts in order to draw attention to the significance of the notion of justice in Dutch corporate law. The first is the notion of reasonableness and fairness in corporate law, and the second notion refers to the way in which the fundamental rights embodied in the European Convention on Human Rights influence the relations between the shareholders within the company. Both notions (reasonableness and fairness as well as the fundamental rights) concern doctrines that continue to be highly relevant despite today's strong focus on the economic basis of corporate law. Should the principles of 'reasonableness and fairness' and 'fundamental rights' find an important place in a newly deregulated Dutch corporate law – and I expect that they will – I predict that the courts and judges generally will play an important role in Dutch corporate governance and law. I expect that a stronger orientation of corporate law on economic efficiency will underline the significance of concepts such as 'reasonableness and fairness' and 'fundamental rights'. Concepts like 'reasonableness' and 'fairness' can correct 'economic outcomes', the result being that parties, in particular minority shareholders, will seek recourse to the courts to determine whether 'reasonableness and fairness' and 'fundamental rights' have been violated in a particular case. Only the courts can fill in concepts like 'reasonableness and fairness' and 'fundamental rights' on a case-by-case basis.

In making these points, it is necessary to state that one of the ideas of which I am convinced is that, with the legislator retreating, the judge will have to take over its role in upholding notions of 'reasonableness and fairness' and 'fundamental rights' as boundaries of what is allowed in corporate law.

It is important to highlight another point as well. With a more liberal corporate law, disputes between shareholders and management in closed corporations will be less frequent. The powers of the management board will be reduced to the extent that the share-

---

Functional Approach (New York, Oxford University Press 2004) – seems to take the same approach: 'more particularly, the appropriate goal of corporate law is to advance corporate welfare of a firm's shareholders, employees, suppliers and customers …' (p. 18).

[6] On this theme, see the excellent essay by the American historian J.C. Kennedy, *De deugden van een gidsland, burgerschap en democratie in Nederland* (Amsterdam, Bakker 2005).

holders' meeting will gain powers. Naturally, disputes between management and shareholders are typical under 'old' Dutch corporate law. However, I expect that conflicts between minority and majority shareholders will become more frequent under the 'new' legislative regime. This is likely to be the case, as shareholders will become more powerful. This will lead to conflicts regarding the division of the newly acquired power. Thus, minority shareholders will appeal to the courts more frequently, invoking concepts such as reasonableness and fairness and fundamental rights. Now, I shall illustrate my expectations with examples taken from the current project to make the legislation applicable to Dutch closed companies more simple and flexible.

3. Reasonableness and fairness

Our company law provisions are located in Book 2 of the Dutch Civil Code. A key provision of this part of our Civil Code (paragraph 8) reads as follows:

> 'Everyone who is involved in the organisation of a company by virtue of the legislation or the articles of association should, in acting towards one another, observe the requirements of reasonableness and fairness.'

In addition to this, paragraph 8 also states that a court may deviate from a statute or the articles of association if the observance of the statute or the articles of association would be unacceptable according to the requirements of reasonableness and fairness. Dutch corporate lawyers consider these paragraphs important, because a private company may have a long existence. As a consequence, the company is often viewed as an 'incomplete contract', as there are few or no adequate provisions to address all kinds of unexpected events or developments, such as misconduct of the majority shareholder. Thus, provisions in the articles of association or the shareholders' agreement that were once fair may through a change in the circumstances and the passing of time become unfair. In turn, judges in the Netherlands may in such cases disregard these contractual or statutory provisions, and in practice they sometimes make such decisions. Because Dutch courts take the principles of reasonableness and fairness seriously, we find that articles of association and shareholders' agreements tend to be much shorter in the Netherlands compared to their Anglo-American equivalents.

In order to fully grasp the importance of the concept of reasonableness and fairness in Dutch corporate law, I should note that, in several of its decisions, the Dutch Supreme Court has stressed that the concept of reasonableness and fairness should not be applied extensively in professional relations. Thus, it should be stressed that something must go seriously wrong before a paragraph of a contractual agreement or the articles of association will be disregarded by a Dutch court.[7]

The Dutch law reform project designed to make Dutch corporate law more simple and flexible currently has no plans to abolish paragraph 8, which establishes reasonableness and fairness as fundamental concepts. In my view, that is also not really possible. The Companies and Business Court in Amsterdam is an important court for Dutch corporate law matters. It adopts decisions that may often be viewed as guiding. Very often these

[7] See, for instance, Hoge Raad 28 May 2004, *Jurisprudentie Onderneming en Recht* (2004) p. 342.

decisions are ultimately inspired by or based directly on the principles of reasonableness and fairness. In this sense, the Companies and Business Court plays a role that is comparable to that of the Chancery Court. Clearly, Dutch corporate law is not able to function well without the concept of reasonableness and fairness as laid down in paragraph 8.[8]

When considering ways to make Dutch corporate law more simple and flexible, it may help to acknowledge that a distinction exists between welfare and economic efficiency, on the one hand, and fairness, on the other hand. I would like to defend the view that ample consideration should be given to this contrast in the proposals. Let me offer an example to support this view. Current Dutch corporate law requires a private company to always include a restriction on the free transferability of shares in its articles of association. At present, the Dutch Civil Code allows a private company two options for such a compulsory blocking clause, of which one should be implemented in the articles of association.

The Ministry of Justice proposes to remove the current obligation to restrict the transfer of shares. This seems to be a good idea. Shareholders may of course still include a restriction on the transfer of shares in the articles of association. For that situation, the Ministry of Justice proposes certain rules as well. The most important of those rules concerns the case in which a shareholder may not transfer his shares to a party of his choice because the articles of association stipulate that he must transfer them to another party. For this situation, the Ministry of Justice proposes an arrangement that is based on a combination of welfare, party autonomy and fairness. Thus, under this proposal, parties may agree in advance on a certain fixed price. According to this approach, this price should be the price for which the shareholder must transfer his shares to a party designated in the articles of association. In addition to this, the Ministry of Justice proposes that, in the case where the shareholder can show that this fixed price is unacceptable according to the principle of reasonableness and fairness, he may request that a court appoint a third-party expert in order to determine a price for the shares. In such a case, the shareholder will be entitled to the market value of his shares. Naturally, the unfairness of the fixed price in the articles of association will not be easy to show. In this light, it is important to recall the decisions of the Dutch Supreme Court in which it decided to apply reasonableness and fairness only in the exceptional circumstances in which a serious violation had occurred. In my view, such an arrangement does do justice to the combination of party autonomy and fairness.

Another important component of the proposals of the Ministry of Justice involves enhancing the exit rights of minority shareholders. I would like to emphasize that it is generally felt that there is a need to improve these sections of our Civil Code.[9] A significant implication of the current proposal of the Ministry of Justice is that majority shareholders will become more powerful compared to the other players within the company, such as the managing directors and the minority shareholders. In cases where a majority shareholder takes a firm stand against disagreeing minority shareholders, the only option for the minority shareholders is to exit the firm. The new Dutch rules for a simplified private company have to provide shareholders with adequate protection in such cases.

---

[8] On this subject, see M.J. Kroeze, 'The Companies and Business Court as a Specialized Court', *Ondernemingsrecht* (2007) pp. 86-91; and J.B. Jacobs, 'The role of specialized courts in resolving corporate governance disputes in the United States and the EU: an American's perspective', *Ondernemingsrecht* (2007) pp. 80-85.

[9] The current exit right for a minority shareholder can be found in section 343 of Book 2 of the Dutch Civil Code.

It has been particularly difficult for the Ministry of Justice to draft new sections determining the value of shares in the case of an exit of a minority shareholder. The new corporate rules provide that the value of the shares should be calculated as stipulated in the articles of association or the shareholders' agreement. Only in cases where the articles of association or the shareholders' agreement do not contain provisions in this regard or the minority shareholder is able to show that the price resulting from the calculation as set forth in the articles of association or shareholders' agreement is evidently unfair in view of all the relevant circumstances, may a judge appoint experts in order to determine the market value of the shares. In such cases, these experts should be paid by the majority shareholder.

4. Fundamental rights

The European Court of Human Rights ruled in 2002 that shares in a company fall under the protection of ownership guaranteed by Article 1 of the First Protocol to the European Convention on Human Rights.[10] According to the Court, shares are an economic position worthy of the protection offered by Article 1 of the First Protocol. As a result, a decision taken by the company to weaken certain powers attached to shares or to weaken other rights, such as financial rights, constitutes a deterioration of title in the share.

Traditionally, the Dutch legislator seeks to protect the shares in a company against dilution. The traditional protection is offered by the statutory pre-emption right. Under flexible corporate law, shareholders may be denied a pre-emption right on the basis of, for instance, a clause to that effect in the articles of association or a resolution of the shareholders' meeting. The protection offered by the traditional pre-emption right may then become rather weak. Will that create problems under Article 1 of the First Protocol? I do not expect so in the case of the Netherlands. Our Civil Code prescribes as a compulsory rule the principle of equal treatment of the shareholders by the company. This principle of equal treatment is nothing more and nothing less than reasonableness and fairness. The Dutch Supreme Court decided in a famous judgment[11] that a selective allotment of shares in principle contravened the statutory equality principle in spite of the fact that the shareholders' meeting had explicitly decided to bypass the pre-emption right. Shareholders holding the same class of shares have to be treated in the same way by the company. When our Supreme Court confirms this decision under a new simple and flexible regime, Article 1 of the First Protocol will not come into view.

Still, there are other questions for which Article 1 of the First Protocol may become of importance. I again refer to the minority shareholder who wishes to exit. The reason for his wish to leave the company may be that the majority shareholder has prejudiced the company's assets, for instance by undertaking competing activities that harm the company. As a result, the shares of the minority shareholder may have decreased in value. Under our present exit rules, the exiting shareholder will obtain compensation for the transfer of his shares that is to be determined as close as possible to the moment at which the shares are transferred to the majority shareholder. This means that the shareholder will not be compensated for the shares' loss of value which was the reason for the minority shareholder to leave and was

[10] European Court of Human Rights, 25 July 2002, *Jurisprudentie Onderneming en Recht* (2003) p. 111; and European Court of Human Rights, 7 November 2002, *Jurisprudentie Onderneming en Recht* (2002) p. 112.

[11] *Hoge Raad* 31 December 1993, *Nederlandse Jurisprudentie* (1994) p. 436.

due to the conduct of the majority shareholder. In my opinion, this outcome is unreasonable, especially if one acknowledges that the majority shareholder can prevent the company from instituting legal proceedings against him. Does Article 1 of the First Protocol any relevance for the solution of this problem?

In 1995, the European Court of Human Rights passed judgment in the *Agrotexim* case.[12] The case concerned expropriation without compensation by Greece of certain assets owned by an English company, called Fixed Brewery. The shareholders of the company, which had been wound up in the meantime, protested against this, alleging that expropriation of any of the company's property resulted in a decrease in the value of shares in contravention of the protection guaranteed by Article 1 of the First Protocol. The European Court of Human Rights did not share this view and decided that only a direct infringement of the title incorporated in a share could constitute an infringement of the right of ownership within the meaning of Article 1 of the First Protocol. It regarded expropriation as a measure related to the possessions of the company and not those of the individual shareholders. According to the Court, the company – not the shareholders – had to take action against the expropriation.

If a majority shareholder harms the company, there can be no question of direct damage to the shares. Accordingly, Article 1 does not seem to be relevant. I doubt whether this is really correct, however. Should the *Agrotexim* judgment apply if the minority shareholder is about to leave the company? In that case, he will no longer be able to benefit from the action taken by the board of the company against the majority shareholder who has prejudiced the company's interest. The decision in the *Agrotexim* case was not about shareholders who wished to leave the company. In addition to this, there is something else. In the case I described above, the majority shareholder prevented the board from functioning properly by preventing the board from taking action against him (as the majority shareholder). In such a case, the majority shareholder is likely to abuse his position as a majority shareholder against the minority shareholder. In my opinion, the Dutch legislator should provide that a minority shareholder who leaves the company can be compensated for the decrease in the value of his shares that has been caused by the majority shareholder (because this is reasonable and in order to prevent problems with Article 1 of the First Protocol). Thus, it gives me some pleasure that the Dutch legislator intends to insert such a clause in our Civil Code.

5. Concluding remarks

In conclusion, welfare and fairness are notions that can clarify and direct the Dutch project to make the private company more simple and flexible. It is my view that reasonableness, fairness and fundamental rights will remain lasting elements of Dutch corporate law. These concepts are becoming increasingly important in the practice of company law. In upholding reasonableness, fairness and fundamental rights, the courts will play a pivotal role, especially in the context of a more simple and flexible private company law.

---

[12] European Court of Human Rights, 24 October 1995, *Nederlandse Jurisprudentie* (1996) p. 375.

Part III

THE EVOLUTION OF HYBRID BUSINESS FORMS IN THE UNITED STATES

Chapter 9

ABOLISHING LLC VEIL PIERCING

Stephen M. Bainbridge*

1. Introduction

Several years ago I wrote an article entitled 'Abolishing Veil Piercing', whose titular thesis called on courts to scrap the doctrine known as piercing the corporate veil.[1] The standard justification for veil piercing argues that it serves as a safety valve allowing courts to address cases in which the externalities associated with limited liability seem excessive.[2]

As such, veil piercing is called upon to achieve such lofty goals as leading shareholders to optimally internalize risk, while not deterring capital formation and economic growth, but while promoting populist notions of economic democracy.[3] The task is untenable. Veil piercing is rare, unprincipled, and arbitrary.[4] Such a doctrine is highly unlikely to consistently effect socially beneficial policy outcomes. Instead, veil piercing achieves neither fairness nor efficiency, but rather only uncertainty and lack of predictability, thus increasing transaction costs for small businesses.[5]

* William D. Warren Professor of Law at UCLA. Professor Bainbridge currently teaches Business Associations, Unincorporated Business Associations, and Advanced Corporation Law. In past years, he has also taught Corporate Finance, Securities Regulation, Mergers and Acquisitions, and seminars on corporate governance. He previously taught at the University of Illinois Law School (1988-1996), where the Class of 1990 gave him the 'Best Instructor Award' as well as at Harvard Law School as the Joseph Flom Visiting Professor of Law and Business (2000-2001), La Trobe University in Melbourne (2005) and at Aoyama Gakuin University in Tokyo (1999).

[1] S.M. Bainbridge, 'Abolishing Veil Piercing', 26 *Journal of Corporation Law* (2001) p. 479.

[2] As a leading text observes: 'Finally, the doctrine of piercing the corporate veil allows courts to impose liability on shareholders in appropriate cases, notwithstanding the limited-liability rule. … As a practical matter, therefore, the piercing doctrine may act as a safety valve that takes some of the pressure off the limited liability rule in cases where the rule is most dubious.' W.L. Cary and M.A. Eisenberg, *Cases and Materials on Corporations*, 7th edn. unabr. (St. Paul, West Publishing 1995) p. 191.

[3] See S.B. Presser, 'Thwarting the Killing of the Corporation: Limited Liability, Democracy, and Economics', 87 *Northwestern University Law Review* (1992) p. 148, at pp. 155–56 (arguing that limited liability was originally rooted in a legislative desire to encourage small and impecunious entrepreneurs to start and grow new businesses); see also Cary and Eisenberg, *supra* n. 2, at p. 190 (explaining that 'state legislatures in particular often seem to put much more weight on promoting local business formation than on requiring the internalization of externalities').

[4] See F.H. Easterbrook and D.R. Fischel, 'Limited Liability and the Corporation', 52 *University of Chicago Law Review* (1985) p. 89 (explaining that veil piercing 'seems to happen freakishly. Like lightning, it is rare, severe, and unprincipled'); cf., *Berkey* v. *Third Ave. Ry. Co.*, 155 N.E. 58, 61 (N.Y. 1926) (Cardozo, J.) (opining that veil piercing is a doctrine 'enveloped in the mists of metaphor').

[5] See Bainbridge, *supra* n. 1, at p. 515 (arguing that the veil piercing doctrine 'is inconsistent with the goals of certainty and predictability').

J.A. McCahery, L. Timmerman and E.P.M. Vermeulen (eds.), Private Company Law Reform

I therefore argued for abolishing veil piercing so as to refocus judicial analysis on the appropriate question, which I posited to be: Did the defendant-shareholder do anything for which he or she should be held directly liable?[6] For example, did the shareholder commit fraud, which led a creditor to forego contractual protections? Or did the shareholder use fraudulent transfers or insider preferences to siphon funds out of the corporation?

In this chapter, my attention turns to limited liability companies (LLCs).[7] Under all LLC statutes, members of a LLC – like shareholders of a corporation – are not personally liable for the firm's obligations.[8] The obvious question is whether courts should export the corporate veil piercing doctrine to the LLC context. Some LLC statutes seem to command courts to do so.[9] Even in the absence of such a statutory command, however, courts are routinely applying the corporate law doctrine to LLCs.[10] Most are doing so in a way that can only be described as unthinking.[11]

My thesis herein is that the case for limited liability – and therefore the case against veil piercing – applies with equal force to LLCs as to corporations. Accordingly, other than in those jurisdictions whose statute commands courts to do so, courts have erred by importing the corporate veil piercing doctrine into LLC law.[12]

Section 2 of this chapter reviews the emerging legal landscape. Section 3 advocates abolishing the veil piercing doctrine in the context of LLCs. Instead, as I proposed with respect to corporations, Section 3 advocates a regime of direct liability: Did the defendant-members do anything for which they are appropriately held personally liable?

2. LAW

In corporate law, the doctrine of limited liability holds that shareholders of a corporation generally are not liable for debts incurred or torts committed by the firm.[13] Shareholder

---

6 Ibid., at p. 516.

7 This chapter assumes familiarity with the LLC form. See generally J.W. Callison, 'Venture Capital and Corporate Governance: Evolving the Limited Liability Company to Finance the Entrepreneurial Business', 26 *Journal of Corporation Law* (2000) p. 97; W.J. Carney, 'Limited Liability Companies: Origins and Antecedents', 66 *University of Colorado Law Review* (1995) p. 855; W.M. Gazur, 'The Limited Liability Company Experiment: Unlimited Flexibility, Uncertain Role', 58 *Law and Contemporary Problems* (1995) p. 135; R.R. Keatinge, et al., 'The Limited Liability Company: A Study of the Emerging Entity', 47 *Business Lawyer* (1992) p. 375; C.W. Murdock, 'Limited Liability Companies in the Decade of the 1990s: Legislative and Case Law Developments and Their Implications for the Future', 56 *Business Lawyer* (2001) p. 499; L.E. Ribstein, 'The Emergence of the Limited Liability Company', 51 *Business Lawyer* (1995) p. 1 [hereinafter Ribstein, Emergence]; L.E. Ribstein, 'The New Choice of Entity for Entrepreneurs', 26 *Capital University Law Review* (1997) p. 325.

8 See, e.g., Unif. Ltd. Liab. Co. Act § 303(a), 6A U.L.A. 590 (2003).

9 See, e.g., Minn. Stat. § 322B.303(2) (2003).

10 See *infra* n. 27 and accompanying text.

11 See *infra* n. 29 and accompanying text.

12 At the outset, however, a distinction must be drawn between veil piercing and enterprise liability. Allocating liability within a business enterprise comprised of multiple corporations and/or LLCs involves far different policy considerations than does holding liable the natural persons who own a limited liability company. These tasks should be unbundled. Intra-corporate group liability issues should be dealt with as a species of enterprise liability, while the liability of individual LLC members is the proper subject of veil piercing law. In this chapter, I propose retaining enterprise liability to deal with allocating liability within business enterprises that include LLCs, including the liability of parent corporations or LLCs for the acts of their subsidiaries, while eliminating the doctrine of veil piercing insofar as it would allow imposition of personal liability on the ultimate owners of the LLC (whether they be natural persons or institutional investors).

13 See, e.g., Model Bus. Corp. Act § 6.22 Supp. (1998).

losses when the firm faces financial difficulties are limited to the amount the shareholder has invested in the firm – i.e., the amount initially paid by the shareholder to purchase his stock.

Despite the statutory guarantee of limited liability for shareholders of a corporation, however, unlimited personal liability may be involuntarily thrust upon a shareholder via the equitable remedy known as piercing the corporate veil.[14]

The 'veil' of the 'corporate fiction', or the 'artificial personality' of the corporation is 'pierced', and the individual or corporate shareholder exposed to personal or corporate liability, as the case may be, when a court determines that the debt in question is not really a debt of the corporation, but ought, in fairness, to be viewed as a debt of the individual or corporate shareholder or shareholders.[15] Or, as a seminal 1912 law review article put it:

> 'When the conception of corporate entity is employed to defraud creditors, to evade an existing obligation, to circumvent a statute, to achieve or perpetuate monopoly, or to protect knavery or crime, the courts will draw aside the web [i.e., veil] of entity, will regard the corporate company as an association of live, up-and-doing, men and women shareholders, and will do justice between real persons.'[16]

LLC statutes likewise provide limited liability for LLC members. Section 303 of the Uniform Limited Liability Company Act (ULLCA), for example, states that:

> 'The debts, obligations, and liabilities of a limited liability company, whether arising in contract, tort, or otherwise, are solely the debts, obligations, and liabilities of the company. A member or manager is not personally liable for a debt, obligation, or liability of the company solely by reason of being or acting as a member or manager.'[17]

Given the corporate precedent, the question inevitably arose whether corporate law's veil piercing rules carried over to the LLC context. Courts and commentators have uniformly concluded that the LLC form does not provide truly unlimited limited liability; rather, the LLC veil may be pierced in appropriate circumstances.[18] In some cases they were com-

---

[14] There is substantial disagreement in the case law as to whether veil piercing is an equitable or legal doctrine. The significance of the issue, of course, is that equitable remedies need not be tried before a jury but parties subject to legal remedies generally are entitled to trial by jury. See also *Wm. Passalacqua Builders, Inc.* v. *Resnick Developers S., Inc.*, 933 F.2d 131, 136 (2d Cir. 1991) (veil piercing has roots in both law and equity, so it was proper for trial court to submit issue to jury); *Am. Protein Corp.* v. *AB Volvo*, 844 F.2d 56, 59 (2d Cir. 1988) (veil piercing is an equitable remedy but issue is normally submitted to a jury); *Compare United States* v. *Golden Acres, Inc.*, 684 F. Supp. 96, 103 (D. Del. 1988) (veil piercing is equitable remedy and affords no right to jury trial), and *Dow Jones Co.* v. *Avenel*, 198 Cal. Rptr. 457, 460 (Cal. Ct. App. 1984) (same), with *Bower* v. *Bunker Hill Co.*, 675 F. Supp. 1254, 1261–62 (E.D. Wash. 1986) (veil piercing a legal remedy because it seeks a money judgment and thus a right to jury trial exists).

[15] S.B. Presser, *Piercing the Corporate Veil* (Chicago, Clark Boardman Callaghan 1991) § 1:1, at pp. 1-6 (footnotes and emphasis omitted). Shareholders may also face personal liability in connection with watered stock or unlawful dividends. In some states, special statutory provisions impose personal liability on shareholders with respect to certain corporate debts. New York and Wisconsin, for example, do so with respect to certain debts to corporate employees. Ibid. and n. 14.

[16] I.M. Wormser, 'Piercing the Veil of Corporate Entity', 12 *Columbia Law Review* (1912) p. 496, at p. 517. For an overview of the modern law of piercing the corporate veil and related doctrines, see S.M. Bainbridge, *Corporation Law and Economics* (St. Paul, Foundation Press 2002) pp. 151-71.

[17] Unif. Ltd. Liab. Co. Act § 303(a), 6A U.L.A. 590 (2001).

[18] See *Kaycee Land & Livestock* v. *Flahive*, 46 P.3d 323, 327–28 (Wyo. 2002) (citing authorities). In some regulatory settings, veil piercing-like standards are mandated by statute or rule. In plant closing litigation arising

pelled to reach this result by statute, but they have done so even when the statute was silent.[19]

2.1 Statutes invoking veil piercing

Minnesota's LLC statute provides that 'case law that states the conditions and circumstances under which the corporate veil of a corporation may be pierced under Minnesota law also applies to limited liability companies.'[20] In *Tom Thumb Food Markets, Inc.* v. *TLH Properties*, LLC,[21] one Hartmann, acting for TLH, agreed to build a building for Tom Thumb on property owned by one Smith. Hartmann represented that he owned the property.[22] In fact, Hartman did not own the property, but believed that he had a deal with one Smith to develop it.[23] After the project fell through, Tom Thumb sued, seeking to pierce TLH's LLC veil and hold Hartmann personally liable.[24] On appeal, the court held that, under the express terms of the Minnesota LLC statute, the law relating to piercing the corporate veil applies to LLCs.[25] On the facts, however, the court held that Tom Thumb had failed to establish the element of injustice or fundamental unfairness necessary to pierce the veil.[26]

---

under the federal Worker Adjustment and Retraining Notification ('WARN') Act, 29 U.S.C. §§ 2101–2109 (2000), for example, the issue often arises as to whether corporate or LLC subsidiaries should be treated as a 'single employer' along with their parents. The federal Department of Labor has promulgated a standard closely resembling corporate veil piercing for use in making that determination. *UAW Local 157* v. *OEM/Erie Westland, LLC*, 203 F. Supp. 2d 825, 832–33 (E.D. Mich. 2002). In addition, courts often supplement the Department of Labor standard with ordinary corporate veil piercing principles. Ibid., at p. 833. These regulatory requirements are beyond the scope of this chapter. Also beyond the scope of this chapter is the use of veil piercing-based theories in procedural settings. See, e.g., *Hesni* v. *Williams & Boshea*, LLC, No. CIV.A. 01-3745, 2002 WL 373273 (E.D. La. Mar. 7, 2002) (holding that because plaintiff would be able to pierce the LLC's veil to hold an individual personally liable consent of that individual was required in order for the case to be removed to federal court).

[19] The statutory language governing LLC member liability 'varies significantly among the states'. R.J. Huss, 'Revamping Veil Piercing for all Limited Liability Entities: Forcing the Common Law into the Statutory Age', 70 *University of Cincinnati Law Review* (2001) p. 95, at p. 101. For a useful taxonomy of the various approaches states have taken to the question of LLC member liability, albeit one whose assignments of individual states to particular approaches is now out-of-date, see R.B. Thompson, 'The Limits of Liability in the New Limited Liability Entities', 32 *Wake Forest Law Review* (1997) p. 1, at pp. 14-18 (analyzing the various state LLC statutes).

[20] Minn. Stat. Ann. § 322B.303(2) (West 2004). At one time, a number of other states had similar provisions, although these have largely faded away. See Ribstein, Emergence, *supra* n. 7, at p. 9.

[21] No. C9-98-1277, 1999 WL 31168 (Minn. Ct. App. Jan. 26, 1999).

[22] Ibid., at p. 1.

[23] Ibid.

[24] Ibid.

[25] Ibid., at p. 3.

[26] Ibid. Minnesota's corporate veil piercing standard is a two-pronged one, requiring proof both that (1) the corporation is a mere alter ego of the shareholder; and (2) that failing to pierce would allow some injustice or fundamental unfairness to the plaintiff to go unremedied. *Gallinger* v. *N. Star Hosp. Mut. Assurance, Ltd.*, 64 F.3d 422, 427 (8th Cir. 1995). In *Gallinger*, the court held that the second prong was not satisfied and that the veil should not be pierced. Student commentator Shaun Klein critiqued *Gallinger* as imposing too demanding a standard for piercing the LLC veil and, accordingly, argued for a legislative change to make veil piercing easier. S.M. Klein, 'Comment, Piercing the Veil of the Limited Liability Company, From Sure Bet to Long Shot: *Gallinger* v. *North Star Hospital Mutual Assurance, Ltd.*', 22 *Journal of Corporation Law* (1996) p. 131. Klein's analysis has been cited with approval by some other commentators, perhaps most notably by David Cohen, who observed that: 'This case is interesting in that it seems to recognize that LLCs are different from corporations and, perhaps as a result, the court argued that although the elements of the first requirement for piercing the veil exist, since the firm was created as an LLC the second prong is weakened to such a degree that no piercing can exist as a matter of law.'

2.2 Silent statutes

Absent a Minnesota-like statute mandating the use of corporate veil piercing precedents in determining the personal liability of members of a LLC, should a court import the corporate law doctrine into the LLC arena? Given the availability of corporate law doctrines as a ready made body of law close at hand, doing so has proven an irresistible impulse.[27] Some courts even refer to the relevant cause of action as being one to 'pierce the corporate veil' of a LLC.[28] The analysis in most of these cases is perfunctory at best; most simply assume the corporate law standard applies and have done with it.[29]

The Connecticut statute, for example, provides that:

> 'a person who is a member or manager of a limited liability company is not liable, *solely* by reason of being a member or manager . . . for a debt, obligation or liability' of the LLC.'[30]

Connecticut courts have read the word 'solely' as permitting imposition of unlimited personal liability on grounds other than mere LLC membership and, moreover, have invoked the corporate veil piercing rules to supply the requisite grounds.[31]

D.L. Cohen, 'Theories of the Corporation and the Limited Liability Company: How Should Courts and Legislatures Articulate Rules For Piercing the Veil, Fiduciary Responsibility and Securities Regulation for the Limited Liability Company?', 51 *Oklahoma Law Review* (1998) p. 427, at pp. 454-55, n. 142. In fact, however, the entity at issue in *Gallinger* was not a limited liability company, at least in the sense that that term is typically used. To the contrary, the entity in question was formed in Bermuda under a statute treating its 'members in a manner analogous to shareholders in a corporation'. *Gallinger*, 64 F.3d at 424. Hence, *Gallinger* should not be treated as precedent in LLC cases.

[27] See, e.g., *Hollowell* v. *Orleans Reg'l Hosp. LLC*, 217 F.3d 379, 385 n.7 (5th Cir. 2000); *Int'l Bancorp LLC* v. *Societe des Bains de Mer et Du Cercle des Estrangers a Monaco*, 192 F. Supp. 2d 467, 477–78 (E.D. Va. 2002); *NetTech Solutions LLC* v. *ZipPark.com*, No. 01 Civ. 2683 (SAS), 2001 WL 1111966 at *11 (S.D.N.Y. Sept. 20, 2001); *GMAC Commercial Mortgage Corp.* v. *Gleichman*, 84 F. Supp. 2d 127, 145 (D. Me. 1999); *In re Sanner*, 218 B.R. 941, 947 (Bankr. D. Ariz. 1998); *Ditty* v. *Checkrite, Ltd.*, 973 F. Supp. 1320, 1335 (D. Utah 1997); *Litchfield Asset Mgmt. Corp.* v. *Howell*, 799 A.2d 298, 309–16 (Conn. App. Ct. 2002); *Bonner* v. *Brunson*, 585 S.E.2d 917, 918 (Ga. Ct. App. 2003); *Hamilton* v. *AAI Ventures, LLC*, 768 So. 2d 298, 302 (La. Ct. App. 2000); *Stauffacher* v. *Lone Star Mud, Inc.*, 54 S.W.3d 810, 815–16 (Tex. App. 2001). Some courts have done even stranger things when it comes to veil piercing in the LLC context. In *New Horizons Supply Cooperative* v. *Haack*, No. 98-1865, 1999 Wisc. App. LEXIS 108 (Jan. 28, 1999), the trial court decided to treat the LLC as though it were a partnership, and imposed personal liability on the members, mainly because the LLC was treated as a partnership for tax purposes. Ibid., at p. 6. The appeals court reversed that holding, but imposed personal liability on the alternative grounds that the member did not follow proper procedures for dissolution and did not prove that the amounts distributed to her on dissolution were less than the amount of the debt to New Horizons. Ibid., at p. 9.

[28] See, e.g., *Stone* v. *Frederick Hobby Assoc. II*, No. CV0001816205, 2001 WL 861822 at 6 (Conn. Super. Ct. July 10, 2001); *Advanced Tel. Sys. Inc.* v. *Com-Net Prof'l Mobile Radio LLC*, 59 Pa.D. & C.4th 286, 289 (Pa. C. P. 2002).

[29] In *Rafferty* v. *Noto Brothers Const., LLC*, No. CV00082596 WL 459073, at * 1 (Conn. Super. Ct. Apr. 17, 2001), for example, the court simply stated: 'The protection afforded by the L.L.C. is not unlimited and may be disregarded, as in the case of a corporation, when the L.L.C. is the alter ego or business conduit of individuals.' (citing other unpublished opinions). In *Ditty* v. *Checkrite, Ltd., Inc.*, 973 F. Supp. 1320, 1355 (D. Utah 1997), the court contented itself with the observation that 'most commentators assume that the [veil piercing] doctrine applies to limited liability companies.' (emphasis added). See also *NetTech Solutions LLC*, 2001 WL 1111966, at * 11 (applying the corporate standard without analysis of difference in entities); *Great Neck Plaza, L.P.* v. *Le Peep Rest., LLC*, 37 P.3d 485, 489–90 (Colo. Ct. App. 2001) (affirming trial court's piercing of the LLC veil without analysis of the LLC issues); *Collins* v. *E-Magine, LLC*, 739 N.Y.S.2d 15, 17 (App. Div. 2002) (rejecting plaintiff's alter ego liability theory for failure of proof rather than as legally insufficient).

[30] Conn. Gen. Stat. § 34-133(a) (2003) (emphasis added).

[31] See, e.g., *Bastan* v. *RJM & Assoc., LLC*, No. CV99-0593189-S, 2001 WL 1006661, at *1 (Conn. Super. Ct. Jun. 4, 2001) (citing the relevant statute and holding that it did not foreclose veil piercing); see also Thompson,

The statute admittedly does not preclude the interpretation given it by the Connecticut courts. Yet, other interpretations were readily available. The legislature's use of the word 'solely' could be understood as suggesting only that a LLC member or manager may be held personally liable on some basis other than his mere status as such.[32] For example, a member who guarantees a LLC debt may be held personally liable if the LLC fails to perform.[33] Likewise, a member can be held personally liable where he committed a tort for which the entity is also liable.[34] Similarly, if the member or manager fraudulently induced a creditor to lend to the LLC, the member or manager could be held personally liable for committing fraud.[35] Perhaps the legislature used the word 'solely' to avoid foreclosing the prospect of direct personal liability of a member or manager arising out of his own conduct in cases such as those just described. If so, there was no need to import the corporate veil piercing rules. Yet, the Connecticut courts have failed to seriously examine this alternative interpretation of their statute.

Securities Investor Protection Corp. v. *R.D. Kushnir & Co.*[36] offers an even better example of just how poor the analysis in many of these cases has been. The original Illinois LLC statute contained a provision pursuant to which members of a LLC were

> 'personally liable for any act, debt, obligation, or liability of the limited liability company or another member or manager to the extent that a shareholder of an Illinois business corporation is liable in analogous circumstances under Illinois law.'[37]

This phrasing plausibly can be interpreted as inviting courts to extend the corporate veil piercing doctrine to the LLC context:

> 'The wording of the statute allows one to make the inferential leap that because a corporate shareholder can be subject to veil piercing and thereby exposed to personal liability, so too can an LLC member.'[38]

Illinois subsequently repealed that statute however, and replaced it with one tracking section 303 of the ULLCA, providing in pertinent part that:

> '(a) Except as otherwise provided in subsection (d) of this Section, the debts, obligations, and liabilities of a limited liability company, whether arising in contract, tort, or otherwise, are

supra n. 19, at p. 20 (arguing that 'the use of "solely" leaves room for other grounds [for setting aside the protections of limited liability] based on traditional common-law corporate principles for piercing the veil').

32 In *Pepsi-Cola Bottling Co. of Salisbury, Md.* v. *Handy*, No. 1973-S, 2000 WL 364199, at * 3-4 (Del. Ch. Mar. 15, 2000), Delaware Vice Chancellor Jacobs reviewed the similar Delaware LLC statute. Interestingly, Jacobs did not seize on the word 'solely' to justify veil piercing. Instead, he parsed the facts and determined that the individual defendants had engaged in at least some of the challenged wrongdoing before the LLC was formed. As such, their liability did not arise solely from their status as LLC members, and plaintiff was entitled to proceed against them individually. This is precisely the sort of analysis which courts ought to undertake in the face of such statutes, as compared to the simplistic assumption that corporate veil piercing standards apply.

33 K. Schwindt, 'Limited Liability Companies: Issues in Member Liability', 44 *UCLA Law Review* (1997) p. 1541, at p. 1549.

34 Ibid., at pp. 1548-49.

35 Cf., Bainbridge, *supra* n. 16, at p. 174 (discussing direct actions against corporate shareholders in such settings).

36 274 B.R. 768 (Bankr. N.D. Ill. 2002).

37 Ibid., at p. 775, n. 1 (quoting statute).

38 Schwindt, *supra* n. 33, at p. 1554.

> solely the debts, obligations, and liabilities of the company. A member or manager is not personally liable for a debt, obligation, or liability of the company solely by reason of being or acting as a member or manager.
>
> . . .
>
> (c) The failure of a limited liability company to observe the usual company formalities or requirements relating to the exercise of its company powers or management of its business is not a ground for imposing personal liability on the members or managers for liabilities of the company.'[39]

If the original wording permitted a pro-veil piercing inference, perhaps one should infer that the subsequent legislative action was intended to preclude extension of the veil piercing doctrine to the LLC setting. The legislature repealed a statute inviting such an extension, replacing it with one containing a flat prohibition of imposing liability on the members of a LLC.

The bankruptcy judge, however, failed even to address this interpretation. Instead, the judge simply quoted the relevant statutes and then opined:

> 'It would seem from the foregoing that "members" or "managers" of an Illinois limited liability company cannot be held liable for the mere failure to observe corporate formalities or repayment, but nothing in the statute bars piercing of the "corporate veil" for other grounds on which that may be done for ordinary corporations.'[40]

Why does the statute have to explicitly bar veil piercing? What else does the judge think the legislature was doing? Granted, the legislative action is not dispositive, because the statutory change in question here was part of a larger package of amendments.[41] In addition, because failure to comply with organizational formalities is a much criticized factor weighed under the corporate veil piercing standard, the legislature's efforts to ensure that failure to observe organizational formalities is not used as a basis for imposing personal liability on LLC members may implicitly recognize the possibility of otherwise applying corporate veil piercing rules to LLCs.[42] At the very least, however, the judge should have joined issue with the alternative interpretation suggested above.

2.3 The leading case

Appropriately enough, the leading case to undertake a substantial analysis, *Kaycee Land & Livestock* v. *Flahive*,[43] comes from Wyoming, the state in which the LLC was born. The Wyoming LLC statute is one of the silent statutes, providing no express authorization for

---

[39] See *Sec. Investor Prot. Corp.*, 274 B.R. at 775 (quoting statute).

[40] Id.; see also C. Brigham, 'Just How Limited is the Illinois Limited Liability Company?', 26 *Southern Illinois University Law Journal* (2001) p. 53 (arguing that the evolution of the Illinois statute history does not preclude application of veil piercing to Illinois LLCs).

[41] W.A. Price, 'A Primer on the Amended Illinois Limited Liability Company Act', *Journal of the DuPage County Bar Association* (Nov. 1998), available at <http://www.dcba.org/brief/novissue/1998/art11198.htm>.

[42] Robert Thompson argues that Illinois-like statutes 'providing general insulation for LLC participants and then an additional provision specifying that a particular piercing doctrine such as failure to follow corporate formalities should not be used to pierce . . . support an inference that other long-developed principles of piercing law remain available for judicial use.' Thompson, *supra* n. 19, at p. 18.

[43] 46 P.3d 323 (Wyo. 2002).

courts to pierce the LLC veil. To the contrary, the statute's text seems clearly to preclude the imposition of personal liability:

> 'Neither the members of a limited liability company nor the managers of a limited liability company managed by a manager or managers are liable under a judgment, decree or order of a court, or in any other manner, for a debt, obligation or liability of the limited liability company.'[44]

Not even the hedge word 'solely', on which the Connecticut courts seized, appears in what looks like a flat prohibition of personal liability. Yet, the Wyoming Supreme Court concluded that the LLC veil may be pierced.[45]

This result was predetermined when the court began its analysis by immediately conflating the LLC with the corporation: 'To answer this question, we must first examine the development of the doctrine within Wyoming's corporate context.'[46] Apparently anticipating this move, Flahive had tried to avoid extension of the corporate doctrine to the LLC by contrasting the LLC statute to the relevant provision of the Wyoming Corporation Code:

> 'Unless otherwise provided in the articles of incorporation, a shareholder of a corporation is not personally liable for the acts or debts of the corporation except that he may become personally liable by reason of his own acts or conduct.'[47]

Flahive pointed out that the LLC statute lacks a comparable proviso for personal liability arising from a LLC member's 'own acts or conduct.'[48]

The court rejected this argument. At the outset of its opinion, the court noted that veil piercing evolved as an equitable doctrine.[49] In response to Flahive's argument, the court then opined that because veil piercing 'is an equitable doctrine' the paucity of statutory authority for piercing the LLC veil was not surprising.[50] Finally, the court invoked the hoary canon of statutory construction under which statutes in derogation of the common law are to be strictly construed.[51] Because the court saw no evidence of legislative intent to preclude application of the common law veil piercing to the LLC context, the court held that the LLC veil could be pierced.[52]

The flaws in this analysis are many and obvious. Most significantly, there was no common law of LLCs. The interpretative canon in question is invoked typically when the legislature adopts a statute in an area of the law where there is pre-existing common

---

[44] Wyo. Stat. Ann. § 17-15-113 (Michie 1977).

[45] *Kaycee*, 46 P.3d at pp. 327-28.

[46] Ibid., at p. 325.

[47] Ibid., at p. 326 (quoting Wyo. Stat. Ann. § 17-16-622(b) (LexisNexis 2001)).

[48] Ibid.

[49] Ibid.; see also Schwindt, *supra* n. 33, at p. 1552 (opining that '[t]he paucity of statutory authority for LLC piercing should not be considered a barrier to its application. The concept of piercing the corporate veil is based on common law, rather than state or federal statutory law.') (footnotes and internal quotation marks omitted).

[50] See *Kaycee*, 46 P.3d at pp. 326-27.

[51] Ibid., at p. 327.

[52] See ibid. (noting the 'dearth of legislative consideration on this issue'); see also *Bastan* v. *RJM & Assoc., LLC*, No. CV99-0593189-S, 2001 WL 1006661, at *1 (Conn. Super. Ct. June 4, 2001) (reasoning that the 'legislature is deemed to have been aware of our deeply rooted common law remedy of imposing personal liability upon a shareholder of a corporation where the corporate shield has been used to promote injustice, and the legislature surely could have expressly created a blanket limitation of member liability had it so chosen').

law.[53] The LLC, however, was an entirely new statutory creation. There was no background of common law against which it was to be implemented. Corporate common law was relevant to the problem at bar only by virtue of judicial fiat.

Even if the court was correct in opining that corporate common law was relevant, its invocation of the canon in question was suspect. Karl Llewellyn famously demonstrated that canons of construction are essentially indeterminate.[54] Further, the canon requiring strict construction of statutes in derogation of the common law is particularly suspect. The canon

> 'can work to ossify an obsolete *status quo* and, in any event, is probably rooted historically in a selfish desire by English judges to limit Parliament's power.'[55]

The authors of the passage just quoted further opine that 'the derogation canon ... is usually treated as anathema by contemporary commentators.'[56]

The *Kaycee* court concluded that it could 'discern no reason, in either law or policy, to treat LLCs differently than we treat corporations.'[57] Section 3 offers some reasons for doing just that. Ultimately, the leading case on the subject utterly failed to offer any compelling reason, in either law or policy, for treating LLCs and corporations the same.

2.4 The emerging standards for piercing the LLC veil

Several formulations of the veil piercing standard compete in corporate law. In light of the predominant trend for courts to import the corporate law regime into the LLC context, it is not surprising that a similar multitude of standards is emerging in the latter setting.

Control is the common (if sometimes implicit) feature of all the concepts used to describe cases in which veil piercing is appropriate. LLC members who do not actively participate in the firm's business or management are rarely held liable on a veil piercing theory.[58] It seems clear therefore that control is an essential prerequisite for holding a LLC member or manager liable.

Standing alone, however, control cannot be a sufficient ground for piercing the veil of either a corporation or a LLC. Granted, *Walkovszky* v. *Carlton*,[59] the leading corporate law decision, indicates that veil piercing is appropriate where the corporation is 'a "dummy" for its individual shareholders who are in reality carrying on the business in their personal

---

[53] See, e.g., *Augusta & Savannah R.R.* v. *McElmurry*, 24 Ga. 75, 78 (Ga. 1858) (noting that '[a]cts relative to railroads cannot be in derogation of the common law, for railroads were unknown to the common law'); see also *Gottling* v. *P.R. Inc.*, 61 P.3d 989, 995 (Utah 2002) (declining to follow the canon where there was no relevant common law when the statute in question was enacted).

[54] K.N. Llewellyn, 'Remarks on the Theory of Appellate Decision and the Rules or Canons About How Statutes Are To Be Construed', 3 *Vanderbilt Law Review* (1950) p. 395.

[55] W.N. Eskridge, et al., *Legislation and Statutory Interpretation* (St Paul, Foundation Press 2000) p. 332.

[56] Ibid. at 334; see also A. Vermeulen, 'The Judicial Power in the State (and Federal) Courts', 2000 *Supreme Court Review* (2000) p. 357, at pp. 429-30 (noting that while '[s]tate courts have often invoked the canon that statutes in derogation of the common law should be narrowly construed . . . that canon may be falling out of favor').

[57] *Kaycee*, 46 P.3d at 327.

[58] See *New England Nat'l LLC* v. *Kabro of East Lyme LLC*, No. 550014, 2000 WL 254590, at *6 (Conn. Super. Ct. Feb. 23, 2000).

[59] 223 N.E.2d 6 (N.Y. 1966).

capacities for purely personal rather than corporate ends.'[60] The problem with this analysis, however, is that a close corporation with, for example, one to three dominant shareholders has no 'corporate ends' separate from those of its owners. In apparent recognition of this fact, courts generally require plaintiffs to show something more than mere control in the corporate law context.[61]

Courts are likewise developing multi-pronged standards for the LLC context. A common formulation, for example, asks whether the LLC member to be held personally liable: (1) controlled the LLC; and (2) abused his control of the firm 'in order to defeat justice or perpetrate fraud.'[62] Another common formulation adapts the three-pronged instrumentality doctrine used in corporate law, under which the plaintiff must show: (1) control of the corporation by the defendant that is so complete as to amount to total domination of finances, policy, and business practices such that the controlled corporation has no separate mind, will, or existence; (2) such control is used to commit a fraud, wrong, or other violation of the plaintiff's rights; and (3) the control and breach of duty owed to the plaintiff was a proximate cause of the injury.[63]

As with corporate law cases,[64] the analysis in LLC litigation frequently collapses into a mere laundry list of factors considered by the court.[65] In *Bonner* v. *Bruson*,[66] for example, the Georgia Court of Appeals set out its 'defeat justice or perpetrate fraud' standard, but then ignored that standard to focus on various specific transactions to determine whether there was 'any evidence that [defendant] Bruson abused the form of the LLC by commingling or confusing LLC business with his personal affairs.'[67]

The *Bonner* decision is particularly troubling because the Georgia court seemingly imported into the LLC context not only the corporate veil piercing doctrine, but also the fetish

---

[60] Id. at p. 8; see F.A. Gevurtz, 'Piercing Piercing: An Attempt to Lift the Veil of Confusion Surrounding the Doctrine of Piercing the Corporate Veil', 76 *Oregon Law Review* (1997) p. 853, at p. 864 ('No corporation in the world has a mind of its own; they are fictitious entities. People control corporations').

[61] See, e.g., *Luis* v. *Orcutt Town Water Co.*, 22 Cal. Rptr. 389, 395 (Cal.Ct. App. 1962) ('It is not true that any wholly owned subsidiary is necessarily the alter ego of the parent corporation.'); *Shafford* v. *Otto Sales Co.*, 260 P.2d 269, 277 (Cal. Ct. App. 1953) ('[C]omplete stock ownership and actual one-man control will not alone be sufficient to impose liability on the individual').

[62] For example, in *Bonner* v. *Bruson*, 585 S.E.2d 917, 918 (Ga. Ct. App. 2003) the court stated: A court may disregard the separate LLC entity and the protective veil it provides to an individual member of the LLC when that member, in order to defeat justice or perpetrate fraud, conducts his personal and LLC business as if they were one by commingling the two on an interchangeable or joint basis or confusing otherwise separate properties, records, or control. See also *Gallinger* v. *N. Star Hosp. Mut. Assurance, Ltd.*, 64 F.3d 422, 427 (8th Cir. 1995) (adopting similar two-pronged standard).

[63] See, e.g., *Zaist* v. *Olson*, 227 A.2d 552, 558 (Conn. 1967); *Collet* v. *Am. Nat'l Stores, Inc.*, 708 S.W.2d 273, 284 (Mo. Ct. App. 1986). A number of decisions, especially in Connecticut, have extended the instrumentality rule to the LLC setting. See, e.g., *Stone* v. *Frederick Hobby Assoc. II*, No. CV0001816205, 2001 WL 861822 (Conn. Super. Ct. July 10, 2001); *Bastan* v. *RJM & Assoc., LLC*, No. CV99-0593189-S, 2001 WL 1006661 (Conn. Super. Ct. June 4, 2001); *Rafferty* v. *Noto Bros. Constr.*, LLC, No. CV000082596, 2001 WL 459073 (Conn. Super. Ct. Apr. 17, 2001).

[64] See Bainbridge, *supra* n. 16, at pp. 157-61 (discussing judicial reliance on a 'laundry list' of factors in corporation law).

[65] See generally E. Fox, 'Note, Piercing the Veil of Limited Liability Companies', 62 *George Washington Law Review* (1994) p. 1143, at pp. 1167-77 (setting out a list of potentially relevant factors and arguing that the relevance of any given factor will depend on the extent to which the LLC's governance and financial structures resemble those of a corporation or an unincorporated firm).

[66] *Bonner*, 585 S.E.2d 917.

[67] Ibid., at p. 919.

for formalities so often found in corporate veil piercing cases.[68] We shall see below that limited liability is a social concern mainly because it permits equity investors to externalize risk.[69] As such, failure to observe organizational formalities is largely irrelevant. Setting aside the rare cases in which failure to observe organizational formalities misleads a creditor into believing it is dealing with an individual rather than a LLC, there simply is no causal link between the creditor's injury and the member's misconduct.

The drafters of the ULLCA recognized the desirability of moving away from an emphasis on compliance with formalities by providing, in section 303(b), that:

> 'The failure of a limited liability company to observe the usual company formalities or requirements relating to the exercise of its company powers or management of its business is not a ground for imposing personal liability on the members or managers for liabilities of the company.'[70]

So too did the *Kaycee* court, which noted that because the LLC is intended to be 'much more flexible' in operation than corporations, the standard for piercing the LLC veil should not emphasize disregard for operational formalities to the extent that the corporate law version does.[71] Unfortunately, as *Bonner* illustrates, not all courts are getting it right; instead, these courts are importing corporate law's insistence on compliance with organizational formalities into the LLC context.[72]

Stone v. *Frederick Hobby Associates II*,[73] decided under Connecticut's instrumentality standard, provides a particularly egregious example of this trend. As is often the case with the instrumentality standard,[74] the court's analysis of the second prong – i.e., the requirement of a showing that

> 'the defendant [exerted such complete control over the corporate entity so as to enable him] to commit fraud or wrong, to perpetrate the violation of a statutory or other positive legal duty, or a dishonest or unjust act in contravention of plaintiff's legal rights.'[75]

---

[68] Cf., Bainbridge, *supra* n. 16, at pp. 159-61 (criticizing the emphasis on compliance with corporate formalities in veil piercing decisions in corporation law).

[69] See *infra* Section 3.1.2.

[70] Unif. Ltd. Liab. Co. ACT § 303(b), 6A U.L.A. 590 (2003).

[71] *Kaycee Land & Livestock* v. *Flahire*, 46 P.3d 323, 328 (Wyo. 2002); see also *Hollowell* v. *Orleans Reg'l Hosp. LLC*, No. Civ.A. 95-4029, 1998 WL 283298, at * 9 (E.D. La. May 29, 1998) (stating that 'analyses between corporate veil piercing and limited liability company veil piercing may not completely overlap . . . '[b]ecause the Louisiana LLC law requires 'fewer formalities' than does corporate law), *aff'd*, 217 F.3d 379 (5th Cir. 2000). Commentators uniformly support deemphasizing organizational formalities in the LLC context. See, e.g., Fox, *supra* n. 65, at p. 1172; Ribstein, Emergence, *supra* n. 7, at p. 9.

[72] See, e.g., *Lincoln Diversified Sys., Inc.* v. *Mangos Plus, Inc.*, No. 98 CIV. 5593 (RWS), 2000 WL 1880338 (S.D.N.Y. Dec. 27, 2000) (citing lack of evidence that formalities were ignored in explaining its refusal to pierce); *Litchfield Asset Mgmt. Corp.* v. *Howell*, 799 A.2d 298, 315–16 (Conn. App. Ct. 2002) (discussing defendant's failure to observe formalities); *Stone* v. *Frederick Hobby Assoc. II*, No. CV000181620S, 2001 WL 861822, at *10 (Conn. Super. Ct. July 10, 2001) (piercing the corporate veil on grounds, *inter alia*, that defendants 'affirmatively acted with disregard for Hobby II's existence as an entity that is separate and distinct'); *Hamilton* v. *AAI Ventures, LLC*, 768 So. 2d 298, 302 (La. Ct. App. 2000) (invoking corporate standard of 'failing to follow statutory formalities for incorporating and transacting corporate affairs' in LLC setting); *Advanced Tel. Sys. Inc.* v. *Com-Net Prof'l Mobile Radio LLC*, 59 Pa. D. & C.4th 286, 305 (Pa. C.P. 2002) (citing the absence of evidence that 'necessary formalities [were] ignored').

[73] *Stone*, 2001 WL 861822.

[74] See Bainbridge, *supra* n. 16, at pp. 153-54 (discussing a leading instrumentality standard precedent).

[75] *Stone*, 2001 WL 861822, at * 8.

– ranged from perfunctory to muddled. The court placed great emphasis on the defendant's failure to follow corporate formalities.[76] The court took the defendants to task, for example, for failing to properly fill out a real estate conveyance tax return.[77] In response to a question asking whether the grantor was a LLC, the principal defendant checked the 'no' box.[78] The principal defendant also signed the return in his individual capacity.[79] But who cares?[80] There was no evidence that these errors harmed anybody.

Aside from the defendants' disregard for organizational formalities, the *Stone* court noted testimony indicating that the LLC was set up 'to shield and protect … the principals of Hobby II, from personal liability.'[81] Granted, some of the defendants were overly colorful – even flippant – in their attitude. Defendants' legal counsel, for example, 'told the plaintiffs to "go ahead and sue [Hobby II]. There is no money in [Hobby II]. Why do you think we set it up as an LLC in the first place?"'[82] But so what? First, setting up a limited liability entity to shield oneself from personal liability is not a fraud or wrong. To the contrary, corporate law expressly 'permits the incorporation of a business for the very purpose of escaping personal liability.'[83] Presumably, LLC law should do likewise.[84] Second, to the extent the lack of resources in the Hobby II LLC troubled the court, undercapitalization alone is not a sufficient basis for piercing the veil in corporate law.[85] Again, the same should be true in LLC law.

---

[76] See ibid., at p. 10 (discussing omitted formalities).

[77] Ibid.

[78] Ibid.

[79] Ibid.

[80] Setting aside the fact that disregard for formalities should be given less weight in the LLC setting, disregard for entity formalities is more directly relevant to the first prong of the instrumentality standard – i.e., whether the defendant treated the firm as his alter ego – than the second. See Bainbridge, *supra* n. 16, at pp. 153-54 (discussing application of the instrumentality standard). Relying on the LLC member's disregard for organizational formalities as a justification for veil piercing is particularly problematic on Stone's facts because it was a contract case. See ibid., at pp. 160-61 (arguing that whether defendant complied with organizational formalities is especially irrelevant when the claim sounds in contract).

[81] *Stone*, 2001 WL 861822, at * 9.

[82] Ibid.

[83] *Bartle* v. *Home Owners Coop., Inc.*, 127 N.E.2d 832, 833 (N.Y. 1955); see also *Northern Tankers (Cyprus) Ltd.* v. *Backstrom*, 967 F. Supp. 1391, 1402 (D. Conn. 1997) (holding that 'the corporate fiction is generally recognized, even when set up for the very purpose of avoiding personal liability', albeit as a matter of federal common law rather than that of Connecticut).

[84] The *Stone* court opined that the misconduct required by the second prong may be found 'even in the absence of fraud or illegality, when the individual in control has, for example, used a corporate instrumentality to avoid personal liability that he had previously assumed.' *Stone*, 2001 WL 861822, at * 8. Even if correct, however, this rule on its face applies only where the corporate (or LLC) form is used to evade a pre-existing obligation. On the facts of *Stone*, there was no such obligation. The original contract was made between plaintiffs and the Hobby II LLC. See ibid. at *1 (noting that 'the plaintiffs allege that: they purchased the premises from the defendant, Hobby II.'). This error has cropped up in other Connecticut trial court decisions. In *KLM Indus., Inc.* v. *Tylutki*, No. CV980062008S, 2001 WL 1098069, at * 5 (Conn. Super. Ct. Aug. 23, 2001), for example, the court pierced the LLC veil where the alleged wrong committed was an effort 'to frustrate the payment of a lawful debt.' This holding is clearly erroneous. In *Campisano* v. *Nardi*, 562 A.2d 1 at * 7 (Conn. 1989), the Connecticut Supreme Court made clear that courts should decline 'to apply the instrumentality rule where the corporations were formed for legitimate purposes and the parties engaging in transactions with those corporations were fully aware of the type of business with which they were dealing. In the absence of a claim that the corporation was formed for an improper purpose, or that the plaintiffs were improperly induced to enter into a contract with the corporation, the mere breach of a corporate contract cannot of itself establish the basis for application of the instrumentality rule.' (footnote omitted).

[85] See, e.g., *Gartner* v. *Snyder*, 607 F.2d 582, 588 (2d Cir. 1979) ('Although Enterprises was thinly capitalized, that alone is not a sufficient ground for disregarding the corporate form. We know of no New York authority

2.5 Enterprise liability involving LLCs

Veil piercing-like issues are frequently presented in cases involving groups of affiliated corporations, including those involving parent and subsidiary corporations. In the leading corporate law decision, *Walkovszky* v. *Carlton*,[86] the defendant was the principal shareholder of a number of corporations operating taxicabs. The plaintiff, who had been injured by a cab owned by one of those companies, claimed that the multiple corporations had no separate existence, but rather were just components of a single business enterprise.[87] The court held that the corporate veil may not be pierced simply because the defendant corporation is part of a larger enterprise.[88] Instead, proof that multiple corporations are part of a single corporate group may give rise to enterprise liability.[89]

If correctly (and successfully) invoked, enterprise liability permits a creditor to reach the collective assets of all of the corporations making up the enterprise.[90] Obviously, this theory is most useful when the responsible corporation is insolvent, but the enterprise as a whole has sufficient assets to satisfy the creditor's claim. Given that enterprise liability is well-established in corporate law,[91] and that borrowing from corporate law is a well-established pattern in LLC cases, it comes as no surprise that courts are extending enterprise liability to corporate groups including LLCs.[92]

2.6 Summation

Benjamin Cardozo long ago observed that veil piercing is a doctrine 'enveloped in the mists of metaphor',[93] a complaint that remains true today. On the one hand, corporate veil piercing cases are highly fact-specific.[94] On the other hand, the facts often tell us little about the likely outcome. Successful corporate veil piercing claims seem to differ only in degree, but not in kind, from unsuccessful claims.[95] Unfortunately, there is no evidence to

---

that disregards corporate form solely because of inadequate capitalization'). The case usually cited for the proposition that undercapitalization alone suffices, *Minton* v. *Cavaney*, 364 P.2d 473 (Cal. 1961), arguably does not in fact stand for that proposition and, in any event, probably is no longer good law even in its home jurisdiction. See, e.g., *Arnold* v. *Browne*, 103 Cal. Rptr. 775, 783 (Cal. Ct. App. 1972) (treating undercapitalization as merely a relevant, but not dispositive, factor); *Harris* v. *Curtis*, 87 Cal. Rptr. 614, 617 (Cal. Ct. App. 1970) (rejecting argument 'that, *per se*, inadequate capitalization renders the shareholders ... liable for the obligations of the corporation').

86 223 N.E.2d 6 (N.Y. 1966).

87 Ibid., at p. 7.

88 Ibid., at p. 9.

89 See ibid., at p. 8.

90 See ibid.

91 See, e.g., *Gartner* v. *Snyder*, 607 F.2d 582, 588 (2d Cir. 1979); *Las Palmas Assocs.* v. *Las Palmas Ctr. Assocs.*, 235 Cal. App. 3d 1220, 1250 (1991).

92 See, e.g., *Litchfield Asset Mgmt. Corp.* v. *Howell*, 799 A.2d 298, 315–16 (Conn. App. Ct. 2002).

93 *Berkey* v. *Third Ave. Ry. Co.*, 155 N.E. 58, 61 (N.Y. 1926).

94 In corporation law, veil piercing claims are treated as pure questions of fact. Accordingly, appellate courts generally defer to the trier of fact and reverse only for abuse of discretion. See *Stark* v. *Coker*, 129 P.2d 390, at * 394 (Cal. 1942). As the California Supreme Court acknowledged, this standard means that appellate opinions typically provide only 'general rules' for guidance. There is nothing to suggest that those principles will change in the LLC context.

95 See generally R.B. Thompson, 'Piercing the Corporate Veil: An Empirical Study', 76 *Cornell Law Review* (1991) p. 1036 (providing a detailed empirical analysis of factors considered in both successful and unsuccessful piercing cases).

date that matters will improve as the vague corporate law standards are exported to the LLC setting.

3. Policy

In the leading *Kaycee* decision, the Wyoming Supreme Court concluded: 'We can discern no reason, in either law or policy, to treat LLCs differently than we treat corporations.'[96] Admittedly, there is a certain intuitive logic to treating LLCs the same way we do corporations. Even so, however, why privilege the assumption that corporations and LLCs are to be treated the same?

Granted, there is little direct evidence that legislatures intended to treat LLCs and corporations differently.[97] Yet, if legislatures had intended to incorporate the corporate law doctrines, they easily could have done so explicitly. Indeed, as we have seen, Minnesota did exactly that.[98] So did a number of other early LLC statutes.[99] Given the ready availability of such models, one could infer that subsequently adopted statutes were not intended to incorporate corporate law rules in the absence of explicit Minnesota-like language. As we have seen, this argument is especially compelling for states like Illinois, which moved away from a Minnesota-like formulation to a more neutral model that neither expressly nor impliedly invokes corporation law's veil piercing rules.[100]

In the absence of dispositive evidence of legislative intent, however, we now turn to the second prong of the *Kaycee* court's pronouncement. Is there good 'reason, in … policy, to treat LLCs differently than we treat corporations?'[101] In an ideal world, at least as defined by my policy preferences, we would treat them the same by abolishing veil piercing as to both. Assuming veil piercing will remain the law as to corporations, however, it is my thesis herein that we should treat LLCs differently by abolishing veil piercing as to them.

3.1 The case for veil piercing

It is surprisingly difficult to find coherent explanations of the policy justifications for piercing the LLC veil, as opposed to mere assertions by fiat that such reasons exist. Two explana-

---

[96] *Kaycee Land & Livestock* v. *Flahive*, 46 P.3d 323, 327 (Wyo. 2002). Many commentators likewise privilege the assumption that LLCs and corporations are to be treated the same. See, e.g., Schwindt, *supra* n. 33, at pp. 1551-52 (opining that: 'Given that corporations and limited partnerships both provide exceptions to the general rule of limited liability, it seems unlikely that LLCs would not also be subject to an exception that would expose their members to personal liability in certain instances'); Thompson, *supra* n. 19, at p. 20 (arguing that courts are unlikely to read LLC statutes as providing 'greater insulation than corporate law ... given the long-standing common law in this area' and the lack of clear legislative intent).

[97] See, e.g., Thompson, *supra* n. 19, at p. 21 (arguing that LLC statutes 'do little, if anything, to change the long-standing and well-developed judicial exceptions to limited liability'); cf., Schwindt, *supra* n. 33, at p. 1552 (arguing that: 'In the absence of statutory authority, courts should strive to develop a common law LLC piercing doctrine just as one was developed in the corporate setting').

[98] See *supra* n. 20 and accompanying text.

[99] See Fox, *supra* n. 65, at p. 1168 (stating that 'Colorado specifically calls for the application of the veil-piercing doctrine to LLCs'); Thompson, *supra* n. 19, at p. 17 (listing California, Hawaii, Minnesota, North Dakota, Wisconsin, and Washington as having statutes that 'specify that corporate law principles should be used to pierce the veil generally').

[100] See *supra* nn. 36-42 and accompanying text.

[101] *Kaycee*, 46 P.3d at 327.

tions tend to crop up most frequently. One depends on a notion of corporate personhood and can be dismissed almost out of hand. The other views limited liability as creating a negative externalities-based market failure. That view is true, but proves too much.

3.1.1 *The entity as separate person*

In *Kaycee*, the Wyoming Supreme Court treated veil piercing as a corollary of the corporation's status as a legal person:

> 'Statutes created the legal fiction of the corporation being a completely separate entity which could act independently from individual persons. If the corporation were created and operated in conformance with the statutory requirements, the law would treat it as a separate entity and shelter the individual shareholders from any liability caused by corporate action, thereby encouraging investment. However, courts throughout the country have consistently recognized certain unjust circumstances can arise if immunity from liability shelters those who have failed to operate a corporation as a separate entity. Consequently, when corporations fail to follow the statutorily mandated formalities, co-mingle funds, or ignore the restrictions in their articles of incorporation regarding separate treatment of corporate property, the courts deem it appropriate to disregard the separate identity and do not permit shareholders to be sheltered from liability to third parties for damages caused by the corporations' acts.
>
> ...
>
> If the members and officers of an LLC fail to treat it as a separate entity as contemplated by statute, they should not enjoy immunity from individual liability for the LLC's acts that cause damage to third parties.'[102]

To be sure, the law treats corporations and LLCs as legal persons separate from their shareholders or members (as the case may be).[103] The entity's legal personhood, moreover, has important real world consequences.[104] Even so, status as a separate legal person is but a convenient legal fiction.[105]

In the present context, the legal fiction that the LLC is a separate entity belies actual practice. A close corporation with a few dominant shareholders has no interests or purposes separate and distinct from those of its shareholders. The same is true of a LLC. To insist to the contrary is simply mindless formalism.

---

[102] Ibid.

[103] *Puerto Rico* v. *Russell & Co.*, 288 U.S. 476, 479 (1933) (noting 'the complete legal personality with which corporations are endowed').

[104] Corporate constituents contract not with each other, for example, but with the corporation. A bond indenture thus is a contract between the corporation and its creditors, an employment agreement is a contract between the corporation and its workers, and a collective bargaining agreement is a contract between the corporation and the union representing its workers. See, e.g., *John Wiley & Sons, Inc.* v. *Livingston*, 376 U.S. 543, 550 (1964) (collective bargaining agreement); *Berman* v. *Physical Med. Assocs.*, 225 F.3d 429, 433 (4th Cir. 2000) (employment agreement); *Lorenz* v. *CSX Corp.*, 1 F.3d 1406, 1417 (3d. Cir. 1993) (bond). If the contract is breached on the corporate side, it will be the entity that is sued in most cases, rather than the individuals who decided not to perform. If the entity loses, damages typically will be paid out of its assets and earnings rather than out of those individuals' pockets.

[105] Cf., *Citizens Coordinating Comm. on Friendship Heights, Inc.* v. *Wash. Metro. Area Transit Auth.*, 765 F.2d 1169, 1173 (D.C. Cir. 1985) (holding that: 'Though a corporation is a person for some purposes, we would be most reluctant to hold that it has senses and so can be affronted by deteriorations in its environment. That is beyond the reach of legal fiction and belongs in the realm of poetic license').

As I have explained elsewhere in more detail, moreover, reifying the firm as a separate entity is inconsistent with the prevailing understanding of the corporation as a nexus of contracts.[106] In this model, the firm is viewed not as an entity separate from its shareholders and other stakeholders, but rather as the nexus of a complex set of contractual relationships between many stakeholders who provide inputs for the corporation's productive processes. In the LLC setting, just as in the close corporation setting, all of these stakeholders know (or should know) that it is those who contribute equity capital that are vested with the power to control the enterprise. They should not be surprised that the equity claimants often blur the distinction between the business of the firm and their personal affairs. At least in the absence of proof that such a blurring of the boundary between the entity and the equity claimants caused injury to another stakeholder, there is no justification whatsoever for judicial intervention. The *Kaycee* court's apparent insistence to the contrary simply cannot be justified.

3.1.2 *The negative externalities of limited liability*

An alternative judicial explanation for veil piercing asserts that courts should pierce the veil when 'the policy behind the presumption of corporate independence and limited shareholder liability – encouragement of business development – is outweighed by the policy justifying disregarding the corporate form – the need to protect those who deal with the corporation.'[107] Clearly, however, not all those who deal with the corporation will receive this protection. As one court opined, 'some "wrong" beyond a creditor's inability to collect' must be shown before the veil will be pierced.[108] What then is the harm against which veil piercing protects those who deal with the corporation? And, does the same harm apply to LLCs?

It is generally accepted that limited liability creates negative externalities.[109] Limited liability allows equity holders to cause the firm to externalize part of the risks and costs of doing business onto other constituencies of the firm and, perhaps, even onto society at large.[110] The point is too well-established to require elaboration. Yet, externalities provide a foundation of sand for the complex edifice of modern veil piercing law.

---

[106] Bainbridge, *supra* n. 1, at pp. 484-86. The nexus of contract model's dominance within corporate law scholarship has been widely recognized by diverse jurists and scholars, including some who are not enthusiasts of the genre. See, e.g., W.T. Allen, 'Contracts and Communities in Corporation Law', 50 *Washington and Lee Law Review* (1993) p. 1395, at p. 1399 (former Delaware Chancellor); B.R. Cheffins, 'Using Theory to Study Law: A Company Law Perspective', 58 *Cambridge Law Journal* (1999) p. 197, at p. 209 ('[O]ne school of thought, law and economics, dominates the academic study of corporate law'); J. Seligman, Foreword to *Progressive Corporate Law* (Lawrence E. Mitchell ed.) (Greeley, Westview Printing 1995) p. ix. ('[T]he dominant recent analytical tool for corporate law analysis has been neoclassical economics … with its by now familiar subtexts of market imperfections, agency costs, and nexus of contracts …').

[107] *Wm. Passalacqua Builders, Inc.* v. *Resnick Developers South, Inc.*, 933 F.2d 131, 139 (2d Cir.1991).

[108] *Sea-Land Services, Inc.* v. *Pepper Source*, 941 F.2d 519, 524 (7th Cir. 1991).

[109] See, e.g., P.I. Blumberg, 'Limited Liability and Corporate Groups', 11 *Journal of Corporation Law* (1986) p. 573, at p. 576 (stating that 'even economists convinced of the utility of limited liability … concede that limited liability raises serious problems because it enables the enterprise to externalize its costs'); Easterbrook and Fischel, *supra* n. 4, at p. 104 (explaining that 'shareholders of a firm reap all of the benefits of risky activities but do not bear all of the costs'); D.W. Leebron, 'Limited Liability, Tort Victims, and Creditors', 91 *Columbia Law Review* (1991) p. 1565, at p. 1586 (asserting that '[l]imited liability does not simply offset positive externalities, but rather encourages excessively risky activity').

[110] See generally Bainbridge, *supra* n. 16, at pp. 132-34 (explaining how limited liability does so).

3.1.2.1 The argument from negative externalities does not justify the veil piercing doctrine

First, the externalities argument proves too much. Indeed, it makes a better justification for repealing the general rule of limited liability than it does for carving out a veil piercing-based exception to the general rule. Professors Hansmann and Kraakman, in fact, famously invoked the externalities argument to justify their proposal that limited liability should be eliminated with respect to tort claims.[111] Their argument has been criticized by a number of commentators.[112] In lieu of rehashing those arguments, it suffices for present purposes to note that their proposal has not been embraced by either legislatures or courts.[113] To the contrary, 'states have been busily expanding the scope of limited liability through the creation of such new enterprise forms as limited liability companies and limited liability partnerships.'[114]

Second, there is no reason to believe that veil piercing causes equity claimants to internalize the risks associated with their business' operations. Both in rhetoric and application, the doctrine focuses on such irrelevancies as observation of organizational formalities and not on whether the equity claimants used their control to externalize risk. After all, it is clear that courts will not pierce the veil whenever the defendant externalized some costs onto third parties. As the leading *Kaycee* decision opined, for example, courts will only impose personal liability on the members of a LLC when they 'fail to treat it as a separate entity as contemplated by statute'.[115]

It seems unlikely that veil piercing even inadvertently addresses concerns over negative externalities. As our review of the doctrine demonstrated, the law of veil piercing is remarkably vague. Indeed, the doctrine is nothing more than analysis by epithet.[116] As a result, application of the doctrine is rare, unprincipled, and arbitrary.[117] Although there are hundreds of thousands of closely held corporations in the United States, according to the leading empirical survey there were only 226 veil piercing cases brought by tort claimants that were reported in Westlaw's various databases through 1985.[118] In only seventy of those did the court pierce the veil.[119] Assuming comparable results for LLCs, the members of a LLC have a far greater chance of being struck by lightning than being held personally liable for their firm's debts and other obligations. Equity claimants of a limited liability entity, moreover, can very effectively insulate themselves from veil piercing-based per-

---

[111] See H. Hansmann and R. Kraakman, 'Toward Unlimited Liability for Corporate Torts', 100 *Yale Law Journal* (1991) p. 1879.

[112] See, e.g., M.P. Dooley, *Fundamentals of Corporation Law* (Westbury, Foundation Press 1995) p. 56; J.C. Alexander, 'Unlimited Shareholder Liability Through a Procedural Lens', 106 *Harvard Law Review* (1992) p. 387; Bainbridge, *supra* n. 1, at pp. 496-500; J.A. Grundfest, 'The Limited Future of Unlimited Liability: A Capital Markets Perspective', 102 *Yale Law Journal* (1992) p. 387.

[113] See Bainbridge, *supra* n. 1, at p. 500 (noting that 'no state has repealed limited liability for mass torts or, indeed, torts of any kind').

[114] Ibid.

[115] *Kaycee Land & Livestock* v. *Flahive*, 46 P.3d 323, 327 (Wyo. 2002).

[116] See P.I. Blumberg, *The Law of Corporate Groups: Procedural Problems in the Law of Parent and Subsidiary Corporations* (Boston, Little Brown & Co. 1983) p. 8 (arguing that veil piercing law amounts to 'metaphor or epithet').

[117] See *supra* n. 4 and accompanying text.

[118] Thompson, *supra* n. 95, at p. 1058, tbl.9.

[119] Ibid.

sonal liability by complying with minimal organizational formalities and providing modest levels of capital and/or insurance.[120] How can such a dysfunctional doctrine possibly create appropriate incentives for the equity claimants of either a corporation or LLC to optimally internalize the social costs of their business activities?

A particularly instructive example of the disconnect between veil piercing law and policy is provided by the treatment of contract claims. There is no externality with respect to parties who voluntarily contract with a limited liability entity.[121] Voluntary creditors can require LLC members to provide a personal guarantee of corporate debts.[122] Where a contract creditor fails to bargain around the limited liability default rule, there is no justification for giving it a second bite at the apple through a veil piercing remedy. At the very least, veil piercing should be limited to cases in which misrepresentations induced the voluntary creditor to do business with the entity without demanding a personal guarantee or where the LLC members subsequently siphoned funds out of the entity through fraudulent transfers.

Based on this analysis one would expect to find fewer contract than tort veil piercing cases and, moreover, that the rate at which courts pierce the corporate veil would be lower in contract than tort cases. In fact, however, the leading empirical study of veil piercing cases not only found that veil piercing claims by contract creditors are more frequent than by tort creditors, but also that contract creditors are more likely to prevail than tort creditors.[123] One can finesse one's way around this result,[124] but there is no denying the disconnect between law and theory.

3.1.2.2 Why abolition is preferable to reform

Could veil piercing be reformed, so as to mend it but not end it? Perhaps veil piercing could be refocused so as to eliminate irrelevancies and be tied more closely to the policy purposes it is intended to effectuate. To answer that question, we must first consider the reasons the veil piercing doctrine is so dysfunctional today.

Determining the availability of limited liability on a case-by-case basis requires courts to balance a number of competing policy considerations. On the one hand, the court must encourage businesses to optimally internalize the costs to society of their activities.[125] On the other hand, courts wish to avoid impeding capital formation and economic growth.[126] Balancing these concerns would require tricky economic analysis, but courts have no staff economists.[127]

---

[120] See generally Bainbridge, *supra* n. 1, at pp. 513-14 (discussing transactional planning implications of veil piercing).

[121] Easterbrook and Fischel, *supra* n. 4, at p. 104.

[122] See W.A. Klein and J.C. Coffee, Jr., *Business Organization and Finance: Legal and Economic Principles*, 8th edn. (St. Paul, Foundation Press 2002) p. 142.

[123] Thompson, *supra* n. 95, at p. 1058 (finding 779 contract veil piercing cases versus only 226 tort claims; contract creditor success rate of 42% versus tort creditor success rate of 31%).

[124] See, e.g., Dooley, *supra* n. 112, at p. 65 (noting that many contract cases likely involve active misconduct by the shareholder affording grounds for direct liability).

[125] See Bainbridge, *supra* n. 1, at p. 506.

[126] See *supra* text accompanying n. 3.

[127] Cf., *Basic Inc.* v. *Levinson*, 485 U.S. 224, 253 (1988) (White, J., dissenting) (observing that 'with no staff economists, no experts schooled in the "efficient-capital-market hypothesis," no ability to test the validity of empirical market studies, we are not well equipped to embrace novel constructions of a statute based on contemporary microeconomic theory').

Generalist judges left to their own devices are hardly likely to strike the correct balance.[128] First, judges are not exempt from the cognitive limitations the theory of bounded rationality suggests afflict all decision-makers.[129] Like all humans, judges have inherently limited memories, computational skills, and other mental tools.[130] Second, judges function under severe time and resource constraints.[131] As a result, judicial decision-making is subject to 'significant institutional constraints providing further incentives for judges to minimize effort.'[132] Third, state court judges (outside Delaware) rarely come to the bench with significant corporate law expertise. State judges likely do not have much interest in developing substantial expertise in this area after they arrive or any incentive to do so, because (outside Delaware) corporate law cases are handled by courts of general civil jurisdiction whose judges decide corporate law issues only episodically. This assumption is confirmed by a study finding that judges who decide consumer credit cases frequently do not even understand the rather basic concept of present value.[133]

Under such conditions, judges would likely seek ways of deciding these cases with minimal effort. A basic way of economizing on limited cognitive resources is to invoke shortcuts – i.e., heuristic problem-solving decision-making processes. On the one hand, the shortcut allows the judge to dispose of the case summarily without dealing with time- and resource-consuming complexities. On the other hand, provided the shortcut is well-accepted, it provides a doctrinally plausible ground for dismissing the case, so the judge is insulated from injury to his or her reputation or self-esteem. When judges rely on shortcuts, however, the result often is skewed and mediocre doctrine.[134]

This pattern, of course, is precisely what we observe in the veil piercing area. Courts rarely, if ever, engage in sophisticated analysis of whether the shareholder used the shield of limited liability to externalize risks. Instead, veil piercing opinions fairly can be characterized as analysis by epithet.[135] Courts may well have a vague intuitive sense of what constitutes an appropriate outcome, but, if so, they seem unable to articulate it. Instead of reasoned analysis, courts typically tack on vague labels such as 'alter ego' or 'lack of separation',[136] which amount to mere conclusory announcements of result – in other words, heuristics. Or, in a different manifestation of the heuristic phenomenon, the courts turn to multi-factor tests even though they appear to have little understanding of why the factors matter (other than the fact that some other court used them).[137]

Given the incentives judges face in the class of cases currently covered by the veil piercing doctrine, it seems highly unlikely that reform will produce any significant improvement on present results. Instead, as I have argued elsewhere:

---

[128] The analysis in this section draws on S.M. Bainbridge and G.M. Gulati, 'How Do Judges Maximize? (The Same Way Everybody Else Does – Boundedly): Rules of Thumb in Securities Fraud Opinions', 51 *Emory Law Journal* (2002) p. 83, at pp. 146-48.

[129] See H.A. Simon, 'Rational Choice in the Structure of the Environment', in *Models of Man* (New York, Wiley Publishing 1957) pp. 261, 271 (developing the concept of bounded rationality).

[130] See C. Jolls, et al., 'A Behavioral Approach to Law and Economics', 50 *Stanford Law Review* (1998) p. 1471, at p. 1477 (identifying such limits).

[131] Bainbridge and Gulati, *supra* n. 128, at p. 85, n. 2.

[132] See ibid., at pp. 100-05 (discussing incentive effects of constraints on judges).

[133] E.A. Posner, 'A Theory of Contract Law Under Conditions of Radical Judicial Error', 94 *Northwestern University Law Review* (2000) p. 749, at p. 758.

[134] Bainbridge and Gulati, *supra* n. 128, at p. 137.

[135] See *supra* n. 116 and accompanying text.

[136] See Blumberg, *supra* n. 116, at p. 8.

[137] See ibid., at pp. 10-12.

'Abolishing veil piercing is thus a necessary step to redirecting judicial incentives towards the correct set of solutions to the problem.'[138]

3.1.2.3 The impact of abolition on the negative externalities created by limited liability

Abolishing veil piercing would not give businesses a license to externalize risk. First, market forces significantly constrain the ability so to do. Granted, limited liability appears to make the LLC a far more attractive choice than the partnership, because equity claimants in the former do not bear the entirety of firm debts and obligations in the way that partners do. On closer examination, however, the advantage of limited liability is easily overstated. As already noted, for example, many contract creditors insist that shareholders of a closely-held corporation or members of a LLC guarantee the firm's debts.[139] In addition, the need to preserve their business as a going concern provides incentives for LLC members to ensure that the firm maintains adequate capital reserves and insurance despite their limited personal liability.[140]

Second, the important category of cases in which a LLC's members externalize business risks through personal misconduct remains subject to sanction under a number of legal regimes. In many nominally piercing cases, the plaintiff could have brought a direct action against the shareholder. In numerous cases, for example, the individual defendant said or did something that misled the creditor.[141] In others, the individual defendant could be held liable either as a joint tortfeasor with the corporate defendant or on a vicarious liability theory.[142] Because these examples capture the cases in which limited liability seems most problematic – namely, misrepresentation in connection with contract claims and deliberate externalization of unreasonable risks in tort cases – abolishing veil piercing would not leave deserving creditors without a remedy.[143]

Finally, in evaluating the externalities-based justification for veil piercing, context is critical. Modern industrial enterprises can do harm on a vast scale. At the same time, the emergence of mass tort litigation means that such enterprises face unprecedented potential liability. In recent years, numerous public corporations have been hit with multi-billion dollar lawsuits, which forced some of them into bankruptcy. Claims have ranged from

---

[138] Bainbridge, *supra* n. 1, at p. 523. John Matheson and Raymond Eby have likewise argued that the veil piercing doctrine is dysfunctional. Instead of advocating abolition of the veil piercing doctrines, however, they have merely advocated its reform. Under their proposed reform statute, however, limited liability would be set aside only where the controlling member committed fraud, transferred firm assets in exchange for less than reasonably equivalent value, or distributed firm property to a member such that the entity was rendered insolvent. J.H. Matheson and R.B. Eby, 'The Doctrine of Piercing the Veil in an Era of Multiple Limited Liability Entities: An Opportunity to Codify the Test for Waiving Owners' Limited-Liability Protection', 75 *Washington Law Review* (2000) p. 182. Because all three criteria involve personal misconduct by the controlling member, the differences in our approaches may be mainly semantic.

[139] See *supra* n. 122 and accompanying text.

[140] See Presser, *supra* n. 15, § 1:7, at pp 1-40 (noting that shareholders, in making an investment decision, are influenced by the amount or character of an entity's capitalization or by the insurance it possesses).

[141] Gevurtz, *supra* n. 60, at p. 870.

[142] See ibid. (citing the example of *Western Rock Co.* v. *Davis*, 432 S.W.2d 555 (Tex. Civ. App. 1968), in which the individual defendants ordered corporate blasting despite knowing that it was damaging plaintiff's property).

[143] See generally Bainbridge, *supra* n. 1, at pp. 514-26 (demonstrating at length that direct liability under rules sanctioning personal misconduct offers a more workable standard than does veil piercing).

products liability, such as those at issue in the Dalkon Shield[144] and breast implant litigation,[145] to environmental, such as those portrayed in *A Civil Action*,[146] to class action discrimination suits. Yet, even though many of the firms involved went through bankruptcy reorganizations, in none of these cases were their shareholders held personally liable for the firm's tortious conduct.

It was concern with precisely this class of cases that motivated Hansmann and Kraakman's proposal to eliminate limited liability with respect to tort claims:

> 'Changes in technology, knowledge, liability rules, and procedures for mass tort litigation have for the first time raised the prospect of tort claims that exceed the net worth of even very large corporations.'[147]

In evaluating my competing proposal to abolish veil piercing with respect to LLCs, however, it is necessary to banish this specter from one's mind. With one important exception discussed below, mass torts and veil piercing simply do not coincide. The appropriate mental image is not Union Carbide's Bhopal disaster, to which so many critics of limited liability point,[148] but rather Walkovszky's injury at the hands of Carlton's driver.

Framing the issue in this manner facilitates cost-benefit analysis. As we have seen, veil piercing has real costs. *Ex ante*, investors are denied certainty and predictability. Some investors will over-invest in expensive precautions, while others will under-invest in insurance and risk reduction. *Ex post*, the vague veil piercing standards lead to expensive litigation and, not infrequently, erroneous results.

Admittedly, there is one situation in which mass tort liability could be externalized. That situation is dealt with *via* veil piercing under current law – namely, the allocation of liability within corporate groups. Some legal scholars argue that courts should be more willing to pierce the corporate veil in the parent-subsidiary context than with respect to an individual shareholder.[149] The point is well-taken. The considerations justifying limited liability insofar as individual shareholders are concerned are far less powerful when ap-

---

[144] See generally R.B. Sobol, *Bending the Law: The Story of the Dalkon Shield Bankruptcy* (Chicago, University of Chicago Press 1991).

[145] See generally J.C. Coffee, Jr., 'Class Wars: The Dilemma of the Mass Tort Class Action', 95 *Columbia Law Review* (1995) p. 1343, at pp. 1404-10.

[146] J. Harr, *A Civil Action* (New York, Random House 1995) (describing litigation against a chemical company charged with contaminating the water table in Woburn, Massachusetts).

[147] Hansmann and Kraakman, *supra* n. 111, at p. 1880. Hansmann and Kraakman also note that firms have sought to evade tort liability through business reorganizations, such as putting hazardous activities in separate subsidiaries. Ibid., at p. 1881. To the extent this is a problem, however, it is better addressed through proper application of the enterprise liability remedy than through general abolition of limited liability.

[148] See, e.g., R.M. Green, 'Shareholders as Stakeholders: Changing Metaphors of Corporate Governance', 50 *Washington and Lee Law Review* (1993) p. 1409, at pp. 1414-15, 1419-20.

[149] See, e.g., F.H. Easterbrook and D.R. Fischel, *The Economic Structure of Corporate Law* (Cambridge, Harvard University Press 1991) p. 56 (arguing that a court's 'greater willingness to allow creditors to reach the assets of corporate as opposed to personal shareholders is . . . consistent with economic principles'). Admittedly, there seems to be little support in the case law for that proposition. See *United States* v. *Bestfoods*, 524 U.S. 51, 61–62 (1998) (citing numerous authorities for the 'bedrock' proposition that parent corporations generally are not liable for a subsidiary's acts or debts). In fact, courts are somewhat less likely to pierce the veil of a subsidiary to reach a defendant parent corporation than when the defendant was an individual. Thompson, *supra* n. 95, at p. 1055, tbl.7.

plied to corporate shareholders.[150] Introducing LLCs into the mix as either parent or subsidiary does not change the result.

In contrast to the veil piercing-based approach, however, I have argued that analytical clarity would be furthered by treating the allocation of liability within corporate groups as a variant of enterprise liability rather than as a species of veil piercing.[151] Doing so would acknowledge that the issue in the parent-subsidiary context is whether the firm has split up a single business enterprise into multiple corporations with the goal of externalizing specific risks. To say that a subsidiary is a parent corporation's alter ego and that the parent is therefore liable for the subsidiary's obligations, after all, differs only semantically from saying that the parent and its subsidiary are a single business enterprise. In either case, a successful plaintiff will be able to reach the combined assets of parent and subsidiary.[152] Put another way, in the corporate group context, what has been labeled 'veil piercing' has been, in substance, enterprise liability all along. That being the case, courts ought to shed the misleading label and call the analysis by its true name.

3.2 The case against veil piercing

3.2.1 *The costs of veil piercing*

As the veil piercing doctrine currently stands, there are two potential associated costs. The first is driven by the prospect of occasional judicial errors. In other words, courts presumably reach the wrong result in some cases because the doctrine is so flawed. Whether a case was wrongly decided, of course, often depends on who one asks. Yet, one can identify some cases in which most observers would likely conclude that the member did nothing for which he should be held personally liable and, accordingly, that the veil should not have been pierced. The *Haack*[153] and *Stone*[154] cases discussed above strike one as highly plausible candidates. If such cases are not infrequent, abolishing veil piercing would force courts to use doctrines such as the law of fraudulent conveyance that go more directly to the issues at hand.

Even if all veil piercing cases are coming out correctly in terms of result, there still is a second cost that arises out of the marginal effect of the doctrine on the incentives of small business owners. As we have seen, veil piercing focuses entrepreneurial incentives on the

---

150 Jonathan Landers has argued that subsidiaries are run for the benefit of their parent corporations, 'not with a view to ensuring that the subsidiary will function as a viable corporate entity.' J.M. Landers, 'A Unified Approach to the Parent, Subsidiary, and Affiliate Question in Bankruptcy', 42 *University of Chicago Law Review* (1975) p. 589, at p. 599. Hence, he criticizes courts for treating enterprise liability 'as an offshoot of the problem of piercing the corporate veil.' Ibid., at p. 633. But see R.A. Posner, 'The Rights of Creditors of Affiliated Corporations', 43 *University of Chicago Law Review* (1976) p. 499 (criticizing Landers).

151 Bainbridge, *supra* n. 1, at pp. 528-34.

152 A distinction may arise at the judgment stage of the proceeding, however. Under enterprise liability, a judgment would be enforceable against the single business enterprise; under alter ego, the judgment could be separately enforced against either firm. In the latter case, moreover, a settlement by one presumably would not foreclose collection of the judgment against the other. See W.M. Fletcher, et al., *Fletcher Cyclopedia of the Law of Private Corporations* (perm. ed. rev. vol.) (St. Paul, West Group 1999) § 43, at p. 727 .

153 *New Horizons Supply Coop.* v. *Haack*, No. 98-1865, 1999 Wisc. App. LEXIS 108 (Jan. 28, 1999); see *supra* n. 27 for discussion of the case.

154 *Stone* v. *Frederick Hobby Assoc. II*, No. CV000181620S, 2001 WL 861822 (Conn. Super. Ct. Jul. 10, 2001); see *supra* nn. 73-85 and accompanying text for discussion of the case.

wrong issues, such as by encouraging them to spend time and effort on organizational formalities that simply do not address the real problem of negative externalities.[155]

Larry Ribstein has suggested that veil piercing's focus on organizational formalities is an information-forcing default rule.[156] But what information does veil piercing elicit, and to whom is the information provided? In other words, what information asymmetry does veil piercing solve?

As to voluntary creditors, recall that there is no externality[157] and, as a result, no information asymmetry that cannot be solved by negotiation. If voluntary creditors want their debtors to comply with specific organizational formalities, they can bargain for such compliance.[158] As to involuntary creditors, the problem is not information asymmetries *vis-à-vis* the equity claimants. By definition, there is no bargaining between the two. Instead, the only question is one of externalization of risk. As we have seen, veil piercing is poorly suited to deal with that problem.

3.2.2 *Tort reform and veil piercing*

Entrepreneurs long could obtain the benefit of limited liability by incorporating. What the LLC brought to the table, however, was the ability to combine limited liability with the governance attributes of a partnership. In many small businesses, possibly excepting those that intend to go public in the short term, the combination of partnership-like governance and corporate-like limited liability is a very attractive option. The corporation's statutorily-prescribed governance structure is a hierarchical one which mandates the separation of ownership and control.[159] Such a structure is particularly well-suited to publicly held entities.[160] In contrast, governance in small businesses tends to be informal, with decisions being made by consensus.[161] Partnership law's default governance rules work well in such settings.[162] Because LLCs initially could not be publicly held, and even today publicly held ones remain quite rare, the combination of partnership governance and corporate limited liability has helped make LLCs the vehicle of choice for small businesses.[163]

---

155 See *supra* Section 3.1.2.

156 See L.E. Ribstein, 'Welcome to Uncorporations' (Apr. 23, 2004), available at <http://busmovie.typepad.com/ideoblog/2004/04/welcome_to_unco.html>.

157 See *supra* n. 121 and accompanying text.

158 Some may claim that most creditors would bargain for such protections. As such, veil piercing emerges as a majoritarian default. Yet, there are at least two problems with this line of argument. First, where is the evidence that creditors demand compliance with the sort of organizational formalities with which veil piercing is concerned? Second, even if obtaining such compliance were the majoritarian default, veil piercing's rare and seemingly arbitrary application makes it an odd choice as a vehicle for achieving such compliance.

159 See M.P. Dooley, 'Two Models of Corporate Governance', 47 *Business Lawyer* (1992) p. 461, at pp. 466-68 (describing the structure of corporate governance as one grounded in a mode of decision-making known as authority).

160 See ibid., at p. 466 (explaining that 'In publicly held corporations, . . . management and residual claimants have sharply differentiated functions. This distinction is codified in all corporations statutes …').

161 See ibid., at p. 467 (explaining that 'an elaborate decision-making structure is unnecessary because the partners will tend to reach agreement informally and largely by consensus').

162 Dooley explains that: Not only is this aspect of partnership governance [i.e., consensus-based decision-making] the one that is most frequently observed, it is also the one predicted by Kenneth Arrow's theories of organizational decision-making. According to Arrow, where an organization's decision-makers have identical information and interests, decisions will be reached by 'Consensus' because each participant, voting in his or her own self-interest, will naturally select the course of action preferred by the others. Ibid. (footnotes omitted).

163 See, e.g., S. Levine, 'LLCs – The Swiss Army Knife of Business Organizations, Partnerships, LLCs, and LLPs: Uniform Acts, Taxation, Drafting, Securities, and Bankruptcy', SJ003 A.L.I.-A.B.A. 1097 (New York,

In an increasingly litigious society, however, expansive tort liability threatens the viability of small business. The Council of Economic Advisers reports that:

> 'With estimated annual direct costs of nearly $180 billion, or 1.8 percent of GDP, the U.S. tort liability system is the most expensive in the world, more than double the average cost of other industrialized nations that have been studied. This cost has grown steadily over time, up from only 1.3 percent of GDP in 1970, and only 0.6 percent in 1950.'[164]

As George Priest has noted, it is

> 'plausible that the expansion of enterprise liability since the 1970s in tort law has imposed differentially burdensome costs on small business,'

albeit one tempered by other government subsidies.[165]

Truly limited liability free of the risk of veil piercing could be viewed as one of the alternative government subsidies that offsets the differential burden of the tort system on small business. Interestingly, Larry Ribstein suggests that the spread of unincorporated limited liability entities, such as the LLC, was a backdoor mechanism for achieving tort reform.[166] One thus may infer that the legislative expansion of the availability of limited liability reflects a shift in legislative intent 'from merely encouraging and protecting passive investors to actively promoting business.'[167]

The benefit of such a subsidy goes beyond the standard rationale of promoting capital formation. Stephen Presser has shown that limited liability was an outgrowth of populist democratic theory.[168] The 19th-century legislators who first adopted limited liability as a central feature of corporate law did so, Presser contends, to encourage small and impecunious entrepreneurs to start and develop new businesses.[169] Entrepreneurs and other small business owners who tie up the bulk of their financial and human capital in their business have limited ability to protect that investment through diversification.[170] Without the shield of limited liability, accordingly, only very wealthy persons would incorporate new businesses.[171] Only persons of pre-existing wealth could afford to tart a new business while

---

Practicing Law Institute 2003) p. 1101 (opining that 'LLCs are now the vehicle of choice for most closely-held business start-up companies'); R. Wild and M. Hirschfeld, 'Check-the-Box Knows no Boundaries (At Least, for the Moment) – 2002 Update', in Tax Strategies for Corporate Acquisitions, Dispositions, Spin-Offs, Joint Ventures, Financings, Reorganizations and Restructurings 2002, 551 P.L.I./TAX 1029 (New York, Practicing Law Institute 2002) p. 1039 (opining that 'The LLC has generally become the vehicle of choice when non-corporate tax status and limited liability are desired').

164 Council of Economic Advisers, *Who Pays for Tort Liability Claims? An Economic Analysis of the U.S. Tort Liability System* (Washington, Government Printing Office 2002) pp. 1-2, available at <http://www.whitehouse.gov/cea/tortliabilitysystem_apr02.pdf>.

165 G.L. Priest, 'Small Business, Economic Growth, and the Huffman Conjecture', 7 *Journal of Small and Emerging Business Law* (2003) p. 1, at p. 9.

166 See L.E. Ribstein, 'The Evolving Partnership', 26 *Journal of Corporation Law (*2001) p. 819, at p. 836. A relationship between the LLC's evolution and tort reform is suggested by the strong opposition LLC statutes faced in several states from the trial lawyers lobby. Ibid. (noting trial lawyers' lobbying efforts in several states).

167 Matheson and Eby, *supra* n. 138, at p. 171.

168 Presser, *supra* n. 3, at pp. 155-56. See generally Cohen, *supra* n. 26, at pp. 442-44 (discussing Presser's argument from democratic principles); Huss, *supra* n. 19, at pp. 103-04 (same).

169 Presser, *supra* n. 3, at pp. 155-56.

170 See Huss, *supra* n. 19, at p. 107 (noting this argument).

171 Presser, *supra* n. 3, at p. 156.

maintaining a diversified portfolio of investments. This situation, Presser argues, was precisely what limited liability was intended to remedy:

> 'The popular democratic justification for limited liability is rarely observed by modern scholars. Nevertheless, it appears that to the nineteenth-century legislators in states such as New York, who mandated limited liability for corporations' shareholders, the imposition of limited liability was perceived as a means of encouraging the small-scale entrepreneur, and of keeping entry into business markets competitive and democratic.
>
> ...
>
> New York's policy of limited liability, and its policy of encouraging incorporation by persons of modest means 'facilitated the growth of a viable urban democracy by allowing a wide participation in businesses that could most advantageously be organized as corporations.' 'More importantly,' . ... New York's general incorporation statutes 'helped equalize the opportunities to get rich. The passage of general incorporation laws for business corporations was the economic aspect of the political and social forces that democratized the United States during the Age of Jackson, 1825-1855.'[172]

Indeed, as Michael Novak has observed, the pursuit of wealth by entrepreneurs has been a major factor in destroying arbitrary class distinctions by enhancing personal and social mobility.[173]

Presser goes on to observe that:

> 'If we consider the evidence from history ..., we see that limited liability came about because of a wish to further economic progress and to maximize state wealth through encouraging investment. Moreover, ... it appears that an equally important factor contributing to limited liability's present stronghold in American corporate law was a desire to encourage individual investment in smaller firms. It is of a piece with other nineteenth-century manifestations of rugged individualism, and reflects a traditional American policy to favor the small-scale entrepreneur. Limited liability, insofar as it reflects a venerable desire to help out smaller investors, those more typical of the people, thus reflects democracy as much as economics. Perhaps, then, limited liability ought to be most sacred for smaller firms, and not those possessing great economic wealth.'[174]

With the LLC having displaced the close corporation as the vehicle of choice for smaller firms, Presser's argument from democratic theory now applies to LLCs even more forcefully than it does to corporations.[175]

---

[172] Ibid., at pp. 155-56 (footnotes and emphasis omitted).

[173] M. Novak, *Toward a Theology of the Corporation*, rev. edn. (Washington, American Enterprise Institute 1990) p. 42.

[174] Presser, *supra* n. 3, at p. 163 (footnotes omitted).

[175] An additional reason for treating LLCs differently than corporations is suggested by the nexus of contracts theory of the firm. Recall that the contractarian model views statutes governing business organizations as a set of off the rack default rules. One advantage to having multiple forms of business organizations is that parties can select the set of rules that most closely tracks their needs and, accordingly, reduces their bargaining costs. Put another way, because investors are heterogeneous the best approach may be to offer them a significant choice. Courts may maximize investor welfare by letting investors choose the form best suited to their business, and different legal rules for LLCs and corporations would do just that.

4. Conclusion

Pro-piercing commentators typically argue that it would be 'unfair to allow LLCs to possess the positive aspects of limited liability ... without also carrying the negative possibility of piercing.'[176] This argument assumes a fact not in evidence – namely, that veil piercing is sound public policy. In this chapter, I have demonstrated that the emerging doctrines for piercing the LLC veil are hopelessly dysfunctional. They encourage inefficient investment in irrelevant precautions, while encouraging expensive and complex litigation. They may discourage capital formation in small businesses by exposing those businesses to a disproportionate share of the burden from the tort liability system, which in turn undermines the valuable democratic contribution – at the risk of being too corny, the American dream – of small business ownership and entrepreneurship.

[176] Schwindt, *supra* n. 33, at p. 1552.

Chapter 10

THE ECONOMICS OF LIMITED LIABILITY: AN EMPIRICAL STUDY OF NEW YORK LAW FIRMS

Scott Baker* and Kimberly D. Krawiec**

1. Introduction

The choice of organizational form for business and professional service firms has been of interest to lawyers and economists for years. The law offers a menu of choices, including general partnerships (GPs), limited partnerships (LPs), limited liability partnerships (LLPs), limited liability limited partnerships (LLLPs), limited liability companies (LLCs), and, of course, corporations. Each organizational form has its own set of default rules, governing everything from the distribution of profits to dissolution. Within each business form, parties can alter most of the default rules governing the arrangement.

One of the most important of these default rules is the extent to which individual firm owners will be held personally liable for the collective debts and obligations of the firm. GPs and corporations are considered polar opposites with respect to this default rule. The corporate default rule is one of limited liability, meaning that, absent special circumstances, corporate shareholders are personally liable for corporate debts only up to the amount of their original investment in the corporation.[1] General partners, by contrast, can be held personally liable for all unpaid partnership debts.[2]

The significance of this difference in default rules, if any, has been hotly debated by legal academics for some time.[3] In addition, both economists and legal scholars have de-

* Professor of Law at Washington University School of Law.

** Professor of Law, Duke Law Faculty.

We thank workshop participants at Harvard, Georgetown, Fordham, Cincinnati, and Florida State University law schools and participants at the conference Uncorporation: A New Age? for helpful input on an earlier draft. Gail Agrawal, Laura Beny, Bill Bratton, John Coates, John Conley, Allen Ferrell, Dan Fischel, Caroline Gentile, Mitu Gulati, Melissa Jacoby, Don Langevoort, Doug Lichtman, Tom Mroz, Mitt Regan, Larry Ribstein, Mike Seidman, Dan Tarullo, and Kathy Zeiler provided useful comments and/or contacts at New York law firms. Finally, we thank Briana Brake, Kim Garrabrant, Rachel Miles, Mike Pawlowski, and Kim Peterson for assistance in gathering the data. This chapter was also published as an article in the *University of Illinois Law Review* (2005).

[1] The exceptions to the general rule of shareholder limited liability are that shareholders will be personally liable: (1) when the corporation is not properly formed; (2) for the amount of any unpaid capital contributions that they have committed to make; and (3) when the veil of limited liability is pierced. J. Bauman et al., *Corporations Law and Policy*, 5th edn. (St. Paul, West Group 2003).

[2] U.P.A §§ 13.15 (1914); R.U.P.A. §§ 304, 306 (1997).

[3] Compare, e.g., R.E. Meiners, J.S. Mofsky and R.D. Tollison, 'Piercing the Veil of Limited Liability', 4 *Delaware Journal of Corporate Law* (1979) p. 351, at p. 364 (arguing that the difference in the limited liability

bated the relative costs and benefits of limited liability, with some observers arguing that the owners' personal liability for the firm's debts provides efficiency benefits that outweigh any costs.[4]

In addition to the rule of full personal liability, many other partnership default rules appear at least at first glance unattractive. For example, the GP default rules include: the rule that profits and losses be split equally among the partners, the one partner/one vote rule, and the guarantee of a partner's right to seek a buyout.[5]

Despite these seemingly unattractive defaults, several theories have emerged regarding the desirability of the partnership form. These theories can be divided into three broad categories: (1) theories based on profit-sharing; (2) theories based on the illiquid nature of a partnership interest; and (3) theories based on the unlimited liability of the GP form. The first two categories of explanations apply to partnerships generally, whereas the third theory – unlimited liability – is a justification for the GP form, in particular.

In contrast to the theories posed by economists and legal academics that assert the benefits of unlimited liability, practicing lawyers cite the high costs of unlimited liability and argue that, given recent innovations in organizational forms, no valid reasons exist for the formation of business or professional enterprises in the GP form.[6] In fact, some legal advisors go so far as to assert that any lawyer who chooses to organize clients as a GP is committing malpractice. If the practitioners are right, one must then question why the GP form exists at all.

In the last fifteen years, all fifty states have passed laws that permit the formation of an LLP.[7] To become an LLP, a general partnership need only file a form with the secretary of

default rule between corporations and GPs is insignificant, because the default rule can be altered through a variety of private mechanisms) with, e.g., F.H. Easterbrook and D.R. Fischel, 'Limited Liability and the Corporation', 52 *University of Chicago Law Review* (1985) p. 89, at p. 93 (arguing that 'the distinctive aspects of the publicly held corporation – delegation of management to a diverse group of agents and risk bearing by those who contribute capital – depend on an institution like limited liability'); H. Manne, 'Our Two Corporation Systems: Law and Economics', 53 *Virginia Law Review* (1967) p. 259 (arguing that the publicly held corporation could not exist without limited liability).

[4] See *infra* text accompanying nn. 23-25.

[5] R.U.P.A. § 401(b) (1997) (default rule on profit and losses); R.U.P.A. § 401(f) (1997) (default rule on management responsibilities); R.U.P.A. § 29 (1997) (default rule on partner buyouts). These default rules can be circumvented or ameliorated in several ways. First, and most obviously, the parties can opt for another organizational regime, such as the LLC or corporation. Second, the default rules other than limited liability can be altered through a detailed partnership agreement. Finally, the rule of unlimited liability can be ameliorated through contract and insurance.

[6] See, e.g., L. Berton and J.S. Lublin, 'Seeking Shelter: Partnership Structure is Called into Question as Liability Risk Rises', *Wall Street Journal* (June 10, 1992) p. A1 (quoting Belverd Needles, former director of DePaul University's School of Accounting as stating, '[w]ith such risks, the partnership may go the way of the dodo'); T. Alleman, 'To LLP or Not to LLP: When Striking Out on your Own, Know the Form of Business your Practice will Take', 229 *The Legal Intelligencer* 47 (5 September 2003) p. 3 (stating that '[f]or most small groups, there really are only two choices – limited liability partnership or some form of corporation'); S. Lovell, 'Few Firms Form Limited: Liability Corporations Inertia and Fear of Client Reaction Breed Reluctance', 163 *New Jersey Law Journal* (12 February 2001) p. 645 (stating that forming a limited liability entity instead of a general partnership should be 'a no-brainer'); J.J. Johnson, 'Limited Liability for Lawyers: General Partners Need Not Apply', 51 *Business Lawyer* (November 1995) p. 85, at p. 87 (urging law firms currently doing business in the GP form to switch to a limited liability entity).

[7] See A.R. Bromberg and L.E. Ribstein, *Bromberg and Ribstein on Limited Liability Partnerships, The Revised Uniform Partnership Act, and The Uniform Limited Partnership Act (2001)* (Frederick, Aspen 2003) p. 15. Some states, including New York, California, Nevada, and Oregon offer LLP status only to professional firms.

state, pay a nominal fee, and comply with a few other formalities.[8] If the partners want, the old partnership agreement can continue to govern the newly formed LLP. The major difference between the GP and the LLP is that, in the LLP, the partners are liable only for debts stemming from their own conduct, or the conduct of someone under their supervision.[9]

The creation of the LLP form allows a natural experiment of the theories advanced regarding the costs and benefits of the partnership form. To test these theories, we collected data on the 147 law firms listed in Martindale-Hubble and NALP as having their primary office in New York City and more than twenty-five lawyers.[10] Since 1994, all of these law firms have had a choice of whether to remain a GP or adopt LLP status. Furthermore, we supplemented the empirical analysis with extensive interviews of three sets of individuals knowledgeable about and active in the debate regarding the choice of organizational form among New York law firms: law firm partners, law firm consultants, and malpractice insurers.

If the profit-sharing or illiquidity theories of partnership fully explain the benefits of the partnership form, then all or nearly all of the firms in our sample should have opted for the LLP form, as it provides all of the same benefits of profit-sharing and lack of liquidity without the costs of unlimited liability. In contrast, if the theories asserting unlimited liability as the primary benefit of the partnership form are true, then a majority of firms should remain GPs, or the firms should break down regarding choice of organizational form on some observable criteria.

Contrary to our expectations, a sizeable number of firms – about 13% – remain GPs. 67% have become LLPs.[11] This mix is puzzling. Overall, our analysis shows no significant variation based on number of lawyers, number of offices, rate of firm growth, level of profits, the level of collegiality, or the level of information asymmetry between the firm and its clients. Furthermore, on the surface, the difference between these firms is minimal. Each has a sophisticated practice, with sophisticated clients. They each provide roughly the same 'product', namely, high-end legal services.

The movement of most firms to LLP status and the lack of a clear relationship between individual firm characteristics and choice of organizational form raise questions about the value of unlimited liability, at least as applied to law firms. However, the fact that a sizeable number of firms remain GPs undermines the profit-sharing and illiquidity-based theories as the sole motivation for the partnership form as well. Because unlimited liability is the only meaningful distinction between the GP and LLP, unless many sophisticated law firms suffer from extreme inertia, it must be unlimited liability, rather than profit-sharing or illiquidity that at least some firms perceive as valuable.

In the end, we argue that law firms today increasingly view the unlimited liability associated with the GP form as burdensome and predict that, at some point in time, nearly all the firms in our sample will file as LLPs. At the same time, however, the perceived benefits of unlimited liability are real to many law firm partners and the public assertions of many

---

[8] See, e.g., *N.Y. Partnership Law* (New York, McKinney 1997) § 121-1500. In New York, a general partnership that renders professional services may become an LLP by filing a registration with the Secretary of State of New York, accompanied by a $200 filing fee. § 121-1500 (a), (c).

[9] See Bromberg and Ribstein, *supra* n. 7, at § 1.02. States differ in the limitations on liability provided by LLP status. Some states limit liability for all claims, whether rooted in contract or tort. Ibid., at pp. 2-17 (discussing the variations among state LLP statutes). Others states limit liability for selected types of tort claims. Ibid.

[10] The sample also includes eight 'foreign' firms whose main US office is in New York.

[11] The remaining firms are PCs or LLCs. For reasons discussed in detail in Section 3, we dropped the PCs and LLCs from the analysis.

lawyers that the GP form provides no countervailing benefits to offset the costs of unlimited liability are patently inconsistent with the behavior of many large and prestigious New York law firms. We conclude, instead, that the choice of organizational form is a complicated matter, dependant on a variety of factors, including the behavior of other similarly situated firms that the decision-makers consider competitors for prestige and clients.

This chapter proceeds as follows. Section 2 reviews six theories traditionally advanced as rationales for the partnership form: (1) insurance; (2) monitoring; (3) generating trust and collegiality; (4) quality signaling; (5) preventing grabbing and leaving; and (6) providing incentives to mentor.

Although there are reasons to approach many of the traditional theories of partnership form with skepticism, each yields a testable hypothesis that we examine in Section 3. Subject to the caveats discussed in Section 3, our data do not support any of the partnership theories introduced in Section 2. To provide insight into the choice of organizational form among New York law firms, we discuss in Section 4 our interviews with three sets of individuals knowledgeable about and active in that choice: law firm partners, law firm consultants, and law firm insurers. In particular, our interview data indicate that unlimited liability is increasingly viewed as a burden to be avoided, but also suggest that, for many law firm partners, the benefits of unlimited liability are real and are not necessarily outweighed by increasing liability fears. Secton 5 concludes that the choice of organizational form is more complicated than either academic researchers or practicing lawyers have recognized.

2. Theories of partnership form

In this part, we discuss six theories advanced by researchers to justify the partnership form. Each of these theories is dependent on one of three characteristics associated with partnerships: profit-sharing, a characteristic of both GPs and LLPs; illiquidity, a characteristic of both GPs and LLPs; and unlimited liability, a characteristic of the GP, but not the LLP.

As we elaborate throughout this section, there are reasons to doubt the explanatory power of many of the traditional theories. For example, contrary to the assumptions of many economists, profit-sharing is not a unique characteristic of the partnership form and can be easily accomplished through an LLC or corporation, albeit with greater transaction costs in the case of the corporation. In addition, illiquidity is a common characteristic of both LLCs and close corporations and, through the use of standard-form restrictions on resale, these investments can be made just as illiquid as the partnership interest. Nonetheless, we test each of these theories of partnership form in the following Section 3 of this chapter.

2.1 Insurance

The insurance theory of partnership form is based on the perceived efficiency benefits of profit-sharing and is frequently invoked to explain the tendency of professionals to organize as partnerships. The insurance theory starts by noting that professionals make a significant investment in human capital.[12] Such investment is hard to diversify and, hence,

[12] For formal articulations of the insurance argument, see K. Lang and P.J. Gordon, 'Partnerships as Insurance Devices: Theory and Evidence', 26 *Rand Journal of Economics* (1995) p. 614, at pp. 615-8; M. Gaynor and

risky. Furthermore, an insurance market for human capital does not exist because of moral hazard and adverse selection. Consider a lawyer who invests heavily to become a skilled bankruptcy attorney. The return on the lawyer's investment is linked to the demand for bankruptcy work. If, for instance, there is a prolonged economic boom, the return on the lawyer's investment is small. The lawyer cannot mitigate this risk through insurance, because any insurer – fearing moral hazard on the part of the attorney – would feel uncomfortable writing a policy that paid out when an attorney's business was slow.

The question becomes, then, how can the bankruptcy attorney insulate herself from risk. According to some economists, she teams up and forms a partnership with other attorneys. The partnership allows the attorney to share profits with attorneys in different areas. Through profit-sharing, the attorneys diversify their individual investments in human capital. Moral hazard remains a problem, however, because one partner might shirk, knowing that she will still recoup income through the profit-sharing arrangement. Nonetheless, economists argue that the partners in a professional firm are better able to monitor (and therefore control) moral hazard than outside insurers.

For the sake of analysis, we accept the premises of the insurance theory of partnership that profit-sharing is useful because it reduces the risk of human capital investment and partners are better than outside insurers at controlling moral hazard. From these premises, however, the choice of partnership form does not inevitably follow. A corporation, LLC, or PC could all share profits in the same way as a partnership. Although such profit-sharing arguably entails higher transaction costs in the corporate form, it is not clear that those costs outweigh the benefits of limited liability provided by the corporate form.

Nonetheless, as discussed in Section 3.1 of this chapter, an examination of New York law firms after the passage of the LLP statute allows at least a partial test of the insurance theory of partnership. If the insurance theory fully explains the advantages associated with the partnership form,[13] then all or nearly all of the firms in our sample should be LLPs,[14] because the LLP provides all of the insurance benefits associated with partnerships without the associated costs of unlimited liability inherent in the GP form.

2.2 Monitoring fellow partners

The monitoring theory of partnership takes two different forms, one based on profit-sharing and the other based on unlimited liability.

P. Gertler, 'Moral Hazard and Risk Spreading in Partnerships', 26 *Rand Journal of Economics* (1995) p. 591, at pp. 594-97.

[13] As an empirical matter, the observed break-down among New York firms allows us only to reject the illiquidity and profit-sharing theories as the sole rationale behind the choice of organizational form among New York law firms. However, as discussed *supra* nn. 10-11 and accompanying text, our interview data, combined with the fact that the partnership form does not provide unique profit-sharing or illiquidity benefits, cause us to doubt that the illiquidity or profit-sharing based theories of partnership are even a contributing factor, much less the sole factor, that explains the benefits of the partnership form.

[14] Although, in theory, if the insurance explanation fully explains the choice of organizational form, all firms in our sample should be LLPs, we phrase the hypothesis as all or nearly all and – without more – would not reject the insurance theory of partnership if we were to observe a few firms still clinging to the GP form. This is because, in reality, there is always a possibility that inertia, lack of attention, or transactions costs prevent a handful of firms from adopting the ideal organizational form.

2.2.1 *Profit-sharing and monitoring*

In an early article on this subject, Armen Alchian and Harold Demsetz proposed that employee-ownership and profit sharing are useful when it is hard to monitor each employee's input in the production process.[15] By, in effect, making each employee a residual claimant, the employee-owned firm with profit sharing induces monitoring of each employee by every other employee.[16] The inability to monitor an individual employee's input, Alchian and Demsetz claim, is the reason why many professional firms are employee-owned partnerships.[17]

More recently, Eugene Kandel and Edward P. Lazear argue that peer pressure can produce higher effort among a firm' members.[18] Because firm members are more likely to apply pressure on other firm members to perform when they empathize with those whose income they affect – i.e., the firm's stakeholders – peer pressure is more likely to be an effective motivating device in firms in which profits are shared among similarly situated individuals.[19] Accordingly, partnerships are more likely to produce higher peer pressure and induce higher effort levels than are firms that are not organized for profit-sharing.

As with the insurance theory of partnership, we accept the premise of the monitoring theory that profit-sharing is desirable for the sake of analysis. Yet the choice of partnership form does not inevitably follow from this premise. As widely discussed in the worker cooperative literature, the monitoring explanation is an argument in favor of employee-ownership rather than investor-ownership of firms.[20] Nonetheless an employee-owned firm does not have to be a partnership. The close corporation and LLC are also typically employee-owned entities in which the residual claimants on profits are directly involved in management.

Nonetheless, we test the profit-sharing based monitoring theory of partnership in Section 3 of this chapter. If profit-sharing through the partnership form fully explains the ben-

---

[15] A. Alchian and H. Demsetz, 'Production, Information Costs, and Economic Organization', 62 *American Economic Review* (1972) p. 777.

[16] Ibid., at pp. 785-86.

[17] Ibid., at p. 786. Henry Hansmann argues that Alchian and Demsetz overstate the monitoring problem associated with professional work. Hansmann points out that professional firms go to great lengths to figure out how much each partner adds to the final product by, for example, tracking billable hours. In addition, Hansmann notes that most profit-sharing agreements reflect the individual productivity of each partner. H. Hansmann, *The Ownership of Enterprise* (Cambridge, Harvard University Press 1996) pp. 70-1. See also, G. Rutherglen and K.A. Kordana, 'A Farewell to Tournaments? The Need for an Alternative Explanation of Law Firm Structure and Growth', 84 *Virginia Law Review* (1998) p. 1695, at pp. 1697-98 (making a similar argument). Others, however, have challenged Hansmann on this point, arguing that monitoring the work-product of professional service providers such as lawyers is not as easy as Hansmann suggests. See, e.g., D. Wilkins and G. Mitu Gulati, 'Reconceiving the Tournament of Lawyers: Tracking, Seeding, and Information Control in the Internal Labor Markets of Elite Law Firms', 84 *Virginia Law Review* (1998) p. 1581, at pp. 1598-9.

[18] E. Kandel and E.P. Lazear, 'Peer Pressure and Partnerships', 100 (4) *Journal of Political Economy* (1992) p. 801, at p. 805 (noting that, although peer pressure guarantees higher effort level, it does not guarantee higher utility, as peer pressure itself is a cost borne by the firm's members).

[19] Ibid., at p. 816.

[20] See A. Ben-Ner, 'The Life Cycle of Worker-Owned Firms in Market Economies', 10 *Journal of Economic Behavior and Organization* (1988) p. 287, at pp. 293-94 (asserting that better monitoring will occur at worker-run firms); H. Hansmann, When 'Does Worker Ownership Work? ESOPs, Law Firms, Codetermination, and Economic Democracy', 99 *Yale L.J.* (1990) p. 1749, at pp. 1762-63 (discussing, but rejecting, the argument that worker control and participation arise primarily to resolve the monitoring problem); G. Dow, *Governing the Firm: Economic Theory and Worker Control* (Cambridge, Cambridge University Press 2003) (discussing evidence on the question of whether worker-run enterprises engage in better monitoring).

efits associated with partnership, then all or nearly all of the firms in our sample should have adopted LLP status, as it provides all of the profit-sharing benefits of the GP form without the associated costs of full personal liability.[21]

2.2.2 *Unlimited liability and monitoring*

Another version of the monitoring theory asserts that unlimited liability encourages monitoring of each partner by every other partner.[22] In the event of another partner's misstep, a partner does not want to be on the hook for any award in excess of the partnership's assets and insurance coverage. Accordingly, under this version of the monitoring theory, unlimited liability induces each partner to pay close attention to the activities of her fellow partners. As a result, effort and care are maximized, resulting in a better product.

Because the ease and effectiveness of monitoring are likely to be a function of the number of offices (geographic dispersion), the number of lawyers (firm size), and the firm's rate of growth, the monitoring hypothesis suggests that the regression results will reveal a statistically significant effect of the number of lawyers variable (LAWYERS), the number of offices variable (OFFICES), and the rate of growth variable (GROWTH) on the choice of organizational form.[23]

In addition, because the unlimited liability version of the monitoring theory asserts that partners of LLPs monitor the quality of the firm's output less vigilantly than do partners of GPs, it suggests that LLPs provide an inferior legal product. If this is the case, and if clients possess some knowledge about the quality of legal services provided by law firms, then law firms that are LLPs must either: (1) charge less for the provision of legal services than would the same firm if it had remained a GP; or (2) charge the same amount, but lose clients to firms that price legal services in accordance with quality.

Accordingly, if the unlimited liability version of the monitoring theory is true, the empirical and interview data should reveal that either: (1) firms that opted for LLPs status were forced to reduce their billing rates, or (2) firms that opted for LLP status experienced less revenue growth (that is, firms that become an LLP experience significant, abnormal, decreases in profits per partner (PROFITS) that the firm would not have experienced if the firm had remained a GP). In addition, if LLPs are actually producing an inferior legal product, then their risk of malpractice liability should be higher and, as a result, their insur-

---

[21] See *infra* Section 3.2.3.2(i) and accompanying text (explaining this hypothesis in more detail).

[22] L.E. Ribstein, 'Ethical Rules, Agency Costs, and Law Firm Structure', 84 *Virginia Law Review* (1998) p. 1707, at p. 1728 (stating that: 'unlimited liability, by substituting for reputational and financial capital, arguably provides an important assurance to clients that law firms will discipline shirking and other self-interested conduct of their members').

[23] Kandel and Lazear, *supra* n. 18, at pp. 812-13 (demonstrating that both the effectiveness of and the incentive to engage in monitoring decrease with increases in firm size and geographic dispersion). We did not predict whether this effect should be positive or negative, because we were unsure of the direction in which size, geographic dispersion, and rate of growth should impact the choice of whether to become an LLP. One might surmise that large firms, geographically dispersed firms, and quickly growing firms find it more difficult to monitor and, therefore, choose to remain a GP in order to induce each partner to monitor every other partner. In this case, we would predict a negative relationship between each of LAWYERS, OFFICES, and GROWTH and the likelihood that a firm is an LLP. Alternatively, one might imagine that large firms, quickly growing firms, and geographically dispersed firms find it so difficult to monitor that remaining a GP in the hopes of inducing more monitoring is pointless. In such a case, the LLP liability shield should be more attractive and such firms should be more likely to form LLPs. Under this scenario, we would predict a positive relationship between each of LAWYERS, OFFICES, and GROWTH and the probability that the firm is an LLP.

ance premiums should be higher than they would be if the firm had remained a GP. As such, the interview data should reveal that law firms that are LLPs pay higher liability insurance premiums than if they had opted to remain a GP.

2.3 Generating trust and collegiality

A third theory of partnership form involves bonding and the creation of trust among partners. A partner, the theory goes, signals trust in her fellow partners by agreeing to personal liability for their actions. This trust creates a more congenial work environment, enhancing the quality of the product.

At first glance, the trust theory of partnership – because of its reliance on the unique unlimited liability characteristic of the GP form – seems a plausible explanation for the choice of GP form. However, as noted in the debate regarding the benefits of limited liability, the GP form is not the only mechanism for placing an owner's personal wealth at stake in a business or professional enterprise.[24]

Nonetheless, we test the collegiality hypothesis in Section 3 of this chapter. Because larger groups, more geographically dispersed groups, and quickly growing groups are typically considered less collegial than small, stable, closely-knit groups,[25] the collegiality hypothesis suggests that the regression results will reveal a statistically significant effect of the number of lawyers variable, the number of offices variable, and the rate of growth variable on the choice of organizational form.

In addition, law firms that have multi-tiered partnership structures (TIER) are considered less collegial than those firms in which partners are treated equally.[26] As a result, one might expect that firms with a multi-tiered partnership structure value collegiality less, and hence are less likely to remain a GP in an effort to maintain firm collegiality. Therefore, the collegiality hypothesis suggests that the regression results will reveal a statistically significant positive effect of the TIER variable on the likelihood that a firm is an LLP.

Finally, some law firms publicize their congenial environment, whereas others do not. If the collegiality theory of partnership is true, we should observe a statistically significant

---

[24] For example, the partners could form a limited liability entity, but personally guarantee debts. They could also post personal bonds, or over-capitalize the corporation, rather than withdrawing funds in excess of that needed for working capital. See, e.g., H. Hansmann and R. Kraakman. 'The Essential Role of Organizational Law', 110 *Yale Law Journal* (2000) p. 387, at pp. 429-30; A.D. Kessler, 'Limited Liability In Context: Lessons From the French Origins of the American Limited Partnership', 32 *Journal of Legal Studies* (2003) p. 511, at p. 546; Easterbrook and Fischel, *supra* n. 3, at pp. 103-04 (arguing that voluntary corporate creditors frequently require personal guarantees or use other mechanisms to alter the default rule of limited liability for shareholders).

[25] See generally M. Olson, *The Logic of Collective Action* (Cambridge, Harvard University Press 1971) (demonstrating that coordination and the resolution of collective action problems are more difficult for larger groups); R. Ellickson, *Order Without Law: How Neighbors Settle Disputes* (Cambridge, Harvard University Press 1991) (discussing the role of extra-legal, collective norms in small, closely-knit groups); C.R. Leslie, 'Trust, Distrust, And Antitrust', 82 *Texas Law Review* (2004) p. 515, at pp. 535-37 (discussing trust and cooperation).

[26] See E.H. Gorman, 'Moving Away From 'Up or Out': Determinants of Permanent Employment in Law Firms', 33 *Law and Society Review* (1999) p. 637 (noting that, in a collegial organization, . . . all are formally equal in status.) and at 650-51 (finding that collegiality, as measured by firms. narrative descriptions, is negatively associated with the presence of a two-tier partnership structure); P.D. Sherer, 'Leveraging Human Assets in Law Firms: Human Capital Structures and Organizational Capabilities', 48 *Industry and Labor Relations Review* (1995) p. 671, at p. 677 (stating that, 'tiers may damage the sense of collegiality and mutual monitoring that exists when partners are coequals').

negative effect of the COLLEGIAL variable on the probability that a law firm chooses to become an LLP.[27]

2.4 Quality signaling

The signaling theory of partnership takes two different forms, depending on the source of the signal. In the initial formulation, firms signal quality by adopting unlimited liability. In the more recent articulation, profit-sharing serves as the signal. According to the quality signaling theory, the need for signaling arises whenever consumers are unable to assess the quality of a product. As a result, they are reluctant to buy the product without some quality assurance.

2.4.1 *Unlimited liability and signaling*

One version of the quality signaling theory asserts that unlimited liability encourages each partner to take more care in the provision of goods and services in order to avoid losing personal assets. In addition, as discussed in Secton 2.2.2, unlimited liability is thought to encourage monitoring of each partner by every other partner. Knowing these facts, consumers feel more comfortable about the quality of the product. In other words, unlimited liability is thought to provide a credible signal of quality.

There are reasons to approach the quality signaling theory with skepticism. Although unlimited liability might serve as a quality signal, it is not the only possible signal of quality. For example, a firm can also signal quality by maintaining a good reputation, established through repeated interactions with consumers. For unlimited liability signaling to work, one must demonstrate that unlimited liability is the cheapest credible signal of quality.

Despite this skepticism, we test the unlimited liability version of the quality signaling theory in Section 3 of this chapter. Because the quality signaling theory depends on information asymmetry between producers and consumers of products (in this case, legal services), we predict that firms whose clients possess less information regarding the quality of legal services they receive should have a greater need to engage in this type of quality signaling than firms whose clients are well-informed regarding the quality of legal services they purchase. Because more sophisticated clients are more likely to possess such information and because clients in the Fortune 250 are more likely to be sophisticated than clients that are not, we predicted a significant, positive effect of the Fortune 250 variable (FORTUNE) on the probability that the firm is an LLP.[28]

In addition, because research shows that more sophisticated clients and clients with a higher number of in-house counsel are more informed about the quality of legal services provided by law firms,[29] this version of the signaling hypothesis suggests that the logit

---

[27] See *infra* nn. 77-86 and accompanying text (describing this variable in more detail.)

[28] Cf., J.C. Coates IV, 'Explaining Variation in Takeover Defenses: Blame the Lawyers', 89 *California Law Review* (2001) p. 1301, at p. 1310, n. 40 (stating that, '[o]lder, larger, and more profitable companies are more likely to have better and larger in-house legal staffs more capable of monitoring outside firms'); A. Chayes and A.H. Chayes, 'Corporate Counsel and the Elite Law Firm', 37 *Stanford Law Review* (1985) p. 277 (discussing the important role of in-house counsel in monitoring and selecting outside counsel, especially at the largest American corporations).

[29] R.L. Nelson, *Partners With Power: Social Transformation of the Large Law Firm* (Berkeley, University of California Press 1988) p. 59; M.C. Suchman, 'Working Without a Net: The Sociology of Legal Ethics in Corporate Litigation', 67 *Fordham Law Review* (1998) p. 837, at p. 856.

model results will reveal a statistically significant positive effect of both the average and the total number of in-house counsel (IN-HOUSE-AVG and IN-HOUSE-TOTAL) and the Fortune 250 variable (FORTUNE) on the probability that a firm is an LLP.[30] Finally, if becoming an LLP really sends a negative signal to clients about the quality of legal services, then firms that become an LLP should either: (1) charge less for legal services than they otherwise could if the firm had remained a GP, or (2) see a significant, abnormal, negative change in profits-per-partner (PROFITS) that the firm would not have experienced if it had remained a GP.

2.4.2 *Profit-sharing and signaling*

Jonathan Levin and Steven Tadelis advance a different signaling theory of partnership, focusing on profit-sharing.[31] They start with the notion that an employee-owned firm engaged in profit-sharing is less inclined than a corporation to hire new workers. In a profit-sharing partnership, each partner cares about profits per partner, not total profits. As a result, a new partner will not be welcomed into the firm unless her contribution to firm profits is greater than the profits produced by the average partner. In contrast, because a corporation cares about total profits, it will bring in new workers if the marginal benefit of that worker is greater than their marginal cost to the firm. Because the partnership focuses on average profits rather than the marginal increase in profits, a profit-sharing partnership has an incentive to hire higher quality workers than the corporation.[32]

In markets where there are informational disparities, however, both the corporation and the partnership have an incentive to hire less able workers, hoping that the consumer will fail to notice the resulting loss in quality. Levin and Tadelis conclude that the incentive to 'cheat' on worker quality is mitigated in a partnership because of the partnership's initial preference for higher quality workers.[33] They argue that this explains why professional firms are more apt than other types of firms to organize as partnerships: the market for professional services (for example, law, medicine, or accounting) contains large informational disparities, making the choice of the partnership form more profitable.[34]

As previously discussed in Sections 2.1 and 2.2 of this chapter, the partnership form is unnecessary to attain the benefits of profit sharing. As a theoretical matter, we thus find it unlikely that any partnership theory based on profit-sharing, including signaling theories, can account for the choice of organizational form among New York law firms. Nonetheless, we test the profit-sharing version of the quality signaling theory in Section 3 of this chapter. If Levin and Tadelis are correct that the partnership form signals profit-sharing to customers, and if this fact fully explains the benefits provided by the partnership form, then all or nearly all of the firms in our sample should be LLPs, as the LLP provides all of the

---

30 See *infra* nn. 49, 60-61 and accompanying text (describing these variables).

31 J. Levin and S. Tadelis, 'Profit-Sharing and the Role of Professional Partnerships', Stanford Institute for Economic Policy Research Paper No. 03-031, available at <http://www.ssrn.com/abstract=500322> (August 2004) ('We take the defining feature of a partnership to be redistribution of profits among partners').

32 Levin and Tadelis demonstrate that this is not always an optimal result. If there is no asymmetric information in the market, the partnership operates inefficiently. It hires workers of too high a quality and provides too high a quality of product. Put another way, in the 'full-information' market consumers prefer to pay less and receive a lower quality product than the profit-sharing partnership produces.

33 Ibid., at p. 2

34 This is the essence of proposition 3 in their paper. Ibid., at p. 10.

profit-sharing benefits of the partnership form without the accompanying costs of unlimited liability necessitated by the GP form.[35]

2.5 Preventing 'grabbing and leaving'

According to the grab and leave theory of partnership, certain types of businesses – specifically, the practice of law – benefit from an up or out system of partnership.[36] This is because, over time, attorneys develop client-specific assets in the form of knowledge and expertise in the handling of specific clients. This expertise gives senior lawyers significant power over their employers. By threatening to 'grab' their clients and leave the firm, these lawyers can extract a higher share of the firm's profits.

To prevent senior lawyers from 'grabbing' their clients and leaving the firm, law firms develop the up or out system of partnership in which associates are either fired before they get a chance to develop a relationship with clients or are promoted to residual claimants on the firm's assets.[37] This system is more important in law firms than in conventional firms because law firms lack the ability to establish property rights in client-specific knowledge.

The partnership structure effectively eliminates the defection of partners, by maximizing profits per partner, rather than total profits.[38] According to Rebitzer and Taylor, only under the partnership structure can senior attorneys be paid enough to prevent them from grabbing and leaving with the firm's clients because the partnership structure results in higher profits per partner, even though the corporation results in higher total profits.[39]

The Rebitzer and Taylor theory, however, is not a convincing explanation of the benefits of the partnership form. Rebitzer and Taylor assume that corporations are, by definition, entrepreneur-owned firms and that partnerships are, by definition, employee-owned firms.[40] Because employee-owned firms are more profitable under certain circumstances that are important to professional firms, many economists believe that this fact explains the prevalence of the partnership structure among professional firms and the prevalence of the corporate structure among industrial firms. However, neither corporations nor LLCs are necessarily entrepreneur-owned firms. In fact, it is quite common in close corporations and small LLCs to see a complete overlap of ownership and management, as is the case in a partnership.

Nonetheless, we test the grab and leave hypothesis in Section 3 of this chapter. The LLP and GP are identical in the extent to which they foster profit-sharing and would thus equally prevent grabbing and leaving. Accordingly, if the grab and leave theory fully explains the

---

35 See *supra* n. 9 and accompanying text (describing this hypothesis in more detail).

36 See, e.g., R. Gilson and R. Mnookin, 'Sharing Among the Human Capitalists: An Economic Inquiry into the Corporate Law Firm and How Partners Split Profits', 37 *Stan. L. Rev.* (1985) p. 313; J.B. Rebitzer and L.J. Taylor, 'When Knowledge is an Asset: Explaining the Organizational Structure of Large Law Firms', IZA Discussion Paper no. 2253, available at <http://www.ssrn.com/abstract=3003> (October 2006); M. Galanter and T. Palay, *Tournament Lawyers: The Transformation Of The Big Law Firm* (Chicago, University of Chicago Press 1991).

37 The firm is unable to write enforceable contracts that effectively prevent grabbing and leaving due to the ABA Model Rules, which prohibit contracts that limit a client's freedom to choose her lawyer. See Model Rules of Prof. L Conduct R. 5.6; R.W. Hillman, 'Law Firms and their Partners: The Law and Ethics of Grabbing and Leaving', 67 *Texas Law Review* (1998) p. 1, at pp. 16-17; Rebitzer and Taylor, *supra* n. 36.

38 Rebitzer and Taylor, *supra* n. 36, at p. 10.

39 Ibid., at p. 12.

40 Ibid.

advantages of partnership relative to other organizational forms, then all or nearly all of the firms in our sample should be LLPs because the LLP provides all of the benefits of profit-sharing without any of the GPs' associated costs stemming from unlimited liability.[41]

2.6 Incentives to mentor

One of the more creative justifications for the partnership form involves mentoring.[42] The mentoring theory begins from the premise that much professional work requires the development of human capital and many professionals require mentoring in order to enhance their skills. The junior associate, for instance, needs a senior partner to teach her how to conduct a trial or close a deal. As the professional ages, however, she has an incentive to horde her knowledge and avoid mentoring new entrants to the profession. She would prefer to take her knowledge and leave the firm, keeping all of the benefits of her knowledge to herself. Partnerships, however, are relatively illiquid forms of investment, making exit difficult. To maintain a pool of skilled workers to promote, the senior professional engages in mentoring. This mentoring is profitable because it increases the return on the partner' illiquid investment in the partnership.

Mentoring is not a wholly satisfactory explanation for the existence of partnership and almost certainly fails to explain the choice of organizational form among New York law firms. Close corporations, LLCs, and LLPs also represent relatively illiquid investments. In fact, such investments can be made just as illiquid as a partnership interest through the use of fairly routine restrictions on the transfer of interests. In addition, although the partnership default rules create an illiquid investment, as an empirical matter most partnership agreements have buyout provisions ameliorating this effect.[43]

Nonetheless, we test the mentoring theory in Section 3 of this chapter. Because there is no liquidity difference between the GP and LLP (in fact, a firm that files for LLP status need not alter the underlying GP agreement, leaving any buyout provisions completely unaltered), if mentoring fully explains the advantage of the partnership relative to other organizational forms, then all or nearly all of the firms in our sample should be LLPs. This is because, like all of the partnership theories based on illiquidity or profit-sharing explanations, the LLP provides all of the purported benefits of the GP, without the accompanying costs of unlimited liability.[44]

3. Empirical analysis

3.1 Data collection

To explore the choice and determinants of organizational form, we collected data on the choice of organizational form among New York law firms – that is, law firms listing New

[41] See *supra* n. 36 (explaining this hypothesis in more detail).

[42] See A. Morrison and W.J. Wilhelm, Jr., 'Partnership Firms, Reputation and Human Capital', Oxford Financial Research Center Working Paper No. 2003-FE-02, available at <http://www.ssrn.com/abstract=373440> (January 24, 2003) .

[43] See L.E. Ribstein, 'Why Corporations?', 1 *Berkeley Business Law Journal* (2004) p. 183.

[44] See *supra* n. 9 and accompanying text (describing this hypothesis in more detail).

York City as their primary office – with more than twenty-five lawyers.[45] We limited our study to New York City firms for a variety of reasons.[46] By restricting our sample to firms in a particular region, we were able to minimize variations in the choice of organizational form based on geographic or cultural differences, differences in the state legal regime or ethics code, and differences in state and local tax codes.[47]

Under the supervision of the two authors, research assistants collected most of the data. The data, along with a detailed memo describing the collection process, are publicly available at <http://www.law.unc.edu/data/economicsoflimitedliability>.

There are 147 firms in the sample. We used seven sources to build the dataset: (1) Martindale-Hubble, both print and web versions; (2) the Directory of Legal Employers (NALP), both print and web versions; (3) filings from the New York Secretary of State; (4) the list of profits per partner for the top 200 law firms published by *The American Lawyer*; (5) American Lawyer Media, Corporate Counsel Division, Directory of In-House Law Departments at the Top 250 Companies (hereinafter, The Directory of In-House Departments);[48] (6) individual law firm websites; and (7) telephone conversations with selected law firms to verify or clarify certain information. We then supplemented this

---

[45] We did not study law firms with fewer than 25 attorneys. These small firms may differ from their larger counterparts in ways that significantly affect their choice of organizational form, rendering them poor subjects for our study. For example, very small firms could differ from large firms in terms of culture, practice area, and the impact of various laws (such as the New York City tax on LLPs). In addition, small associations of lawyers may be less a 'firm' than a grouping of lawyers that share office space and resources, but lack a common goal, history, and culture. See B.M. Price, 'How Green Was My Valley? An Examination of Tournament Theory as a Governance Mechanism in Silicon Valley Law Firms', 37 *Law and Society Review* (2003) p. 731, at p. 742 (excluding law firms of fewer than ten lawyers from an empirical study of Silicon Valley firms for similar reasons).

[46] Bob Hillman, who constructs a nationwide database of law firms, has done one of the two other major empirical studies examining the choice of organizational form by law firms. See R.W. Hillman, 'Organizational Choices of Professional Service Firms: An Empirical Study', 58 *Business Lawyer* (2003) p. 1387, at pp. 1397-1402. Although a welcome addition to the literature, Hillman does not use the data to test the economic theories concerning partnerships. Eric Talley and John Romley also conduct a major nationwide empirical study. J. Romley and E. Talley, 'Uncorporated Professionals', USC Law and Economics Research Paper No. 04-22; and USC CLEO Research Paper No. C04-18, available at <http://www.ssrn.com/abstract=587982>. We discuss their results in detail *infra* n. 77.

[47] For example, converting from a PC to an LLP has significant negative tax consequences. Johnson, *supra* n. 6, at p. 85, n. 19 (stating that, '[w]hile a PC may also convert to an LLC or an LLP, there are significant tax impediments to such a conversion in that it will be treated as a liquidation under I.R.C. § 336 (1988)'). In addition, many firms in states whose PC statute (unlike New York's) provided an advantageous liability shield converted from GPs to PCs some time ago. As a result, these firms are effectively prohibited from filing as an LLP, even if they might desire to do so. Similarly, in some jurisdictions, local tax codes may affect the choice of organizational form. For example, New York City and New York State taxes PCs more heavily than partnerships. See T.A. Oved, 'New York State Limited Liability Partnerships', *New York State Bar Journal* (March-April 1995) p. 39 (noting that '[g]eneral partnerships do not pay . . . state tax on their profit but rather a 4% unincorporated business tax to New York City' and 'a law firm organized as a professional corporation must make an annual tax payment of up to 1.8% and approximately 9% of its net income, respectively, to New York State and New York City'). Presumably because of these tax considerations, as well as the fact that New York's PC statute is not a superior liability shield to the LLP, only two firms filed for PC status after the LLP statute was enacted.

[48] A searchable version of The Directory of In-House Departments is available at <http://solis.365media.com/alm/search.asp?cat=987223>. The Directory of In-House Departments includes information collected and printed in the November issue of American Lawyer Media's Corporate Counsel magazine in the article entitled 'Who Represents America's Biggest Companies?' as well as additional biographical data that was independently compiled by American Lawyer Media's Corporate Counsel Division. We compiled a list of the number of each firm's *Fortune 250* clients, if any, and the number of in-house counsel employed by those clients by searching the directory in May 2004.

empirical data with a series of interviews of individuals active in and knowledgeable about the choice of organizational form by New York law firms.

1. Number of Lawyers (LAWYERS), Number of Offices (OFFICES), and Growth Rate (GROWTH) Martindale-Hubble and NALP provided firm names, number of lawyers (LAWYERS), number of offices (OFFICES), choice of organizational form (FORM), and was used to calculate each firm's growth rate (GROWTH). We verified the Martindale-Hubble and NALP information through the New York Secretary of State's office, by consulting firm websites and, in a few cases, by calling the firm's offices to verify information that remained unclear after consulting the website.

LAWYERS is the total number of attorneys at each firm in 2004. OFFICES is the total number of each firm's separate offices in 2004. LAWYERS and OFFICES were collected from the Martin-dale-Hubble website.[49] OFFICES was then cross-checked against each firm's website.[50]

GROWTH is the yearly percentage change in each firm's total number of attorneys, averaged from 1994-2003.[51] For reasons detailed below, GROWTH was calculated using two sources: the print versions of NALP and Martindale-Hubble. This calculation was done by dividing the firms into three categories: (1) firms that NALP listed in every year for the period 1994.2003; (2) firms that NALP did not list for any year during the period 1994.2003; and (3) firms that NALP listed in some years during the period 1994.2002, but not in others.[52]

For a variety of reasons, NALP is both a more reliable and more user-friendly source for calculating law firm growth rates.[53] Accordingly, we used NALP to calculate GROWTH whenever possible. For the first category of firms (those listed in NALP every year for the period 1994.2003), we used NALP data for every year.[54] For the second category of firms

49 See <http://martindale.com/xp/Martindale/home.xml>.

50 When the number of offices listed on the firm's website conflicted with the number of offices provided by Martindale-Hubble, we used the number of offices listed on the firm's website. Both the Martindale-Hubble search and the website cross-checks were conducted in March 2004.

51 Except as otherwise noted, we include within the attorney count for GROWTH all firm members with a J.D. degree, including partners, associates, counsel, and of counsel, but do not include retired partners. We include individuals regardless of whether the individual has been admitted to a bar or whether bar passage is still pending. Data on the number of lawyers is not available for all firms for every year between 1994 and 2003. In such cases, 'GROWTH' is the average growth rate for the subset of years for which growth data is available. In addition, for the years 1994-2003 we did not collect data on the number of lawyers for PCs and LLCs. Hence, GROWTH is defined for GP and LLP firms only.

52 Due to inconsistencies and apparent errors in reporting by NALP and/or Martindale-Hubble during the time frame of our study, various firm-specific decisions were made about how certain information on GROWTH would be treated. These decisions are detailed in a memo available on our web-site, which is available at <http://www.law.unc.edu/data/economicsoflimitedliability>.

53 For example, NALP provides information on firm demographics that includes the number of lawyers (although, as discussed *infra* n. 54, this number is sometimes a firm-wide number and at other times an office-wide number). In contrast, Martindale-Hubble lists lawyers within a firm by name and does not provide a total number, thus increasing the likelihood of error caused when individual names (in some cases, more than 1000) must be counted by hand. Furthermore, Martindale-Hubble sometimes lists all of the firm's lawyers under the heading for the New York office. At other times, it lists only the New York lawyers under this heading. As a result, every office for every firm must be cross-checked against every other office for that firm to determine whether lawyers have been double-listed under both New York and a branch office.

54 NALP lists each firm's number of attorneys under 'Firm Demographics'. Sometimes this number represents each attorney employed by the firm. At other times, it represents only the number of attorneys in the New

(those that NALP did not list for any year during the period 1994-2003), we used Martindale-Hubble data for every year.[55] For the third category of firms (those listed in NALP for some years, but not for others), we compared the available NALP data to the Martindale-Hubble data for any missing NALP years and determined whether the Martindale-Hubble data followed the yearly trend in growth rates calculated from the NALP data. If consistent, we used the Martindale-Hubble data for the years the firm was not listed in NALP. If inconsistent, we disregarded the previously collected NALP data and recalculated the firm's growth rate using Martindale-Hubble data for every year.

2. Organizational Form (FORM), Filing Date (DATE), Whether the Firm Is Domestic or Foreign (FOREIGN), and Designation of New York City as the Firm's Main Office We verified each firm's organizational form (and, for firms that were organized as LLPs, LLCs, or PCs, collected filing date information) from filings with the New York Secretary of State's office.[56]

We considered a firm's main office to be located in New York City if the Martindale-Hubble website designated the New York City office as the firm's 'main office'. If Martindale-Hubble reported a firm as having multiple main offices, we concluded that the firm's main office was in New York City, so long as one of the main offices was located in New York City.

FOREIGN indicates those firms headquartered outside of the United States, but who report to Martindale-Hubble that their main United States office is located in New York City. All main office results were cross-checked against each individual firm website. If the individual website conflicted with the designation in Martindale-Hubble, we listed the main office as it appeared on the firm's website.[57]

3. Profits Per Partner (PROFITS)
The American Lawyer magazine provided the partner profit data. American Lawyer has two series of profit data. One series reports profits per partner on the 100 most profitable firms in the United States (the AmLaw 100). A second series, the AmLaw200, provides profit data on the second 100 – firms that rank between 101 and 200 in terms of profitability – [58] Thirty-six firms in the sample are among the 200 most profitable law firms in the country.

York office. When the 'Firm Demographics' listed only the New York attorneys, attorneys from other offices were added in from the firm's 'Narrative Description' or from the 'Other Offices' category.

[55] As noted *supra* n. 53, in order to calculate GROWTH from Martindale-Hubble, we had to hand-count the attorneys that were listed by name in every office for each firm. On some occasions, Martindale-Hubble did not list associates, but instead listed only partners, counsel, and of-counsel. In order to maintain a consistent counting method for each firm across time, if the firm did not list associates in any single year, we did not count associates – even if they were listed – in any other year.

[56] We gathered this information in March 2004, from a searchable website maintained by The New York Secretary of State, located at <http://appsext5.dos.state.ny.us/corp_public/enter_search>. In several cases, the choice of organizational form indicated by Martindale-Hubble or NALP varied from information provided by the law firm's website and the New York Secretary of State's Office. In these cases, we used the information provided by the New York Secretary of State.

[57] For example, Martindale-Hubble lists Milberg, Weiss as having its main office in New York. However, the firm's website indicates that its main office is in San Diego. Accordingly, we adopted the Website's designation of the firm's main office and excluded Milberg, Weiss from our sample. This cross-check was conducted in March 2004.

[58] *The American Lawyer* publishes the AmLaw 100 in the July edition of the magazine and the AmLaw 200 in the August edition of the magazine. See, e.g., The Amlaw 100, 2004, *The American Lawyer*, July 2004, at 91;

4. Average Number of In-House Counsel (IN-HOUSE-AVG), Total Number of In-House Counsel (IN-HOUSE-TOTAL), and Number of Clients in the Fortune 250 (FORTUNE)

The number of a firm's clients in the Fortune 250 (FORTUNE) was used as a proxy for client sophistication and, thus, for the level of information asymmetry between lawyer and client. The theory behind the FORTUNE variable is that firms that have more clients in the Fortune 250 have clients who are more informed regarding the quality and pricing of legal services than do law firms with fewer numbers of clients in the Fortune 250. As a result, there is a lower level of information asymmetry between the lawyer and client in these firms than in others and they, therefore, have less need to signal quality by being a GP.

In addition, both the average number of in-house counsel (INHOUSE-AVG) and the total number of in-house counsel (INHOUSE-TOTAL) were used as a proxy for the level of client-lawyer information asymmetry.[59] Consistent with prior research on the role of in-house counsel in reducing this asymmetry, our theory was that firms with a higher number of both average and total in-house counsel should have lower levels of information asymmetry and, therefore, less need to signal quality by remaining a GP. The Directory of In-House Departments provided client information and information on each client's number of in-house counsel.[60] Of the 118 firms that are LLPs or GPs, only forty firms have clients in the Fortune 250.

5. Starting Associate Salaries (SALARY), Multi-Tiered Partnership Structure (TIER), and Collegiality (COLLEGIAL)

NALP provided starting associate salaries, whether the firm used a multi-tiered partnership structure, and whether the firm self-identified as collegial. TIER indicates whether or not the firm employs a multi-tier partnership structure. TIER was collected from the NALP On-Line Directory of Legal Employers for the fifty-four firms in our sample that are included in the on-line directory.[61]

COLLEGIAL indicates whether or not the firm self-identifies as collegial. Firms can identify themselves as collegial through the narrative description that they provide to NALP for publication. A research assistant labeled the sixty firms in our sample that were listed in the 2002-2003 NALP directory (print version) as congenial/collegial or not congenial/collegial. To determine which category the firm best fit in, we examined the narrative information included in their NALP entry. Descriptions of the firms that stressed 'teamwork', a 'congenial' or 'collegial' environment, and 'friendly' or 'close-working relationships' were coded as collegial. Firms that did not mention any of these characteristics in their narrative description were coded as uncollegial.[62]

The Amlaw 200, 2004, *The American Lawyer*, August 2004, at 83. Data on the AmLaw 100 was available for the years 1993-2003. *The American Lawyer* only published data on the AmLaw 200 for the years 1999-2003.

[59] See R. Lancaster and B. Uzzi, 'From Colleague to Employee: Determinants of Changing Career Governance Structures in Elite U.S. Law Firms', in A. Grandori (ed.) *Corporate Governance and Firm Organization: Microfoundations and Structural Forms* (Oxford, Oxford University Press 2004) (using this same variable to test the level of information asymmetries in the market for legal services).

[60] The searchable directory is available at <http://solis.365media.com/alm/search.asp?cat=987223>. The variables were constructed by searching for each firm's name in the directory. If the firm has *Fortune 250* clients, then the directory provides the client names, along with the number of in-house-counsel employed by each client.

[61] This information was collected from the NALP web directory in June, 2004. The NALP web directory is located at <http://www.nalpdirectory.com/>. There is an entry on each form entitled 'Partnership Data'. One item under this heading is 'Two or more tiers?' to which firms respond 'yes' or 'no'.

[62] See Gorman, *supra* n. 26 (using the NALP narrative descriptions to construct a dummy variable for whether or not the firm was collegial).

One might expect that every firm would advertise its congeniality as a marketing tool, rendering firms' narrative statements a poor proxy for collegiality. In fact, however, there is great variation in the narrative descriptions and only 44% of the New York firms in our sample were coded as collegial.[63] In addition, COLLEGIAL was negatively associated with TIER as one would expect if these two variables are acting as a proxy for the firm's level of collegiality.

SALARY measures each firm's starting associate salary as reported in the NALP On-Line Directory of Legal Employers.[64] All salaries are those reported for 2003, except in the case of two firms that provided only 2004 salary information.[65] SALARY was calculated for the fifty-seven firms in our sample for which such information was provided in the On-Line Directory.

6. Raw Data

The raw data for New York law firms are attached as Appendices A.D to this chapter. Appendix A lists LAWYERS, FORM, OFFICES, DATE, and GROWTH for all firms in the sample. Appendix B reports TIER, SALARY, and COLLEGIAL for the subset firms for which such information was available.[66] Appendix C lists INHOUSE-AVG, IN-HOUSE-TOTAL, and FORTUNE for the subset of firms for which such information is available. Appendix D contains the PROFITS data.

3.2 Empirical results

3.2.1 *General results*

Tables 1, 2, and 3 report summary statistics for the data collected on New York law firms. As is evident, the large majority of firms (67%) are LLPs, whereas only 13% are GPs.[67] The average number of offices is higher for LLPs than for GPs, as is the average number of lawyers. As demonstrated in the logit model in Section 3.2.3.2, however, neither of these variables is a statistically significant predictor of the choice of organizational form.

Table 1. Overall Statistics

Firm Type	Total Number	Percentage of Sample
GP	19	13%
LLP	99	67%
PC	27	18%
LLC	2	1%

[63] Similarly, in a national study of collegiality at law firms using this same coding method, only about 20% of the firms were coded as collegial, and collegiality was negatively associated with a multi-tiered partnership structure. See Gorman, *supra* n. 26 .

[64] This information was collected from the NALP web directory in June, 2004. The NALP web directory is located at <http://www.nalpdirectory.com/>.

[65] The firms are Thacher, Proffit, and Wood; and Friedman, Kaplan, Siler, and Adelman.

[66] Note that information on each variable is not available for all firms in Appendix B. A blank space indicates that information on this variable was unavailable for the firm in question.

[67] The remaining firms are PCs and LLCs. See *infra* n. 69 (breaking down these numbers).

Table 2. GP Summary Statistics

Avg. Number of Offices	4.263158
Std. Dev. Number of Offices	3.841905
Avg. Number of Lawyers	181.1579
Std. Dev. Number of Lawyers	214.7811

Table 3. LLP Summary Statistics

Avg. Number of Offices	5.232323
Std. Dev. Number of Offices	6.54471
Avg. Number of Lawyers	240.798
Std. Dev. Number of Lawyers	446.6612

3.2.2 *Filing patterns*

In order to examine law firm filing patterns, we divided the firms in our sample into large firms, small firms, and elite firms.[68] Information regarding the LLP filing dates of large firms, small firms, and elite firms is graphically depicted in Chart 1.

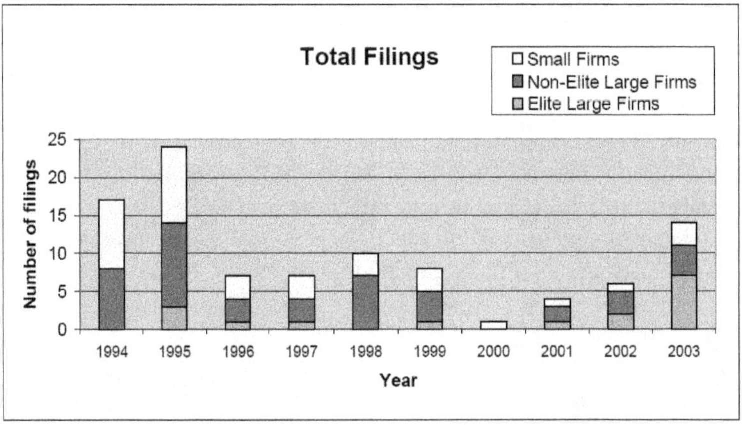

Chart 1.

As the bar chart shows, LLP filings peaked in 1994.1995, the two-year period after New York's LLP statute became effective, and were distributed roughly equally between large and small firms. Few elite firms filed during this time period. LLP filings then tapered off, but began rising again between 2001 and 2003. Unlike the 1994.1995 filing period, large firms dominate the LLP filings during the 2001-2003 period. In particular, a large number of elite law firms filed during this period, roughly coinciding with two events: the Arthur Andersen trial and bankruptcy, and the large numbers of securities fraud suits accompanying the stock market downtown associated with the burst of the 'dotcom' bubble.

---

[68] 'Large firms' are firms with more than 50 lawyers. 'Small firms' are firms with between 25 and 50 lawyers. 'Elite firms' are defined as firms with more than $1 million in profits per partner for 2002.

Given the large numbers of securities offerings in which these firms are involved, and the corresponding liability fears that may result, we theorized that many large and elite law firms may have consciously chosen this time frame in which to seek liability protection.

This conjecture is supported by our interview data. Our follow-up interviews reveal that both rising liability fears and the Arthur Andersen bankruptcy were salient factors associated with many firms' decisions to opt for LLP status.[69]

LLP filing dates plotted against 2003 PROFITS are graphically depicted in Chart 2.[70]

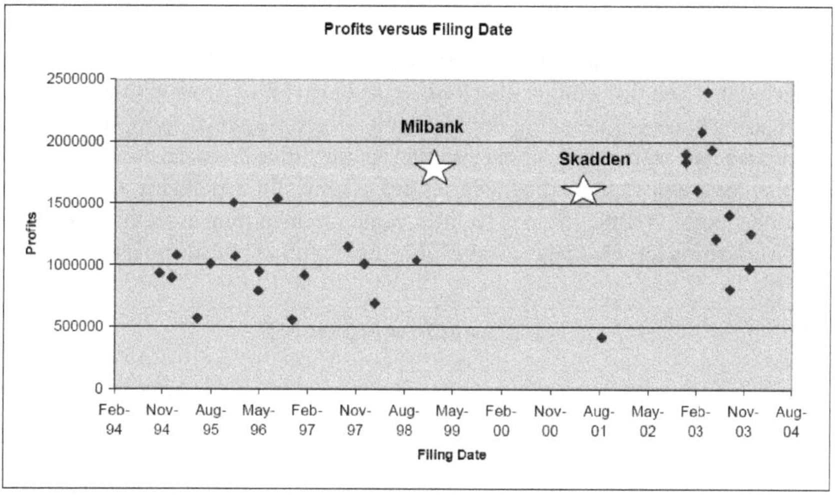

Chart 2.

The chart shows a rough bunching of LLP filings that corresponds with PROFITS. As discussed in more detail in Section 4, we believe that this is attributable to a concern by firms with the negative signal that may accompany an LLP filing. However, as more firms that the decision-making firm considers to be a competitor convert to LLP status, the negative signal is muted. For this reason, firms tend to file with their cohort. The interview data supports this notion that firms account for the actions of competitor firms when making a decision regarding organizational form.[71]

Two apparent outliers in Chart 2 are noteworthy: the LLP filing of Milbank, Tweed on February 1, 1999, and the LLP filing of Skadden, Arps on May 25, 2001. Both of these firms filed early relative to firms with comparable profits-per-partner, and both filings were noted with interest by their cohort firms. The Milbank filing closely followed the conviction and sentencing of Milbank partner John Gellene in the summer of 1998 to fifteen months in federal prison for filing false declarations in a bankruptcy proceeding.[72] Al-

[69] See *infra* nn. 120-23 and accompanying text (discussing Arthur Andersen and rising liability fears as salient factors in law firms' choice of organizational form).

[70] Because per partner profit data is reported in *The American Lawyer* for only the 200 most profitable firms in the United States, only 36 of our original sample of 147 firms are included on this chart.

[71] See *infra* nn. 118-19 and accompanying text (discussing this phenomenon).

[72] See M.C. Regan, *Eat What You Kill: The Fall of A Wall Street Lawyer* (Ann Arbor, University of Michigan Press 2004); L. Perlman, 'Trading One Striped Suit (With Cuffs) For Another', 20 *The American Lawyer* (October 1998) p. 10 (discussing the Gellene incident).

though several partners at New York firms surmised during interviews that the Gellene incident may have made liability matters more salient at Milbank and prompted the firm's early filing, our interviews with Milbank suggest that this was not the case.[73] The Skadden filing in 2001 gained the attention of many elite New York firms and, according to our interviews, caused many firms to begin reevaluating the decision of whether to become an LLP.[74] Although many interviewees indicated that the firm eventually decided to wait until firms within their cohort other than Skadden were prepared to file before their own firm was willing to file, the event was clearly a salient trigger in many firms' decision-making processes.[75]

Another area in which law firms compete is starting associate salaries.[76] Accordingly, we predicted that law firms might also look to the behavior of firms with whom they compete on starting salaries in making decisions about organizational form, resulting in clusters when associate starting salaries are plotted against filing dates. LLP filing dates plotted against first year associate starting salaries are graphically depicted in Chart 3. Unfortunately, at this point in time, there is so little variation in starting associate salaries among the New York firms for which data is available that the chart reveals no useful information.

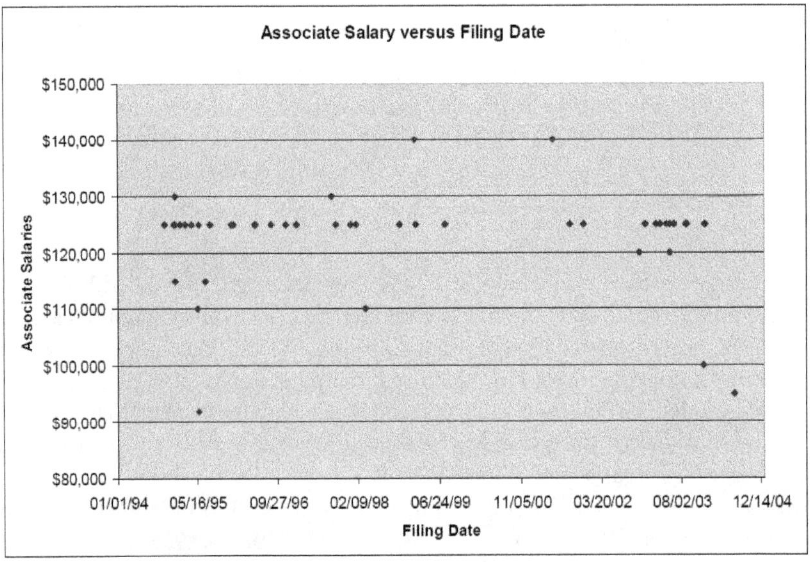

Chart 3.

[73] Confidential interview with Milbank partner (interview notes on file with the authors) (attributed with permission of interview subject).

[74] Confidential interviews with law firm partners (interview notes on file with the authors).

[75] Idem.

[76] See B.M. Price, 'A Butterfly Flaps Its Wings in Menlo Park: An Organizational Analysis of Increases in Associate Salaries', 2005 *Wisconsin Law Review* (2005) p. 713 (demonstrating that law firms compete on associate salaries, even when doing so appears to make little sense as an economic matter).

3.2.3 *Testing the partnership theories*

3.2.3.1 Profit-sharing and illiquidity-based theories

In Section 2 of this chapter, we discussed four theories of partnership that are based on the purported benefits of profit sharing through partnership: insurance, monitoring, quality signaling, and preventing grabbing and leaving. In addition, we discussed one partnership theory – mentoring – that relies on the illiquidity benefits of the partnership form. As noted, there are reasons to approach each of these theories with suspicion because, assuming that profit-sharing and illiquidity are valuable attributes in at least some business and professional organizations, the partnership form is unnecessary to provide these benefits. Both profit-sharing and illiquidity can be, and frequently are, replicated through a variety of organizational forms, including the LLC, PC, and corporation.

Nonetheless, each of these theories generates a testable hypothesis. If any of these partnership theories fully explains the benefits of the partnership form, then all or nearly all of the firms in our sample should be LLPs, because the LLP provides the same illiquidity and profit-sharing features of the GP, without the accompanying costs of unlimited liability. Contrary to the predictions of the illiquidity and profit-sharing based hypotheses, a sizeable number of firms in our sample remain GPs.

Standing alone, however, our empirical data allow us only to reject the illiquidity and profit-sharing based theories of partnership as the sole motivation for the choice of organizational form among New York law firms. However, our theoretical objections to these theories, detailed throughout this chapter, cause us to doubt that they are even contributing factors in the choice of organizational form, much less decisive ones.

3.2.3.2 Limited liability, monitoring, and collegiality

(i) Results

As discussed in Section 2 of this chapter, several partnership theories rely on the purported benefits of unlimited liability. Under the monitoring theory, unlimited liability induces partners to more carefully scrutinize each other. This monitoring becomes more difficult with increased size, rate of growth, and geographic dispersion of the firm.

In contrast, the collegiality theory of partnership asserts that the willingness to face personal liability for a partner's acts generates trust and collegiality within the firm. Larger groups, quickly growing groups, more geographically dispersed groups, and firms with multi-tiered partnership structures are considered less collegial than small, closely-knit groups, in which all members are treated equally. In addition, some law firms self-identify as collegial in their NALP narrative statement whereas others do not. Accordingly, the monitoring and collegiality partnership theories each yield a testable hypothesis: if either of these theories is a significant rationale for the choice of organizational form among New York law firms, then regression results should reveal a statistically significant effect of LAWYERS, OFFICES, and GROWTH, and in the case of the collegiality theory, TIER and COLLEGIAL, on the choice of organizational form.

In order to test this hypothesis, we estimated a logit model with the dependent discrete variable being whether the firm was an LLP or GP. The independent variables are LAW-

YERS, OFFICES, GROWTH, and whether the firm is domestic or foreign (FOREIGN). The model had 117 observations. Although there are a total of 118 GPs and LLPs in the data, GROWTH was unavailable for one firm.

As Table 4 reports, the coefficients on all variables are insignificant.[77] Note, however, that OFFICES and LAWYERS are correlated, raising the possibility of a multicollinearity problem. Without using additional independent variables or collecting more data, we cannot correct for this problem.[78] With this qualification in mind, the initial indications from the data are that neither the monitoring nor the collegiality hypotheses find much support.

Table 4.

Logit estimates — Number of obs = 117
Log pseudo-likelihood = -49.7556 — Pseudo R2 = 0.0414

	Coef.	Robust Std. Error	z	P>|z|	[95% Conf. Interval]	
LAWYERS	.0003985	.0007504	0.53	0.595	-.0010723	.0018693
OFFICES	.0283613	.0524437	0.54	0.589	-.0744265	.1311491
GROWTH	.0011623	.01928	0.06	0.952	-.0366258	.0389503
FOREIGN	-1.748595	.9146515	-1.91	0.056	-3.541279	.0440886
CONST	1.566562	.3697773	4.24	0.000	.8418118	2.291312

The logit results are based on a relatively small number of firms, an unavoidable problem for this population. Although we collected data on all New York City firms listed in Martindale-Hubble and NALP with more than twenty-five lawyers, rather than drawing a sample of such firms, this is, nonetheless, still a limited number of observations.[79]

As an additional check on the robustness of the significance results, we bootstrapped the sample, a process that involves re-sampling from the data. The computational technique randomly draws with replacement a new sample from the data at hand.[80] The logit model is then run on each of the bootstrapped samples.[81] Because bootstrapping re-samples

[77] We also ran a probit model, which assumes a slightly different structure. See W. Greene, *Econometric Analysis*, 5th edn. (Upper Saddle River, Prentice Hall Publishers 2002) pp. 814-15. As in the logit model, the coefficients on all variables were insignificant. In a provocative new working paper, Eric Talley and John Romley conduct a nationwide inquiry into law firm choice of form. They find that a firm's size measured in terms of number of lawyers in 1993 is a statistically significant predicator of the law firm's choice of organizational form as of 1999. Romley and Talley, *supra* n. 46, at pp. 31-32 and Table 11.

[78] Dropping one of the correlated variables is a common but incorrect fix for multicollinearity. See P. Kennedy, *A Guide To Econometrics*, 5th edn. (London, Blackwell Publishers 1992) p. 182. Because this incorrect correction is frequently used, however, we also ran two additional models. In the first model, we dropped LAWYERS as an independent variable, but kept OFFICES. In the second model, we dropped OFFICES, and kept LAWYERS. Neither OFFICES nor LAWYERS was significant when run without the presence of the other in the regression.

[79] Some firms, especially smaller firms, may choose not to list in Martindale-Hubble or NALP because such listing involves a fee. So, while we are confident that our dataset includes most New York law firms, the data set may not include all New York firms. This potential selection bias among smaller firms is one reason that we did not include in our sample firms with fewer than 25 lawyers

[80] See C.Z. Mooney and R.D. Duval, *Bootstrapping: A Nonparametric Approach To Statistical Inference* (Newbury Park, Sage Publications, Inc. 1993) pp. 9-15 (describing how bootstrapping works generally)

[81] Bootstrapping is useful in developing confidence intervals. Ibid., at p. 60. However, the parameter estimates from bootstrapping are unreliable, a problem that does not concern us here, as we are concerned only with the significance of the results. Ibid.

from the same data, it is only appropriate when certain assumptions are met. Specifically:

We must be prepared to assume that the empirical distribution function represented by the sample is a good estimator of the population distribution function that generated the sample in the first place. That is, we must believe that a representative sample of all possible distinct values of the population is found in the data.[82]

We believe that our dataset meets this assumption because of the method of data collection. As previously noted, our dataset represents the entire population of New York City firms with more than twenty-five lawyers, as reported by Martindale-Hubble and NALP.[83]

Table 5 summarizes the bootstrapping results. The coefficients on GROWTH, LAWYER, and OFFICE are insignificant for all three methods for constructing bootstrap confidence intervals.[84] The coefficient on FOREIGN was insignificant for two of the methods for constructing intervals and significant for one of the methods.[85]

Table 5.

bootstrap statistics

Number of obs = 117
Replications = 1000

Variable	Reps	Observed	Bias	Std. Err.	[95% Conf. Interval]		
B_LAWYERS	1000	.0003985	-.00004	.0015948	-.002731	.0035279	(N)
					-.0031016	.0037558	(P)
					-.0030128	.004021	(BC)
B_OFFICES	1000	.0283613	.0253877	.0859417	-.1402856	.1970082	(N)
					-.0809225	.2596718	(P)
					-.1091741	.1871728	(BC)
B_GROWTH	1000	.0011623	.0054339	.0309361	-.0595449	.0618694	(N)
					-.0491735	.0783014	(P)
					-.0584999	.0620802	(BC)
B_FOREIGN	947	-1.74859	-.22967	1.334121	-4.366775	.8695839	(N)
					-4.961497	-.0081233	(P)
					-4.125079	.086775	(BC)
B_CONST	1000	1.566562	-.048501	.4290887	.7245433	2.408581	(N)
					.7236955	2.400121	(P)
					.8607135	2.549127	(BC)

Finally, as an additional test of the collegiality hypothesis, we estimated a logit model for the subset of fifty-three firms for which data on both COLLEGIAL and TIER was available. Table 6 reports the logit results from this subsample. As with the other models, the coefficients on all variables were statistically insignificant.

However, one cannot make a strong inference from the results in Table 6. The sample size is too small, making heavy reliance on the results unjustifiable.[86]

---

[82] Ibid. at p. 61 (emphasis added).

[83] See *supra* n. 79 (discussing the dataset).

[84] See Mooney and Duval, *supra* n. 80, at pp. 33-42 (describing the different ways to construct bootstrap confidence intervals).

[85] The replication for FOREIGN occurred only 947 times. This means that in 53 of the resamples, the sampling did not draw any foreign firms, making it impossible to run the logit on those resamples.

[86] We also bootstrapped this smaller sample. The coefficients on all variables were insignificant when bootstrapped. However, we are not confident about these results, because the smaller sample is not representative of the population under study. See Mooney and Duval, *supra* n. 80, at pp. 60-1 (discussing the limitations of the bootstrap technique).

Table 6.

Logit estimates — Number of obs = 53
Log pseudo-likelihood = -19.406266 — Pseudo R2 = 0.0619

	Coef.	Robust Std. Error	z	P>|z|	[95% Conf. Interval]	
LAWYERS	.0002044	.0007751	0.26	0.792	-.0013147	.0017236
OFFICES	.0511103	.0785404	0.65	0.515	-.1028261	.2050466
GROWTH	-.0692595	.0474476	-1.46	0.144	-.1622552	.0237361
FOREIGN	-1.390741	1.368034	-1.02	0.309	-4.07204	1.290557
COLLEGIAL	.2180422	.8244907	0.26	0.791	-1.39793	1.834014
TIER	-.002586	1.052599	-0.00	0.998	-2.065643	2.060471
CONST	1.979628	.7010438	2.82	0.005	.6056078	3.353649

(ii) Section summary

To summarize this subsection, given the results on the entire sample, the bootstrapping results, and the preliminary results on firms reporting TIER and COLLEGIAL information, the indications from the data are that neither the monitoring nor the collegiality hypotheses find much support in the data. Although the coefficient on FOREIGN was insignificant, except in one method for constructing intervals in the bootstrapping results, three out of eight foreign firms were GPs, a much higher proportion of GPs than in the total sample.

Although we hesitate to read too much into this result because of the small number of foreign firms in the sample, our interview results provide some insight into why the filing patterns among foreign firms, especially UK firms, may differ from the filing patterns of domestic firms.

For most law firms based outside of the United States, the New York office represents a relatively small percentage of the total partnership. Accordingly, were the firm to seek liability protection, most would prefer another avenue, such as filing as a limited liability entity in their own country, to accomplish it.[87] Although many jurisdictions have recently modernized their limited liability laws available to professional associations, making them more attractive, there are still impediments to limited liability in many jurisdictions.[88] Accordingly, although many large law firms based outside of the United States are currently considering the issue of becoming a limited liability entity and many of our interview subjects predicted that all of the major international firms based outside of the United States would soon follow the lead of the domestic firms, these practical impediments have slowed the process among many foreign firms.[89]

[87] Confidential interview with senior partner at foreign firm (interview notes on file with the authors).

[88] For example, UK law firms that choose to limit their liability must make their financial statements publicly available, a requirement that has caused many UK firms to forgo the benefit of the statute. Confidential interview with senior partner at foreign firm (interview notes on file with the authors). In addition, law firms with a substantial German practice must contend with German tax laws that deem partnership goodwill recognized if the firm changes its organizational form. Although it is apparently possible to get a firm-specific ruling waiving the statute, the ease and speed with which this occurs varies by jurisdiction. Confidential interview with senior partner at foreign firm (interview notes on file with the authors).

[89] One of the UK's leading law firms, Allen and Overy, recently announced that it would become a UK LLP effective on May 1, 2004. Many predict that other major UK firms will soon follow suit. See B. Sherwood, 'Limited Liability: A Question of Protection', *Financial Times* (Apr. 26, 2004).

3.2.3.3 The relationship between profits and choice of form

Recall that the unlimited liability version of the monitoring theory suggests that, because LLPs provide an inferior legal product, they must either (1) charge less, or (2) suffer reduced revenues. As discussed below in Section 4, our interview data allow us to reject the first possibility. This subsection considers the second possibility, investigating the link between choice of organizational form and profits-per-partner.

As noted previously, we collected profit per partner data for the years 1993-2003 on the thirty-six firms in our sample that were listed among the 200 most profitable in the country. The goal of this section is to determine whether a switch in form from a GP to an LLP had any effect on firm profitability. This is a panel data set, in which we observe the same firms over a ten-year span. During this span, thirty-one firms changed from a GP to LLP; five firms remained GPs.

To tell whether a change of form had any effect on profits, we ran a fixed effects model that accounts for unobservable firm-specific traits and secular trends, both of which – if unaccounted for – might affect profitability.[90] The independent variables include dummy variables for the filing date and the lags of the filing date.

The variable, FILING, equals one if the firm filed for LLP status in that year and zero otherwise. The variable, FILLAG1, equals one if the firm filed as a LLP in the previous year and zero otherwise. The remaining variables, FILAG2, FILAG3, FILAG4, FILAG5, FILAG6, FILAG7, FILAG8, are defined in a similar fashion. These lags of the filing date allowed us to examine whether the switch in form had a persistent and/or delayed impact on profits.

Tables 7 and 8 summarize the results. The dependent variable in Table 7 is the level of profits. The dependent variable in Table 8 is the log of profits. The log function compresses the profit data, reducing the impact of outliers on the results.[91] In both tables, we suppress the estimates on the time dummy variables, which account for the secular trends.

As Table 7 reports, many of the filing variables are statistically significant and negative. One must be careful, however, in interpreting the point estimates. Take, for instance, the estimate on FILAG6, which is 185,928.1. Roughly speaking, this means that, all else being equal, a firm that files for LLP status in 1997 will have $185,928 less profits in 2003.

In Table 8, none of the filing variables are statistically significant and the point estimates flip signs, starting negative and turning positive as the length of the lag increases.[92] The results in Table 8 caution us against reading too much into the results from Table 7.[93] Given the results in Table 7, however, we cannot completely dismiss the possibility that a switch in form from a GP to an LLP reduces profitability, at least in the first few years.

---

[90] For a non-technical discussion of the fixed effects model, see J.M. Wooldridge, *Introductory Econometrics: A Modern Approach*, 2nd edn. (Stamford, Thomson Learning/South-Western College Publishers 2003) pp. 461-69.

[91] See *infra* n. 96 (discussing the effect of the log function).

[92] When the dependant variable is the log of profits, the coefficient estimates represent the percentage change in profits. So, for example, in Table 8, the estimate on FILAG2 equals -.09. This means, all else equal, a switch in form from a GP to an LLP in 1999 leads to 9% less profits in 2001.

[93] The results from Table 7 do not seem to be the result of outliers. We reran the model with profit levels as the dependant variable, but dropped the firms, which had, in 2003, the three highest profits per partner and the three lowest profits per partner. The same results occur: The filing date coefficients are all negative and many of the lag variables are statistically significant.

Table 7.

Regression with robust standard errors

Number of obs = 344
R-squared = 0.9469
Adj R-squared = 0.9370
Root MSE = .13263

(standard errors adjusted for clustering on firm)
(firm | absorbed (36 categories))

PROFITS	Coef.	Robust Std. Error	z	P>|z|	[95% Conf. Interval]	
FILING	-21609.24	44451.99	-0.49	0.627	-109099.9	65881.45
FILAG1	-87122.87	66141.12	-1.32	0.189	-217302.3	43056.51
FILAG2	-174052.5	83941.33	-2.07	0.039	-339266.4	-8838.649
FILAG3	-188951.5	101717.4	-1.86	0.064	-389152.3	11249.25
FILAG4	-160853.2	94466.6	-1.70	0.090	-346783	25076.56
FILAG5	-189750.6	81612.24	-2.33	0.021	-350380.3	-29120.87
FILAG6	-185928.1	79855.69	-2.33	0.021	-343100.6	-28755.63
FILAG7	-152261	88270.91	-1.72	0.086	-325996.4	21474.34
FILAG8	-164291.1	85617.34	-1.92	0.056	-332803.7	4221.523
CONST	602903.7	40501.57	14.89	0.000	523188.2	682619.1

Table 8.

Regression with robust standard errors

Number of obs = 344
R-squared = 0.9469
Adj R-squared = 0.9370
Root MSE = .13263

(standard errors adjusted for clustering on firm)
(firm | absorbed (36 categories))

Ln_PROFITS	Coef.	Robust Std. Error	z	P>|z|	[95% Conf. Interval]	
FILING	-.009777	.0432551	-0.23	0.821	-.094912	.075358
FILAG1	-.0536235	.0581945	-0.92	0.358	-.1681624	.0609154
FILAG2	-.0913073	.0690882	-1.32	0.187	-.2272872	.0446725
FILAG3	-.039976	.0660399	-0.61	0.545	-.1699561	.0900042
FILAG4	.0460658	.0732625	0.63	0.530	-.09813	.1902616
FILAG5	.0579672	.0644386	0.90	0.369	-.0688611	.1847956
FILAG6	.0793543	.0772123	1.03	0.305	-.0726155	.231324
FILAG7	.1238531	.0881448	1.41	0.161	-.049634	. 2973402
FILAG8	.1079902	.0796176	1.36	0.176	-.0487137	.2646941
CONST	13.23827	.0369417	358.36	0.000	13.16556	13.31098

3.2.3.4 Unlimited liability and signaling

As discussed in Section 2.4.1 of this chapter, unlimited liability is thought to send a positive signal to customers by indicating that, because each partner's personal assets are at stake in the event of her own or another partner's blunder, each partner will take more care in the provision of legal services and will more carefully monitor other firm members. Because the quality signaling theory depends on information asymmetry between the firm and its clients, the signaling theory suggests that firms whose clients possess less information regarding the quality of legal services they receive should have a greater need to engage in this type of quality signaling than firms whose clients are well-informed regarding the quality of legal services.

To test this hypothesis, we predicted a positive, significant relationship between each of IN-HOUSE-AVG, IN-HOUSE-TOTAL, and FORTUNE on the probability that a firm is an LLP. Tables 9 and 10 report the results on signaling. In Table 9, FORM again serves as the discrete dependent variable. The independent variables include GROWTH, OFFICES, and FOREIGN, plus FORTUNE. The coefficients on LAWYERS, OFFICES, and FORTUNE are all insignificant.[94] However, the coefficient on FOREIGN was significant in this model.[95]

Table 9.

Logit estimates Number of obs = 117
Log pseudo-likelihood = -47.700453 Pseudo R2 = 0.0810

	Coef.	Robust Std. Error	z	P>|z|	[95% Conf. Interval]	
LAWYERS	.003625	.0029158	1.24	0.214	-.0020897	.0093398
OFFICES	-.0196299	.063816	-0.31	0.758	-.144707	.1054471
GROWTH	-.0016844	.0195909	-0.09	0.931	-.0400818	.0367131
FOREIGN	-2.266825	1.073779	-2.11	0.035	-4.371393	-.1622578
FORTUNE	-.2088203	.1224337	-1.71	0.088	-.4487859	.0311453
CONST	1.638935	.4037346	4.06	0.000	.8476294	2.43024

Table 10 summarizes the results from the last logit model. The sample for this model contains only thirty-nine observations and, hence, the results are suggestive at best. The sample includes only those firms who represent clients in the Fortune 250. In this model, we add as an independent variable the log of the average number of in house counsel (IN-HOUSE-AVG) and the total number of inhouse counsel (IN-HOUSE-TOTAL).[96] The coefficients on all variables are statistically insignificant.[97]

---

[94] We also ran a model with whether the firm had any clients in the Fortune 250 as a dummy variable. In this model as well, all the coefficients were statistically insignificant.

[95] Although we hesitate to read too much into this result because the data set includes so few foreign firms, the proportion of foreign firms that are GPs is much higher than in the total sample, and our interview results indicate that foreign firms face different issues concerning the choice of organizational form than do domestic firms. See *supra* nn. 88-89 and accompanying text (discussing the foreign firms.)

[96] The log is used because the figures on the average number of in-house counsel are skewed. The log operator minimizes the impact of this dispersion. Consider an example: Shearman and Sterling represents six companies among the Fortune 250 with an average number of in-house counsel of 438. Morrison and Cohen represents one company with an in-house counsel office of 17 people. Using just the average number of in-house counsel implies that the information asymmetry between Shearman and its clients is 25 times less than the information asymmetry between Morrison and Cohen and its clients. This seems unreasonable, and the log operator minimizes this difference. See S. Choi and M. Gulati, 'Choosing the Next Supreme Court Justice: An Empirical Ranking of Judicial Performance', 78 *Southern California Law Review* (2004) p. 23 (noting that the 'use of the log transformation . . . helps reduce the skewness in the distribution due to the superstar effect (resulting in a more normal distribution').

[97] FOREIGN does not appear in this table because, for the firms in this small dataset, FOREIGN perfectly predicted the choice of form. As a result the logit model could not run with FOREIGN.

Table 10.

Logit estimates Number of obs = 39
Log pseudo-likelihood = -14.818863 Pseudo R2 = 0.1150

	Coef.	Robust Std. Error	z	P>|z|	[95% Conf. Interval]	
LAWYERS	.0004058	.0029048	0.14	0.889	-.0052875	.006099
OFFICES	.167362	.1000963	1.67	0.095	-.028823	.3635471
GROWTH	-.1034546	.0860331	-1.20	0.229	-.2720763	.0651671
IN-HOUSE-AVG	-.5099148	.6412853	-0.80	0.427	-1.766811	.7469813
IN-HOUSE-TOTAL	-.0006731	.0008786	-0.77	0.444	-.0023951	.0010489
CONST	4.375029	3.180182	1.38	0.169	-1.858014	10.60807

In contrast to the statistical tests of the other theories, the data here is weaker. As a result, our conclusion is more tentative. The proxies for information asymmetry are just that: proxies.[98] That said, when combined with insights from our interview data, the data suggest that firms are not retaining unlimited liability to signal quality to the market.

3.2.4 *Testing the theories revisited – a duration analysis*

3.2.4.1 Motivation for the duration analysis

The duration model is a time event study that measures the time that has elapsed before a certain event occurs.[99] Unlike the logit model, which analyzes a firm's choice of form at a particular moment in time, the duration model permits an analysis of choice of form as it changes over time. In other words, whereas the logit model asks whether there are significant differences between firms that are GPs and firms that are LLPs, the duration model asks whether there are significant differences in the speed with which firms with certain characteristics became LLPs. Unlike the logit model, the duration model thus allows us to examine whether the length of time it takes a firm to switch from the GP to LLP form correlates with the variables that economists predict are important in determining the choice of form. Did, for example, larger firms or more geographically dispersed firms adopt LLP status more quickly than small firms with only one office? This question can only be answered by looking at the firms over time.

The duration model provides two other benefits as well. First, the logit models discussed above may suffer from a problem of endogeneity. The logit model assumes, for

[98] In addition, if information asymmetry causes firms to remain a GP and information asymmetry causes clients to increase the number of in-house counsel, then, there is a simultaneity problem. In this case, treating the number of in-house counsel as an exogenous variable will lead to incorrect results. See Greene, *supra* n. 77, at pp. 652-53. We thank Allen Ferrell for bringing this to our attention.

[99] For complete and more technical treatments of the duration model see J.M. Wooldridge, *Econometric Analysis of Cross Section and Panel Data* (Cambridge, MIT Press 2002) pp. 685-715; N.M. Kiefer, 'Economic Duration Data and Hazard Functions', 26 *Journal of Economic Literature* (1998) p. 646.

example, that the number of lawyers is exogenous. In other words, it assumes that the number of lawyers is not influenced by the choice of form.

As noted above, the hypothesis we would like to test is that the number of lawyers in the firm significantly impacts the probability that the firm will limit its liability.[100] However, it is also possible that the firm's choice of form determines the number of lawyers. In other words, an LLP may have more lawyers precisely because it has limited its liability. If this is the case, then it is the choice of form that drives the number of lawyers, rather than the other way around as hypothesized. This same type of endogeneity problem is possible with the variables OFFICE, GROWTH, and FOREIGN as well, rendering the logit estimates potentially unreliable.

To address this problem, we gathered data on the number of offices and the number of lawyers from 1994 to 2003. Next, we used the fact that each firm filed for LLP status on a different date to control for endogeneity.

To see how this works, consider Skadden Arps Slate Meagher & Flom LLP. Skadden filed for LLP status on May 25, 2001. The duration analysis asks whether the number of lawyers at Skadden in any one year influences the probability that Skadden files for LLP status in that same year, assuming that Skadden had not filed for LLP status up to that point in time. The number of lawyers at Skadden after the filing date thus plays no role in the analysis, as the duration analysis ends with the filing date. The temporal nature of the analysis mitigates the chance of endogeneity. In contrast to the logit model (which is based on a snapshot of firm characteristics), endogeneity will be a problem in the duration model only if the firm adds or subtracts lawyers in anticipation of the switch in form.[101]

The final benefit of the duration model relates to sample size. Although we collected data on every New York law firm listed in Martindale-Hubble as having 25 or more lawyers, the logit models are based on a small sample size. The duration analysis takes the same small sample and expands it by looking at each firm over a ten-year period. This increase in the sample size gives us more confidence in the results.

3.2.4.2 Description of methodology

(i) The duration model

The duration model originated in medical studies in which researchers desired to study the length of time a patient survives after a particular treatment.[102] For this reason, the duration model is sometimes referred to as a survival model. In a duration model, the key variable is the hazard rate. The hazard rate is the probability that the event of interest occurs, given that the event has not occurred up to that point in time.[103]

To see this more clearly, consider an economic problem that has been subject to duration analysis: unemployment.[104] In a duration analysis of unemployment, the event of interest

---

[100] For reasons discussed *supra* n. 23, we did not predict whether this impact would be positive or negative.

[101] M.A. Cleves, et al., *An Introduction To Survival Analysis Using Stata* 166 (College Station, Stata Press 2004) (noting that in duration analysis, 'researchers often ignore anticipation or delay effects').

[102] Wooldridge, *supra* n. 99, at p. 685.

[103] See Kiefer, *supra* n. 99, at p. 649.

[104] For an early study of this sort, see T. Lancaster, 'Econometric Methods for the Duration of Unemployment', 47 *Econometrica* (1979) p. 939.

is finding a job. The hazard rate for a particular week is the probability the person finds employment that week, given that the same individual has been unemployed for the previous weeks. One policy issue is how unemployment benefits affect the hazard rate.[105] If unemployment benefits decrease the hazard rate, this means that more benefits increase the chance of continued unemployment.

In this same context, a researcher might be interested in whether certain characteristics of the unemployed person influence the hazard rate, say, whether the person is male or female. These sorts of characteristics are called covariates. Some covariates change over time. Unsurprisingly, these covariates are called time-varying covariates. In the unemployment context, an example of a time-varying covariate is underlying economic conditions.

(ii) Application to the choice of organizational form

In our model, the event of interest is the switch from the GP form to the LLP form. Our covariates are the number of lawyers and the number of offices in any year and whether the firm is a foreign or domestic firm, as we are interested in whether these characteristics impact the probability that the firm switches form, given that it had not switched form before. Based on the economic theories discussed above in Section 2, we would predict that a firm's number of lawyers and number of offices will impact the speed with which the firm switches form. That is, the hazard rate (the probability of switching to the LLP form at a specific moment, conditional on the firm not switching up to that point) will change with the number of lawyers and the number of offices. Both OFFICES and LAWYERS are time-varying covariates in the analysis. FOREIGN, by contrast, is a constant covariate.

(iii) Results

The starting date of the study is 1994 – the year that New York's LLP statute became effective. Although the model is based on 110 firms, only 90 firms switched from the GP form to the LLP form during the course of the study.[106]

Each firm has multiple observations. For example, we observe the number of lawyers and the number of offices for Kelley Drye & Warren LLP in 1994, 1995, and 1996. We discarded all observations after Kelly switched form in 1996, and, in effect, exited the study.

We used the Cox method for estimating the model.[107] For ease of interpretation, the estimates on LAWYERS, OFFICES, and FOREIGN are reported as hazard ratios. Hazard ratios have a simple interpretation. If the hazard ratio equals two, this means that a one-unit increase in the covariate increases the hazard rate by 100%.[108]

---

105 See G.J. van den Berg, 'Search Behaviour, Transitions to Non-Participation and the Duration of Unemployment', 100 *Econimic Journal* (1990) p. 842, at pp. 855-56 (1990) (discussing unemployment benefits as a policy lever).

106 The model is based on 110, not 118, firms because complete data was unavailable for eight firms.

107 The Cox model assumes that the .covariates multiplicatively shift the baseline hazard function. See Cleves, et al., *supra* n. 101, at p. 121. The baseline hazard function is the hazard function when all the covariates equal zero. Id. The Cox method is a common way to estimate a duration model. We also estimated the effects using various other models, which make different assumptions about the distribution of the hazard function. These models include, for example, the exponential and Weibull models. Ibid., at pp. 213-50. Neither LAWYERS nor OFFICES was significant in any formulation of the model.

108 For a fuller discussion of hazard ratios, see Cleves et al., *supra* n. 101, at pp. 122-27.

So, for example, if the number of lawyers increases by one and the estimated hazard ratio is two, this means that, at any point in time, a law firm with 200 lawyers has twice the conditional probability of adopting LLP status as a law firm with 199 lawyers.[109] If the hazard ratio equals one, a one-unit increase in the covariate of interest has no impact on the hazard rate.

Table 11 reports the results. We cannot reject the hypothesis that LAWYERS and OFFICES have no effect on the probability of a switch in form from a GP to an LLP (i.e., that the hazard ratio for each of these variables is equal to one.) In other words, we cannot reject the possibility that, contrary to theory, the number of lawyers and the number of offices play no role in a law firm's decision to limit its liability. This finding provides another check and adds robustness to the logit model findings presented above.

Table 11.

No. of subjects = 111 Cox regression -- Breslow method for ties
No. of failures = 90
Log likelihood = -371.20846 Number of obs = 585

	Haz. Ratio	Std. Error	z	P>|z|	[95% Conf. Interval]
LAWYERS	.9997929	.0007201	-0.29	0.774	.9983825 1.001205
OFFICES	1.024761	.0359544	0.70	0.486	.95666 1.09771
FOREIGN	.6540692	.340994	-0.81	0.415	.235427 1.817152

4. Interview data

We sought clarification and confirmation of the implications of our empirical results through a series of interviews with individuals active in and knowledgeable about the choice of organizational form by New York law firms. Specifically, we interviewed: (1) partners at law firms in our sample who had been involved in their firm's decision regarding organizational form; (2) legal consultants, who advise law firms on a variety of matters, including the choice of organizational form; and (3) insurers, who base malpractice liability insurance rates on a variety of factors thought to correlate with the probability of a malpractice judgment and, thus, collect data from law firms regarding those factors.[110]

4.1 **Law firm partners**

4.1.1 *Methodology*

In order to shed light on the results of our empirical analysis, we interviewed partners at many of the law firms in our sample. We interviewed partners at many firms across a range of sizes and practice areas that had opted for LLP status. More importantly, we interviewed at least one partner at every law firm in our sample that had chosen to remain a GP. To add

[109] We also did the same analysis but changed the units on lawyers. With the changed units, a one-unit increase meant an increase of ten lawyers at the firm. Under this modification, we could not reject the possibility that the hazard ratio equals one.

[110] All interview subjects were ensured confidentiality and are not identified by name or firm name in this Article. For purposes of verifiability, redacted interview notes are available from the authors.

depth and understanding to our analysis, we also interviewed a limited number of in-house counsel and partners at law firms that are not in our sample, but that we felt were sufficiently similar to our sample of firms to provide useful information concerning issues relating to the choice of organizational form by firms in our sample.[111] In total, we interviewed seventy-five partners at sixty firms.

Interviewees were encouraged to freely discuss the choice of organizational form at their firm, without prompting or leading from the interviewer. When necessary, interviewees were prompted to discuss particular issues of interest to the authors through a list of questions. The list of questions designed for GP partners is attached to this chapter as Appendix E. The list of questions designed for LLP partners is attached to this chapter as Appendix F.

4.1.2 *Findings*

Although the explanations offered for the choice to remain a GP vary across firms and law firm cultures are undoubtedly idiosyncratic, several general themes arose from our discussions with law firm partners. First, neither apathy nor lack of attention to the costs and benefits of LLP status seem to explain the choice of organizational form in any of the firms in our sample. Second, the most frequently-cited issues that arose in connection with the LLP debate at most firms were: concerns over lost collegiality, concerns over the perceived negative signal to clients associated with limited liability, whether a sufficient number of the filing firm's peer firms had filed, the 'Arthur Andersen effect' and the connection between limited liability and lock-step compensation. In addition, nearly every partner that we interviewed indicated a belief that the ultimate movement of law firms to limited liability forms was inevitable. This was true even among partners at firms that had decided to remain a GP, at least temporarily. Third, intra-firm economics had caused a handful of firms to struggle with the move to a limited liability entity, although each of those firms was eventually able to overcome that struggle and file for LLP status. Finally, some law firm partners cited the size, decentralization, and specialization of modern law firms as relevant factors motivating the decision to become an LLP.

4.1.2.1 Ruling out apathy and lack of sophistication

It is worth noting at the outset that neither lack of sophistication, failure to appreciate the costs and benefits of limited liability, nor simple apathy can explain the lack of movement into LLPs by those New York law firms that remain a GP. As is evident from the many large and successful firms listed in Appendix A as a GP, partners at the GP firms are quite sophisticated. Our interview data reveal that, in these firms, the partners have debated (and rejected) LLP status. The existence of the debate reveals that: (1) partners know about LLP status, and (2) the LLP is not the preferred choice for every partner. At least some partners perceive costs as well as benefits to the LLP form.

This is not to imply that the conversion to a limited liability entity entails no transaction costs for law firms. Simply garnering agreement from, in some cases, hundreds of busy and

[111] As an example, one large foreign firm whose main US office is in New York City did not appear in our sample due to a quirk in the method by which the firm lists with Martindale-Hubble. We felt that partners at this firm faced issues regarding the choice of organizational form sufficiently similar to those faced by firms in our sample to provide useful information.

opinionated law firm partners doubtless can be difficult. However, in almost every case the reason for this difficulty stems from the fact that many law firm partners perceive real costs to the conversion to an LLP form, as discussed throughout this Section 4.

In addition, some firms did attribute their slow movement to the LLP form to the fact that limiting liability 'simply was not a priority' for the firm.[112] However, at every firm we spoke to, this view changed substantially after the Arthur Andersen bankruptcy, as discussed in more detail in Section 4.1.2.5.

4.1.2.2 Collegiality

Every partner we interviewed identified fears regarding a loss in firm collegiality as an issue that arose in their firms' debates over whether to become an LLP.[113] When pressed to describe exactly what was meant by a loss of collegiality, it became clear that 'collegiality' takes on several different meanings.

For some partners, particularly older partners, a loss of collegiality resembled a form of nostalgia. These partners often lamented the increasing commercialization of law practice and yearned for the days when all partners knew and trusted each other and all clients knew and trusted their legal counsel.

At other firms, concerns over lost collegiality took on a decidedly economic cast. A commonly-asserted fear was that partners would hesitate to advise fellow partners or pitch in on matters if doing so would create additional liability risk. A handful of partners at firms that had become LLPs believed that this fear had been well-founded at their firm and that certain partners now avoided helping out on other partners' projects, out of a desire to limit their personal exposure.[114] Most partners, however, indicated that becoming an LLP had not impacted in any way the relations among partners. As stated by one law firm partner,

> 'partners who were uncollegial before [the firm became an LLP] are still uncollegial and partners who were collegial before are still just as collegial [after the firm became an LLP]'.[115]

4.1.2.3 Signaling

Our interviews with law firm partners revealed that, at nearly every firm, partners feared the negative signal that any limitation on personal liability might send to their clients and competitors. This fact was particularly true when very few of the firm's competitor firms had opted to limit their liability. As stated by one law firm partner,

> 'at the time we first debated becoming an LLP, none of the firms that we consider similar to us had limited their liability. We didn't want to be path breakers on this'.[116]

---

[112] Confidential interview with law firm partner (interview notes on file with the authors).

[113] Ibid.; See also A. Lin, 'After Enron, Firms Rethink Partnership', *New York Law Journal* (April 15, 2002) p. 1 (quoting an unnamed partner at a major New York law firm as stating that his firm deadlocked over the decision of whether to become an LLP because of the 'tremendous fear that the partnership would lose its collegiality').

[114] Confidential interviews with law firm partners (interview notes on file with authors).

[115] Ibid.

[116] Ibid.

At the same time, as more firms within a given cohort opt for LLP status, the perceived negative signal associated with limited liability diminishes, and the arguments in favor of limited liability are more persuasive. As stated by one partner,

> 'We're currently reconsidering the issue and my prediction is that we.ll switch [to an LLP] at some point in the near future. Now that most of the other firms like us have switched, the arguments against it seem weaker.'[117]

Interestingly, it is not at all clear that this fear is well-founded. Every LLP partner that we spoke to believed that the firm's relations with clients had not been altered by the decision to become an LLP.

4.1.2.4 The importance of cohorts

Our interview data reveal that law firms are extraordinarily conservative and are reluctant to take actions that may distinguish them in a negative manner from their competitor firms. This fact is especially true of the large, elite law firms that we interviewed. For those firms who were slow to file for LLP status (as noted, this is true of the majority of elite firms), one of the most commonly-cited rationales for the firm's hesitation in filing was the fact that the firm did not want to file until a sufficient number of peer firms had also decided to file.[118] Similarly, in addition to the Arthur Andersen effect, the most commonly-cited motivation behind the eventual decision to file was the fact that a sufficient number of peer firms had finally determined to file. Our interview data also reveal that law firm partners were in regular communication with peer firms about the decision to file and, in some cases, coordinated the timing of their filings.[119]

4.1.2.5 The Arthur Andersen effect

In our interviews with partners at firms that had recently chosen to limit their liability or were currently considering whether to do so, one factor was mentioned repeatedly as being relevant to the firm's decision: the demise of Arthur Andersen.[120] This fact was especially true at large, elite law firms, many of whom only opted for LLP status after 2001. Apparently, for many of these firms, the threat of a liability judgment that exceeded the firm's malpractice insurance seemed relatively remote.[121] Given the perceived losses associated with limited liability, many firms simply felt that the benefits of LLP status were insufficient to overcome the costs.[122] For many firms, however, this perception changed with the trial and subsequent bankruptcy of Arthur Andersen. Suddenly, the possibility of a liability

---

117 Ibid.

118 Ibid.

119 Ibid.

120 Ibid.; see also Lin, *supra* n. 113, at p. 1 (noting that, '[i]n light of the potentially crippling liability faced by Arthur Andersen, Vinson and Elkins, and Kirkland and Ellis for their roles in the collapse of Enron Corp., major law firms are considering again whether to form themselves into limited liability partnerships'.)

121 Confidential interviews with law firm partners (interview notes on file with authors). See also Lin, *supra* n. 113 (quoting Ward Bower, a principal at the law firm consultancy Altman Weil, as saying that, prior to Enron, many law firms assumed that malpractice was an insurable risk, but that 'you can't insure againt 10-figure liability').

122 Confidential interviews with law firm partners (interview notes on file with authors).

judgment that would not only exhaust the firm's liability insurance, but its partners' personal assets as well, seemed very real. Apparently, the fact that a firm as large and reputable as Arthur Andersen could simply disintegrate was a sobering experience for many law firm partners, and one that changed their outlook on limited liability. In fact, several partners asserted their belief that their firms never would have switched to an LLP had the Enron and Arthur Andersen debacles not occurred.[123]

4.1.2.6 Ruling out the monitoring theory

Many, if not most, of the law firm partners with whom we spoke were familiar with the theory that placing each partner's personal liability at stake for the blunders of every partner induces more careful monitoring among partners. However, law firm partners with whom we spoke tended to scoff at this theory of partnership form. First, most partners cited the size, decentralization, and specialization of the modern law firm as a factor that prevented the effectiveness of such attempts to monitor.[124] In addition, many partners were offended by the notion that partners fail to attempt such monitoring to the best of their ability absent the threat of full personal liability.[125]

As noted by most partners, the fear of a liability judgment so large that it wipes out the partnership's assets and insurance is not the factor that motivates careful legal work and monitoring of fellow partners and associates. Instead, it is concern with maintaining the firm's reputation and maximizing the firm's billable rates that motivates monitoring of partners by other partners.[126]

4.1.2.7 The partnership penalty

Despite the ongoing debate within many law firms regarding the choice of organizational form, the interview data reveal a feeling among many law firm partners that those partners pushing to remain a GP may some day lose the intra-firm debate. At that time, the remaining GP firms – like most of their competitors – will opt for a limited liability form of some sort.

These statements, combined with the other interview data discussed in this Section 4, cause us to conclude in Section 5.1 of this chapter that, if the GP form continues to exist, it will not be as an organizational form voluntarily chosen by firm participants after weighing the costs and benefits. Instead, we predict that the only function of the GP form in the coming years will be as a penalty default rule that forces parties contemplating the formation of a business or professional enterprise to reveal relevant information to courts and interested third parties. At the same time, however, the fact that many law firm partners have aggressively pushed to remain a GP indicates that, at least for many law firm partners, the benefits of unlimited liability are real, a phenomenon explored in Sections 4.1.2.2-4.1.2.4 of this section.

---

123 Ibid.

124 Ibid.; see also *infra* nn. 131-33 and accompanying text (discussing size, decentralization, and specialization as impacting the choice of organizational form).

125 Confidential interviews with law firm partners (interview notes on file with authors).

126 Ibid.

4.1.2.8 The lock-step connection

The decision to switch from a GP to an LLP seemed particularly difficult at firms that still practiced some version of lock-step compensation. As noted both by partners at lock-step firms and by those that are not, the concept of differentiated personal liability is inconsistent with the foundational principal at a lock-step firm that all of the partners 'sink or swim together'.[127] In addition, because partners at a lock-step firm can only succeed if every other partner succeeds, a willingness to pitch in and help out partners on any project on which help is needed is especially valued.[128]

4.1.2.9 Intra-firm economics

Our interviews revealed that intra-firm economics had caused a handful of the law firms in our sample to struggle with the move to a limited liability vehicle, although in every case the firm was eventually able to overcome those issues and adopt the LLP form. According to some partners we interviewed, problems with renegotiating the division of profits within the firm before moving to a limited liability entity caused negotiations over the move to LLP status to stall.[129]

Although LLP law permits partners to use their old GP agreement without modification to govern their relationship once they become an LLP, at least some firms feel that modification is necessary. This is because the GP form requires partners to share all profits and all liability risks, despite the fact that some partners are in high-risk, high-return practice areas. Presumably, GP agreements are premised on the notion that such high-risk, high return partners are willing to give up some portion of those returns, in exchange for the opportunity to share the risk of personal liability with all firm partners.

Once a firm adopts limited liability status, however, partners are no longer sharing the risk of personal liability for the acts of fellow partners. As such, some high-risk, high-return partners expect to receive a greater share of the division of firm profits if the firm becomes an LLP. Debates over whether and how much more some partners would receive under an LLP form and how much other partners would, in turn, be forced to give up caused some law firms to struggle with the move to LLP form, in some cases for as long as a year or two.[130]

4.1.2.10 Size, specialization, and decentralization

Although neither the number of lawyers variable nor the number of offices variable were significant predictors of the choice of organizational form in our logit regression,[131] law firm partners frequently cite the increasing size, decentralization, and specialization of the

---

127 Ibid.

128 Ibid.; see also *supra* nn. 113-15 and accompanying text (discussing firm collegiality).

129 Confidential interviews with law firm partners (interview notes on file with authors).

130 Ibid.; see also Lin, *supra* n. 113 (quoting Kenneth J. Laverriere, a Sherman and Sterling partner involved in the organizational form decision, as stating that Sherman's negotiations over the move to LLP status took several months or longer, in part because of concerns over the division of profits under the LLP structure when some partners were in high-risk, high-return practice areas.)

131 See *infra* nn. 77-78 and accompanying text.

modern law firm as a factor impacting the choice to limit the partners. personal liability.[132] To many partners, the notion that a trust and estate partner in Texas could or would more carefully monitor a bankruptcy partner in New York simply because of personal liability fears is absurd, given the realities of modern law firm life.[133]

4.1.2.11 Summary

As noted by law firm partners, no single factor is a determinant of the choice of organizational form.[134] Instead, as stated by many partners, a .confluence. of events has dictated the decision. Those events include the number of similarly situated firms that have chosen to become LLPs, rising liability fears associated with Arthur Andersen, larger transaction sizes, more frequent malpractice awards, the failure of malpractice insurance to keep pace with these risks, and the intricacies of internal firm economics and culture.[135]

4.2 Law firm consultants

Law firm consultants work for consultancy firms that advise law firms on a variety of matters relating to law firm structure, operation, and profitability, including the choice of organizational form. Our interviews with law firm consultants reinforced the information gathered through interviews with law firm partners.

4.3 Law firm insurers

Insurance companies insure business and professional enterprises, including law firms, against a variety of risks, including the risk of liability arising from legal advice rendered to clients. In determining what rates to charge law firms for such insurance, insurance companies consider a variety of factors that are thought to correlate with an increased risk of such liability.

If the theories proposed by economists and legal scholars that assert that unlimited liability results in the provision of higher-quality legal services are true, then insurance companies should charge GPs lower premiums than LLPs, in order to reflect the decreased risk of liability among GP firms.[136] In other words, if unlimited liability really causes partners to better monitor each other, then that reduced liability risk should be reflected in lower insurance rates.

Our interviews with law firm insurers reveal that insurance companies do not consider organizational form in setting liability insurance premiums.[137] This is supported by our

---

[132] Confidential interviews with law firm partners (interview notes on file with authors).

[133] Ibid.; See also 80 *ABA Journal* (September 1994) pp. 54, 56 (quoting Robert R. Keatinge, Chair of the ABA Business Law Section Partnership Committee's Subcommittee on Limited Liability Companies, as stating '[w]hen you think about it, there is nothing I as a tax lawyer can do that will protect against someone from another department within the firm screwing up a water law issue'.)

[134] Confidential interviews with law firm partners (interview notes on file with the authors).

[135] Ibid.

[136] This is in contrast to theories such as signaling, which predict higher profitability but not a lower liability risk, and profit-sharing, which predicts higher per-partner profitability, but not a better product.

[137] Interviews with insurers (interview notes on file with authors); see also J. Hanna, 'Legal Malpractice Insurance and Limited Liability Entities: An Analysis of Malpractice Risk and Underwriting Responses', 39 *S.*

interviews with law firm partners. Although not every partner we interviewed was familiar with the firm's insurance rates, those who were indicated that the decision to become an LLP had been made after consultation with the firm's insurance company and had not altered liability insurance premiums.[138] Accordingly, insurance companies apparently do not believe that unlimited liability causes law firms to render higher quality legal services. Unless insurance companies have erred in their actuarial calculations or have failed to consider the possible connection between organizational form and liability risk, this fact undermines the economic theories asserting that unlimited liability results in a better legal product.

5. Conclusion: explaining the New York law firm market

In today's litigious age, legal practitioners understandably are concerned with the costs associated with liability, including liability for legal malpractice. According to many sources, malpractice actions against law firms are increasingly common and judgments are becoming larger.[139] In addition, malpractice insurance is more expensive, covers less, and by all accounts has not kept pace with the increased liability risks associated with larger transaction sizes and volatile markets.[140] This is particularly true in high-risk legal fields, such as banking, securities, and other heavily regulated industries.[141]

As a result, it is not uncommon today to see law firm bankruptcies or law firm partners who incur personal liability as a result of malpractice judgments or other law firm debts.[142]

An analysis of the empirical and interview data collected for this chapter, however, indicates that, at least with respect to New York law firms, the costs and benefits of limited

Tex. L. Rev. (1998) p. 641, at p. 645 (stating that, '[o]nly if the insurer provides coverage for prior affiliations of the attorney constituents of a limited liability entity will there conceivably be a reduced incident of loss as a result of limited liability status'); R.W. Hillman, 'The Impact of Partnership Law on the Legal Profession', 67 *Fordham Law Review* (1999) p. 393, at p. 409 (noting that 'LLP status does not reduce the liability of the partnership itself, which means the need for insurance underwriters to insist on implementation of monitoring mechanisms is largely unaffected by conversion of a firm from a general partnership into an LLP').

138 Confidential interviews with law firm partners (interview notes on file with authors).

139 Johnson, *supra* n. 6, at pp. 85, 87; M.R. Ramos, 'Legal Malpractice: The Profession's Dirty Little Secret', 47 *Vanderbilt Law Review* (1994) p. 1657, at pp. 1674-80; App. B and D (demonstrating that malpractice claims have sharply increased); C.R. Goforth, 'Limiting the Liability of General Partners in LLPs: An Analysis of Statutory Alternatives', 75 *Oregon Law Review* (1996) p. 1139, at p. 1142; R.E. Mallen and J.M. Smith, *Legal Malpractice* § 1.6, 5th edn. (St. Paul, West Publishing 2000) (noting the rise in malpractice suits is proportionally larger than the increase in the number of practicing attorneys); ABA, *Standing Committee on Lawyers. Professional Liability, The Profile of Legal Malpractice Claims: 1996-1999* (Chicago, American Bar Association 2001) (finding that insurers expect more frequent and severe lawsuits against attorneys following economic downturns).

140 Johnson, *supra* n. 6, at p. 88; R. Henley Jensen, 'For Third Straight Year Malpractice Rates Rise Again', *National Law Journal* (April 12, 1993) p. 3; E. Ainsworth, 'Malpractice Insurance: A High Priced Headache for Lawyers', *New Jersey Lawyer* (March 10, 2003) p. A2; S. Saab Fortney, 'Legal Malpractice Insurance: Surviving the Perfect Storm', 28 *Journal of the Legal Profession* (2003-2004) p. 41, at pp. 41-42 (citing various factors that 'have contributed to fewer insurers writing legal malpractice insurance, limited coverage offered by those insurers who remain in the market, and dramatic premium increases for those policies that are available'); Institute of Management and Administration, *Managing Risk: What Law Firms Must Do to Control Liability Insurance Costs* (2003), available at 2003 WL 2068161 (stating that firms, especially larger firms, are likely to see substantial rises in liability insurance rates); see also Confidential interviews with law firm partners (interview notes on file with the authors); Confidential interviews with law firm insurers (interview notes on file with the authors).

141 Johnson, *supra* n. 6, at p. 88.

142 Coates, *supra* n. 28, at pp. 354-55, n. 183 (discussing law firm dissolutions); Johnson, *supra* n. 6, at pp. 88-9.

liability are more complicated than either the academics or legal practitioners would like to believe. The rapid movement of firms into the LLP structure and the failure of the empirical tests in Section 3 of this chapter to return the results predicted by existing partnership theories cast doubt on arguments that the unlimited liability of the GP form provides the unqualified benefits asserted by many researchers. At the same time, the fact that a substantial number of large and sophisticated law firms have opted to remain a GP despite the availability of a quick, inexpensive, and easy alternative undermines the arguments of legal practitioners who suggest that the GP form provides no benefits to those considering the formation of a business or professional enterprise.

5.1 The future of GPs: a penalty partnership theory

Our empirical results indicate that most New York law firms have, in fact, abandoned the GP regime and our follow-up interviews with law firm partners whose firms are represented in our study indicate that the rest may at some point in time follow suit. The asserted reasons for each firm's choice of organizational form are telling and indicate that, for many partners, the perceived benefits of unlimited liability are real. At the same time, however, the interviews indicate that this view is changing, and that most of those interviewed believe that full movement into the LLP form is inevitable. If this is true, then the New York law firm market has not yet reached equilibrium.

Consistent with these views, we predict that, with the advent of the LLP form, if the GP form is to continue to exist in the future, it will not be as an organizational form voluntarily chosen after carefully weighing the costs and benefits. Instead, we predict that, as is the case with the New York law firms in our sample, parties in business and professional relationships will abandon the GP form altogether, and it will continue to exist primarily as a penalty default regime that forces the revelation of information to the state and interested third parties. Accordingly, we add a new theory of partnership to those already advanced by lawyers and economists: a penalty default theory of partnership.

The penalty default theory of partnership arises from the fact that the GP is the ultimate default regime for businesses operated by more than one person. If two or more parties run a business for profit and do nothing else, the GP default rules apply.[143] The case law is full of situations where parties entered into a business and unintentionally ended up a partnership.[144]

We propose that the GP default rules may make sense – and may, in fact, be socially desirable – because they penalize parties who fail to formalize their arrangements, either by affirmatively choosing an organizational form that requires notification to the state, or through elaborate contractual drafting. In the terms familiar to contract law scholars, the entire general partnership regime may operate as an information-forcing default rule.

---

[143] See *White Consul. Indust., Inc.* v. *Waterhouse*, 158 F.R.D. 429, 434 n.7 (D. Minn. 1994) (stating that, 'whether a legally binding partnership has been formed is a question of fact which can be inferred from the partners. actions. We are aware of no requirement that, in order to verify its formation, a partnership agreement must be filed with the State'); Uniform Partnership Act (1914) (U.P.A.) § 6 (defining 'partnership'); Revised Uniform Partnership Act (1997) (R.U.P.A.) §§ 101(4), 202 (defining 'partnership').

[144] See *Reddington* v. *Thomas*, 45 N.C. App. 236, 262 (1980); *Bass* v. *Bass*, 814 S.W.2d 38 (Tenn. 1991); *Howard Gault and Son* v. *First Nat.l Bank*, 541 S.W.2d 235, 237 (Tex. Civ. App. 1976). On the formation of partnerships, see generally Bromberg and Ribstein, *supra* n. 7, at § 2.05.

The state may desire such information-forcing from business and professional service firms for a variety of reasons. First, by forcing parties to file as an LLP, LLC, or corporation, the state encourages the parties to acknowledge they are a business association. This recognition, then, pushes parties to explicitly resolve (or at least think about) many important issues – such as, for example, the division of profits through careful negotiation and drafting – and this, in turn, reduces the information gathering burden on courts and creditors.

Second, state notification of the existence of a for-profit firm enables the state to take certain actions with respect to that firm. For example, the state can more easily tax and regulate for-profit firms when it has been alerted to their existence.[145]

5.2 Innovation and diffusion: status, networks, and signaling

In addition, if the New York law firm market has not reached equilibrium, this leads to two questions: (1) why has full movement into the LLP form been so slow; and (2) why have some firms moved relatively quickly, while others have taken their time? Our interview data reveal that law firms will go to great lengths (in this case, risking full personal liability) in order to avoid being perceived in a negative light relative to firms that they consider competitors for prestige and clients. This finding is consistent with prior research on the importance of signaling and status when the quality of output is difficult for consumers to judge,[146] and with research on herding behavior among law firms and other professionals.[147] This insight is also consistent with prior research on network effects and innovation, as (at least for the elite firms) it is only after a sufficient number of peer firms have become an LLP that the benefits of limited liability are judged to outweigh the perceived costs.[148]

This finding also provides insight into two aspects of change and innovation that have interested lawyers and social scientists for some time, but which have received minimal

---

145 See Ribstein, *supra* n. 43, at p. 223.

146 Price, *supra* n. 76, at p. 25 (stating that law firms decided to match Gunderson.s salary increases because to fail to do so would signal that they were not a top tier firm); C. Jones, 'Signaling Expertise: How Signals Shape Careers in Creative Industries, in Career Creativity: Explorations In The Remaking Of Work', in M.A. Peiperl, M.B. Arthur, and N. Anand (eds.), *Career Creativity: Explorations in the Remaking of Work* (Oxford, Oxford University Press 2002) pp. 224-25 (discussing the importance of signaling in the movie industry); J.M. Podolny, 'A Status-Based Model of Market Competition', 98(4) *American Journal of Sociology* (1993) p. 829 (discussing the importance of status as a signal of quality).

147 See Price, *supra* n. 76, at p. 5 (noting that professional organizations, especially law firms, tend to copy each other); R.S. Burt, 'Social Contagion and Innovation: Cohesion versus Structural Equivalence', 92 *American Journal of Sociology* (1987) p. 1287 (demonstrating that whether or not an individual adopts an innovation is a function of whether or not prominent peers have done so).

148 See M. Kahan and M. Klausner, 'Standardization and Innovation in Corporation Contracting (Or, 'The Economics of Boilerplate')', 83 *Virginia Law Review* (1997) p. 713; M. Klausner, 'Corporations, Corporate Law, and Networks of Contracts', 81 *Virginia Law Review* (1995) p. 757; R.B. Ahdieh, 'Cueing Transition in Sovereign Debt Contracts: Network Effects, Coordination Games, and Focal Points in the Choice of Mandate Versus Contract' (February 14, 2004) Emory Public Law Research Paper No. 03-23, available at <http://www.ssrn.com/abstract=503542>; S. Choi and M. Gulati, 'Innovation in Boilerplate Contracts: The Case of Sovereign Bonds', *Emory Law Journal* (2004), available at <http://www.ssrn.com/abstracts=515542>. But see B. Kobayashi and L.E. Ribstein, 'Choice of Form and Network Externalities', 43 *William and Mary Law Review* (2001) p. 79 (finding that network externalities 'in the form of an established body of law' have only a minimal impact on the choice of organizational form) (unpublished draft on file with the authors); M.J. Whincop, 'An Empirical Analysis of the Standardization of Corporate Charter Terms', 23 *International Review of Law and Economics* (2003) p. 285 (finding similar evidence with respect to the evolution of Australian charter provisions).

empirical study: (1) how new standards are adopted by particular market actors; and (2) how those changes then diffuse throughout the market.[149] Our data indicate that elite firms adopted the new LLP form far more slowly than did their less elite New York counterparts. Only after an exogenous shock, the Enron and Arthur Andersen debacles, along with other corporate scandals, prompted some 'higher bracket' firms to file as LLPs did the elite firms feel comfortable making this move. In addition, our interview data reveal the mechanisms by which this diffusion occurred. Not only did firms observe and copy the organizational form of their peer group, they explicitly coordinated their actions so as to minimize any potential negative signal associated with differentiating themselves from their cohort in terms of organizational form.[150]

In short, markets in equilibrium are frequently studied by social scientists. The adoption of the New York LLP statute, however, provides a rare opportunity to study a market in flux. In 1994, the New York state legislature provided law firms with a viable alternative to the organizational form that most firms had been using for many years, in some cases, for centuries. An analysis of how the market responded to this change provides valuable insights into the mechanisms by which change occurs and spreads across a market.

---

[149] See W.S. Frame and L.J. White, 'Empirical Studies of Financial Innovation: Lots of Talk, Little Action?', XLII *Journal of Economic Literature* (2004) p. 116, at p. 121 (lamenting the lack of empirical research on the impact of network effects on innovation).

[150] Confidential interviews with law firm partners (interview notes on file with the authors); see also J. Farrell and G. Saloner, 'Coordination Through Committees and Markets', 19 *Rand Journal of Economics* (1988) p. 235 (studying the function of standards committees in achieving coordination).

APPENDIX A

NAME	FORM	DATE	LAWYERS	OFFICES	GROWTH
Aaronson Rappaport Feinstein & Deutsch LLP	LLP	01/03/95	58	2	6.5
Abelman Frayne & Schwab	GP		29	1	4.9
Afridi & Angell LLC	LC	07/01/02	30	6	
Amster, Rothstein & Ebenstein	LLP	05/19/03	43	1	3.4
Anderson Kill & Click PC	PC	05/04/73	121	6	
Barnes, Richardson & Colburn	GP		27	3	-0.1
Barry, McTiernan & Moore	GP		30	3	3.3
Bernstein Litowitz Berger & Grossmann LLP	LLP	09/28/95	34	4	13.8
Bivona & Cohen P.C.	PC	01/10/79	37	5	
Borah, Goldstein, Altschuler, Schwartz & Nahins PC	PC	11/14/79	45	1	
Brauner Baron Rosenzweig & Klein LLP	LLP	12/23/94	28	1	-0.6
Brown Raysman Millstein Felder & Steiner LLP	LLP	05/24/95	220	5	19.2
Cadwalader Wickersham & Taft LLP	LLP	02/26/03	411	5	6.2
Cahill Gordon & Reindel LLP	LLP	04/29/03	225	3	1.9
Carter Ledyard & Milburn LLP	LLP	11/14/02	118	3	4.5
Chadbourne & Parke LLP	LLP	08/08/95	428	7	4.2
Cleary Gottlieb Steen & Hamilton	GP		798	12	5.7
Clifford Chance US LLP	LLP	01/28/98	3500	32	19.9
Cohen, Weiss and Simon LLP	LLP	12/02/99	31	1	0.8
Condon & Forsyth LLP	LLP	05/07/98	51	3	3.8
Conway, Farrell, Curtin & Kelly PC	PC	01/05/71	38	3	
Cooper & Dunham LLP	LLP	12/28/94	38	1	3.2
Coudert Brothers LLP	LLP	09/05/01	630	25	7.9
Cowan, Liebowitz & Latman PC	PC	12/01/72	50	1	
Cravath Swaine & Moore LLP	LLP	03/25/03	499	3	5.6

NAME	FORM	DATE	LAWYERS	OFFICES	GROWTH
Curtis Mallet-Prevost Colt & Mosle LLP	LLP	07/28/99	156	12	3.4
D'Amato & Lynch	GP		84	2	0.6
Darby & Darby Professional Corporation	PC	12/27/73	73	2	
Davidoff, Malito and Hutcher LLP	LLP	12/22/94	42	4	5.6
Davidson, Davidson & Kappel LLC	LLC	04/01/98	26	1	
Davis & Gilbert, LLP	LLP	03/10/98	84	1	9.0
Davis Polk & Wardwell	GP		624	9	5.6
Debevoise & Plimpton LLP	LLP	12/30/03	514	8	6.3
Dewey Ballantine LLP	LLP	09/26/97	550	13	5.5
Dreier LLP	LLP	10/17/97	28	1	75.5
Eaton & Van Winkle LLP	LLP	09/04/02	27	2	6.1
Emmet Marvin & Martin LLP	LLP	12/30/94	62	3	1.5
Epstein Becker & Green PC	PC	06/23/80	355	12	
Esanu Katsky Korins & Siger LLP	LLP	07/18/97	33	1	4.5
Fischbein Badillo Wagner Harding	GP		79	3	3.9
Fish & Neave	GP		173	3	4.4
Fitzpatrick Cella Harper & Scinto	GP		142	3	7.1
Flemming, Zulack & Williamson LLP	LLP	11/23/94	28	2	2.4
Ford Marrin Esposito Witmeyer & Gleser LLP	LLP	03/02/95	27	2	2.2
Fragomen, Del Rey, Bernsen & Loewy LLP	LLP	06/29/04	141	17	19.7
Frankfurt Kurnit Klein & Selz PC	PC	09/24/80	41	1	
Fried Frank Harris Shriver & Jacobson LLP	LLP	12/23/03	550	5	4.0
Friedman Kaplan Seiler & Adelman LLP	LLP	04/13/95	47	2	11.1
Frommer Lawrence & Haug LLP	LLP	09/02/97	52	2	19.3
Fross Zelnick Lehrman & Zissu PC	PC	04/02/82	49	1	
Gianni Origoni Grippo & Partners	GP		270	7	9.4
Gibney, Anthony & Flaherty LLP	LLP	11/30/94	34	4	-1.5
Goldberg Weprin & Ustin LLP	LLP	11/21/96	27	1	7.3
Goldfarb & Fleece	GP		26	1	4.9

NAME	FORM	DATE	LAWYERS	OFFICES	GROWTH
Golenbock Eiseman Assor Bell & Peskoe LLP	LLP	08/29/03	35	1	9.5
Goodkind Labaton Rudoff & Sucharow LLP	LLP	10/26/94	46	2	3.5
Gordon & Silber PC	PC	07/03/79	29	2	
Graubard Miller	GP		28	1	-3.4
Grubman Indursky Schindler & Goldstein PC	PC	10/01/74	30	1	
Granfeld, Desiderio, Lebowitz, Silverman & Klestadt LLP	LLP	03/16/95	32	4	4.1
Hahn & Hessen LLP	LLP	05/23/95	48	2	-0.6
Hawkins Delafield & Wood LLP	LLP	12/18/03	111	7	1.1
Healy & Baillie LLP	LLP	08/22/96	27	3	4.3
Heidell Pittoni Murphy & Bach LLP	LLP	12/15/98	64	2	4.1
Herrick Feinstein LLP	LLP	12/27/94	124	3	13.7
Herzfeld & Rubin PC	PC	09/29/71	100	6	
Hughes Hubbard & Reed LLP	LLP	05/14/96	303	7	2.9
Jacobowitz, Garfinkel & Lesman	GP		32	1	9.3
Jones Hirsch Connors & Bull PC	PC	01/29/97	50	5	
Kane Kessler PC	PC	02/01/71	32	2	
ECasowitz Benson Torres & Friedman LLP	LLP	03/14/95	150	5	17.0
ECaufman Borgeest & Ryan LLP	LLP	03/14/03	67	5	29.2
Kaye Scholer LLP	LLP	12/29/95	400	9	4.1
Kelley Drye & Warren LLP	LLP	05/09/96	305	8	0.2
Kenyon & Kenyon	GP		198	3	11.4
Kleinberg, Kaplan, Wolff & Cohen PC	PC	10/27/75	26	2	
Kopff, Nardelli & Dopf LLP	LLP	07/24/96	28	1	-3.1
Kramer Levin Naftalis & Frankel LLP	LLP	10/23/98	260	2	9.0
Kronish Lieb Weiner & Hellman LLP	LLP	03/01/95	101	1	4.8
Kurzman Eisenberg Corbin Lever & Goodman LLP	LLP	02/14/95	27	2	13.6
Ladas & Parry	LLP	11/21/03	50	5	1.3
Landman Corsi Ballaine & Ford PC	PC	09/18/95	46	3	
LeBoeuf Lamb Greene & Macrae LLP	LLP	10/24/94	650	22	1.7

NAME	FORM	DATE	LAWYERS	OFFICES	GROWTH
Lester Schwab Katz & Dwyer LLP	LLP	06/16/99	65	2	-3.7
London Fischer LLP	LLP	05/11/99	50	2	30.1
Martin Clearwater & Bell LLP	LLP	10/17/02	70	3	4.3
McAloon & Friedman PC	PC	10/07/77	37	1	
McLaughlin & Stern, LLP	LLP	11/15/94	47	2	10.0
Mendes & Mount LLP	LLP	12/11/95	160	3	0.1
Milbank Tweed Hadley & McCloy LLP	LLP	02/01/99	496	9	4.4
Morgan & Finnegan LLP	LLP	12/19/94	98	2	1.6
Morris Duffy Alonso & Faley	LLP	09/06/95	80	1	
Morrison Cohen Singer & Weinstein LLP	LLP	12/23/94	83	1	7.7
Morvillo, Abramowitz, Grand, Lason & Silberberg PC	PC	09/06/79	38	1	
Moses & Singer LLP	LLP	05/24/95	65	2	3.8
Vlound Cotton Wollan & Greengrass	GP		73	5	3.2
Newman Fitch Altheim Myers PC	PC	06/25/75	41	2	
Nicoletti Hornig Campise Sweeney & Paige	GP		28	2	28.9
Ohrenstein & Brown LLP	LLP	04/27/95	56	3	8.7
Olshan Grundman Frome Rosenzweig & Wolosky LLP	LLP	07/10/95	54	2	6.8
Ostrolenk, Faber, Gerb & Soffen, LLP	LLP	06/08/95	28	2	1.4
Otterbourg Steindler Houston & Rosen PC	PC	06/09/70	58	1	
Patterson, Belknap, Webb & Tyler LLP	LLP	12/30/94	181	1	4.2
Paul Weiss Rifkind Wharton & Garrison LLP	LLP	12/23/02	500	7	4.4
Pavia & Harcourt LLP	LLP	07/30/01	34	1	-4.4
Phillips Nizer LLP	LLP	05/11/95	78	3	-2.7
Proskauer Rose LLP	LLP	01/26/95	600	7	4.1
Pryor Cashman Sherman & Flynn LLP	LLP	03/27/98	125	1	4.3
Putney, Twombly, Hall & Hirson LLP	LLP	12/04/98	29	4	2.8
Quirk and Bakalor PC	PC	09/14/71	29	2	
Richards Spears Kibbe & Orbe LLP	LLP	12/31/02	55	2	14.4
Roberts & Holland LLP	LLP	11/09/94	40	2	-0.4

NAME	FORM	DATE	LAWYERS	OFFICES	GROWTH
Robinson Brog Leinwand Greene Geno-vese & Gluck PC	PC	02/14/72	50	1	
Rosenberg & Estis, P.C.	PC	06/02/76	36	1	
Sabin, Bermant & Gould LLP	LLP	12/20/95	36	1	5.4
Salans	GP		400	14	21.2
Satterlee Stephens Burke & Burke LLP	LLP	12/30/94	58	2	-0.5
Schulte Roth & Zabel LLP	LLP	08/23/96	300	2	7.2
Seward & Kissel LLP	LLP	01/26/99	115	2	3.6
Shearman & Sterling LLP	LLP	06/16/03	697	18	7.7
Simpson Thacher & Bartlett LLP	LLP	05/23/03	602	6	6.7
Skadden Arps Slate Meagher & Flora LLP	LLP	05/25/01	1750	21	5.9
Smith Mazure Director Wilkins Young Yagerman & Tarallo PC	PC	12/09/88	32	1	
Snow Becker Krauss PC	PC	02/21/80	26	1	
Sokolow, Dunaud, Mercadier & Carreras LLP	LLP	02/03/98	38	4	44.3
Stroock & Stroock & Lavan LLP	LLP	01/24/97	345	3	0.2
Sullivan & Cromwell LLP	LLP	12/20/02	661	12	10.6
Sullivan Papain Block McGrath & Can-navo PC	PC	09/23/74	35	3	
Tannenbaum Helpern Syracuse & Hirschtritt LLP	LLP	06/13/95	46	2	9.1
Thacher Proffitt & Wood LLP	LLP	09/02/03	191	5	6.7
Thelen Reid & Priest LLP	LLP	11/19/96	408	6	4.3
Torys, LLP	LLP	11/30/01	280	2	4.0
Wachtel & Masyr, LLP	LLP	12/13/94	34	1	1.0
Wachtell Lipton Rosen & Katz	GP		181	1	7.0
Warshaw Burstein Cohen Schlesinger & Kuh LLP	LLP	03/02/95	34	1	-0.3
Watson Farley & Williams	GP		220	7	-1.8
Weil Gotshal & Manges LLP	LLP	12/18/95	1000	17	5.5
Weitz & Luxenberg PC	PC	02/01/91	45	4	
White & Case LLP	LLP	12/29/97	1700	37	8.1
White, Fleischner & Fino	LLP	11/09/00	30	3	2.7

NAME	FORM	DATE	LAWYERS	OFFICES	GROWTH
Willkie Fair & Gallagher LLP	LLP	08/29/03	507	8	4.5
Wilson, Elser, Moskowitz, Edelman & Dicker LLP	LLP	02/26/98	225	19	3.8
Windels Marx Lane & Mittendorf LLP	LLP	12/22/99	100	5	9.1
Wolf Haldenstein Adler Freeman & Herz LLP	LLP	11/16/94	55	5	3.7
Wollmuth Maher & Deutsch LLP	LLP	03/31/98	26	2	40.1
Wormser, Kiely, Galef & Jacobs LLP	LLP	02/05/97	36	2	-0.1
Zeichner Ellman & Krause LLP	LLP	04/26/99	27	3	-0.6

APPENDIX B

FIRM	SALARY	TIER	COLLEGIAL
Amster, Rothstein, & Ebenstein	120,000	no	N
Anderson Kill & Olick PC	115,000	yes	C
Brown Raysman Millstein Felder & Steiner LLP	125,000	yes	N
Cadwalader Wickersham & Taft LLP	125,000	no	C
Cahill Gordon & Reindel LLP	125,000	no	N
Carter Ledyard & Milburn LLP	120,000	no	C
Chadbourne & Parke LLP	125,000	no	N
Cleary Gottlieb Steen & Hamilton	125,000	no	C
Clifford Chance US LLP	125,000	yes	C
Cooper & Dunham LLP	115,000	yes	N
Coudert Brothers LLP	125,000	yes	N
Cravath Swaine & Moore LLP	125,000	no	N
Curtis Mallet-Prevost Colt & Mosle LLP	125,000	yes	N
Darby & Darby Professional Corporation	125,000	no	N
Davis Polk & Wardwell	125,000	no	C
Debevoise & Plimpton LLP	125,000	no	C
Dewey Ballantine LLP	125,000	no	C
Epstein Becker & Green PC			N
Fish & Neave	125,000	no	N
Fitzpatrick Cella Harper & Scinto	125,000	no	N
Fragomen, Del Rey, Bernsen & Loewy, LLP	95,000	yes	C
Fried Frank Harris Shriver & Jacobson LLP	125,000	no	C
Friedman Kaplan Seiler & Adelman LLP	125,000	no	C
Frommer Lawrence & Haug LLP	130,000	no	N
Hahn & Hessen LLP	110,000	no	C
Hawkins Delafield & Wood LLP	100,000	yes	C
Herrick Feinstein LLP	130,000	yes	N
Hughes Hubbard & Reed LLP	125,000	no	N
Kasowitz Benson Torres & Friedman LLP		no	C
Kaye Scholer LLP	125,000	no	N
Kelley Drye & Warren LLP	125,000	no	C
Kenyon & Kenyon	125,000	yes	N
Kramer Levin Naftalis & Frankel LLP	125,000	no	C
Kronish Lieb Weiner & Hellman LLP	125,000	no	C
LeBoeuf Lamb Greene & Macrae LLP	125,000	no	N
Milbank Tweed Hadley & McCloy LLP	125,000		N
Morgan & Finnegan LLP	125,000	no	N
Morrison Cohen Singer & Weinstein LLP			N
Moses & Singer LLP	92,000	no	
Olshan Grundman Frome Rosenzweig & Wolosky LLP	115,000	no	C
Otterbourg Steindler Houston & Rosen PC	115,000	no	N

FIRM	SALARY	TIER	COLLEGIAL
Patterson, Belknap, Webb & Tyler LLP	125,000	no	C
Paul Weiss Rifkind Wharton & Garrison LLP	125,000	no	N
Proskauer Rose LLP	125,000	no	N
Pryor Cashman Sherman & Flynn LLP	110,000	no	N
Salans	112,500	yes	N
Schulte Roth & Zabel LLP	125,000	no	N
Seward & Kissel LLP	140,000	no	N
Shearman & Sterling LLP	125,000	no	N
Simpson Thacher & Bartlett LLP	125,000	no	C
Skadden Arps Slate Meagher & Flom LLP	140,000	no	N
Stroock & Stroock & Lavan LLP	125,000	no	N
Sullivan & Cromwell LLP	125,000	no	N
Thacher Proffitt & Wood LLP	125,000	no	C
Thelen Reid & Priest LLP	125,000	yes	C
Torys, LLP	125,000	no	C
Wachtell Lipton Rosen & Katz	140,000	no	C
Weil Gotshal & Manges LLP	125,000	no	C
White & Case LLP	125,000	yes	N
Willkie Fair & Gallagher LLP	125,000	no	C
Windels Marx Lane & Mittendorf LLP			N

APPENDIX C

FIRM	FORTUNE	IN-HOUSE TOTAL	IN-HOUSE AVERAGE
Amster, Rothstein, & Ebenstein	1	34	34
Anderson Kill & Olick PC	1	120	120
Brown Raysman Millstein Felder & Steiner LLP	1	50	50
Cadwalader Wickersham & Taft LLP	5	745	149
Cahill Gordon & Reindel LLP	2	396	198
Chadbourne & Parke LLP	1	76	76
Cleary Gottlieb Steen & Hamilton	6	1512	252
Clifford Chance US LLP	9	1884	209.3333333
Cowan, Liebowitz & Latman PC	3	457	152.3333333
Cravath Swaine & Moore LLP	9	1886	209.5555556
Davis & Gilbert LLP	1	27	27
Davis Polk & Wardwell	16	1677	104.8125
Debevoise & Plimpton LLP	7	843	120.4285714
Dewey Ballantine LLP	2	208	104
Epstein Becker & Green PC	5	713	142.6
Fish & Neave	6	1383	230.5
Fitzpatrick Cella Harper & Scinto	3	337	112.3333333
Fragomen, Del Rey, Bernsen & Loewy LLP	1	154	154
Fried Frank Harris Shriver & Jacobson LLP	6	761	126.8333333
Friedman Kaplan Seiler & Adelman LLP	1	73	73
Hughes Hubbard & Reed LLP	3	357	119
Kasowitz Benson Torres & Friedman LLP	1	11	11
Kaye Scholer LLP	3	417	139
Kelley Drye & Warren LLP	1	89	89
Kenyon & Kenyon	1	246	246
Kramer Levin Naftalis & Frankel LLP	2	1050	525
Ladas & Parry	6	1598	266.3333333
LeBoeuf Lamb Greene & Macrae LLP	7	1616	230.8571429
Milbank Tweed Hadley & McCloy LLP	2	1050	525
Morgan & Finnegan LLP	1	174	174
Morrison Cohen Singer & Weinstein LLP	1	17	17
Patterson, Belknap, Webb & Tyler LLP	2	320	160
Paul Weiss Rifkind Wharton & Garrison LLP	7	2143	306.1428571
Proskauer Rose LLP	7	2084	297.7142857
Shearman & Sterling LLP	6	2632	438.6666667

FIRM	FORTUNE	IN-HOUSE TOTAL	IN-HOUSE AVERAGE
Simpson Thacher & Bartlett LLP	14	2047	46.2142857
Skadden Arps Slate Meagher & Flom LLP	32	4337	135.53125
Stroock & Stroock & Lavan LLP	4	331	82.75
Sullivan & Cromwell LLP	7	1606	229.4285714
Thelen Reid & Priest LLP	6	172	28.66666667
Wachtell Lipton Rosen & Katz	13	1562	120.1538462
Weil Gotshal & Manges LLP	7	2380	340
White & Case LLP	3	335	111.6666667

APPENDIX D

FIRM	YEAR	PROFITS
Brown Raysman Millstein Felder & Steiner LLP	1993	
Brown Raysman Millstein Felder & Steiner LLP	1994	
Brown Raysman Millstein Felder & Steiner LLP	1995	
Brown Raysman Millstein Felder & Steiner LLP	1996	
Brown Raysman Millstein Felder & Steiner LLP	1997	
Brown Raysman Millstein Felder & Steiner LLP	1998	
Brown Raysman Millstein Felder & Steiner LLP	1999	
Brown Raysman Millstein Felder & Steiner LLP	2000	
Brown Raysman Millstein Felder & Steiner LLP	2001	
Brown Raysman Millstein Felder & Steiner LLP	2002	530000
Brown Raysman Millstein Felder & Steiner LLP	2003	565000
Cadwalader Wickersham & Taft LLP	1993	505000
Cadwalader Wickersham & Taft LLP	1994	425000
Cadwalader Wickersham & Taft LLP	1995	565000
Cadwalader Wickersham & Taft LLP	1996	645000
Cadwalader Wickersham & Taft LLP	1997	785000
Cadwalader Wickersham & Taft LLP	1998	820000
Cadwalader Wickersham & Taft LLP	1999	935000
Cadwalader Wickersham & Taft LLP	2000	1040000
Cadwalader Wickersham & Taft LLP	2001	1105000
Cadwalader Wickersham & Taft LLP	2002	1250000
Cadwalader Wickersham & Taft LLP	2003	1610000
Cahill Gordon & Reindel LLP	1993	1210000
Cahill Gordon & Reindel LLP	1994	1200000
Cahill Gordon & Reindel LLP	1995	1250000
Cahill Gordon & Reindel LLP	1996	1400000
Cahill Gordon & Reindel LLP	1997	1445000
Cahill Gordon & Reindel LLP	1998	1600000
Cahill Gordon & Reindel LLP	1999	1710000
Cahill Gordon & Reindel LLP	2000	1610000
Cahill Gordon & Reindel LLP	2001	1805000
Cahill Gordon & Reindel LLP	2002	1845000
Cahill Gordon & Reindel LLP	2003	2405000
Chadbourne & Parke LLP	1993	525000
Chadbourne & Parke LLP	1994	515000
Chadbourne & Parke LLP	1995	545000
Chadbourne & Parke LLP	1996	610000
Chadbourne & Parke LLP	1997	535000
Chadbourne & Parke LLP	1998	615000
Chadbourne & Parke LLP	1999	815000

FIRM	YEAR	PROFITS
Chadbourne & Parke LLP	2000	940000
Chadbourne & Parke LLP	2001	980000
Chadbourne & Parke LLP	2002	1000000
Chadbourne & Parke LLP	2003	1010000
Cleary Gottlieb Steen & Hamilton	1993	890000
Cleary Gottlieb Steen & Hamilton	1994	885000
Cleary Gottlieb Steen & Hamilton	1995	910000
Cleary Gottlieb Steen & Hamilton	1996	975000
Cleary Gottlieb Steen & Hamilton	1997	1060000
Cleary Gottlieb Steen & Hamilton	1998	1075000
Cleary Gottlieb Steen & Hamilton	1999	1225000
Cleary Gottlieb Steen & Hamilton	2000	1250000
Cleary Gottlieb Steen & Hamilton	2001	1325000
Cleary Gottlieb Steen & Hamilton	2002	1445000
Cleary Gottlieb Steen & Hamilton	2003	1445000
Coudert Brothers LLP	1993	260000
Coudert Brothers LLP	1994	370000
Coudert Brothers LLP	1995	310000
Coudert Brothers LLP	1996	315000
Coudert Brothers LLP	1997	380000
Coudert Brothers LLP	1998	395000
Coudert Brothers LLP	1999	425000
Coudert Brothers LLP	2000	390000
Coudert Brothers LLP	2001	455000
Coudert Brothers LLP	2002	475000
Coudert Brothers LLP	2003	420000
Cravath Swaine & Moore LLP	1993	1410000
Cravath Swaine & Moore LLP	1994	1225000
Cravath Swaine & Moore LLP	1995	1340000
Cravath Swaine & Moore LLP	1996	1515000
Cravath Swaine & Moore LLP	1997	1790000
Cravath Swaine & Moore LLP	1998	2050000
Cravath Swaine & Moore LLP	1999	2110000
Cravath Swaine & Moore LLP	2000	2245000
Cravath Swaine & Moore LLP	2001	2135000
Cravath Swaine & Moore LLP	2002	1960000
Cravath Swaine & Moore LLP	2003	2080000
Curtis Mallet-Prevost Colt & Mosle LLP	1993	
Curtis Mallet-Prevost Colt & Mosle LLP	1994	
Curtis Mallet-Prevost Colt & Mosle LLP	1995	
Curtis Mallet-Prevost Colt & Mosle LLP	1996	
Curtis Mallet-Prevost Colt & Mosle LLP	1997	
Curtis Mallet-Prevost Colt & Mosle LLP	1998	615000
Curtis Mallet-Prevost Colt & Mosle LLP	1999	655000
Curtis Mallet-Prevost Colt & Mosle LLP	2000	700000
Curtis Mallet-Prevost Colt & Mosle LLP	2001	

FIRM	YEAR	PROFITS
Curtis Mallet-Prevost Colt & Mosle LLP	2002	
Curtis Mallet-Prevost Colt & Mosle LLP	2003	
Davis Polk & Wardwell	1993	1020000
Davis Polk & Wardwell	1994	940000
Davis Polk & Wardwell	1995	975000
Davis Polk & Wardwell	1996	1125000
Davis Polk & Wardwell	1997	1295000
Davis Polk & Wardwell	1998	1530000
Davis Polk & Wardwell	1999	1610000
Davis Polk & Wardwell	2000	1740000
Davis Polk & Wardwell	2001	1775000
Davis Polk & Wardwell	2002	1775000
Davis Polk & Wardwell	2003	1925000
Debevoise & Plimpton LLP	1993	685000
Debevoise & Plimpton LLP	1994	805000
Debevoise & Plimpton LLP	1995	890000
Debevoise & Plimpton LLP	1996	1020000
Debevoise & Plimpton LLP	1997	1105000
Debevoise & Plimpton LLP	1998	1200000
Debevoise & Plimpton LLP	1999	1225000
Debevoise & Plimpton LLP	2000	1225000
Debevoise & Plimpton LLP	2001	1105000
Debevoise & Plimpton LLP	2002	1085000
Debevoise & Plimpton LLP	2003	1260000
Dewey Ballantine LLP	1993	510000
Dewey Ballantine LLP	1994	515000
Dewey Ballantine LLP	1995	530000
Dewey Ballantine LLP	1996	650000
Dewey Ballantine LLP	1997	780000
Dewey Ballantine LLP	1998	860000
Dewey Ballantine LLP	1999	950000
Dewey Ballantine LLP	2000	1035000
Dewey Ballantine LLP	2001	1075000
Dewey Ballantine LLP	2002	1125000
Dewey Ballantine LLP	2003	1150000
Fish & Neave	1993	
Fish & Neave	1994	
Fish & Neave	1995	
Fish & Neave	1996	
Fish & Neave	1997	
Fish & Neave	1998	740000
Fish & Neave	1999	700000
Fish & Neave	2000	675000
Fish & Neave	2001	725000
Fish & Neave	2002	800000
Fish & Neave	2003	730000

FIRM	YEAR	PROFITS
Fried Frank Harris Shriver & Jacobson LLP	1993	400000
Fried Frank Harris Shriver & Jacobson LLP	1994	400000
Fried Frank Harris Shriver & Jacobson LLP	1995	495000
Fried Frank Harris Shriver & Jacobson LLP	1996	615000
Fried Frank Harris Shriver & Jacobson LLP	1997	580000
Fried Frank Harris Shriver & Jacobson LLP	1998	760000
Fried Frank Harris Shriver & Jacobson LLP	1999	855000
Fried Frank Harris Shriver & Jacobson LLP	2000	1045000
Fried Frank Harris Shriver & Jacobson LLP	2001	875000
Fried Frank Harris Shriver & Jacobson LLP	2002	930000
Fried Frank Harris Shriver & Jacobson LLP	2003	980000
Hughes Hubbard & Reed LLP	1993	300000
Hughes Hubbard & Reed LLP	1994	325000
Hughes Hubbard & Reed LLP	1995	335000
Hughes Hubbard & Reed LLP	1996	350000
Hughes Hubbard & Reed LLP	1997	400000
Hughes Hubbard & Reed LLP	1998	420000
Hughes Hubbard & Reed LLP	1999	450000
Hughes Hubbard & Reed LLP	2000	520000
Hughes Hubbard & Reed LLP	2001	640,000
Hughes Hubbard & Reed LLP	2002	820000
Hughes Hubbard & Reed LLP	2003	950000
Kaye Scholer LLP	1993	535000
Kaye Scholer LLP	1994	490000
Kaye Scholer LLP	1995	475000
Kaye Scholer LLP	1996	445000
Kaye Scholer LLP	1997	525000
Kaye Scholer LLP	1998	620000
Kaye Scholer LLP	1999	690000
Kaye Scholer LLP	2000	795000
Kaye Scholer LLP	2001	890000
Kaye Scholer LLP	2002	980000
Kaye Scholer LLP	2003	1070000
Kelley Drye & Warren LLP	1993	255000
Kelley Drye & Warren LLP	1994	200000
Kelley Drye & Warren LLP	1995	275000
Kelley Drye & Warren LLP	1996	400000
Kelley Drye & Warren LLP	1997	430000
Kelley Drye & Warren LLP	1998	515000
Kelley Drye & Warren LLP	1999	575000
Kelley Drye & Warren LLP	2000	840000
Kelley Drye & Warren LLP	2001	625000
Kelley Drye & Warren LLP	2002	810000
Kelley Drye & Warren LLP	2003	790000
Kenyon & Kenyon	1993	
Kenyon & Kenyon	1994	
Kenyon & Kenyon	1995	

FIRM	YEAR	PROFITS
Kenyon & Kenyon	1996	
Kenyon & Kenyon	1997	
Kenyon & Kenyon	1998	550000
Kenyon & Kenyon	1999	500000
Kenyon & Kenyon	2000	565000
Kenyon & Kenyon	2001	615,000
Kenyon & Kenyon	2002	770000
Kenyon & Kenyon	2003	685000
Kramer Levin Naftalis & Frankel LLP	1993	
Kramer Levin Naftalis & Frankel LLP	1994	
Kramer Levin Naftalis & Frankel LLP	1995	
Kramer Levin Naftalis & Frankel LLP	1996	
Kramer Levin Naftalis & Frankel LLP	1997	
Kramer Levin Naftalis & Frankel LLP	1998	685000
Kramer Levin Naftalis & Frankel LLP	1999	710000
Kramer Levin Naftalis & Frankel LLP	2000	750000
Kramer Levin Naftalis & Frankel LLP	2001	795000
Kramer Levin Naftalis & Frankel LLP	2002	935000
Kramer Levin Naftalis & Frankel LLP	2003	1040000
LeBoeuf Lamb Greene & Mac Rae LLP	1993	340000
LeBoeuf Lamb Greene & Mac Rae LLP	1994	365000
LeBoeuf Lamb Greene & Mac Rae LLP	1995	360000
LeBoeuf Lamb Greene & Mac Rae LLP	1996	400000
LeBoeuf Lamb Greene & Mac Rae LLP	1997	450000
LeBoeuf Lamb Greene & Mac Rae LLP	1998	550000
LeBoeuf Lamb Greene & Mac Rae LLP	1999	620000
LeBoeuf Lamb Greene & Mac Rae LLP	2000	645000
LeBoeuf Lamb Greene & Mac Rae LLP	2001	705000
LeBoeuf Lamb Greene & Mac Rae LLP	2002	855000
LeBoeuf Lamb Greene & Mac Rae LLP	2003	935000
Milbank Tweed Hadley & McCloy LLP	1993	540000
Milbank Tweed Hadley & McCloy LLP	1994	575000
Milbank Tweed Hadley & McCloy LLP	1995	590000
Milbank Tweed Hadley & McCloy LLP	1996	735000
Milbank Tweed Hadley & McCloy LLP	1997	860000
Milbank Tweed Hadley & McCloy LLP	1998	1105000
Milbank Tweed Hadley & McCloy LLP	1999	1275000
Milbank Tweed Hadley & McCloy LLP	2000	1450000
Milbank Tweed Hadley & McCloy LLP	2001	1600000
Milbank Tweed Hadley & McCloy LLP	2002	1785000
Milbank Tweed Hadley & McCloy LLP	2003	1820000
Patterson, Belknap, Webb & Tyler LLP	1993	
Patterson, Belknap, Webb & Tyler LLP	1994	
Patterson, Belknap, Webb & Tyler LLP	1995	
Patterson, Belknap, Webb & Tyler LLP	1996	

FIRM	YEAR	PROFITS
Patterson, Belknap, Webb & Tyler LLP	1997	
Patterson, Belknap, Webb & Tyler LLP	1998	470000
Patterson, Belknap, Webb & Tyler LLP	1999	550000
Patterson, Belknap, Webb & Tyler LLP	2000	620000
Patterson, Belknap, Webb & Tyler LLP	2001	600000
Patterson, Belknap, Webb & Tyler LLP	2002	730000
Patterson, Belknap, Webb & Tyler LLP	2003	900000
Paul Weiss Rifkind Wharton & Garrison LLP	1993	610000
Paul Weiss Rifkind Wharton & Garrison LLP	1994	655000
Paul Weiss Rifkind Wharton & Garrison LLP	1995	675000
Paul Weiss Rifkind Wharton & Garrison LLP	1996	745000
Paul Weiss Rifkind Wharton & Garrison LLP	1997	865000
Paul Weiss Rifkind Wharton & Garrison LLP	1998	825000
Paul Weiss Rifkind Wharton & Garrison LLP	1999	1050000
Paul Weiss Rifkind Wharton & Garrison LLP	2000	1210000
Paul Weiss Rifkind Wharton & Garrison LLP	2001	1680000
Paul Weiss Rifkind Wharton & Garrison LLP	2002	1740000
Paul Weiss Rifkind Wharton & Garrison LLP	2003	1840000
Proskauer Rose LLP	1993	400000
Proskauer Rose LLP	1994	420000
Proskauer Rose LLP	1995	480000
Proskauer Rose LLP	1996	510000
Proskauer Rose LLP	1997	600000
Proskauer Rose LLP	1998	660000
Proskauer Rose LLP	1999	740000
Proskauer Rose LLP	2000	915000
Proskauer Rose LLP	2001	965000
Proskauer Rose LLP	2002	1025000
Proskauer Rose LLP	2003	1080000
Schulte Roth & Zabel LLP	1993	
Schulte Roth & Zabel LLP	1994	
Schulte Roth & Zabel LLP	1995	
Schulte Roth & Zabel LLP	1996	610000
Schulte Roth & Zabel LLP	1997	670000
Schulte Roth & Zabel LLP	1998	725000
Schulte Roth & Zabel LLP	1999	825000
Schulte Roth & Zabel LLP	2000	875000
Schulte Roth & Zabel LLP	2001	950000
Schulte Roth & Zabel LLP	2002	1090000
Schulte Roth & Zabel LLP	2003	1540000
Shearman & Sterling LLP	1993	590000
Shearman & Sterling LLP	1994	625000
Shearman & Sterling LLP	1995	595000
Shearman & Sterling LLP	1996	815000
Shearman & Sterling LLP	1997	920000
Shearman & Sterling LLP	1998	1045000
Shearman & Sterling LLP	1999	1135000

FIRM	YEAR	PROFITS
Shearman & Sterling LLP	2000	1350000
Shearman & Sterling LLP	2001	950000
Shearman & Sterling LLP	2002	1275000
Shearman & Sterling LLP	2003	1215000
Simpson Thacher & Bartlett LLP	1993	925000
Simpson Thacher & Bartlett LLP	1994	930000
Simpson Thacher & Bartlett LLP	1995	1110000
Simpson Thacher & Bartlett LLP	1996	1155000
Simpson Thacher & Bartlett LLP	1997	1285000
Simpson Thacher & Bartlett LLP	1998	1495000
Simpson Thacher & Bartlett LLP	1999	1655000
Simpson Thacher & Bartlett LLP	2000	1740000
Simpson Thacher & Bartlett LLP	2001	1690000
Simpson Thacher & Bartlett LLP	2002	1845000
Simpson Thacher & Bartlett LLP	2003	1940000
Skadden Arps Slate Meagher & Flom LLP	1993	690000
Skadden Arps Slate Meagher & Flom LLP	1994	820000
Skadden Arps Slate Meagher & Flom LLP	1995	885000
Skadden Arps Slate Meagher & Flom LLP	1996	990000
Skadden Arps Slate Meagher & Flom LLP	1997	1290000
Skadden Arps Slate Meagher & Flom LLP	1998	1380000
Skadden Arps Slate Meagher & Flom LLP	1999	1600000
Skadden Arps Slate Meagher & Flom LLP	2000	1600000
Skadden Arps Slate Meagher & Flom LLP	2001	1565000
Skadden Arps Slate Meagher & Flom LLP	2002	1605000
Skadden Arps Slate Meagher & Flom LLP	2003	1600000
Stroock & Stroock & Lavan LLP	1993	490000
Stroock & Stroock & Lavan LLP	1994	495000
Stroock & Stroock & Lavan LLP	1995	485000
Stroock & Stroock & Lavan LLP	1996	500000
Stroock & Stroock & Lavan LLP	1997	560000
Stroock & Stroock & Lavan LLP	1998	595000
Stroock & Stroock & Lavan LLP	1999	630000
Stroock & Stroock & Lavan LLP	2000	685000
Stroock & Stroock & Lavan LLP	2001	785000
Stroock & Stroock & Lavan LLP	2002	800000
Stroock & Stroock & Lavan LLP	2003	920000
Sullivan & Cromwell LLP	1993	1275000
Sullivan & Cromwell LLP	1994	1185000
Sullivan & Cromwell LLP	1995	1310000
Sullivan & Cromwell LLP	1996	1330000
Sullivan & Cromwell LLP	1997	1450000
Sullivan & Cromwell LLP	1998	1645000
Sullivan & Cromwell LLP	1999	1790000
Sullivan & Cromwell LLP	2000	1715000
Sullivan & Cromwell LLP	2001	1670000
Sullivan & Cromwell LLP	2002	1720000
Sullivan & Cromwell LLP	2003	1900000

FIRM	YEAR	PROFITS
Thacher Proffitt & Wood LLP	1993	
Thacher Proffitt & Wood LLP	1994	
Thacher Proffitt & Wood LLP	1995	
Thacher Proffitt & Wood LLP	1996	
Thacher Proffitt & Wood LLP	1997	
Thacher Proffitt & Wood LLP	1998	415000
Thacher Proffitt & Wood LLP	1999	480000
Thacher Proffitt & Wood LLP	2000	480000
Thacher Proffitt & Wood LLP	2001	475000
Thacher Proffitt & Wood LLP	2002	640000
Thacher Proffitt & Wood LLP	2003	810000
Thelen Reid & Priest LLP	1993	
Thelen Reid & Priest LLP	1994	
Thelen Reid & Priest LLP	1995	
Thelen Reid & Priest LLP	1996	
Thelen Reid & Priest LLP	1997	
Thelen Reid & Priest LLP	1998	405000
Thelen Reid & Priest LLP	1999	465000
Thelen Reid & Priest LLP	2000	500000
Thelen Reid & Priest LLP	2001	560000
Thelen Reid & Priest LLP	2002	510000
Thelen Reid & Priest LLP	2003	555000
Wachtell Lipton Rosen & Katz	1993	1350000
Wachtell Lipton Rosen & Katz	1994	1400000
Wachtell Lipton Rosen & Katz	1995	1595000
Wachtell Lipton Rosen & Katz	1996	1390000
Wachtell Lipton Rosen & Katz	1997	2200000
Wachtell Lipton Rosen & Katz	1998	3105000
Wachtell Lipton Rosen & Katz	1999	3385000
Wachtell Lipton Rosen & Katz	2000	3285000
Wachtell Lipton Rosen & Katz	2001	3165000
Wachtell Lipton Rosen & Katz	2002	2920000
Wachtell Lipton Rosen & Katz	2003	2585000
Weil Gotshal & Manges LLP	1993	745000
Weil Gotshal & Manges LLP	1994	700000
Weil Gotshal & Manges LLP	1995	705000
Weil Gotshal & Manges LLP	1996	735000
Weil Gotshal & Manges LLP	1997	805000
Weil Gotshal & Manges LLP	1998	890000
Weil Gotshal & Manges LLP	1999	980000
Weil Gotshal & Manges LLP	2000	1025000
Weil Gotshal & Manges LLP	2001	1130000
Weil Gotshal & Manges LLP	2002	1300000
Weil Gotshal & Manges LLP	2003	1505000
White & Case LLP	1993	530000
White & Case LLP	1994	555000

FIRM	YEAR	PROFITS
White & Case LLP	1995	565000
White & Case LLP	1996	565000
White & Case LLP	1997	625000
White & Case LLP	1998	665000
White & Case LLP	1999	725000
White & Case LLP	2000	775000
White & Case LLP	2001	865000
White & Case LLP	2002	935000
White & Case LLP	2003	1010000
Willkie Fair & Gallagher LLP	1993	720000
Willkie Fair & Gallagher LLP	1994	740000
Willkie Fair & Gallagher LLP	1995	760000
Willkie Fair & Gallagher LLP	1996	915000
Willkie Farr & Gallagher LLP	1997	900000
Willkie Farr & Gallagher LLP	1998	955000
Willkie Farr & Gallagher LLP	1999	1100000
Willkie Farr & Gallagher LLP	2000	1015000
Willkie Farr & Gallagher LLP	2001	1170000
Willkie Fair & Gallagher LLP	2002	1295000
Willkie Farr & Gallagher LLP	2003	1410000
Wilson, Elser, Moskowitz, Edelman & Dicker LLP	1993	405000
Wilson, Elser, Moskowitz, Edelman & Dicker LLP	1994	275000
Wilson, Elser, Moskowitz, Edelman & Dicker LLP	1995	320000
Wilson, Elser, Moskowitz, Edelman & Dicker LLP	1996	330000
Wilson, Elser, Moskowitz, Edelman & Dicker LLP	1997	305000
Wilson, Elser, Moskowitz, Edelman & Dicker LLP	1998	290000
Wilson, Elser, Moskowitz, Edelman & Dicker LLP	1999	270000
Wilson, Elser, Moskowitz, Edelman & Dicker LLP	2000	270000
Wilson, Elser, Moskowitz, Edelman & Dicker LLP	2001	370000
Wilson, Elser, Moskowitz, Edelman & Dicker LLP	2002	605000
Wilson, Elser, Moskowitz, Edelman & Dicker LLP	2003	690000

APPENDIX E
Questions for GP partners

1. Has your firm discussed becoming an LLP?

2. What were the reasons asserted in favor of remaining a GP?

3. What were the reasons (other than limited liability) asserted in favor of LLP?

4. Was there an age division?

    a. I.e. did older partners favor the status quo more than younger ones?

5. Do you think that you'll eventually move to become an LLP?

6. Was there any talk of redoing the partnership agreement to reflect higher profits for high risk/ high-return partners if you moved to LLP?

7. Does your firm have a lock-step partner compensation structure?

APPENDIX F
Questions for LLP Partners

1. Your firm didn't take advantage of the LLP statute right away. In fact it took you ___ years to make the LLP filing. What took so long?

OR

Unlike many New York firms, your firm opted to become an LLP fairly quickly after the statute became effective. Why was the choice so easy for you? Why do you think other firms struggled with the decision and your firm did not?

2. What were the primary arguments made against the LLP filing?

   a. Monitoring?

   b. Collegiality?

   c. Signaling?

   d. Intra-firm economics?

   e. Were there age differences in these arguments? i.e. did older partners favor the traditional GP structure more than younger partners did?

3. What were the factors that caused the arguments in favor of LLP to finally win out?

4. Has your firm had any regrets about the choice to become an LLP?

   a. Has it altered your practice or relations with clients in any way?

   b. Has it altered relations among the partners in any way?

   c. Has it altered relations with your insurance company in any way?

5. IF APPLICABLE . I notice that you filed at the same time as _____ [similar firms].

Was that a conscious decision? Did their decision to file affect your decision in any way?

6. Does your firm have a lock-step partnership structure?

Chapter 11

ETHICS IN THE AGE OF UN-INCORPORATION: A RETURN TO AMBIGUITY OF PRE-INCORPORATION OR AN OPPORTUNITY TO CONTRACT FOR CLARITY

Richard W. Painter*

1. INTRODUCTION

The age of un-incorporation presents both a problem and an opportunity in the field of professional responsibility. The problem is that the ethical obligations of lawyers representing un-incorporated entities are uncertain. This ambiguity harkens back to an earlier pre-incorporation era when lawyers were retained principally by individuals and groups of individuals, not entities, and when lawyers were often confused as to which individuals behind an enterprise were in fact their clients. One of the most famous lawyers to confront this ambiguity was Louis Brandeis, who tried to solve this and other conflicts in his law practice with his intuitively appealing, if only marginally useful, concept of 'lawyering for the situation'.[1] Today, lawyers representing partners, joint venturers, and participants in other un-incorporated entities are often still viewed as representing the individuals behind these entities, rather than exclusively representing the entities themselves. However, exactly which individuals the lawyers represent is often ambiguous.[2]

The later age of incorporation brought some clarity to lawyers' obligations by elevating a client entity, itself a legal person, above the interests of its individual shareholders, officers, and directors. Incorporation created a client entity that lawyers could purport to represent, while professing not to represent the individuals behind it. The ABA's Model Rules of Professional Conduct now embrace this concept of entity rep-

---

* S. Walter Richey Professor of Corporate Law, University of Minnesota Law School.

[1] See generally R.W. Painter, 'Contracting Around Conflicts in a Family Business: Louis Brandeis and the Warren Trust', 8 *University of Chicago Law School Roundtable* (2001) p. 353, at pp. 353-4; see *infra* text accompanying nn. 9-14.

[2] In some cases, a lawyer representing a partnership is assumed to represent at least some individuals behind the partnership. See *Prisco* v. *Westgate Entm't, Inc.*, 799 F. Supp. 266, 272 (Conn. 1992) (granting motion by former general partner in a limited partnership to disqualify a law firm from representing limited partners in a dispute with the former general partner on the grounds that the law firm had previously been general counsel to the limited partnership and had drafted the partnership agreement). In other circumstances, representation of individuals behind a partnership while representing the partnership itself is an impermissible conflict. See *Braumstein* v. *Statewide Grievance Comm.*, No. CV9904973N8S, 2001 Conn. Super. LEXIS 462 at 26 (Conn. Super. Ct. Feb. 9, 2001) (affirming Grievance Committee finding that lawyer violated Rule 1.7(a) where lawyer simultaneously represented a limited partnership and its general partner in his individual capacity, when the personal interests of the general partner were at odds with the interests of the limited partner investors).

J.A. McCahery, L. Timmerman and E.P.M. Vermeulen (eds.), Private Company Law Reform

resentation,[3] although the specific professional responsibilities of lawyers representing corporations sometimes remain unclear.[4] Two nagging questions in the age of un-incorporation are whether the supremacy of the entity as client could disappear, and, if so, whether the pre-incorporation ambiguity of representing individuals and groups of individuals behind business enterprises could return.

The opportunity created by the new age of un-incorporation grows out of a possible response to this problem. Lawyers, individual owners, and managers behind un-incorporated entities could define the lawyer-client relationship through private ordering *ex ante* rather than rely on public ordering to define that relationship in judicial and bar association opinions. Without definitive case law, ethics opinions, or other precedent specifying what a lawyer's obligations are in the context of un-incorporation, public ordering is at a disadvantage, and lawyers presumably should encourage clients to contract for their own solutions *ex ante* rather than submitting to an uncertain *ex post* determination of the lawyer's professional responsibilities. Private contracts that define professional responsibilities of lawyers for un-incorporated entities could bring clarity to the age of un-incorporation; indeed more clarity than public ordering has, through decades of judicial decisions and ethics opinions, supplied to corporations. If lawyers and clients in the age of un-incorporation contractually define their relationships more often, legal representations will more closely correspond with expectations of both lawyers and clients, and there should be less litigation over conflicts and other matters. Only time will tell whether this contractarian vision of lawyers' ethics in the age of un-incorporation will prevail, or whether public ordering will, as it did in the age of incorporation, slowly and unpredictably, but eventually, prevail in establishing norms of professional ethics that most lawyers and clients presume to be immutable.

2. Ethics in the Age of Pre-Incorporation

The corporate form has been recognized in England and the United States for centuries. The corporate form, however, has not always been easy to use. The Bubble Act of 1720, for example, required an Act of Parliament to establish a corporation.[5] Before the early 20th century, some states denied limited liability to, or refused to recognize, shareholders of foreign corporations doing business within their borders.[6] The corporate form, largely be-

---

[3] See Model Rules of Prof'l Conduct R. 1.13 (organization as client) (specifically stating that the lawyer for an organizational client represents the organization, not its individual constituents such as managers or shareholders).

[4] As recently as 2003, for example, controversy continued within the ABA over when a lawyer must report known illegal conduct to the board of directors or other highest authority within an organizational client, and Model Rule 1.13 remained unclear on this point. Indeed, the ABA only revised Model Rule 1.13 in 2003 to clarify this issue after Congress imposed an 'up-the-ladder' reporting requirement on securities lawyers under the Sarbanes-Oxley Act of 2002. See *infra* text accompanying nn. 51-52.

[5] An Act to Restrain the Extravagant and Unwarrantable Practice of Raising Money by Voluntary Subscriptions for Carrying on Projects Dangerous to the Trade and Subjects of This Kingdom (Bubble Act), 6 Geo. 1, c. 18 (1719) (Eng.).

[6] See generally A.M. Alger, 'Consequences of Illegal or *Ultra Vires* Acquisition of Real Estate by a Corporation', 8 *Harvard Law Review* (1894-95) p. 15, at p. 16 (describing and criticizing '[t]he view expressed, either directly of inferentially, in the authorities in question, that corporate realty unlawfully acquired may be seized by the State'); A.M. Alger, 'The Doctrine of Public Policy as Applied to Ownership of Real Estate by Foreign Corpo-

cause of its limited liability feature, was also viewed as suspect by private parties, and many businesses resorted to other forms of organization. Sometimes a partnership was used, but variations on the trust, and for family enterprises the dynastic trust, were also popular.[7] Sometimes a lawyer's ethical obligations in representing such entities and their owners and managers were clear, but often they were not.

A poignant example of muddled ethical obligations in the age of pre-incorporation was Louis Brandeis's representation of the Warren Trust (Trust) from 1889 to 1910. Brandeis designed this dynastic Trust to run a large paper mill in Maine and to be inherited by Samuel Warren,[8] Warren's mother, and his four siblings.[9] Brandeis set up the Trust with three trustees: Sam, Sam's mother, Mrs. Warren, and a cousin, Mr. Mason. Brandeis represented the Trust and apparently also represented Sam in his capacity as trustee. In order for Sam to run the paper mills (trust law apparently prohibited him from paying himself for doing so in his capacity as trustee of the Trust), Brandeis set up a separate operating firm owned by Sam, Sam's brother Fiske Warren, and Mr. Mason. The firm would lease the paper mills from the Trust, pay rent to the Trust contingent on the profits of the business, and distribute the remainder of its profits to its principals as compensation for their work. The Trust in turn would make distributions to its beneficiaries who, as passive investors, did not want to participate in operating the paper mills. Two entities, the Trust and the firm, were thus required to operate the business, compensate the persons who operated it, and distribute profits to its owners. Sam Warren, because he was both a trustee of the Trust and a principal of the firm, faced a potential conflict which, apparently, was consented to by the various members of the Warren family. Brandeis also faced a potential conflict because he represented both the Trust and the firm even though they were on opposite sides of the lease. Members of the Warren family apparently consented to Brandeis's conflict as well (although not in writing). What was not clear was whether Brandeis also represented the members of the Warren family in their individual capacities. He probably did not represent them all individually as Trust beneficiaries, although he drafted a will for one of Sam's brothers, Ned Warren, and there was no written clarification of whether Brandeis represented the Trust beneficiaries individually.[10]

These entities that Brandeis cobbled together for the Warren family functioned relatively smoothly for over fifteen years. Trouble started, however, when Ned demanded increased distributions from the Trust to satisfy his insatiable appetite for collecting antiques in Europe. Sam's dispute with Ned had much to do with sibling rivalry. The brothers also disagreed over matters of business judgment such as whether more profits should be rein-

---

rations', 9 *Harvard Law Review* (1895-96) p. 91 (describing state statutes that prohibit a foreign corporation from taking or holding land within its borders and the prospect of judge-made law imposing a similar prohibition); J.W. Lilienthal, 'Non-Public Corporations and *Ultra Vires*', 11 *Harvard Law Review* (1897-98) p. 387 (describing legal consequences of a corporation exceeding the powers granted in its charter, including in some jurisdictions forfeiture of the charter); G.W. Pepper, 'The Unauthorized or Prohibited Exercise of Corporate Power', 9 *Harvard Law Review* (1895-96) p. 255 (describing the *ultra vires* doctrine and its impact on the enforcement of contracts against a corporation and hence on the ability of a corporation to contract).

[7] See generally L.M. Friedman, 'The Dynastic Trust', 73 *Yale Law Journal* (1965) p. 547, at pp. 554-5.

[8] Samuel Warren was Brandeis's law partner and his coauthor of the famous 'Right to Privacy' article in the *Harvard Law Review*. See L. Brandeis and S. Warren, 'The Right to Privacy', 4 *Harvard Law Review* (1890-91) p. 193.

[9] See Painter, *supra* n. 1, at p. 355.

[10] Ibid., at pp. 371-77.

vested in the business for the benefit of future generations, as Sam wanted, or instead be distributed to the Trust beneficiaries.

When Ned was still unsatisfied, he became convinced that Sam was self-dealing in his dual roles as trustee of the Trust and principal in the firm. In 1910, Ned sued Sam. In the middle of a gruelling trial in 1910, Sam shot himself after days of giving testimony, and the matter was settled by the remaining members of the Warren family who hoped it would come to rest.[11]

Sam's situation would have been easier had he been chief executive officer, and perhaps a director, of a corporation – a form of organization in which managers are fiduciaries for shareholders but which is also flexible enough to allow a certain degree of self-interested behavior by managers. In the corporate context, Sam would have been compensated directly by the corporation acting through its board of directors, instead of through a mechanism much more prone to self-dealing accusations: a separate firm under his control that transacted with a trust of which he was a trustee. Most of the issues that Sam and Ned disagreed about also would have been subject to the presumption of the business judgment rule rather than the very strict prohibition on conflicts of interest in the law of trusts.[12] Warren family members who did not like the way the corporation was being run, by majority vote, would have been able to replace Sam as a director at the next shareholders' meeting, a governance feature not available in a trust (the Warren Trust had self-perpetuating trustees). In the pre-incorporation context, the principal remedy for passive investors thus lay in court rather than in the Trust's governance structure; they could sue for breach of fiduciary duty, and trustees charged with self-dealing were judged by a very strict standard.[13]

Brandeis was not named in the suit and was never subjected to a formal allegation of conflict of interest or a motion to disqualify, even though his law firm represented Sam against Ned (another potential conflict if he had in fact represented Ned in connection with the Trust). In 1916, however, the entire episode was brought up, along with other ethics allegations, by Brandeis's opponents at his confirmation hearings for the Supreme Court. His dual representation of the Trust and the firm was alleged to breach professional standards, even though the Warren family members had probably consented. The issue of whether Brandeis's firm could defend Sam in his role as Trustee against Ned's lawsuit also came up. Anti-Semitism perhaps colored the way Ned's Boston lawyers described Brandeis's role in the transaction to the Senate Judiciary Committee. The full Senate, possibly seeing through the motives of Brandeis's accusers, confirmed his nomination to the Court by one vote.[14]

Brandeis's role, like Sam's, would have been clearer had the business been set up as a corporation. Instead of representing a Trust and a firm, and perhaps also the individuals behind these entities, Brandeis would have had a single entity as his client. He would have represented the corporation with Sam as an officer directing the representation under the supervision of a board of directors annually elected by the Warren family shareholders. Unless Sam was clearly breaching his fiduciary duty, a matter that Brandeis would have had to have taken up with the directors, Brandeis would have been relatively safe following Sam's directions. Only if the directors themselves insisted on a clear breach of Sam's fidu-

[11] Ibid., at pp. 369-71.
[12] Ibid., at pp. 364-66.
[13] Ibid., at p. 363.
[14] Ibid., at pp. 354, 373-78.

ciary duty, or in ignoring Sam's breach, might Brandeis have to resign. Otherwise, so long as Brandeis did not also represent Sam individually, as well as the corporation, most of the conflicts problems that plagued this representation would have been avoided.

3. Ethics in the age of incorporation

Later in the 20th century, the Warrens' paper mills probably would have been run as a corporation, a single entity that could have done the work of both the Trust and the firm. Although Brandeis's life would have been easier, the age of incorporation has not been a panacea for lawyers' ethics. One area of continued confusion arises when investors who are previously clients of a lawyer form a new corporation or convert a partnership into a corporation. It is not always clear whether the lawyer represents the individuals, the corporation, or both.[15] Confusion also arises over whether the lawyer for a corporation also represents parent, sibling and subsidiary corporations.[16] Confidentiality also is a concern when shareholders demand access to communications between a corporation and its lawyers, access which is often, but not always, granted in the close corporation context and more often than not denied in the context of a large public corporation.[17] Yet another area of difficulty has been lawyer response to corporate fraud.[18] Although corporate statutes are clear that directors, not officers, are the legal authority in charge of a corporation, it took until 2003 for the ABA to recognize in Model Rule 1.13 that a lawyer for a corporation must report unrectified criminal acts and fraud to its directors[19] – and this was only after Congress mandated the same in section 307 of the Sarbanes-Oxley Act of 2002.[20]

The age of incorporation thus has by no means eliminated confusion surrounding the ethical obligations of lawyers representing corporations. Part of the problem is that public ordering has sought to define the lawyer's ethical obligations with one-size-fits-all rules such as the ABA's Model Rule 1.13. Because particulars differ depending on the representation, these rules have been worded so generally that many questions of professional responsibility are left to *ex post* determination, usually by judges but occasionally by bar disciplinary boards. Conflicts rules worded as if they applied to individual clients are applied to corporate representations, and these rules also are very general.[21] Here also, much

---

[15] See L.E. Mitchell, 'Professional Responsibility and the Close Corporation: Toward a Realistic Ethic', 74 *Cornell Law Review* (1989) p. 466.

[16] See generally C.W. Wolfram, 'Corporate-Family Conflicts', 2 *Journal of the Institute for the Study of Legal Ethics* (1999) p. 295 (discussing the lateral and lineal dimensions of the client-identify problem in corporate families).

[17] See *Garner* v. *Wolfinbarger*, 430 F.2d 1093, 1104 (5th Cir. 1970) (articulating a 'good cause' exception to a corporation's attorney-client privilege under which shareholders in suits accusing a corporation of acting against their interests have an opportunity to show good cause why the privilege should not be invoked).

[18] R.W. Painter and J.E. Duggan, 'Lawyer Disclosure of Corporate Fraud: Establishing a Firm Foundation', 50 *Southern Methodist University Law Review* (1996) p. 225, at pp. 261-3 (discussing lack of clarity in this area and proposing legislative provisions resembling the subsequently enacted § 307 of the Sarbanes-Oxley Act).

[19] See T.D. Morgan, 'Sarbanes-Oxley: A Complication, not a Contribution, in the Effort to Improve Corporate Lawyers' Professional Conduct', 17 *Georgetown Journal of Legal Ethics* (2003) p. 1, at p. 22 (criticizing Congress for enacting this up-the-ladder reporting rule).

[20] Ibid., at pp. 15-16.

[21] See, e.g., Model Rules of Prof'l Conduct R. 1.7 (concurrent conflicts) and R.1.9 (successive conflicts) (2003).

is left to *ex post* adjudication, perhaps to the benefit of law professors opining as expert witnesses on conflicts and other matters of legal ethics, but hardly to the benefit of the lawyers and clients subjected to these uncertainties.

This author has suggested elsewhere that corporate representation could improve significantly if ethics rules were the subject of more *ex ante* contracting between lawyers and their clients.[22] This is true for rules on whistle-blowing in response to corporate fraud,[23] conflicts rules,[24] and rules governing the scope of a representation and lawyer use of client information, and other rules.[25] Although corporate clients contract with their lawyers more frequently now than they used to,[26] the contractarian paradigm is relatively weak in the field of legal ethics. Lingering doubts about the enforceability of such contracts, even with sophisticated clients, and doubts about whether seeking to contract around ethical obligations is itself unethical, continue to give a strong advantage to public ordering, however vague the rules it chooses to impose.

Despite these and other problems with corporate representation, however, ethics questions are simplified by the fact that there is a generally agreed upon analytical starting point: a corporation is an independent legal person entitled to the undivided loyalty of its counsel.[27] The corporation is not to be confused with the interests of the persons who manage the corporation or the individual interests of its shareholders. The corporation, like an individual client, has an expectation of confidentiality,[28] loyalty,[29] communication,[30] and representation free of conflicts from its lawyer's representation of persons having interests adverse to its own.[31] Unlike Brandeis in the Warren Trust matter, the corporation's lawyer can represent the entire business enterprise by representing only the corporation and by refusing to embroil himself in parallel roles that compromise this representation.

4. Ethics in the Age of Un-Incorporation

What will happen in the age of un-incorporation? We could go back to the confusion that plagued Brandeis and his contemporaries when persons, not entities, usually retained lawyers, and entities often were not treated as legal persons entitled to legal representation apart from the individuals who owned and managed them. The member managed LLC and some other forms of un-incorporation, particularly partnership based organizations, raise this possibility. In these situations, even if the entity is recognized as a separate legal per-

---

22 R.W. Painter, 'Rules Lawyers Play By', 76 *New York University Law Review* (2001) p. 665, at p. 666.

23 See R.W. Painter, 'Toward a Market for Lawyer Disclosure Services: In Search of Optimal Whistleblowing Rules', 63 *George Washington Law Review* (1995) p. 221 at pp. 256-57; see also Painter and Duggan, *supra* n. 18, at p. 266.

24 See R.W. Painter, Advance Waiver of Conflicts, 13 *Georgetown Journal of Legal Ethics* (2000) p. 289, at pp. 289-92.

25 See R.W. Painter, 'Professional Responsibility Rules as Implied Contract Terms', 34 *Georgia Law Review* (1999) p. 953; Painter, *supra* n. 22, at pp. 708-12.

26 See Painter, *supra* n. 22, at p. 680.

27 See generally S.A. Schane, 'The Corporation is a Person: The Language of a Legal Fiction', 61 *Tulane Law Review* (1987) p. 563.

28 Model Rules of Prof'l Conduct R.1.6.

29 Model Rules of Prof'l Conduct R.1.3.

30 Model Rules of Prof'l Conduct R.1.4.

31 Model Rules of Prof'l Conduct R.1.7, 1.9, 1.10.

son, its managers and owners are sometimes one and the same. A court may determine, and perhaps rightly so, that the intent of the owners and managers of the entity was that the lawyer would represent them all. Once, however, conflicts and other ethics questions turn on individuals' intentions and other factual considerations rather than on strong presumptions arising out of the organizational form itself, confusion is likely. On the other hand, rules tied to a specific organizational framework may not work because there are so many different forms of un-incorporation and because most of these forms allow significant deviation from statutory norms in the articles of organization, operating agreement, or other governing instrument.[32] The confusion that public ordering has been unable to eradicate from the age of incorporation could pale by comparison with the potential uncertainties each time an un-incorporated entity retains a lawyer without clarifying who the client is and how the lawyer's specific responsibilities to that client are to be performed.

4.1 Existing commentary and case law

So far, the ethical obligations of lawyers in the un-incorporation context are not very clear. Relatively sparse academic commentary[33] and practitioner materials[34] tend to focus on the role of lawyers in representing the individuals who set up an LLC or other un-incorporated entity at the formation stage. In situations where the lawyer is retained before the entity itself even exists, entity representation is at this stage precluded, and these commentators are right to point out that the lawyer must make clear whether he is representing all of the organizers of the entity or just some of them.[35] More difficult questions, however, arise once the entity is formed. First, it must be decided whether the lawyer who originally represented some or all of the organizers now represents the entity alone or also represents

---

[32] These include the Limited Liability Company (LLC), the Limited Liability Partnership (LLP), the Limited Liability Limited Partnership (LLLP), and various forms of statutory trusts, new and old. The statutes governing these various entities contain a large number of default rules that organizers can contract around in organizational agreements if they wish. Statutes for these un-incorporated entities are also designed to give organizers maximum contractual freedom. In its LLC statute, for example, Delaware provides a forum selection clause, absent from the Delaware General Corporation Law, which specifically allows members or managers to agree in the LLC agreement, or in another writing, for arbitration of claims under the agreement. See Del. Code Ann. tit. 60, § 18-109(d) (2004) ('In a written limited liability company agreement or other writing, a manager or member may consent to be subject to the nonexclusive jurisdiction of the courts of, or arbitration in, a specified jurisdiction, or the exclusive jurisdiction of the courts of the State of Delaware, or the exclusivity of arbitration in a specified jurisdiction or the State of Delaware . ...'). The Delaware Supreme Court interpreted this provision broadly in *Elf Atochem North America, Inc.* v. *Cyrus A. Jaffari and Malek LLC*, 727 A.2d 286 (1999), emphasizing that freedom of contract is an essential element of the Delaware LLC statute. 'The Act's basic approach is to permit partners to have the broadest possible discretion in drafting their partnership agreements. ...' Ibid., at p. 291 (quoting M.I. Lubaroff and P.M. Altman, *Delaware Limited Partnerships* (Denver, Aspen Publishers 1999) § 1.2, and stating that this same 'observation relating to limited partnerships applies as well to limited liability companies').

[33] See, e.g., R.R. Keatinge, 'The Implications of Fiduciary Representations in Representing Limited Liability Companies and Other Unincorporated Associations and Their Partners or Members', 25 *Stetson Law Review* (1995) p. 389. For more general discussion, see J.S. Dzienkowski, 'Lawyers as Intermediaries: The Representation of Multiple Clients in the Modern Legal Profession', 1992 *University of Illinois Law Review* (1992) p. 741; A.C. Rollock, 'Professional Responsibility and Organization of the Family Business: The Lawyer as Intermediary', 73 *Indiana Law Journal* (1968) p. 567.

[34] See, e.g., J.M. Cunningham, 'The Professional Responsibilities of Lawyers Who Represent Multiple Clients in LLC Formations', available at <www.Cunningham-Seminars.com>; J.A. Reed, 'Ethical Issues In Business Law Practice' (2003), available at <www.wlaw.com/Reed>.

[35] The importance of clarifying this in advance is made clear in all of the articles cited in *supra* nn. 32-34.

some or all of its organizers. This question might, or might not, be answered differently if the entity is represented by a new lawyer having no prior relationship with the organizers. Even if the lawyer represents the entity alone, is the lawyer necessarily precluded from representing some of its organizers at some later point in time? Second, it must be decided what specific obligations arise from the lawyer's representation of the entity. From whom shall the lawyer take instructions, with whom shall the lawyer share confidences, and to whom shall the lawyer report concerns about illegal activity or breaches of fiduciary duty?

The little case law that exists on these questions is confusing. Perhaps most problematic is the fact that courts seem reluctant to treat un-incorporated entities as separate persons that can alone be represented by counsel. *Chaiklin* v. *Bacon*[36] is an example of how easy it is for courts to hold that a lawyer's fiduciary obligations to an un-incorporated client flow through to an individual member, even absent evidence that the lawyer represented that individual member in connection with the entity.

Here, the plaintiff was independently represented by private counsel during his negotiations with Boise LLC for a buyout of his interest in a dissolution of Boise that he had requested.[37] The Superior Court in Connecticut still disqualified a different attorney who had previously represented Boise LLC from representing its remaining members in litigation over the sale of Boise's assets and the buying-out of the plaintiff's interest.[38] Even though there was insufficient evidence from which the court could conclude that the Boise attorney had been involved in the formation of the company – the time period during which its members would have had the greatest expectation that the attorney was representing each in their personal capacity[39] – the court held that the attorney could be disqualified from representing the remaining members of Boise in this dispute over their alleged breach of fiduciary duty to the plaintiff.

> '[W]hile [the attorney] represented Boise he also must be seen to have represented the interests of the plaintiff concerning his membership in that partnership, pending perfection of his contract for discharge … . Until the completion of the plaintiff's discharge from Boise then, while he remained a member in fact, if not a member in name, of that company, the plaintiff was entitled to the fiduciary obligations of [the lawyer], who served as Boise's attorney.'[40]

The court cited Rule 1.13 of Connecticut's rules of professional conduct in support of this holding,[41] even though the Connecticut Rule, like the ABA's Model Rule 1.13, concerns the lawyer's obligations to the organizational client itself, not to its individual constituencies. Nowhere does Rule 1.13 state that fiduciary obligations owed to an entity flow through to its individual members. Indeed, Rule 1.13 emphasizes that the lawyer is not the personal attorney for the organization's various constituents and should favor the interests of the organization over the interests of those constituents. Rule 1.13 arguably might be a basis for disqualifying an attorney from representing some members of an LLC in a dispute over buying out another member, but disqualification under Rule 1.13 should require that the proposed representation of the remaining members be adverse to the LLC as an entity, not

---

36 No. CV990594039, 2000 Conn. Super. LEXIS 1729 (Conn. Super. Ct. July 3, 2000).
37 Ibid., at p. 6.
38 Ibid.
39 Ibid.
40 Ibid., at pp. 22-24.
41 See ibid.

simply adverse to the interests of one of its former members. The court's equation of Boise's interests with the interests of its individual members is made even more transparent by the court's reference to Boise as a 'partnership' even though it was in fact an LLC.[42]

Even absent a finding of a client relationship with individual members of an LLC, a court might still assume that the attorney for the LLC has a heightened duty to disclose information to members, and may hold the attorney liable if he does not. In *Exposition Partners, LP and ICMC Investors, LLC* v. *King, Leblanc & Bland LLP*,[43] a Louisiana court held that the lawyer for an LLC could be sued for fraud by Exposition Partners when the partners of Exposition mistakenly believed that Exposition had become a member of the LLC.[44] Because Exposition's partners were themselves members of the LLC, they had the right to expect disclosure by the attorney to them of whether Exposition had in fact been made a member of the LLC, as the other defendant members of the LLC apparently misrepresented to Exposition that it had:

> 'Because the law classifies CRG [LLC] as a distinct business entity, [the defendants, CRG's lawyers] allege that at no time were they retained to represent [CRG's members] Mr. Ryan, Exposition or ICMC. Nevertheless, CRG can only act via Messrs. Dawley, McPhail, Ryan, etc. The premise of the defendants' argument is that representing CRG posed no conflict of interest *vis à vis* the distinct members of CRG.'[45]

In rejecting the defendants' argument, the court held that the lawyers could be liable for fraud allegedly committed by some of CRG's members against others, if the lawyers negligently furthered the fraud by acts such as incorrectly naming Exposition as a member of the LLC on official correspondence:

> 'Without proving fraud, the fact that ICMC was excluded and Exposition was included in CRG's official correspondence gives it [Exposition] a right to allege fraud or that it was being misled, even if in fact this amounted to nothing more than documentary confusion.'[46]

The most troubling aspect of the Exposition holding is that, while the court does not directly say so, it assumes a greater duty to communicate with individual members of an LLC, even absent a lawyer-client relationship with those members, than the lawyers themselves probably believed they had at the time. While no lawyer can sit idly by and allow some members of an LLC client to commit fraud on other members of the LLC, it is troubling to see a fraud claim against a lawyer representing an LLC predicated in part on a supposed duty to communicate to a member of the LLC specific information, particularly apart from something rising to the seriousness of the lawyer's knowledge of an impending fraud. If there is an affirmative duty on the part of a lawyer for an LLC to communicate all material facts to all of its members, a statute or ethics rule at least should say so *ex ante* rather than a court saying so *ex post*.

These two cases on the ethical obligations of lawyers representing un-incorporated entities underscore the inadequacy of public ordering as a mechanism for defining these obli-

---

42 Ibid.

43 869 So. 2d 934 (La. Ct. App. 2004).

44 Ibid., at p. 944.

45 Ibid., at p. 942.

46 Ibid., at pp. 943-44.

gations. Basic questions remain unresolved, including when a lawyer for an un-incorporated entity also represents its members, what duties the lawyer owes to those members even when there is no lawyer-client relationship, and to whom the lawyer should communicate important information about the entity. Lawyers who do not know the answers to these questions will find it difficult to effectively and ethically practice law, and their un-incorporated clients, as well as the individuals behind those clients, will not know what to expect of the lawyers.

4.2 Private ordering and the opportunity to contract for clarity

Resolution of all of these questions is made difficult by the fact that un-incorporation is an organizational framework that is remarkably fluid compared with the more rigid and hierarchical organizational framework of corporations. Corporations for the most part all have directors, officers, and shareholders with specific statutory rights and duties, although individuals may perform more than one of these functions.[47] Some un-incorporated entities are run by their members (member-managed entities). Others are run by designated managers (manager-managed entities),[48] although the method for choosing and removing these managers may differ depending on the entity. Statutes and case law seek to define precisely the function and fiduciary duties of members and managers in each context, as well as prohibitions on their conduct (such as related party transactions), but public ordering does not provide anywhere near the volume of precedent that it does in the field of incorporation. Furthermore, because un-incorporated entities can differ so much from each other, precedent may not even be particularly valuable.

In the context of representing incorporated entities, as pointed out in Section 2 above, ethics questions have often been overlooked *ex ante*, and often dangerously so, because lawyers and clients far too often assume that default rules are clear, even when they are not. In the un-incorporation context it should be obvious that, with legal precedent at this point being so thin, it is even more dangerous to assume that certain default rules apply. Private ordering, in which the responsibilities of the entity's lawyers are clearly defined in advance along with the rights and responsibilities of the entity's members and managers, has a clear advantage over blind reliance on what little clarity public ordering provides. Lawyers and clients who do not define ethics rules *ex ante* proceed at their own peril.

The age of un-incorporation is thus an opportunity to advance in the direction of clearer professional obligations for lawyers rather than to regress into the muddled ethics of the pre-incorporation era. At least in situations where managers and owners of an un-incorporated entity are sophisticated, contracting parties should agree *ex ante* on questions such as whether the individual members of an entity are also the clients of the entity's lawyer, to whom the lawyer should communicate important information and other specific responsibilities of the lawyer. In this 'contractarian' regime, the intent of clients and lawyers would be defined by themselves rather than by courts, and confusion, as well as subsequent litigation, over conflicts and other ethics matters would be minimized.

---

[47] Modern statutory provisions in some jurisdictions allow for the elimination of the board of directors in close corporations, although, perhaps because of the traditional rigidity of the corporate form, these provisions are rarely used.

[48] Keatinge, *supra* n. 33, at p. 407.

4.3 Setting the default rules

What, if any, default rules should public ordering supply for a regime in which it is expected that most un-incorporated clients and their lawyers would contractually define the lawyers' professional responsibilities themselves? The most frequently tried approach to setting defaults would be for the rule drafter to determine what rule would satisfy the majority of lawyers and clients (a majoritarian default rule).[49] Because, however, of the wide variety in governance structures used for un-incorporated entities, majoritarian default rules for one type of entity (such as a rule that the lawyer must disclose all relevant information to all members of a member-managed LLC) would not be suitable for another type of entity (for example, a large manager-managed LLC).

There could be different default rules for different types of un-incorporated entities, and some of the possibilities are explored further below. Nonetheless, because of the difficulty of setting majoritarian defaults in the un-incorporation context, rule drafters should not overlook the possibility of using penalty default rules instead. These might include a rule that a lawyer for an un-incorporated entity automatically also represents all of its members unless otherwise agreed, and a rule that the lawyer's duty to communicate under Model Rule 1.4 extends to all of the entity's members unless otherwise agreed. Presumably the majority of entities and their lawyers would not want these rules and would contract to avoid them. If the objective of the contractarian regime is to encourage private ordering instead of misplaced reliance on the vagaries of public ordering, penalty default rules might help accomplish this objective.

Going back to possible majoritarian default rules, the most basic rule from which others flow is that which identifies the lawyer's client. The majoritarian rule would probably be the same for un-incorporated entities as for incorporated entities under Model Rule 1.13: that the lawyer representing an entity represents the entity alone unless otherwise agreed (for example, the lawyer may have a prior client relationship with one of the entity's members). The case is somewhat stronger for a default rule that the lawyer also represents the individual members of smaller entities that are also member-managed, although this rule would, even in this context, probably not be favored by the majority of users because of the prospect of the lawyer having to resign in the event of a conflict between the entity and one of its members.

A majoritarian rule concerning the duties to communicate and keep confidences, like those in Model Rules 1.4 and 1.6, is particularly difficult to set. Communication of confidential information to individual members of an un-incorporated entity might be expected in one case, accepted in another, and considered a breach of confidence in a third. The majoritarian rule would probably require communication with managing members (although not necessarily all of them) of a manager-managed entity and with members (although once again not necessarily all of them) of a member-managed entity. In each case, the entity could contract around the rule by designating in advance a group of managers or members with whom the lawyer is required to communicate. The majoritarian default rule might allow, but not require, communication of confidential information also to non-manager

---

[49] For discussion of majoritarian default rules in the professional responsibility context, see Painter, *supra* n. 22.

members of a manager-managed entity;[50] if the entity wished to prohibit such communication, the entity could contract around the rule.

Concerning the identity of the person(s) from whom the lawyer should receive instructions, default rules once again are difficult to set. Model Rule 1.13 appears to impose a duty to take instructions from the individual constituent of the organization with whom the lawyer deals in the ordinary course unless the lawyer knows that the constituent is acting improperly. This is often the person who retained the lawyer on behalf of the entity (this person may or may not also personally be a client of the lawyer, a situation which often gives rise to a thorny set of conflicts). Given the non-hierarchical structure of many unincorporated entities, Model Rule 1.13's flexible approach may be the only workable default rule. In the absence of a board of directors or other supreme authority within the organization, even the revised Model Rule 1.13 provisions concerning consultation with the organization's highest authority may not always work well in the un-incorporation context. Whatever the default rule, clients should thus specify in advance the identity of the person from whom a lawyer representing an un-incorporated entity should take instructions.

This brings up a final question, which is to whom the lawyer should report fraud and breaches of fiduciary duty. Section 307 of the Sarbanes-Oxley Act and the ABA's 2003 revisions to Model Rule 1.13 provide an answer that is relatively clear in the context of incorporation: 'up-the-ladder' reporting should be made first to a corporation's officers and general counsel, and if that does not work, to its board of directors.[51] The SEC rules under section 307 pay some heed to contractarian proposals by allowing the corporation *ex ante* to designate a committee of its directors (a Qualified Legal Compliance Committee) to whom the report can be made instead.[52] These rules also apply to lawyers for un-incorporated entities, such as LLCs, that issue securities to the public.

This arrangement, however, may not work well for un-incorporated entities that have no board of directors. In this context, the default rule for a manager-managed entity would probably require only a report to the managers (probably to all of them). Requiring a report also to the members would thus be a penalty default rule, although it is understandable why some clients might want such a rule. The default rule for a member managed entity would probably be a mandatory report to all of the members, if the lawyer's prior report to other constituents of the entity is of no avail. Once again, as recognized by the SEC's rules under section 307, the entity should be allowed some degree of contractual flexibility to have the report made to a special committee of managers or members that has been designated in advance and charged with the responsibility to deal with fraud, breach of fiduciary duty and similar violations.

---

[50] This would be the rough equivalent of allowing a lawyer for a corporation to communicate confidential information to shareholders who are not also officers or directors, which in a publicly held corporation is probably prohibited outside the exception for crime or fraud. See Model Rules of Prof'l Conduct R.1.6.

[51] Painter, *supra* n. 22, at p. 718.

[52] A similar 'contractarian' proposal – that up-the-ladder reporting to directors be required as a default rule, but that the report may be to a committee of directors designated by the corporation in advance – had in 1996 been made in Painter and Duggan, *supra* n. 18.

5. Conclusion

Lawyers representing un-incorporated entities face uncertain default rules defining their professional obligations to individuals behind client entities. Lawyers and clients should not wait for unpredictable rules to be imposed on them by public ordering; rather they should define their lawyer-client relationships as much as possible through private ordering. Wherever possible, courts and bar associations should enforce those contracts when ruling on the professional responsibilities of lawyers for un-incorporated entities.

For different un-incorporated entities there are likely to be different answers to questions such as who is the lawyer's client for conflicts purposes, whose confidences must be kept by the lawyer and from whom, to whom the lawyer may communicate information in some circumstances, to whom the lawyer must communicate information in other circumstances, and whose instructions the lawyer should follow. If lawyers and un-incorporated clients contractually define their relationships more often, the conduct of lawyers will more closely correspond with expectations of clients. There should also be less litigation over conflicts, misrepresentation, failure to follow instructions, and other matters of professional responsibility. As a result, lawyers and clients will be better off.

Chapter 12

THE SOCIAL-WELFARE BASED LIMITS ON PRIVATE ORDERING IN BUSINESS ASSOCIATION LAW

Allan W. Vestal*

1. INTRODUCTION

The topic I was asked to address is 'private ordering within closely held companies'. The issue is whether we ought to have limits on the extent to which participants in business firms can re-order their relations *inter se* from the statutorily-defined relationship. I would like to suggest that we begin to consider a different way of approaching the issue, looking to restrictions based on social-welfare, and not traditional fairness, concerns.

The conventional wisdom on this point is fairly clear: (a) we are all adults; (b) the society is benefited by the creation of value, by having efficient economic arrangements in firms; (c) private ordering allows the parties to come to such efficient arrangements; and, (d) the only appropriate restrictions on such private ordering are a fairly minimal range of fairness-based limitations, looking to the capacities and behaviors of firm participants.

It is natural that the welfare *versus* fairness debate invites us to argue for traditional limits on private ordering as a function of fairness. Certainly there are cases in the business associations area which call for decisions based on fairness considerations, and surely one may assume that such fairness-based situations are not infrequently found in the private firm context.

Take, for example, the case of *Alexander* v. *Sims*.[1] Alexander and Sims were partners in a jewelry store from 1942 until Sims' death in 1950. Shortly before Sims' death, at a time when Alexander but not Sims knew of Sims' terminal illness, Alexander got Sims to sign an agreement which provided that upon the death of either of them, the deceased's partnership interest would become the property of the survivor. Some forty-five years before the Revised Uniform Partnership Act (RUPA), using the Uniform Partnership Act (the UPA) and the common law, the court refused to enforce the agreement based upon 'the rule which requires partners to exercise the utmost good faith in their dealings with each other.'[2] There is a reasonable argument that the outcome of the case would be different

---

* Dean and Professor of Law, Drake University Law School. I would like to thank Bill Callison, Biff Campbell, and Tom Rutledge for their comments.

[1] *Alexander* v. *Sims*, 249 S.W.2d 832 (Ark., 1952).

[2] Ibid., at p. 836.

J.A. McCahery, L. Timmerman and E.P.M. Vermeulen (eds.), Private Company Law Reform

under the 'pinched and almost mean-spirited vision' of the fiduciary obligations of partners[3] under the RUPA.[4]

I suspect many people would agree with the *Alexander* court's decision, feeling that some fairness or good faith obligation should render the agreement ineffective. But I also suspect that most of those people would silently add that Sims should have known better than to sign the agreement in the first place.

So we use the fairness, the good faith rule, in the private ordering area to shield firm participants from their own frailty. But at the same time, we hope for better from the participants in business firms. After all, to paraphrase the Court of Appeals, '[firm participants] are not – like sailors or idiots or infants – wards of the judiciary.'[5]

It would seem bad policy to make basic business organization law policy decisions based on the needs of sailors, idiots or infants. In the end, although one can make a fairness-based argument for limitations on private ordering, the argument is far too small, and results in only minor restrictions on private ordering.

Indeed, it can be argued that the welfare *versus* fairness discussion is the approach taken in the drafting of RUPA in the United States, which resulted essentially in a plenary private ordering regime, tempered by minor restrictions based on fairness. RUPA provides for the primacy of the partnership agreement over the statutory provisions,[6] except for a limited number of statutory provisions as to which the power of the parties to modify is constrained.[7] These are fairly characterized as trifling fairness restrictions.

I decline to make the fairness argument in this forum, suggesting rather that we consider the appropriateness of having some limits on private ordering based on social welfare considerations.

---

[3] Letter from Melvin A. Eisenberg to The Commissioners on Uniform State Laws, 4 (July 27, 1992), cited in A.W. Vestal, 'Fundamental Contractarian Error in the Revised Uniform Partnership Act of 1992', 73 *Boston University Law Review* (1993) p. 523, at p. 579, n. 241.

[4] Rev. Unif. P'ship Act §§ 403(c)(1), 404(b), (d), 6 U.L.A. Pt. I at 140, 143; Allan W. Vestal, ibid., at pp. 563-64.

[5] *Guttmann* v. *Ill. Cent. R. Co.,* 189 F.2d 927 (2nd Cir., 1951).

[6] Rev. Unif. P'ship Act § 103(a), 6 U.L.A. Pt. I at 73: 'Except as otherwise provided in subsection (b), relations among the partners and between the partners and the partnership are governed by the partnership agreement. To the extent the partnership agreement does not otherwise provide, this [Act] governs relations among the partners and between the partners and the partnership.' R.W. Hillman, A.W. Vestal and D.J. Weidner, *The Revised Uniform Partnership Act* (St. Paul, Thomspon West 2006) pp. 41-3.

[7] Rev. Unif. P'ship Act § 103(b), 6 U.L.A. Pt. I pp. 73-4: 'The partnership agreement may not: (1) vary the rights and duties under Section 105 except to eliminate the duty to provide copies of statements to all of the partners, (2) unreasonably restrict the right of access to books and records under Section 403(b), (3) eliminate the duty of loyalty under Section 404(b) or 603(b), but: (i) the partnership agreement may identify specific types or categories of activities that do not violate the duty of loyalty, if not manifestly unreasonable; or (ii) all of the partners or a number or a percentage specified in the partnership agreement may authorize or ratify, after full disclosure of all material facts, a specific act or transaction that otherwise would violate the duty of loyalty; (4) unreasonably reduce the duty of care under Section 404(c) or 603(b)(3); (5) eliminate the obligation of good faith and fair dealing under Section 404(d), but the partnership agreement may prescribe the standards by which the performance of the obligation is to be measured, if the standards are not manifestly unreasonable; (6) vary the power to dissociate as a partner under Section 602(a), except to require the notice under Section 601(1) to be in writing; (7) vary the right of a court to expel a partner in the events specified in Section 601(5); (8) vary the requirement to wind up the partnership business in cases specified in Section 801(4), (5), or (6); (9) vary the law applicable to a limited liability partnership under Section 106(b); or (10) restrict rights of third parties under this [Act].' Hillman, et al., *supra* n. 6, at pp. 43-58. Rev. Unif. P'ship Act § 401(f), 6 U.L.A. Pt. I at 133.

I readily acknowledge that in questioning plenary private ordering, I am clearly on the wrong side of recent history, at least within the context of contemporary business associations law in the United States. In form after form we have allowed private ordering which changes what people a generation ago would have seen as essential elements of the familiar business forms. For example, under contemporary American business associations law I can modify allocation of management rights in a partnership to create a 'partner' who has no rights in management,[8] or eliminate the consent requirement for the admission of new partners.[9] Under the Model Business Corporation Act (MBCA) I can have a corporation without a board of directors,[10] while under RUPA, I can have a partnership with a board of directors.[11]

Perhaps the best indication that I am on the wrong side of history on this matter is the new statutory business association forms which have been created. An extension of plenary private ordering in existing forms has been the creation of new statutory business forms such as the limited liability company (LLC), the limited liability partnership (LLP), and the limited liability limited partnership (LLLP).

Like a sideshow performer in a cheap carnival, an American practitioner can take a wide range of mixes of participants, contributions, powers, profit and loss participations, and tax status, and often achieve all of the points with a limited liability company, a limited liability partnership, a limited partnership, a limited liability limited partnership, or a corporation.

Clearly, with what I would argue are extremely limited fairness-based restrictions, we have bought into the conventional wisdom that we are all adults, the society is benefited by the creation of value – by having efficient economic arrangements in firms – and private ordering allows the parties to come to such efficient arrangements. The important corollary – into which we have also bought – is that there are no external costs created by the plenary private order regime – in short, that 'private ordering' is truly private.

I think the conventional wisdom is wrong. Or at least that it is incomplete. I would suggest that plenary private ordering causes external inefficiencies. My suspicion is that these external inefficiencies, appropriately evaluated, outweigh the level of value creation from plenary private ordering. I think we should no longer assume that the external, social costs are trivial. At the very least, it is a topic worthy of study and discussion, which we have not yet had at a policy level.

2. AN AGGREGATE, NET ANALYSIS OF THE VALUE OF PRIVATE ORDERING

The first step in this discussion ought to be an acknowledgement that we are not choosing between two absolutes, one a mandatory system under which the terms of the deal are fixed by statute and nothing is subject to private ordering; the other a default system under which the statutory terms are simply a starting point and everything is subject to private ordering.

No serious commentator would suggest a mandatory system, as the parties need to be free to change certain statutory defaults to reflect the calculus of their deal. For example, everyone agrees that the parties should be free to change the statutory defaults of equality

---

[8] Ibid.

[9] Rev. Unif. P'ship Act § 401(j), 6 U.L.A. Pt. I at 133.

[10] Model Bus. Corp. Act § 7.32(a)(1).

[11] Rev. Unif. P'ship Act § 401(f), 6 U.L.A. Pt. I at 133.

in the distribution of profits[12] and the management of the firm[13] in favor of unequal participation in profits and management to reflect unequal capital contributions.

As to the other absolutist position, a default system under which the statutory terms are simply a starting point and everything is subject to private ordering; while it might be that some serious commentators would advocate such a position, it seems clear from the statutes which have been enacted that some level of restrictions on private ordering will typically be included, if only some fairly minor fairness-based limitations.

What level of private ordering is appropriate? Is it the plenary private ordering option, where the participants are constrained only by fairly minor fairness-based limitations. What we need to do is to compare the value created by a given level of private ordering against the costs incurred, looking for an appropriate balance. In the following discussion, I use the term 'plenary private ordering' to indicate the starting point for the analysis, consideration of the least restrictive of the range of possible levels of such private ordering. If the analysis of that least-restrictive version suggests it cannot be justified, then a series of aggregate, social calculations of costs could be done so that an appropriate balance might be found.

In searching for such a balance, we should remember that the comparison is an aggregate, net calculation. The appropriate comparison is an aggregate one. One must look across society, not within individual firms. If an occasional firm benefits from plenary private ordering but other firms face uncompensated costs from the practice, then it would be necessary to balance the aggregate benefits and costs to see whether plenary private ordering could be justified. The question, after all, is the social question of whether to institute a legal system of plenary private ordering. The answer needs to be an aggregate, social one.

Since the public policy determination is based on aggregate, social calculations of benefits and costs, the intra-firm calculation has to be a net calculation. The conventional wisdom, remember, is that we are all adults, the society is benefited by the creation of value – by having efficient economic arrangements in the firm – and private ordering allows the parties to come to such efficient arrangements. I don't for a moment deny that value can be created when private ordering is allowed. In the first order, intra-firm analysis, the conventional wisdom ignores the cost of negotiating the private ordering, assumes perfect information and rational parties. This all makes sense since rational parties would not incur the costs of negotiation if the value created wasn't greater than the cost. In the intra-firm analysis we don't need to quantify the costs of private ordering since the equation for firms which engage in private ordering will always be positive.

Perfectly reasonable within the firm, but the question of whether to institute a system of private ordering is a public policy decision – a social determination. To make that balance, we need to quantify the net gain across all participating firms, and we need to add in the costs imposed on firms which do not participate in private ordering. Again, I don't for a moment deny that net value can be created when private order is allowed, but we need to acknowledge that there is a net in firms for which value is created. And, perhaps more importantly in terms of the public policy calculation, we need to acknowledge that there may be costs for firms which decide not to engage in private ordering, as well as costs for those who deal with both participating and non-participating firms.

---

[12] Rev. Unif. P'ship Act § 401(b), 6 U.L.A. Pt. I at 133. Hillman, et al., *supra* n. 6, at p. 217.

[13] Ibid., at p. 219.

3. THE COSTS OF PLENARY PRIVATE ORDERING

What costs are incurred in plenary private ordering? Ignoring the fairly small fairness issues, there are at least two types of costs from plenary private ordering: the search and negotiation costs of firm participants; and the monitoring costs of third parties.

The first cost of plenary private ordering is search and negotiation costs imposed on firm participants. When we allow parties to redefine the basics of the partnership form, we impose search and negotiation costs on participants during the formation period. For example, if we allow partnerships to change the traditional fiduciary rules, then thereafter parties negotiating to form a firm will predictably spend some amount of time – perhaps a large amount, perhaps a small amount – on that point. This is true whether or not they end up engaging in private ordering of that specific type.

The key here is the real-world cost savings that come from having language which means something predictable, constant, and narrow. If firm participants cannot vary a given rule, they won't incur costs in searching the alternatives or negotiating a variation from the statutory provision. Note that the costs – particularly the search costs – are not limited to firms which actually make use of private ordering; the fact that a firm could engage in plenary private ordering imposes search and may impose negotiation costs, even if only to confirm that the members don't want to engage in private ordering.

This is not to say that the costs of plenary private ordering may not be justified; surely firms can realize efficiencies through private ordering. It is merely to observe that there are costs which have to be considered in the social decision as to whether plenary private ordering should be allowed.

A simple illustration: consider a universe of one thousand firms being formed. As to each firm, it costs the members in aggregate $1,000 to go through the individual analyses of whether plenary private ordering will be to their advantage and then come to an agreement among the participants; across the universe of firms a cost of $1,000,000. If one out of the thousand firms will use plenary private ordering, and if that use will generate $900,000 in value, one could compare the $1,000,000 aggregate cost and the $900,000 value and conclude that a policy allowing plenary private ordering was not justified.[14]

The second cost of plenary private ordering is monitoring costs imposed on third parties. When we allow parties to redefine the basics of a business form we impose monitoring costs on third parties which deal with such firms.[15] Note that the monitoring cost is not limited to third parties which deal with firms which actually make use of private ordering;

---

[14] The more difficult decision, of course, is when the $900,000 in widely distributed costs yields $1,100,000 in value to one firm. A policy decision would need to be made about the wealth transfer from the non-participating firms to the participating firm.

[15] True, the reordering is internal as a formal matter. Rev. Unif. P'ship Act § 103(a) ('relations among the partners and between the partners and the partnership are governed by the partnership agreement'); (b)(10) ('The partnership agreement may not . . . (10) restrict rights of third parties under this [Act]'); § 103 cmt. 12; 6 U.L.A. Pt. I pp. 73, 74, and 76. But a reordering which is internal in form could nevertheless be of importance to third parties. For example, the allocation of management rights under RUPA, '[e]ach partner has equal rights in the management and conduct of the partnership business', is subject to the modifying agreement of the parties under § 103. Rev. Unif. P'ship Act § 401(f); § 401 cmt. 1 ('All of these rules are . . . subject to contrary agreement of the partners as provided in section 103'); 6 U.L.A. Pt. I pp. 133, 133-34. But the external agency authority of a partner, as to which a third party might be very interested, is inextricably bound up in the internal allocation. Rev. Unif. P'ship Act § 301; 6 U.L.A. Pt. I p. 101.

the fact that a firm could engage in plenary private ordering imposes on third parties a monitoring cost, even if only to confirm that the firm hasn't reordered.

Now, it may be that we are willing to make the tradeoff in some of these cases, that it is important enough to us to have intra-firm creation of value that we are willing to accept the external costs. The key, however, is that private ordering does impose costs, and these costs have not been sufficiently addressed.[16]

4. STRIKING THE SOCIAL BALANCE

Does the aggregate of value produced within firms from plenary private ordering exceed the total costs of such plenary private ordering – both internal and external? We don't know enough to even begin making this determination, but we may know – or at least suspect – one thing which bears on the discussion. This relates to the rate of use of the various plenary private ordering tools.

Because we are seeking to make an aggregate determination of value and costs, not simply a determination within a single firm, we need to have some sense of whether the ability to do plenary private ordering actually – not theoretically – is used and creates value. To make such a determination, we need to have some sense of the frequency with which parties are using plenary private ordering.

I suspect the case for plenary private ordering may be sufficiently disconnected from actual behavior as to call into question the entire exercise, at least as to the most extreme private ordering variations. Having been in practice, dealing with a fair number of clients who used partnerships, I find the case for plenary private ordering to be descriptively inaccurate: real parties, in real firms, don't act the way the model suggests. Put another way, real parties in real firms don't particularly want – and for the most part have not used – the plenary private ordering possibilities we've provided.

Take the ability to almost completely eliminate the fiduciary duty of loyalty and the associated obligation of good faith and fair dealing. RUPA allows partnership participants by their agreement to almost completely eliminate the fiduciary duty of loyalty and the non-fiduciary obligation of good faith and fair dealing.[17] I have made a point of asking lawyers in any number of different types of practice whether they can recall a partnership-related negotiation in which their client wanted to completely eliminate the protections of loyalty, good faith, and fair dealing. I've yet to find one. Even if you could find one, or a handful, of real parties in real firms who wish to used the most extreme private ordering examples, we need to debate whether it is appropriate to structure and entire body of business organization law to cater to their bizarre desires.

---

[16] My colleague, Professor Biff Campbell, suggests another social cost from plenary private ordering. It is his observation, and intuition, that when we allow plenary private ordering, some parties will use that flexibility and their superior position to negotiate purposefully inefficient deals. An example would be the general partner of a limited partnership which inserts and maintains a gross negligence standard in a limited partnership investment vehicle aimed at a group of dentists. The calculus of the deal is optimal for the general partner, who gets a limitation on liability without having to give up a corresponding pricing benefit to the unskilled investors. It is suboptimal for the dentists, but they perhaps deserve the deal they negotiate. From Professor Campbell's perspective, however, the deal is socially suboptimal, since society gets a limited partnership with a skewed liability-pricing arrangement.

[17] Rev. Unif. P'ship Act § 103(b)(3), (5), 6 U.L.A. Pt. I at 73. Hillman, et al., *supra* n. 6, at pp. 41-51.

It is important in the analysis to strike a balance to remember that the benefits are isolated while the costs are widely distributed. Some level of cost – bargaining costs within firms and monitoring costs on the part of parties which deal with firms – is imposed on all parties when the ability to engage in plenary private ordering is present. Therefore, the frequency with which plenary private ordering is used becomes terribly important. If it is rare, then the entire exercise may be unjustifiable.

On the other side of the equation, it may be that the widely distributed costs are *de minimis* because real firm participants and their lawyers – in the formation process – and real third parties who deal with firms, and their lawyers, routinely ignore the private ordering possibilities, driving the search, negotiation and monitoring costs toward zero. Of course, such conduct would itself be fairly strong evidence that plenary private ordering is not justified by widespread use.

Note that I have dealt with this so far as a unitary question: is plenary private ordering justifiable as a whole. Of course, the question should be broken down under further analysis: as to each statutory provision, what level of private ordering is justified. It might well be that as to some points – fiduciary duties or the admission of new partners – broad private ordering is not warranted, but as to others—the standard of conduct under the duty of care – it is. Further, it might well be that as to some points – fiduciary duties, again – restrictions but not elimination of private ordering would be justifiable.

5. The related question of multiple business forms: how many are too many?

How does the suggestion that we evaluate plenary private ordering using an aggregate, net, social calculation of value and cost relate to default forms? I mentioned earlier that an extension of plenary private ordering in existing forms has been the creation of new statutory business forms. The same analysis obtains.

It matters what your statutory default forms are in terms of the need for and efficiency of bargaining and monitoring. It is reasonable to assume that the universe of transactions – of firms – potentially within the coverage of our business association laws is reasonably limited, and that the firms tend to cluster in a relatively small number of fairly well-defined patterns. This is to say that there are only so many dimensions along which these fact patterns differ. The trick is, I suspect, to have our statutory forms and within each form the statutory defaults, approximate the clusters of arrangements to which the parties would bargain. We do this in the recognition that the closer we can bring the statutory provisions to the endpoints to which the parties would bargain, the more efficient we make the system.

But because of the internal bargaining and external monitoring costs, you don't want to have an infinite number of statutory forms any more than you want to have only one, even with plenary private ordering. In the case of an infinite number of statutory forms, your bargaining costs approach zero – there being an off the rack form for every fact pattern – but your search costs escalate. In the case of one statutory form, your search cost is zero – there being only one option – but your bargaining and monitoring costs escalate.

Take for example the situation we have created in the United States with the limited liability company and limited liability partnership forms. There are differences between the two, from jurisdiction to jurisdiction, but I have yet to hear a convincing rationale for having both forms in every jurisdiction.

We need to address the question of how many business forms is it socially optimal to have. At what point are the distributed search, negotiation and monitoring costs, and the narrowly distributed marginal gains such that one cannot justify additional forms. The answer, of course, lies in part in the level of private ordering we allow within each of the forms.

6. The Related Question of Multiple Jurisdictions: Should Business Entity Law Be Federal?

Another related question is the efficiency effects of having business entity law made at the state, not the Federal, level. Apart from the question of whether having business entity law made at the state level promotes any type of meaningful competition among the states, is the simple observation that a lack of uniform adoption among the states – especially on key points such as fiduciary duties – creates monitoring, search and bargaining costs.

We need to address the question of how many state-based variations of each business form is it socially optimal to have. At what point are the distributed search, negotiation and monitoring costs, and the narrowly distributed marginal gains such that one cannot justify additional state-based variations.

As with the basic private ordering policy question, it may be that on the issue of state-based variations, the widely distributed costs are *de minimis* because real firm participants and their lawyers – in the formation process – and real third parties who deal with firms, and their lawyers, routinely ignore the state-based variations, driving the search, negotiation and monitoring costs toward zero. Of course, such conduct would itself be fairly strong evidence that state-based variations are not justified by widespread use.

7. Cross National Developments: Social Inefficiencies from Plenary Private Ordering Writ Large

How does the suggestion that we evaluate plenary private ordering using an aggregate, net, social calculation of value and cost relate to cross national development of the law?

I start from the assumption that this is a common area of inquiry. I am unconvinced that – putting aside for a moment factors such as tax codes and securities regimes – there is a unique and immutable French way to organize a restaurant, or an American way to organize a pharmacy. I am unconvinced that the universe of private businesses in America, France, Poland and Norway requires us to have diverging business organization laws. The law of Germany on the organization of a small firm to renovate and sell residential properties need not differ from the law of Netherlands applicable to a similar firm.

Similarly, I assume that there is no reason why our defaults, or the extent to which we permit private ordering, need differ.

I am not, of course, suggesting a single law, or even the global equivalent of the type of harmonization that may be possible within the European community. But it does make sense to see if we can have a generally common set of forms, and a common approach to private ordering. It makes sense for us to have a common language. And we can acknowledge that we impose costs when we do not have as much commonality as possible.

I would not be so presumptuous as to suggest that this common approach be based on the American experience: frankly, I don't think we have done well enough to serve as a model. I would be presumptuous enough to suggest that we attempt to move toward a common nomenclature and parallel concepts of private ordering.

8. Where do we go from here?

Where do we go from here? A constructive start would be to acknowledge that private ordering generates costs, some of which are social. Having done so, we could agree that an aggregate, net, social calculation of value and cost is appropriate to see if plenary private ordering is justified and, if not, to determine the appropriate level of private ordering.

One of my colleagues asked if I knew that I was 'tilting at windmills' in this exercise. His point was that the calculation of the costs and the benefits of plenary private ordering in closely held firms is too difficult to attempt, much less to attempt repeatedly for subtly different permutations of a private ordering regime. I readily concede the point. It is enough for my purposes simply to seek the acknowledgement that there are costs associated with plenary private ordering, and that if, as to some provisions of the law, the ability to engage in private ordering isn't used, or doesn't result in substantial value, then those provisions ought not be subject to plenary private ordering. If that is tilting at windmills, then I can think of no better venue for the exercise than here in the Netherlands, at The Hague.

Perhaps the most valuable reminder from the private ordering policy discussion is of the value in commonality in these matters. We benefit when we adopt common modes of analysis, shared nomenclature, and harmonious statutes. That value of commonality, I believe, has been too often put aside as we have been guided by a market-oriented conceptualization which focuses too heavily on the presumed benefits to individual participants and firms and ignores the social dimensions of public policy formation. The private ordering discussion is of value if it signals a renewed consideration of the social costs of the contemporary paradigm.

In closing, I would be remiss if I did not acknowledge with gratitude the role that the Netherlands has played in these discussions. Starting with the rich contemporary scholarship of Dutch academics, judges, practitioners, and policymakers; through the landmark 2001 Tilburg roundtable conference;[18] and continuing with this timely and valuable conference, the Netherlands has made essential contributions to the international development of private company law. Those contributions have been marked by a special sense of creativity and openness, and by a willingness to thoughtfully examine and re-examine fundamental issues.

The leadership of the Netherlands in this regard is greatly appreciated.

---

[18] The Tilburg roundtable conference – officially the Conference on Close Corporation and Partnership Law Reform in Europe and the United States – was held in May of 2001, under the auspices of the Tilburg University Faculty of Law and the Center for Company Law, and with the sponsorship of the Anton Philips Fund. Articles from the roundtable conference were published in a symposium issue of *The Journal of Corporation Law* (Symposium: Unincorporated Business Entities, 26 *J. Corp. L.* (2001)) and in book form by J.A. McCahery, T. Raaijmakers and E.P. Vermeulen (eds.), *The Governance of Close Corporations and Partnerships: US and European Perspectives* (Oxford, Oxford University Press 2004).

Chapter 13

THE EUROPEAN PRIVATE COMPANY BEFORE ITS PENDING LEGISLATIVE BIRTH

Peter Hommelhoff*

1. Introduction

In the summer of 2008, the EU Commission will present the draft regulation for a European private company. The Commission indicates by this announcement of the internal market commissioner,[1] after prolonged hesitation that it wishes to comply with the urgent and detailed request of the European Parliament (EP)[2] and to initiate the legislative process. Apparently, the arguments directed at the small- and medium-sized enterprises (SME) and their specific interests have now, after the EU parliamentarians, also convinced the Commission. In fact, the significance of this group of enterprises in the economy of the Community cannot be overestimated. The Commission therefore acts with appropriate responsibility in not confining itself to taking up the draft regulation[3] prepared ten years ago by business practitioners and academic lawyers (CCIP/CNPF working group) but being prepared (as can be seen in the Consultation Paper of the General Directorate Internal Market of July 2007)[4] to develop its own statute for a European private company. This paper is intended, mainly on the basis of that Consultation Paper but also on the basis of the EP resolution,[5] to introduce the main issues and central regulatory elements of the new legal form of community law.

1.1 The necessity for an EPC

In spite of the legislative initiative promised by the Commission, the practical necessity for the EPC as a supra-national legal form in addition to those already in existence is still an

* Professor of Law, University of Heidelberg. The chapter was originally delivered as a lecture to the Industrial Law Seminar at Bonn University. The author wishes to thank Austin Dunne, Solicitor, Munich for the translation of the text. Email: peter.hommelhoff@igw.uni-heidelberg.de.

[1] E.H. Fietz, in: *GmbH-Rundschau* 321 (2007).

[2] Accessible at <www.eurparl.europa.eu/registre/recherche> through 'advanced search' in the document type 'texts adopted' as of 1 February 2007; in this text, see also the reference to almost identical draft of the European Parliament legal committee with the exception of the co-determination passages.

[3] Reproduced in J. Boucourechliev and P. Hommelhoff (eds.), *Vorschläge Für Eine Europäische Privatgesellschaft* (Köln, Otto Schmidt Verlag 1999) p. 281 (mainly in the area of creditor protection). See also the revised version by C. Teichmann, *European Company Law* (2006) p. 279.

[4] Accessible at <http://ec.europa.eu/internal_market/company/epc/index_de.htm>.

[5] See *supra* n. 2.

J.A. McCahery, L. Timmerman and E.P.M. Vermeulen (eds.), Private Company Law Reform

open political question. The necessity for the EPC has to be justified even if only for the reason that all 27 Member States deciding the matter in the Council of Ministers according to Article 308 EC[6] must be convinced in favor of the EPC and its statute.

1.2 A single organization

If a SME wishes to be active in the entire European internal market as well as in the three EEA states, by means of local companies as is the norm, it must concern itself in the most extreme case with 29 legal systems, meaning that for the formation of national companies and their operation it must deal with that number of national company laws. On the principle that good advice is expensive, this legal fragmentation leads to very high advisory costs – equally in money and time.[7] This expense, to which the Consultation Paper openly refers,[8] is confirmed by the German Chamber of Industry and Commerce (*DIHK*) in a survey of its member companies and discussions in its working groups and committees published in October 2007.[9] While many of the companies replying did not confirm impediments in cross-border business, a quarter of them nevertheless see in the variety of national regulations a massive problem for their businesses.

The percentage of companies which confirmed the necessity for an EPC, i.e., 75%, greatly exceeds this number.[10] They see many advantages in the legal form of the EPC, including simpler formation of foreign subsidiaries, a single legal form recognized and known in the entire EU and having the same conditions in each state, consequent simplification in internal management in medium-sized groups,[11] increased legal certainty in case of the formation of subsidiaries abroad, increased company mobility, externally effective internationalization (European label), reduction of advisory costs on formation and ongoing management.[12] On the whole, apparently many enterprises see in the EPC an extremely attractive vehicle for their cross-border activities in the European internal market. In their opinion, the EPC is tailored to the need of SMEs.[13]

---

[6] In its judgment of 2 May 2006 (Rs. C-436/03, Coll. 2006, I-3733), the European Court of Justice [ECJ] specified this provision as the legal basis for companies of Community law; see hereto C. Teichmann, *Binnenmarktkonformes Gesellschaftsrecht* (Berlin, Walter de Gruyter 2006) p. 192; in contrast, see P-C. Müller-Graff, 'Rechtsgrundlagen im Gemeinschaftsrecht für die Europäische Privatgesellschaft', in P. Hommelhoff and D. Helms (eds.), *Neue Wege In Die Europäische Privatgesellschaft* (Köln, Otto Schmidt Verlag 2001) pp. 289, 294, who suggests resort to Art. 95 EC as the legislative basis.

[7] See already P. Hommelhoff, 'Die 'Société fermée européenne' – eine supranationale Gesellschaftsform für kleine und mittlere Unternehmen im Europäischen Binnenmarkt', *Wertpapiermitteilungen* 2102 (1997), pp. 2102-3; see further C. Steinberger, 'Die Europäische Privatgesellschaft – Schaffung einer europaweiten Gesellschaftsform für kleine und mittlere Unternehmen', *Binnenmarkt, Betriebsberater* 7 (2006), p. 28 with figures in fn. 16 (drawing on the experience of the *Verband Deutscher Maschinen- und Anlagenbau*)

[8] See *supra* n. 4, at p. 4 under II.

[9] Statement of 31 October 2007 at the occasion of the EU consultation on the European Private Company, accessible at <www.dihk.de> through the link '*Recht und Fairplay*' on the '*DIHK-Positionen zu Gesetzesvorhaben*' in answer to Question 1 to the EU Commission

[10] Ibid., see the answer to Question 3.

[11] In comparison see A. Brandi, 'Diskussionsbeitrag Einsatzmöglichkeiten einer EPG und ihre Akzeptanz in der mittelständischen Wirtschaft', in P. Hommelhoff and D. Helms (eds.), *Neue Wege In Die Europäische Privatgesellschaft* (Köln, Otto Schmidt Verlag 2001) p. 79, after consultation of a number of medium-size enterprises in east Westphalia; see also H. Kallmayer, 'Einsatzmöglichkeiten einer EPG im Konzern', ibid., at p. 84

[12] Specifically on the assessment of the engineering company *Verband Deutscher Maschinen- und Anlagenbau,* see Steinberger, *supra* n. 7, at p. 28; in comparison see also P. Hommelhoff in S. Kalss, C. Nowotny, and M. Schaeuer (eds.), *Festschrift Für Peter Doralt* (Vienna, Manz 2004) p. 201, 202.

[13] See the DIHK Statement, *supra* n. 9 in the answer to Question 3.

1.3 Alternative national forms?

The existing legal forms of community law fall more or less far behind as the Consultation Paper accurately reports.[14] In particular, the European company (SE) is said to be directed at a widely distributed shareholding, is too inflexible and too expensive for smaller enterprises and is not a genuine unitary instrument because ultimately of the major influence of national regulations.[15] Contrary to the original aspiration for the SE,[16] it is, as a legal form, entirely unsuitable for the organization of a SME in a cross-border manner in the internal market. The same applies to the European Economic Interest Group and the European Co-Operative – alone because of their very narrowly regulated objectives.

Encouraged by the *Überseering* judgment of the ECJ[17] and by the possibility existing in many Member States, or shortly to be introduced there, of transferring the registered office of the company abroad without liquidation,[18] many SMEs will initially consider using the legal form with which they are familiar at home for their foreign activity. An engineering company from Bielefeld may conduct its French, Italian and Spanish subsidiaries in the form of a German *GmbH*. That outweighs all advantages of the EPC at a single stroke. But the problem lies on the other side of the market.[19] The customers of the Bielefeld company in France or Italy are uncertain and cannot be really confident in what is for them a foreign legal form.

With the EPC this would be different because after its introduction it would also be familiar in these states. From the political perspective of community law, the specific aspect of equality must also be considered: the SME from Riga could not use the Lithuanian *GmbH* with which it is familiar as its cross-border organization.[20]

For this reason also, the English Limited is also excluded as a functioning substitute for the EPC.[21]

---

[14] See *supra* n. 4 in the answer to (1), II p. 4.

[15] In detail R. Gutsche, *Die Eignung Der Europäischen Aktiengesellschaft Für Kleine Und Mittlere Unternehmen In Deutschland* (1993) summarized p. 239; consult also Teichmann, *supra* n. 6, at p. 273 with further references in fn. 249 of the text; for an emphatically positive contrasting view, although not fully convincing, see H. Heckschen, *Die SE als Option für den Mittelstand, in: Wirtschaftsrecht. Festschrift Für Westermann* (Rainer, Albertz & Eberhard (eds.) 2008) p. 999.

[16] SE Statute recital 13 sentence 2 (*OJ* EC of 10 November 2001, L 294/1), also reproduced in H. Neye, *Die Europäische Aktiengesellschaft* (2005) p. 265; see also F. Blanquet, *'Das Statut der Europäischen Aktiengesellschaft (Societas Europaea).* Ein Gemeinschaftsinstrument für die grenzüberschreitende Zusammenarbeit im Dienste der Unternehmen', *Zeitschrift fur Unternehmens und Gesellschaftsrecht* 20 (2002), p. 52.

[17] C-208/00, Coll. 2002, I-9947 '*Überseering*'; see also Teichmann, *supra* n. 6, at p. 89.

[18] In the government bill (MoMiG) § 4a GmbHG new version, a German *Gesellschaft mit beschränkter Haftung* (Limited Liability Corporation) (*GmbH*) is also able to seek permission to move its registered office abroad (details Hofmann, *ZIP* 2007, 1581). The transfer of registered office, according to established judgements, still involves the dissolution of the company (for a critical view of this, consult C. Teichmann, *supra* n. 6, at p. 171). A solution may be provided in the soon to be anticipated codification of international company law: see H-W. Neye, 'Casenote on a decision by the *Oberlandesgericht* [OLG]' (Higher Regional Court) Munich of 4 October 2007), *EwiR*, 716 (2007).

[19] See Hommelhoff, *supra* n. 12, p. 204; Steinberger, *supra* n. 7, pp. 29-31; O. Vossius, 'Die Europäische Privatgesellschaft – *Societas Europaea Privata'*, *EWS* 438 (2007) p. 440.

[20] See A. Radwan, 'European Private Company and the Regulatory Landscape in the EU – An Introductory Note', 18 *European Business Law Review* 769, 771 (2007); Steinberger, *supra* n. 7, at p. 29.

[21] See Vossius, *supra* n. 19, at p. 440.

1.4 Models

For what purposes should the EPC be provided and on what should it be modeled? From the perspective of medium-sized businesses, sales and service subsidiaries abroad are concerned.[22] This gave rise in the Consultation Paper to the question of whether the EPC should be structured as a one-man company or as a company with several shareholders.[23] German businesses argue in favor of freedom: it should be possible to form an EPC with one or more shareholders, whether natural or legal persons.[24] This should be accepted because the EPC must also be available to be used as a joint venture.[25] In addition, this supra-national legal form should also acquire the specific strength typical of all 'second' corporate forms in the EU Member States, namely as 'utility furniture'[26] for all thinkable purposes (including immaterial or charitable) which are not legally forbidden. Major businesses must also be able to use the EPC as part of their groups.[27]

The EPC Regulation should therefore be tailored to the specific interests of the SMEs in the Community and be structured on the model of both a sales and service subsidiary abroad as well as that of a joint venture in the medium-sized economy. However, these models must not be inscribed in stone. The EPC shareholders must rather retain complete flexibility[28] provided that the protection of creditors or similar interests is adequately provided for.[29]

1.5 Interim conclusion

To summarize: in the European internal market, a supra-national EPC tailored to the specific concerns and interests of small and medium-sized companies would be advantageous for many reasons. Neither the already existing legal forms of community law nor any one of the national legal forms can perform its function. The draft regulation for the EPC should provide the maximum possible flexibility in accordance with the typical applications in the medium-sized economy.

2. Principles

The Consultation Paper of the General Directorate Internal Market[30] lists in detail the areas which should in its opinion be regulated in an EPC statute, namely formation, sharehold-

---

[22] See Steinberger, *supra* n. 7, at p. 28; see also Brandi, *supra* n. 11, at p. 81.

[23] *Supra* n. 4, see (1) III p. 5 (Model A and B).

[24] DIHK Statement, *supra* n. 9, at p. 4 in answer to Question 7.

[25] In detail H-J. Hellwig, 'Zum Einsatz einer EPG als Jointventure', in P. Hommelhoff and D. Helms (eds.), *Neue Wege In Die Europäische Privatgesellschaft* (Köln, Otto Schmidt Verlag 2001) p. 89; see also Brandi, ibid., at p. 81.

[26] This description is known to come from H. Wiedemann, 'Unternehmensrecht und GmbH-Reform', *Juristenzeitung* (1970), p. 596.

[27] This idea was also the basis of the European Private Company (EPC) Draft Regulation of the CCIP/CNPF Working Group, *supra* n. 3, at Preamble, p. 282.

[28] On company law freedoms see the seminal book by F. Rittner, *Die Werdende Juristische Person* (Tübingen, Mohr-Siebeck 1973) p. 248.

[29] On the protection of individuals and minorities see *supra* n. 4, at s. II p. 4; on commercial codetermination of employees, see *supra* n. 4, at s. II p. 6.

[30] See *supra* n. 4, in answer to s. (2) IV see Question 11 p. 12; most of the companies asked did not answer, see DIHK Statement, *supra* n. 9, at s. IV p. 5.

ers, capital and management, but then asks business whether these areas should each be regulated in the Regulation or in the statutes of the individual company or by the Member State. What the content of such regulation may be is hardly mentioned although this itself requires discussion to the greatest possible extent throughout the community. Some approaches and principles are therefore dealt with here.

2.1 Limitation of liability and creditor protection

Precisely since they are not intended to be organized as mere branches, foreign subsidiaries require legal personality[31] in order to take their place on the market. Logically, the parent finds it important that the contractual partners and creditors of its subsidiaries cannot have recourse to it. This insulation of the group against risks is implemented by the limited liability function of the subsidiary. It is also significant for SMEs in the internal market, because, while risks arising within a foreign subsidiary and therefore from a strange jurisdiction are incalculable and cause apprehension, owners of SMEs who are averse to risks, are particularly sensitive.[32]

The indispensable protection of creditors (stable and effective) could then be modeled on the limited partner liability[33] with limited liability of the shareholders and exclusion of liability if the shareholder's contribution has been fully paid up. This system of protection should be adequate from the point of view of creditors. The parent SME on the other hand would not be able to accept this because it would lead to a direct confrontation with an unspecified number of creditors of the subsidiary. That is extremely burdensome, results in a disorganized competition between subsidiaries and is not completely balanced because of the ultimate limited liability of the parent SME.

Contrasted with the above is internal liability between the companies,[34] i.e., the channeling of liability through the foreign companies in the interests of the parent SME without neglecting the protection of the creditors of the subsidiary. This protection is initially and solely organized and dealt with at the level of the subsidiary and its assets. That is only logical because, unlike in a branch, the subsidiary itself acts independently of its parent abroad.

The corporate law protection system to be prescribed for the EPC requires even more intensive discussion: the continental asset protection system with statutory minimum capital[35] (admittedly without its acknowledged gaps)[36] or the Anglo-Saxon liquidity protection

---

[31] Teichmann, *supra* n. 6, at p. 328 correctly sees the grant of legal personality as the key to the integration of a *supra*-national legal form into the legal systems of the Member States.

[32] Hommelhoff, *supra* n. 7, at p. 2104.

[33] This solution is suggested by Vossius, *supra* n. 19, at p. 443, for further discussion.

[34] For the legal position under German law, see the *Trihotel* decision by the *Bundesgerichtshof* (Federal Court of Justice – FCJ), published in *GmbH-Rundschau* 927 (2007), p. 931, where the FCJ applies the valid fundamentally preventative *'Basisschutzkonzept'* (Base Protection Concept) of §§ 30, 31 *GmbHG* and thereby rejects to 'lift the veil' which would in many cases be extremely excessive and would seriously undermine the basis for the *GmbH* legal form.

[35] This is recommended by the European Parliament. Hereto, see the commentary by P. Hommelhoff, in P. Hommelhoff, P. Rawert, and K. Schmidt (eds.), *Festschrift für Hans-Joachim Priester Zum 70. Geburtstag* (Köln, Otto Schmidt Verlag 2007) p. 251, however, with mediating compromises.

[36] See V. Röhricht, 'Insolvenzrechtliche Aspekte im Gesellschaftsrecht', *ZIP* 505 (2005), 514; see the decision by the *Bundesgerichtshof*, published in *GmbH-Rundschau* 927 (2007), p. 929, fn. 16 with further references.

system.[37] It is not intended here to set these systems against each other – all the more so because the European Parliament on the basis of the asset protection system, has suggested a considerable number of concrete details.[38] To say only the following: a choice given to the states as to the system to be used for the EPC in the state where it is registered would contradict the basic principle of community-wide uniformity and would, for the SME, considerably complicate the management of its group in the internal market.[39] Likewise, the combination of both protection systems as a political compromise is not to be recommended. Such cumulative protection could overload the EPC which is intended to be simply constructed and burden it to an excessive extent compared with other legal forms.[40] However, the Commission and the Council of Ministers will not be able to avoid a clear decision in principle on creditor protection in the EPC.

2.2 Insolvency law

According to the General Directorate, liquidation and insolvency law should not be provided for in the EPC Regulation. While the first may be based on an omission,[41] insolvency is intentionally not included.[42] For two reasons, this requires greater in-depth discussion. Firstly, the instruments of creditor protection between company law and insolvency law as shown in recent legal developments in many Member States are functionally practically interchangeable;[43] politically preventative or reactive protection of creditors, effectiveness and the associated extent of rules and administration are concerned.[44] And secondly, in several Member State legal systems, the stage prior to insolvency, i.e., the company crisis, is regulated with increasing precision and legal obligations.[45]

A clearer demarcation (distinction) between company law and insolvency law in the EPC statute must therefore be considered again, in particular, if the demarcation would condemn those responsible in the foreign subsidiaries, their management as well as that of the parent, to degrees of uncertainty varying from one Member State to another, as to how

---

[37] See the report by R. Veil, 'Kapitalerhaltung. Das System der Kapitalrichtlinie versus situative Ausschüttungssperren', in M. Lutter (ed.), *Das Kapital Der Aktiengesellschaft In Europa* (Berlin, de Gruyter Recht 2006) pp. 96-113; D. Joost, 'Die Gmbh-Reform', in P. Behrens, P. Hommelhoff, and D. Joost (eds.), *Der Diskussionsondertagung Der, Gesellschaftsrechtlichen Vereinigung* (Köln, Otto Schmidt Verlag 2006) p. 46.

[38] *Supra* n. 35.

[39] *Supra* n. 11.

[40] Such a combination is recognized in USA and New Zealand law, see Veil, *supra* n. 37, at p. 96.

[41] The DIHK Statement is more open on this, *supra* n. 9, in answer to Question 12.

[42] See the Consultation Paper, *supra* n. 4, in answer to Question (1) III p. 5.

[43] On creditor protection by insolvency law in England see T. Bachner, 'Gläubigerschutz durch Insolvenzrecht in England', in M. Lutter (ed.), *Das Kapital Der Aktiengesellschaft In Europa* (Berlin, de Gruyter Recht 2006) p. 526.

[44] See for example, the discussion on the approach to protection of (deemed capital) shareholder loans: U. Huber and M. Habersack, 'GmbH-Reform: Zwölf Thesen zu einer möglichen Reform des Rechts der kapitalersetzenden Gesellschafterdarlehen', *Betriebs Berater* (2006), p. 1; M. Habersack, 'Gesellschafterdarlehen nach MoMiG: Anwendungsbereich, Tatbestand und Rechtsfolgen der Neuregelung', *ZIP* 2145 (2007), pp. 2146-7 on the one side, and Hommelhoff, in 'Die Gmbh-Reform In Der Diskussion' (*supra* n. 37), at p. 1; and R. Bork, 'Abschaffung des Eigenkapitalersatzrechts zugunsten des Insolvenzrechts?', *Zeitschrift fur Unternehmens und Gesellschaftsrecht* 250 (2007), at pp. 252, 254 on the other.

[45] H. Drenckhan, *Gläubigerschutz In Der Krise Der GMBH* (Baden-Baden, Nomos Verlagsgesellschaft 2005); R. Veil, 'Krisenbewältigung durch Gesellschaftsrecht', in M. Lutter and H. Wiedemann (eds.), *Zeitschrift für Unternehmens und Gesellschaftsrecht* (Berlin, de Gruyter Recht 2006) p. 374; S. Kalss, N.J. Adensamer, and J. Oelkers, in M. Lutter (ed.), *Das Kapital Der Aktiengesellschaft In Europa* (Berlin, de Gruyter Recht 2006) p. 134.

they should behave in a crisis, pending insolvency and insolvency itself.[46] There are therefore many indications that these points of contact in the ongoing management to insolvency law (up to and including the obligation to make an insolvency application and liability for delaying to do so) should, for reasons of legal uniformity and legal certainty, be regulated in an EPC Regulation as has been recommended by the European Parliament.[47] This does not in the least aim at the entire Europeanisation of insolvency law on the occasion of the establishment of a new legal form of community law.

2.3 Structural freedom

SMEs are usually strongly characterized by the personality and individuality of their owners, by the relationship of the owners between themselves, by their particular objectives, but also strongly by the markets on which the individual SME is active and by its products and services. SMEs therefore require the maximum possible structural freedom for the drafting of their statutes.[48] This applies to the EPC and similarly to major companies and regional public bodies if they wish to avail of this legal form and tailor it to their requirements.

Nevertheless, the Consultation Paper for the EPC again proposes for discussion an intensive and very detailed legal framework from which the founders and shareholders can deviate in the statutes only to a limited degree.[49] The Consultation Paper lists, as possible advantages of such a concept, the greater uniformity among all European Private Companies within the Community together with the comprehensive overall regulation, greater legal certainty and less advisory costs. On the contrary, the companies through the *DIHK* statement[50] demand the greatest possible freedom in the statutes for the internal organization in the EPC, this being of the greatest significance for SMEs.

One's own opinion must concern itself with clear distinctions. The extent of regulation in the EPC Regulation has nothing to do with the freedom of design. Only the question of what is optional is decisive. Detailed complete regulation can even provide major freedom of design provided that its provisions are to a great extent susceptible to change. The EPC Regulation, however strictly or loosely its provisions may be construed, must provide the greatest possible scope to design the statutes freely in the actual individual case. Only by this means, will the specific concerns of potential users of this community legal form be catered for.

On the other hand, freedom of design also necessarily involves renunciation of certain options. The EPC may not, for example, participate on the capital markets, because inves-

---

46 See K. Schmidt, *Das Kapital Der Aktiengesellschaft In Europa*, *supra* n. 43, at p. 188; emphasizing preventative creditor protection by insolvency law; specifically on the EPC see U. Ehricke, 'Die Überwindung von Akzeptanzdefiziten als Grundlage zur Schaffung neuer supranationaler Gesellschaftsformen in der EU', 64 *RABELS Z* 497 (2000), at pp. 503-4.

47 *Supra* n. 2, Recommendation 11.

48 For more details see W. Zöllner, 'Inhaltsfreiheit bei Gesellschaftsverträgen', *Festschrift 100 Jahre Gmbh Gesetz* (Lutter/Ulmer/Zöllner (eds.) 1992) pp. 85, 88; K. Schmidt, *Gesellschaftsrecht* (4th ed., 2002) p. 114. and Hommelhoff, 'Gestaltungsfreiheit im GmbH-Recht', *Gestaltungsfreiheit Im Gesellschaftsrecht* (Lutter/Wiedemann (eds.) 1997) p. 38.

49 See, *supra* n. 4, in answer to (1) III2 option 1, p. 6.

50 See, *supra* n. 9 in answer to Question 10; see also Steinberger, *supra* n. 7, at p. 29.

tor protection requires a wide range of mandatory provisions. The General Directorate Internal Market ultimately agrees.[51]

2.4 Protection of minorities and individuals

Freedom of design demands responsibility on the part of the drafter of the statutes. It is therefore logical to leave the protection of minorities and individuals in the EPC to him or more precisely, whoever wishes to enter the company as a minority shareholder should himself ensure his own protection at the time of the formation or his entry. This concept suggests itself where a company is a minority shareholder usually having the necessary expertise either itself or through its advisors. One could, in parallel, argue for a joint venture statute.

The Consultation Paper adopts a different approach.[52] It sees a need to regulate minority protection in an EPC statute, if there are a number of shareholders. According to the General Directorate, it must also be ensured that the decisions in the company are properly made, i.e., by resolutions of general meetings. All of this can only be dispensed with if the EPC, according to the statutory plan, is intended to be used exclusively as a wholly owned company. The *DIHK* in its statement does not deal with the protection of minorities but argues for the admission of several shareholders[53] and relies for the powers of the general meeting on the provisions in the statutes.[54]

Ultimately, one has to agree with the General Directorate as to the configuration of an EPC which has exclusively companies as shareholders,[55] because, apart from the lack of awareness of problems which is often found and the occasional limited power of individual founders or shareholders to enforce their will, it is above all the aspect of legal certainty and security which indicates the necessity to regulate in the EPC Regulation a minimum of majority and individual protection. For joint ventures, on the other hand, there is no room for such precaution. Self-regulation is indicated.

2.5 Obligatory more than one State

Since the EPC should, above all, facilitate the cross-border activity of the SME in the internal market,[56] it could be advisable that the cross-border element of the connection between the EPC on the one hand and its founders and shareholders on the other be made obligatory as a condition for formation. The principle of subsidiarity also favors this.[57] It cannot be the task of the Union to offer a supranational legal form for the economic activity within only one Member State and that in competition with the national legal forms. With

---

[51] Consultation Paper, *supra* n. 4, in answer to question (1) II, p. 4: here the EPC is distinguished from the SE as a 'public company'.

[52] *Supra* n. 2, in answer to question (1) III 1, p. 6.

[53] *Supra* n. 4, in answer to Question 7.

[54] *Supra* n. 4, in answer to Question 10.

[55] See Hommelhoff, *supra* n. 7, at p. 2106; K. Heider, 'Gesellschafterpflichten nach dem EPG-Statut', in P. Hommelhoff and D. Helms (eds.), *Neue Wege In Die Europäische Privatgesellschaft* (Köln, Otto Schmidt Verlag 2001) p. 138.

[56] Consultation Paper, *supra* n. 4 in answer to question (1) IV, p. 8.

[57] On the principle of subsidiarity see only Streinz, in: Streinz, EUV/EGV, 2003, Art. 5 EC, see note in the margin p. 30 with further references.

the obligatory cross-border element, the EPC Regulation would only continue the reservation which already applies to other corporate bodies of community law.[58]

The Consultation Paper apparently assumes an obligatory cross-border element and, logically therefore, does not enter into any discussion thereof. On the other hand, greater liberality was demanded earlier in the literature:[59] if the founding company is active in the economy of at least two Member States, that must be adequate. This should be accepted, because firstly, a subsidiary EPC could then already be formed if business involvement abroad is still only intended and secondly, at the location of the founder or founders with subsequent transfer of registered office and management centre to the target Member State. If the EPC (in a certain limited sector) enters into competition with a national legal form, the Member States will be able to live with that. Since the *Centros* judgment of the ECJ, the company forms are, in any event, in competition with each other.[60]

2.6 Company co-determination

Due to the conflict about co-determination, decades were required until the statute for the European Company was finally passed at the Nice summit.[61] Many feared that the EPC project would suffer the same fate, in particular in the Commission.[62]

The Consultation Paper therefore obligingly lays down the cornerstones:[63] It would have been difficult to retreat from the compromise found for the SE. The EPC should not be available to be used as an instrument to avoid co-determination. On the other hand, the solution for the EPC should respect the need of SMEs for flexibility and not burden them with undue difficulty. The *DIHK* is very reserved on the question of co-determination (not particularly surprising).[64]

In the legislative process for the EPC, co-determination cannot be circumvented. Three reasons for this can be urged. Firstly, this legal form should be available as a group element for major companies[65] and may therefore employ a greater number of people. Secondly, it will be intended to enable the EPC to be formed by the transformation of a national company. This possibility should not be denied to companies under national law already subject to co-determination. And thirdly, the European Parliament, in its resolution, has requested the Commission[66] to take account of the co-determination implication and not to fall below the standard already reached at Community level in this respect.[67]

One could imagine that co-determination provisions would only apply when the number of employees of an EPC exceeds a certain threshold. As a number of states with quite

---

58 Art. 4 ss. 2 EEIA Regulation; Art. 2 SE Regulation; Art. 2 European Cooperative Regulation (SCEVO).

59 See for example Steinberger, *supra* n. 7, at p. 29 following the high level group on company law (Winter Group).

60 On company law competition between legislatures in detail most recently, see Teichmann, *supra* n. 6, at p. 320.

61 On the troubled history of the coming into being of the SE in detail, see F. Blanquet, *Zeitschrift fur Unternehmens und Gesellschaftsrecht*, 20 (2002), p. 21; see also S. Grundmann, *Europäisches Gesellschaftsrecht* (2004) p. 480; G.C. Schwarz, *Europäisches Gesellschaftsrecht* (2000) p. 643; Teichmann, *supra* n. 6, at p. 249.

62 Notably K. van Hulle, 'Geleitwort Die EPG – ein Blick aus Brüssel', in P. Hommelhoff and D. Helms (eds.), *Neue Wege In Die Europäische Privatgesellschaft* (Köln, Otto Schmidt Verlag 2001).

63 *Supra* n. 4 in answer to (1) V p. 8.

64 *Supra* n. 9 in answer to Question 13.

65 *Supra* n. 27.

66 Consultation Paper, *supra* n. 4, in answer to (2) Question 13.

67 See Hommelhoff, *supra* n. 35, pp. 253-4.

low thresholds meanwhile belong to the EU,[68] the minimum for the EPC could be fixed at 50 employees. That would leave most SME sales and service companies free of co-determination. Above that threshold, the Regulation could proceed according to the Community law basic precedent[69] of a co-determination agreement with default solution (however, emphatically more simple than in the case of the SE). Naturally, founders must be enabled to structure their groups active throughout the Community in the various Member States according to uniform principles.[70]

In order to further facilitate and stimulate the formation of an EPC, a co-determination moratorium according to the Danish example[71] could be allowed. For the first three years after its formation, the EPC (with the exception of the transformation of a national company already subject to co-determination) could be free of co-determination. Only after the expiry of this moratorium is the introduction of co-determination in the company to be negotiated, if the number of employees in the EPC exceeds the thresholds (here suggested to be 50). The then necessary coordination between the co-determination agreement and the powers of the shareholders under the statutes is not a special problem for the EPC.[72]

3. The regulatory system

At a time when the EU Commission has committed itself to reducing bureaucracy, there is everything in favor of intensive efforts towards a lean and easily understandable EPC Regulation in its construction and systems with practically convenient provisions. From a regulatory point of view, concentration on general principles and avoidance of excessively intensive detail in the Regulation must be considered. The experience gained in the 1970s with the draft statute for the SE is an argument for such a regulatory concept.[73] Its comprehensive regulation with the objective of regulating the organization and functioning of the SE autonomously and independently of national law did not, even among the then small number of Member States, find the necessary support.[74]

3.1 Comprehensive regulation

The General Directorate has been well advised to survey companies as to their preferred regulatory concept: That of a comprehensive regulation by the EPC Regulation itself or the

[68] For a review of the co-determination regimes in the EU see G. Mävers, *Die Mitbestimmung Der Arbeitnehmer In Der Europäischen Aktiengesellschaft* (Baden-Baden, Nomos Verlagsgesellschaft 2002) p. 58; see also the contributions in Unternehmens-Mitbestimmung Der Arbeitnehmer Im Recht Der Eu-Mitgliedstaaten, Zhr Sonderheft No. 72 (T. Baums and P. Ulmer (eds.) 2004).

[69] On similarities and the (few) differences between the negotiation solution of the SE Directive and the 10th Directive, see Teichmann, *Der Konzern* (2007) p. 89.

[70] *Supra* n. 11.

[71] See Hommelhoff, *supra* n. 12, at p. 209.

[72] On this problem in the SE see M. Habersack, 'Grundfragen der Mitbestimmung in SE und SCE sowie bei grenzüberschreitender Verschmelzung', 171 *ZHR* 613 (2007), p. 613; for a contrasting view see Teichmann, *supra* n. 69, at p. 93; both authors argue different positions on freedom of the social partners in the structure of an agreement on worker participation.

[73] See F. Blanquet, *Zeitschrift fur Unternehmens und Gesellschaftsrecht* (2002) 20, at pp. 23-4; Teichmann, *supra* n. 6, at p. 249.

[74] Consultation Paper, *supra* n. 4 on (1) III 2, p. 6 points this out explicitly.

alternative of a Regulation limiting itself to some (mostly mandatory)[75] core provisions indispensable for the functioning of a company, and otherwise to stating areas of regulation in the Regulation which must be provided for in the statutes by the founders in accordance with their own preferred design.[76]

For both regulatory concepts, the Consultation Paper lists the advantages and disadvantages of each in detail. The answer of the companies in the statement of the *DIHK*[77] is surprising. The majority prefer in principle the comprehensive regulation because this provides the legal certainty favored by the companies, simplifies the formation of the company in other Member States and the formation of group structures. Ultimately, only a uniform statute for the EPC can achieve the objective of facilitating cross-border activity.

Seen accordingly, the change of concept from the Community law full regulation to half regulation[78] in the case of the SE was, from the point of view of the companies, a serious error which must not be repeated.[79] The EPC requires a uniform statute solely with rules of community law without the addition of national law rules. That of course means in practice no single uniform for all private companies. It must rather be reserved to their founders in the exercise of design freedom to give each company its own character. Within individual groups this will in any event take the same form, so that group subsidiaries will have the same structure. Distinction must therefore be made between the uniform EPC statute and the uniformity of all EPC statutes in any particular group.

The plea of the companies for comprehensive full regulation corresponds noticeably with the experience in France after the introduction of the *SAS* with its open design.[80] The wide-ranging lack of statutory regulations led to considerable legal uncertainty among companies, including major companies, and initially scared them off from using this new legal form. It follows therefore that the acceptance and practical application of the EPC as a new organization form of community law would be very severely inhibited if the EPC Regulation did not offer comprehensive regulation. The regulatory concept is a prerequisite for success – namely among SMEs and their owners who are particularly sensitive to legal risks. The European Parliament agrees. In its first recommendation, it clearly listed those areas which should be regulated in the EPC Regulation as conclusively as possible. They extend from the legal nature of the EPC and its legal capacity and capacity to act, to liability of a shareholder in an EPC for its debts.[81]

3.2 Regulatory instructions and discretionary law

Complete regulation does not necessarily mean uniform regulation. Even with comprehensive regulation, the legislature does not need in the least to regulate everything itself. Conceptually, it would be adequate if the legislator intended only to ensure that a certain complex (for example, the right of individual shareholders to information) be regulated in the statutes. For such complexes, the legislator could impose an obligation to regulate them in the

[75] See Vossius, *supra* n. 19, at p. 441.

[76] Consultation Paper, *supra* n. 4, to (1) III 2, p. 6.

[77] *Supra* n. 9, in answer to Question 10, p. 5.

[78] *Supra* n. 73.

[79] For a pointedly critical view of the EP decision see also *supra* n. 2, recommendation 1 sentence 1; see also Hommelhoff, *supra* n. 35, at p. 246.

[80] I thank RA Dr. Dietmar Helms, Frankfurt, for the information on French corporate practice

[81] *Supra* n. 2, recommendation 1; see also Hommelhoff, *supra* n. 35, at p. 246.

articles,[82] the precise compliance therewith together with the regulations prescribed by the legislature would ultimately result in comprehensive regulation. By imposing the task of self-regulation, the legislature also avoids deprivation of choice, to a greater extent than with discretionary law, and considerably strengthens the exercise of design freedom with self-responsibility of the drafter of the statutes.

The businesses surveyed do not seem to wish to evade this self-responsibility. They name a whole list of areas which should be provided for in the articles,[83] the general meeting, shareholders' resolutions and voting rights, the sale and repurchase rights, capital increase, but, above all in questions of management, the surveyed companies see room for the design of articles, the nomination of the managing directors and their rights and duties including conflicts of interest, the structure of management and its publication obligation. However, with this list it remains open whether the companies request for these complexes only the freedom to regulate or expect such self-regulation tasks to be imposed in the EPC Regulation.

Recently sharp criticism from notaries has been made of the instrument of statutory imposition of self-regulation.[84] If the legislature, by statutorily prescribed drafting tasks, wishes to deflect the real problems to practitioners, this is, in their view, a case of inadequate fulfillment of the legislative task. This, however, can also be seen in reverse: The instructions to regulate as an expression of respect owed by the legislator to the variety of the individually characterized SME.

Be that as it may – for the founders of the EPC, the problem of prescribed self-regulation lies elsewhere. They cannot be sufficiently certain whether the provisions of the articles made by them in accordance with the regulatory instructions, are legally sound. In addition, the development of such provisions in the articles costs quite a bit in time and money and stands therefore in contradiction to the basic aims of the EPC.[85] Whether a precedent articles (Table A)[86] issued by the legislature can constitute a politically convincing way out requires critical reflection again against the background of the debate conducted on the planned precedent articles in the German *GmbH*.[87] Instead, the legislature could incorporate the content of such precedent articles immediately in the EPC Regulation. The Table A solution could be a fallback position if the issue of a precedent articles on the English model were a condition for the approval of Great Britain of the EPC Regulation.

---

[82] For a seminal book on prescribed self-regulation, see C.H. Beier, *Der Regelungsauftrag Als Gesetzgebungsinstrument Im Gesellschaftsrecht* (Köln, Carl Heymanns Verlag 2002), specifically on the EPC, p. 256.

[83] DIHK Statement, *supra* n. 9, at section IV, p. 5.

[84] Vossius, *supra* n. 19, at p. 441.

[85] *Supra* n. 7.

[86] On their function see D. Helms, 'Mustersatzungen für die Europäische Privatgesellschaft', in P. Hommelhoff and D. Helms (eds.), *Neue Wege In Die Europäische Privatgesellschaft* (Köln, Otto Schmidt Verlag 2001) p. 259; and recently R. Drury, *European Company Law* (2006) pp. 267, 268.

[87] For information on the current political discussion see W. Bayer, J. Schmidt, and T. Hoffmann, 'Satzungskomplexität und Mustersatzung', *GmbH-Rundschau* 953 (2007); A. Heidinger, 'Fluch und Segen der privatschriftlichen Mustersatzung', *Status: Recht DB* 07/2007, p. 243; K. Schmidt, 'Kann man eine GmbH auf einem Bierdeckel gründen?', *GmbH-Rundschau* 958 (2007).

3.3 Instruments for closing gaps

The legislative concept for the EPC is therefore heading for a complete and comprehensive provision in the Regulation – although certainly not in the detail of a listed SE. Against this background, the most controversial issue can be addressed, namely how can gaps in the EPC statute according to the Regulation be filled: exclusively at the level of community law or by recourse also to national law of the Member States in which the EPC has its registered office?[88]

The consequences of recourse to Member State law are known. Contrary to the basic concept of the EPC, the individual national companies would be partially repatriated. For the parent company, this would result in lack of transparency and in legal uncertainty. The legal uniformity would be endangered. That would be diametrically opposed to the urgent wish of the SMEs surveyed for a Europe-wide uniform and legally secure EPC.[89]

Nevertheless, the suggestion that gaps in the statute be closed by recourse to the principles of the statute, namely the principles of European company law, and if that is not adequate, to the common principles of Member State law,[90] meets with wide rejection in German literature.[91] European community law, according thereto, is not at present sufficiently developed to the extent that general principles, which would contribute to the solution of practical problems, can be identified. And even with deduction from such principles of community law, their result is not as predictable as is the case with national law.

To this I reply: of course legal uncertainty is associated with closing gaps by resort to principles. However, for the SME active throughout the internal market, the total of legally uncertain issues is not greater than would be the case with resort to each national law. It would therefore be politically indefensible to allow the EPC project to fail because of a dispute as to how to deal with closing gaps. It would be equally indefensible to reject the uniformity so urgently demanded by businesses[92] and thereby to reduce the acceptance of this legal form. The SE concept with its mixture of community and national law is completely intolerable for SMEs.[93] This should not even in reduced form be imposed on the EPC. A political balance must be found between closing gaps by recourse to national law and European law. The scales should be tipped in favor of community mechanisms.

3.4 Interpretation committee and European jurisprudence

The scales should be tipped in favor of community mechanisms even if only because, on the coming into force of the EPC Regulation with community law provisions for closing

---

[88] See the controversial discussion reported by D. Mattheus, 'Die EPG: Grundkonzept und rechtspolitische Eckpunkte', in P. Hommelhoff and D. Helms (eds.), *Neue Wege In Die Europäische Privatgesellschaft* (Köln, Otto Schmidt Verlag 2001) p. 97.

[89] DIHK Statement, *supra* n. 9, s. III in answer to Question 10/VII, p. 6.

[90] This is the formula originally proposed for the SE Regulation; having regard to the common principles of the laws of the Member States, it will only be sustainable for the EPC without this part because English and Irish law on the one hand, and Scandinavian law on the other, are not part of the continental European legal family. The expansion of the EC must be taken into account in any event in the formula for closing gaps for the EPC. A first attempt to develop legal principles and regulatory concepts in European Company Law is made by Veil, *supra* n. 35, at p. 799.

[91] Most recently H. Wicke, 'Die Euro-GmbH im 'Wettbewerb der Rechtsordnungen', *GmbH-Rundschau* 356 (2006), at pp. 357 8 (with further references).

[92] *Supra* n. 10.

[93] *Supra* n. 79.

gaps, many academics in legal faculties will extract solutions from the principles of the Regulation, community company law and possibly[94] the company law of the Member States, on many of the problem issues. Why should there not be (as for international accountancy law)[95] a private interpretation committee on European company law? It is certainly needed. It is certain that, even before the first closing the gap case reaches the European Court in Luxembourg through the national courts in their function of community courts,[96] academics together with practitioners will have developed a stock of arguments on general principles of company law in the community. The judges in Luxembourg will then be able to consider these in order to themselves establish principles of European community law on the basis mainly of the EPC Regulation.[97] As an additional security, in this respect it might be advisable to establish a specialized company law chamber in the European Court of First Instance.

4. Interim conclusion

I come to my conclusion. The idea of a community-wide uniform European Private Company has now, after a long run-up, been adopted by the EU organs – first by the European Parliament and now by the Commission. In the coming summer, they will present a draft of an EPC Regulation. Whether this can serve any of the Member States as a basis for the modernization of its own company law, we will see. In any event, this is not the objective of the EPC Regulation drafters, so that nothing is prejudged.

The draft Regulation will provide company lawyers in the Union and beyond it with a unique chance to engage with each other in an intense discussion on many stimulating questions of company law in a constructive search for EU-wide acceptable solutions, in a manner which has so far not taken place with the inclusion of practitioners from business and associations, the legal professions, the courts and ministerial bureaucracy. The project of a uniform EPC could provide a strong impetus to real Europeanisation of company law in the Community. Legal faculties in the EU and EEA should not miss this opportunity of contributing to the design of company law of the Community in conformity with the internal market.

---

94 *Supra* n. 90.

95 *Bilanzrechtsmodernisierungsgesetz* (BILMOG), <www.der-betrieb.de/pdf/081107_bilmog_refe.pdf> (§ 342 ss 1 p. 1 No. IV HGB – Commercial Code) wishes to impose an additional (national) task on the private accountancy committee DRSC

96 On the interaction of national and European courts, see U. Everling, 'Das Europäische Gesellschaftsrecht vor dem Gerichtshof der Europäischen Gemeinschaften', in U.H. Schneider, P. Hommelhoff, K. Schmidt, W. Timm, B. Grunewald, and D. Tim (eds.), *Festschrift Für Marcus Lutter zum 70. Geburtstag* (Köln, Otto Schmidt Verlag 2001) p. 33.

97 See G. Bachmann, 'Grundtendenzen der Reform geschlossener Gesellschaften in Europa', in M. Lutter and H. Wiedmann (eds.), *Zeitschrift fur Unternehmens und Gesellschaftsrecht* (Berlin, de Gruyter 2001) p. 373; on closing the gaps in connection with the EPC Statute in general see A. Hatje, 'Lückenschluss im Europarecht', in P. Hommelhoff and D. Helms (eds.), *Neue Wege In Die Europäische Privatgesellschaft* (Köln, Otto Schmidt Verlag 2001) p. 247; H. Völter, *Der Lückenschluss Im Statut Der Europäischen* (Köln, Otto Schmidt Verlag 2000).

5. Summary – concluding theses

1. Medium-sized companies welcome the introduction of the EPC for many reasons – in particular, cost and time reasons.
2. Neither the existing forms of community law nor national forms can match the advantages of an EPC.
3. Based on the model of sales and service companies of an SME abroad, the EPC should be legally open as 'utility furniture' with one or more shareholders.
4. The EPC should be designed as a legal personality with limited liability. The necessary creditor protection should not follow the KG model but the model of internal liability in company law. Whether this should be according to the continental European concept or that of the Anglo-Saxon legal world requires further discussion in preparation for a political decision.
5. Contrary to the ideas of the Commission so far, it should again be considered whether certain points of reference with insolvency law such as the duties and obligations to make an insolvency application should also be included in the EPC Regulation.
6. The EPC must, as far as at all possible, be flexibly designed as an organization instrument primarily for medium-sized businesses but also as an element in a group for major companies and for the public sector. Logically therefore, access to the capital markets must be declined.
7. In the interest of legal certainty and legal consistency, a certain minimum protection for minorities and individuals should be included in the EPC Regulation.
8. In the EPC Regulation, it should be an adequate condition for formation that at least one of the founders is already active in business in at least two EU Member States in any form whatsoever.
9. Co-determination in the EPC should arise only from a certain threshold (e.g., 50 employees) and then only three years after foundation (with the exception of the transformation EPC). In addition, the principle of negotiation with the default provision should apply.
10. Only a comprehensive regulation provides the legal certainty which SMEs require and demand.
11. For reasons of legal certainty but also for reasons of cost, the EPC Regulation should grant structural freedom mainly by means of discretionary provisions and less by prescribing drafting tasks. Model articles of association like the English Table A can be dispensed with.
12. Gaps in the EPC statute should be closed by recourse to community law principles or common principles in the EU Member States. Legal uncertainty thereby arising would not be greater than that in the case of recourse to various national laws of Member States.
13. The development of principles of European company law is the task of the European Court. Legal academics in the Member States should assist in this process – possibly organized in an interpretation committee.
14. The EPC provides a unique chance for company law academics of continuous discourse in the EU.

Chapter 14

THE EUROPEAN PRIVATE COMPANY

Robert Drury*

1. THE ORIGINAL RATIONALE FOR THE EUROPEAN PRIVATE COMPANY

In planning how a European private company (EPC) might facilitate enterprise one tends to think firstly of trade within the internal market. If a European private company form became widely known and used throughout the Union those dealing with it would not have to worry about the still substantial differences that exist today between the various national forms of private company. Private company law has been much less touched by harmonization than that regulating the public company. These differences are still significant but to gain information about these different national forms requires an investment of time and expertise that many businessmen do not have. For lenders and suppliers, doing business across borders would be facilitated by the ability to deal with a familiar European private company. For marketing of products across borders, a company that has a European rather than a national identity could have distinct psychological benefits. Marketing and image could be a very significant attraction. The setting up of European subsidiaries could also be assisted by the use of a European private company. For a group holding company, the facility to incorporate a set of subsidiaries in each of the Member States with a reasonably uniform and relatively uncomplicated constitution and management structure would be a distinct advantage. Discussions with French, English and German lawyers in private practice and with representatives of European scale groups of companies have confirmed that this is the case. This idea has been discussed with representatives of the Daimler Chrysler group and with high-level executives of US multinational corporations and the possibility was very well received, particularly by the former. Also, small businesses as well as large ones should have access to a European vehicle that will facilitate their cross-border collaboration in running a joint enterprise. The *Societas Europea* is primarily designed for larger businesses, and its structure and attendant employee participation rules render it unsuitable for smaller firms wishing to collaborate in a joint project. Certainly experienced lawyers could draft a suitable joint-venture framework, but this may well be just too expensive for smaller firms to contemplate. Hence the provision of an 'off the peg' rather than a 'tailor made' structure would give a much cheaper alternative for small and medium sized enterprises, especially if a form of model constitution was available which could be easily adapted by the entrepreneurs themselves or by their usual local legal advisers.

---

* University of Exeter; Member of CREDA / MEDEF Drafting Group for the EPC Regulation.

All of this could be particularly relevant to countries that have recently joined or are about to join the EU. For these countries, all of the potential advantages of a European private company suggested above could be beneficial. As former centrally planned economies endeavor to create an infrastructure of capitalist business law, the provision of a European private company could be very effective as a partial means of filling any legal vacuum. The marketing advantages for former Eastern bloc countries selling their products into the internal market or beyond, under the neutral banner of a European private company, could also be very important.

However, although trade within the existing and expanded single market can benefit from this proposal, it is just as important to consider the relevance of a possible European private company to trade flows outside the EU and the competitive position of the EU in world markets. Again there might be marketing advantages for European exporters selling products throughout the world under a collective European banner. While exporting is crucial, so too is inward investment. An efficient and universal European private company vehicle could be a major benefit in this respect. Instead of lawyers having to know the peculiarities of twenty seven or more separate systems of company law and then having to choose between them, they would only need to be aware that the European private company will have the same structure in every Member State and could move to a different state if the nature of the original business changes.

There is a further rationale for the EPC that takes the form of a political statement of a kind. We have seen the political agenda, either hidden or on the table, that was created for the European Company (*Societas Europea*), and that one of the mainsprings for its realization was the perceived need to provide a vehicle within the European Community that was compatible with the size of the internal market that industry had to serve. A vehicle was felt to be needed to enable European enterprises to achieve a size that would enable them to compete on equal terms with vast US or Japanese corporations. This led to the use of the merger method of formation and also the incorporation of provisions for the construction of groups of European Companies that existed in the earlier drafts of the *Societas Europea* Regulation. Much of this thinking has now been seen to be somewhat dated in its orientation, and in any case can have no real application to the proposal for a European private company. This leads to the question 'what is or should be our political agenda, if any?' It could be suggested that there is a need to provide a completely European vehicle through which trade can be carried on even at a modest level by small- and medium-sized enterprises. It could have the effect of blurring boundaries and frontiers and diminishing their importance. When the public deals with a large commercial company there is always a label attached to it such as *AG*, *NV*, *SA*, *PLC* or *AE*. Such labels give that company a distinctive national flavor in the minds of the public. The more informed know that in fact a supposedly French, English or Belgian public company may well be owned by interested parties from a wide variety of different countries. While the nationality of those nominally owning or even controlling the company is not normally an issue, it can in exceptional circumstances become crucial.[1] In the case of private companies, the nationality of the company and its owners corresponds much more closely, and probably matters more than

[1] As it did when the US owners of the French Fruehauf company wanted to sacrifice it in response to US foreign policy. The French decision is reported at Paris, 22 May 1965, J.C.P. 1965 II 14274 *bis*, conc. av. Gén. Nepven: D. 1968, p. 147 Note R. Contin, and the case is commented on by P. Leleux, 'The Affaire Fruehauf', [1972] *JBL* 66.

in public companies. One item on the political agenda therefore could be to provide a completely European vehicle so that anyone dealing with it can recognize that it is above all European, and is not indissolubly associated with a particular national origin. These were some of the thoughts in the minds of the drafting team at the time of the original proposal, but the position in the European Union has not stood still, and we need to consider the impact of recent developments.

2. The impact of recent developments

Recent years have brought a number of potentially important changes to the position of companies in the Union wishing to engage in cross border activities. The decisions of the European Court of Justice in the cases of *Centros*,[2] *Überseering*,[3] *Inspire Art*[4] and *Sevic Systems*[5] in the field of freedom of establishment have initiated a regime of wider recognition and acceptance of corporate movements across frontiers by a variety of different mechanisms. *Centros* has shown that the establishment of a company in a foreign jurisdiction immediately followed by the registration of a branch in what can be regarded as the home state of the enterprise can facilitate the creation of *de facto* pseudo-foreign corporations, in particular by its acceptance of the fact that such a device is not to be regarded as an abuse or fraudulent conduct. *Überseering* has required Member States to recognize the capacity that a foreign company enjoys in its state of incorporation in circumstances where it moves its head office to another jurisdiction. *Inspire Art* has limited greatly the extent to which a jurisdiction can take steps to impose its own rules on pseudo-foreign corporations, and *Sevic Systems* has in certain circumstances facilitated cross border mergers by preventing Member States from refusing to register the resulting merged entity on the grounds that one of its original component parts is a foreign but European Union corporation. Taken together these decisions constitute an endorsement of cross border movement of companies by various means. When these are combined with the transposition of the provisions of the Tenth Directive on cross border mergers[6] by December 2007, coupled with the eventual adoption of a Fourteenth Directive enabling the movement of a company's head office without loss of legal personality it becomes obvious that we are now living in a different climate from that in which the project of the European Private Company was conceived.

However, there are many reasons to doubt whether this particular 'climate change' is as profound as appears at first sight. While some of these developments may have marginalized some of the advantages sought by the European Private Company project, they do not

---

[2] Case C-212/97 of 9 March 1999 [1999] *ECR* I-1459.

[3] Case C-208/00 of 5 November 2002 [2002] *ECR* I-9919. See, *inter alia*, M. Andenas, 'Free Movement of Companies', 119 *Law Quarterly Review* (2003) p. 221; W-H. Roth, 'From *Centros* to *Überseering*: Free Movement of Companies, Private International Law, and Community Law', 52 *International and Comparative Law Quarterly* (2003) p. 177; E. Micheler, 'Recognition of Companies Incorporated in Other EU Member States', 52 *International and Comparative Law Quarterly* (2003) p. 521.

[4] Case C-167/01 of 15 November 2003 [2003] *ECR* I-10155. See C. Kersting and C.P. Schindler, 'The ECJ's Inspire Art Decision of 30 September 2003 and its Effects on Practice', *German Law Journal* Vol. 4 No. 12 – 1 December 2003, at <http://www.germanlawjournal.com> (accessed 12 July 2007), and see Micheler, *supra* n. 3. See also S. Rameloo, 'At Long Last Freedom of Establishment for Legal Persons in Europe Accomplished …', 11 *Maastricht Journal of European and Comparative Law* (2004) p. 379.

[5] Case C-411/03 of 13 December 2005 [2005] *ECR* 10805.

[6] 2005/56/EC of 26 October 2005 *OJ* 2005 L 310/1.

actually touch the core issues that lie behind the case for a transnational corporate vehicle designed essentially to be friendly to small businesses. We now have the fact that recognition can be sought, hopefully not after an expensive court action, for a small business moving its head office from one Member State to another. This does compete with the benefits derived from the immediate and unquestionable recognition that must be accorded by all Member States to a European Private Company that is the product of a binding European Regulation, moving its head office under the terms of that Regulation. In fact, some of these developments may well have improved the potential for a European Private Company in so far as that after *Überseering* it will no longer be necessary for the EPC Regulation to follow the line taken in the *Societas Europea* Regulation and stipulate that the entity's registered office must correspond to the location of its central administration. Registered office and head office can now be located wherever commercial advantage dictates, although if there is a common set of rules governing the EPC throughout the Union there should be no real need to have these in different locations.

If we look at one of the major potential functions of the EPC we can see that not much has been changed by these developments. Consider two small businesses in different Member States that have an interest in each other's activities and compare them to two young people in the same situation. They have a series of meetings to get to know each other and discover a mutual attraction. Neither wishes to make a commitment at this stage and so they get together in mutually interesting activities. For the young couple this may be conventional courtship activities such as dating or going on holiday together. For the businesses this may be negotiating a joint venture contract or, if this is successful, entering into a European Economic Interest Grouping under which each party retains their autonomy while collaborating in certain fields with the other partner. These days young people like to see if they can make their relationship work by living together for a while before making the ultimate commitment – marriage. Prudent businesses are the same. While a full-blown merger represents the ultimate commitment, a trial run might prove a good idea. Cross border mergers are becoming a practical reality, but the trial period can still be a problem for businesses as well as people. They face the same problem, will he go to her country or will she go to his? The conditions for setting up a home could well be very different in the two countries. After *Überseering* small companies may be able to take their head office across borders and link it up with that of another company, but if they want to have some degree of commitment or permanence in their liaison they will need to set up home with their business partner in the form of a jointly owned corporation. Doing this can lead to difficulties and each may well feel that they would be unnecessarily sacrificing their own interests on the altar of cooperation if they subject the business venture to the company law of a foreign jurisdiction with which they are unfamiliar. None of the recent developments can assist in this dilemma. What is needed is a neutral or mutually accepted set of conditions for the liaison. Only something like the European Private Company can provide this. The European Economic Interest Grouping is not an efficient platform from which to run a joint business and was never intended to be, the *Societas Europea* is too cumbersome, expensive and unwieldy and a cross border merger too permanent and potentially divisive. Something more familiar, flexible and user friendly is required, and the EPC fits this description very well.

Many of the other rationales for the EPC remain untouched by these recent developments. Providing a uniform structure for a Europe wide group of companies, facilitating inward investment by providing a vehicle that can operate in and move to any part of the

Union under a single and unchanged set of regulations and giving a European identity to a business that wants to penetrate markets on other continents for the first time all remain advantages provided by the EPC that are not affected by these recently increased possibilities for internal migration or merger.

3. Particular problems for a common law jurisdiction

The question of which law to apply where an issue cannot be finally determined by the EPC legislation is one of the most difficult and pressing problems connected with the project. Private company law is generally much more nationally distinctive, in terms of its detail, than public company law. As mentioned earlier, the law concerning private companies has been less affected by the EU harmonization programme than that relating to public companies. Public companies are listed on European stock exchanges and the freedom of movement of capital, one of the main driving forces for harmonization, applies especially to such companies. As it does not apply to private companies, they have been less regulated by this aspect of the harmonization programme. Therefore more remains of their distinctive national flavor. An example is the rule in German *GmbH* law that the company's constitution can require members to put in more capital at a later stage of the company's existence.[7] French law has a requirement that intending transferors of shares in an *SARL* must obtain the consent of the other members before transferring their shares.[8] However, to prevent intending transferors from being locked into the company, the other members must either approve the transfer, buy the shares themselves at an agreed price (the machinery being provided by the law), or get the company itself to buy back the shares. Because private company law is more nationally distinctive than that applying to public companies, the technique of referring substantial areas of regulation to the law applicable in the state in which the company's registered office is located has to be used very sparingly, and preferably only in specified situations such as those involving accounting rules, employees' rights and matters such as winding up, liquidation, and insolvency. If this is not done then there is a very great risk of extreme diversification in the varieties of European Private Company emerging from this exercise. The key to the distinctiveness and success of the European Private Company project is that it should provide as complete and independent a system of company law as possible, free of reference to or dependence upon the individual domestic laws of the Member States. The unattractive alternative is that such companies would become individually dependent upon the national laws of a particular Member State and be a uniform European company in name only.

The solution proposed is to refer matters not covered by the provisions of the Regulation and the provisions of the EPC's articles of association to a hierarchy of rules. These envisage the successive application of the general principles of the Regulation and then the general principles of Community company law and the general principles common to the national laws, provided that they are not inconsistent with the Regulation. No subsequent, residual or fall-back reference to national law is proposed. It is felt that the danger from the

---

[7] See §§ 26 – 28 of the *GmbHGesetz* (Law pertaining to companies with limited liability) of 1892 amended most recently by the Act of October 28, 1994.

[8] See Article L.223-14 of the *Code de Commerce* as amended by Ordonnance n°. 2000-912, 18 September 2000.

reference out of key areas of European Private Company law with the potential for the creation of 27+ types of such company considerably outweighs the difficulties that judges would be faced with in their search for an appropriate solution. With no possibility of a reference out to national laws Judges would be forced to come up with solutions in keeping with the concepts inherent in the European Private Company project.

This technique though will pose particular problems for Judges from Common Law jurisdictions who are bound by statute and the precedents of previous cases from higher courts, and who are traditionally not encouraged to be individually creative in their search for solutions. Instead they would derive these from the application of materials from their Common Law heritage. Blocking off this source of authority from such a Judge will impose certain strains on the system. However, if the applicable law which binds them, the proposed EPC Regulation in this case, very clearly instructs the Judge to seek a solution in a particular way, there is no doubt that they will rise to the challenge. Cases decided before the national courts of other Member States will be available to provide guidance, and such cases have been cited increasingly in Common Law Courts. This lack of access to the Common Law as a source of inspiration may of course mean that these Judges may well have to have recourse to the available academic literature. On occasion this has been done before in the UK, but not often or perhaps willingly. An available precedent here could be the way in which Courts in Civil Law jurisdictions have been doing this for many years without noticeably catastrophic effects!!

One response to the need for expensive court intervention might be to make provision for alternative dispute resolution in the Regulation setting up the EPC. It is possible that use might be made of a provision resembling Article 337 of the Netherlands Civil Code, Book 2, which states that a shareholder in dispute with another shareholder shall have no *locus standi* unless the dispute resolution machinery in the company's constitution or an agreement cannot be applied. There are though some disadvantages in recommending such a course because it would inhibit the growth of a body of case law that could be used to guide judges in future cases.

4. The model articles of association

4.1 The function of the model articles

A small team from Exeter and Heidelberg has drafted a set of model articles for the European Private Company as envisaged by Article 13 and Schedule 1 of the CREDA/MEDEF draft Regulation. In approaching the task of drafting these articles a number of ideas have been influential. If those founding a European Private Company wish to use it as a subsidiary in a group of companies, or as a vehicle for a joint venture they will very probably have access to fairly sophisticated legal advice. Such types of European Private Company are likely to require constitutions that have been very specifically designed to meet the particular needs of their participants. On both of these counts there seems very little utility in providing a standard format for such articles of association, and in any event, drafting such a form catering for such a wide range of possibilities would be all but impossible.

Two broad classifications have been targeted where it was felt that a standard form could have a useful part to play. The first category is the small owner-managed business incorporated by a limited number of participants operating in many ways as a quasi-partnership. It was anticipated that the owners of such an enterprise would wish to have a hands-on rôle in its management. Those running such a business would probably not have access to sophisticated and therefore expensive legal advice. Thus, providing them with a ready made, but still flexible form of constitution seemed to be a worthwhile objective.

The second classification is that of a business with a larger and more diverse group of participants. Here the possibility was envisaged of at least one passive investor – a person or company who contributes to the capital, but who does not necessarily contemplate playing a major part in the day-to-day management of the business. For such an enterprise a more defined managerial structure will usually be necessary, imposing certain obligations on the managers to report to, and if desired take instructions from, the full body of shareholders. Again, this is essentially a small- or medium-sized enterprise where the margins, or the initial investments may not be that great, and where expensive advice from lawyers skilled in the international corporate scene is simply either not available or is too expensive to justify. In such a case, providing a model format for the constitution could be particularly valuable.

Another thing that these models do is to demonstrate that this type of entity could actually work in practice. It will, hopefully, give the whole project greater credibility. The models will help to show the flexibility of such a legal form to lawyers in Europe who are not always totally accustomed to such freedom. In many ways the idea to be conveyed is that this Regulation as a whole starts from the characteristic British approach that everything is possible unless the law prohibits it, rather than the approach which characterizes some European systems, the German *AG* or public company for example, which take the general line that the company's constitution can only do what the relevant law permits it to do and where flexibility is somewhat limited.

4.2 Common provisions

It was very interesting to find that the much vaunted British Table A model articles[9] were actually of very limited use in the drafting process. Both German and particularly French precedents were of considerable help, and the statute for the French *Société par Actions Simplifiée*,[10] the most recent legislation available, was the most use of all. The British model articles were so completely linked to and integrated with the British legislation that they did not provide particularly useful precedents for a constitution that in many ways had to stand up on its own. The philosophy of the EPC is that it is an entity that is largely contractual in nature and the Regulation would make only a minimal provision covering the essential elements of a system of company law. Everything else is left to be regulated by the terms of the foundation contract or constitution. In consequence there was no reservoir of basic concepts to fall back on that a national system of company law would provide, and therefore it was necessary to cover many of these issues in the contract itself. This is a strength rather than a weakness because it enables the easy adoption of this EPC format by businesses from very diverse national backgrounds. Hence the model articles cover things like the following:

---

[9] Contained in The Companies (Tables A to F) Regulations 1985 (SI 1985/805).

[10] *Société par Actions Simplifiée*; SAS Loi of 3 January 1994.

- the fiduciary duties of directors, in particular the obligation to avoid a conflict between their personal interest and their duty to the company;
- a business judgment rule providing a defense against a negligence claim where the directors acted 'honestly and reasonably having duly obtained sufficient information before making any relevant decision';
- pre-emption rights of shareholders on an increase in share capital;
- the requirement of a three-quarters majority resolution to dissolve the company or to alter those terms of the articles which do not require unanimity for this purpose;
- the ability of the shareholders, by a special majority resolution, to give the directors binding instructions on the exercise of their management powers;
- relieving shareholders from the effects of any alteration in the articles requiring them to contribute further capital unless they have consented in writing; and
- the ability of the shareholders to ratify a breach of the 'no conflict' rule and so on.

The articles also cover such standard matters as the company's name, objects, registered office, duration, share capital, transfer and transmission of shares, procedures for meetings and voting as one would expect. Because a close company or a family company is envisaged as using the EPC form the articles provide a restriction on the free transfer of shares. In doing this two options are given. Basically the consent of the remaining shareholders is required to any transfer of shares, but special provision is made for alternative ways of dealing with the situation which arises when a majority shareholder wishes to transfer part only of their holding. This might happen for example, where the founders wish to bring their children into the business, and the other shareholders may not approve. The draft provides alternative avenues through which either all or a three-quarters majority of the other shareholders must approve a transfer, thus excluding the potential transferor from this decision. A realistic *pro rata* valuation method is given which comes into operation if the remaining shareholders reject the potential transferee and become entitled, or in the final analysis obliged, to buy the shares themselves.

4.3 The micro-business model

The matters referred to above were dealt with in both of the models that were drafted. Where the models diverge is primarily in the matter of management structure and shareholders' proceedings. In the first model, where a very limited number of participants was envisaged, there is a relatively simple structure which recognizes that the owners of the business are actively involved in its management at all levels. Quite properly they do not separate out what they are doing in running the business from what they do in managing the company or in acting as its shareholders. Hence there is no need to differentiate these roles with great formality in the structure provided, and that structure should incorporate a certain amount of flexibility. In consequence the articles provide that the business is to be managed by the shareholders acting as a management board unless a unanimous decision is taken to appoint a manager. In family companies, as some members of the family get older and more frail, they may wish to leave the active day-to-day management to the younger and more dynamic elements, while still retaining some measure of control. Thus one or more of these younger members may be appointed managers, or an outsider can be appointed to fulfill this function. If a manager is appointed then certain crucial decisions are reserved for a collective decision of the shareholders. These decisions can be taken at a meeting or by way of written consultation (including electronic communication). If no manager is appointed then the shareholders as a body run the business and make all of the management decisions.

4.4 The more capacious model

The second model contemplates a slightly larger and more diverse body of shareholders, with the possibility that one or more of them will take a passive rather than an active role in the day-to-day management of the business. Therefore a more formal corporate structure was required which makes provision for the managing team to report back to the shareholders and which clearly puts the shareholders themselves in the driving seat as far as major decisions are concerned. In addition, the drafting team was aware of the major differences in European private company management structure between a single or very small group of managers, as found in the *SARL*, the *GmbH* and similar types of company, and the board of directors which typifies the British and Irish types of private company or both board and management as can be the case in Denmark. In order to promote the wide acceptability of this form and to maintain some measure of familiarity for the users alternative structures in the body of the model articles were provided. The first possibility is for a manager or managers to be responsible for the management of the company's business. These are to be natural persons because the complexity of having one company to manage another is scarcely called for in a standard model for this type of company. Some formality is required in the conduct of the business in the interests of any passive shareholders, and thus written minutes need to be kept of all formal decisions. Managers are required to devote their whole time and attention to the affairs of the company and must have their service contracts approved by the shareholders. Dismissal is by way of a simple majority collective decision of the shareholders. While the manager may be one of the shareholders, no express provision is made for this, indicating the slightly more detached and less cosy nature of the management's position in this type of company. The alternative structure that is provided places management responsibility in the hands of a board of directors, acting essentially as a board. The board may appoint a managing director and enter into a service contract with them, as is very common practice in the UK. Removal of any director is by collective decision of the shareholders taken by simple majority. Provision is made for major decisions affecting the company to be taken, not by the managing body, but by the shareholders acting collectively. Because maximum freedom for those running the company was felt desirable and because the need for some informality in the conduct of the company's affairs was recognized, these decisions are not required to be taken at a formal shareholders general meeting, but can be taken by written consultation if wished. However, to protect the passive shareholders at least one formal meeting each year is required, but this can be dispensed with if the shareholders voted unanimously for it. Provisions were also made for the conduct of any meeting and alternative ways of resolving a deadlock by giving or prohibiting a casting vote.

ANNEX

The European Private Company: Model Articles

Abstract

This set of model articles was produced by several members of the research team assembled by CREDA to investigate the prospects for a European Private Company. It emerged as an offshoot from the main project and was conducted as a separate exercise. The drafting team came from the Universities of Exeter (Robert Drury and Andrew Hicks) and Heidelberg (principally Professor Peter Hommelhoff and Dietmar Helms). The idea, as mentioned in the chapter by Robert Drury on the European Company above, was to give practical substance to the concept of a European Private Company, and provide model articles that could be used by quasi-partnership and small to medium sized enterprises wishing to emphasize their European credentials.

Schedule 1: Standard Form Articles of Association

Model A

Form

1. The company is a European Private Company formed pursuant to European Union Regulation number [ ] ("the Regulation").

Name

2. The name of the company is "[ ] European Private Company".

Object

3. The object of the company is to [ ].

Registered Office

4. The registered office of the company is at [ ].

Duration

5. The duration of the company is indefinite.

Share Capital

6.1 The company's share capital is [ ] divided into [ ] shares of [ ] each which shall be subscribed for and paid in full at the time of subscription in cash or in kind but not in work or services.

6.2 Any increase of capital shall be paid for in full at the time of subscription.

6.3 No shareholder shall be bound by any alteration to these articles requiring them to take or subscribe for more shares in the company or increasing their liability contribute to the company's share capital or otherwise pay money to the company unless such shareholder has agreed in writing to be so bound.

Contributions

7 The founding shareholders shall contribute the share capital in the following proportions:

In cash... Mr. [ ] [ ] Euros

Mr. [ ] [ ] Euros

Total [ ] Euros, which amount was deposited on [/ /] to the credit of an account opened in the name of the company [in formation] at [ ] Bank as is proven by [receipt no. [ ]].

In kind in the form of [ ] which the founding shareholders value at [ ] Euros, and which has been put at the disposition of the company as is proven by the receipt of [ ] as agent for the company in formation. A report valuing the contribution(s) in kind is appended to these articles.

Transfer of Shares

8.1 Shares are transferred by a written form of transfer signed by or on behalf of the transferor and transferee.

8.2 Shares are freely transferable to other shareholders but shares or any interest in them may only be transferred to third parties with the written approval of [other] shareholders representing [three quarters of] the shares not subject to the proposed transfer.

Note: The words in square brackets represent alternative ways of dealing with the problem which arises where a majority shareholder wishes to transfer part of their holding to a third party of whom the remaining shareholders may not approve. Such a transfer should be subject to the approval of either all of the other shareholders (in which case all of the words in the brackets could be removed) or of a three quarters majority of the other shareholders (in which case the brackets themselves should be removed).

8.3 Within 28 days of receiving a written request to transfer shares the company shall notify the applicant of the decision of the shareholders.

8.4 If a shareholder requests approval to transfer some or all of their shares, the continuing shareholder or shareholders who so wish are entitled to take a transfer of the shares at a fair valuation determined in accordance with article 8.6 below, and if more than one such shareholder, to take them in proportion to their existing shareholdings.

8.5 If the shareholders refuse approval of a transfer of shares the shareholder requesting transfer shall make reasonable endeavours to find a transferee willing to take a transfer who is acceptable to the continuing shareholders. If such endeavours fail to find an acceptable transferee, the continuing shareholders shall at the expiration of six months from the refusal of the original transfer take the shares of the shareholder requesting transfer in proportion to their existing shareholdings at a fair valuation for an immediate or deferred payment.

Note: *While it may be desirable to find an exit route for disappointed transferors, they should not have too immediate a right to offload their shares on the continuing members as a sudden withdrawal of capital would threaten the survival of many small businesses.*

8.6 A fair valuation shall be found by taking the market value of all the company's shares, assuming a sale by a willing seller to a willing buyer as at the end of the six month period referred to, and by multiplying that market value by the fraction of the whole share capital of the company which the shares to be transferred represent.

8.7 Failing agreement on valuation, a fair valuation on the basis set out above shall be decided by an independent person acting as an expert valuer. The independent valuer shall be the company's statutory auditor if one is appointed, or if none, shall be nominated by agreement between the parties, or in the event that they fail to agree the valuer shall be nominated by [the President for the time being of the [ ] Chamber of Commerce].

Note: *This should result in a pro rata valuation rather than one discounted by reason of the shares being a minority holding nor one giving a premium for control.*

8.8 Any share or shares may only be held in the name of a single shareholder and the company shall not be bound by or recognise any interest in shares except the absolute right of the holder to the whole interest therein.

Note: *This provision, which is usual in English companies, is inserted to deal with the problem of shares being held by trustees, or an administratiekantoor in the Dutch system or possibly under a usufruct in this and other systems*

Management and Representation

9.1 The business of the company shall be managed by the shareholders exercising all the powers of the company as a management board unless by unanimous decision they appoint a manager or managers to act in their place for a fixed period. The manager or managers may be appointed from among the shareholders or not, as the shareholders shall decide.

9.2 If no manager or managers are appointed the members shall conduct such business by majority decision, each having one vote. The quorum required for taking such decisions shall be two. If so requested by any one member or members together holding at least 20% of the shares of the company they shall vote on the basis of one vote per share. Otherwise, subject to the requirements of the Regulation and these articles, they may conduct their business as they think fit.

9.3 Any two members acting jointly shall represent the company in making commitments to third parties and before the courts. If a manager or managers are appointed, a sole manager acting alone or, if more than one manager is appointed, any two acting jointly, shall so represent the company.

<u>Shareholders' Rights</u>

10.1 Profits allocated for distribution and surplus assets in a liquidation shall be distributed to shareholders in the proportion in which they hold shares in the company.

10.2 Where the share capital of the company is increased the shares shall first be offered to the members of the company in proportion to their existing holdings. If any member declines to purchase any such shares they shall be offered to the other members of the company in proportion to their existing holdings. If any of the shares then remain unsold they shall be offered to any members willing to purchase them. Any remaining shares shall be issued in accordance with a collective decision of the members.

10.3 Shareholders shall be entitled to one vote per share on decisions taken collectively by them.

10.4 If a manager or managers are appointed the following decisions shall nevertheless be taken collectively by the shareholders:

i) the dismissal or re-appointment of a manager;

ii) the appointment of a new manager or managers;

iii) the approval of the annual accounts and other documents required by the applicable national law;

iv) the allocation of profits;

v) the appointment of a statutory auditor as required by the applicable law;

vi) any variation of the articles of association;

vii) any increase, redemption or reduction of capital;

viii) any merger or division of the company;

ix) the mortgaging or charging of any assets of the company;

x) the disposal of all or a substantial part of the company's business undertaking;

xi) decisions, other than those in the ordinary course of business, which may materially affect the company or its shareholders;

xii) that the company be dissolved or enter into insolvency proceedings.

10.5 The shareholders may at any time by unanimous resolution in writing notify the manager or managers of any further matter that is to be decided by the shareholders collectively or upon which they wish to be consulted.

10.6 One or more shareholders holding at least ten per cent (10%) of the votes may at any time call for a consultation of the shareholders holding voting rights. This consultation may either take place at a meeting in respect of which all shareholders have been given sufficient notice to enable them to attend or, if no member dissents, by written or other permanent means of communication signed or otherwise authenticated by them.

10.7 Collective decisions may either be taken at a meeting in respect of which all shareholders have been given sufficient notice to enable them to attend or, if no member dissents, by written or other permanent means of communication signed or otherwise authenticated by them and acceptable as good evidence of the decision made. Such communication shall be returned to the registered office of the company within a reasonable time of receipt of notification of the decision to be taken.

10.8 Members may vote at any meeting either in person or by proxy. Members may appoint a shareholder or a manager to act as their proxy, and the instructions in such proxies shall be binding upon the person so appointed. An instrument appointing a proxy shall be in writing, executed by the member and must be delivered to the registered office of the company at least 48 hours before the meeting in respect of which it is to be exercised.

10.9 The quorum for any meeting at which a collective decision is to be taken shall be two members present in person or by proxy.

10.10 Except as otherwise provided in these articles, collective decisions shall require the approval of shareholders holding a majority of the votes attaching to the shares of the company.

10.11 Collective decisions adding, removing or amending the terms of the articles of association provided for under Articles 20, 21 and 22 of the Regulation may only be made by the shareholders acting unanimously.

Note: A reference to the articles of association would be preferable to a reference to the Regulation if this document is adopted.

10.12 A collective decision of the members to dissolve the company or to make any alteration to the articles of association other than those specified above may only be made by shareholders representing three quarters of the shares in the company.

10.13 Minutes of the collective decisions of the shareholders shall be recorded in writing or other permanent legible form.

10.14 Collective decisions of the shareholders are binding on the manager or managers and other officers if any.

10.15 Whether a manager or managers are or are not appointed, the shareholders shall have access at all reasonable times to the company's principal management documents and to such books, accounts and other documents and records of the company as are necessary to enable them to carry out their managerial duties and to assert their rights under the Regulation and these articles.

Financial Year

11. The financial year of the company runs from [ ] to [ ] each year.

Transmission of Shares

12. On the death of any shareholder, the surviving shareholders may not object to the transmission of shares to a spouse, an ascendant or descendant of the deceased shareholder, but in the case of transmission to any other person they may exercise the same rights over these shares as if the personal representatives of the deceased shareholder had requested approval of a transfer of shares under article 8 above.

Compulsory Assignment and Withdrawal of a Shareholder

13.1 If a shareholder has seriously damaged the company's interest or if the continuation of the shareholder as a member of the company is detrimental to its proper operation, the shareholder may be required to assign their shares as appears below and one or more shareholders holding a majority of voting rights in the company may apply to the Court of competent jurisdiction for an order that the offending shareholder assign their shares as directed.

13.2 The continuation of a shareholder as a member of the company shall be considered detrimental to its proper operation *inter alia* in the following circumstances:

i) if a creditor of a shareholder becomes entitled to any interest in the shares or in their proceeds of sale by reason of a legal process for the enforcement of a debt or other obligation;;

ii) if any insolvency proceedings or proceedings for the realisation of any security are instituted against any shareholder;

iii) if a shareholder pledges all or part of their shares without the prior consent of the other shareholders;

iv) if a shareholder commits a serious breach of any obligation arising under these articles;

v) if there is any change in the control of any corporate shareholder, except where the new shareholders of that corporate member to whom control passes are either the spouses or descendants of the previous shareholders.

13.3 In the circumstances specified in article 13.2 above, or in the event that an order of a competent Court under article 21.1 of the Regulation requiring the assignment of any shares is not immediately complied with, the non-pecuniary rights attaching to those shares may immediately be suspended by a collective decision.

13.4 A shareholder who considers their interests to have been damaged may petition the Court of competent jurisdiction for the acquisition of their shares in the circumstances and in the manner appearing in Article 21.2 of the Regulation.

13.5 Where shares are assigned or acquired under this article the price shall be determined in accordance with articles 8.6 and 8.7 above, but may not be less than the actual value of the shares.

Redemption of Shares

14. **Either** The shares issued by the company shall not be redeemable.

or Without prejudice to article 15 of the Regulation, the company may redeem its shares in compliance with the laws of of the place of its registered office regulating the equivalent form of company specified in Schedule 2 of the Regulation.

Auditors

15.1 In the circumstances required by the legislation in force in the state of the company's registered office applicable to the equivalent form of company in that jurisdiction specified in Schedule 2 of the Regulation, the company shall appoint an auditor

15.2 In other cases the company may appoint an auditor if the members by collective decision so decide.

15.3 Every appointment of an auditor shall be made by a collective decision of the members.

15.4 The terms of appointment, qualifications, function and duties of such auditors shall be as required by the applicable legislation.

Formation Expenses

16. The reasonable expenses of forming the company shall be borne by the company.

Dispute Resolution

17. In cases other than where a shareholder is entitled under the Regulation or these articles of association to bring a matter before a Court of competent jurisdiction, in any dispute arising between members or between members and the company the parties will use their best endeavours to settle it by voluntary mediation involving the non-binding intervention by a neutral third party who helps the disputants to negotiate an agreement [*for alternative wording see below*] and no party may commence any court procedings in relation to any such

dispute until they have in good faith attempted to settle it by mediation and that mediation has terminated.

Note: *Reference to a more precise procedure for such a mediation may be thought desirable in some cases e.g. for a British EPC, and a clause like the following which refers to the known and established rules of the Centre for Dispute Resolution even though it is a commercial organisation may be used as an alternative e.g. {in accordance with the Centre for Dispute Resolution (CEDR) Model Mediation Procedure or such other procedure having effect to employ the services of a suitably qualified mediator in the settlement of the dispute}.*

Model B

Articles 1 – 8 are the same as in Model A

Management and Representation

9.1 The first members of the management body are [ ]. They are appointed for a period of three years, but are eligible for re-appointment. The shareholders may remove, appoint or re-appoint any member of the management body by a simple majority of votes cast at a collective decision, each member to be voted upon individually.

EITHER

9.2 The management body is the manager or managers, natural persons, who is/are responsible for the management of the business of the company.

9.3 Subject to the provisions of these articles and to the matters reserved by them for the collective decision of the shareholders and to any direction given to the manager(s) by collective decision of the shareholders restricting their authority or limiting their discretion in management, each manager shall have the most extensive powers to act in all circumstances in the name of the company.

9.4 Each manager may represent the company in making commitments to third parties or before the courts.

9.5 The manager or managers may delegate any of their management functions (except those that are required to be performed by the management body as a whole either by the Regulation or by these articles) to such person or persons as they choose.

9.6 The manager(s) shall ensure that written minutes are kept of all formal decisions.

9.7 The managers shall devote their whole time and give their undivided attention to the affairs of the company.

9.8 Any decisions by the company to enter into a contract of employment with a manager and to determine the terms of such a contract shall be taken collectively by the shareholders.

9.9 The office of manager is vacated on:

- removal by collective decision of the shareholders;
- on being made bankrupt or otherwise entering formal insolvency proceedings;
- on being prohibited by the law of any Member State from holding office as a director or manager of a company;
- on suffering mental incapacity.

OR

9.2 The management body is the board of directors which is responsible for the management of the business of the company. The board of directors shall transact business as a board, the directors acting together by board resolution.

9.3 Subject to the provisions of these articles and to the matters which are reserved by them for the collective decision of the shareholders and to any direction given to the board of directors by collective decision of the shareholders restricting their authority or limiting their discretion in management, the board of directors shall have the most extensive powers to act in all circumstances in the name of the company.

9.4 The board of directors may appoint a member of the board to be chief executive on such terms as it thinks fit and may delegate any management functions to such person or persons as it chooses.

9.5 The board of directors acting as a board may represent the company in making commitments to third parties or before the courts. However, if a sole chief executive is appointed, such a person shall so represent the company. If more than one chief executive is appointed, any two acting jointly shall so represent the company.

9.6 The board of directors may regulate its proceedings as it thinks fit except that it shall ensure that written minutes are kept of all formal decisions.

9.7 The board of directors may enter into a contract of employment with a chief executive on such terms as it thinks fit.

9.8 The office and employment of a chief executive shall terminate if the chief executive ceases for any reason to be a director.

9.9 The office of director is vacated on:

- removal by collective decision of the shareholders;
- on being made bankrupt or otherwise entering formal insolvency proceedings;
- on being prohibited by the law of any Member State from holding office as a director or manager of a company;
- on suffering mental incapacity.

ALL

9.10 The management body and each member of it shall act in the interests of the company.

9.11 No member of the management body or any other officer of the company shall put themselves in a position where their interest may conflict materially with the interest of the company.

9.12 If any member of the management body or any other officer of the company profits from any circumstance in which their interest conflicts with that of the company they shall be liable to account to the company for all profits arising.

9.13 If any member of the management body or any other officer of the company enters into a contract or other transaction with the company whereby their interest conflicts with that of the company, the company may in its discretion affirm or avoid the contract or other transaction.

9.14 A transaction entered into by any member of the management body or any other officer with the company shall be valid and such persons may retain the benefit of any transaction notwithstanding a conflict of interest in either case if at least seven days before its conclusion they gave notice in writing to the management body, the person specified in Article 29.2 of the Regulation and the shareholders of their interest and of the nature of the transaction and no shareholder within that period of seven days requests the board to call a meeting of shareholders to resolve as a collective decision that the company shall not enter into that transaction or that such a person may not retain the benefit of the transaction.

9.15 If such a transaction referred to in article 9.14 is not within the ordinary course of the business of the company the period of seven days in that article shall run from the time of the receipt by the shareholders of a copy of the report referred to in Article 29.2 of the Regulation.

9.16 By a resolution of shareholders representing a majority of the share capital, the liability to the company of any member of the management body or of any other officer of the company in respect of a conflict of interest may be waived and any contract with the company affirmed either prospectively or retrospectively.

9.17 The members of the management body are jointly and severally liable to the company in respect of serious management errors where they fail to exhibit the care, skill and diligence reasonably to be expected of a business person under the circumstances, except that they shall not be so liable if they acted honestly and reasonably having duly obtained sufficient information before making any relevant decision.

9.18 On any collective decision of the shareholders to exempt a member of the management body from liability for any breach of duty to the company, such a member, being a shareholder, shall be disqualified from voting and shall not be counted in the quorum present at any meeting at which they are so disqualified.

9.19 The management body is responsible for ensuring that the company complies with the accounting rules referred to in Article 32 of the Regulation and that the shareholders are consulted in the circumstances set out in Article 28 of the Regulation.

Shareholders' Rights

10.1 Profits allocated for distribution and surplus assets in a liquidation shall be distributed to shareholders in the proportion in which they hold shares in the company.

10.2 Where the share capital of the company is increased the shares shall first be offered to the members of the company in proportion to their existing holdings. If any member declines to purchase any such shares they shall be offered to the other members of the company in proportion to their existing holdings. If any of the shares then remain unsold they shall be offered to any members willing to purchase them. Any remaining shares shall be issued in accordance with a collective decision of the members.

10.3 Shareholders shall be entitled to one vote per share on decisions taken collectively by them.

10.4 The following decisions shall be taken collectively by the shareholders and not by the management body:

i) the dismissal or re-appointment of a member of the managing body;

ii) the appointment of a new member of the managing body;

iii) the approval of the annual accounts and other documents required by the applicable national law;

iv) the allocation of profits;

v) the appointment of a statutory auditor as required by the applicable law;

vi) any variation of the articles of association;

vii) any increase, redemption or reduction of capital;

viii) any merger or division of the company;

ix) the mortgaging or charging of any assets of the company;

x) the disposal of all or a substantial part of the company's business undertaking;

xi) decisions, other than those in the ordinary course of business, which may materially affect the company or its shareholders;

xii) that the company be dissolved or enter into insolvency proceedings.

10.5 The shareholders may at any time by a three quarters majority resolution notify the management body of:

- any further matter in addition to those listed in article 10.4 that is to be decided by the shareholders collectively;
- any matter, whether specific or general, about the occurrence of which they wish to be individually informed.

10.6 The shareholders may by a three quarters majority resolution give a direction which shall be binding on the management body with regard to the exercise of its management powers or discretions.

10.7 One or more shareholders holding at least ten per cent (10%) of the votes may at any time require the management body to arrange for a meeting or other consultation of the shareholders holding voting rights, and shall have the right to propose any item to be considered. The management body shall either call a meeting in respect of which all shareholders have been given at least fourteen days notice or, if no member dissents, arrange for a consultation of all of the shareholders by written or other permanent means of communication signed or otherwise authenticated by them.

Shareholders' Proceedings

11.1 Except where procedures are specifically provided by these articles or the law applicable under the Regulation, collective decisions may either be taken at a meeting in respect of which all shareholders have been given at least fourteen days notice or, if no member dissents, at a meeting held with shorter notice or by a consultation in writing of all of the shareholders.

11.2 When a decision is taken by consultation in writing the text of the resolution proposed is sent by the managing body to each shareholder by a letter sent by recorded delivery [*lettre recommandée* AR]. Shareholders shall indicate their acceptance or rejection of the resolution so communicated by written or other permanent means of communication signed or otherwise authenticated by them and acceptable as good evidence of the decision made which shall be returned to the registered office of the company within fourteen days of receipt of notification of the resolution.

11.3 Shareholders may vote at any meeting either in person or by proxy. Shareholders may appoint another shareholder or a member of the managing body to act as their proxy, and the instructions in such proxies shall be binding upon the person so appointed. An instrument appointing a proxy shall be in writing, executed by the member and must be delivered to the registered office of the company at least 48 hours before the meeting in respect of which it is to be exercised.

11.4 The quorum for any meeting at which a collective decision is to be taken shall be two members present in person or by proxy.

11.5 Except as otherwise provided in these articles, collective decisions shall require the approval of shareholders holding a majority of the votes cast at that collective decision.

11.6 Collective decisions adding, removing or amending the terms of the articles of association provided for under Articles 20, 21 and 22 of the Regulation may only be made by the shareholders acting unanimously.

> *Note: A reference to the articles of association would be preferable to a reference to the Regulation if this document is adopted.*

11.7 A collective decision of the shareholders that the company be dissolved or enter into insolvency proceedings or to make any alteration to the articles of association other than those specified above requires the approval of shareholders holding a three quarters majority of the votes cast at that collective decision.

11.8 Minutes of the proceedings including the collective decisions of the shareholders shall be recorded in writing or other permanent legible form.

11.9 Collective decisions of the shareholders are binding on the management body and on all other officers of the company.

11.10 A general meeting in respect of which all shareholders have been given at least twenty one days notice shall be held once each year for the approval of the annual accounts and other documents required by the applicable national law unless by a unanimous collective decision the shareholders elect to dispense with holding annual general meetings for this purpose. A collective decision made by shareholders holding a majority of the votes cast may subsequently require the holding of annual general meetings for the approval of the accounts and other documents specified above.

11.11 The shareholders shall have access at all reasonable times to the company's principal management documents, including minutes of the decisions and proceedings of the management body and of the shareholders and to such books, accounts and other documents and records of the company as may be necessary to enable them to carry out their managerial duties and to assert their rights under the Regulation and these articles.

11.12 Any period of notice of any meeting or other proceeding referred to in these articles shall be exclusive of the day upon which the notice is given and of the day upon which or by which the meeting or other proceeding is to take place.

11.13 Any requirement for the giving of notice under these articles shall mean the service of notice in writing, and a notice sent by facsimile transmission to a number given by the shareholder to the company for that purpose or by any other electronic process approved for the purpose by unanimous decision of the shareholders shall be deemed to be in writing.

11.14 Where a meeting is called under these articles the chairman shall be as follows:

- a chief executive if appointed or the sole member of the management body (where there is only one), if present within fifteen minutes of the time appointed for the meeting, shall preside as chairman;
- failing which the members of the management body present at the meeting shall appoint a chairman;
- failing which the shareholders present at the meeting shall appoint a chairman.

11.15 In the case of an equality of votes at any such meeting the chairman <u>shall/shall not</u> be entitled to a casting vote in addition to any other vote that they may have.

Articles 12 – 17 are the same as Articles 11 – 16 in Model A apart from the numbering.

<u>Dispute Resolution</u>

18. In cases other than where a shareholder is entitled under the Regulation or these articles of association to bring a matter before a Court of competent jurisdiction, in any dispute arising between members or between members and the company the parties will use their best endeavours to settle it by voluntary mediation involving the non-binding intervention by a neutral third party who helps the disputants to negotiate an agreement. [*for alternative wording see below*]

Note: *Reference to a more precise procedure for such a mediation may be thought desirable in some cases e.g. for a British EPC, and a clause like the following which refers to the known and established rules of the Centre for Dispute Resolution, even though it is a commercial organisation, may be used as an alternative e.g. "in accordance with the Centre for Dispute Resolution (CEDR) Model Mediation Procedure or such other procedure having effect to employ the services of a suitably qualified mediator in the settlement of the dispute".*

INDEX

GPSR Compliance
The European Union's (EU) General Product Safety Regulation (GPSR) is a set of rules that requires consumer products to be safe and our obligations to ensure this.

If you have any concerns about our products, you can contact us on

ProductSafety@springernature.com

In case Publisher is established outside the EU, the EU authorized representative is:

Springer Nature Customer Service Center GmbH
Europaplatz 3
69115 Heidelberg, Germany

www.ingramcontent.com/pod-product-compliance
Lightning Source LLC
Chambersburg PA
CBHW071238230926
51849CB00001B/144
* 9 7 8 9 0 6 7 0 4 2 5 1 2 *